G

THE NORTHERN ISLES:
Orkney and Shetland

THE NORTHERN ISLES:
Orkney and Shetland

ALEXANDER FENTON

Director European Ethnological
Research Centre, Edinburgh

TUCKWELL PRESS

Published in Great Britain in 1997 by
Tuckwell Press
The Mill House
Phantassie
East Linton
East Lothian EH40 3DG
Scotland

First Published in 1978 by John Donald
Publishers Ltd
Copyright © Alexander Fenton 1978

ISBN 1 86232 058 6

British Library Cataloguing in Publication Data

A catalogue record for this book is available
on request from the British Library

Printed and Bound by
Cromwell Press, Melksham, Wiltshire

Preface

ORKNEY and Shetland, the Northern Isles, have the satisfying quality of all islands. The sea delimits the land. It is possible to view as a mental concept the amalgam of land and sea, fields and houses and boats, cliffs and sheep holms, sea-birds and fishing boats, wind and mist, wide skies and changing clouds and lights on the water. Language adds its appeal, as well as the consciousness of the people of many nations who have come here, each contributing a little of themselves to the total picture. Others will come in the future.

My approach in writing is to try to show the details of the amalgam, how the elements interlock in different ways and degrees. This involves looking at the functioning of the island communities in relation to the organisation of the land and the resources of the sea and the shore and the cliffs, for subsistence, rent and commerce. Because things interlock, the full story is not always outlined in one place and the book must be read as a whole to get the full flavour. For special topics dealt with in more than one place the index provides a guide. The shape of the book is dictated by the character of the islands and one topic has been allowed to flow into another, with no attempt to fit them into a pre-determined structure. This approach, though not without its difficulties, may reflect the complex life of the islands more truly.

The book does not include the story of oil, the latest incident in the long saga of the islands. Its intention is to provide explanations of the earlier processes of change, so that the present may be seen in the perspective of what has gone before. Sources of all kinds have been used, books and manuscripts, notebooks compiled during visits to different islands, letters and information from the many people who have willingly imparted their knowledge. Of special value have been the Dictionary of the Older Scottish Tongue and especially the Scottish National Dictionary, with whose Editor, David Murison, I worked for four years. From him I learned the critical, analytical use of language as evidence in historical research. Throughout the book, full and deliberate use is made of dialect terms and their etymologies, as a convenient and often essential way of assessing the relative strength of Norse and Scots influence within the subjects treated, and as between the Orkney and Shetland island groups.

Though this volume is an analysis of material assembled over many years, I am conscious that it is no more than the thin end of the wedge. Each chapter and many of the sections could be developed into a full-scale book, and many subjects that might have been treated more fully have been barely touched. Throughout, the emphasis is on what might be called 'pre-industrial' conditions, whether they belong to the past or exist at present, and on placing them in the context of the Northern world. For this reason, much use has been made of comparative material from Scandinavia, especially Norway and the Faroe Islands. The contents form a base on which others can build, without the need for again searching through many sources for the innumerable tiny points brought together here to create as accurate a picture as possible.

If the book helps to give insight to those drawn to the Northern Isles and can help to interpret the historical environment, it will have served its purpose; but no amount of writing can ever replace the virtue of coming to these islands, and experiencing them *in natura*.

ACKNOWLEDGEMENTS

I am indebted to Gordon Donaldson and to Roy Linklater for reading the draft and suggesting many improvements; to David Brown, Margaret Alma Grant and Barbara Robertson for technical help; to Gavin Sprott for help with illustrations and for comments on the text; to Mrs Helen Bennett, for commenting on the textiles section; to John Brown (Figs 113, 125, 126–7, 152, 226), Colin Hendry (Figs 131, 135–6, 153, 195), Helen Jackson (Figs 1–4, 6, 7, 9–11, 15, 18, 19, 22, 39, 40, 41, 48, 49, 51, 87, 92, 93, 102–4, 156, 170, 181, 183, 198, 220, 225–6, 249, 252, 259, 281) and Bruce Walker (Figs 52, 53, 57, 58, 205, 207–9, 237) for drawings; to Tom Henderson, James Troup and Bryce Wilson for photographs; to the many people who have contributed to the Country Life Archive in the National Museum; and above all to those who spent so much time showing me their islands and telling me about them, in particular J. H. Johnson and James Laurenson, whose contributions to the Archive are monuments to their knowledge. I am grateful to all those from whom the basic inspiration for this book has come.

ALEXANDER FENTON 1978

THIS book has been long out of print. Nevertheless it appears to have become something of a classic, and there is a continuing demand for it. I was happy to agree when Tuckwell Press proposed a photographic reprint, and I dedicate it to the memory of my many Orkney and Shetland friends who have passed on since the book was written nearly twenty years ago.

ALEXANDER FENTON 1997

Contents

Fuel for the Fire

Back Transport, Harness and Straw Working

Baskets and Ropes

The Land and its Produce

Draught Animals and Transport

Cereal Crops

Pigs, Rabbits and Geese

The Shore and the Sea

1

The Shape of Things

THE islands of Shetland and Orkney are the most northerly units of land in the British Isles. Shetland is as far north as Cape Farewell in Greenland, and Helsinki in Finland, and Orkney as far north as Bristol Bay in Alaska. Lerwick in Shetland is 340 km from Bergen in Norway, and an equivalent distance from Aberdeen in Scotland. A sailing ship could cover this distance in two days and two nights if the wind was favourable[1]; a modern ship takes around 12 hours. In the exposed waters around these islands, however, wind and weather can make remarkable differences in these timings, whatever the motive power of the vessel. Winds and more favourable tides could often make the Bergen to Lerwick passage easier than that from Lerwick to Aberdeen.

To the people of mainland Britain, especially those in the south, such factors will tend to confirm an impression, as yet only slightly deflected by the coming of oil, that the Northern Isles are distant, inaccessible, isolated areas, not quite part of the British Isles, and seeming to defy central authority with some success. They have remained separate Island Authorities under the regionalisation scheme that became law in May 1975, and in particular played havoc with the creation by parliament of a joint Water Board for Shetland, Orkney and the mainland counties of Caithness and Sutherland, with headquarters at Wick in Caithness. They have been able to lay down their own terms regarding the landing of oil.[2] The Scottish parliament annexed the earldom of Orkney and lordship of Shetland in 1472 in favour of King James III, after King Christian I of Denmark and Norway had pledged his land and rights in Orkney for 50,000 florins on 8 September 1468 and those in Shetland for 8,000 florins on 20 May 1469, in an attempt to make up the dowry of 60,000 florins of the Rhine he had promised to his daughter Margaret as her dowry on her marriage to James III. Nevertheless the thought is often aired that redemption remains a possibility, and that the islands might again become part of Scandinavia, though it may well be that redemption of the wadset was not really envisaged at the time.

Isolation and remoteness are relative concepts, however, and in terms of the ebb and flow and intermixture of culture, these islands have been more like busy crossroads than remote backwater areas, even though changes in politics, communications, and economic-geographical interrelationships have left them, and especially Shetland, on the fringe, with few economic relations or ship connections with Scandinavia.[3] Yet in Viking times they were stepping stones towards northern and western Britain, Ireland, the Faroe Islands and Iceland, and highly favoured places of settlement. Orkney stood out like a fertile jewel amongst these northern lands, and became the heart of the Norse kingdom in northern Britain to such an extent that some of the Mainland place-names are seen from the viewpoint of Orkney. The most northerly county in Britain is Sutherland, the 'southern land', and the Hebrides the *Suðreyjar*, the 'southern isles',[4] a word preserved in the title of the Bishop of Sodor and Man.

There are many similarities between Orkney and Shetland, yet what becomes more and more striking the more the life and culture of the Northern Isles is studied, is the range of differences at many levels. Some of the standard ones are summarised in the following table.[5]

	Year	Shetland	Orkney
Total Area	—	352,319 acres	240,847 acres
Arable Percentage	1931	3.4%	37.3%
Farming	1931	2,636 persons	4,611 persons
Fishing	1931	938 persons	234 persons
Cattle/Sheep Ratio	1880	1:4	1:1.2
	1935	1:17	1:1.8
Average Size of Holding	1930	8.2 acres	33.1 acres

The features picked out here point to the economic emphasis of Shetland on fishing and sheep, and of Orkney on arable farming. Between the 1861 and 1961 censuses, the population of Shetland moved from 31,670 to 17,809, and of Orkney from 32,395 to 18,743.

To attempt to interpret and understand these differences – given the common factors – is to try to unravel the history of the two island groups in terms of their physical nature and environment, and of their differing rates of development arising from this. For comparative detail, and as a yardstick for assessing differences, the adjoining Mainland, especially Caithness, must be taken into account, as well as the nearest comparable island group, the Faroes, and Scandinavia, especially western Norway.

Several studies of the history of the Northern Isles exist, and it is enough here to provide a brief outline to set the scene. From the ninth century AD till the third quarter of the fifteenth century, a period of over 500 years, the Northern Isles were Norse, though Scottish influence was having its effect long before the end of this period. Their pledging and annexation did not mean that all communication with the parent country was cut off. The continuing strength of the connection is shown by the way in which business transactions in land continued. A Norwegian called Olaff Perszøn, living near Bergen, sold udal land he owned in Whalsay in 1567, a hundred years after the islands ceased to be Norse politically.[6] Trading links with Norway remained strong until the

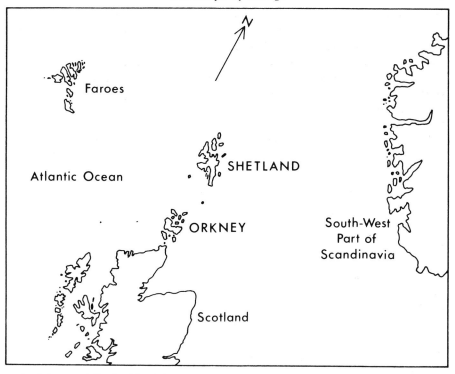

1. Orkney and Shetland in their Northern European crossroads setting.

nineteenth century, providing the treeless islands with essential timber for boats and to some extent for house-building and for ploughs and plough-parts. Trade was a means of maintaining and renewing culture contacts with Norway long after 1468–9.

Besides these long-continued links with Norway, trading links with Germany and the Low Countries were also close from the late fifteenth century onwards. Merchants from the great Hanseatic trading towns, mainly Bremen, Lübeck and Hamburg, came each year and set up their trading booths[7] where they exchanged goods for the produce of the islands. The traders brought fishing requirements such as hooks, lines, and herring nets; brandy, mead, and strong beer; foodstuffs such as biscuit, wheat- and rye-meal, barley, salt, pease and fruit of various kinds; tobacco; and textiles such as the coarser kinds of linen and muslin, and Monmouth caps. In return they got sun-dried fish; the hides and skins of oxen, sheep, goats, seals and otters; knitted stockings, woven gloves, garters, and coarse cloth or wadmal made from the wool of native sheep; fish oil, butter, mutton, birds' feathers. An important Orkney product was corn, and there were quantities of rabbit skins. Scots and English merchants also had their trading booths. Dundee merchants had their booths along the south side of Grutness Voe, where the 'Dundee vessel' loaded up with fish, butter, oil, beef, hides and tallow.[8]

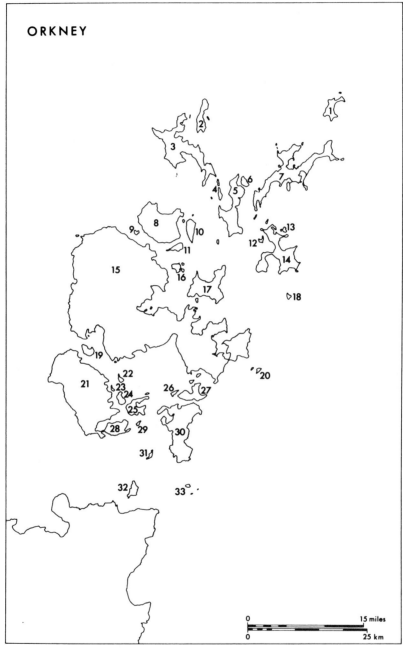

2. The Orkney Islands: 1 North Ronaldsay. 2 Papa Westray. 3 Westray. 4 Fara. 5 Eday.
6 Calf of Eday. 7 Sanday. 8 Rousay. 9 Eynhallow. 10 Egilsay. 11 Wyre. 12 Linga Holme.
13 Papa Stronsay. 14 Stronsay. 15 Mainland. 16 Gairsay. 17 Shapinsay. 18 Auskerry.
19 Graemsay. 20 Copinsay. 21 Hoy. 22 Cava. 23 Rusa Little. 24 Fara. 25 Flotta. 26 Hunda.
27 Burray. 28 South Walls. 29 Switha. 30 South Ronaldsay. 31 Swona. 32 Stroma. 33 Pentland
Skerries.

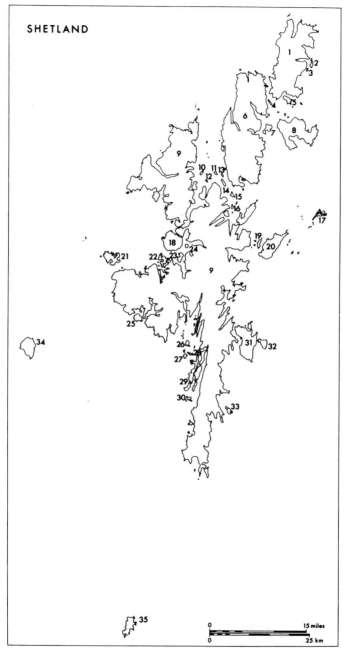

SHETLAND

3. The Shetland Islands: 1 Unst. 2 Balta. 3 Huney. 4 Linga. 5 Uyea. 6 Yell. 7 Hascosay.
8 Fetlar. 9 Mainland. 10 Lamba. 11 Brother Isle. 12 Little Roe. 13 Unarey. 14 Bigga.
15 Samphrey. 16 Linga. 17 Out Skerries. 18 Muckle Roe. 19 West Linga. 20 Whalsay.
21 Papa Stour. 22 Vementry. 23 Papa Little. 24 Linga. 25 Vaila. 26 Hildasay. 27 Oxna.
28 Trondra. 29 West Burra. 30 South Havera. 31 Bressay. 32 Isle of Noss. 33 Mousa.
34 Foula. 35 Fair Isle.

Because of such trade links the people of the Northern Isles had a wider experience in eating and drinking habits than many of their inland contemporaries on Mainland Scotland, but the foreign influence on the islanders' diet was seasonal, annually renewed, and not constant throughout the year. It depended more on barter than on a supply of ready money. The culture of the visitors also affected the dress of the local fishermen.

By the middle of the eighteenth century, details of the trade outlets become more readily available. Shetland saithe was sold in Dundee and Leith. Fish, fish-oil, butter, stockings and worsted stuffs went mostly to foreign markets. About 1733 ten to twelve ships were coming annually from Hamburg and Bremen, their crews drying and salting the fish at the booths from May till August. This trade was ended by the imposition of a salt-tax, and the establishment of a customs-house at Lerwick. Thereafter a new emphasis developed, for the landlords themselves became the merchants.

The centres of trade began to change. Whereas Scandinavia, the Hanse towns, and the Low Countries, along with Scotland, had been the main trading partners, now the trade of Shetland was with Leith and London, Hamburg and Spain, and that of Orkney with Leith and Newcastle (especially because of the production of kelp), and to a lesser extent with Hamburg, Norway, Spain and Portugal. Shetland continued to get 'some of their best Boats' from Norway, and corn and flour came from Orkney and Scotland, clothes and better linen from Leith, groceries and household furniture (at least for the lairds' houses) from London. In Shetland as in Orkney, the butter exported was from the rent that was paid in kind at Lammas, and the grain, malt and meal from Orkney came largely from payment of the crown rent.[9]

Trading contacts brought the Northern Isles into the orbit of the Hanseatic League of North German towns that grew up in the thirteenth century and came to dominate commerce and to some extent politics in the Baltic and North Sea areas in the fourteenth and fifteenth centuries.[10] Dutch fishermen started to flock around the coasts of the Northern Isles and especially Shetland, from about 1500, reaching a peak about 1640, and tailing off in the course of the eighteenth century.[11] German merchants had an effect on the local fishing industry, for the native fishermen caught cod and ling for them. The Dutch made little impact on the island fishery, but had more importance for the domestic economy, for they purchased large quantities of knitted stockings for cash. A good deal of foreign money was got in this way, which helped to pay the rent and buy necessities, as long as the sale of stockings for ready money lasted.

In spite of the advantage to the domestic economy, Hollanders and others were not always favoured by the authorities. For example, an act was passed in 1615, forbidding anyone to go to the island of Bressay 'for furnishing of beir, vivoris and uther necessaris to the Hollandaris and utheris foirrenn[eris] committing thairby villanie, fornicatioun and adultrie', under the pain of a £20 fine, and the owners of the ground were required to demolish all houses built for such people.[12] Problems could scarcely be avoided when they came in great numbers. In the 1770s, a traveller counted 400 herring boats in Bressay Sound, half of them Dutch, and the remainder Danes, Prussians, French and Ostenders, with two English and one Scottish boat. As late as 1806, Dutch and Danish coins were more common in Lerwick than British money. It is not surprising, therefore, that in the clothes of the man who died in a peat bog at Gunnister in Shetland in the seventeenth century, there was a woollen purse containing a Nijmegen 6-stuiver piece of 1690, an Overijssel 2-stuiver piece of 1681, and a Swedish $\frac{1}{6}$ øre of 1683.[13]

A strong international flavour remains to the present day. In Lerwick a fisherman from Esbjerg in Denmark may be seen mending his net on the quay, there may be a German trawler with spitted fish being smoked in a barrel on the deck, ships from Baltic and Russian ports may be around, English and Scottish fishing boats will be mingling with the local ones, and American accents will identify the oil-men. A Danish vessel may be chartered as readily as a Scottish one for carrying sand and gravel for the building of a new island road or pier.

The kind of free-trading marked by the ready use of international currency came to an end during the eighteenth century, when local merchant lairds began to develop and exploit the fishing industry with the encouragement of the Government and of the Fishery Societies or Companies that had been founded.[14] Two main lines were followed: the expansion of the herring fishery, taken over where the Dutch left off, and the organisation of the white fishing. The consequences were very great in relation to land use, and indeed land and sea cannot be studied in isolation from each other by anyone concerned with the historical development of the Northern Isles.

The Norse phase lasted directly for 500 years from the ninth century and indirectly for two or three centuries longer; that of the Hanse traders and Dutch fishermen covered about 300 years from the fifteenth century; but it cannot be doubted that the strongest and most pervasive element in this cultural mélange was the part played by the islands' closest neighbours, the Scots, at all levels, and at all periods, though the main impact on language and culture came after the fifteenth century. Political change brought a fairly fundamental re-arrangement of the economic and administrative organisation, though not necessarily all at the same time and often only incompletely. The story of the influence of the kind of central direction applied by the Scots who came and settled on the best available land, and who gradually substituted feudal for udal forms of landholding, is a main key to an understanding of the changes in the life and culture of these islands during the last 500 years and more.

There were two main periods of scotticisation. In the first period, starting before the fifteenth century, the lords and earls, the civil servants, the ministers of the church (often the younger sons of landed gentry), and others involved in administration arrived. The church had almost as big a part to play as the state, and the concern was with land ownership, tenancy, rents, taxes, tithes, and other dues, and general regulation of estates, even down to details like the allocation of seaweed on the foreshore for manuring the fields. The status of these incomers is made clear in many ways, not least in the inventories in the Testaments they left behind them. Whereas the household goods and clothes of the native inhabitants are often lumped together in a phrase such as 'the insicht and plenishing and the defunct's abulziements' (furnishings, equipment, clothes) and a single value given for all together, those of the Scottish landlords, burgesses, merchants, factors, and ministers include lists of pewter, glass, silver, linen, beds, and so on, with individual valuations.

The effect was a new kind of social dichotomy in the islands, the incomers introducing forms of middle- and upper-class culture that had been little known before. They represented a commercial outlook on a scale that had never been considered previously, and it was out of this class, with education and money, that the entrepreneurs came, the merchant lairds who in the eighteenth and nineteenth centuries developed the fishing and kelp industries, and introduced new commercial breeds of sheep. Though merchant lairds, capable of trading with Scotland, England, Scandinavia, and elsewhere, were later replaced by ordinary merchants, nevertheless their activities had a decisive influence in effecting extensive changes in land-use, housing, equipment, and social organisation.

This period affected Orkney and Shetland equally, but the second period of influence, in the mid-nineteenth century, related mainly to Orkney. It was brought about by a different class of people, farmers, many of them from the North-East of Scotland, who moved to Orkney and rented farms just when draining and liming improvements were beginning to take good effect. These were not upper-class farmers. Socially they were in no way superior to the Orkney farmers amongst whom they settled, but they had a farming tradition of hard work behind them, they had already learned and practised improvement techniques, and they used their experience to tame the Orkney soil for their own benefit. They prospered, and by their example influenced the standards and techniques of farming in Orkney. They have left their mark on the language as well, so that the names of some parts of the byre, and the methods of roping down grain stacks, for example, are North-East Scottish, and no longer Norse, as they are in Shetland. At present Orkney farming is as advanced as anywhere in Scotland, and it may be something of an irony that Orkney farmers, some of them perhaps descendants of the Scottish incomers, have been returning to the North-East and buying large farms there.

There was a saying that the Orkney man is a farmer who fishes, but the Shetlander is a fisherman who uses the land to supplement his livelihood. Nevertheless, the further back in time, the more closely the island groups approximate to each other in these respects, though Orkney has always been more fertile than Shetland, the preferred area of settlement for the Vikings, and a centre of grain production.

During the nineteenth century, agricultural improvements, and especially draining and liming, made possible much successful reclamation in moorland Orcadia, so that the productive acreage increased greatly. In Shetland, on the other hand, the cultivated arable remained mostly confined to the restricted coastal areas where it had been carried on for centuries. Though some attempt was made to cultivate farther into the moorland than before in the sixteenth

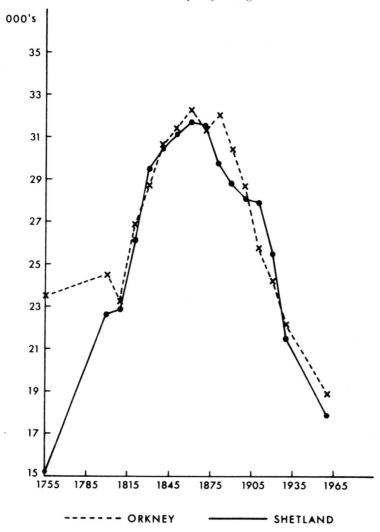

000's

4. Population graph, 1755–1931. After O'Dell 1939. See also Barclay 1965. C5846.

century, the grain yields did not justify the effort,[15] which has not been repeated till this present century, when improvements in grazing – but not directly in arable – have been made by re-seeding moorland areas.

The Northern Isles have a culture with a Norse basis made firm by over 500 years of Norse occupation. Overlying and mingling with this is the overlay of Scottish culture, also at least 500 years old, with a dash of influence from Germany and the Low Countries. Allied to this is the position of the islands, which has made them a maritime cross-roads, where men of many nations met and became acquainted with each other. The term 'isolated' can scarcely be applied. The relative distances of the two island groups from the Scottish

Mainland are responsible, in combination with the different degrees of fertility, for the fact that it is as much the differences as the similarities between the groups that have to be studied. It is the study of such differences – having taken the similarities into account – and of the reasons for the differential rates of change that have produced the present degree of difference, that provides a historical tool for disentangling the story of the life and culture of the Northern Isles.

Farm and Township: Pattern of Settlement

2

The Early Settlement

ACCORDING to *Egils Saga Skalla-Grímssonar*, many men fled from Norway in the time of King Harold Fairhair and settled in many deserted places, amongst which are mentioned the Hebrides, Ireland, Caithness, Orkney and Shetland, and the Faroes.[16] Since the comment can scarcely mean that these places were totally deserted, it must refer to stretches that had not yet been settled. The eventual Norse colonisation of the Northern Isles was so intensive that there is hardly any way of getting back to the immediate pre-Norse, Pictish, period, except by the spade of the archaeologist. If Egils Saga indicates that the first Norsemen came as fugitives who were glad to occupy hitherto unsettled land, then the likelihood increases that they did not seize their land by force of arms. None of the excavated Norse settlements in Scotland – Birsay, Buckquoy, Skaill and Westness in Orkney, Jarlshof and Underhoull in Shetland, the Udal in North Uist, Drimore in South Uist, and Freswick in Caithness[17] – gives any indication of anything other than a peaceful colonisation. There are no destruction layers of burnt or broken materials in the first settlement period, no mangled bodies and bent and broken swords.

Some have thought the colonisation peaceful because the Pictish population of the Isles was not able to make an effective resistance.[18] In a discussion of a small rectangular building at Jarlshof, the suggestion was made that the difference between its construction and that of other Norse outhouses there reflected a pre-Viking building technique. The domestic equipment found in it also showed a mixture of pre-Norse and Norse, and 'it would seem reasonable to suppose that this building housed native serfs.'[19] Here again is the implication that the native population was made subservient to the new Viking masters.

But if the first settlers were fugitives seeking asylum, and if – as is likely – the Norse and the Picts were no strangers to each other before settlement began in the ninth century, then relatively peaceful co-existence, without any special thrall and master relationship, may have been the real state of affairs. In this connection, the Viking farm at Underhoull in Unst was erected on an Iron Age site that had already been deserted for a while. At Jarlshof there is no apparent break in continuity from the Iron Age settlement, but at the Point of Buckquoy in Birsay, Orkney, the Pictish buildings had been abandoned for some time before the site was re-occupied by the Vikings.[20] It is possible that the Vikings were *given permission* to settle on these farms that the native inhabitants had left for some reason. At any rate, the quality of the Pictish house that underlay the Viking farm at Buckquoy shows that the natives included men of status, capable of negotiating with fugitives seeking new homes. Another factor that demonstrates easy integration is the relative lack of specifically Norse material amongst the finds from excavated Norse buildings. This is also true of the Norse settlements in Greenland, and at L'Anse aux Meadows in Newfoundland,[21] where Norse farmsteads dating to around AD 1000 have been excavated.

The Vikings readily adopted native artefacts, no doubt because the material culture of their everyday economy at home was similar. Even the food they ate hardly had to change, and analysis of food debris from the Viking and pre-Viking layers at Buckquoy shows 'that there was no significant difference between the economic life-styles of the Pictish and succeeding Norse home-steads; the proportions of cattle, sheep and pig remained the same, and it is unlikely that shell fish were ever an important item of diet'. In the course of the four centuries before the Vikings came, the native inhabitants were also moving by a gradual process of indigenous development of their building techniques towards a long, rectangular house form similar to the kind the Vikings brought (see pages 113–14 below), and there was parallelism not only in the house-plans, but also in the walling techniques, the use of turf, the long central hearths, and the benches alongside them.[22]

If the people of Buckquoy had the status that the last of their houses indicates, then it is reasonable to assume that they had a working land organisation. Because of factors of functionalism related to similar environments, this need not have been very different from the land organisation in Norway at the same period. This may be one good reason why the intensive Norse colonisation has hidden it so completely – it was almost the same thing. Pre-Norse buildings and artefacts provide few clues, and the main evidence may be the numerous massive dykes, many surviving in part or remembered only through place-names, that seem to have a special status. In a perambulation of the township of Clouston in Stenness in February 1681, the inquest took the declaration of the heritors of the land 'anent the mairches of the uppa balk, beginning at the entrie of the little burne at the loch within the picka dyke, and up throw Quoy Anna following the old balk to the turne of the picka dyke at the grip or little burne of the Fidges, containing nyne faddomes to each two fardings balk'.[23] It is these 'picka' or 'pickie' dykes, that may show a little of the land organisation of the Picts, to whom the adjective given in common speech relates them. There is no doubt that such dykes, which are made of turf with stone footings, are very old. In some cases they are older than the growth of peat. Examples at Birsay run down into peat which may be up to 8 ft (244 cm) deep.[24]

The way in which entire islands are divided into sections by such dykes could be interpreted as having a territorial or 'tribal' function. North Ronaldsay, for example, is traversed by the Matches Dyke and the Muckle Gersty, which split the island into three unequal parts. According to a local legend that appears to reflect the udal system of division of an inheritance, it was a man with three sons who divided the island into three, with one son at Holland, one at Finyerhoose, and one at Breck. The upper and lower divisions are called Northyard and Southyard. Papa Westray is also divided by a dyke into the North Yard and South Yard.[25] In these examples, 'yard' must be a scotticisation of Old Norse *garðr*, Norwegian *gard*, a dyke, so that these dividing dykes were used for orientation in the same way as the township dykes.

It may be assumed that the 'pickie dykes' are amongst the oldest of the numerous dykes in the Northern Isles. The fact that some of them are older than the peat confirms this, but however far they go back, their basically agricultural function must remain. Recent discoveries in Ireland have brought to light both stone enclosure walls and cultivation ridges deep below blanket peat and old pasture land in County Mayo, marking what seems to be a kind of planned enclosure system already in the Neolithic period, about the nineteenth century BC.[26] There is, therefore, nothing inherently impossible in the concept of an organised land economy in the Northern Isles long before the Vikings came.

In the Northern Isles, the term commonly used for old dykes is *gersty* or *gorsty* (Old Norse *garð-staðr*, Norwegian dialectal *gardstøde, gardstad*). Less common and now obsolete is *gerbick* or *gorback* (Old Norse *garðr*, fence + *bálkr*, partition, Norwegian *gardbolk*, a length of dyke). These are undoubted Norse terms. But a third term, confined to Orkney, may have a Celtic origin. The evident age of the dykes naturally supports such a view. This name is *treb*, *treve* or *thrave*, found in the adjacent islands of Westray, North Ronaldsay, Sanday and Stronsay. It is so common in Sanday that the generic term *treb-dyke* has come to be used there. In Blaeuw's map of Orkney for c. 1650 a house called Treb is shown in Sanday, lying on or near one of the dykes. According to a perambulation of the farm of Haghquoy in Stronsay in 1738, the minister Mr John Scollay had built a house on ground 'lying near to the *Treve* which is part of said balk of North Strenzie'. The argument is that *treb* is related to Welsh *tref*, a homestead, Irish *treb, treabh*, place of abode, Gaelic *treabh*, to plough, and that since the land of the Treb farms is usually fertile, they may therefore mark centres of settlement of Pictish times.[27] However, the resemblance to the Celtic words may be no more than a coincidence. The suggestion has been made that *treb* is an extension in sense of Old Norse *þref, þrep*, a loft, ledge, platform, Norwegian *trev*, loft, shelf, *trip*, a step, gap.[28] If this is so, the idea of a Celtic origin, however tempting, and however well it seems to suit the situation, must be discounted or at least held to be not proven.

This interpretation of the first stage of Norse settlement in the Northern Isles points to relatively peaceful integration, involving the use of areas not hitherto settled, or the re-use of farms that had been deserted for some reason. If this is so, then the initial colonisation of the Northern Isles must have differed in some degree from that of the Faroe Islands and Iceland. There, the *landnám* was absolute from the start, for the Celtic monks who had been there since the late eighth century did not 'take land' in the later sense.[29] But the Northern Isles were becoming increasingly familiar with Vikings from south-west Norway in

5. A Viking ship drawn on a piece of slate, found at Jarlshof. It has a mast with a rigging, and a steering oar. In the National Museum, Edinburgh. HSA 790.

particular, and some were already migrating from Agder and Rogaland by the end of the eighth century to find new homes. With them, the integration of Norse and natives was probably well under way as a prelude to the main migration period in the ninth century. As far as Shetland and Orkney are concerned, the settlers were probably farmers of a similar social level to the natives, moving out because of overpopulation and pressure on land, which helps further to explain how little impression the colonisation has left in tradition or printed sources. The likelihood is that the Norsemen, coming from a comparable environment and social milieu, were able to slot into a farming system like the one they knew at home, with cattle and sheep, a little grain-growing, and access to sea birds, seals and whales. It was not difficult, therefore, for the Norse colonisation to have a blanketing effect on the foregoing culture,[30] and to absorb it.

How the colonisation proceeded after these early days is not clear. In Iceland, it can be seen from the *Landnámabók* that the 400 or so primary settlers can be divided into three groups: the first arrivals, who took possession of considerable areas, using a ritual of going round the land with fire to make the seal of ownership; men who got land within these possessions with the

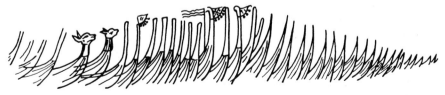

6. The prows of a Viking fleet, from a wood-carving found at Bergen. After Foote and Wilson 1970. 233.

consent of the owners; and men who got land as a gift, or who bought it or acquired it through fighting.[31] The situation in the Faroe Islands was no doubt the same, but in Orkney and Shetland, the first stage may well have been the peaceful occupation of farms – as at Underhoull and Buckquoy – with the consent of the native population. The second stage may have been grimmer for the islanders, as the Norse came in increasing numbers. This is the view of the late twelfth century *Historia Norvegiae*, which tells that relations of the mighty chieftain Rognvald, who crossed the sea from Norway, ejected the natives from their homes, exterminated them, and took the islands for themselves.[32] The hiding of a native chieftain's considerable and highly civilised treasure under the floor of the church in St Ninian's Isle in Shetland is a sure sign of troubled times,[33] when raiding and plundering was part of the Viking way of life. Even Norway herself was subject to Viking attacks, from the Northern Isles and elsewhere, in the late ninth century. Truth, as always, is relative. There were here no absolutes. Periods of peacefulness sufficient for the needs of the farming year no doubt alternated with raiding, with attack and defence, but the important point is that the Northern Isles came out as Norse to such an extent that 99 per cent of all place names there are Scandinavian.[34]

There are other factors that point to a state of relatively peaceful co-existence, at least for much of the time. Of the 400 settlers in Iceland named in the *Landnámabók*, 130 are said to have come from Norway and 50 from the British Isles (usually the Hebrides or Ireland). Many of the others may also have come from Norway via Britain, moving from there especially after being defeated in Wessex and Mercia, and thrown out of Dublin in 902. At the same time they were being hard pressed in the Hebrides and Scotland. There is, however, an undoubted element of Celtic intermixture in Iceland, though it left only a small number of loan words and a few personal names and place names, such as Bekansstaðir and Brjanslœkr, commemorating the Irish personal names Beccan and Brian.[35] A proportion of these Celts must surely have come from the Northern Isles. Even anthropological facts are relevant, for the cranium indices of Viking Age Icelanders are said to agree closely with bone finds from Ireland and Scotland. The distribution of bloodgroups in the population of modern Iceland is also closer to that of the Irish and Scots than of modern Norsemen. Though there are references to Irish and Scottish slaves, these are relatively few, perhaps too few to justify an old insinuation that the Icelanders derived from slaves and bandits.[36] Probably many Celts, and people of mixed Norse and Celtic parentage, were numbered amongst the followers of the 400 settlers of the *Landnámabók*, and were of a status above or even well above that of slave, but not high enough for them, whether Norse or Celt, to deserve specific mention in the sources.

Another point of potential linkage, as yet not extensively studied, is the fact that some Icelandic place names have their counterparts in the Hebrides. One group of names in a small area of Lewis recurs in another small area near Reykjavík, stated in *Landnámabók* to have been settled by people who came at least in part from the Hebrides. It is quite possible that these names were first brought from Norway to the Western Isles, and thence to Iceland. Such parallels can also be found in Shetland and the Faroe Islands – for example the Faroese names Kaldbak, Kollafjørður, Lorvík, Hvalvík, Viðvík, Mjóvanes, Streymnes, Saltnes, Kallanes, Mykines, í Kirkjubø, correspond to Shetland Calbak, Collafirth, Lerwick, Hwalek, Widwick, Mjoness, Stromness, Saltness, Kalliness, Migeness, Kjorkabi. There is also a Kollafjørður in Iceland. Mykines looks like a naming after some place in Norway. Here too, there appear to be compound names brought to the Faroes and Iceland directly or via the Northern Isles or other parts of Scotland.[37]

All this gives a picture of what might well be regarded as one widespread northern community, within which, in spite of the seasonal relaxations of raiding and plundering, people and families could move from one place to another, making new settlements or taking over old ones, carrying with them the names of places for which they may have sometimes been homesick. Within this community the Northern Isles had their own part to play.

3

Consolidation of Settlement

THE possession of a ship, or ships, was alone a mark of standing. A ship was both a symbol of power and wealth, and a means of transport. Though ships were known and used long before the Viking era, it was the eighth century development of the sail that gave easier means to the migrations. The earliest known sailing boat, excavated at Äskekärr near Göteborg in Sweden, is radio-carbon dated to AD 830±75 (AD 755–905). The Gokstad ship from Norway, of which a replica sailed the Atlantic between 30 April and 27 May 1893, dates to AD 850–900. Its light, flexible hull, built of strakes that were first nailed together and then lashed with pliable spruce roots to the frame, gave such elasticity that the gunwale could twist up to 15 cm (6 in.) out of true, whilst the ship remained watertight. It was 23·3 m (76 ft 6 in.) long × 5·25 m (17 ft 3 in.) wide amidships, and could carry a load of about 18 tons. The crew numbered up to 70.[38] The sheer size of the Viking ships must have been a matter of marvel and terror when they appeared.

The Orkneyinga Saga contains a good deal of information about the ships that were sailing around the Northern Isles. About 1046, Earl Rognvald with 30 large ships was opposed in the Pentland Firth by Earl Thorfinn with 60 ships, most of which were small. Eighty dead men were carried ashore from one ship. In 1046–7, Thorfinn sailed from Orkney to Norway with two twenty-oared ships, and over 100 men. Valthjof Olafsson and nine others were drowned in Stronsay Firth when coming in a ten-oared boat to Earl Paul's Yule feast in his great hall at Orphir, in 1135. When Uni sailed to Fair Isle with three Shet-landers in 1136 with some stores and fishing tackle, he did so in a six-oared boat. A merchant ship with 30 men was mentioned in 1136, and another from Orkney had a crew of 10 when it was at Banff about 1143–8. Sweyn Asleyfsson of Gairsay collected his rents with three other men in an eight-oared boat in 1151.[39] The variety, therefore, was considerable.

From Skuldelev at Roskilde in Denmark come five sunken Viking ships, now undergoing conservation in the Viking Ship Museum at Roskilde. These include two cargo vessels, 16·5 m (54 ft) and 13·5 m (44 ft 4 in.) long, and one with a rounded bottom, about 12 m (39 ft 5 in.) long, which may have been a fishing boat for net-fishing, or a ferry for short distance transport of passengers and goods. Their length to beam ratio was approximately 4:1. The remaining two, with a ratio of about 6 or 7:1, were warships, one 28 m (92 ft) long and capable of taking 50 to 60 warriors, the other 18 m (59 ft) long. All had been fitted with masts. Radio-carbon dating puts them to a period between AD 900 and 1100, the more precise bracket probably being AD 950 to 1050.[40]

It is hardly necessary to spell it out that a single ship of any of these types required several men in the crew, so that the requirements of a one-ship group could be considerable in terms of accommodation and land. For this reason alone, too much should not be made of the concept of plain farmers settling quietly, even if this did happen sometimes, for even a single ship's load was a force to be reckoned with, with a skipper capable of directing it both on sea and on land. The men who came in their ships, with goods and gear and families, lesser kinsmen, servants and dependants, were leaders, of some wealth and substance, capable of organising their groups on land in a way that was beyond the capabilities of most plain farmers. As in Iceland, the names *agætr* and *göfugr* were applied to such men, showing that they had the status of chieftains, even if they were not necessarily of ancient family. They also had the name *bóndi*, proprietor of farming land (though the term was later restricted to the lowest land-owning class). Such a chieftain was Sweyn Asleifsson of Gairsay, who had the greatest drinking hall in Orkney, kept a retinue of 80 men with arms, went around the islands in a boat collecting his rents, and on his own land sowed a great deal of seed, doing much of the work himself.[41] These were the men who shaped and consolidated the settlement pattern of the Northern Isles, who from their manor farms or *heid-bules* ran their udal estates not as single-family farms but as multiple-family farms or groups of multiple farms of patriarchal type.

The fact that the Northern Isles were inhabited before the Norse came must have dictated a pattern of settlement adapted in some degree to existing local conditions. The earliest settlers might have occupied single farms, as the evidence of Underhoull and Buckquoy may suggest. The number that a ship could contain probably implies that they were more than unorganised refugees, but even if they were, the situation must have changed rapidly when immigration reached full flood.

What happened in the Northern Isles may be guessed at from what happened in the almost empty lands of Iceland and the Faroes. There, the Viking leaders, with their boat-loads of followers and servants and slaves, took over large areas of land for themselves. They organised its settlement, allocating units to their followers and associates in such a way that the basic needs were observed of access to the sea, land for crops, and grazing for animals. An examination of settlement areas that are environmentally suitable in these terms in Shetland and the Faroes has shown, on the basis of excavated sites and saga evidence, that this was primarily where the farms stood, even though the seven farms named in the Faereyinga Saga, for example, are difficult to reach by sea, and a Viking farm at Seyrvágur stands high on the steep slopes.[42]

Though the Vikings were farmers, they probably liked the rough side of farm-work no more than anyone else, leaving it in part to their servants and slaves. In the Norse poem, the Rígsþula, the different castes of early society, the slaves, the farmers, and the warriors (þræll, Karl, and Jarl), are outlined. The thralls were dirty, they did the rough work, building dykes, spreading dung, seeing to the swine and goats, digging peat. The farmers did joinery work and drove the plough, whilst their wives had a cloth on the table and saw to the weaving. But the warrior class did no work. They were the planners.[43] It is not known where the *Rígspula* was composed, but – allowing for the flattery of a poet who was singing for his supper in warriors' halls – the attitude of the times to work of different types comes through clearly. It is also worthy of note that a slave who was given a certain element of freedom, but without the full official status of freed man, was called *grefleysingi*, interpreted as 'one freed from digging', or one who was allowed to carry a mattock as a weapon.[44] Either way, there is the association of these lowliest people with the task of tilling the soil with hand tools, and it is likely that much of the first breaking in of land at new settlements, and later reclamation, was done by means of slaves. The Northern Isles were already partly under cultivation, but it can scarcely be doubted that the native population was pressed into service for carrying on, for and alongside the incomers, the basic tasks of digging or ploughing and harvesting, and above all fishing, in which context the Norn language – the form that Norse developed in these islands – survived for long in a relatively pure form.[45] It is hard to say whether the use of slaves was as usual in the Northern Isles as it evidently was in all the Scandinavian countries, as well as Finland and Estonia, for there is little or no reference to thralls in the *Orkneyinga Saga*.

In the early stages, therefore, the settlement pattern of the Northern Isles, and possibly also the social stratification, differed to some extent from that of the Faroes and Iceland. It is even possible, though it is not easy to prove, that the Pictish land divisions, perhaps the areas demarcated by the old 'pickie' dykes, became the basis for the Scandinavian fiscal units known as *eyrislands* or ouncelands.[46] This is not inherently impossible, if the methods of land-use were comparable, and if the very beginnings of colonisation were reasonably gradual.

If there were differences at the beginning, they were soon ironed out within the freemasonry of the Viking world, though for a time only, for the influence of the Scottish Mainland was real and strong. Already by 1261 King Alexander III of Scotland had raised with King Haakon IV of Norway the question of ceding the Western Isles to the Scots – an idea that became fact in 1266, by the Treaty of Perth that followed the Battle of Largs in 1263. The negotiations were in part conducted from Orkney.[47] Even before that date Orkney earls were intermarrying with those from Scotland. The father of Harald Maddadson, who in 1139 at the age of 5 became ruler of half the Orkney earldom, was the son of Matad, Earl of Atholl. Harald's first wife was the daughter of Earl Duncan of Fife, his second the daughter of Malcolm MacHeth who held the earldom of Ross. The direct line of Norse earls is usually taken to have ended with the death of his son, Earl John, in 1231, when the earldom passed to Magnus, a son of the Earl of Angus, but in fact the male line of Norse earls had more or less died out with Earl Rognvald already in 1158. Scottish influence was strong at the top levels, long before the period when the islands became to all intents and purposes part of Scotland. This factor, too, must be borne in mind when considering the form of land organisation.

In looking at the consolidation of the settlement pattern, therefore, the main factors are the pre-existence of a Pictish pattern, the superimposition of the Norwegian pattern, and influence from Scotland. It is not possible to get at the precise details of the consolidation, but a generalised picture can be worked out on the analogy of other areas, especially Iceland and the Faroe Islands.

The Orkneyinga Saga tells a great deal about the Northern Isles. The Norse earls, the leading men of the time, had their drinking halls, at Orphir, in Gairsay, and elsewhere, and those who wished to make a name for themselves in their life-time through great hospitality as well as great feats of arms and daring might, like Earl Thorfinn, entertain their bodyguards and men of rank with meat and ale all winter through, so that there was no need to go to the ale-house, emulating and outdoing the Yule feasts provided by kings and earls in other countries. Orkney could not always provide fully for such top-class subsistence, so that about 1046 Thorfinn had to get provisions for his own use from Caithness. The spoils of spring and autumn raiding in the Hebrides and farther afield gave a necessary base for such conspicuous consumption, but these leaders of society also had to have an internal organisation for the conversion of the land's produce. If they overdid their raiding and warfaring, the land suffered. When Earl Einar, who had two-thirds of Orkney, wanted to impose a levy around 1016–18 to keep six ships at sea, this was considered too oppressive by the farmers, who had to find men, and food to keep them, so Einar had to agree to three ships only. Too much service on board ship irked the farmers, and a large levy for summer raiding could lead to a bad harvest because few hands were left behind for cutting and leading the corn. Einar's brother Brusi, on the other hand, was a peaceful man with no lust for raiding. The farmers on this one-third share of Orkney prospered and their harvest was fine.[48] As in later times, the activities of the leading men had a strong effect on the land.

The land itself was held according to the udal form of tenure. About the year 894, when King Harald Fairhair laid a tax of 60 gold marks on Orkney, Earl Torf-Einar offered to pay it on behalf of his fellow Orcadians if they made over their udal rights to him. They agreed, fatalistically, for the rich farmers thought they could buy back their rights, and the poor ones had no money to pay anyway. These udal rights constituted a form of freehold tenure, according to which inherited land was held in absolute ownership, with no superior of any kind. Nevertheless the Orkneyinga Saga shows some ambivalence in the system. From the time of Torf-Einar, the Earls are said to have held the udal rights, until about the year 995 when Earl Sigurd gave them back to the Orkney men in return for war service. Yet it is also said that King Harald Fairhair had taken all the udal rights in Orkney – so that by implication those who were already settled there regarded themselves as absolute owners – and that the Earls had since held the land from him *i lén*, in fief, in a kind of non-heritable feudal tenure of a piece of land or of the income from it, but never in absolute ownership, which is an essential part of udal tenure.

A century and a half later, in 1137, when the expense of building St Magnus cathedral was proving excessive, Earl Rognvald was advised by his father Kol 'to bring in a law to the effect that Earls had in the past inherited all of the udal lands from their owners, but the heirs might redeem them'. This proposal was considered too hard, so Rognvald summoned a court (Thing), where he told the farming proprietors to buy the udal lands outright, so that there would be no need for the heirs to redeem them. They agreed, but the condition was that 1 mark should be paid to the Earl for every ploughland, *plógsland*, throughout the Isles. In this way money enough was got for the church. It appears from this that udal proprietors formerly had to buy themselves in again at the entry of each heir. Such payment of relief at entry does not sound like outright udal ownership.[49]

Whatever the accuracy of these details in the Saga, the fact remains that the udal form of tenure was not absolute. Here and there a decidedly feudal impression is given, and in terms of the organisation of land for production and taxation, the differences between the two forms of land-holding were not very great.

The special features of udal tenure were the holding of land in absolute ownership without a superior, and the system of inheritance whereby an udal property was divided on the proprietor's death between his legitimate children or their successors, daughters' shares being half those of sons. The eldest son was entitled to the heid-bule or main house, or had first choice of the available lots of land. Udal property could be sold, but could then be redeemed within a prescribed period by the relatives of the vendor, as heirs of the antecedent proprietor. It was subject to the payment of the land-tax known as *skatt* to the Crown or its representative (skatt is said not to be the same as feu-duty), and of ecclesiastical teind.[50]

Inheritance and kinship had a primary part to play in udal tenure. According to the older Norse laws, udal rights were acquired by undisturbed possession of a piece of land for three to five generations, after which the rights were transmitted by hereditary descent. Because of this time qualification, it has been argued that the existence of udal tenure in Orkney in the time of Harald Fairhair showed that Orkney had been settled for several generations before Fairhair's time. It might equally well be argued that the settlers simply took it for granted that their rights to the new land they occupied were of a udal nature, and carried on from where they had left off in Norway. It is even possible that an allodial system preceded the arrival of the Vikings, for many authorities on the law assume that the feudal system in Scotland was preceded by an allodial system.[51] This again would have made it easy for the Norsemen to carry on their own system in the Northern Isles.

Udal tenure meant that the land was held in units of individual ownership, as a rule consisting of farm groups to which the relatively modern name 'township' may be applied. The formation of such farm groups is an almost inevitable result of the udal division of an inheritance among the members of a family. At the present day, the result of such division is best seen in the Faroe Islands, where fragmentation of units can be extreme. One farmer in the island of Sandur, for example, held nearly a hundred small patches of land scattered over the township area in 1908.[52]

It is likely that the multiple farms or townships were in origin single farms that later split up, partly because of division of the inheritance, partly because the leaders gave units of their own land to kinsmen and associates, and partly through the growth in size of the original families. At the time of an initial settlement, the number of folk who could arrive in one or two boat-loads might have led to the almost immediate appearance of multiple-farm settlements, as has been postulated for the Faroe Islands.[53] Jarlshof gives one indication of a possible course of events, for the expansion of the Viking settlement can be followed from its establishment in the first half of the ninth century until the beginning of the eleventh century. The original dwelling-house stood by itself, with separate outhouses for the animals. Then, 'the parent dwelling which continued to play a dominant role underwent expansion, a byre being added to the living quarters. The secondary farmsteads lying at right angles down the slope were either abandoned or converted to outhouses. At the same time as the parent house drew around it the outbuildings from which it was previously separated, the yard area to the west was given over to new buildings. Here, on the foundations of the old outhouses, new dwellings were erected. Though these dwellings are smaller, they are of the same rectangular type as those abandoned, but differ from the latter in being sited in close proximity to one another without intervening yard-walls'. The buildings gradually expanded to incorporate store rooms and byres. As further farmsteads were added, a pattern of close-knit settlement appeared, similar to multiple farm groupings at Birsay in Orkney and at Freswick in Caithness.[54]

This tight clustering, which in a Viking context is said to be peculiarly Scottish,[55] is significant in terms of the early settlement techniques. In the Faroe Islands, the building ground was one of the three primary elements of a village settlement, along with a landing place for boats, and cultivable ground. It was called *skattegrund*, *heimrustir*, or, in the island of Sandoy, *rustari*, defined as an open area in a settlement reserved as building ground for houses or outhouses, as well as grazing for heifers kept around the houses. Another Faroese name, *ruddstaður*, 'cleared place', emphasises that this was originally a cleared area – possibly the first part to be cleared or levelled off in the settlement process. It also played a part in tax assessment at one time, as the term *skattegrund* shows. In Shetland the name is found as *hamerest*, common pasturage or hill pasture adjoining enclosed land or a farm, which corresponds in sense to Norwegian dialectal *heimrast*. The Icelandic equivalent, *heim-röst*, can mean a lane leading up to houses, or a homestead.[56] It is in this nub of the settlement, with associated grazing for the household animals, that the multiple farm clusters developed.

The special characteristics of this nuclear area are further emphasised by the

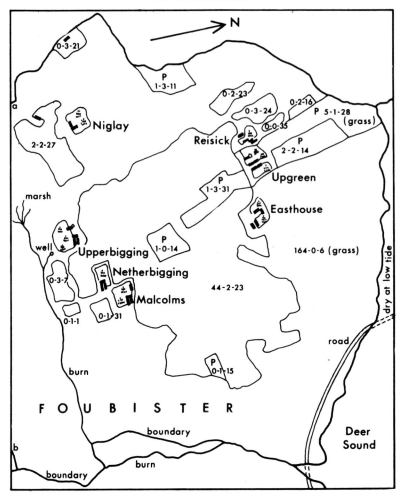

7. Foubister, Orkney, in 1766 to 1769, showing arable areas, houses and
yards with stacks, tounmals and grazing areas. P=planked areas. After Clouston
1932. 351, from a William Aberdeen Estate Plan. C5843.

tounmal, from Old Norse *tún-vǫllr*, 'a strip of the infield'.[57] The second element
means 'field'. The tounmal was held in continuity by the tenant, or might
sometimes be shared between two, especially if they were related, but it was
never shared with all the tenants in the same way as the other land – the
tounland – in a township. It lay outside the communal runrig system, hard by or
around the houses.

There was a difference between Orkney and Shetland tounmals. In Orkney,
it was the best piece of infield land, continuously cultivated and heavily
manured in the manner of a garden. Because bere was grown on the best land,
the Orkney tounmals were cropped with bere, and paid tax in bere. The

Balance Sheet of the Elsness Estate in Sanday shows that in 1721, the 'Cottar Tounmal of hetle' paid 2 meils of bere a year, the 'tounmal of Istagarth' 1 meil of malt and 2 meils of bere, and the 'Cottar tounmal of Crouana' 4 meils. A meil of bere amounted to approximately $3\frac{1}{3}$ imperial bushels. The firmness of the tradition that the tounmal was the best land in Orkney is emphasised by a division of the township of Inner Stromness in 1624, when six tounmals were ordained, one for every sixpenny land, all near named houses. All but half a tounmal lay amongst the best of the old arable land in the township.[58]

In Shetland, however, the tounmal was a piece of grazing or rough land, never dug up, used for such purposes as tethering horses that were wanted for immediate use. Where farms lay close together, or side by side, the tounmals could be together in a continuous strip. This was so for the farms of Thoft, Nurgie, and Sutherhouse in the township of Funzie in Fetlar, and the tounmal of Stentaft lay only a short distance away. A fifth farm, Gardie, was a secondary creation outside the township dyke, and its tounmal was separate from the others. In contrast to Orkney, the Shetland tounmals did not pay tax.[59]

It is not easy to say whether or not the difference in the nature of the tounmal in Orkney and Shetland indicates original differences in the character of the settlement. Probably the superior quality of Orkney soil led to a situation whereby the field near the houses became so well fertilised with the droppings of stock grazed on the tether that it was natural to break it in for cultivation.

The same kind of progression is implicit in the equation of tounmal and *hill balk* in a perambulation of the township of Paplay in South Ronaldsay in 1677, though elsewhere in Orkney the hill balks were usually strips or patches of waste or rough pasture above the arable.[60] The hill balk, frequently referred to in Orkney records, appears to equate in part with the Faroese *heimrustir*, for it was an area on which houses could be built. In Paplay, all the houses were sited there, but this was exceptional, and more often balks began or ended at points where houses had been built. A 'balk for bigging houses on' is mentioned in 1626, and in the seventeenth century, balks were actually bought for house-building. Even if houses on balks are secondary to the first settlement, nevertheless it is likely that they repeat some of the characteristics of the first settlement in their analogies with the hamerest and tounmal.[61]

In seventeenth-century Orkney, tounmals had ceased to be sacrosanct to individuals and they could sometimes be brought into the general runrig system of a township, for a time at least. In 1642, Uray was divided, 'alsweill *tounland* as *towmale land*, being maid all *tounland*'. In 1677, a tounmal at Paplay had been in runrig for some time. The same happened with hill-balks, though it is not suggested that these were originally in individual ownership in the same way as tounmals. Indeed, the use of them could rotate between farms. At Clouston in Stenness, there were in 1681 six balks or heather strips stretched end to end round three sides of the township, between the upper houses and the 'picka' dyke. Each balk was divided into two sections by a cross division, and each section in turn split into a series of small balks which were given to the various farms in rotation.[62]

The tight clustering and the relatively restricted yard space of the Jarlshof farms may have been due to an unwillingness to build on good, cultivable land, and the use of hill balks for secondary house sites seems to be part of the same line of thought. There were, however, limits to the tightness of the packing, and the time came when new settlement sites began to appear as offshoots from the parent one. It is wrong to try to express the dynamics of settlement expansion in too simple terms, for changes and adaptations of several kinds went on simultaneously. Whether Jarlshof is typical or not, nevertheless it seems to reflect a general truth, that the communal housekeeping and farming of the first settlers gradually gave way to individual housekeeping combined with communal farming, as numbers increased. The same increase led concurrently to a growth in the number of farms, and to a spread of settlement through the migration to neighbouring areas of those who were being crowded out, or who had been given units of land by the chieftain.

The parent farmhouse at Jarlshof was probably a heid-bule, the main farm in a unit of settlement, to which the eldest son had the right under udal succession. At a court held in Shetland in 1602, support was given to the claim of Jhone Murray and his son that the 'sax merk land of Gruting wes thair heid buile and could nocht be giftit nor disponit fra the principall air'. This was repeated in 1603.[63] In 1576, it was noted that according to the use and custom of Shetland, when a man or woman died who had land, goods or gear to be divided amongst the heirs, the underfoud or bailie of the parish or island came, along with a number of honest neighbours, 'to the principall houss quhair the persoun deceissit, callit the Heidbull', to divide the inheritance. This inquest was called a 'scheind'.[64]

Heid-bule is a direct translation of Norwegian *họfuðból, –bæli*, the head farm on which the udal owner lived, and which always went to the eldest son. Equivalent terms in Denmark, Sweden and Finland are translated into Latin as *mansio, curia, curia principalis* or *-residentalis, villa, manerium*. Early Swedish also had the term *bo* (or *bol* for smaller places). Whatever their origins, these became the noblemen's seats, but in Norway and in Iceland, as well as in the Northern Isles of Scotland, they remained at a more modest level.[65]

In Orkney, *bule* (Old Norse *ból*) was a general term for a homestead, like the 'bull of Skaile', referred to in 1502, and the principal dwelling of an udal estate was the heid-bule, or *heyd chymys*, a Scottish word of French origin also used in Orkney documents. The late sixteenth century sources all bring into emphasis the central part played by the heid-bule in a system of udal inheritance.[66] In the Orkneyinga Saga, thirty *bows* are explicitly or implicitly mentioned. Twenty of these were in Orkney, the rest in Caithness, Sutherland, and Shetland (Fair Isle), surviving in place names like the Bu of Hoy and the Bu of Orphir.

A distinction has to be made between such heid-bules, and the bu which was the manorial farm of an earl or chief, with its dwelling house and land. One authority says the word is from Old Norse *bú*, a farmstead, estate, and that the form *bule* or some variant with *-l* is a false anglicisation, on the analogy of 'pu'' for 'pull', 'fu'' for 'full', etc. In Iceland, *bú* has the sense of a household, the stock of a farmstead, an estate. There is a notion of property and produce in it, and here, as in Norway, the sense of 'home-farm' is also implicit. In Sweden, *bo* (the East Norse form) was used of a manor-house or farm with administrative responsibilities, and in place names sometimes has the sense of bailiwick. In Norway it can form part of the name of a jurisdictional district, a *härad*.[67] The word, therefore, involves the concept of control and administration, which also applies to the earldom bus in Orkney.

But this is only part of the story. Bule can equally well derive from West Norse *ból*, East Norse *bol*. In Norway, though rare in farm-names, it usually means a dwelling-place, farm, and this is in keeping with the sense of heid-bule in Orkney. It is relatively common in the names of farms and small settlements in Denmark, often referring in the Middle Ages to a group of farms within a farming village, the land of which was gathered into a block.[68]

An extension of this word is West Norse *bólstaðr*, Middle Danish *bolsted*, Norwegian dialectal *bolstad* (*ból* + *staðr*, place, 'stead'). Though its precise sense is not clear, it has been thought to have in Western Norway the same significance as the medieval Danish *bol*.[69] It is common in Western Norway as a place name element, and was so fertile over a long period in the Northern Isles as well as in the Hebrides and the North and West Mainland of Scotland, probably from the time of the original setting down of farmsteads, that 'one can fairly and without exaggeration state that a distribution map of names containing *bólstaðr* . . . is the map of Norse settlement in the Northern and Western Isles and on the adjacent mainland when such settlement was at its most extensive and Norse power at its height'. It is represented by the element -*bist*, -*bust*, -*bister*, or -*buster* in present-day names.[70] There is little difficulty in seeing it simply as a common noun, scilicet the 'farm-place', which became a proper name by prefixing a descriptive element. This need not make such names secondary to those with personal names as the first element, for in an udal farming context, where the family rather than the individual was important, it would be natural to prefer descriptive names.

In the *bólstaðr* compound, *staðr* is used in the singular; but its plural form, *staðir*, has also given rise to numerous place names. In Shetland it results in the -*sta* ending, as in Gunnista, Sotersta, Wethersta. In Orkney it can be disguised as -*ston*, from the dative plural *stǫðum*, as in Herston, Grimeston, Tormiston, though the -*sta* ending is also found, for example Costa, Gangsta. Because there are many such names in Norway, and because there is no linguistic reason against it, -*staðir* names could have been used immediately by the first settlers and can be equal in age to the *bólstaðr* farms.[71] However, there is a good case for thinking that they do not belong to the primary settlement phase. Both in Norway and in Iceland, they are usually compounded with a personal name, and tend to lie in the secondary or peripheral parts of their districts. The same seems to be true of Orkney, where not only are they rare in the very fertile islands of Sanday, Stronsay, Westray and Shapinsay, where early settlement took place, but also in the Mainland, to which they are largely confined, they have an inland rather than a coastal distribution. There is a concentration of them between the Lochs of Harray and Stenness, and one historian, noting that they were sited between two of the main bus in Orkney (at Birsay and Orphir), has thought that they originate in land given as udal land or in *veizla*, in fief, to followers of the families associated with these bus. Veizla was a gift of an estate, with its rents, on a non-hereditary basis.[72] But since this area of Orkney was the longest surviving stronghold of the udallers in Orkney, it is simpler to think in terms of udal land from the start, even if the giving of it was at first on a semi-feudal basis, of such a kind that it allowed the use of the occupants' personal names in a way that was not otherwise common. This alone points to a close link with the nearby bus, just as the plural form of the name may indicate the giving of the land in small farm-groups rather than as single farms. As in Norway, where farms with names in *-staðir* and *-heimr* (home) already indicate the progress of inner expansion in pre-Viking times, usually marking newly reclaimed areas that were offshoots from the first centres,[73] so the tradition seems to have continued in Orkney.

The dependence of such secondary settlements on the bus helps to emphasise an important point in the early Viking society – that it was highly aristocratic in its organisation. The nature of the bus shows this clearly, though by the time documentary evidence begins to be available about them, so many changes had taken place, as in all the Scandinavian countries, that it is not easy to get back to the early situation. Certain features can be identified. The bus were large, extending to a half or whole *urisland*, and were not affected by udal division. Some of them had a number of small, attached farms which they kept in their own hands, and did not lease separately, to provide a reservoir for labour services, especially during harvest and at the peat-cutting season. The same thing happened in Sweden, where manor farms were served with day-labour by small-scale farmers settled on the poorer land around them. The Bu of Skaill, for example, consisting of half an urisland, had twenty farms of various qualities attached to it, including eleven small *quoyland* farms, from which such a labour reserve could come.[74]

A further feature of the old earldom lands was that part of them paid no skatt. A rental made at the 'bull' of Hoy in 1503 noted 'That all the Ile of Hoy is of the ald erldome & bordland quhilk payit nevir scat'.[75] *Bordland*, a term used generally in Scotland, appears to have the sense of land that provided supplies for the lord's table or 'board',[76] something like the home farm or mains farm on an estate. The special nature of such land is also indicated by the fact that in the endowing of bishopric lands, an earldom bu and its bordlands were frequently excluded. There were, therefore, two types of earldom land: the unskatted bordland, with great internal stability, and the old earldom land, which was skatted and could be more easily alienated.[77] The bordland may be considered a form of aristocratic tounmal, directly geared to the household subsistence of the earl or chief; the other earldom lands had the duty of supporting the earl and his men as they moved around. The bordlands, therefore, must have formed a basic part of the central core around which the early settlement pattern grew.

The picture is becoming clearer. The noble earl set up his pattern for living, with a decent mansion house, and land to keep his domestic pot boiling. This can be reckoned as a single farm unit, unaffected by division due to udal inheritance. Alongside such farms, and indeed an essential part of their operating, were the udal farms, and there were also farm units kept in the hands of the earl for men who provided labour for the bus. These men were tenants, not udal proprietors. It has been said with some justice that in the twelfth century the bus were in a state of transition, half-way between life fiefs and family's udal property – which they eventually became.[78] The mixture of tenantry and udal proprietors is part of the same phenomenon.

On this basis, settlement could expand in two main ways around the fixed core, by a natural spread due to population growth and the functioning of a farm, especially where large families, including daughters, were involved. Amongst place name elements that indicate spread through functioning are *quoy* and *-setter*. *Quoy* (Old Norse *kví*, Norwegian *kvi*, a fold, animal enclosure) was used of an enclosure where animals were gathered, overnight, for milking, and so on, and can be a first or second element in place names: Quoyangry, the duplicative Quoyfaulds, Quoyloo, Beaquoy, etc. Sometimes a quoy-farm might be found within the dykes of a township, in which case it reflects a pre-township expansion phase, but usually they are outside the dykes, and no doubt developed on places where the soil had become enriched by animal droppings. The farms of Stedaquoy, Cumlaquoy, Quackquoy and Leequoy, for example, form a fringe on the slopes of Marwick Head, on the outskirts of the bigger farms of Langskaill and Netherskaill in Marwick township, Birsay. In the early rentals, quoyland is used of land not subject to skatt, and as a rule quoy-farms were untaxed. Those that were, however, had evidently been taken in at an early date, as early extensions of the older settlements. Some of these were quite large, like the 24[d] land of Southerquoy to the south and west of Skaill loch, and Tuquoy in Westray.[79]

Nowadays quoy, as a noun meaning a stock-enclosure, is obsolescent, if not obsolete, but it is undoubtedly 'the longest-lived and latest-used of Norse farm-name elements in Orkney'. It can be compounded with Scots as well as Norse names. In Shetland, it is much less common; 47 examples have been counted as against 160 in Orkney. The usual Shetland equivalent is *pund* (pound), of which the place name Stourapund (big pound) provides a sixteenth-century example. It has been noted that Shetland quoys are generally nearer the parent settlement than punds.[80] Here, as in so many other points, there is a difference between Orkney and Shetland.

The extent of quoyland in Orkney, and its frequency in the rentals, pinpoints the importance of this means of extending the cultivable acreage. Other terms were in use too. In 1595, a definition was given in a Rental: 'Ane Quoy Land or Outbrek is ane peece of land newly win without the dykis, and payis no scatt'.[81] The word outbreak is equated here with quoyland. There was a rig of outbreak called the 'ryg of the gait' (path) at Thurrigair in South Ronaldsay in 1509.[82] In 1536, the tenants who laboured the lands of Weyland, Grain, Hatston, Yarsay and Saverock were granted the right to dig peat and turf for their own use 'et cum potestate illis agrum sibi proximum frangiendi (id est) to mak outbrekes on their awin bakes haudque aliter'.[83] Similarly, in 1597, Williame Mairteine, bailie in Kirkwall, got 4 marks of udal land in Hobbister, Orphir, with 'power to mak outbrekis, to ryve out corne land and girse, and to alter, flit, and remufe dyikis, quoyis, and fauldis from ane part to ane wther within the propper boundis of the saidis landis'.[84] Here something of the working of a piece of land whose arable content was being expanded by reclamation, can be clearly seen. Once broken in, outbreaks paid taxes and teinds and could be allocated in rigs just like any other arable.[85]

Other Orkney terms with similar senses are *outcast*, and *owtchist*, which may be an irregular or erroneous form of *outcast*. *Out-teling* (tilling) appears to be similar and in a reference dated 1565–6, teinds were paid for such pieces of land in proportion to the amount of 'inlands' that was held.[86] A term used in Shetland as well as in Orkney, and certainly brought in from Scotland, is *outset*, recorded from 1600 in the Northern Isles.[87] It goes with a mainly eighteenth century expansion phase (see page 55ff.).

Whereas such names show expansion of the settlement mainly as a result of farming needs, the word *outland* is more closely related to the system of inheritance. It is defined as land held in addition, but lying outside the principal holding or heid-bule. Under udal tenure, the heid-bule passed to the eldest son, and if there was a daughter, her share of the land had to be taken in the form of outlying pieces, so as not to break up the possession. This is what lies behind a decree of a court held in Harray in 1578, when Margret Cargell was found to have got her lawful share in land and movables, at her father's death, and that her brother William had bought out her share. Margret Cargell's heirs, her son and daughter, made a claim as they were entitled to do under udal law, but the purchase was sustained, and the heirs were not allowed to try to reclaim the land in the future, 'becaues the said land lay under the haid bwile or Howis, and thair wes na owtlandis to outred (pay off) the sister, except the wit off the cuntre brak the samin'.[88] That is to say, the only way Margret Cargell's male heir could have got a share of land was by the splitting up of the principal farm. A daughter could only claim a share of the outlands, and if there were none, as here, she had to be content with movables, and money in lieu of land.

Where outlands were available, daughters could take them, and a new centre could be established in this way through the female line. Even though the farm units or 'home-towns' that developed in this way were quite small, nevertheless the family dignity remained. It has been noted, for example, that two classes were represented amongst the *roithmen*, the 'best landed men' or the 'best and worthiest of the land' who composed the head courts in Kirkwall in the sixteenth century. First there were the men who owned the bus, and then came small landowners, not representing the largest farms after the bus, but quite small townships, or single farms within townships, or, though rarely, large townships with relatively little udal land. Only two of the more substantial udal townships were involved, Redland and Grimbister, even though several families of standing were to be found in such townships. It therefore appears that the right to serve on the *ráð* or council, and to be a *roithman*, was an inherited right that could remain with branch families sprung on the female side from those on the bus. Again, the aristocratic nature of the society of the period is made evident, and though the growth of new, smaller centres around the original centre is comparable to the smaller *býlingar* that grew around the original farm village settlements of the Faroe Islands,[89] nevertheless the mixture of udal and what might be called semi-feudal in the Northern Isles does not appear to be paralleled in the Faroes.

Where no outlands were available, and where there was more than one son, internal division of the original single units became inevitable, so that a younger son could have his share, where he could build a new head-house and start a cadet branch of the family. Such divisions can be pinpointed from place name evidence. In the Northern Isles, if an old township was split up, its name still remained, like a territorial designation. Examples are Over-, Mid- and Nether-bigging in the township of Grimbister, Firth; Over-, Nether-, and West Linklater at Linklater in Sandwick; and at Mirbister in Harray are Nisthouse, Midhouse, and Northbigging. Significantly, the 'home-towns' of nearly all the recorded township-owning families are of this type, with 'house' or 'bigging' farms distinguished by directional first elements. The fact that relatively few of the townships show this evidence of having been original units may indicate that the majority were group-townships from an early stage of settlement.[90]

Another name or name-element that helps to throw light on the consolidation and spread of settlement is 'setter', or '-ster', as in Setter, Voxter, Gunnister (Shetland), Setter, Mossetter, Inkster (Orkney). Two original Norse words are involved, *setr*, a dwelling-place, homestead, and *sætr*, a hill area for the grazing of stock. Phonologically, it is impossible to distinguish between these cognate terms, though 'if the first element is the name of an animal like cow, sheep, or horse, and if the name applies to a site (or settlement) far from the beaten track, the word it contains is likely to be *sætr*'. The majority, however, are likely to derive from *setr*, a homestead, and chronologically they appear to follow the *-staðir* names. The relatively small size of the *setter* farms, as indicated by the rentals, suggests secondary settlement, marking a thickening of the settlement pattern. It is also significant that half of the 25 examples of such names noted by Hugh Marwick in Orkney were applied to quoylands that were untaxed, and therefore of relatively late date. A more recent writer boosts the number of setter names in Orkney to 34, but this is far fewer than the 170 examples from Shetland.[91] Possibly this statistical difference points to the generally later nature of Viking settlement in Shetland, seen from the perspective of the two island groups together.

Curiously, *setr* or *sætr* names are completely lacking in the Faroes and Iceland.[92] However this is to be explained, there is nevertheless some evidence for summer grazing areas, for in Suðuroy there is a group of names, Argir, Argisá, Argisfossur, Ergibyrgi, Ergidalur, all referring to places high in the mountains. At Ergidalur, 200 m above sea-level, a stone building measuring

5.3×3.5 m was excavated, presumably a shieling-hut. These names incorporate Old Faroese *ærgi*, Modern Faroese *argi, ergi*, derived from Gaelic *airigh*, Early Irish *airge*, a shieling.[93] Evidence of a similar nature comes from Orkney. In the island of Sanday there was a farm called Arie, near the present farm of Grindally. There is another called Airy in Stronsay, and a house with the same name near Greeny Hill in Birsay. The form Arian at Stromness incorporates the Norse enclitic definite article, *-in*, that is *ærgin*, the shieling. The hill Errival in Papa Westray, paralleling Airafea in Sanday and Stronsay, probably contains the same Gaelic element.[94] It is possible that such names are pre-Viking, even if Viking elements are added to some of them. At any rate, they demonstrate that sites did exist to which the Norse name *sætr* could have been given.

4

Scattald and Hagi

IN the Faroe Islands, the grazing area beyond the dyke was known as *uttan-garðs jørð*, *udmark*, or more often *hagi*. An individual's share in the *hagi* was normally proportional to his holding in the *indmark* or township land, but whereas the *indmark* units were definite, demarcated and demonstrable, those in the *hagi* were not. The Faroese and Old Norse word *hagi* was used in Shetland and survives in place names and some common nouns, though it has been replaced by the word *scattald*, in the sense of hill-grazing. Place names the form 'the Hoga', 'the Hoga of —', 'the Hogen of —', or are compounded as in Lambhoga, Hogaland, Hogali, Hogapund.[95] In most examples hagi or its variant hoga has the approximate emphasis of a noun. It occurs in a number of noun-compounds.

Haglet (*hagi* + Norwegian dialect *leite*, a particular place, spot) is an enclosed piece of hill pasture, a piece of ground habitually grazed by a flock of sheep or herd of cattle. A comparable Swedish dialect word, *haglet*, is used, however, of infield pasture.[96]

A mark or boundary stone set up to indicate the dividing line between two hill pastures is a *hagmark*, *hagmet*, or *hogsten*.[97] Such marks played a part in a special ceremony, *to ride the hagri* (*hagi* + Old Norse *reið*, ride). A scattald could have several townships with rights in it, 'and the inhabitants of the towns within the same scattald are called Scat brethren. In the memory of man, there was a Judicial procession of the Inhabitants once in every 3 or 4 years, to inspect and recognise the boundaries of these Scattalds. Upon this occasion the Baillie of the parish presided, the Heritors and inhabitants were convened . . . ; all the marches and ancient boundaries were inspected and described, with their names bearings and distances, in a book kept for that purpose; this procession was called riding the hagra. It seems to have been indissuetude, at least neglected in many parts of the Country before the abolition of heritable jurisdiction (1746). But it was solemnised in one or two parishes in or about the year 1745'.[98] Here, the use of a book marks official documentation; but that the custom had a long weight of tradition behind it is suggested by the fact that on these occasions, at the end of the corn-harvest, the men took one or more of the tenants' young sons round with them, and at each mark stone a boy 'got a sair treshin sae as he sood mind weel whaur da hagmets stude'. Different boys took their punishment each time, so that there were always witnesses with indelible memories of the boundary stones.[99] In this way, oral tradition could be used to reinforce documentation, according to the old country act which stated that 'the bailiff of each parish, with twelve honest men, should annually ride the marches of the parish betwixt the first of October and the last day of April, or at any other time when required by the scattlers, the penalty of non-performance being Forty pounds Scots'. Here, however, the whipping custom is not specifically mentioned, nor was it referred to in a description of the surveying of the scattald marches in Yell, by Gilbert Neven, Bailie, in 1667, though he was accompanied by 31 persons, mostly portioners or co-tenants, and 'many other Witnesses'.[100]

Though some sources define hagi as unenclosed pasture ground, others define it as enclosed pasture or specify it as that part of the hill pasture nearest the township.[101] In this sense it was equivalent to the *heimrast* (hamerest) of Austland and Trondelag in Norway.[102] However, it could also be a remoter area, perhaps equivalent to 'the garths called wolmemning or common garths' in Snabrough scattald in Unst, a *garth* being enclosed pasture, especially for cattle or a small patch of enclosed cultivated ground surrounded by waste land.[103] A further possible parallel from Yell is the 'waste ground not strictly marched, which is anciently called Woll-mennis-hoga, or the hill wherein all the Scattalds of Strand and Nebeback may as fairly pasture, as any in Windhouse Scattald may do'. Here, 'wolmemning' and 'Wollmennis . . .' are versions of Old Norse *almenning* or *almenningr*, the former a feminine form meaning common land, the second a masculine form meaning common pasture.[104] The Shetland examples seem to cover both these senses, and the second one shows that part of the hagi could be common pasture shared between a number of scattalds.

Since the root sense of hagi (cognate with hedge) is that of a fence, enclosure, the idea of it as an enclosed part of the grazings is probably original. In Old Swedish, *haghi* was enclosed pasture, and in Sweden, Norway, and Iceland, it is frequently compounded with the names of domestic animals, as in the Swedish place-names Horshoga (1361), Hästhoga (1498), Svinhoga (1481), and in Iceland, Hrosshagi, Lambhagi (cf. Lambhoga in Fetlar), Sauðhagi.[105]

The hagi could be divided into specific areas. In the Faroes, the nearer part was the *húshagi* or *undirhagi*, the remoter the *fjallhagi*. In Norway, there could be found the *heima hagha* (1411), *wthagha* (1457), *hushage*, *fjellhage*, *sæterhage*, though even a fairly remote enclosure for grazing domestic stock could simply be called *hagi*. There was also a distinction relating to summer and winter use, hence the Icelandic *sumarhagi* and *vetrarhagi*.[106] Such distinctions were hardly necessary within the strait-jacket of Shetland's geography, where the stock never went any great distance from home and seasonal variations in climate were not extreme. Nevertheless parts of the hagi were differentiated in Shetland too, for example in Foula with its *doon-hogin* and *ophogin*, and in Yell with its *hemhoga*.[107]

In Unst, *hogaland*, pasture for cattle, survived as a noun into the twentieth century, and elsewhere as a place name. The word has its analogues in Old

Norse *haglendi*, Norwegian *hageland*, *hag(e)lende*, Faroese *hagalendi*,[108] and may therefore be almost as old as *hagi* itself in Shetland.

Finally, there is the compound *hogaleave*, leave or permission, given in return for payment, to graze cattle or sheep, to cast peats, or to cut coarse grass and heather for thatch, on a hagi belonging to another. This happened if some of these essential resources were lacking in a particular place. Examples are numerous. In Unst, 'in the point of the Ness of Wedbister lies the little room called Oganess or Saxaburness, which has no priviledge without its dykes, as it pays no part of the scatt of Wedbister scattald, but by allowance from the heritor of Wedbister, to whom it pays yearly an agreed sum for peats and pasture'. The room of Gardon paid hogaleave for peat and thatch from Snabrough. The town of Voesgarth in Balista or Midparish scattald had no privileges outside its dykes or on the shore, except by permission of the neighbouring heritors. The room of Northdeal had no scattald, but got peat, thatch and pasture from Norwick, for payment. Clibberswick also paid hogaleave to Norwick. The town of Hagdealt had no privileges outside the dykes on either side of it, except 'by tolerance' of the neighbouring proprietors. Haroldswick paid hogaleave to Ungersta and Sotland, and Cliff's Setter, a town of 4 marks belonging to the Grays of Cliff, had no privileges apart from its known fourth part of the ness called Kewsaness, to the north of it. The same applied to islands. Balta and Huney had no privileges on the shore or isle of Unst, and Uyea island, with half of Gruna and Weather Holm, 'have had and contend yet to have privileges of peats, thatch and pasture on the shore of Unst, on the west side of Orwick, being called Uya, now Clivocast and Muraster scattald, *which is refused them by the inhabitants of these two rooms*' (deleted in pencil). The custom was still going on in the early nineteenth century. The actual payment itself also came to have the name hogaleave.[109]

Whatever the range of senses contained in the word hagi, it was always purely a grazing area. Scattald, on the other hand, usually etymologised as *skat* and *hald*, holding, is more complicated. The word dates to the sixteenth century.[110] In origin it seems to have applied to a settlement group, apparently covering the whole of the lands available to the group. In support of this view, it has been noted that there is a link between chapels and scattalds, for the chapel distribution seems to correspond to a marked degree with scattalds and with the earliest Norwegian settlements.[111] The comprehensive nature of the scattald is suggested by a source of 1575–6 which talks of clearing, burning and reclaiming new corn lands on 'ony part or partis of the inscattell callit infeild or outscattell callit outfeild', and of making 'habitationis saittis and quoyis thairupoun'. Similarly, those who had shares in a *scattald* were *inscattalders*, and those who had none were *outscattalders*.[112]

As far back as the sixteenth century, therefore, the scattald was thought of as a unit, with elements distinguished by their functions. This explains the idea of tax or skatt in the name, for it is hard to understand how this could happen if the scattald had always had the current meaning, used at least since the late eighteenth century, of the common or shared pasture-land of a township community or set of communities. Though such grazing was essential to the working of such communities, tax seems always to be applied primarily – even in communities where the pastoral emphasis is dominant – to the cultivable land, to which the value of the grazings is then made proportionate. The Rentals of the Northern Isles show that if a farm was out of cultivation, no skatt was levied. That the hill grazings were unskatted until cultivated is demonstrated by the fact that quoylands were unskatted, at least before a certain period. The tradition in Shetland that skatt was levied for the use of the scattalds is scarcely tenable, unless the term is taken to cover the township area as well. A reasoned comment was made in the late eighteenth century, in a discussion of the nature and origin of skatt, about which opinions differed:

'... if the following facts are attended to, there will appear to be very little ground for that difference. Though Tradition alone is a blind guide, and more so in Countries which like these have so often changed masters and Inhabitants yet where in spite of these changes, a tradition is uniform and universal, not contradicted by any positive evidence, it is entitled to a considerable degree of credite. Now there is not a man in Shetland or in Orkney neither who hath heard of and known that Scatt was paid to the King or Overlord, who, if he is asked the question will not answer "that Scatt was paid for the hills or commons in Shetland called Scattalds, and here too they sometimes add for the meadows". Such they call those Boggs from which they take considerable quantities of coarse hay. In conformity to this Tradition we find that the Scatt in Shetland though more or less from -/2^d to -/12^d or more per merk land generally is in some proportion to the extent and goodness of pasture and other accommodations in the Scattald. Small Islands though inhabited from early times, if they have no right of commonage upon the mainland or next adjacent large island pay no Scatt. Where they possess this right of commonage on the next adjacent large island they do pay Scatt but still not in proportion with their Scatt brethren upon the large island. Of both these there are instances, of the former a great many. *Setter-lands* as hath been said, which are numerous and at different periods enclosed from or upon the Scattalds already paying Scatt, never paid Scatt to the Crown, but very often pay a subsideary Scatt to the dominant tenant called a Tulbert Scatt, There are many lands which though they are not now understood to be setter lands, nevertheless pay no Scatt to the Crown; but then they pay a Hogaleave – much the same with the *Tulbert Scatt* to the proprietors or possessors of the lands upon whose common they pasture their cattle and from whence they take their peats, Earth and turf for manure, etc. .... To this tradition supported by these facts the only thing that is opposed here is, that though the Scatt is for the most part in proportion to the benefits arising from the Commons, yet in several instances it is directly otherwise. To this it is answered though this may be the case at present, we do not certainly know how it stood anciently ...'[113]

The writer of this note thought these facts proved that skatt was originally paid from the commons. Hogaleave was a payment for access to some of the hill's resources. Tulbert Scatt is here a payment by a sub-tenant who had broken in part of the hill-grazing to make a homestead, though originally it may have been a fine or rent exacted from unentitled squatters. The origin of this curious word is uncertain, but it may be from Norwegian *til-*, to, in addition, plus *bot*, plural *bøter*, compensation, perhaps paralleling Icelandic *tilbót*, addition, extra.[114] In the first case, it is rent rather than tax that is involved. In the second, the use of a piece of common or shared land for a private purpose could be regarded as an infringement of the rights of the community as a whole, so that the payment was compensation rather than rent. These features, therefore, need not affect the argument, for skatt was applied to the unit and not to its parts.

Whatever the origin of the name, it undoubtedly meant more than simply the common or shared hill-pasture. In the eighteenth century it was noted that lands were divided into parishes, and these in turn into scattalds, each with '1, 2 or more often 12 to 20 towns or Hamlets, the lands of which have a right, pro indiviso, to pasture, Peats, etc. in one and the same common called in common speech, "The Scattald"'. Several records of scattalds survive, so that it is possible to work out the boundaries in some instances. Those of Unst have been reconstructed.[115]

Gifford's MS Rental of Shetland, 1716–17, mentions thirteen scattalds in Fetlar.

Funzie totalled 81½ marks of land, and was divided into two rooms:
>   1. Funzie, 71½ mk. (7 tenants)
>   2. Litlaland, 14 mk. (1 tenant)

Aith, 81½ mk. (13 tenants)
Town and Velzie, 28 mk. (2 tenants)
Grutton, 81 mk. (6 tenants)
Unnamed scattald (1 tenant)
Tresta, 81 mk.

Rusater, 54 mk., divided into three rooms:
>   1. Russeter, 18 mk. (1 tenant)
>   2. Culbinstoft, 18 mk. (2 tenants)
>   3. Crossbister, 18 mk. (4 tenants)

Oddsta, 136 mk., divided into eight rooms:
>   1. Urie, 60 mk. (6 tenants)
>   2. Udsta, 24 mk.
>   3. Oddsetter, 12 mk. (2 tenants)
>   4. Frackaseter, 6 mk. (1 tenant)
>   5. Hamer, 17 mk. (4 tenants)
>   6. Snabrough, 8 mk. (1 tenant)
>   7. Uraseter, 6 mk. (1 tenant)
>   8. Fogravell, 6 mk. (1 tenant)

Dale, 65 mk., divided into six rooms:
>   1. Southdale, 18 mk. (2 tenants)
>   2. Northdale, 18 mk. (3 tenants)
>   3. Uckaseter, 8 mk. (1 tenant)
>   4. Sand and Brough, 13 mk. (2 tenants)
>   5. Forland or Fourland, 3 mk. (1 tenant)
>   6. Clodon or Clothan, 7 mk. (1 tenant)

Houbie, 89 mk., divided into five rooms:
>   1. Gord, 23 mk.
>   2. Setter, 8 mk. (1 tenant)
>   3. Goodmanshuss, 23 mk. (2 tenants)
>   4. Baela, 13 mk. (2 tenants)
>   5. Feal, 20 mk. (2 tenants)

Strand, 81 mk., divided into five rooms:
>   1. Kirkhouse, 21 mk.
>   2. Bigtoun, 14 mk. (1 tenant)
>   3. Langhouse, 8¼ mk. (1 tenant)
>   4. Toft, 24 mk. (3 tenants)
>   5. Everland, 13½ mk. (3 tenants)

Baelagord, 2½ mk.

Heliness, 3 mk.[116]

The thirteen scattalds, therefore, contained a total of 34 rooms or multiple-farm townships. It is easy to imagine these scattered spots of cultivation, green areas with golden-yellow patches when the corn was ripe, set amongst deep peat-bogs with pools of dark water glistening at the bottom of cuttings, or on the slopes of hills clad with heather and rocks. From the details reported in the course of surveying scattalds, a lively picture of the landscape is conjured up, as in an example from Yell, dated 1667:

'*Houlland Scattald*. Being the first Northmost Scattald, is bounded to the West and North with the Sea, to the East and South with Brugh Scattald and the Sea. The first March Mark dividing these Scattalds, stands upon the top of the little Hill or Hillock, be-east the little piece of dyke, which is builded from the North end of the Loch, or water, beside the Kirk or North Yell, to the head of the gooe, at the North Sea banks (called commonly Dyelda-gooe), upon which Hillock be-east the said Piece of dyke as said is; there has anciently been as it seems, a Warder or Watch Place is to be found; the first dividing March Stone standing near about in the middle of the waste grounds between the dykes of Houlland and Brugh, acknowledged to be from the said Watch place, the second March Stone, from which stone the line of the March was found to go, straight to a great Flat-Stone which lies at the distance of an pair of Butts or thereby, from the Northmost crooke or bught of the ancient hill dykes between Houlland and Brugh, which by the consent of all present was found to be a March Stone, and accordingly was renewed by laying a heap of stones upon it, from which March, the March goes to the hill or hillock called Houlnahoule, and from the line of the March inclining a little more Westward to the hill or hillock called the westmost Mossahoule, which was by all foresaid acknowledged to be a March, and was renewed by rearing an heap of Stones upon it, from thence west to the head of the mire called Kinna-loiahe or the dividing Mire, and from the foot of that with a straight line to the little hill or hillock called Tonglafeyll, and from that to a great flat rock (which is called the Heilla) lying at the south side of the Slack, called Marka or Merkeiesmoode at the Neep or West Sea banks, which the last or Westmost March pointing out the Southmost bounds of the Scattald of Houlland, and the Northmost of the Scattald of Brugh'.[117]

Because the nature of the records and of the areas differ, it is easier to see the settlement pattern in Shetland through the scattald or hagi than through the bu or heid-bule. Grazing needs predominated, though this did not prevent the growth of secondary settlements which had no grazing rights outside their dykes, just as could happen with the *býlingar* of the Faroe Islands.[118] This demonstrates clearly that hill-grazing was not an *essential* attribute of a township, even though the resources of the hill were essential to the proper working of a township, and hogaleave had to be paid if these were lacking.

5

The Township and its Functioning

TOWNSHIPS were close-knit communities of people who depended on each other and on the resources of the area for their subsistence. They varied in character according to the natural resources, but all shared common features. The buildings generally clustered at the edge of the cultivated ground, as elsewhere in Scotland, sometimes being 'so close and intermixed that it was impossible for a stranger to distinguish which belonged to the different holdings'. In Orkney, long-surviving examples were to be seen at the Biggings of Stove and Quoyloo in Sandwick,[119] and in Shetland, at Aith in Fetlar, and Fladdabister near Lerwick. The individual farm units consisted of a dwelling house and offices – always a byre and barn, and sometimes also a corn-kiln, stable, or in Shetland a lambhouse. Each unit had a stackyard close to it for oats, bere and hay, and, at least from the late eighteenth century, a kailyard.

8. The township of Sound, Lerwick, with its clustered buildings and fields being harvested. Per E J F. Clausen. 3.10.9.

Also individual to each tenant, or occasionally shared by close relations, was the tounmal, consisting of rough grazing in Shetland, and of arable in Orkney. To these exclusive rights can be added the *plantiecrues* in the hill-grazing, where kail or cabbage was grown from seed before being transferred to the kailyard (see page 101 ff.).

The main element was the townland, shared between the tenants. This covered everything within the dyke that enclosed the township, grass and meadow as well as arable, other than the tounmal. The tenants held their land in a number of rigs and strips or patches scattered amongst those of their neighbours, or sometimes in individual groups of rigs. This kind of land use was called *rendal* or *rig and rendal* in the Northern Isles and Caithness, equivalent to the Scottish *runrig*. The first reference noted dates to 1519, when certain lands in Orkney were described as not lying in 'curig (? co-rig) nor rendell' with neighbouring land. In 1775, the Rev John Mill 'obtained a life-rent tack of Sumburgh's ten marks land in Skelberry, which lies Rigg and Rendal, (as called) with my glebelands' – that is, the lands were intermixed. In Dunrossness, which formed part of John Mill's parish, the small farms in general were parcelled out in discontinuous plots called there *rigg* and *rendale*.[120]

Rigs or ridges formed part of larger *sheeds* (Old Scots *schedd*, piece of ground, 1473), or fields. Information from Orkney shows that sheeds were sometimes divided between two or more proprietors, but more often were held by one only. At Netherbrough in Harray, in 1787, most of the sheeds extended to one *plank* (Old Scots 1584; cf. French *planche*, strip of land) of approximately 40 fathoms square, though some were of two planks and others a plank and a fraction. Thus, when the township of Inner Stromness, consisting of 36 pennylands (two urislands) was divided among the heritors in 1624, all the sheeds in the town were divided into six, in conformity with the number of tounmals and therefore with the number of occupants, or into three, for the three sixpenny lands of one of the urislands. A large meadow lying amongst the sheeds was divided into two, for the two urislands to use year about. This marks a considerable degree of regulation of the division of land amongst the members of the township. Not only the arable, but also the grass was laid out in sheeds. In a perambulation of Graves in Holm in 1631, preserved amongst the Graemeshall Charters, there is a reference to a whole plank of grassland on which all the houses of Easter Gravis stood. In this case the plank of grass, and 8 rigs of arable next to it, lay alongside the rendal land and appear to have been apportioned individually.[121]

On this evidence, arable sheeds were fields divided into numbers of rigs proportionate to the number of farm-units in the township. In theory each unit had a share in each sheed or plank. This was the effect at Inner Stromness in 1624, and following a perambulation at Clouston in 1666, the heritor, Thomas Omand, who had acquired land amounting to a ninth of the township, was given the ninth rig of every nine rigs in every sheed there. But by 1680, one of the sheeds mentioned in 1660 had become the joint property of two men. It seems, therefore, that Omand 'got a *theoretical* collection of ninth rigs and then adjusted matters with his neighbours on more common sense lines'. This almost instinctive move towards independent units was not smooth flowing. It led to irregularities that were not officially approved. At Kirbister, for example, it was ordered that 'because of the great enormities that they have found quhilk formerly has been committed within the said toun', all the arable formerly rendalled as outbreak and planked land should be rendalled again, and the sheeds again divided into rigs, the first one on the East side in each case being called the *uppa* or upper rig.[122]

A further point that emerges from the 1666 perambulation of Clouston is that though 50 sheeds are listed, and also named, a fact which gives them firm territorial status, yet the ones associated with the old 'Head House' were not mentioned, though known from other sources. These must have stood outside the communal part of the townland, as what in Orkney was called *inskift*, 'a parcel of land not lying in runrig with other lands but belonging solely to one owner'. In 1509, the ninepenny land of Sabay lay 'in ane inskeyft withtin hyttselff in lentt and breyd', and in South Ronaldsay a distinction was made between inskift, townland, outbreks, and tounmals. The Skaill Charters show that soon after 1600, James Louttit and his nephew Alexander in the township of Mirbister in Harray had their inskifts dyked around. Other references dated 1643 and 1677 show that the individually held inskifts were a mixture of arable and grass, like the rest of the townland.[123] The inskift (cognate with Old Norse *einskipta*, to divide as a unit, Icelandic *einskifta*, to reduce to a unit) is evidently to be seen in relation to udal inheritance, with reference to the land of heid-bules that was not to be split up (see page 26 ff.).

The inskifts seem to point back to an older Norse form of land organisation. The same may be true of the way in which pennylands are sometimes differentiated within a township, being sometimes treated as individual operative units. Mirbister consisted of three pennylands. But in a sasine of 1643, land sold there included half a mark of udal land in the pennyland of Nether Mirbister, specified as the 'third rig of every aucht rig of the said pennyland'. The two other pennylands were not involved, and the Nether Mirbister pennyland was runrig within itself. At Hoxa in South Ronaldsay, two pennylands were divided individually in 1645, starting as known divisions of land within the township. The division was done in a precise and workmanlike way, using a pole or shaft measuring 'seven futtis of ane futt in measure and four inches mair', ie each 'foot' was 1 ft 4 in. (41 cm) long, making a total of 9 ft 4 in. (2.8 m). First the hill balks of Hoxa were divided in halves, laying 109 shafts to each pennyland, which gave its width along the top end. Then the north pennyland was divided in halves according to the quality of the land and mark stones set up. Finally one of these halves was divided into four parts by boundary lines. The one pennyland of Lythes in the same island was split into four exact farthing lands, one of which was 84 ft (25.6 m) wide at the lower end, expanding to 98 ft (30 m) wide in the middle, keeping to this where it touched the lower end of a quoy, and expanding again to 112 ft (34 m) wide at the quoy's upper end. The next two farthings were similar in size, and the fourth a little wider when it reached the quoy. This individuality of the pennylands was still evident in 1787, when in planking the township of Netherbrough in Harray the oversman 'compared the pennylands as they stood planked'. Similarly in Caithness, there are examples, as at Scarmclet in 1773, of land lying in a plank by itself and not runrig with the land of other tenants.[124]

Such individual treatment of planks and pennyland units was not ubiquitous. A deed relating to Paplay in South Ronaldsay, dated 1677, helps to balance the picture. The townships contained nine pennylands, and in the townland, 'we found the peney land of Laley to have the first rig of the towne, and the seconde rige to the peneyland of Birstone, and swa fwrth to ewerie heritor conform to their proportions in ewerie each peneyland'.[125] This arrangement is to be seen as the rule rather than the exception.

The individual treatment of pennylands and planks may have something to do with earlier division of an udal inheritance, but the surprising feature is the amount of symmetry and careful division dating at least from the sixteenth century. In parts of Orkney, the common concept of scattered, irregular patches of arable as a standard ingredient of runrig can scarcely be maintained. Planks or sheeds were often remarkably precise, as must have been the division of rigs within them. The standard size of about 40 fathoms (73 m) square gives an area of 1600 square fathoms (5329 square m) or 1⅓ English acres. Though it has been suggested that the 40 fathom square was chosen just because it was the size of the Orkney fields, nevertheless there may be a more general reason for it, for the area amounts to approximately 1 Scots acre. This being so, the Orkney plank – the term was little used in Shetland[126] – corresponds to the Scots *acre-dale*, a sixteenth century term for land divided into units of one acre each. However, a further correlation can be observed, for 1600 square fathoms was reckoned in Orkney to be what one *markland* should contain.[127] There was much more regularity about the Orkney marklands than those of Shetland, where every mark of land 'consists of so much arable ground, and of another part which is only fit for pasturage, but the arable part alone varies in extent from less than one to two acres'. The process of planking, therefore, which in general distinguishes Orkney from Shetland, may be seen in relation to the adoption of the division or valuation of lands by marks in the fourteenth and fifteenth centuries.[128]

The constituent elements of the sheeds or planks were the rigs. Rigs varied in size, 'long rigs' and 'short rigs' being often mentioned. At an inquest on the lands of Swartaquoy in Holm in 1678, two rigs were said to be 30 ft (9.1 m) wide at the lower end and 33 ft (10 m) at the upper end. This may be a measurement of both rigs together, not of each separately. In 1623, a rig near St. Margaret's Hope was 330 ft (101 m) long, 33½ ft (10.2 m) broad at the top end, 25½ ft (7.8 m) broad at the middle, and 17½ ft (5.3 m) at the lower end. At Clouston in 1666, the numbers of rigs were given for every sheed, and ranged from 6 to 18 in 12 sample sheeds. The variation, therefore, was considerable. The township of Skeatown in Deerness in 1707 had 31 sheeds, on which over 198 rigs and spelds can be counted. In 1849, Sir Arthur Nicolson estimated that there were

800 to 1000 small ridges of arable within the dykes of the single townland in Papa Stour, with interspersed holding.[129]

Small rigs were dug with the spade, but larger rigs were cultivated by the plough. In the nineteenth century, a width of 18 ft (5.5 m) was said to be most suitable for most Orkney soils. Rigs of 17 ft (5.2 m) broad are mentioned for Shetland. They were often crooked and irregular in shape. An example of plough rigs can be seen at Mossetter, north of the Loch of Brockan in Evie and Rendall. Here, they run up to and then swing round the old farmhouse. At Noss in Shetland, rigs could vary in width from 6 to 30 ft (1.8–9.1 m). In Fetlar, about 1829, the good quality rigs averaged 15 ft (4.6 m) across, and the longest rig noted was 180 yards long (165 m). Rigs of poorer quality, however, were rarely half that length.[130]

From seventeenth century Orkney sources, it can be seen that the first rig in a sheed, especially at the beginning of a township, on the north or east side according to the lie of the ground, was called the *uppa* or *uplay*. The last one was the *nulay* or the unreferenced forms *nulla(y)*, *nurley*, *ulla*, whilst in between came the *midla* if there were three, or simply the second, third, etc., if there were several. The names are from Old Norse *uppi*, up, *meðal*, between, and probably *neðarla*, *neðarliga*, low down, far below.[131] Significantly, udal land and feued land could be grouped together, as in a 1689 source:

'The said James Ewensone to have the first rigg thereof beginning at the north, and Bracoes tennent to have the next rigg, commonlie called the uplay, as being udall land; and the said Oversanday to have two riggs both closs together thereafter as the so comonly called the nulay, as fewed land, thorowout the haill town land as the samen is planked'.[132]

Rigs had various names, some of which amounted to firm place names, but because of the nature of the unit itself, many were liable to change and to vanish as rigs were subdivided or amalgamated. Probably some of the names point to rigs of particular kinds. A *speld* or *spell* (Norwegian dialectal *spjell*, a strip of ground, *spol*, plural *spelir*, a narrow ridge of a field) may be a small rig, or perhaps one with grass on either side of it. In 1758 in Shetland, 'two Spelds or little Rigs' were delved with spades. There is a rig called Spelds at Biggins in Papa Stour. In Orkney, a Mirbister sasine of 1643 mentions '9 riggs or spelds called Quoynabrenda', and at Easter Voy, two rigs called the Pockie Spelds are mentioned in 1664. At Upper Briggan in Clouston in 1666, there were 10 rigs and 4 spelds in the same sheed divided into 9 pieces. Each rig and speld was measured with a line during a perambulation of Wideford in 1674. The Orkney evidence does not make clear whether a speld was a special type of rig or not, though the use of both terms together suggests a distinction.[133]

A rig-name element in Shetland, common in Norway, but less so in Orkney, is *teg* or some variant, as in Staen Tigs (Setter), Boo Taegs or Butegs (Hurdiback) in Papa Stour, and Tegenagrüna, Smirkeyldatig, Gyoddatig, Whamstig, in Fetlar.[134] It derives from Old Norse *teigr*, Norwegian dialectal *teig*, used of strips or patches of arable or meadow, but in Scandinavian contexts has a rather wider sense than simply that of rig. The Orkney form is *tie*. An old man in Rousay told that he cut a tie 3 or 4 ft (91 cm–1.2 m) broad, producing only six or seven sheaves.[135]

A frequent name was *dall* or *deld* (Old Norse *deild*, a portion, Faroese *deild*, a plot of land in the home-field). Some of the forms, however, may be Scots, which has the parallel word *dale*, a share, portion, or piece of land, from Old English *dāl*, *dǣl*. Papa Stour examples, such as Baeni Daelds, Aander Daelds, etc., number twenty. At Noss in the South Mainland of Shetland the name appears as Dalls, Hellidalls, Firvidals etc.[136] In a document of about 1851 relating to the process of division of commonty in Papa Stour, it was stated that 'a mark of land is not so much a definite measure as a proportionate share of arable in run-rig and of meadow cow grass lying pro indiviso, or in patches called dyelds, and of the Scattald or Common'.[137] A 'dyeld', therefore, could be a patch of either arable or grass in the home-field.[138]

Of a different origin though similar in appearance is *dellin* (Shetland), *dello(w)* (Orkney), a small patch of arable cultivated by the spade, sometimes with the extended sense of the site of a dwelling. This is from Scots *dell*, to delve, dig, and is traceable in Orkney back to 1841. By 1829 in Fetlar there was a number of small patches for cultivation amongst the grass area. These dellings were quite small, many being little more than 10 yards (9.1 m) long. The fact that they were reckoned as part of the grass sections suggests that they were then of a recent nature.[139]

As might be expected at this most intimate level of all in a township, the number of names descriptive of the shape, quality, or situation of rigs is considerable – 'bits, beds, brods, dels, ditches, flets, riebs, tegs, tongs, skaaps, skurpins, etc'.[140] A *bit*, *bed*, *bøti*, or *bødi* is a strip of grass-land, also found in place-names referring to small patches of tilled ground.[141] *Flet*, as in Flitts at Noss, a strip of grass or arable, could sometimes be bigger than a rig, for it could be cultivated by different occupants in alternate strips.[142] It is cognate with Old Norse *flöt*, a plain, Faroese *fløttur*, a strip of grass or arable, Norwegian dialectal *flot*, a flat, level field. *Rieb* may be from Norwegian *rep*, a strip of arable ground; the Orkney form *rap* is closer to Norwegian *rabb*, a ridge of land. *Tong* is a tongue of arable projecting into grassland, as in Tunga (Setter), Kjurkatungs (Biggins), and Tunga Daelds (Hurdiback) in Papa Stour.[143] Other rig-names from Orkney are *reevo* (Norwegian *rive*, a strip), *skutto* (perhaps from Old Norse *skott*, fox's tail), and *flaa*, a strip of green grass standing out against the heather, now usually found in place-names, such as 'The Flaas o' Rusht'. According to a Rousay lawsuit of 1825, 'David Cray of Hammer has two flaws of land which run across said road, making two riggs on each side of the road, or in other words the road divides the riggs in two, the ends touching the road on each side ... John Inkster has two riggs in one place and a tae or half a rig which cross the road ... all the rest of the land on each side of the road belongs to the petitioner consisting of eight flaws crossing the road and from these flaws extend riggs parallel to the road towards the shore lying on each side of it also belonging to petitioner ... that the lands belonging to Lord Dundas ...

do not lie together but are intermixed and runrig with the flaws above deponed to belonging to the petitioner'. This word, from Old Norse *flá*, strip of meadow land, Norwegian dialectal *flaa*, a ledge on a hillside, a flat area between steep slopes, probably referred originally to a stretch of grass. It is first recorded in 1597 in the island of Westray, with reference to nine large 'lie (ley) flawis' of land.[144]

Some of these terms, such as *d(y)eld*, *flet*, and *flaa*, referred originally to patches of grass, as does the element *-ing*, 'meadow', in the names of cultivated rigs. This fact reflects the mixture of arable and grass within the townland, and the spread of arable at the expense of the grass. It was evidently common for rigs or sheeds to be separated by strips or patches of grass, and when portions of these were taken in for cultivation, various names were given. In Orkney, an *inbreck* was a piece of pasture land newly broken up or tilled.[145] A *merkister* was a strip of unfenced grass separating arable patches or left as unsuitable for cultivation. The importance of this for stock feeding is emphasised by a case judged at the Bailie Court at the Kirk of Deerness in 1706, where:

'It is complained by the parishioners that a great Cwstom by severall in the paroch to take ther beasts in mercisters and roads for eating the Gras yrof by doing qrof the corns are eaten troden down & abused & it likways occassons great disorder & discord among neighbours. Qrfor the Baillie discharges all persons in tym coming to goe in to the saids rods & mercsters with ther beasts untill the tym the corns be skrewt or at least shorn under the pain of 4 sh. toties quoties'.[146]

The equivalent in Shetland is *merkigord*, allied to Old Norse *merkigarðr*, a dividing dyke or hedge. The Orkney form is related to Faroese *merkisgarður*, Norwegian dialectal *mærkjisgar*, with the same sense.

Another term, *ger*, *gyr(o)* or *garrick*, is used for a narrow, grass-grown piece of land between two cultivated patches, an odd piece of land, especially one of angular shape, a green spot among heather, or 'sward on hillside where heather has been exterminated by water'.[147] The source is Old Norse *geiri*, a triangular strip, Norwegian dialectal *geire*, *grasg(j)eire*, whilst the forms *gair*, *gare* found in southern Scotland are from Old English *gāra*, a gore, triangular piece of land.

The complicated mixture of grass and arable in the townland is made clear by the situation in Funzie, Fetlar. There, in 1829, the land was divided into 459 separate pieces, exclusive of numerous small outbreaks, of which 439 lay runrig, and all was unenclosed. Detailed surveying was carried out as part of an exercise to separate the intermingled lands of the three proprietors. From this it appears that 24 patches of meadow, averaging 0.76 acres, were each held by groups of 3 tenants; 2 pieces of meadow, averaging 3.09 acres, by groups of 7; 1 piece of meadow measuring 1.25 acres by 2; 2 pieces of corn averaging 0.49 acres were held in lieu of meadow shares; 92 patches of grass averaging 0.74 acres were held by individuals; 9 averaging 0.98 acres by groups of 3; 1 patch of 9.49 acres was held by a group of 9. There were 92 infield rigs averaging 0.28 acres, and 215 outfield rigs averaging 0.17 acres, along with an outfield unit of

0.80 acres shared by a group of 9. In addition there were 9 pieces of tounmal grass averaging 0.77 acres.[148]

Though the re-allocation to tenants of arable rigs at regular intervals is often regarded as an element in the runrig organisation, nevertheless the evidence is not strong. At Funzie, rigs only changed hands as a result of dispute, or a change in the number of tenants, or the moving of tenants. This was a general situation, and though re-allocation annually or every three years did occur in parts of Scotland, it was not frequent in the Northern Isles.[149] Seventeenth century Orkney records suggest that rigs changed hands as a rule only when a whole township was re-organised. Even then change seems to have been minimal. A source of about 1600 mentions rigs in the possession of one family over four generations, divided by march stones from the rigs of neighbours. However, exchanges of arable did take place until the 1830s in the five townships of North Ronaldsay.[150]

When it comes to grass, the situation is otherwise. The sharing of grass could be done either by joint use, or by rotation of units. Where tenant groups shared a piece of meadow, the individuals cut and cured the hay jointly, afterwards dividing it equally. A similar system operated at Uyea Sound in Unst, but here a woman from another township was usually asked to do the dividing. At Tresta in Fetlar, four small sections of meadow rotated annually amongst four crofters until 1965, and at Sandness in the West Mainland the meadow is still held in shares, though the hay has not been cut on it for many years. At Noss in the South Mainland, the custom was to cast lots each May for the 20 to 30 pieces of grazing in the township. The boundaries were marked out afresh each year by digging lines of holes. The grazing land on the back slope of the Noup of Norby was used in 1964 by 10 tenants holding 3 strips each, changed annually. The grass was unfenced, and the stock grazed on the tether.[151]

In Orkney the system can be traced back to the seventeenth century, when, following a perambulation in 1686, the meadow grass of a township was divided, 'and the saids haill meadowis to goe about yeirlie according to the said division, according to the vulgar country terme called meadow skift'. In a Sheriff Court Record of a division of lands in Kirbuster in 1691, it was ordained that all the grass and meadows within the dykes of the township should in all time coming go 'in Rapaskift and meadowskift' yearly, this formula being repeated as 'Kappaskift and meadows Skift'.[152] *Rapaskift* or *kappaskift* are clearly the same as meadow skift, though it is not certain which of the forms is a ghost word.

The townland, therefore, was a mixture of individually and communally held fields or sheeds of grass or meadow and arable divided into rigs, the former changing hands regularly and the latter remaining in one tenant's hands, often over several generations. The example of William Henderson, who had the farm of Thoft in the township of Funzie, Fetlar, in 1829, shows the individual's place in the system, though exactly the same organisation need not have applied in other areas. His house and one other shared the yard, and he had half of the tounmal, about 0.8 acres, which was under grass. As one of nine tenants, he had an infield rig in each of nine blocks of rigs, amounting in all to about 2.85 acres. His twenty-three outfield rigs were much smaller, and totalled 2.64 acres. He had a seventh share in each of the large meadows of Smirkeylda and Backadyeald, and co-operated with his neighbours at Thoft and at Gardie in haymaking on eight sections of the area called the Heart of the Mires. He had nine patches of grass, a third share in three patches of 'halvers' grass, and shared Noustaness with all the other tenants. Finally, he had access to the scattald, like the others, for his sheep, cattle, ponies, pigs and geese. His total holding within the dykes amounted to about 20 acres, giving him a farm that was bigger than average for Shetland at that period.[153]

In many of the respects mentioned here, the form and joint economic working of the townships of Orkney and Shetland paralleled patterns found elsewhere in Scotland, including Lowland Scotland before the days of agricultural improvement, and in many parts of Europe. It is in no way an isolated phenomenon, but a pattern of settlement and land-use that functioned regardless of the form of legal organisation. Although it has been suggested that Orkney runrig was introduced by Scottish lairds in the sixteenth century,[154] this is scarcely likely, for as a means of exploiting the resources of an area through communal activity it was geographically very widespread. Regional studies show how it could evolve to meet local situations. At the same time the strong non-runrig element traceable in Orkney is a reminder that there were alternatives, as long as land could be worked by means of people providing labour and services in exchange for a small piece of ground.

6

The End of Runrig

THE end of runrig means different things in different places. In much of
Orkney, it involved a rather complete transformation of the farming landscape,
and the disuse of the hill-dyke that separated the townlands from the moor and
common grazings. In Shetland the dyke has remained, as in other crofting
counties, and though the crofts within the dyke are now usually separate,
standing on their own units of land, nevertheless the grazings are held in
common. The change is less complete than in Orkney, because of the terrain,
and as a result of a different set of economic factors.

In Orkney, most of the corn lands lay runrig in 1760.[155] In the late 1760s,
there was a division of lands in the parish of Evie and Rendall, but the planks of
ground given to the farmers were scattered over a wide area, and not grouped.
There were 1200 planks of 40 fm. or 80 yds (73 m) square, the farms having 6,
10, or 12 planks of arable, besides grass and pasture. Before that the whole
parish was runrig, and remained so in part in the late 1790s.[156] In 1805 it was
still said to be largely runrig, with grass common to many tenants. The pasture
extended to 4800 planks, four times as much as the arable. There was still some
runrig in Shapinsay. In 1836 'rig-tenures' were still to be seen. In Holm and
Paplay, the Graemeshall Estate, the property of Alexander Sutherland
Graeme, was surveyed in 1828, cleared of runrig, and laid out in a considerable
number of farms of various size.[157]

In North Ronaldsay, the land was divided in 1832 apart from 200 acres at the
North End that remained in runrig till the 1880s, and is still marked by the
layout of unfenced fields in parallel strips. Runrig was abolished in Braeswick,
Sanday, in 1850.[158] St Andrews parish remained runrig in 1841, with the arable
of several farmers intermixed. Such a situation meant that no tenant could
improve his land without the consent and co-operation of both his neighbours
and the proprietor. By this date, too, more than half of the parish of Sandwick
had been 'lately' divided under a process of division of runrig.[159] By the middle
of the nineteenth century, Orkney was poised for a leap forward. Though
runrig remained in places, a great deal of it had been re-organised into separate
farms, as a logical extension to the planking process that had been going on
from at least the early seventeenth century.

The story in Shetland differs from that in Orkney. There, the arable was
mostly in cultivated spots by the coast,[160] and in only a few places would there

have been much advantage to the proprietors in separating their holdings of land. In one of the more fertile areas, Dunrossness, the arable, which was by the shore, was parcelled out '*rigg* and *rendale*'.[161] In Aithsting and Sandsting, it was reported that each of the twelve or fourteen tenants within the townships had their lands lying undivided and often runrig.[162] The qualification 'often', however, suggests that runrig was not quite universal, and that some blocking out of rigs was to be found in some if not all townships. In 1841, the rental land in Bressay, Burra and Quarff lay runrig, as did most of the farms in Unst.[163] In 1874, *rigga-rendall* still survived in places, for example at Burrigarth near Westing (three proprietors), though much planking had taken place in the preceding 10 years.[164]

Runrig lasted in Shetland into the twentieth century, for example at Brough in Bressay, Netherdale and Finnigart in Walls and Huxter in Sandness,[165] and in Fetlar, where, under the Fetlar Townships Scheme, proposed in 1963 under the Crofters (Scotland) Act 1961, a measure of consolidation would reduce the 59 crofts held in 218 separate parcels of land to 54 crofts held in 117 parcels.[166]

This long survival, in places up till the present day, does not alter the fact that Shetland was subjected to as much change as Orkney, and in fact change in runrig had become pervasive at an even earlier period, coinciding with the development of the fishing industry in the second half of the eighteenth century. Where conditions were suitable, however, the factors that influenced Orkney also influenced Shetland; and whatever the underlying economic causes of change, it is certain that the end of the runrig form of township organisation came about not through the re-allocation of the arable, but through the absorption of the common grazings which were all-important to the proper working of farming communities.

In 1695, a second Act of the Parliament of Scotland under William and Mary smoothed the path towards the division of commonties between heritors,[167] and the ramifications of this were felt in the Northern Isles. The sequence can be followed in outline. In some places it was straightforward, in others it was more complicated, as where an undivided common was shared by Holm and the four adjoining parishes.[168] Two thirds of the island of Stronsay were commons, and three quarters of Eday. In Stronsay, however, a first step was taken in the 1760s, when on the advice – or perhaps insistence – of Thomas Balfour of Huip, the hill-dykes of earth were allowed to fall into disrepair. The only dykes still maintained at the end of the century were those across the nesses or headlands, where the sheep could be kept from straying into the growing corn in summer, without herds. Shapinsay's hill-ground was all commonty in the 1790s, and St Andrews and Deerness contained much waste and undivided common.[169] In Evie and Rendall in 1805, the hills were mostly common, supporting 3000 sheep without a shepherd, and 400 to 500 swine.[170] About this period, much thinking about commons was going on, from the amount of statistical data that appears. In 1805, only one ninth of Stromness and Sandwick, an area of 31 square miles, was reckoned to be under cultivation, and one ninth under grass. The 18 square miles of South Ronaldsay had more arable and grass than most other places. Eday had less tillage in proportion to pasture than elsewhere, but Sanday was nearly all cultivated. Less than a sixth of Westray was cultivated, and only a narrow strip on the shore of Rousay.[171] For Orkney as a whole, the estimate in 1808 was as follows, Orkney being assessed at 600 square miles or 384,000 imperial acres.[172]

	Acres	% of Area
Heath and moss used as common	294,000	76.6
Green pasture occupied in common	30,000	7.8
Infield pasture and meadow	30,000	7.8
Arable (including gardens)	24,000	6.3
Houses, roads, walls, ditches, etc	2,000	0.5
Fresh water	4,000	1.0

This may be compared with the situation in June, 1969, when Orkney had 199,288 acres of agricultural land, a total of 52 per cent of the whole, composed of 81,000 acres of rough grazing (21.1 per cent) and 94,673 acres of grassland

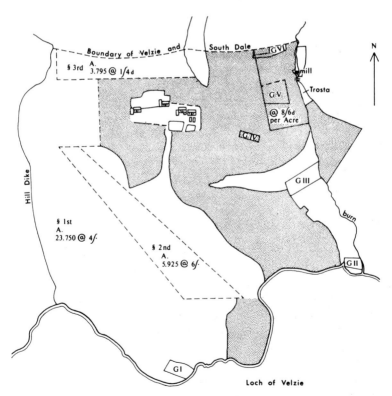

9, 10, 11 (10 and 11 on following pages). Examples of surveys dating from the second half of the nineteenth century in Fetlar, showing re-allocations of the townlands and scattald. From the Nicolson Papers. C5036–8.

(24.7 per cent) and 21,604 acres of tillage crops (5.6 per cent).[173] For accurate comparison, it has to be borne in mind that the present day grassland is cultivated, and should be counted along with the tillage percentage. The nature of the road Orkney farming has travelled in a century and a half is clear, but though it started on that road in the eighteenth century, it needed the impetus of systematic draining and liming, as well as dividing of commons and enclosing, for a real push forward into modern times.

Though in 1841 2850 acres of Holm and Paplay were divided into farms, including the Graemeshall estate, there still remained 4767 acres of undivided common. There was much undivided common in Evie and Rendall, though that in Rendall was about to be divided. Eday had 979 acres of arable, 126 acres of arable improved since 1838 and 72 acres of green pasture. Little improvement had taken place on the small farms of Birsay and Harray. Westray had 14,579 imp. acres of undivided common, 882 of improvable land, 4284 of land never cultivated, and 3616 of arable. Papa Westray had 441 acres of improvable land, 1215 never cultivated, and 1205 of arable. Stromness had 1865 acres of arable, 908 of infield pasture, and 5387 of undivided common. Here the problem of

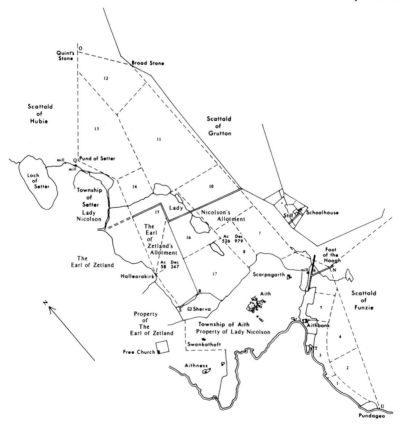

improvement was made more difficult because much of the useful surface had been removed for fuel and for byre-bedding, a process that was still going on. There was an early division of the common in Orphir, under Sir William Honeyman, resulting in 26 farms where there had been none before, in part occupied by a few families who came from neighbouring parishes to settle. Rousay had 2200 acres of arable, 10,440 of uncultivated land or pasture, and 7500 of undivided common, Shapinsay 748, 2386 and 3134 acres respectively,

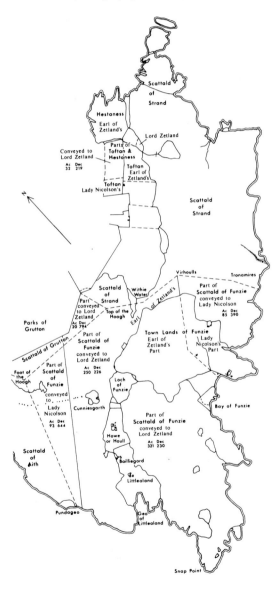

Sandwick 2294, 3224 and 5202 acres respectively. In Kirkwall and St Ola few estates had been surveyed or measured and the commons remained undivided.[174]

About 1818, 26 new farms were set up on the old common grazings at Orphir. The Birsay commons, divided in 1856, gave land for 40 squatters, 50 new farms, and additions to neighbouring farms. In Shapinsay, farms of 30 to 200 acres were established, alongside holdings of 5 to 10 acres for fishermen and tradesmen. The interior of Stronsay was made into 10 to 30 acre farms, and in Sanday, lots of 16 to 20 acres were squared off.[175]

These statistics show that there were considerable possibilities for an extension of the settlement pattern in Orkney in the mid nineteenth century, though not without an accompanying re-organisation of the existing arable. A runrig community could not otherwise survive the loss of the common grazings.

Shetland lagged behind Orkney in regard to the abolition of runrig and the division of the commons. Though division was much discussed, no effective steps to implement it had been taken by 1808. By the 1840s, Mr Hay had made improvements at Laxfirth by draining and liming. Tenants then got enclosed areas of 10 acres, each divided into 5 long strips for oats, potatoes, barley and grass-seeds, hay, and pasture, at a rent of £1 a year.[176] This, however, was not a widespread phenomenon, and the major influence on the Shetland farming landscape was the subdivision of farms and the creation of outsets on the scattald to provide homes for the men needed by the lairds to carry on the fishing industry.

7

Outsets and Outbreks

FROM the beginning of the Norse period, the common grazing areas were being constantly nibbled away by the expansion of settlement. Enclosures for animals became the sites of farms with their quoylands, some of them old enough to be skatted like the land within the dykes, others more recent and not subject to skatt.[177] In sixteenth and seventeenth century sources, especially for Orkney, quoylands and outbreks are equated, and the power to make outbreks was one of the pertinents usually specified in legal documents.

Whether outbrek is of direct Norse descent or not is uncertain. The second element may be from Old Norse *brekka*, a slope, from which comes *breck(s)*, used in the Northern Isles and Caithness for thin, shallow soil, hardly worth cultivating, or common pasture ground. Parallels are the Roxburgh *brekk(s)*, *braiks*, *brack*, uncultivated or fallow land lying between patches of arable, and Shetland *utbroggs*, 'hilly soil in the outskirts of the home-field'. Since *breck*, *break*, occurring in some English dialects with a similar meaning, probably comes from Old English *bræc*, *brec*, an English origin cannot be entirely excluded, especially since outbrek is much commoner in Orkney than in Shetland, and is also found in Caithness.[178]

In Shetland, on the other hand, the usual term is *outset*, and it was the rapid increase in the number of outsets in the eighteenth and nineteenth centuries, allied to fragmentation or subdivision amongst tenants of the townlands, that did most to change the old settlement pattern there. In Muckle Roe, a few spots were brought under cultivation along the sea-coast between about 1740–90.[179] In Yell, the population was increasing, partly because inoculation had begun to be practised, and partly because of the parcelling out of land for fishermen. A young married couple given a piece of land, needed no more than 'a cow, a pot, a spade, a tusker (peat-spade), a buthie (basket), fishing rods, and a rug, or blanket'.[180] The practice in Dunrossness was to give a couple 2 marks of land at first, of about 1600 square fathoms each, increasing it to 3 or 4 marks as the family developed.[181] In Aithsting and Sandsting, many outsets had been enclosed from the common in the later years of the eighteenth century, and set to tenants for money rents only, as opposed to rents in kind. Because of this, and the splitting of tacks, the population of the parish had increased. One farm that had only 2 tenants in 1742 now had 7 tenants and 3 outsets. On other farms, the number of families had trebled. Because of the outsets too, the amount of land under cultivation had increased in relation to 60 or 70 years before.[182] Nevertheless, as noted for Unst, the subdivision of farms was bringing about a decline in the standard of agriculture.[183] In Kirkwall and St Ola there were 50 farms, exclusive of cottars, with an average of 10 people per family in spite of the small size of the farms. Around Kirkwall itself, there was some reversal of the general trend, for some amalgamation of holdings was taking place there.[184] In Bressay, Burra and Quarff, farms had been reduced in size by being split up, and an increase in population was encouraged by persuading young folk to marry, even if they had no stock.[185] In North Yell and Fetlar, farms had been broken into small parcels, due to the needs of fishing.[186] In Northmavine, about 100 new outsets had been made, at 3 marks each, but exempt from skatt, cess, and corn-tiend.[187] In Nesting, the population had become high because of the efforts of Steuart Bruce of Symbister and Mr Hunter of Lunna in creating outsets, to increase the number of fishermen.[188] Since 1770, the population of Walls and Sandness had risen to too high a level, due to the splitting of farms, often into three, during the 40 years from about 1750.[189]

The nineteenth century pattern was a continuation of this. 'The soil in Shetland', said one writer, 'is no farther valuable in the estimation of the proprietors, than as it furnishes settlement to fishers'. Such fishing tenants got about 3 acres, at a rent of 10/– an acre, but land rents were the smallest part of the revenue of Shetland lairds, whom fishing had turned into traders, and whose land had become subservient to commerce. Subdividing of farms went on, outsets were reclaimed on the wastes and the old Country Act that had prohibited marriage unless the couple had £40 Scots of free gear was ignored. Now four families were commonly found on a farm that had supported only one in the 1770s. Yet the landlords were not to be entirely blamed, for they had to be at the same time landlord, merchant, farmer, fish-curer, and banker for their tenants.[190]

By the 1840s, Sandsting and Aithsting had 104 outsets, and farms that had formerly had one or two tenants now had five or six. Three or four acres was the maximum size of most farms. In Dunrossness, Alexander Sinclair was unfortunate with his estate of Brow, which had been overblown by sand except for some small outsets or pendicles, and there were a few recent outsets in Fair Isle, part of the same parish. In Mid and South Yell, the small size of the holdings was said to be the biggest drawback to agriculture. The scale of things can be gauged from the fact that of the 70,000 acres of land, including 33,000 acres of pasture, only 1500 acres were cultivated. Yet considerable additions to the area of arable had been made, so that few people had to buy meal before the beginning of August, their own stocks of corn having run out. Northmavine showed a population increase from 1009 in 1755 to 2500 in 1831, housed in about 400 farms, due to the fragmentation of farm units to house fishermen, and the taking in of small farms from the undivided common. Here, as in Unst, it was said quite specifically that fishing and farming were incompatible, and that because the land for feeding families was so limited, fallowing was impossible. In the relatively fertile parish of Tingwall, Whiteness and Weisdale much wasteland had been lately reclaimed, some of it by tenants who got outsets on condition that they brought the land under crop, and who were allowed to sit rent-free for 7 years. Fetlar had few outsets, but North Yell, the other half of the same parish, had several. It was noted that the reclaiming of hill ground curtailed the pasture for those in the rental land within the dykes. In Yell, the farms averaged 2 to 3 acres, and none was larger than 6, at a rent of £1 an acre. Meadow and pasture were not subject to rent. Some of the people lived poorly, because they had married too soon to be able to stock a farm, or because they had settled on patches of ground that were too small. In Bressay, Burra and Quarff the arable had been increased by outsets. In Unst, the 2000 arable acres consisted of farms averaging 6 acres each. Because of a population growth from 1368 in 1755 to 2909 in 1831, most farms held more people than were necessary to work them. At the same time farms had become smaller since the 1790s, just adequate to keep the fishers in meal, potatoes and cabbage, and to graze enough stock. Nesting, the population of which rose from 1941 in 1801 to about 2250 in 1841, contained more people in proportion to the rental land than any other Shetland parish, because of the number of outsets.[191]

By the 1870s, the fisher-farmers of Unst had adopted rotations, but in general little change was to be seen. Because the fishermen were bound to the landlord, usually without a lease, the overall result was 'the multiplication of small holders, the general reliance upon the industry of the sea rather than upon that of the farm, the substitution of the spade for the plough (see page 285 ff.), and – a gradual "letting down" of the farming. While all other districts have been advancing, Shetland has remained stationary, if it has not retro-graded'. The establishment of what is here called 'offsets' had been continuous as new land was broken in. By this date, a tenant paid an average of £1 per cow for his land, house, byre and barn. A unit of 6 to 7 acres arable with unlimited access to the scattald allowed about 4 or 5 cows, milking or dry. For such tenants, there was no possibility of initiating improvements. These had to come from the laird.[192]

The net result of this continuous and long-extended activity was that though the arable acreage increased, the standard of farming fell. There was a wide-spread fragmentation of units, which in turn affected the implements and methods of working. Because of the small size of the units, Shetland came fully within the terms of the Crofters Holdings Act of 1886, which applied to crofts in the parishes in the seven crofting counties of Argyll, Inverness, Ross and Cromarty, Sutherland, Caithness, Orkney and Shetland, where there were or had been in the preceding 80 years holdings of arable land with rights in the common pasture, and where there were tenants paying money rents of under £30 a year.[193] The effect was to freeze the croft sizes, even though machinery was incorporated to permit enlargement of holdings. In Orkney on the other hand, the sequence of events had created many units that fell outside this definition, so that though technically one of the crofting counties, it is as much a farming county as any other part of Scotland. For a time, however, events in Shetland were paralleled by those in Orkney, but for a different, though equally commercial reason – the burning of kelp.

8

Kelp

The Influence of Kelp Burning on Orkney Farms

AROUND the shores of Orkney, and to a much lesser extent in Shetland, a great deal of seaweed was available. This was an important source of manure for the soil (see page 274 ff.), but when in the course of the eighteenth century it came to be burned to make kelp as a source of iodine and potassium salts, a conflict of interests arose, in relation both to the amount available for fertiliser, and to the degree to which kelp working absorbed farm-labour. James Fea of Whitehall, Stronsay, said to have introduced the manufacture of kelp into Orkney with the help of a man from Peterhead, sold his first cargo in Newcastle in 1722.[194] By 1757, kelp had been producing an income of about £2000 a year for the previous 20 years. Kelp was plentiful in Walls, and in Flotta, where the kelp burners played fiddles and danced in the evening to relax after their day's work. It could provide useful employment for poor old men and women. Holms that had formerly served only for pasture now greatly increased in value to the proprietors where, like the Greenholms in Egilsay, they provided plenty of tang for kelp making.[195]

By this period kelp burning was a flourishing industry in Orkney. In Shetland, on the other hand, it was on a much smaller scale, and was established only in the second half of the eighteenth century, after a number of landlords had employed someone from Orkney to survey their shores. The whole county produced only about 200 tons in 1780.[196] The 1791 estimate was 200 to 300 tons a year. Lerwick produced only 6 tons a year. The Aithsting and Sandsting shores, let to farmers for kelp, gave 40 to 50 tons a year. Burning had been only lately introduced. Kelp was tried in Unst in 1780, and yielded about 10 tons a year. Bressay, Burra and Quarff produced only a few tons. Yields gradually increased to about 400 tons a year, with a record 600 tons in 1808.[197] In 1814, production was only 400 to 500 tons, at which low level the trade was 'not so hostile to agricultural improvement' as in Orkney. Kelp burning had declined greatly in Shetland by the mid nineteenth century. It gave employment to 20 to 30 boys and girls in Bressay, and still towards the end of the century a few hundred tons were made each year, mainly in Unst, Yell and on the Mainland by Yell Sound. The kelp shores were not worked by the proprietors, as in Orkney, but were let on royalties to the fishcurers of the district, who employed

12. Gathering kelp in Papa Westray, *a*. 1912. Per Miss M. Harcus. C3021.

women to collect and burn the seaweed. At one time before 1800, however, the Shetland lairds did sometimes keep the kelp shores in their own hands, not letting them to the tenant along with the land. The procedure then was for the proprietor or tacksman to employ a man who knew how to make kelp, paying him £2 to £2.10/– a ton. This man in turn hired women and boys at a low rate per month, or sometimes by the tide, to cut and gather tang.[198] Such prices remained static almost till the twentieth century.

The story of kelp in Orkney was much more commercial, after a slow start, though as early as 1688 it had been pointed out that Orkney produced plenty of the tangle which was used in other places to produce kelp for making soap.[199] When kelp making started in the 1720s, little was made at first, and the price was low. But by the 1760s it was a staple commodity, with the price rising from 40 to 50/– a ton to £5 to £8 a ton in the 1770s. At first only tang that grew on the rocks was used, until skill was learned in using other kinds of seaweed. Sanday was amongst the most prolific areas, giving 500 to 600 tons a year, about a quarter to a fifth of the Orkney output. The North Ronaldsay average was 90 to 100 tons. There was a demand for Orkney kelp in Newcastle, for the manufacturers of crown glass who used alkaline salts in the processes.[200] In Kirkwall and St Ola, there was at first positive opposition to kelp burning. It was work to which the people were not accustomed, and 'they represented to the proprietors, how hurtful that new business was likely to be, for they could have no doubt of its driving the fish from the coast, and it would therefore ruin the fishing; they were certain it would destroy both the corn and the grass, and they

13. Burning kelp in Papa Westray, 1920–1930. Per T. Mackay.

14. Burning kelp at Black Craig, Stromness, Orkney. Per W. Morrison. C5517.

were much afraid, that it might even prevent their women from having children'. Even a sea-monster with the name of Nuckelavee was so offended by the burning of seaweed that he vented his wrath by smiting the horses in the island of Stronsay with a deadly disease which then – so it is said – spread over all the islands where kelp was made. The disease got the name of 'mortasheen'. Such fears had already led to positive action at an earlier date. For a time James Fea in Stronsay was the only kelp burner in Orkney, but when profits were seen others joined in, till the smoke of the Stronsay kelp kilns made the island look like an active volcano. Eventually, Patrick Fea of Dinnatoun, along with John Fea in Cleat, gathered the islesmen together on 17 May 1762 and went around the shores destroying the tang and kelp, quenching the kilns, and removing the implements. There was some rioting and bloodshed during the apprehending of Patrick Fea. It was pleaded in mitigation at the Court on 28 October 1762 that 'it is the common opinion of Orkney and others that the burning of Tang in this Country had not only been the cause of bad crops of corn these three years past, but also that the same has been prejudicial to their persons and cattle when in a sickly condition, and made them in a worse condition, and some of the cattle dyed by the smoke thereof, and for want of wair the fish have gone from the shores, and the lempods growing upon the rocks, being sometimes the food of the poor, for want of wair blades, their covering, have fallen from the said rocks by the heat of the sun, so that the poor people were deprived of that part of their food'. The farmers considered they had a right to protect their interests. In the event, Peter and John Fea were found guilty and fined.[201]

It was an effect of the kelp industry in Stronsay, as elsewhere, that all the spring work of farming had to be squeezed in after March, including the repairs to the hill dykes, before the kelp season began in May, which meant that extra men and horses were necessary.[202] The seasonal round of work was unbalanced.

The amount made at first was small, a reflection not so much of fear of such calamities as of the low price of kelp. At 45/– a ton between 1740 and 1760, about £2000 a year was brought into Orkney. It then rose to 4 guineas a ton, giving an income of £6000 a year between 1760 and 1770. The next 10 years produced £10,000 a year at £5 a ton and from 1780 to 1793 an average of £6 a ton brought in £17,000 a year. The proprietors therefore got, in 50 years, an aggregate of £370,000; but in pursuing this industry, which employed nearly 3000 hands in June and July, both fisheries and farming were neglected. The income from kelp tided the people and estates over during the semi-famine years of 1780 to 1787, and led in general to an improvement in the food, clothing, and houses of the lower classes, allied with a spirit of independence. At the same time, increases in wages pushed up the prices of provisions, trebling them since 1760.[203]

Firth and Stenness made 80 tons a year, Sandwick and Stromness 50, and Westray 280 tons, with a further 70 from Papa Westray. Here, kelp put agriculture firmly into a secondary place. A good deal also came from Rousay and Egilsay, Stronsay and Shapinsay, which produced about 120 tons a year.

Birsay and Harray made 17 to 18 tons a year. Information on kelp wages is available from St Andrews and Deerness. Here, where kelping was one of the reasons for a scarcity of farm-servants, men got 13 to 16/– a month and 4 stones of meal, whilst women got 8/– and 3 stones of meal. In Walls and Flotta, where 80 tons a year were produced, the rate was £1.5/– to £1.10/– per ton of 24 cwt. for burning. The Orphir report again shows that fishing as well as agriculture was being hindered by kelp making, which was the main article of commerce. Fifty tons a year were produced in this parish. From Evie and Rendall came 70 tons a year, the work of it taking up the farm-hands in the summer. The value of kelp to Orkney is made very clear by the fact that between about 1720 and 1790, the worth of kelp estates rose seven- or eight-fold. In Shetland, by contrast, kelping affected the rents not at all. The range of the business further demonstrates the importance of kelp in Orkney. Between 1789 and 1795, 15,768 tons were exported to Glasgow, Leith, Newcastle, Whitby, Stretton and Hull, with smaller quantities going to Dundee, Sunderland, London, Bristol and Liverpool. The biggest amounts went to Newcastle.[204]

In 1805, the people of Orphir made their living by burning kelp as well as by farming and supplying peat to their neighbours. Shapinsay was producing 100 tons a year, Stronsay 300, Eday 80, Sanday 550, North Ronaldsay 100, Westray 300, Papa Westray 80, Egilsay 70, Rousay 30. In fact, a seasonal routine developed, with farming in spring and harvest, kelping in summer, and fishing in the intervals. By this date, 2 to 3000 tons a year were produced in Orkney, and the prices at Leith, Newcastle, etc., were £7 to £10 per ton of 21 cwt.[205]

The prosperity that kelp brought was not without its critics. Kelp had changed the state of society by making more money available. As a result, many country gentlemen had begun to move into Kirkwall, especially in winter. Concentration on kelp had made the state of agriculture as a whole very low, and the fisheries were being neglected – 'kelp will be the ruin of Orkney'. Kelp employed about 3000 people in summer, each of whom made an average of 24 cwt. and earned from 30/– to £3 between July and August, and this had improved living standards.[206] As long as circumstances were against land improvement, there was good reason for making the most of kelp manufacture, but after the obligation to pay feu-duties in kind was removed, and as runrig lands began to be laid out in individual units, the need increased for owners to give serious thought to improving their property as a source of revenue more certain than kelp. Landholders had come to be supported entirely by their kelp shores, and though revenue from kelp had helped to preserve many estates intact, 'yet the agriculture of the country is not improved, and the situation of the farmer is as wretched as ever'. The laird could survive on the kelp income, but the tenant had no such base and agriculture suffered accordingly. Even the principal farms were retained only for the profit from their kelp shores.[207]

Such doubts were justified. The year of the greatest kelp yield was 1825, when 3500 tons were processed at £7 a ton, yielding £24,500. During war years, however, prices rose to £18 to £20 a ton,[208] for the economics of kelp were closely related to events in Spain. Kelp is an alkaline ash used in various industrial processes, and especially in the manufacture of soap, and of crown and bottle glass. The alternative was barilla of which Spain was the main supplier, and since barilla, made from the ash-residue of glasswort, *Salicarnia*, yielded four times more per ton it was preferred if it could be got, even though government import duties were applied, starting at 5/2½ per cwt. in 1782, rising to 42/– in 1824, and falling to 2/– a ton in 1831.[209] The cutting off of supplies during the Napoleonic Wars, and especially after Napoleon's invasion of Spain in 1809, pushed up home prices. So did the taxation of salt (abolished 1825), which became the basis of the alkali industry in the nineteenth century. At the same time, though the gathering and burning of kelp was a laborious process, yet there was a plentiful supply of raw materials with no need for elaborate equipment to process it locally, and the concentrated product could be transported cheaply. As long as external conditions were favourable, profits were high and home production costs were low.[210] The effect of the war is clearly seen from the prices. Between 1740–1805 there was an increase from £2.5/– to about £10 a ton, from 1806–10 it ran from £16 to £20, and from 1815, after the French Wars ended, the price steadily dropped – though pegged somewhat by the high import duty on barilla that lasted till 1828 – to £2.10/– by 1840.[211] Throughout the whole period, the cost of production ranged between £2 and £3 a ton, and the cost of transport was similar. There was, therefore, a considerable amount of cash left over for the organisers of the industry, and though it is beyond doubt that kelping had led to a decline in both farming and fishing, nevertheless it must have provided some proportion of the cash basis for the improvements in Orkney farming that came after the middle of the century. For example, one crofter paying a rent of £8 earned up to £34 a year from kelp. At the same time, the laird's share of the profits helped him to help his tenants to improve houses and land, in a way that might not otherwise have been possible.[212]

From a maximum of 3500 tons in 1825, the yield fell to 500 tons by 1840, and the industry remained depressed till about 1880. Relatively little mention of it is made in the Second Statistical Account in the 1840s, though the ministers of St Andrews and Cross and Burness parish still thought its production worth describing. Kelp was on the way out in Stronsay and Eday, where 215½ tons and 161 tons respectively were made in 1841. The kelp cutting and carrying in North Ronaldsay was done to a great extent by women. Here, one large farm paid £80 rent, the next highest was £25, and the majority paid much less, because of the sub-division of the land for kelp. The five townships there were finally squared off into small farms in 1832. In 1841, kelp was still paying about a third of the annual rent. Kelp was on the decline in Westray, and little was being made in Stromness and Orphir, where production had dropped from 70 to 20 tons. In areas like Lady parish, where there were large farms, the pattern of farm-service was affected by kelp. Amongst the workers was a class known as *bollmen* or *bowmen*, paid in kind with a monthly allowance of grain and oatmeal during winter and spring. In summer, however, after May, they worked on kelp at a stipulated price per ton. A little kelp was made in Firth and Stenness, in Sandwick it was almost out, and in Kirkwall and St Ola it had declined.[213]

Following this period, the industry picked up slightly because of a price increase, due to the extraction of iodine from the ash of tangles. The discovery of iodine was made by French kelp burners who were extracting potassium carbonate from seaweed, in the latter years of the Napoleonic Wars. For this, the oarweeds, *Laminaria*, were used, and several iodine extraction factories sprang up around Glasgow. This industry was eventually ended by the discovery of the Chilean saltpetre deposit from which cheaper iodine could be made. Generally speaking, driftweed was preferred for the production of iodine, bromide of potassium, and chlorate of potassium, whilst cut weed was best for glass making. In latter days when the demand for kelp for glass making had ceased, care had to be taken to prevent the gatherers from substituting cut for drift seaweed. Kelp was sent from Orkney to Mr Hughes at Bo'ness, or to Messrs W and M Paterson, Glasgow. The British Chemical Company, Glasgow, continued to get kelp from Orkney into the twentieth century. To encourage production, an advance of 10/– a ton was offered for the kelp made in Orkney in 1913, chiefly for iodine.[214]

Kelp burning still lies within the period of living memory. One of the last occurrences was recorded in 1925:

'On a small scale this season kelp burning was tried at Innertown, Stromness, when Mr Allan of Pow made about a couple of tons or better. Not for over a dozen years has it been tried in Innertown, and this small parcel was in the nature of a trial to see how it would pay. Last year Mr Stout, the Laird of Leger, in Outertown, made some kelp, but no one tried it there this year.'[215]

The Kelp Making Process

The types of seaweed preferred for kelp were the wracks, *Fucus* and *Ascophyllum*, known by such names as, for example, yellow, black and prickly tang. Cutting was done by means of hooks and sickles, whose blades were toothed like harvest hooks.[216] Collecting could start as early as mid-November, when the winter gales had torn the red-ware loose and cast it ashore. A two-pronged fork, with prongs at right angles to the shaft, was used. This was a *pick* (Orkney) or a *taricrook* (Shetland), the first part of the latter name coming from Norwegian *tare*, *Laminaria*.[217] With this implement, the kelpers worked urgently in the white, rushing surf, dragging the wet, heavy ware out of the sea's grasp, before a change of wind should wash it away again. Summer work, cutting with the toothed sickle and gathering, was infinitely more pleasant.

The gathered seaweed was spread out to dry on the grass or on stone foundations or *steethes* (Old Scots *stede*, place, site, 1375) at the head of the beach. The heaps, which had to be turned sometimes to prevent fermentation, had various names. A *beek* was, in Stronsay, a pile of tangles for kelp making, laid in tiers at right angles to each other. Other Stronsay names are *build* (cf.

Swedish dialectal *bål*, heap of stuff) and *kes* or *kace*, with *kyest* (Norwegian dialectal *kas*, *kos*, a heap, Old Norse *kasa*, to heap earth on, *kǫs*, a heap, *kǫstr*, a pile) in Rousay and *kokk* (cock) in Birsay. When the tangles were being heaped up to dry the broad fronds were stripped off, a process called 'to klokk tangles'. In Walls, each man's tangle was heaped in a *kossel* (from Norwegian dialectal *kǫs*, heap), 'a round place above high water mark, a hollow where each man's seaweed is collected'. On the Sanday shores, a mark-stone set up between the plots of ground used by kelpers for spreading their seaweed was a *dull* (Old Scots *dule*, boundary mark, 1563), or in North Ronaldsay a *met* (Old Scots *met*, measure, 1426).[218] The ware was piled in conical heaps, and when drying greens were used for spreading it out, they had to be grassy and not sandy.[219] In winter only the tangles could be dried, till they became hard and wrinkled, but the fronds and softer parts went to manure the fields. In an area as rich in seaweed as Orkney, it was seldom that the manuring of fields suffered because of the kelp industry, since the produce of the sea could be shared between farming and industry in this kind of way. The real problem that affected farming was the absorption of manpower by the kelp industry.

When dry, the tangle was burned in a kelp kiln. In Shetland this took the form of a pit 5 ft long by 3 ft broad by 2½ ft deep (1.5 m × 91 cm × 76 cm) of the same form as those commonly used in the Hebrides. The Orkney preference, on the other hand, was for round kilns, stone lined, about 5 ft in diameter by 2 ft deep (1.5 m × 61 cm).[220] An example excavated at the North end of North Ronaldsay in 1964, one of several dozen kilns there, was 5 ft (1.5 m) in diameter by only 1 ft (30 cm) deep. Here the sides were level with the surrounding grass or had become so, whereas an example in the Calf of Eday had stone sides rising above this level. These kilns dot the sides of the grassy drying places.

It was generally acknowledged that a lot of impurities resulted from the open kelp kiln. Slivers were apt to split off the heated stone lining, sand got mixed in, burning was imperfect. It was impossible in this way to produce kelp of a quality that could rival barilla, and some experiments were tried with reverberatory furnaces, for example by Captain Bichan, who erected several at the holm of Rousholm, after the plan of Col. Fullarton in Ayrshire. This allowed the drying and burning of tangle in winter, and he got purer kelp and a higher price. This, however, had to be balanced against the scarcity of coal for fuel.[221]

To start the fire in an open kiln, handfuls of dry ware or a smouldering peat or

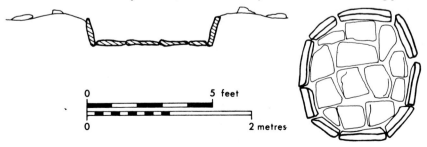

0   5 feet

0   2 metres

15. A circular kelp kiln in North Ronaldsay, excavated by A. Fenton, 1964. C5845.

a handful of lighted straw or straw simmens (ropes) were laid in the bottom, placed centrally if there was not much draught, but otherwise nearer to the windward side. A sack could be held up at one side to draw up the fire. Once the fire was going all over, the dry ware was piled on, slowly at first, then more rapidly. Sometimes ware and tangles were burned separately, but more often they went into the same kiln. Tangles made the best kelp. In laying them on, the system was to place them first round about, then across the middle, then round again. The filled pit rose about 2 ft (61 cm) above ground level. For six or eight hours the kiln was left to burn, new fuel being piled on to prevent a burst of flame, and from it rose 'pale blue smoke-drifts, which cast over the low, sloping shores a certain charm of remoteness and of mystery'. If tangles alone were being burned, dried ware was used to finish off the process, to make sure that no bits of the last stems to be added would remain. The alternative was to remove such pieces with rakes.

By the time the fire had smouldered low, the kiln was filled with about half a ton of semi-fluid, oily-looking, dark bluish-grey kelp, which was then raked vigorously with iron rakes, with up to four rakes going in one pit. The process was called 'rinnin-oot' in North Ronaldsay. One man worked a small-bladed spade with a 7 ft (2.1 m) long handle, the lower half of which was of iron. Two other workers, who might be women, had 'rakes' with equally long handles, 'not unlike a rough caricature of a golfer's iron'. They were used to mix and smooth the kelp, whilst the man with the spade turned it up from the kiln bottom. 'Hard work it is and hot, great jets of flame shooting out under the spade from what looks like gray crumbling earth mingled with black ashes and white quarz; for the kelp assumes so many colours and forms that to describe it accurately were impossible. As the kelper turns and tosses the glowing mass on a warm June evening, he knows he has come near the end of that labour which began in the gray winter dawn, when the rolls of red-weed lashed about him amid the soaring backwash of the waves'.

After the raking, the kiln was levelled over, and scattered ashes swept in with a handful of dry ware. The kiln was left to cool and harden, sometimes being left for several weeks till it was ready to be broken up for transport. Then it was raised with crowbars, and either lifted in a solid cake or broken into lumps of a grey colour, with rainbow streaks of blue and white and brown. It was more easily broken if it could be got out whole first and turned upside down. Big lumps were carried on their own, the dross was put in sacks. Since rain could spoil it, lairds often built storehouses to which the kelp was carted, pending shipment, and there the kelp grieve weighed it, paying a fixed amount per ton. The standard of weight in the kelp trade was the *weigh*, a unit of 2 cwt. The old kelp store at Bridesness in North Ronaldsay was broken down by the sea, and the stones were built into a tower that served as a guide for fishermen. From the store, when a ship's load had been gathered, the kelp was flitted out to a chartered vessel, or loaded from a pier if there was one, and the year's work, the produce of the sea metamorphosed by fire and the labour of man's hands, went off to serve the industrial processes of the south.[222]

9

Surveys and Surveyors

IN the eighteenth and nineteenth centuries, the old joint farm or township organisation, with its use of the natural resources in a seasonal rhythm and balance based on the experience of hundreds of years, was being adapted and changed through the pressure of a new world of commercialism. The changes were not the result of a long, slow process of indigenous, small-scale evolution, but were imposed with positive intent. Some aspects, such as the creation of outsets, can only be plotted after the event because no paper planning was involved. Others have been put on record through the activities of land surveyors, commissioned by the lairds to survey and map their holdings as a prelude to reorganisation.

Amongst the earliest of such surveyors were Alexander Aberdeen who worked for the Earl of Morton, owner of the Orkney Earldom Estate, and William Aberdeen who worked for Morton's successor, Sir Laurence Dundas, who became owner of the Earldom lands in 1766. They produced numerous plans of parts of Orkney and Caithness, showing how the lands were owned and the countryside divided at the time, with vignettes of animals, buildings, farming and fishing activities, and archaeological sites. Their plans are sources of much value, especially for the appearance of the Orkney settlement pattern in the 1760s. The purpose of these plans is undoubted, for a carefully drawn 'Chart of the Orkney Islands' is subtitled 'Scheme of the Division of Land in the Earldom of Orkney'.[223]

In Shetland, Andrew Dishington Mathewson was appointed surveyor and divider for the division of the lands of Funzie in Fetlar. He was a young parish schoolmaster in South Yell, and lived for a time in Fetlar after his father was evicted from his croft in Yell. At the age of 14 he was schoolmaster in Urie, Fetlar. Land surveying was a regular means by which he added to his slender income. The very detailed map of Funzie township made in 1829 was his work.[224]

One of the best-known surveyors was Thomas Irvine of Midbrake in Yell. His manuscript notes give a lively picture of the work of a surveyor, tramping with his notebooks, measuring chain, and assistant, through bog and hill and arable, in rain and sun and mist, noting measurements and making field notes and plans. In November 1848, at Lunna, he divided Lower and Upper Skelberry, after measuring and setting up marches. Friday the 17th November was 'not field weather laid down the Plan of Laxo', but the marches were set up at Laxo on the next day, and surveying of Flugarth began, with Grunafirth and Lunning to follow. The grass belonging to the Town of Upper and Lower Skelberry was also measured.

In June 1849, he surveyed Firth, Laxobigging and Gravin in Delting. On 6 July, the rooms of Upper and Nether Sound in Weisdale were measured. Neep was surveyed on 13 July. On 26 September 1849 he travelled to Unst at the request of R. N. Spence to sketch and measure Burgagarths or Burragarths near Lund, and in October he went with chain and map-case to Seter in Weisdale, then to Neep. Following 10 October, South Hammerslund and Easthouse were perambulated, and plans drawn. Later in the month he was in the Town of Minn in West Burra Isle, and mapped and made a valuation of Fitch.

In July 1850, five witnesses were named for establishing the Culswick scattald boundary. Saltness was surveyed and valued, marches set up, and division lines laid down. Wick in Gulberwick was surveyed, and a map and report prepared for Forratwat.

Between 14 October 1850–28 January 1851, he carried out a survey of Uradale, and prepared notes on Mathieson's report on East Quarff and Sievwright's plan of the outsets there. Trondra Island was surveyed between 13 to 30 November. A piece of unenclosed scattald on the south side of Uradale was measured, the lines of division through the hill ground extended within the dykes, and marches set up. At Gulberwick, he laid down the lines of division in the 'Room of Wick', set up marches, and straightened the boundary between Gilbert Newlson's pund and the 'So. Allotment' in Wick. Noss of Trebister was surveyed.

In 1852, he went around the town of Firth, and pointed out the division lines of proprietors and farms, and the head and foot marches of each. Marches for the division and sub-division in Udhouse and in the two Punds were completed. He also went to Nashian and showed the lots to the tenants.

In 1853, he surveyed the scattald of South and North Hammerslund, Easthouse and Wadbuster. According to his Journal, on 10 June and the days following, he reached the point of Ness of Wadbuster along the east side; then across to Wadbuster along the town dyke to the south-east corner, and to the top of the hill of Stova; from Wadbuster to the north-west point of Ness and across to the north-east point; from the south-east corner of the dyke of Wadbuster to the march at the top of Gilsa Burn; from the top of Gilsa Burn to the march on Bodhoull, and thence to Geo Stones. A map of the enclosures was drawn up. He also surveyed the hill or scattald of Berry, near Tingwall, Muckle Ure, the south Town of Culswick, and Scord at Vaila. The Town of Westerwick was divided into six farms.

In 1855, the Manor Farm at Bigton, consisting of five parks (fields), the garden, and farmyard, was measured. In the Town of Papa lines of division were laid down, including the marches between the proprietors Sir Arthur Nicolson and Mr Gifford, 'within the Town dike – and carried the line on to the hill from Town dike to South end of Gorda water and set up the marches thereon and from West side of Gorda Water near the south side of the Well of Klink Hammer to East side of Dutch Loch ... set up marches from Gorda Water to Dutch Loch 5 in all—continued the line on west side of Dutch Loch over Mawns Hill—worked upon line for Hamnavoe—Finished Hamnavoe line and North line between Mr Gifford and Sir Arthur to the West sea banks. ... Laid down lines for the Reader and Minister and completed Mr Gifford's line to the West between him and the Minister and School m! ...'

Later, in August, Irvine had a meeting at Voe about the division of the Hogan, and started to divide the seaside portions into proportional shares for merkland. The survey of Dale scattald was begun, and there was a meeting of Commissioners and parties concerned at the north-east end of the Loch of Gossawater, with witnesses, to perambulate the line between the scattald of Dale and those of Sound and Greemaster. Surveying was also done in the Hill of Herraslee.

In 1856 came a survey of Houlland scattald. In the Town of Papa, however, some problems had arisen. Mr Gifford of Busta objected to the Reader's allocation. Eventually the Papa scheme was approved, 'Mr. Gifford's agent Mr. R. N. Spence reserving the effect of objections on Mr. Gifford's part to the position of the Reader's Allocat.ⁿ as laid down in the middle of his ... Mr. Gifford being willing to pay the value of or rebuild the Reader's house and exchange the ground.'

At Trebister, there was a meeting of heritors and agents on the allocation of the hamerest portion of 'our Skathold'. The Earl of Zetland's 6 merk farm at Trebister was measured. This came to 6 acres 1 rood 18 falls Scots measure according to a survey of 1824 by Mr William Sievwright, Land Surveyor, but Irvine's assessment was 8.29371 imperial acres, equal to 6¾ Scots acres, from hill to sea. The whole Town of Trebister amounted to 24 merks, which came to 33 acres 20 falls Scots.

Irvine made measurements at Berry, and noted signs of encroachment, especially by the Scotts of Scalloway. He 'took the oath de fidele before Mr Sievwright the Commissioner as a valuator in the Weisdale Skathold', and in carrying out his work noted some 'unprescribed outsets' at Setter in Weisdale. All the sections were measured from Kirgord to the scattald boundary at Marafield, along with the outsets on the north and east of Kirgord. The boundary was set between Whiteness and Weisdale, and all was valued from the Clubb of Stromford to the Scord of Tuby, then to the Stone of Comba. There were two outsets at Cott.

Further undated entries refer to a meeting of parties about Dale scattald, the line of division between Symbister and Sumburgh, the surveying of Toab, and the finishing of the Scatness division, with J W Spence of Symbister in Scatness wanting his allocation divided into four farms. Irvine also surveyed at Sweenaster, Houll, Break, Setter, and Ness, with both grass- and corn-land being divided at Sweenaster.

In the island of Fetlar, Irvine did a good deal of surveying. On 30 April 1850 he submitted a report on his perambulation of the scattalds of Strand, Funzie, Aith, Grutton, Houbie, Dale, Oddsta and Urie, and Russeter. For the latter, the marches were traced on the east from Funzie Girt dyke end to the 'Ting or green Knoll' upon Turvafield or Turrafiel, and on the west from Ogans Gio at the old dyke end of Uraseter to the crook of the dyke of Crossbister, and from there to the dyke of Newerhouse. The skatt brethren here, those who shared the scattald, alleged they had a right to take up driftwood in Tempa Gio and that their line should go there. Andrew Johnson, reputedly the oldest man in the island, said that at the last riding of the hagri 30 years before (*c.* 1820), at which he was present, the line from the Ting on Turvafield was adopted.

Five years earlier, on 1 October 1845, Irvine collaborated with Robert Bain, teacher in Fetlar, in a *Report of Valuation of runrig lands in the Room of Hestaness.* They divided it into nine sections of arable and four sections of grass.

In June 1850, Irvine submitted a *Report to the Lord Ordinary* on the measurements of the boundary lines and the setting up of march marks. The description has a special interest, since it has a bearing on possible archaeological misinterpretation:

'At the head of Tempa Gio 136 Imp! Links from the present edge of the cliff ... I placed the first March mark, being the Southernmost, consisting of one large stone set upright in a pit with coal under it and 3 smaller stones round it, one on the east, one on the south and one on the north side respectively as supporters, a pile of turf built round them in the form of a cone, the whole surrounded by a circular trench 6 ft (1.8 m) in diameter cut deep in the soil.'

Other march stones were similar, but without the coal.[225]

Other surveyors worked in Fetlar too. I W Hepburn spent twelve days on valuation and surveying the marches in 1881, prior to an action of excambion between Lady Nicolson and the Earl of Zetland. The excambion was to proceed on the footing that the Earl of Zetland should convey to Lady Nicolson the whole of his infield lands in the scattalds of Oddsta, Urie, Dale, Russater and Grutton, with the outsets and right of commonty effeiring thereto (which clearly demonstrates the original sense of 'scattald'); and Lady Nicolson was to convey her infield lands of Litlaland, Baelagord and Houll in the scattald of Funzie, with outsets and rights of commonty, and such portion of her infield lands of Toftan and in Strand as would complete the equivalent (July 1875).

Hepburn's account, which was queried, was:

1875, Sept.	To 12 days on Valuation and Surveying of Marches @ £1.1 p.d.	£12.12/–
1881	To division of 4336.664 acres @ 3½d p.ac.	£63.4.8
1881	To paid expenses	£8.7.2
		£84.3.10[226]

In spring 1875, Thomas Irvine surveyed the Town of Velzie in Fetlar. Six detached pieces of glebe land lay within the Velzie hill dyke. Velzie itself amounted in all to 77 acres 3 roods imperial measure, and the glebe land, consisting of 3 arable patches, 2 meadow, and 1 grass or outfield, were valued as follows:

	Area	*Valuation*
1.	.31110 square links	12/– per acre
2.	.19947 square links	6/– per acre
3.	.49686 square links	1/4 per acre
4.	.09945 square links	
5.	.55128 square links	£6.16.1 total relative value
6.	.17476 square links	

1.83292 square links, ie 1 Acre 3 Roods 13 Poles

In proportion to the rental of the Town of 31 merks, 3 merks share of this value for the glebe amounted to 13/1¾ slg., which, added to the total relative value of the 6 pieces, amounted to £1.8.2¾ slg. relative value. This calculation then gave the basis for allotting a single piece, instead of six, in the north-east quarter of Velzie.[227]

PAPA STOUR: A CASE STUDY

Thomas Irvine also carried out the survey of the island of Papa Stour. Details of his work and of the whole process of division were preserved in the Nicolson Papers, now unfortunately destroyed. These notes indicate the value of the evidence, for what was a time of primary importance in the history of the island. What happened in Papa Stour gives much insight into what was happening in other parts of the Northern Isles in the mid nineteenth century.

On 9 Feb. 1846, Sir Arthur Nicolson wrote from his home at Brough Lodge in Fetlar, to Arthur Gifford of Busta. Between them, they owned Papa Stour, except for the shares of the Minister and Reader. Though differing on the details, both proprietors were anxious for division: 'It is a measure indispensible not say for improving the property, but saving it from destruction ... The property is extensive and from the minute subdivisions of the present allotments will require a surveyor of great experience and habits of minute accuracy ... In Papa where there is such gross mismanagement of the lands I submit that no correction of existing abuses to say nothing of improvement or comfort of management could be made with detached holdings'.[228] Gifford, in his reply of 16 Feb. 1846, said he had been seeking division for 25 years. He approved of T. Irvine as a competent surveyor, who could act as valuator and would be able to suggest re-allocations. He considered a correct plan and measurement of the present state of the island to be a basis for discussing changes, though he did not accept Sir Arthur's desire for the concentration of the lands of each proprietor. The reason was clear and understandable: 'I will not blindly incur the hazard of having 30 houses and as many steadings to rebuild out of a rental of £50.' Gifford's willingness to settle things independently of the court and Commissioner was clearly due to this economic consideration. The 30 holdings on Gifford's 72 mks. of land averaged $2\frac{1}{3}$ mks. or little more than an acre, according to Sir Arthur who had been told that Papa Stour merks were only about half an acre. 'I also have some such labourings which I wish to abolish; for I think that a man who has only an acre in 20 morsels some of them $1\frac{1}{2}$ miles distant, must live in a constant conflict with starvation . . . Had he $4\frac{1}{2}$ or 5 mks. laid together his subsistence would be secured'.[229]

This exchange of correspondence followed a Summons of Declarator initiated by Sir Arthur in 1845. Gifford claimed that the Summons was grounded on Sir Arthur's belief that all the Papa land lay runrig, whereas he himself maintained that it was only a small proportion.[230] The Summons stated that the pursuer, Sir Arthur, was 'heritably infeft and seized in All and whole one hundred and forty-four merks Udal land in the island of Paper Stour, ... conform to charter under the Great Seal in his favour, written to the seal and registered 19th, and sealed at Edinburgh the 21st September 1808, and instrument of sasine following thereon, dated 13th September, and recorded in the particular register of sasines at Lerwick the 6th October 1809: THAT the said island of Papa Stour consists of arable land and cows' grass, surrounded by one dyke, termed merks land, or rental land, and of commonty or scattold, lying without the said dyke, and of the room and lands of Hamnavoe and North Banks, these last being the exclusive property of the pursuer THAT the said arable lands, situated within the aforesaid dyke, lie runrig, and are possessed by the pursuer and his tenants, and by other proprietors and their tenants, all of them having alternate patches of land everywhere over the whole space enclosed by said dyke; and the cows' grass within said dyke having been possessed by the pursuer, his predecessors and authors and their tenants past the memory of man, and by the other proprietors and their tenants, *pro indiviso*, and occupied by them in common: THAT the remainder of said Island, excepting the crofts of Hamnavoe and North Banks, lying without the said dyke, and forming the commonty or scattold of Papa Stour, has been possessed by the pursuer, his predecessors and authors, and their tenants, past the memory of man, as their common property, and part and pertinent of their said 144 merks of rental land, and of the said room or lands of Hamnavoe and North Banks . . . by pasturing cattle and using other acts of commonty thereon: THAT, therefore, the pursuer, in terms of the Acts of Parliament 1695, chap. 23, entitled, "Act anent lands lying runrig", and 1695, chapter 38, entitled, "Act concerning the dividing of commonties", has good and undoubted right, title, and interest to prosecute and insist in the action of division underwritten: AND ALTHOUGH the pursuer has often desired and required Arthur Gifford, Esq. of Busta, heritor, and also the Reverend Archibald Nicol, minister of the united parishes of Walls, Sandness, Papa, and Foula, and James Irvine, reader in Papa Stour . . . to concur with the pursuer in a division thereof;

YET they refuse, at least delay so to do: THEREFORE, the said defenders, and all others having, or pretending to have, any right or interest in the premises, OUGHT and SHOULD EXHIBIT and PRODUCE their several respective writs and titles, in virtue whereof they claim right to the said runrig lands; and in virtue of which they claim any right either of property in, or of servitude over the said cow's grass and commonty or scattold: And it OUGHT and SHOULD be FOUND and DECLARED, by decree of the said Lords, that the pursuer is entitled to prosecute the said action of division of the said runrig lands and cow's grass and commonty or scattold, against the defenders ... And thereon the same OUGHT and SHOULD be divided by the said Lords betwixt the said parties; and for that purpose, a commission OUGHT and SHOULD be granted by the said Lords to the Judges Ordinary, or other persons, to perambulate the said runrig land and cow's grass, and also the said commonty or scattold, and take a proof of the extent, limits, quality, and marches thereof respectively, as the same have been reputed, possessed, and enjoyed for forty years byegone, or past the memory of man, by the pursuer and such of the defenders as shall produce their rights in manner foresaid, and to describe the marches of the said runrig lands, cow's grass, and common ground respectively, and set up march stones therein, and to take a proof of the number of merks land in the said Island of Papa Stour, belonging to the pursuer and such of the defenders as shall appear and instruct their right as heritors or proprietors of merks land, or who shall instruct any other right thereto, or interest in the said runrig lands, scattold, or commonty, and to appoint a proper person or persons to value the several parts and parcels of the said runrig lands and of the said cow's grass, and also the said commonty or scattold, on due consideration of the different qualities of the soil and ground thereof, and to appoint a surveyor or surveyors to measure and survey the said arable lands, cow's grass, and commonty or scattold respectively, and the several parts and pertinents thereof, so to be valued, and thereafter to divide the said lands ... according to the number of merks land in the said Island ... as the established and recognized rule of division in Zetland, in such cases, or according to any other rule or valuation which our said Lords may prescribe, and to draw out a plan thereof, and of the several divisions made of the same, and to mark off, by stones, or otherwise, the several divisions and shares to be allocated to each person, with instructions to the said Commissioners that in making the said division, the parts and portions to be allotted to each heritor, be such as may be next adjacent, or as near as possible to his property lands; and with power also to the said Commissioners, to cause divide the mosses lying within the said Island ... or if it shall be instructed that the said mosses cannot be divided, to leave the same still common, with free ish and entry thereto ... and such of the defenders as shall not produce their rights and titles, and instruct their possession of the said runrig lands and cow's grass, and common ground, OUGHT and SHOULD be FOUND and DECLARED, by decree foresaid, to have no right thereto, or interest therein, and discharged from claiming or exercising such right or interest in all time coming: And the said defenders OUGHT and

SHOULD be DECERNED and ORDAINED, by decree foresaid, to make payment to the pursuer of £50 sterling each, or such other sum, more or less, as the said Lords shall ascertain to be their respective portions of the said expenses to be disbursed in prosecuting and obtaining the said division . . .'[231]

Following this, the Lord Ordinary granted commission to the Judge Ordinary of the Bounds to perambulate the lands, grass, and commonty, to establish boundaries and values, and to carry out the required divisions.[232] A survey was carried out between 10 June and 23 July 1846 by T. Irvine, which established, inter alia, that the average of the arable for each mark of the 226 mks in Papa was 0.92496 square links. Sir Arthur's 144 mks averaged 0.84784, and Gifford's 72 mks, 1.09126 square links. The 7 mks of the Minister averaged 0.94091 and the 3 mks of the Reader 0.59873 square links. This disparity in the merks was one of the factors that made division more difficult. It appears to have arisen because some spots of grass had been turned into arable in the course of the previous 40 years.[233]

Meantime, there was another problem: was Papa Stour one township or more than one? Gifford claimed that the greater part of his arable lay in separate and distinct 'Towns or Rooms', of a certain number of merks each, with distinctive names, and his exclusive property according to the number of merks in each. In his Title Deeds they were contained as distinctive townships, and were so possessed by his tenants. Since these exclusive arable farms consisted of plots of ground from 5 to 20 acres in extent, they were not legally subject to division; but he did not object to the division of the detached portions of ground belonging to his tenants, that lay runrig with the land of Sir Arthur's tenants.[234]

The other parties, the Rev. Archibald Nicoll, and James Irvine, Schoolmaster and Reader, were also consulted. They agreed to a fair and legal division. The Minister however, obviously a canny man, asked that the surveyor should mark on the map the position of the three geos at or near Bragasetter, called Riversand, Ministers' Gio and Outer or Kirk Gio (and perhaps also Thistlebysand – evidence of H. Scott, 4 March 1846), from which the minister, from time immemorial, had had the exclusive right of taking seaweed.[235]

Next, all the parties involved submitted their claims. Under a Sasine dated 10 July and recorded at Edinburgh on 15 July 1841, proceeding on a Crown Charter of Resignation in his favour, Gifford claimed for himself and his tenants a proportional share, by merkland, of the scattald and cow's grass relative to the 12 mks each of Bragasetter, Midsetter, Setter and Evrigarth, the 6 mks of Olligarth, and the 18 mks of Hurdiback. He also claimed isolated patches separated and laid adjacent to his principal arable farms, which were not divisible, and besides this, the Punds of Evrigarth and Olligarth as a separate and distinct property, together with the booth at the west end of the beach of the West Voe, and water mills and water courses then possessed by his tenants.[236]

The supporting documents produced by Gifford, as required by law, were:

1. Disposition and Deed of Entail by Thomas Gifford of Busta to and in favour of Gideon Gifford his grandson ... of 12 merkland ninepenny land in Bragasetter, 12 merkland ninepenny land in Midsetter, 18 merkland ninepenny land in Hurdiback, 12 merkland ninepenny land in Setter, 12 merkland ninepenny land in Evrigarth, 6 merkland ninepenny land in Olligarth, dated 1 Nov. 1752, recorded in Register of Entails 17 June and in Books of Council and Session 5 July 1757.

2. Deed Correctory and Explanatory of the Disposition above executed by the said Thomas Gifford, excluding his daughters from the succession—15 May 1756.

3. Extract Instrument of Sasine in favour of Gideon Irvine following in the Deeds above, dated 4, 5,—16, 17 June 1761, in the Particular Register of Sasines for Zetland, Lerwick 1 July 1761.

4. Extract Register of Disposition and Settlement by said Gideon Gifford in favour of himself, or Arthur Gifford his eldest son ... 10 August 1792, in Books of Council and Session 13 Dec. 1813.

5. Retour of the Service of Arthur Gifford, 6 March 1837.

6. Instrument of Sasine for Arthur Gifford—19–22 April 1837, in General Register of Sasines, 31 May 1837.

7. Decree of Declarator, Arthur Gifford of Busta versus Arthur Gifford, Purser, Royal Navy—20 Nov. 1839.

8. Crown Charter of Confirmation for Arthur Gifford—21 Dec. 1840 written to the seal, registered and sealed 15 March 1841.

9. Procuratory of Resignation by Arthur Gifford—14 April 1841.

10. Crown Charter of Resignation for Arthur Gifford, written to the seal etc.—7 June 1841.

11. Instrument of Sasine for Arthur Gifford—General Register of Sasines, 15 July 1841.

Sir Arthur claimed a proportional share of land, cow's grass and commonty in relation to his 144 mks of rental land; the room and lands of Hamnavoe, with access; a 'right or servitude over the scattald in favour of Hamnavoe and the Pursuer as Proprietor thereof, of pasturage of cattle, sheep, and horses, cutting, winning and drying peats or turf for fuel, cutting feal and divot, quarrying stones, and using other acts of common property thereon; the room and lands of North Banks, with a similar servitude; the Punds of Gardie, an old enclosure lying south of North Banks, which he claims as exclusive to him, not part of the rental lands of Papa but paying a separate rent to him for a period much beyond 40 years; and the fishing booths and fishing stations at Westair, Cullivoe and Northhouse, with free access, as also water and water mills and drift sea weed whenever it came ashore, with free access to it.'[237]

In support of these claims, title deeds and writs were produced. They were:

1. Extract wadset disposition by Patrick Mowat of Balquholly in favour of A. Nicolson of Ballister, 19 May 1715, of Papa Stour, consisting of 224 mks

udal land, with the room and lands of Hamnavoe and North Banks, and the 'Booth, Air, and Strands thereto belonging'. Extract dated 22 Nov. 1763.

2. Attested copy Instrument of Sasine thereon, dated 11 June and recorded at Kirkwall, 30 June 1715 (Certificate dated 12 May 1768).

3. Tack or lease by Thos. Gifford·of Busta in favour of William Nicolson of Lochend of his 72 mks, 2 May 1748.

4. Instrument of Sasine, to Arthur Nicolson of Lochend, 22 May 1782 (General Register of Sasines, Edinburgh, 13 June 1782), proceeding on a charter under the Great Seal, 20 Aug. 1781.

5. Rental of A. Nicolson's property in Papa as set in lease by Public Roup at Lerwick, 14 Mar. 1800, and carried by Mr. Gideon Henderson and certificate subjoined thereto all holograph of the deceased Thomas Bolt Esq. of Cruister.

6. Instrument of Sasine to A. Nicolson, 13 Sept. 1809, in the Particular Register of Sasines, Lerwick 6 Oct. 1809, proceeding on a charter under the Great Seal, registered 19 Sept. and sealed 21 Sept. 1809.

For the Minister and Reader, no titles could be produced, but they claimed 'under the immemorial possession of their predecessors'. The Rev. A. Nicoll's claim was for 7 mks with relevant proportional shares. Most of the land was next to Kirkhouse, which had a good steading of houses, except for 'the Minister's merk' which lay in Bragasetter and was the best land there. He claimed equal quality, or quantity for quality, adjacent to the Kirkhouse, as well as his seaweed rights in three geos, with access to them. The Reader claimed his 3 mk share, including the Schoolhouse and offices. The only change he wanted was to have his runrig patches laid together.[238]

The valuations worked out in detail by J. Irvine have considerable interest when averaged out for the different kinds and qualities of ground.

Nature of Ground	Place	No of Patches	Average Value	Extremes
Arable	Northhouse	4	12/2	9/—15/–
	East Town	28	12/0	4/6–15/–
	East of Biggins, and North Meadows to Kirk Path	3	15/–	All 15/–
	West the Biggins to Midsetter south of the road	21	11/5	3/4–15/–
	North the road	4	13/5	10/6–15/–
	Setter	8	11/–	7/6–14/3
	Bragasetter	7	13/3	11/7–15/–
	North Biggins to Olligarth	11	11/9	6/—15/–
	Gardie, Evrigarth and Hurdiback	16	13/3	8/3–15/–

Nature of Ground	Place	No of Patches	Average Value	Extremes
Unprescribed encroachments on cow's grass	—	11	9/2	3/9 (uncultivated piece) or 6/9–11/3
Punds	of Evrigarth and of Gardie	2	11/8	10/10–12/7
Cow's grass	Between Wart of North House and Forwick	3	7/9	4/10–10/6
	Loch Meadow	2	10/5	9/9–11/3
	North Meadow	1	11/3	—
	Kirk Sand to Gor'sendy Gio	5	7/8	4/10–10/6
	Bragasetter to Setter and Northward to Dale	16	4/2	1/6–12/–
Scattald	Including Kollaster's Pund and Borda	18	1/4	0/6–2/6
Within dykes but equal to commonty in quality	North Ness and Little Ness	5	1/2	0/7½–1/9

From the detailed figures, it can be seen that the areas given the highest values, up to 15/–, are in and around the Biggins, leaving little doubt about the position of the original core of settlement. Other parts, however, including Bragasetter, were not very far behind. The unprescribed encroachments on the cow's grass had in general a higher value than the average suggests, since this includes a low-priced, as yet uncultivated portion. In valuing grass, the cost could be considerably affected where the depth of soil was enough to admit of cutting turf and laying the sward down for grass. The highly priced patch of grass, 10/6, between Wart and North House and Forwick, was the Mailins north of North House, presumably the farm's tounmal.[239]

A further factor that had to be considered was the stock-carrying capacity. In assessing the allocation of commonty for Hamnavoe and North Banks, which had servitudes of pasturage, it was pointed out that they could pasture 9 and 5 head of cattle respectively. Sir Arthur's 144 mks could fodder 432 head, Gifford's 72 mks, 288 head, the 7 mks glebe land 5 to 6 head, and the Reader's 3 mks 2 to 3 head. The island could support 728 head of cattle. The surveyor was asked, on this basis, to work out the extent of ground in the commonty that would be considered a suitable equivalent for the two servitudes.[240] Thomas Irvine did this on the assumption that these servitudes were the same as for the rental land farms, a fact which, taken with the reference to the room and lands of Hamnavoe and North Banks in the wadset disposition of 1715, solidly establishes these places as early outsets. In making his assessment, Irvine had to consider the whole contents of the commonty without and within dykes, cow's grass excepted, the average relative value per acre, the number of cattle foddered, the value of a cow's pasture over the commonty, and the established value per acre of the fee simple of the common according to its relative annual value. This gave '5$\frac{8}{10}$ acres per merk over the whole common, 1$\frac{3}{4}$ acres for each cow, 3/–slg. for the net annual value of the privilege of a cow's pasture on the commonty, 1/1$\frac{1}{4}$.^{d} per acre of average relative value and 20/– per acre as the average price of the commonty in fee simple'. Accordingly, 27 acres of average commonty in absolute property was considered a full equivalent for the Hamnavoe servitude, and 15 for North Banks.[241]

At the same time, the question of whether Papa Stour contained one or more townships was under review. In support of Gifford's contention that there was more than one, five documents were produced to show that the 'respective townships' in Papa were held to consist of a certain number of merks land *in each* as far back as the early part of the eighteenth century.[242] These were:

1. Power of Attorney by George Mowat of Hamnavoe and Margaret Mowat his spouse in favour of James Mowat of Stennis their son inter alia empowering him to collect the rents of their 12 mks land in Bragasetter, 12 in Midsetter, and 9 in Setter, 17 Dec. 1706.

2. A Rental with tenants' names, number of merks held by each, and distinguishing the towns in which the merks lay. Holograph of George Mowat, Hamnavoe.

3. Tack, James Mowat of Stennis to James Hay in Hurdiback and others, of a fixed number of merks land in certain towns in Papa, 29 Oct. 1716.

4. Order by Arthur Nicolson to Papa tenants to pay their poultry to "Stennis", 18 Aug. 1721.

5. Extract Register of Instruments of Sasine in favour of deceased Gideon Gifford of Busta (containing inter alia the lands in the respective townships in Papa referred to in the Defender's claim), June 1761.

Witnesses were called by Sir Arthur to prove the contrary. The first was Alexander Ewanson, farmer and Sheriff Officer in Papa, aged 57. He was then a tenant of Sir Arthur, but had been a tenant of Arthur Gifford also. He was born in Papa, and had farmed there for 30 years. He said Papa consisted of the 'hametown' within dykes, and scattald without dykes, plus the farms of Hamnavoe and North Banks, and that the arable lands lay in runrig in all the merk land of Papa: 'I do not mean in drafts regularly up and down, but in separate patches. This has been the nature of possession by the tenants of the respective proprietors during all my recollection and in so far as I have heard in all time before also. The Cows Grass within the Hill dyke was possessed in common by all the tenants of the respective proprietors. The North Banks tenants were in the habit of possessing exclusively the grass within their own dyke during the 6 months the crops were on the ground, thereafter their cattle pastured promiscuously over the whole town with those of other tenants.' The scattald had been held in common, though the tenants observed some kind of marches among themselves for firing. Their possession of it was proportionate to their possession of rental land, and this applied also to the tenants of Hamnavoe and North Banks.

Sir Arthur had claimed the Pund of Gardie, but this was said to be erroneous. He had no separate title to it, and therefore this and the Punds of Evrigarth were to be taken as part of the rental lands, and subject to division. In his evidence, Ewanson said that Sir Arthur's tenants in Gardie had always possessed the Pund of Gardie till Mr Henderson took it off them. He was Gideon Henderson, merchant in Papa, whose dwelling house had been erected by Arthur Gifford's father for Gideon Henderson's father, with a sufficient supply of peat moss set aside for its firing. This house, though built by the Giffords, stood on the lands of Gardie which belonged to Sir Arthur.[243]

There was a booth and fishing station belonging to Sir Arthur at Westair, as well as 3 booths and 3 curing stations at Cullivoe, though one of the booths there was not then in repair.

Ewanson also stated that the 'merk land in Papa used to pay scatt at the rate of 4.^{d} per merk', but this was now included in his 'slump rent'. The corn teind was also paid by the merkland up till the time the teinds were valued, since when a 'slump rent' had also been paid.

Speaking for the Minister and Reader, Ewanson said that the Rev. A. Nicoll had possessed the glebe lands for 18 years. They were all runrig, with one patch at Bragasetter and another at Eastown, with seaweed rights in Kirk gio, though this was of little use because the sand was quicksand and the seaweed could not be saved. The Minister had built a good steading at Kirk house on entry, about 1829. The Schoolhouse stood on undivided or common property, to which it had been moved about 1807. It had a yard enclosed from the cow's grass.[244]

The next witness was William Henry, Freefield, Lerwick. He was 57, and born in Papa where he lived till he was 43. He and his father had tenanted North Banks since 1792, being joint tenants from 1823 till 1833. He agreed with Ewanson's statement, and made an additional point relevant to the unity of the merk lands of Papa Stour: that for the division of seaweed, they were divided into 12 lasts of 18 merks each, exclusive of the Glebe and the Reader's lands, of which two thirds of the last belonged to Sir Arthur Nicolson, and the rest to Arthur Gifford.[245]

William Georgeson, 45, tenant of Sir Arthur in Gardie for 3 years and in North Banks for 14 years before that, agreed with the others, and said he did not know the number of merks for Arthur Gifford but thought they must be more than half the number Sir Arthur had, since Gifford's lands drew more than half the amount of seaweed that went to Sir Arthur's lands.[246]

Jas Mowat, Jnr., merchant in Lerwick and factor for Sir Arthur in Papa since 1840, also appeared. He said that North Banks was separated from the townlands by the remains of an old dyke; that in 1846 Sir Arthur had 35 tenants in his rental lands, the possessions averaging 3 to 5 mks, and 8 mks of these were lying vacant; and that the public burdens of cess, prison money, schoolmaster's salary, and minister's stipend, were charged on Papa by the merk land, at a uniform rate per merk. Sir Arthur paid £2.8/– yearly as skatt, at 4.^{d} per merk.[247]

In the following spring, more evidence was taken. James Greig, Writer in Lerwick, compeared for Sir Arthur. He explained that in Shetland public burdens, land tax, rogue money and prison money, as well as other incidental county expenses and parochial burdens, school salary, stipend, teind, assessments for repair of kirk and manse, and skatt, were always rated by the merk. Even though merk lands might vary in size and value, public burdens were still paid equally on all, which was why Sir Arthur's tenants, in paying rents, complained that their lands were of less value than those of Gifford. As Commissioner during the valuation of teinds in Papa, he knew that since then they had been paid by the merk land. He had come across no instance of judicial division of runrig other than by the merk land, nor had Alex. Nicoll, Sheriff Clerk Depute of Shetland, who examined the Sheriff Court Records and found that all the 20 runrig division cases since 1813 had been divided by the merk land.[248]

Sir Arthur, therefore, was taking his stand on a belief that Papa Stour constituted one township, and on the principle of division by merk land. Gifford, however, had witnesses to summon on his side.

The first was Hugh Scott, 60, tenant in Evrigarth. He stated that Gifford's 72 marks were in separate "Towns or Rooms", Bragasetter, Midsetter, Setter, Hurdiback, Evrigarth and Olligarth, each with patches of land scattered runrig within the town dykes on account of the seaware which was almost the only manure. Cow's grass, held in common by all tenants, separated the different steadings of these towns. The scattald was common, but the water-mills and courses were possessed by the tenants of each proprietor. The Pund of Evrigarth, separate from other lands and lying within dykes, belonged to Gifford, whilst Gifford's Pund of Olligarth was in the possession of Gideon Henderson and his father. The manor-house of Papa, belonging to Gifford, was possessed by Henderson, who cut peat for it in the common scattald, as his father did before him.

A booth had been set up by Mr Henderson for his own use at the west end of West Voe, but Scott did not know to which proprietor it belonged.

He said the lands of the proprietors lay intermingled: Sir Arthur had land near Bragasetter and in Midsetter, but not in Setter. The land was also mixed at Hurdiback and Olligarth. The Reader had a piece of land in Setter and the Minister in Midsetter. For many years, Gideon Henderson and his father had been tenants of Sir Arthur in the 8 mks at Gardie and the Punds of Gardie, and of Gifford in the Punds of Evrigarth and Olligarth. Henderson and his father were tacksmen of Sir Arthur in Papa, where no Nicolson had ever resided, any more than the Giffords. The house and garden at Gardie stood on the common grass, as did the extension added by Henderson to the south end in 1810. Gifford's tenants possessed 4 mks of land each, paid a rent of about 14/- a merk, and generally foddered 3 cattle and a calf. Two of Sir Arthur's tenants had 6 mks each, the rest 2 to 5 mks, and they were understood to pay 15/- a merk.[249]

John Henry, 53, tenant in Olligarth, agreed in the main with Hugh Scott. He said he understood that the Westair Booth had been erected by Henderson for Gifford's behoof, but did not know if Gifford had repaid the expenses. He agreed with Scott that Bragasetter, Setter and Midsetter contained some of the best ground in the island. This was borne out by the fact that where most of Gifford's tenants could fodder 3 head of cattle and in a good year a calf besides on their 4 mks, Bragasetter and Setter could fodder a head more, and Midsetter a young beast more than the other towns. The Nicolson tenants could fodder 3 head per 4 merks.

The Reader, it appeared, had been making his own encroachments, for in the preceding few years, he had broken out a rig and some outfield land near his house, in addition to his yard.

An important point was his definition of a town, as a steading of houses with its tounmal, the grass around it, and such part of the arable close to it as was possessed by the tenant in the steading, the rest of the lands lying intermixed.[250] To him, therefore, a town was a single farm-unit, and not the group of units as a whole within a single dyke.

Alexander Ewanson was called again, this time on behalf of Gifford. At Bragasetter, Gifford had 12 merks of land, of which 6 were runrig through the island. He had 3 tenants in Midsetter and 3 in Setter, with 4 merks each, runrig throughout the island. Ewanson had himself resided at Setter for 25 years and knew that most of the land lay runrig or in separate patches. Sir Arthur had no tenants in Setter or Midsetter, but had lands near there, runrig with Gifford's land. Gifford had 18 mks at Hurdiback, and 12 at Evrigarth, by which was meant that the tenants there had their merks lying runrig throughout Papa. Nicolson had neither tenants nor merks there. He did have lands at Bragasetter, 'but I never heard that he had merks land there', and did not know if they were merks land or not. The two main proprietors each had 6 merks at Olligarth, scattered runrig throughout Papa. Nicolson's 18 mks at North House, and the remainder at Biggins, were also runrig, and were all said to be merks land. Ewanson also emphasised that the scatter of small patches of ground in different parts of Papa was for the convenience of seaweed manure. This was why Gifford's 3 tenants at Bragasetter had 2 mks each near their houses, and their other 2 mks runrig through the island.

He differed from John Henry in defining a town as a collection of houses called by their various names and occupied by tenants who possessed lands throughout the island.

The Pund of Evrigarth belonged to the land of Evrigarth. He had never heard the term pund being applied to a piece of ground called Enalie broken out by Mr Henderson (who, like his father, had been tacksman of both Nicolson and Gifford at the same time), from the common grass between Olligarth and Hurdiback.

Ewanson's information on stock-holding differed from that of his colleague. He considered that the 4 merks of Gifford's tenants could fodder 4 to 5 cattle, whilst Sir Arthur's land could scarcely fodder 3 per 4 mks.[251]

William Henry produced further evidence. He understood that the houses, cornyard, kailyards, and tounmals at Bragasetter belonged to Gifford, whose 3 tenants there possessed the tounmals according to a division made among themselves. The same applied at Midsetter, Setter, Hurdiback and Evrigarth. The tounmals were defined as small pieces of unlaboured grassland near the houses on which they fed their milking cattle occasionally, but which were pastured promiscuously once the crops were off the ground. In Papa the tounmals were not divided by dykes from the arable.

Mr Henderson cut about 3 times more fuel than any of the other tenants, because he had more fires. He was also in the habit of importing peat and coal. Hugh Scott, compearing again, said Mr Henderson no longer cut more peat than any other tenant, but imported peat and coal.[252]

Once all the evidence had been examined, the Commissioner, Robert Bell, found that next Sir Arthur's houses of North House, the Biggins, and at East Town and Gardie, with the Punds of Gardie bordering on North Banks, there were contiguous masses of land, belonging to Sir Arthur, which exceeded 4 acres. These, with Hamnavoe and North Banks, were therefore not subject to division under the 1695 Act. There were similar masses next Gifford's houses of Setter, Midsetter, Bragasetter, Hurdiback and Evrigarth.

The lands of Olligarth etc. were to be held runrig and were to be divided and valued, 'giving the several proprietors according to their respective interests, which are to be ascertained by the state of their possessions ... and by a due consideration of the quality of the lands'. The allotments were, as far as possible, to be adjacent to the indivisible lands.

For Hamnavoe and North Banks, Sir Arthur was entitled to have 27 and 15 acres of average commonty, set apart as a deduction from the whole common, and the surveyor and valuator was to divide the rest.

The Commissioner considered that 'the case of Papa is in many respects peculiar'. Gifford's lands were generally considered more valuable than those of Nicolson, and Hamnavoe and North Banks were very different from ordinary outsets, having been held as distinct rooms at least from the beginning of the eighteenth century, with an unrestricted right of servitude over the whole commonty. He thought it fair, therefore, that the arable lands subject to division should be divided according to the interests of the parties therein, as ascertained by reference to the comparative extent and value of the lands possessed by each.

Another point was that the Surveyor should reserve sufficient means of access to the Northha', the booths and beaches, and geos for seaweed, as claimed by the various parties.[253]

In this question of division according to interests, the Commissioner was departing from the usual form of division by the merk land, which happened even where the lands of different townships lay intermingled, and was reasonable when such intermingled lands consisted of a number of merks presumed to be of equal value. If rooms were distinct, however, the case was different, because adjacent rooms of the same number of merks could be of different values. Since in Papa there were various distinct townships, groups of houses with yards and tounmals, belonging to the pursuer and defender, with contiguous and indivisible masses of land around them, the Commissioner thought the only fair way to divide the smaller, detached runrig portions was by measurement and valuation, and by placing equivalents alongside the undivided portions. In this way, account could be taken of the fact that Gifford's lands were in general more valuable than those of Sir Arthur. He should not be deprived of a fair equivalent for property possessed beyond the years of prescription, 'and the natural presumption appears to be that his Towns or Rooms were either originally more valuable and extensive or that more attention has been paid to their improvement and enlargement to which after the years of prescription no objection can be taken'.[254]

Thomas Irvine was therefore asked to 'report a plan of division for carrying out the Interlocutor of the Commissioner of 27 August 1849 as now confirmed by Lord Cowan's Interlocutor and note of 12 November, having regard to the principle fixed above according to which the heritors are to draw value, and also to the claims of exclusive property in arable lands set up for Mr Gifford, ruled in his favour by the Commissioner but still in pendente in the Court of Session, and also in the plan of division to the collocating of lands to be given each party ... except that Gifford limits his claim of lands to be excluded from division at Bragasetter, Mid Setter, Setter, Evrigarth and Hurdiback to certain portions ...'.[255] Sir Arthur, not quite satisfied with this, added a memorandum, pointing out that though this implied that only Gifford's tenants resided on the places mentioned, nevertheless four of his were also to be found there. He was making it quite clear that the lands of the two heritors were intermingled.

Discussions went on into the 1850s, with much exchanging of letters and repetition of what had gone before. The difference in the size of the merks was a source of difficulty, though Sir Arthur noted in an undated Memorandum that they were originally all of one denomination, believed to be the ninepenny merk. Continued appropriation of grassland had increased the value of Gifford's merks.[256] This difference seems to have been in part responsible for Sir Arthur's objection to division of the runrig lands according to the interests of the proprietors, 'which are to be ascertained by the state of their possessions', and that the 'remaining Commonty of Scattald and Cowsgrass there are to be divided according to the number of merklands belonging to each'. Sir Arthur explained that the normal Shetland practice was to divide runrig, where an attempt at equality was made, by dividing alternate rigs, with reference to the merkland. This was difficult where adjacent rooms or townships were distinct, since the same number of merks in each could be of different values. The rule of division by merks was sometimes departed from in dividing commonty and common grass, but there was no evidence for this in the case of arable. It was claimed that the merkland, itself a form of valuation, was the only legitimate basis for valuation.

'All of Shetland consists of merklands, about 14,000, thrown together into towns consisting of 2 or 300 merks, each town bounded by a dyke. Within is the arable, meadow, and cow's grass, and what is occupied by the cottages, corn, and cabbage yards. Outside are the commons divided into scattalds, with well known boundaries registered in the Bailie Books, and which have been rode, and the Marches kept up by authority. A large town has a scattald to itself, a number of small contiguous towns, one between them, each merk having an equal share of the scattold, as it has of each of the different descriptions of ground within the dyke. A merk of land is not so much a definite measure as a proportionate share of arable in runrig and of meadow cow grass lying pro indiviso, or in patches called dyelds, and of the Scattald or Common.'

He emphasised that Papa Stour did not consist of separate townlands as assumed in the Deliverance. Apart from the outsets of Hamnavoe and North Banks, the island formed one townland, under one dyke, measuring 226 or 224 merks. Possession was said to have been always 'promiscuous' with 800–1000 ridges of arable. The Crown Charter conveyed 144 mks to Sir Arthur, Gifford had 72, the Minister 7, and the Reader 3.[257]

Irvine's surveys gave the size of the arable patches belonging to each proprietor, possibly equivalent to *sheeds*, and subdivided into rigs:

Proprietor	Place	No. of Patches	Area (Acres)
A. Gifford	Bragasetter	1.	5.16962
		2.	4.40479
	Setter	1.	0.82597
		2.	1.30920
		3.	2.39907
		4.	1.97811
		5.	0.60557
		6.	0.58331
		7.	0.41624
	Setter (west the Biggins)	1.	0.26205
		2.	2.92519
	Midsetter	3.	1.33265
		4.	1.64192
		5.	1.86319
		6.	3.80151
	Bragasetter	1.	0.14526
	Hurdiback	1.	0.06578
		2.	0.05054
	Evrigarth	1.	4.57706
		2.	0.88853
		3.	0.79268

Proprietor	Place	No. of Patches	Area (Acres)
	Hurdiback	1.	1.33275
		2.	0.79268
		3.	0.69086
		4.	2.47610
		5.	1.12936
		6.	0.50401
		7.	1.43115
Sir Arthur Nicolson	Biggins (east the Biggins and west the Biggins)	1.	4.12834
		2.	2.92277
		3.	3.57943
		4.	1.38414
		5.	1.26302
		6.	3.03358
	North House	1.	0.13860
		2.	5.32336
		3.	1.64115
		4.	6.17459
	Biggins	1.	0.42662
		2.	0.06960[258]

It was because of the doubt about division according to merklands, that the Commissioners laid down the principle that division should not be by the merk of land, but by possession, all units of land over 4 acres being indivisible. As an almost predictable by-product of the long drawn-out negotiations, tenants who had been waiting for changes which could have put them on different land, had been neglecting to manure their patches and the land was beginning to deteriorate.[259]

If the principle of division by valuation was chosen, the relative value of arable falling to Sir Arthur for 144 mks was £82.16/–. The allocation of this required all the land around North House, the East Town, the North Biggins and Olligarth, all the land at Hurdiback, Evrigarth and Gardie, and as much from East the Biggins as made £6.14.0½. In getting some of Gifford's land at Hurdiback, Evrigarth and Olligarth, he would have to relinquish some at the Biggins. Sir Arthur's relative value of cow's grass came to £38.5/–, which required as an equivalent the Mailins of North House, all the grass between the Wart of the North House and the point of Forwick Ness, the Loch Meadow, the North Meadow, and from Dale (round by the west) southward, with as much more in the same direction or at the Meadow as amounted to £3.18.2. To this should be added the amount of unprescribed encroachments on the cow's grass. In the commons, the North and Little Nesses, inter alia, would be allocated to Sir Arthur.

The Minister's relative value of arable was £4.0.6, and the Reader's, £1.14.6. These would come next to Sir Arthur on the south.

Gifford would get the rest of the arable and grass in one continuous field, including Bragasetter, Mid Setter and Setter, and his proportion of common would be laid in contiguity.

If possession, however, were to be the basis for division, each heritor would retain any units of land he had over 4 acres in size, and contiguous to his steadings. In order to tidy detached runrig portions, an exchange would have to be undertaken – Gifford would have to exchange ground at Hurdiback, Evrigarth and Olligarth for an equivalent in value for the smaller portions and an equivalent in quantity and quality (measure and value) for the land at Hurdiback and Evrigarth. The grass, meadow, and encroachments would be sorted out by a valuation scheme.

Mr Cheyne, however, disapproved of division by possession, since it ignored the judgement of the Commissioners and proposed excambion, not division.[260] In the end, division was by possession, though Nicolson pressed for division according to his merks. Gifford still maintained his point of view that there were different townlands in Papa, though he could not deny that a great part of the nominal lands were not adjacent to the hamlets of these names but were widely scattered, and that residents in other hamlets possessed lands adjoining these alleged townlands, and that the whole mass was really one runrig town. He insisted, however, that in his hamlets that lay alongside the township dyke he possessed masses of land of 4 acres and above, which he held were not divisible. He considered that the remainder should be divided by possession.

The Court decided in his favour, and Sir Arthur appealed. After Court proceedings it was settled that each should have the whole of his property laid in a mass, Gifford abandoning his claim to the 4 acres on Sir Arthur's side, but the division being according to possession and not by the merkland, Gifford getting an equivalent for what he held in excess. A line of division was struck at right angles to the township dyke in 1851, giving the tenants of both proprietors access to the common, and to the cow's grass adjoining the arable inside the dyke. This was at first refused by Gifford and only accepted by him when it seemed to be in accordance with the judgement of Lord Cowan. Mr Cheyne wanted to make Sir Arthur responsible for paying all expenses subsequent to the Deliverance of the Commissioner.[261] The costs of the exercise, from the Commissioner's first judgement on 27 August 1849, till November 1856, amounted to £160.[262] In 1857, the long process finally ended. Gifford's claim for expenses was maintained. The Lord Ordinary found him entitled to expenses incurred by him in making up and closing the Record ordered by the Lord Ordinary on 18 Nov. 1851, and closed on 8 March 1853. No other expenses were due to either party,[263] but for the general expenses the Lords found both parties liable, according to the number of merks land belonging to each.[264]

Two months later, Thomas Irvine's accounts were presented – £23.3/– and £13.2.5.[265] He had worked hard for his money. The job of a surveyor and valuator was one that demanded technical skill, mental ingenuity, diplomacy, responsibility, and an ability to stand the rigours of travel. By a lucky chance, part of Irvine's travel diary for 1846 has survived. It speaks for itself:

'Monday, April 20th 1846. Set out from Midbrake at 10 o C A.M. Boat to Vatseter 2/6 or 3/–. Landed there at ¼ past 1 oC. Ulsta at 4 – Mossbank at 6 — 1/6 – Serv! Girl at Mossbank 1/–. Geo. Fraser 2/– to carry him home 2/–.

'Tuesday 21st. Left Mossbank at near 11 A.M. Scatsta 3 miles to Brae 2. Boat to Brinister 3/– to Mellby 6 or 7 m. Boy 1/6. Boat to Papa 1/6 – 8 o C P.M. Met at Mr. Henderson's house. Mr. Bell Commiss.ᵉʳ Mr. Sievwright Mr. R. N. Spence and Mr. A. Greig agents of Mr. A. Nicoll Clerk. Servant 1/–.

'Thurs. April 23.ᵈ Set out from Papa at 11 o C A.M. in a six-oared boat to Killister thence by Bayhall by land 2 m. thence to P. Peterson's house – Vadelea – Thence to Whitesness a short mile. Boat up to Gruting Voe to Olla's Voe, walked 3 long miles to Reawick. Boat to Scalloway – arrived in Lerwick at 11 o'C at night.

'Papa Wednesday 22 April. 10 o'C A.M. Perambulation began. The Dike begins at the Ollerhad on the east geos — to Hundy Shun where the outset dike begins – old dike Stieth marked by Dots westward to the Grind – next to which is Sir Ar.'s piece. – E!ward Mr. G. – next E.ward Sir A – next E.ward Mr. G. – on the Longbrakings between Hundy Shun & the Grind of Mid Setter.

'North House. A piece formerly occupied by Mr. H. now Ley — perambulated – a part of D.º occupied in the Same way by N.º house tenants – Oppen to all.

'North Banks. W! boundary from E! side to little Gio or sindrins to stone at L. E! ward along — to Bombe Gio.

'Gardie E! of N.º Haa. a piece of Ley – broken up by Mr. H. outside the dike of Gardie – Sir Arthur Nicolson.

'No E. of No Haa. a piece outbroken from Grass – Mr. Gifford.

'Punds of Gardie. By the dike Stieth – by north banks line – By the sea banks – by the path up by Gardie & along Mr. H.'s Garden.

'Hamnavoe. W! Dike end begins at the Gio of Combe.

'Bragaster. 3 Gioes – Skrivers Sand Kirk Gio, Minister's Gio – excluding Glebe right to take up ware ...

'The upper portion of Out f.ᵈ taken from the Grass – not proven within the 40 years — Small but at the well along the E! side a piece marked by dots. — belongs to the arable.

'A long Dole broken out from the Grass on the E! side of B. by Sir Arthur's tenants in Biggins – On the N.º end of the said Dole a piece occupied by the Schoolmaster to the edge of the Grass E! of the School House a piece in the occupancy of the Schoolm.ʳ taken from the Grass.

'W.ᵗ side a small bit for the Glebe.

'Biggins. W! – Small patch unworthy of notice ⎤
         Russigil a pretty large piece   ⎬ broken out on
         N.º from Russigill a Dole   ⎬ grass by Sir
         Partly Ley and part cultivated ⎦ Arthur Nicolson.

'A piece of Stubble ground N° the — Site of House & 2 yards on the common – called Hardlabor.

'Olligarth – a part of the yard taken from the Grass.

'Punds of Everagarth – excluding Mr. Gifford – pointed out.

'Near Ollagarth a Pund of Mr. G's called "Enalu" – exclusive not pointed. N.B. at Bragaster is a house & yard of Mr. G's in the same circumstances at "Hardlabor".'[266]

In 1856, Sir Arthur Nicolson raised the rents of his Papa Stour tenants by 21%.[267]

10

Dykes and Enclosures

THE Northern Isles are full of dykes, new and old, from the old 'pickie' dykes to the sheep-dykes and field walls of more recent times. Most important for the townships was the hill dyke that made a division between the townland and the common grazing, in the summer time. It was not a fortress wall that encapsulated the community, not a dividing line, but a link between the elements of the township. As soon as the crops were off the ground in the autumn, the dykes were breached, and the stock were free to roam on the townland, which now became common grazing too. The Shetland phrase was *to slip de okregert* (Old Norse *akr(a)gerði*, enclosure of arable land), to leave the okregert or enclosed arable open for the animals[268] by leaving the *grinds* (Old Norse *grind*, gate) or gates open. The date for opening the dykes was not precisely fixed, and would vary with the state of the weather and date of harvest, but the slipping of the okregert was a strong incentive to the slower tenants to get their crops off the ground and into the stackyard at the same time as their neighbours.

Such hill dykes were of stone or of turf, which crumbled in the winter, and had to be repaired in spring when the young corn started to green. All the proprietors or their tenants had a duty to repair and maintain a part of the hill dyke, in proportion to the extent of their holdings.[269] In many places, such as Fair Isle, stone dykes of recent date march straight and true alongside the old dykes of stone and turf, which meander from point to point, taking advantage of large earthfast stones and natural outcrops, and providing shelter for animals from a range of different angles. In some cases the top of a turf or *feelie* (Old Scots *fayle, faill*, turf, *c* 1420; Gaelic *fàl*) dyke was railed with a row of sticks linked by rope or wire and set to slope outwards, away from the township land, to deter sheep from crossing. A turf dyke topped with a line of sticks and two strands of wire remained in use at Noss in the South Mainland of Shetland till 1948, and examples could be found later. The Shetland name for fixing such a fence was to *revel* (Old Scots *revel*, railing, 1633; cf. Faroese *revil*, fillet of wood, Danish dialectal *revel*, strake of a boat). This feature was also frequent on the dykes around the *plantiecrues* (see page 101 ff.) in the common grazings. If, however, hunger or the desire for a tasty bite encouraged the sheep or cattle to leap the dyke, they were attacked with sticks and stones and chased by dogs to drive them out again.[270]

Some dykes have alleged supernatural origins. On the north and west sides of

16. Early division dykes in North Ronaldsay. From William Aberdeen, *Chart of Orkney*, *c*. 1770, in Kirkwall Free Library.

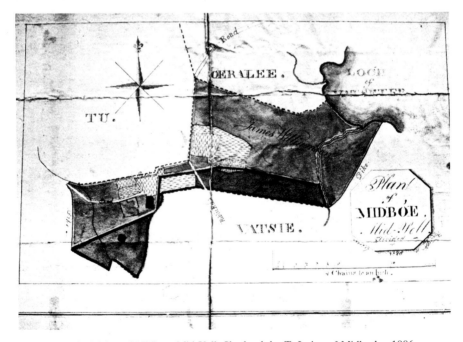

17. Plan of Division of Midboe, Mid Yell, Shetland, by T. Irvine of Midbrake, 1886.

the Vord Hill in Fetlar, there are the remains of an old wall. The tenant who lived in the farm of Culbinstoft was troubled by the inroads of his neighbours' cattle, and vowed one night that he would give one of his best oxen if there was a wall built there in the morning. When he got up the wall was there, and his best ox lay dead in the byre.[271]

In terms of relative chronology, the pickie dykes may be oldest, followed by the gairsties, and then by the hill dykes as farm settlement spread. However, there is a lot of overlapping. Gairstie or gorstie (see page 14) must refer to dykes with a number of functions, and in Shetland – for example, in Papa Stour – the hill dyke can also be called the gorstie. Hill dykes were smaller than those with a presumed territorial rather than a farming function, like the Green Gairsty in Rousay which was 4 to 5 yds (3.7–4.6 m) broad at the base, and 3 to 4 ft (91–122 cm) high.[272] The breadth is partly due to slumping and spread over a long period of time, and the original height would have been greater. Hill dyke dimensions were specified in an agreement of 1761 between the tenants and heritors of Onston in the township of Clouston, Stenness. Here, part of the commonty called Bryascow was to be enclosed along the foundations of a new dyke lately built by the heritors. This turf dyke was 6 ft (1.8 m) high, and a 30 ft (9 m) breadth of ground to the south side of it was allotted for its building and repair,[273] a clear indication of the enormous consumption of turf for building purposes in such communities.

In the Northern Isles, as elsewhere in Scotland, the earliest enclosures were for grazing purposes, even if such quoys later became arable. The Acts of the Parliament of Scotland in 1695 relating to runrig and division of commonties, promulgated to help land improvement through enclosing, gave heritors an easier means of separating out their runrig lands from each other, and of splitting up the common grazings, though encroachments on the latter had been going on for as long as settlement existed. With the filling in of the settlement pattern, encroachments came to be resented. There was in Orkney, for example, an expression *ringit quoy*, for a dyke-enclosed area in the hill ground, and 'it is said scornfully to one who has a possession of this kind 'You have nothing but a *ringet-quoy*''; as signifying that he has as it were stolen what he calls his property; that he has no right to hill pasturage in common with his neighbours, as not paying *scatt* for his *quoy*, and no right to poind the cattle which trespass on this inclosure'.[274] The feeling that the hill land really was common property was strong.

Apart from quoys, outbreks and the like, enclosures associated with the ending of runrig were slow to begin. Enclosed fields producing much grass were noted in Orkney in 1777.[275] By the same year, the farm of Bu in Burray, managed by the estate factor for Sir Thomas Dundas, had been enclosed and subdivided into fields with dykes of stone and earth. In the fields Dutch white clover and rye grass were grown, fifty or sixty cows were grazed, and twenty-five to thirty calves reared. Butter and cheese were sold, and hay when there was any to spare. Though this was amongst the first improvements in Orkney, other farmers had not followed the example.[276] It took some time for such improvements to spread, and in the 1790s, the majority of the Orkney parishes were still bare of enclosures, and therefore unable to make use of sown grasses as at Bu. The same was true of Shetland.[277]

In Birsay and Harray, an area with a high concentration of small udal holdings, it was said that every farmstead was enclosed by an outfence of earth, but not divided. There had been some amalgamation of holdings around Kirkwall.[278] In Stronsay, where the hill dykes had been allowed to fall into desuetude, Thomas Balfour of Huip tried improvements on the farm of Links-ness, where the soil was poor through having been much cut up for fuel by cottars and subtenants. They failed here, as at another place where he had enclosed 50 acres with earthen dykes. Some dyke enclosing was carried out at North Strynzie by Robert Laing, a Kirkwall merchant. Edward Chalmers took a 15-year lease of South Strynzie from John Scollay, and sowed grass seed on an area of 8 to 9 acres that he enclosed with an earthen dyke. He also moved the farmhouses. In Eday, John Murray and his son James built several hundred fathoms of stone dyke enclosures, repaired the farmhouses, and improved the quality of the cattle.[279] The money built up by the kelp industry was beginning to show results, as in Shapinsay, where Major Balfour was the only resident heritor. Between about 1788 and 1786, he had totally changed his estate of Cliffdale. Patches of arable with scattered hovels were replaced by an elegant house, an extensive garden, and enclosed land where modernised agricultural practices and implements were adopted. At the same time, he set up a village at Elwick, following the fashion of lairds in many parts of Scotland, for joiners, carpenters, weavers, tailors, shoemakers, coopers and labourers, to provide goods and services for the island. In Shetland at the same period, enclosures tried by two gentlemen in Unst had been found useful,[280] but these appear to have been exceptions rather than rules.

The first part of the nineteenth century saw little change in the Northern Isles. In Deerness parish, some small patches on the farms had been enclosed for artificial grasses by 1805, and a female proprietor in Stronsay had brought a man from England to enclose and improve the waste. Few enclosures appeared on townland, however, for such land often lay runrig and became common pasture in winter. At Malseter, Major Moodie built a ring-fence round an extensive area of grass near his house, to feed his sheep in winter. The dyke was of freestone, in the Galloway style which was very suitable for sheep.[281]

In Shetland, the only enclosures were near the proprietors' houses. In fact, enclosing of the small units resulting from fragmentation of holdings and the establishment of outsets would have been both costly and impractical. Though the need for enclosures was acknowledged, and though stone examples existed by the 1840s in Tingwall, Whiteness and Weisdale, in general little advance was made until well into the second half of the nineteenth century, even though large proprietors had begun to employ surveyors from the 1820s, as a pre-liminary to having the scattalds divided and fenced. Tenants, however, had no love of enclosures, which reduced the grazing area and involved new regu-lations. Mr Hay's 10-acre enclosures at Laxfirth and Dale, each with five two-acre fields for rotational cropping, were resented; but he 'carries out his places with a high hand, and the refractory tenant is turned off without mercy'. A small enclosure of 2 to 3 acres was made by George Lyle in North Yell, where he grew improved crops. A few years before 1841, the proprietor of Bressay brought in a Berwickshire grieve to manage his home farm. Later he took a small farm nearby and did well on it. In Unst, the landowners had good stone fences round their farms, each of which was subdivided into enclosed fields of 6 to 7 acres for rotational crops. A 40-acre common around Lerwick had been enclosed and divided into 31 parks since about 1820, most of them cultivated and laid down to grass.[282]

Later in the nineteenth century, the Shetland pattern was changed chiefly by the innovation of sheep farming. Former arable land in the valley of Dale, Tingwall, provided the best grass for sheep on G H B Hay's land. By 1874, 200 acres had been ploughed to make permanent pasture on G. Bruce's land in Veensgarth Valley, to allow an increase in his flock of ewes. Extensive sheep farming had been introduced by Major Cameron's agent, John Walker, in the Holm of Noss and on eight farms in Delting and Yell. Andrew Umphray at Reawick had reclaimed 75 of his 90 acres of sheltered land since 1860, mostly from peat. Here and on a nearby outlying farm, he had 14 fields each of 12 acres, 5 of which were cultivated. A J Grierson at Quendale (Fitful Head) had 400 acres of enclosed pasture. David Shepherd at Symbister, an 'energetic Scotch farmer', had the only sheep farm in Whalsay, including 100 acres of former arable, mostly laid down to grass. It was said of Unst that the enclosure of scattald and the division of fields was more advanced than in any other part of Shetland. Here, as a sign of the changing times, it had become possible for someone like Joseph Monsel, a cottar tenant, to build a house and small shop and divide his farm of 7 merks of land into four fields with stone dykes and wire fences – and this even though he rented the land from Major Hamilton, and did not own it. Furthermore, because the neighbouring scattald, which he once would have used, was enclosed, he had to pay in money for the use of Lord Zetland's unenclosed scattald. In general, however, tenants of 7 to 8 acres had to depend on their landlords, on whom the onus of initiating improvements normally had to rest.[283]

Progress in Orkney, on the other hand, was quicker, and of a different character. In 1828, Mr Graeme's property in the parish of Holm and Paplay was surveyed, cleared of runrig, and laid out in farms of a variety of sizes which were given on 15-year leases. The common of Rendall was about to be divided in 1841. Some stone dykes had been built lately in Stronsay, and Mr Laing of Papdale had reclaimed 200 acres of moor, though the amount of peat was a bar to improvement. In Cross and Burness, much of the land had been sorted out between heritors, marches ascertained between farms and estates, and some good division fences erected. As an associated improvement, money rents were being adopted, and feu duties formerly payable in grain, butter and meal could be purchased or redeemed, so releasing energy for the raising of cattle and sheep, which were more suited to the area. At the same time, the middleman or tacksman system of letting, involving numerous cottars and sub-tenants at the mercy of the principal tenant, was ending. As part of the improvements at Stove, S. Laing allocated a separate part to such people, giving each 3 Scots acres of arable and an equivalent in grass. They paid a money rent, and were themselves paid for the work they did, for example as kelpers. Papa Westray was enclosed with stone dykes, within which red and white clover, and good turnips, were grown. A tenant who wished to enclose and break in part of the waste in Papa Westray was allowed by Mr Traill to sit rent-free for seven years. Mr Pollexfen's estate of Cairston in Stromness was well enclosed and improved, though otherwise enclosures were few. Sir William Honeyman's division of the Orphir common in 1818 led to the creation of 26 farms. In Sandwick, W G Watt of Breckness had enclosed and reclaimed parts of the waste, and Mr Heddle had enclosed all the property he had bought at Clumlie in 1836. The Glebe, enclosed and drained between 1838–41, was the only farm under a regular 6-year rotation of crops.[284]

By the 1870s, most Orkney farms were occupied by their proprietors or let directly to tenants, with no intermediate tacksmen.[285] This meant they got much more individual attention, as a result of what had amounted to a revolution in Orkney agriculture since the 1840s, following the pioneer work of Alexander Sutherland Graeme in Holm, and of the factor Robert Scarth on some estates in his charge. Farm sizes also were increasing by the addition of hill land. However, it was Colonel Balfour, of Balfour and Trenabie, in Shapinsay, who really got the movement for agricultural improvement going. He began in 1848, when 700 acres of the island were cultivated. By 1859, there were 5000 acres, and over 6000 acres by 1874. Scattered patches gave way to a continuous tract of cultivation. Colonel Balfour's factor, Marcus Calder, divided the island into 10-acre squares, by means of open drains, in a geometrical grid pattern, with farm sizes varying between 30 and 200 acres, and a few holdings of 5 to 10 acres for fishermen and tradesmen. The home-farm of Balfour Castle extended to 700 acres, mostly of new or reclaimed land. In Stronsay, Colonel Balfour's farm of Huip was also of 700 acres, half of it reclaimed by the tenant since about 1859. The tenant had also enclosed some of the fields with stone walls. At the late George Traill's farm of Houseby, improvements started in 1845, and 700 arable acres had been enclosed with flagstones set on edge as in Caithness. The farm of Huntown, owned by Colonel Balfour and tenanted by Mr Hume, was also enclosed to a great extent by stone fences.

In Sanday, Braeswick townland was squared off into lots of 16 to 20 acres each, and runrig abolished. Colonel Balfour's tenant at Warsetter, John McKay, had enclosed much of his farm with stone dykes, like Messrs Jerome and Walter Dennison at West Brough. In North Ronaldsay, Robert Scarth, factor to Dr Traill of Woodwick, abolished payment of rents in kind in 1832, along with all kains and services, and squared off the runrig fields. He allowed half of the new money rent to be laid out by the tenants on well-planned drainage and enclosures. In Westray, the land around Colonel Balfour's village of Pierowall had been squared and put in good order, and his farm of Trenabie was squared, subdivided, and partly enclosed. T. Traill had laid off and fenced the farm of Brough, and Mr Stewart had subdivided and enclosed Cleat with stone fences. In the island of Eday, the land of the small tenants was squared and laid off in separate farms by Robert James Hebden, who bought Eday from the Trustees of the late S. Laing. In Wyre, Robert Scarth introduced the same improvements as in North Ronaldsay.

A leading improver in the West Mainland of Orkney was Archer Fortescue, a Devonshire man who bought the Swanbister Estate, Orphir, in 1845, when there were no roads or enclosures, and the tenants held the land in runrig. He squared off the land for each tenant, dividing each square into five equal parts. Much fencing went on from 1846, and 80 acres of salt marsh, reclaimed from the sea, made into 12- to 15-acre fields, with stone dykes $4\frac{1}{2}$ ft (1.4 m) high. Fortescue's work was not appreciated at the time. His squaring off of the tenants' land was opposed, and because of his insistence on getting the cattle herded on the hill, and his poinding of trespassing cattle and taking of poind money, he earned the title of 'the Devil of the Hills'. On the hill behind Stromness, where all the available surface had been removed in the course of time for 'midden-feal' for compost middens, trenching by the spade was carried out by the Stromness feuars, amongst whom it was divided. The stones dug up were used for making fences. Much of Sandwick had been improved by W W G Watt, in particular the farms of Skaill and Keirfiold. In the 1850s, Keirfiold had been a rabbit warren and commonty. On the Swannay estate in Evie parish, R. Brotchie had carried out improvements, with stone dykes and intermediate wire fences. At Binscarth, bought by Robert Scarth in 1841, 20-acre fields were made with stone dykes. The whole farm was enclosed so that trespassing by animals was no longer possible. Two new farms of 150 acres each, made by Scarth from the waste in Firth, were laid out in 10-acre squares, divided by ditches 5 ft (1.5 m) wide × 3 ft (91 cm) deep.

In the East Mainland, Mrs William Balfour's 300-acre mains farm at Birstane House, St. Ola, was subdivided into suitable fields not only by stone dykes, but also by thorn and beech hedges. In 1848, Mr Traill of Holland bought 1200 acres of the commonty lands of Holm, to make New Holland. Since 1858, 450 acres of this had been reclaimed and made into 20-acre fields, mostly enclosed with stone dykes. The work was still going on.

South Ronaldsay on the other hand, though well farmed, had a general lack of fences. Boys were needed to herd cattle by day, which by night were kept in small enclosed yards.

There is much truth in the comment, that 'it is doubtful... whether any part of the United Kingdom has been improved in so remarkable a manner as Orkney within the period mentioned'.[286]

From this digest of the progress of enclosure and the creation of the modern landscape, it can be seen that with the exception of the pickie dykes and gairsties, all the dykes in the Northern Isles are of relatively recent origin, few being more than a century old. There were a number of methods of building

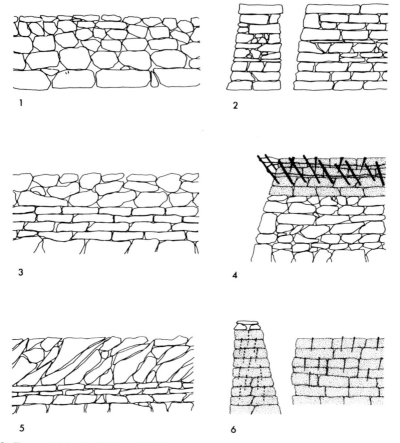

18. Types of dykes in Fetlar: 1 single stone dyke; 2 double stone dyke; 3 single and double dyke; 4 a 'feelie tap dyke', with turf on top, containing wooden stobs and ropes to keep off sheep; 5 a 'lean-to' dyke, with a slantwise coping; 6 a 'feelie' turf dyke, with pinned turves. From drawings by J. Laurenson. C5039.

dykes. At Uyea in Shetland, there were stone dykes with turf copings. To beat down the turf and force it into position, a conical piece of sandstone called a *clapper* was used. It tapered from $3\frac{1}{4}$ in. (8 cm) diameter at its flat end to 2 in. (5 cm) diameter at its rounded narrow end, and was $8\frac{1}{2}$ in. (26 cm) long. It weighed $5\frac{1}{2}$ lbs.[287] The technique of topping a dyke with turf was common on plantiecrues, and was called in Fetlar a *feelie tap dyke*. This gave more height as a defence against sheep, and sticks and ropes could be added easily. The latter were placed 18 in. (46 cm) apart, at an angle outwards of 10°.[288]

The turf or feelie dyke proper was made of sods cut with the spade. The foundation sods were cut large, about 18 in. long by 12 in. broad by 9 in. deep (46×30×23 cm) laid in double tiers. Any available stones were added to augment the material, and in fact few dykes were of turf alone. Wooden pins were driven in to hold the sods together, and their decayed stumps are often found when old dykes are being cut into to get dry mould for bedding in the byre. Little finesse was used in building feelie dykes. Sods were piled up regardless of whether the joints overlapped, and 'it was a case of get on with the job and never mind the looks'.[289] Though turf is still used in dykes, and even for patching fallen parts of stone dykes, the day of the turf dyke came to an end with the agricultural improvements. The scalping of the ground for turf and sods conflicted too sharply with grazing requirements, and dykes of stone, and fences of stob and wire, were the successors.

Stone dykes took various forms. Single dykes were built very open, so that the wind could pass through freely. Though loose and ramshackle in appearance, they could, like the one put up by P. Manson at Blobersburn in Foula, stand up in places where the wind would have damaged a more solid construction. Single dykes were also used on plantiecrues, since the wind passed through without creating a back-draught and did not blast the growing plants. Plantiecrue walls of this kind had the biggest stones at the foot, medium sized ones in the middle, and the smallest on top, but single dykes noted in Foula and in the Dunrossness area were of evenly sized stones throughout, laid to overlap each other with considerable gaps between.

Another form was the combined double and single dyke, with the lower half of double thickness, and the top single. This was a good sheep dyke. Some dykes near Brough Lodge in Fetlar are topped by large stones set slantwise on edge, hence the name 'lean-to' dyke. In none of these dykes in Shetland were stones of white quartz used, nor would they be included in a building, or as ballast in a ship, since they were regarded as unlucky.[290] Stone dykes were built in the Galloway style, as at Malseter in Orkney, for a sheep enclosure. In Rendall parish, Mr Sinclair of Kirkwall built limestone walls about 5 ft (1.5 m) high. This made 'a beautiful and substantial fence ... to be coped with flagstones set on their edge, and, when finished, would effectually secure sheep and every other domesticated animal'.[291]

19. A dyke at Blobersburn, Foula, built very open to let the wind pass through, and also to help to deflect the force of the wind from the thatched roofs of the houses. From a photograph. C5408.

20. A flagstone dyke near Stromness, Orkney, *a.* 1911. Ellison collection. Per J. Troup.

21. Sheep-dyke at Urie on the Nicolson estate, Fetlar, built in the second half of the nineteenth century. 1963.

22. A Shetland harr-hung *grind* in a hill dyke. From a photograph by S F Kjellberg, 1934. C5407.

The advantage of stone over turf dykes was that they could stand up to water. It was possible to use them as dyke-ends, built on the ebb-shore and running seawards so that animals were prevented from reaching the arable by way of the ebb.[292]

In parts of Orkney, for example around Stromness, stone dykes of a special kind were used for field boundaries. These consisted of a row of upright flagstones embedded in the earth. They go back in time to the second half of the nineteenth century, when Mr Traill used them to enclose 700 acres at Houseby.[293] It is possible that the Caithness practice of erecting such dykes had some influence here, and that in Orkney they are little, if at all, earlier in date than the introduction of stob-and-wire fencing.

Gates or grinds in the dykes had more than one form. One type was of horizontal bars that slotted at each end into hollows in two upright stakes or an adjoining wall,[294] like one noted at Barkland in Fair Isle in 1972. More common was the harr-hung type, with the main upright of the gate passing through a hole in a projecting stone or bar of wood, whilst the lower end pivoted in a hollow in a stone, or even the inverted base of a bottle. Such pivot stones are known from prehistoric times. As a complement to the gate was the stile or *stiggy* (Norwegian *stige*, Old Norse *stigi*, ladder, steps), which let people cross the wall without opening the gate or having to make a detour to the gate.

The importance of the dykes in the old communities, and the collective responsibility of the community for their maintenance, is fully underlined by the Country Acts from Shetland, dating as they stand to the seventeenth century, but likely to be older. The relevant passage is:

'6. – That good neighbourhood be observed and kept by timeous and sufficient bigging (building) of dikes, and putting up of grinds and passages, keeping and closing the same and that none big up accustomed grinds or passages through towns, or any way close up the king's high road, under the pain of £10. That all dikes be sufficiently built, before the first of March, so as that all cattle may be kept without dikes from the times that the labouring begins; and whatsoever person shall wilfully allow their cattle to tread upon their neighbour's land or meadows before the first of May, shall pay for each swine 10 s., for each sheep 2 s., for each horse, mare, or nolt, 6 s.; doubling the same fines after the first of May, besides payment of the damages, and that they pay 40 s. Scots besides the damages. That all within one dike keep good neighbourhood to others, by tethering, herding, or folding, as well by day as by night, and not to pasture upon or overlay others with their cattle, nor unlawfully hound or drive upon others, under the pain of 40 s. for each fault, *toties quoties*, besides damages; and that none have more swine than effeiring to their land labouring: And that none have swine pasturing upon their neighbour's lands, meadows, grass commonty and pasturage, neither within nor without dikes, that hath no swine pasturing upon them; and that they kept their swine upon their own grounds, under the pain of £10, besides damages; and that building (making shelters), punding and herding be used in a lawful way, before or a little after sun setting; and that none scare, hound or break up their neighbour's punds and buils, under the pain of £10 Scots, besides damages.'[295]

Within the old townships, the only parts that might be enclosed were the individually held tounmals, and the kailyards and stackyards. It was the individual's own responsibility to maintain the dykes around these areas, as paragraph 27 of the Country Acts makes clear. It laid down that:

'. . . all persons have sufficient corn yard dikes, and that no mends be made for corn eaten within corn-yards, except where more than one is concerned in the yard. He that hath insufficient dikes, must pay the other damages; as also for all marks, the owner whereof must pay the damage.'[296]

The kailyards by the houses were complemented by the plantiecrue in the common grazings, outside the hill-dyke. They were also individually held by the tenants and played a considerable part in the domestic economy.

11

Plantiecrues, Cabbage and Kail

KAIL, grown from at least the fifteenth century in Scotland, was a valuable food because it could to some extent act as a specific against the prevalent disease of scurvy, especially in the days before potatoes, a source of vitamin C, were grown. That it was popular is beyond doubt, for it appears frequently in law cases where offenders were charged with the theft of kail. It was under this head that the first reference appeared in Shetland, in 1615, but evidently not enough was eaten to prevent scurvy, which was still common in the Northern Isles at the end of the seventeenth century. An excess of salt fish in the diet was said to be the cause.[297]

In 1693 cabbage was noted as a garden crop in Orkney and in 1733 it was in wide use in Shetland.[298] By the 1790s there is no doubt that a Brassica crop was being grown everywhere, though the exact variety cannot always be certain since the dialectal usage of the Northern Isles and of Caithness is to give the name 'cabbage' to kail. A farmer in Sanday, Patrick Fea, recorded the details of the work:

> 1766　9 April: All my other People mucking and delving the Kealyard Sett that day 300 plants of my own growth.
> 10 April: Had 3 men delphing all day in the Garden and done with Setting all thereof except a part of the New ground.
> 12 April: Set the yard in the little Links with 4 Hundred Plants.
> 1769　8 April: Sown some seeds in the Park Viz.' Carret, parsnips, Spinage Curled Keal and Savoys. [299]

The town of Kirkwall itself created a big enough demand for Brassica to be grown in fair quantities on the outskirts, on land for which the inhabitants were prepared to pay fully £3 an acre. The old palace garden was rented out in small patches, called *hundreds*. The *hundred* or *hundersgrund* was 'a measure of garden-ground in Orkney, 15 ft by 18 ft (4.6×5.5 m) in extent: ground sufficient for the growth of a hundred plants of kail. In each plot or hundred the plants are set 18 inches (46 cm) apart or in ten rows of twelve each. *Hundred*, therefore, means the long hundred or six score'.[300] In effect, these were kail-yards for finishing off the plants.

For starting off the plants from seed, a small 'penn or bught' was used, such enclosures being made by even the poorest of the people. It was around 1804

23. Plantiecrues of turf on stone foundations, in Foula, *c*. 1902. Photo. H B Curwen.

24. Kail growing in a square plantiecrue in Papa Stour, 1967. 3.38.12.

that a visitor to Stronsay 'first saw the small inclosures for raising cabbage-plants called *planty-cruies*. They are merely little square penns, or *bughts*, inclosed by a dry-stone wall: black mould, or more frequently a mixture of clay and ashes, is laid on the inclosed area, and here cabbage-plants are raised, to be set out in the spring. These *planty-cruies* are always situated on the flattest part of the shore, close by the sea, where the frost is best avoided'.[301]

Plantiecrues are still very much part of the Shetland and to some extent of the Orkney scene. Tenants could have more than one, and there was little or no restriction on anyone who wished to choose a spot for a plantiecrue on the common grazings. They make a remarkable landscape feature in a place like Fetlar, where a long row of them marches across the hill ground in parallel with the hill dyke. Some were round and some were four-sided, ranging as a rule from 5 to 10 yards (4.6–9 m) across. Some were oblong, about 10 to 12 ft (3–3.7 m) long by 4 to 5 ft (1.2–1.5 m) broad.[302]

There is no significant pattern of distribution for square, rectangular, and round plantiecrues. All three varieties can appear in the same area. Rectangular examples with rounded corners, noted in Fetlar, averaged 16×14 ft (4.9×4.3 m) outside and 12×9½ ft (3.7×2.9 m) inside. The smallest was a rectangle of stone from which a capping of turf had vanished, 13×9½ ft (4×2.9 m) outside, and 8×6 ft (2.4×1.8 m) inside. The biggest, a 'halvers crue', 21 ft (6.4 m) square, was shared by two crofters, and had a low green

25. Kail transplanted from a plantiecrue to the kailyard at the Biggins, Papa Stour, 1967. C3911.

bank across the middle as a division. In general, round crues appeared to be younger than the four-sided ones. The best of the crues had stone walls 6 ft (1.8 m) high. Some had bottom courses of stone and upper courses of turf set with a fence of wooden stakes.

Inside, the ground level was about 18 in. (46 cm) higher than outside, resulting from the accumulation of turf dug from the scattald, laid inside and chopped up with the blade of a spade to improve the tilth. In theory the old earth from the crue was supposed to be taken out and replaced in the scattald where the fresh turf had been removed.[303] Fresh turf was put in every two or three years, a necessary measure because Brassica is very exhausting to the soil. For the same reason, the roots had to be removed each year, otherwise they would sprout again and use up more of the soil's fertility. Kail seed was prepared by being placed in a cup of water, when the light, useless stuff floated to the surface and could be thrown away. The good seed was then put into the mouth and blown over the surface of the plantiecrue with a series of sharp, firm blasts to get an even spread. In Fetlar this was to 'frush (Norwegian dialectal *frøsa*, *frusa*, Icelandic *frussa*, to spurt, sputter) da seed', and in Papa Stour it was to 'sprone (Norwegian dialectal, Old Norse *sprœna*, squirt, spit out) da seed'.[304] Red peat ash was sometimes spread over the seed as a fertiliser.

In 1963, only one plantiecrue remained in use in Fetlar, dug by the Shetland delving spade. Several were seen in use in 1967 in Papa Stour, where the kail was a good source of winter fodder for the animals. This was not a novelty, for in the 1840s the farmers of Sandsting and Aithsting were planting late or winter cabbage, sometimes up to 3000 plants or more, as food for both man and beast, but as a rule the plants were for domestic use rather than for stock.[305] In Papa Stour, most crofts had one or two crues, and sometimes more when an amalgamation of crofts had taken place. The Busta tenants were not supposed to use plantiecrues on the Nicolson estate, and vice versa.

Seed was sown in the plantiecrues in July to August, and transplanted to the kailyards in April to May of the following year. The plants were ready in November. The stronger plants were removed first, allowing their weaker brethren to develop a little before their turn came for transplanting. In Holm, plants were transplanted a second time, from the kailyards to the fields, in mid-June, but this was not common.[306]

In Orkney, plantiecrues at Dennis Head in North Ronaldsay are square or round, about 17 ft (5.2 m) square or 17 ft (5.2 m) in diameter. In 1964 none were used in the traditional manner, though the lighthouse keepers were using some of them as gardens for potatoes, cabbage and peas. For this, the plantiecrues had been adapted by having gates knocked in the sides – an innovation unknown to earlier generations. Rhubarb is also a common replacement for kail in surviving plantiecrues in the Northern Isles.

A comparable technique for kail and cabbage growing was in use across the Pentland Firth in Caithness. Here, both before and after the introduction of potatoes, every farmer and cottager had a kailyard supplied from seed nurseries known as *plant tofts* or *plant cots*. These were made in June in the common, by enclosing an eighth to a tenth of an acre with a turf dyke about 6 ft (1.8 m) high. In July the surface of the enclosure was pared with a spade and the turf dried and burned as a fertiliser, before the seed was sown.

A new bed was made each year, the dyke at one side serving as one side of a new one. The cottagers and small farmers who made and worked these plant tofts sold the young plants to farmers at 3[d] to 8[d] per 100 in the early 1800s. Until the island of Stroma in the Pentland Firth was vacated in the twentieth century, the inhabitants bought their plants in bundles of 50 from the Skarfskerry district on the mainland of Caithness.[307] The remains of disused plant cots can still be seen on the slopes of Dunnet Head.

This form of cultivation now survives sporadically in the Northern Isles, as a relic of what once was an important part of the older community life, closely linking the land around the houses with the commons. At a time when the arable land of the community was laid open as common grazing for the animals once the crops were off the ground, it was important that the Brassica crop, of which the seeds had to shoot and develop throughout the period when all the land lay open for grazing, should be protected in the stoutly built enclosed plantiecrues or nurseries that now form a relict feature of the landscape.

12

The Finishing Touches:
Drainage and Liming

THOUGH recognised as a major means of improvement, drainage was slow in coming to the Northern Isles. It was in any case a difficult task, especially where the soil overlay sandstone or sandstone flag that was impervious to water, so that in wet weather it remained spongy and water laden. The only solution was to make the plough ridges high so that the furrows gave better drainage. A suggestion that auger holes should be bored at intervals in the ridges to let water through to a porous substratum was scarcely practical.[308]

Improvements were certainly taking place in the late eighteenth century, yet drainage was never mentioned. As long as the arable was scattered in small patches, systematic drainage was difficult. In summer in Shetland, a farm was frequently a curious collection of irregular plots of corn divided and bordered by strips of pasture. The corn was full of boulders, and was fringed with thistles and docks, which were useful for making baskets. Wet spots were often laid dry by gathering the earth from a wide area into beds with small ditches and rows of weeds between,[309] evidently a kind of lazy-bed technique. The abolition of runrig and the creation of individually held land units was a prerequisite to drainage. Furthermore, drainage was an expensive operation, beyond the purse of the majority of farmers in the Northern Isles.

By the 1840s, some activity was taking place in Shetland. Covered stone drains had lately appeared in Delting, there was a little draining in Tingwall, in Northmavine not a dozen fields in the parish were properly drained, and drains were few in Sandsting and Aithsting. Mr Hay had been draining and liming at Laxfirth, before handing the land over to tenants in 10-acre blocks. St Andrews parish had no covered drains and in Westray it was said there was little draining of the waste lands. These negative statements may both imply the existence of drains of some kind. Draining and enclosing of the glebe had taken place since about 1837 in Sandwick. Open drains were used as lines of division for 10-acre squares of land in Shapinsay. The field drains, which were of stone or of tiles, were usually set 18 ft (5.5 m) apart. Two-inch (5 cm) diameter tiles, a type that began to spread in Scotland in the late 1840s, were preferred. Minor drains were laid 33 to 36 in. (84–91 cm) deep, and main drains 6 in. (15 cm) deeper. The cost of drainage was about £7.10 an acre. In North Ronaldsay, half of the commuted rent money was allowed to the tenants for draining and enclosing after the re-organisation of 1832, and in Westray, the proprietor, Mr Traill, of Clifton, had much ditching and draining done. Archer Fortescue began a drainage programme from 1846 on the Swanbister Estate in Orphir. He laid the drains 18 to 20 ft (5.5–6 m) apart, and $3\frac{1}{2}$ to 4 ft (1.1–1.2 m) deep. At Binscarth in Firth, Robert Scarth spent £100 on draining one point only, having to lay drains 9 to 10 ft (2.7–3 m) deep, through hard rock. The drains kept choking due to bog-iron ore concretion, and to clear the ore deep trenching and liming were required. Two farms were made out of the waste here, with divisions of 10-acre squares divided by open ditches as in Shapinsay, 5 ft (1.5 m) wide by 3 ft (91 cm) deep. At Wideford Farm in the East Mainland, Mr Iverack carried out systematic field drainage, using stone drains rather than tiles. Reclamation of a 450-acre area started at Graemeshall in 1858 by Mr Traill involved the dyking, draining and liming of 20-acre units. In South Ronaldsay, 340 acres, reclaimed by William Cromarty on Carra Farm, were well drained.[310]

The sequence of types of drainage, therefore, though not in strict chronological order and with much overlapping, was, first, the furrows of the ridge and furrow system of cultivation, and the open ditches alongside rigs. Then came stone drains, which long continued to be made. As late as 1923–6, W S Tait, farmer at Ingsay, was recording in his Diary the carting of stones and turf for drains opened in the Meadow.[311] Next came tile drains from the late 1840s, but the expense of transporting them across the sea was enough for stone drains to be given the preference for some time by most improvers.

The use of lime for fertilising the fields followed much the same pattern, except that parts of Shetland were better off than Orkney. In 1814, lime from beds at Beness in Sanday, Kerbuster in Stronsay, and Linton in Shapinsay was a source of quicklime, but only for building purposes. The kilns were inverted cones, about 6–8 ft (1.8–2.4 m) in diameter and of equivalent depth. They were built of turf and constantly needed repair. Since the only fuel was peat, the limestone had to be broken into small pieces about the size of a hen's egg.[312] Kilns were found in Shetland on the limestone veins from Unst to Dunrossness. In 1771, there was in Unst, on the west side of Snarravoe, a lime-kiln and lime-house built there by order of William Mouat, proprietor of Wadbister.[313]

In the 1830s, a lime quarry and kilns at Fladdabister supplied Lerwick and district with lime,[314] and at some date in the second half of the nineteenth century, Irvine of Midbrake bought 40 barrels of lime from Robert Jamieson of Fladdabister for £1.13.2, discount 2.^{d}[315] A kiln at Girlsta was built by local masons in 1872, set back in a slope to facilitate filling. It had a brick lining 15 ft (4.6 m) in diameter below and 12 ft (3.7 m) above, and could burn 70 tons of lime at a time, using 14 tons of coal and 10 tons of peat. Before the First World War there were five burnings a year, producing 350 tons, but by the 1930s only 40 to 50 tons were being sold each year. It was mainly used on land within a 15-mile radius. At Ukensetter, there is an older kiln, of a round, open shape, built within 50 yds (46 m) of the shore. The limestone was broken into pieces

26. An improved and partly enclosed landscape of twentieth century Shetland, at Spiggie, South Scousburgh. Photo. J B Ratter. 3.44.31.

the size of road metal, and the kiln was filled with peat fuel and limestone in alternate layers. After the burned lime had been removed from the peat ash, it was slaked. At each burning, 30 to 36 barrels of lime were got, 13 barrels weighing a ton. Three 'kilns' a year were burned before the First World War. In Weisdale, there had also been several kilns, but by the 1930s, the importation of cement and hard plaster for building purposes, the increasing difficulty of getting peat fuel, and a diminution of the amount of liming of the ground, had led to their disappearance.[316]

With these improvements, the final touches were added to the long series of events that led up to and through the disappearance of runrig and the division and enclosing of substantial parts of the commons. The effect on Orkney was remarkable. In Shetland, it was more partial.

Homes and Working Places

13

The Raw Resources

ONLY in recent times has new settlement and the positioning of houses become independent of the environment. Man-made walling and roofing materials and fuels like gas, electricity and oil have broken the former close relationship between settlement and the resources of the region. It is no longer necessary to seek a place where fuel and water can be found, for wires and pipes do all that is necessary. Formerly, however, the presence of essential raw resources was decisive with regard both to location, and the structural appearance of buildings.

The underlying geology had much influence on the nature of buildings and enclosure dykes, as well as on their age. Where building stone was not easy to get, turf was used, but turf structures are perishable, easily affected by frost and moisture, and surviving examples are of no great age. Though turf buildings may incorporate old building techniques, it is stone that lasts longest. In Orkney, as in Caithness, the flagstone beds provide building stone of a good, enduring quality, and as a result, Orkney contains a number of farms that are probably older on the average than in any other part of Scotland.

Orkney is predominantly an old red sandstone area. The most fertile districts overlie flagstone, which usually weathers down to good soils made productive by liming and draining followed by manuring. Small quarries are frequent, none of them ever having been exploited for anything other than local use. Slate and millstone quarries were found at Firth (not much worked in the 1790s), at Yesnaby, the Black Craig at Stromness, and near the house of Skaill; in Eday, from which the Kirkwall houses got not only their grey slates, but also mullions and decorative work from the red and yellow sandstones on the hill of Midland next to Houton in Orphir, from which 6000 slates went to Kirkwall and South Ronaldsay in 1834, and 12,000 in both 1835 and 1836. A quarry was opened at Mustardquoy about 1843 for building the church, men from the different districts taking it in turn to get out the stones.[317] In many parts of Orkney there was no need to open a quarry because the flagstone layers were exposed on the shore. There, they could be readily split with hammers and wedges into suitable sizes.

In Shetland a species of rough stone, long-grained, greyish in colour, and suitable for lintels, was found at Muness and Norwick. Quarries were opened in Fetlar when required, then closed. Those in Bressay employed twelve men and boys. Bressay slates, really thin flagstones, were used on some of the Lerwick roofs, and were shipped as far as Baltasound. They were no longer worked by 1939. Stones of squared grey granite from Nesting were used for Symbister House. Stone from Eday was used for the lintels of Scalloway castle, and the Bruce Hostel in Lerwick has corner and lintel stones from Orkney.[318]

There were plentiful resources in turf and stone, but timber was lacking. Wood had to be imported, as in the Faroe Islands and Iceland, though there and in the Northern Isles, driftwood could be got in quantity. Trees probably existed at one time, for the roots of birch and other trees are found in peat bogs, and place names like Scockness, Skuan in Sourin, and Skuanie in Wasbister, all in Rousay, may preserve the Old Norse *skógr*, Norwegian *skog*, a wood.[319] But to an Orkney man, fuchsia-bushes along a dyke-side make a row of trees, and the main supplies of timber were what boats or the sea brought in.

About 1567, Shetland boats carried from Sunnhordland in Norway 36 dozen deals, 59 dozen fir beams each 9 ells long, 9850 young trees for making barrel hoops, and 700 'Hjeltespirer', literally 'Shetland spars', probably for building; Orkney boats carried deals, fir beams, wood for barrel hoops, and *knapholt* (Low German *klappholt*, clapboard, planks of split oak).[320] This name was widespread in Scotland from the fifteenth century.

In 1576, four Fetlar men complained that the Laird, Laurence Bruce of Cultmalindie, had taken from them a piece of sea-driven tree, two fathoms long, worth 'nyne babies' (9 halfpennies).[321] When Captain Frobisher sailed from Orkney towards Iceland in 1577, in *The Aide*, of 9 score tons, with two barks, *The Gabriel* under Maister Fenton, and *The Michael* under Maister York, he kept meeting 'great Firre trees', which were said to provide most of Iceland's fuel, and were probably driven from Newfoundland.[322] In 1587, Gilbert Irvine of Sabay brought a thousand deals from Norway to Orkney.[323] In the parish of Walls, Shetland, in 1602–3, 'sevin greit fallin treis out of the wod cum in at Futabrughe, thrie fallin treis of timmer of fir cum in at Litilvie, twa daillis cum in at Quhytsness'.[324] The inhabitants of Unst had a bark with which they traded to Norway in 1633, getting 'Timber for Houses ready framed, also Deal-Boards, Tar, Ships, Barks, and Boats of all sorts'.[325] This is the first specific reference to the import of wood for building purposes. Orkney had a nearer source of supply, for there is a reference in the Sheriff Court Records for 1670 to 'great birkin Kaiberis, forkschafts, flailes and other great tries'. The cabers of birch were probably from Caithness and used as untrimmed roofing timbers. In 1683, several of the chimney-pieces seen in Sanday were made of driftwood. A letter from George Traill to David Traill, Kirkwall, 18 June 1718, mentioned a cargo of '9 or 10 dozen large firr balks, 500 double deall 16 foot (4.9 m) long 2 inches (5 cm) thick, 2000 single deall 14 foot (4.3 m) long, 800 deall of 10 foot (3 m) long ...'[326]

A further major source of wood was shipwreck, and on many crofts panels of doors and beds, or fireplace surrounds, come from ships that met their end on the rocks of these islands. Examples are numerous. In January 1800 the *Three Friends of Montrose* was wrecked on South Ronaldsay. She was carrying a cargo of timber from Danzig to Messrs. Garrioch and Black in Aberdeen – balks of timber, fir deals, oak planks, oak staves. All the timber that came ashore was measured by Mr Omond, merchant in Kirkwall, and sold legally. An unknown woodship carrying 15 to 40 ft (4.3–12.2 m) logs of over 4 ft (1.2 m) girth was wrecked in January 1804. The *Two Sisters*, or the *Prudentia*, with timber from Porsgrund in Norway, was wrecked in Hoy Sound in April 1811. Her main mast, and the logs, balks and deals were sold.[327] The treeless state of the Northern Isles, therefore, can scarcely be regarded as inhibiting to the buildings.

It sometimes happens that a building technique adapted to one type of material is carried over into another. One example is the way in which stones are laid sloping in alternate directions to produce a herring-bone effect in the walling of the Stone Age burial chambers at Blackhammer, Lairo and Midhowe on Rousay. Admittedly there could be cultural influence from far afield here, for mud-bricks were laid in this way in Mesopotamia about 2700–2400 BC, and herring-bone masonry was popular around the Aegean in the third millennium, but the same technique was used in turf much nearer home. In Iceland herring-bone turf walling may still be seen, and examples have been photographed in Aberdeenshire. In Orkney, peat was set up to dry in dykes of this form in damp weather. It is at least possible that herring-boning in stone is a reflection of a turf antecedent.[328]

In Viking and immediately pre-Viking times turf was in common use for composite walls, about 1 to 1½ m thick, usually with an inner stone facing, a turf core, and an outer facing of turf or of alternating courses of stone and turf. This technique is found at most of the excavated buildings, at Underhoull and Jarlshof in Shetland, Birsay, Buckquoy, Skaill and Westness in Orkney, and elsewhere in Scotland (see page 12). The same applied in other areas of Viking settlement. In the Faroes, walls could be found made of two stone faces with a core of turf or earth between, as in Iceland. They also occur in south-west Norway and survive in the 'blackhouse' of north-west Scotland, now with outer and inner facings of stone, but up till the mid-nineteenth century with outer facings of turf as in Viking times.[329]

It has been suggested that the use of alternating courses of turf and stone in wall faces, as found at Jarlshof, is a Viking innovation but this need not be so. The technique was widespread in Scotland in later times, in areas which lay both in place and time outside Norse influence.[330] Examples have been photographed in recent years in Angus and Inverness-shire.

14

The Longhouse

PROBABLY the most significant feature in the layout of early farms, and one that has continued sporadically till the present day, is the close association between the accommodation for people and animals, resulting in the 'longhouse' or 'byre-dwelling'. The date at which the longhouse evolved, with byre and living quarters end on to each other within a framework of rectangular walling, is not quite sure. At Jarlshof, the earliest dwelling house, dating to the first half of the ninth century, stood by itself, with outhouses including a barn or byre and a smithy nearby. It was only in the eleventh century, when considerable changes were taking place in the settlement, that a byre was added to the living quarters of the parent dwelling. The original house was 70 ft (21 m) long by 16 ft (5 m) wide internally.[331] It is possible that the addition of a byre came when the house ceased to be the main dwelling house, for longhouses of the same size built down the slope from it in the ninth and tenth centuries appear, on the evidence of facing in the lower half of each, to have included byres.

The farmhouse at Underhoull is smaller, 60 ft (18 m) long by 15 ft (4.9 m) wide. It seems to have been first built as a longhouse, but was later upgraded to a dwelling house only, with separate outhouses.[332] This, inter alia, makes it difficult to accept its dating to the same period as the parent dwelling at Jarlshof.

The evidence of Buckquoy shows a separate dwelling house, with a combined barn and byre alongside in Pictish times. At Kvívík, one of the early farms in Streymoy in the Faroe Islands, the conjoint barn and byre are behind and parallel to the hall. In Iceland this simplicity began to be replaced by tight clusters of dwelling house and outhouse units sometime during the fourteenth century and Reformation period. Farm buildings excavated at Gjáskógar and Gröf, dated to the eleventh and mid-fourteenth centuries respectively, contain dwelling house units alone. In Greenland the earliest farmhouses, though built on an elongated plan, do not include byres. These appear with the later clustered type of house. The splitting of the undivided hall into separate rooms for cooking, living, and sleeping seems to date to about the start of the twelfth century, and the further adding of outhouse units to the nuclear block is later still. Even farther afield, the late tenth to early eleventh century Viking settlement at L'Anse aux Meadows, Newfoundland, has no evidence for byres as part of the houses, but for an expeditionary party, as this must have been, the lack of byres here is scarcely diagnostic.[333]

Even if the Viking leaders kept their halls free of cows, and the longhouse with a byre is a phenomenon of the lower classes, the evidence suggests that the evolution of the longhouse is secondary in all the main Norse colonies. It may have appeared in the Northern Isles, as Jarlshof shows, earlier than elsewhere. Since the longhouse is or was a marked feature of several parts of Scotland as well as Ireland and Wales, there is at least a possibility that its eventual adoption in the Norse colonies is in part a reflection of Scottish building traditions. On the other hand, it is considered, on the evidence of paved areas in excavated houses, that men and animals lived under one roof in the Iron Age in south-west Norway.[334] The Norse settlers were probably not strangers to the idea. At all events, there is at least a thousand years of tradition behind the longhouse in the Northern Isles.

For 800 of these years, further evidence is almost non-existent. It was so much the standard form, apart from upper class houses, that no one thought to make comments until the sophistication of the nineteenth century caused writers and travellers to look askance at these old ways. There is here and there a possibility of making inferences, however. In an Orkney charter of c. 1536 to 1537, the listed features of the udal estate of Sabay included 'housses, biggines, yairds, barnes, stabells ...', but no specific mention of byres was made. The same was true of a $2\frac{1}{2}$ merk unit at Fiblasetter, Northmavine, with 'buithis, barnes, yairdes', in 1626.[335] Perhaps in such cases the byre was part of the house.

A minister travelling in Shetland was one of the first to make a direct reference to the lower ranks inhabiting houses in common with their cattle.[336] In Dunrossness, it was noted that the byre usually adjoined the house, with a common door for man and animals.[337] The entrance to a blacksmith's house across from Vailey Sound was through the byre, with the smithy at the far end of the house. The entrance to the house was often through the byre in Sandsting and Aithsting and in Walls, where it was in front of the dwelling house, and contained calves, sheep, young pigs, dogs and fowls.[338]

About this period, houses originally built by poor tenants in Westray were byre-dwellings. The animals lived in one end and the family or the domestic servants at the other. In St Andrews, the people sometimes shared the houses with poultry, pigs, calves, dogs and cats.[339] One of the reasons for the survival of such places was no doubt the regulation Anent Demolishing of Houses in The Acts of Bailiary for executing of Justice through the County of Orkney of 1615:

'*Item*, It is statute and ordained by the Sherreif-depute, with consent forsaid, that no removers from housses shall demolish the samen, in haill or in pairt, nor take timber doors nor windows furth thereof, although bigged by themselves, under the pain of 20 pund Scots, the one half to the Sherreif, and the other to the pairty interest, and that by and attour the reedifying of the houses, under the like paine'.[340]

From these sources, it is evident that there are different types of longhouses. Some, especially in Orkney, are linear in form, with dwelling-house, byre, and other units end on to each other. Others, especially in Shetland, have the byre lying parallel to the house, and it is the barn that is end on to the dwelling house.[341]

By the first quarter of the nineteenth century, the longhouse, of whatever form, was on its way out, though modified examples have survived till the present day. By 1822, the pattern of change had already been set, as in the Quendale area where such houses were scarcer than elsewhere in Shetland, 'and the antiquary will be often chagrined in observing such provoking modern improvement as slate roofs, regular windows, and detached cow-houses, all of which have been introduced into the country by that foe to archaeological sources of pleasure, ever stimulating to innovation, – a sense and desire of increased comfort'.[342]

15

Twentieth Century Survivals:
Some Detailed Examples

IN 1911, old farms in Orkney were described as long straggling rows of buildings, with a barn, stable, house with but- and ben-ends, and byre all in a line. Other buildings often stood parallel, but separated by a narrow close. Another possible sequence of units was barn, stable, byre, and dwelling house.[343]

Besides the diagrams in these two sources, a number of examples can still be seen in Orkney. Some of these were examined by J S Clouston in the 1920s,[344] and several of his plans were reproduced in 1934 by the Dane, Aage Rousell, in his study of *Norse Building Customs in the Scottish Isles*. When these plans were made, some of the houses were still occupied, and it was not easily possible to look behind box-beds and furniture for straight joints and other structural evidence. In 1968 a fresh survey of a number of these buildings was made, and as a result, earlier plans and conclusions must be modified.

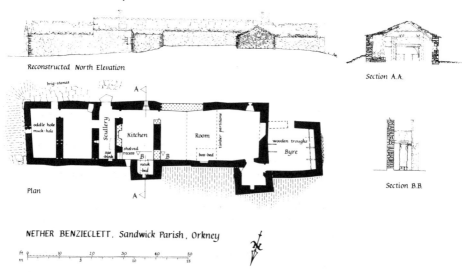

27. Nether Benzieclett, Sandwick, Orkney, surveyed 1968. Copyright: Royal Commission on Ancient Monuments, Neg. no. ORD/3/1.

Nether Benzieclett in Sandwick is a good example of a simple longhouse, with two dwelling-house units and a byre in line, roughly on an east–west axis. A small, windowless, 9 ft (2.7 m) square building formerly stood separately at the west end, but by 1923 it had been joined on,[345] and now serves as a byre with an outer door, and an inner door knocked through the wall of a small outshot store-room, which leads into the house through the ben-end. The byre at the east end is divided in two by an inserted partition wall of stone, to make a stable and a byre. A small floor-level opening, the *oddle-hole* (Norwegian dialectal *aale*, Danish dialectal *ajle*, *adel*, *al*, cattle urine), leads liquid manure from the byre into the stable. Another oddle-hole in the east gable underlies a *muck-hole*, 1 ft 8 in. (51 cm) square, through which the manure was graiped to the midden outside. The stable door is likely to be a later insertion. Originally, one front door served for men and animals. The animals turned left on entering to pass through a door in an inserted partition wall. The angle is awkward, and as a result of continued rubbing and pressing by animals or from deliberate building, the inner door has a curved, cow-shaped look, widening as it rises.[346] Though this is an inserted partition, butting against the back wall, it is likely to be original, since it is stepped down externally to serve as the east gable to the house. The roof of the byre, as commonly happens, is at a lower level than that of the house.

The first unit is the scullery, with a shallow recess in the back wall, a low stone table or *sae-bink* (Old Norse *sár*, cask, Old Scots *say*, bucket + *bink* = bench) for water tubs or buckets, and in an east wall a narrow recess and a row of wooden pegs that supported slate shelves. The west wall of the scullery is the back of a stone gable containing, at the kitchen side, a hearth with an iron swey, topped by a slab lintel or *breast-stone* of a type common in Orkney. Alongside is a press with two flagstone shelves. About head-height at either side of the fireplace are two rectangular openings 7½ in. (19 cm) high by 4 in. (10 cm) wide by 5 in. (13 cm) deep. They may have been sockets for short beams to carry a part loft, supported at their outer ends by a beam across the side walls. This is more likely than the suggestion that there was once an upper storey here, the joist-holes for which had been blocked up and the side-walls lowered.[347] According to Alfred Work, who lived here until 1942, this gable and fireplace were inserted by his grandfather about 1870–80. The original wide hearth was later built up with stone to make it narrower, no doubt reflecting a change from peat to coal.

The flagstone lintel of the kitchen door is recessed to make a shelf inside. Two small windows light the kitchen front and back, and on the north side a *neuk-bed* (Scots *neuk*, corner) projects as an outshot in a manner that characterises some of the older Orkney farms. The bed is 5 ft 4 in. (1.62 m) long by 3 ft 10 in. (1.17 m) deep. The front is narrowed to 2 ft 2 in. (0.70 m) by an upright flag at one side, though other examples have a flagstone at each side. At the head and foot of the bed are stone benches about a foot (30 cm) high to hold the bed boards. The outshot has a catslide roof of flagstone, in continuation of the main roof.

The kitchen is divided from the ben-end by another stone cross-wall. At present, the door, which has been narrowed by a foot (30 cm), runs through in line with the one leading into the kitchen, but because there is a blocked door opening, with a recess above its lintel, at the other end beside the neuk-bed, it has been suggested that this was the original door. If so, it could have been blocked up when a rebuilding of much of the south wall and west gable was done about the 1860s,[348] or when the gable hearth was built, no doubt as a replacement for a fire in the centre of the floor.

The ben-end was divided into three by two wooden partitions, the doors of which were in line with the others, to form a long passage along the front of the house. There is a rebuilt break in the front wall. In the back wall of the middle section, a large flagstone, set slantwise into the wall, is associated with a flagstone floor or base that immediately underlies the present one. Formerly this was concealed by a box-bed. It must belong to an earlier phase of the house's existence, and is part of the evidence, together with the comment on an 1860 rebuild, for a possible extension of the house westwards. There is a tendency for the house to widen out towards the west end, but nothing like as much as in the earlier diagram. The part of the but-end nearest the kitchen formerly held a box-bed, end on to the back wall, against the wooden partition; one in the middle unit lay along the back wall; two in the third unit, which contains a gable fireplace, were at right angles, one against the partition and one against the back wall. This made a total of five beds.

Opposite the small window in the third unit, a door leads into a store-room or larder which buts against the back wall and has its own double-pitched and gabled roof of flagstone. There is a blocked up square niche in the middle of the back wall, and a triangular recess for a shelf 1 ft 6 in. (46 cm) deep in the south-east angle. The back-door that leads into the west byre has a latch opened by a string that leads from an inside wooden thumb-grip through a finger-hole.

This byre was presumably built when the house was extended, and the store-room could have been added at the same time. The byre contains flag-stone partitions for cows along the west gable and for calves along the east wall.

If the added features are removed, including the stable door, Nether Ben-zieclett appears as a simple three unit longhouse, with byre, kitchen or ben-end, and but-end. The adaptations date from the second half of the nineteenth century, and an eighteenth century date for the original building is likely.

Mossetter, a farm in the parish of Evie and Rendall, situated NNW of the Loch of Brockan, is similar, but with fewer alterations. One door serves the whole range, which has a byre at the west end, a ben-end divided into a scullery and kitchen by an inserted cross-wall containing a fireplace, and a but-end with a gable fireplace. The roof of the byre is at a lower level than that of the house. The most noteworthy feature is the long continuous outshot on the north wall under a catslide roof. It contains two neuk-beds, a smaller unit that may have held peat or else was for general storage, and two in the scullery end with flagstone shelves, which probably housed small animals. In one of the latter is a fastening for an animal, probably a calf.

The house is 73 ft 6 in. long (22.4 m) externally, by 15 ft (4.6 m) wide across

the east gable and 17 ft 3 in. (5.25 m) across the west, with walls varying from
2 ft (61 cm) to 2 ft 6 in. (76 cm) thick. The byre has a muck-hole and oddle-hole
in the west gable, and there was a range of stalls formed by flagstone partitions,
now marked by grooves in the north wall. Inside the door, a part circle of stones
has been built in the scullery, apparently to direct the animals more easily into
the byre. In the wall to the right of the door is a low square recess, probably a
nest for a broody goose, and just along from it is a sae-bink, a rounded niche 2 ft
3 in. (69 cm) deep by 8 in. (20 cm) deep, with a curved flagstone sill projecting
8 in. (20 cm). The bink, now awkwardly placed at the side of the doorway, may
have gone out of use when the internal gable and hearth were inserted.

The east gable fireplace is formed by stone cheeks protruding into the room
in such a way as to make a press 2 to 3 ft (61–91 cm) wide by 1 ft (30 cm) deep at
each side. Wooden pegs in the plastered walls show that these press alcoves
were wood-lined. The fireplace cheeks are bonded into the wall, not simply
butting against it. This suggests either that the house does not antedate the
introduction of this type of fireplace to Orkney, probably in the early

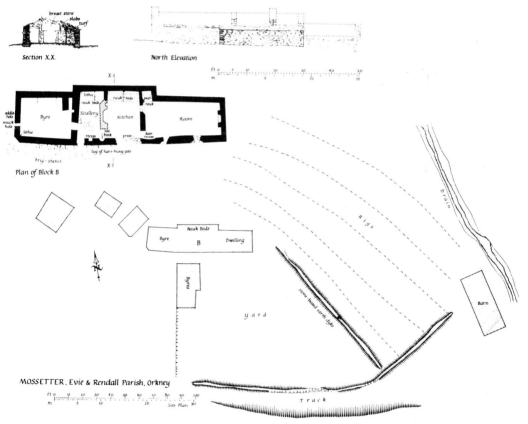

28. Mossetter, Evie and Rendall, Orkney, surveyed 1968. Copyright: Royal Commission on
Ancient Monuments, Neg. no. ORD/1/1.

nineteenth century, or that there has been a rebuilding or extension at the east end. The only two wall windows in the whole complex are in the south wall of the ben-end. They are placed at unequal heights, and are not recessed down to floor level as is usual in later buildings. The actual light area is very small.

The flagstone catslide roof of the outshot is supported by stout untrimmed tree branches in the but-end. The kitchen neuk-beds are divided by a central upright flagstone, on top of which stones have been crudely corbelled to provide the necessary height. Though the tumbled front wall, and the substantial buttress against the south wall of the byre, show that the stonework was not eternally enduring, yet the method of its use in the neuk-bed is in keeping

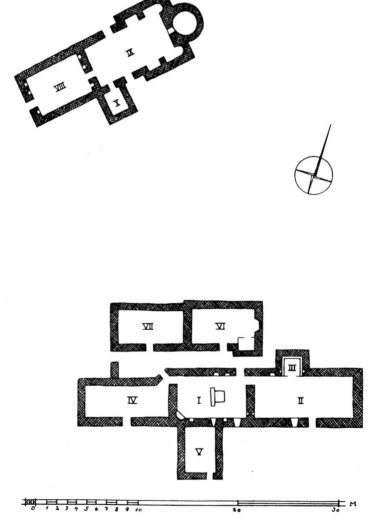

29. Winksetter, Orkney. From Roussell 1934. 97.

with the nature of the material, in a way that was already known to the prehistoric people who made corbelled stone structures in these islands and elsewhere in Europe. Such a technique does not, however, mean that the farm is particularly old. The exterior of the south-east byre gable is neatly splayed back, as at other farms in Orkney – e.g. Quina near Stromness – to let loads and animals turn in more easily along the *brig* (bridge)-*stanes* or paved path that leads to the entrance. Such a feature is not likely to be older than the late eighteenth century. Even the fact that plough ridges and furrows of the old high-backed style, about 20 ft (6.1 m) across the crowns, run up to and then swing round the house, does not mean an early date, since this is a wet area not amenable to systematic underground drainage. A deep open drain runs through the fields, which are enclosed by tumbled dykes of stone and turf. The general three unit plan is similar to Nether Benzieclett, and a late eighteenth to early nineteenth century date is perfectly feasible. It could be regarded as a kind of improved byre-dwelling, since the byre is separated from the but-end by a stout mid-gable, even though the entrance is common for man and beast. The farm of Mossetter, vacated about 1920, was around 30 acres in size.

Winksetter in the parish of Harray has been ascribed to the fifteenth century, because of a reference of 1503 to Johne Ismond's son, tacksman of the penny land of Winksetter. In 1665 the farm was leased to a Kirkwall burgess.[349] The site, at least, has a long continuous history, but it is not likely that the buildings as they stand are so old, though a high social level is suggested by the traces, no longer evident, but unique on Orkney farms, of a decorative framework of hewn stones around the main door on the north gable, and by the height of the side walls. However, the longhouse farm is the basic three unit one. The byre, originally 10 ft (3 m) wide, has been widened to about 16 ft 6 in. (5 m), wide enough to hold two rows of animals instead of one. It is offset to the central line of the building. The roof was heightened at the same time, but remains lower than that of the house. The but-end has an inserted gable and hearth, replacing the central hearth with stone back which is included hypothetically in published plans.[350] In the south-west angle of the *ootbye* or scullery area is a semicircular recess with a flagstone base. This is the *quern-ledder* (Old Norse *luðr*, floor round a mill-stone), where grain was ground on the hand-mill. The inserted gable contains a small fireplace, set well to one side so as not to coincide with the bigger fireplace in the kitchen on the other side of the wall. At the same time, this gable has been built 3 ft (91 cm) thick to accommodate the two fires.

Inside the kitchen or *inbye*, the fireplace has had a wooden surround. By the entrance door, there is a half-round sae-bink in the wall, and along from it a slate-sided wall press with two shelves. A recess for a goose nest is at floor level below it. The blocked up front door has been turned into a press. The south wall contains a blocked goose nest, and a window recessed to floor level. A second, unrecessed, blocked window to the east of this one is partially obscured by the internal gable that divides the but- and ben-ends, making the gable clearly secondary. This gable contains another goose nest, making three in all.

The but-end, which has a step up into it from the kitchen, has a window in the

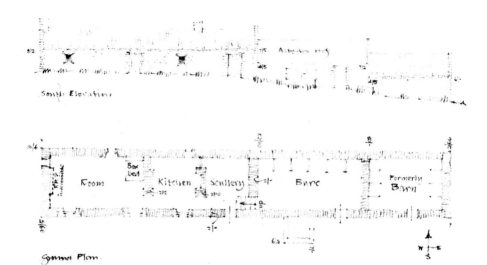

ESTABIN — sketch drawing (only accurate in room proportions & dimensions stated.)
Firth Parish, Orkney. 16/10/68

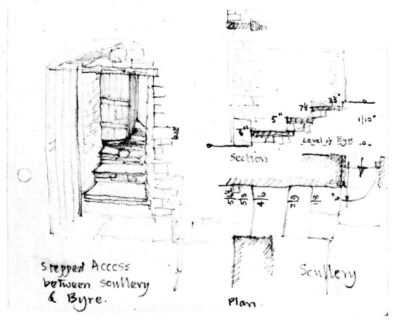

30. Estabin, Firth, Orkney, surveyed 1968. Copyright: Royal Commission on Ancient Monuments, Neg. no. ORD/5/2. Sketches by G. Hay.

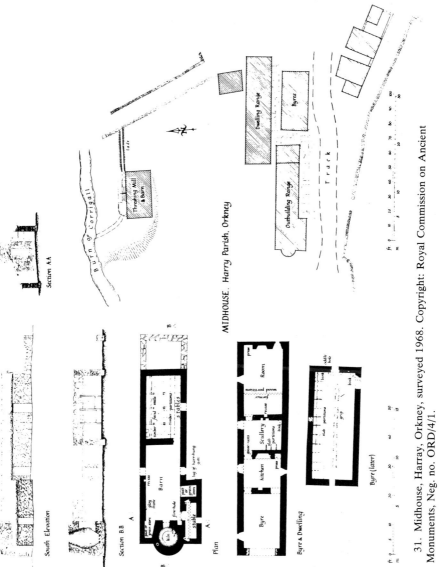

31. Midhouse, Harray, Orkney, surveyed 1968. Copyright: Royal Commission on Ancient Monuments, Neg. no. ORD/4/1.

back wall, opposite an outshot store-room at the front. The store-room formerly had a low bench of earth along its outer wall,[351] but no trace of this remains. A gable with a hearth has been built across here, with a blocked up door that gave access to a part that has been demolished. The north wall contains a press with a single shelf.

There are no neuk-beds here, which may be a further indication of superior status. Across a narrow close to the north, a block containing a stirks' byre and a chaumer lies parallel to the byre-dwelling. This chaumer contains a fireplace, and a 'half-neuk' bed in a shallow outshot recess. Here, some of the farm servants slept.

Estabin in the parish of Firth is a longhouse of a more sophisticated type, which appears to be of one build. The line of intercommunicating units consists of a ben-end with a box bed, a but-end equally divided into kitchen and scullery areas by a mid-gable with a hearth, and a byre entered by a flight of three steps from the scullery. There are separate doors leading into the but-end (possibly a later insertion), the scullery, and the byre. At the east end is a former barn, now converted into a byre, with a separate entrance. The overall size is 99 ft 5 in. (30.3 m) long by 16 ft 4 in. (5 m) across, and the walls average 2 ft (61 cm) in thickness.

Midhouse in the parish of Harray is on a bigger scale than Estabin. A barn with its corn-drying kiln, and a stable, lie near the byre-dwelling, which has three units as at Estabin. The east gable has a fireplace with stone cheeks like the one at Mossetter, flanked by a press at one side and a small gable window at the other. Three goose nests are low in the north wall of the scullery, and against the mid-gable wall that divides the kitchen and scullery, behind the hearth, are three low stone partitions that possibly housed pigs. Both Estabin and Midhouse, though incorporating traditional building features, are well-squared, regular structures, with regularly set and relatively numerous windows. There are no neuk-beds in them. They are likely to be later in date than Nether Benzieclett and Mossetter. Midhouse has been tentatively dated to about 1735–40,[352] but this may be too early.

Because of the uniform character of Orkney stonework, it is difficult to date it. Known alterations to earlier buildings look exactly the same as the older parts. The farm of Appiehouse in Stenness, therefore, with its datable phases, is of particular interest. The two-storey part was built first about 1815, to the order of Nicol Leith who had been invalided out of the navy. Presumably prize-money from the Napoleonic Wars enabled him to build in such style, for this was only the second two-storey house in the parish. He had bought the farm at that time, and built his new house about 200 yds (183 m) up the hill from the old house and steading.

The building has a roof of grey slates, and a flagstone floor. The roofing couples were linked with wooden pins, as were the slates, but the laths were fixed with iron nails and the rusting of these made re-roofing necessary in 1955. The wooden pins were then still in good condition. For symmetry, two chimneys were built, but the lower one was a dummy. The water berges at the chimney bases were made to project in the manner used on a thatched roof.

Later, the building was extended by the addition of a kitchen in traditional style with a central fire and a smoke-hole at the gable, with no external chimney. This kitchen has a sae-bink, quern-ledder, and two presses with stone shelves. By the outer door is a small opening which may have been for cats or hens. Wall-fastenings or *lithies* (cf. Danish dialectal *lejd(e)*, Swedish *lejd*, a wall-plate, Low German *lehde*, a sill, sleeper) for calves are still in position in the kitchen gable. This kitchen extension must have been in the original plan, since a guttering had been left for it in the gable to the two-storey part. Apart from skylights, it had only one window about 18 in. (46 cm) square at the back. A small byre was added at the end about the same time. About 1880, the back wall of the two-storey unit showed signs of weakness, and a room was added to strengthen it.

When the central hearth got out of date, the back was replaced by a mid-gable and the whole section from this point back to the two-storey house was raised to incorporate an attic. The small window was taken from the back and put into the front wall, and a larger one inserted at the back. The byre was also lengthened. The fireplace now had a mantelpiece. The hearth area was about 6 ft (1.8 m) wide by 5 ft (1.5 m) high, and an iron fire-crane was incorporated. A small recess at the side held the 'guidman's' pipe and tobacco. The next stage in evolution was the insertion of a smith-made fire grate, the sides being built up to a height of 18 in. (46 cm) to accommodate it. Later the sides were built right up, leaving a relatively narrow opening like a modern grate. Finally this opening was closed with an iron sheet and a cast-iron stove set in front of it. The last stage has been to take out the stonework built into the hearth, and to recess the stove back into it.[353]

From these examples of various periods and different sizes, and others previously published, the basic characteristics of the Orkney longhouse can be seen. It is a one-storey building with a dwelling area divided by a cross-wall into a but- and a ben-end, the but-end being later (in the nineteenth century) split into a scullery and a kitchen by an inserted gable with a hearth, replacing the older central fire with a stone back that divided the living room less formally into the ootbye and inbye. Young animals could be kept in the inbye, but the cattle, especially the milking stock, were in the byre that opened off the scullery. The byre is often lower than the dwelling house, and may be narrower. In some examples a stable forms part of the line, sometimes also a barn and corn-drying kiln, but usually the barn and kiln block, jointly with a stirks' byre or stable, stands separate from the main block. On bigger farms there is a chaumer for servants, built by itself or as part of a parallel block, including a byre, across a narrow close.

The pattern in Shetland is much less complicated, partly because farms were small and partly because the buildings are younger. The oldest is the late thirteenth or early fourteenth century medieval farm at Jarlshof. The foundations show two buildings in parallel in the earliest phase, one a dwelling house and the other a barn, at least in part, for a corn kiln was built into the north-west angle. In later stages of existence in the fourteenth and fifteenth centuries a new kiln replaced the old one, and the dwelling house became a byre. There is no indication, however, that this was originally a longhouse.[354]

It is likely that the kiln reflects influence from Orkney (see page 380), and indeed it may be said that the farms of Dunrossness are closer in form to those of Orkney than anywhere else in Shetland. An example is South Voe, now restored and preserved as a museum. It is built in two linked blocks, so that the units cluster together in a way reminiscent of the much older farm of Conglabist in North Ronaldsay, the Orkney island that lies nearest to Shetland.[355] The entrance to the dwelling was through the byre, by a door in the middle of the gable opening into the but-end. This door was later blocked, and a fireplace and chimney built against the gable behind it. The original fireplace was against the internal gable that divided the but- and ben-ends, and the mantelpiece and side-pieces from it were re-used on the new one. At the same time, a central door was made, opening into a short passage made by the insertion of a bedroom recess. This turned the house into a conventional but-and-ben and bedroom. Before this, two *biggit* (Old Scots *big*, Old Norse *byggja*, to build) *beds* or box-beds stood end to end against the back wall of the but-end, and an iron-framed bed along the mid-gable. The present restoration has replaced the old arrangement of gable door and mid-gable.

The byre, when examined in 1965, was used as a sheep-house, but still contained four wall-dooks or *veggels* (Norwegian dialectal *vegg*, Old Norse *veggr*, wall, + Norwegian *vol*, Old Norse *vǫlr*, round stick, stake) for cattle. It

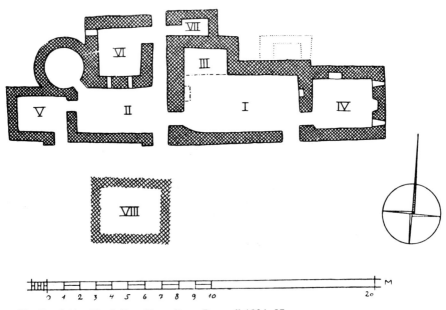

32. Conglabist, North Ronaldsay. From Roussell 1934. 87.

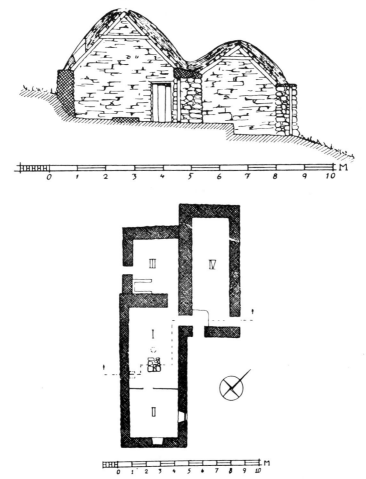

33. Effirth, Shetland. From Roussell 1934. 53.

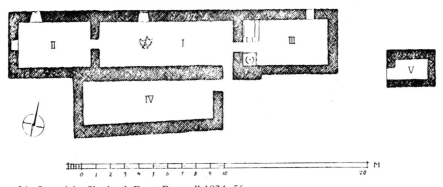

34. Stanydale, Shetland. From Roussell 1934. 56.

has a separate door, and a wooden partition cuts off the end of the byre. A passage leads through to the barn behind, with a potato store, tattie hoose, at one end and a corn-kiln at the other. An opening in the back wall of the barn was for sheaves to be thrown in from the stacks outside, and also provided a draught for the kiln if necessary. A building forming an extension of the barn, with a separate entrance, originally had a small fireplace in the gable between it and the barn. An old lady lived in it for some time. Latterly it was used as a

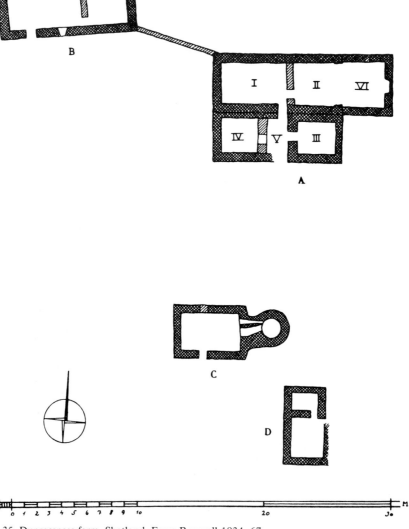

35. Dunrossness farm, Shetland. From Roussell 1934. 67.

lammiehoose for sheep and lambs. This unit, like the barn, has its own separate inner wall, though it is built hard against the dwelling house and byre.

The general layout characterises a number of farms in the Dunrossness area. South Voe was the last building to be put up in a spell of new house building by the Dunrossness estate. Though incorporating features of Shetland building, it is not entirely characteristic, except for its own area and period.[356] The same way of setting units in parallel, with the walls touching, can be seen at Effirth, Stanydale, Dunrossness farm, Skelberry, and elsewhere. In some cases the byre lies alongside the house unit, with access through it. However, though the byre and house are so closely associated, these are not longhouses sensu stricto. Nevertheless, the linear form is so strongly entrenched in the building tradition

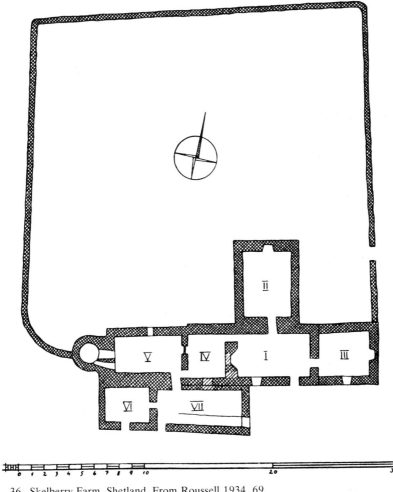

36. Skelberry Farm, Shetland. From Roussell 1934. 69.

37. A Foula Croft, Brakins, with the byre in parallel with the house. Coalfish are drying against the gable. H B Curwen 1902.

that the unit consisting of a dwelling house with a byre at one end and a barn at the other, though without internal communication, may be considered standard, for crofts, if not farms, and a fairly direct successor to the longhouse form.[357]

16

Farms in General

KIRBISTER in the parish of Birsay was built, according to a lintel above what was probably the original front door, in 1723. The dwelling house is unorthodox in layout, for a partition gable roughly at the mid point divides the range into two rooms to the west serving as bedrooms, and two to the east, one of them a kitchen with a central hearth, and the other with an exterior door.

The unit of main interest is the kitchen, which includes several features of early type. To the left of the entrance door is an upright flagstone about 3 ft (91 cm) wide by 3 ft (91 cm) high. Behind this, against the internal gable, there formerly stood a box-bed, and beyond it, against the back wall, a stone bench for buckets etc. about 7 ft (2.1 m) long by 1 ft 6 in. (46 cm) deep and 1 ft 3 in. (38 cm) high. A holed peg in the wall just behind the upright flag may indicate that calves were formerly tied up here, and a plan made in 1947 gives this whole area the name of 'calf box'.[358] However, the peg is slim and the hole in it is an exact circle, with none of the characteristic one-sided wear caused by constant rubbing with a rope. It almost certainly served another purpose.

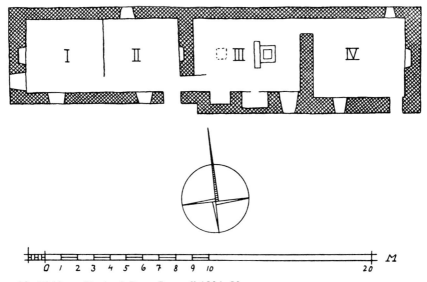

38. Kirbister, Shetland. From Roussell 1934, 83.

To the right of the door is a recess in the thickness of the wall, 3 ft 4 in. (1 m) wide at the front, 4 ft 3 in. (1.3 m) wide at the back, 6 ft 2 in. (1.9 m) high and 4 ft (1.2 m) deep. This was the peat neuk, in which peat fuel for the central fire was kept. Along from it is a much larger recess, the front of which is partly closed by two flagstones. The total length is approximately 6 ft 3 in. (1.9 m), the width varying from 2 ft 5 in. (74 cm) to 2 ft 11 in. (89 cm). Unlike most neuk or half-neuk beds in Orkney, which are accommodated in outshots, this recess lies within the thickness of the wall, like wall-beds in some of the old blackhouses of the Hebrides. It is built open up to the roofing flags, giving a height of 6 ft 7 in. (2 m) to the timber lintel spanning the opening above. At the corners there are rough corbel stones 2 ft 4 in. (71 cm) above floor level, which probably supported the framework of the bed. A wooden front board is still in position. At the west end of the recess, 3 ft 5 in. (1.1 m) above floor level, is a 3½ in. (9 cm) deep ledge with a square storage recess a foot (30 cm) above it, 1 ft 4 in. (70 cm) wide by 10 in. (25 cm) deep by 8 in. (20 cm) high and a smaller one immediately below, 9 in. (23 cm) wide by 1 ft 1 in. (33 cm) deep by 10 in. (26 cm) high. In the 5 ft (1.5 m) thick wall to the east of the bed recess is a four-paned window whose commodious embrasure contains a solid bench sill.

The internal gable at the far end of the kitchen has two recesses, one of them wood lined, with a shelf and door. Roughly in the middle is a wooden swey, like one from a gable hearth, that supported the lamp.

A door in the back wall leads into a milk house, which was added in the twentieth century. Near it, a 3 ft (91 cm) long recess in the wall contains a wooden plate rack, like the back of a Dutch dresser.

The room is split into the inbye and ootbye by the fire-back, a dwarf wall lying north–south, 4 ft 8 in. (1.4 m) long by 1 ft 6 in. (46 cm) thick and 3 ft 6 in. (1.1 m) high. Lying on top of it is a 5½ in. (14 cm) thick slab which gives a stepped profile. The wall is built of small rubble masonry, evidently consolidated from time to time with plaster, and through the base of it is a hole 1 ft 7 in. (48 cm) wide by 1 ft (30 cm) high. In front of the hole on the east or inbye side is a square hearth, paved and now stepped up 2 in. (5 cm) round the sides with brick. The hole was closed by an upright flag. To make the fire a large sandy peat was laid against the flag, and good black peat in front. The wall was kept whitewashed. When a visit was paid to the house whilst it was still occupied in the 1950s, there was a mist of smoke rising from behind the back, shot through with white light from the window in the wall and the smoke-hole in the roof. Above the hearth a charred and soot-blackened beam, the *pan-tree* (Old Scots *pane*, 1520, Middle English *panne*, wall-plate, French *panne*, Medieval Latin *panna*), 7 in. (18 cm) deep by 5½ in. (13 cm) wide, spans the wall-heads. The crook and links for pots and kettles is slung from it, and consists of a chain of hook-and-eye links fixed at the top to an iron rod cranked over the beam, and at the bottom to four links with an iron crook.

The smoke escaped through a square smoke-hole in the roof, reconstructed in recent years but conforming to the dimensions of the old one. It is set not immediately above the fire, but about 4 ft 6 in. (1.37 m) west of it, and takes the form of a square box protruding about 18 in. (46 cm) above the roof-ridge. A flat board sticking out above it could be moved from side to side to control draught by means of a long handle hanging down into the kitchen (see page 198).

Like Winksetter, Kirbister is a farm of reasonable status. It is not a long-house, and the walls are 8 ft 3 in. (2.5 m) high internally instead of the more usual 6 ft (1.8 m). The floor is flagged, and the kitchen is relatively well lit. There is a good set of detached outbuildings, including a barn with a corn kiln, a pig-sty, and a lean-to with a forge for smithing.

Langalour is a much smaller farm in the parish of Firth, which now, like Estabin, belongs to Redland farm. It consists of two blocks of buildings, both aligned east–west, in parallel but stepped so that the outbuilding block lies to the west and south of the other. The entrance to the house block is through the scullery, by the east gable. Just to the right of the entrance there is in the east gable a blocked doorway, the top part of which has been made into a recess. In the middle of the gable a foot (30 cm) square opening cuts right through to the outside, with a foot (30 cm) square recess just above it. This opening, and the blocked door, suggest that another unit lay beyond. Conceivably, it was a byre, demolished when the road was made alongside.

In the north-east corner there is a half-round recess 3 ft 9 in. (1.1 m) across by 3 ft 4 in. (1 m) high with a flagstone base 2 ft 5 in. (74 cm) deep and 3 ft (91 cm) above floor level. This is a quern-ledder. Above the door that leads past the mid-gable is a flagstone shelf. In the stonework at the back of it, the clay mortar with a mixture of straw that cements the stones is clearly visible.

The mid-gable is built in such a way that it is cheeked out to make a set-back at the north side, matching the door opening on the south. The set-back contains three recesses, one above the other, and of decreasing sizes from bottom to top, respectively 1 ft 4 in. (40 cm) wide by 1 ft 2 in. (36 cm) high by 10½ in. (27 cm) deep, 1 ft 1 in. (33 cm) wide by 2 ft 6 in. (76 cm) high by 9 in. (23 cm) deep, and 8 in. (20 cm) wide by 8 in. (20 cm) high by 11 in. (28 cm) deep. There is a substantial breast-stone above the fire, with a massive chimney of masonry, 4 ft (1.2 m) wide by 3 ft 10 in. (1.1 m) across, standing 2 ft 6 in. (76 cm) above the ridge. Chimneys of this kind are common on Orkney houses. The hearth opening is 4 ft (1.2 m) wide. The west gable has a similar, but smaller fireplace, with an opening 3 ft 2 in. (97 cm) wide. The cheeks make two presses, each of which has had two flagstone shelves. The heavy chimney has been removed.

The south wall has two window openings, both recessed to the floor. The easterly one replaces a blocked door. Less than 2 ft (61 cm) west of it are traces of what must have been a cross-wall. Perhaps this marks the original place of the mid-gable, if the present one is an insertion replacing a central fire with a back. It is matched in position on the north wall by the division between the two neuk-beds there.

At Langalour, the bed outshot roof, though formed of flagstone in the same way as the house roof, is at a slightly lower level and is not a catslide continuation. It covers two units, both of which were neuk-beds originally, though one was made into a storage space. The neuk-bed was in use within living memory. A number of wooden spars that made a base under the straw are still lying lengthways in it. The storage unit is fully open, but the bed-space is narrowed by two upright flagstones, leaving an entrance 1 ft 6 in. (46 cm) wide by 4 ft 6 in. (1.4 m) high. The east side of the neuk-bed has a 9 in. (23 cm) deep shelf at a height of 3 ft 6 in. (1.1 m), and the west side contains a recess 1 ft (30 cm) square by $7\frac{1}{2}$ in. (19 cm) deep at a height of 3 ft (91 cm).

The outbuildings lie 6 ft 4 in. (1.93 m) to the west. The unit nearest the house was a stable, and has a recessed manger with a flagstone front in each of its four corners. The stable door in the centre of the east gable has a 9 in. (23 cm) step up, and above it there are four pigeon holes. A little above them is a protruding flag that would have served both as a landing platform and as a shelter for the nest below. A door in the middle of the inner gable has been blocked up. The westerly unit is a small barn. This is shown by the stone protruding at a height of 3 ft 8 in. (1.1 m), from the south wall near the door, used as a gloy-stone (see page 358) for threshing sheaves by hand. In the north wall opposite the door is a 1 ft 10 in. (56 cm) square opening to provide a winnowing draught.

No other buildings are present, and it must, therefore, be taken as certain that the byre lay beyond the east gable of the house. Langalour was originally a longhouse.[359]

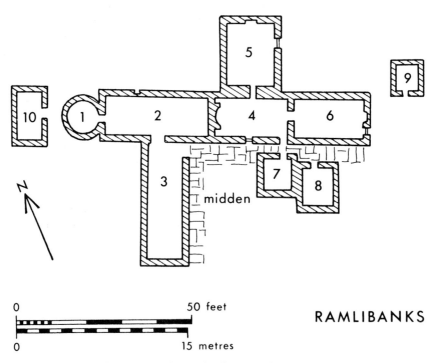

RAMLIBANKS

0   50 feet

0   15 metres

39. Ramlibanks, Dunrossness, Shetland. After Tait 1951. II. 78. C5840.

A Shetland example is the farm of Ramlibanks in Dunrossness, built in 1817 and vacated in 1882. It is a long building with a kiln and barn, and dwelling house in line, but not intercommunicating. A byre lies at right angles to the south wall of the barn and a bedroom at right angles to the north wall of the but-end, as at Skelberry.[360] Parallel to the house and across a narrow, partly roofed close are two buildings, one described as a porch or *ander* (Norwegian *anddyr*, back door; Old Norse *anddyri*, porch), the other a stable. On the west side, in line with the barn and house, is a lambhouse, and on the east a small shed or skeo for storing meat. The cornyard is on the north side of the house behind the barn, in the wall of which there is an opening 2 ft 3 in. (69 cm) square for putting in sheaves.

In the but-end is a massive fireplace with two protruding stone cheeks that form press recesses at each side. The north side press is 2 ft 6 in. (76 cm) high by 2 ft 6 in. (76 cm) wide by 1 ft 9 in. (53 cm) deep; on the south side there are two, a lower one 2 ft 6 in. (76 cm) high by 2 ft (61 cm) wide by 1 ft 6 in. (46 cm) deep, and an upper one 3 ft (91 cm) by 1 ft 9 in. (53 cm) wide by 1 ft 6 in. (46 cm) deep.

The byre is narrow, and has a 3 ft (91 cm) wide channel for urine along one side. The animals, therefore, were fastened along one wall only. There is no trace of a muck-hole, but the midden lies in the angle between the byre and the house. The barn entrance is through the byre door.[361]

North Banks in Papa Stour was altered like the rest of the houses there about the middle of the nineteenth century, so that the house roof is now higher than the roof of the barn and byre alongside. The barn and byre unit, separated by an internal wooden partition with a door, is a foot (30 cm) narrower than the house. The house has two windows in front only, a porch with two doors covering the entrance, and is 33 ft (10 m) long by 16 ft (4.9 m) wide externally. The outhouses are 15 ft (4.6 m) wide by 39 ft (11.9 m) long, giving a total length of 72 ft (21.9 m). A muck-hole at the end of the byre debouches on a partly stone-sided midden about 3 ft (91 cm) deep.

Across the paved close are two sheds, one for general storage, one a lamb-house, each roofed by half of a boat cut in two. At the end of the lambhouse is a small sod-roofed hen-house. The remaining buildings are at the bottom of the yard – a small half-underground tattie hoose for storing potatoes (see page 418), and a lambhouse and byre built half into the face of the sloping yard. The lambhouse is 20 ft 2 in. (6.14 m) long by 7 ft 10 in. (2.39 m) wide internally, and the byre 14 ft 10 in. (4.5 m) long by 7 ft 10 in. (2.4 m) wide.[362]

17

Orkney Houses and Plenishings

APART from excavated sites, the earliest information about Orkney houses appears in the Orkneyinga Saga. A feast held by Earl Thorfinn about 1020 was in a large hall, *skáli*, with a door at either end. There were fires (the word is used in the plural) in the middle of the floor, with seats alongside. Thorfinn's house appears to have had a loft floor at the back. Earl Paul's large drinking hall in Orphir had, about 1135, a door in the south wall under the east gable. There was a large flagstone on the left inside the hall – reminiscent of the one at Kirbister – with a number of large ale-casks behind it. Opposite the outer door was a small room with a small window. The greatest drinking hall in Orkney was Sweyn Asleifsson's, at Gairsay. After his death in Dublin about 1172, his sons Olaf and Andrew divided his estates, and split the hall between them by putting a partition across the middle. Other building details in the Saga are the half-doors in a house in Papa Stronsay in 1046, and the wicker-partition in part of a house in Sanday in 1154,[363] but otherwise nothing is said about the ordinary run of houses and information remains sparse and fragmentary over the following centuries.

The essential buildings and building materials are listed in a charter of James V, probably dated 1536 to 1537, confirming James Irving of Sabay and his heirs in their possession of their udal estates. These were 'housses, biggines, yairds, barnes, stabells, ... sklett and skletthews, sten and stenquarrell, lym and lymkilles, dowes, dowcketts', as well as a mill.[364] Lime mortar was in use, therefore, for better class stone-built houses, and they were roofed with slate or thin flags. In Sanday in 1535, a 'sufficient mansion house' had a hall, chamber, kitchen, barn, byre and doocots (sufficientem mansionem cum aula, camera, coquina, horreo, boscari, columbariis ...).[365]

The internal layout of such a mansion house is further suggested by a list of the household gear of the place of Essinquoy in St Andrew's Parish in 1550: 'ane stannand bed, ane small buking cownter; in the selleris, ane meit amrye, ane seller dowr; in the hall, ane he buird maid of buirdis of aik, twa sait buirdis maid of fowr buirdis of rawcheter, ane old scheir ane fire hall dur'.[366] There was a hall, and apparently a fire hall (kitchen?) too, and *sellers*, which were merely rooms and not halls, though the word has been erroneously interpreted as 'hall' because of its fancied but etymologically and semantically untenable resemblance to Old Norse *salr*. This list clearly differentiates between 'hall' and 'seller'.

A point of some importance also is the way in which farm buildings are changed and adapted from time to time. They are never static, and any survey of existing buildings, as in the examples studied above, involves the unravelling of chronological sequences. The same is true of the remains of excavated buildings. Change is here a constant factor, and in documentary sources change can also be illustrated. When the houses of Clouk in the town of Inner Stromness were divided between Marion and James Beaton in 1566, they got the innermost part of the fire house (ie the inbye) and two sellers or rooms, presumably the but-end, next to it. Of the sellers one was totally and one partly in ruins. They also got a kailyard, cornyard, barn, kiln, and stables which had been turned into a kailyard. The byre that belonged to William Beaton, late father of James, was on the west side of the new chamber of Clouk and had been made into a long barn.[367]

In 1575, an adjudication regarding the dimensions of a house in the Midtown of Kirkwall, belonging to Janet Guid, gave the line measurement as 22 ft (6.7 m) plus a hand's breadth along the road in front, 'foir gate'.[368] The house, therefore, was gable-end on to the road.[369] The long, narrow character of Kirkwall houses is further indicated by a grant in 1620 of a piece of waste ground, 73 ft (22.3 m) long by 18 ft (5.5 m) broad, for building a house and kailyard.[370]

All such sources tell of upper class or town houses. A mansion house on an estate in the seventeenth and eighteenth centuries was small, plain, and of two storeys. There were four rooms, with two small chambers behind the stairs. Usually there was an attic, and often a one-storey annex. Its farm-steading was close by, but not attached. Smaller mansions of udal proprietors were of one storey with a two-storey end. Houses of Kirkwall dignitaries were comparable. The majority had slate roofs, like the 'new Sclaitt house or tennement' built by William Gow at Rennies (or Ranies) Ness, later called Gow's Ness, in Kirkwall, about 1716,[371] or Hugh Clouston's house, at 72 Victoria Street, Kirkwall, described in a 1714 valuation as a double house, slate roofed, very old. The west gable on the street was 3 ft 6 in. (1.1 m) thick, the side walls 3 ft (91 cm), the east gable 3 ft 3 in. (99 cm), and the mid-gable, containing a fireplace, 4 ft 6 in. (1.4 m). There were three rooms below, and three above, reached by a one flight stair. There was also an attic. Two of the ground floor rooms measured 15 ft 6 in. (4.9 m) by 15 ft (4.6 m) internally, and the one behind the mid-gable 15 ft 6 in. (4.9 m) by 10 ft (3 m). An inventory of 1657 identified the rooms and listed the contents. The 'laigh west chalmer' contained two beds with one cover, one of wainscot (oak), and one of fir, a fixed table, and a lock on the door. The 'great hall' in the middle had a high table of wainscot with 'firmes' and 'branders' front and back, a fir table with a wainscot 'tresse', two wainscot cupboards with a 'portal' partition (inner porch) on the door at the hall entrance, a 'lang settle' of fir, three presses for vessels, and a lock on the door. The 'east chalmer' had two wainscot beds and a round table. The 'heigh west chalmer' had two fir beds 'with boddom and back', a table with a 'brander' and 'form', and a door lock. The loft contained a bed and had a door lock. The 'laigh- and heigh cellars' each had a door lock. There was also – showing that this was a merchant's house – a 'chop upon the foreway' with two long presses, a little press, a great chest, a 'long boord of thick daill' for a counter, and a door lock. On the south side of the close was a house with two beds, a table, a 'lang settle', an 'almerie', and a 'fat' in the kitchen. 'Jean Gadie's house' contained a bed. She was, presumably, a servant.[372] About this period, the beginning of the eighteenth century, Kirkwall consisted of one street with houses on each side, mostly slated.[373]

In 1729, James Traill wrote from Edinburgh to his wife, discussing amongst other things a house he was having built:

'I expect the litle house is somewhat advanced in the building. I have no alterations to the scheme I left with Cussine George of it, only lett the side stair to the second storie be on side nixt to my mothers house about the midle in place of putting it on the end nixt the guarden, because there I cannot dispense with so much room. The under storie must be full 9 ft (2.7 m) high from the foundation to the loft, because I fear underwater which will perhaps obleige me to raise the ground floor a foot or two. And lett the side wall be full six foot (1.8 m) above the loft beside the beam filling. The jeasts must be laid withon a foot (30 cm) of other of the best of Baillie David Traills trees, and let Cuss George or Papa (a merchant, originally from Papa Westray) see to gett home the 1500 scleat I payd the child for at Firth . . . The dealls may be laid louse upon the jeasts for the loft but not nailed till I come home. I designe by first occasione from this to send naills, locks, and all other iron work for it'.[374] Such merchant lairds evidently kept a close personal control over these activities.

The Commissariot Records for Orkney and Shetland provide a key to status. Only people above a certain social level would have their testaments included in any case, but for the most part the inventory covers stock, crops, lying money, debts, and occasionally items that had special value, like an old sword estimated at £1.4.0 that the late James Craigie had at Brandaquoy in 1685. For the most part, however, the 'insight & pleneshing of the houss with the defuncts abulzie[ts]' (abulziements), the domestic goods, furnishing, and clothes, were lumped together under one estimated figure. But for the upper classes, the case was very different, and the inventories of their goods underline the great gulf not only between them and those whose goods and chattels were not worth listing, but even more between them and those who did not even reach testamentary status. An example is the inventory of Jon Elphingstoune of Lopnes, given by George Ritchie Chamberlain of the Stewartry of Orkney, dated 19 October 1685:

Imp.	6 Kyne at 5 lib. pr. peice is	30.00.00
It.	3 ffeather bedds wt. their whole furnitur	36.00.00
,,	ane Cunning (rabbit) nett est. to	04.00.00
,,	of neaprie in the hous worth	06.00.00
,,	six chists and ane girnell	12.00.00
,,	2 Looking glass	04.00.00

,,	ane old yoall est. to	06.00.00
,,	12 old guns & 4 swords est. to	40.00.00
,,	of peuther pleats stoups & chalmer potts	12.00.00
,,	ane Little Kettle worth	40.00.00
,,	2 fatts 6 lib & of brewing weshells worth—	
	6 pounds is	12.00.00
,,	of other weshells & a quearne worth	04.00.00
,,	a pair of bellowes & a studie (anvil)	12.00.00
,,	12 trenchers ane salt foot and lume work	02.00.00
It.	threttie head of sheip young & old	20.00.00
,,	6 chairs, 2 tables & 2 furmes	06.00.00
,,	ane Cupboard	02.00.00
,,	3 potts ane pair raxes & 2 speits	06.00.00
,,	ane old cairt worth	04.00.00
,,	12 silver spoons & 2 dishes	40.00.00
,,	2 candle stickis	01.04.00
,,	ane malt pundler worth	02.00.00
		301.04.00

This was comfortable living in Sanday, but it came nowhere near the wealth of Mr Thomas McKenzie, minister of Shapinsay, whose testament is dated 12 Oct. 1688. The domestic equipment of his house alone was valued at £133.06.08. For the rest, he had:

It.	ffyve old gunns est. all to	15.00.00
,,	of pleat peuther in the houss weighand ffyve	
	pund weight at 8^s pr. pund is	20.00.00
It.	of pleat peuther in the houss 12 pund weight	
	at 6 s 8 d. pr. pund is	4.00.00
It.	ffourscoir head of sheip est. to	80.00.00
It.	ane old fishing yoall w^t her furnitur est. to	10.00.00
,,	ane brewing kettle est. to	40.00.00
,,	of lyeing money in the houss	470.13.09
,,	ane silver Dish, six silver spoons, a signet	
	ring of gold and a small gold locket qch.	
	was impignorat to the defunct be ffrancis	
	murray Comiss^r of Zetland & Elizabeth Mudie	
	spouss for the somme of 200 mks. scots. est. to	109.10.00
It.	2 Little silver Dishes ane Duzone of	
	silver spoons and a silver ... Cupp	
	belonging to the Defunct	75.06.00
		0952.16.00
[Debts owing to him]		4915.16.08
		5868.12.08
[He owed – including cost of funeral, £100]		0455.12.00
	Free gear	5413.00.08

Here was a rich man, well able to act as banker by lending money to his more needy neighbours. The average run of lairds, however, was more like Jon Elphingstoune in Lopness, and the merchant burgesses of Kirkwall were on a similar level. The difference between them and a farmer of fairly reasonable means is demonstrated by the inventory of Andro Peatrie in Foubister, in the parish of St Andrews, dated 27 July 1685:

Impris. ane Dinn horss 6 yeir old est.^at to		14.00.00
It.	ane black horss 16 yeir old estimet to	04.00.00
It.	ane redd shaltie of 21 yeiris old	02.00.00
It.	two old Kyne estim. both to	10.00.00
It.	Two young oxen strickis estim. to	04.00.00
It.	ane quoyack in halveris estim. to	02.10.00
It.	ane young weather sheip	01.06.00
It.	in the barne yaird of bear 2 meils pryce is	06.00.00
It.	in the barne of oats j meils pryce	02.00.00
It.	in the houss ane meill of meall pryce is	05.00.00
It.	Two gees & a ganner is	01.00.00
It.	the insight & pleneshing of the houss with the defuncts abulzie.^is estim. to	12.00.00
		70.16.00

Ffollowis the debts restand to the dead

It.	be Jon peatrie in Tankerness	02.18.00
It.	be Margaret werk in Deirness	00.11.00
		03.09.00
	Inv. & debts is	74.05.00

Debts owed

It.	to James grahame of groundshall pr. bond	35.10.00
It.	to Wm. Robertsone shoemaker in Kirkwall	00.12.00
It.	to George Ritchie chalmerlane	03.06.08
It.	for the defuncts funerall	10.00.00
		39.08.08
	Ffrie gear is	44.17. 4
	Divyde in thrie pts.	14.17.00

If the cost of the funeral is any criterion, this farmer had ten times less social standing than the minister of Shapinsay.

The hard realities of the lower end of the social scale appear in travellers' reports rather than in official documents. When Dionyse Settle visited Orkney in 1577, he saw and put in words these realities:

'Their houses are verie simply buylded with pibble stone, without any chimneys, the fire being made in the middest thereof. The good man, wife, children, and other of their familie, eate and sleepe on the one side of the house, and their cattell on the other, very beastly and rudely, in respect of civilitie. They are destitute of wood, their fire is turffes and Cowe shardes.'[375] Here, beyond doubt, is the longhouse of the humbler classes, seen in an island such as Sanday or North Ronaldsay, where fuel was scarce.

The mortality rate of such buildings was probably high, sometimes through casual building, sometimes through casual treatment. This explains the Act of Bailiary of 1615, Anent Demolishing of Houses, referred to on page 114 above.[376]

Another aspect is the clustering of houses, usually at the side of the arable and even the sharing of houses by more than one family. In 1633, M. Richart's house and that of her grandmother were close together, and Robert Drever had a house in the same building as another.[377]

An early seventeenth century visitor, Richard James, added some details to Settle's account. He noted that the houses were built underground, with only the heather covered roof protruding. A barrel or such like served as a smoke-hole for the central hearth, and around this there were broad benches to lie on. He also noted that in recent years the better sort had begun to have 'faire greate houses of stone',[378] a comment which may in itself suggest that surviving stone built farms, especially those of longhouse type, may not much antedate this period.

The custom of building partly underground, or at least against slopes, continued for some time, though increasingly characterising the lower social scales. In 1773 houses were still said to be half underground, and 'like most other farm houses in Orkney, most ordinary hutts, where people and cattle all sleep under the same roof, and sometimes the calf has a better apartment than the heir of a family that can boast of twenty-four generations of uninterrupted lineal succession'.[379] A century after this, the farm-servant or cottar class in the North Isles of Orkney were said to have chosen sites for their houses on the south sides of rising ground. The earth was dug away until a perpendicular face was made on the north side, equal in height to the north wall of the house. In this way the house got shelter, and it saved stones, since the north wall only had to be built 'one face' against the soil. The side walls were $4\frac{1}{2}$ to 5 ft (1.4–1.5 m) high, and the gables were often built of turf. Mortar was rarely used, but loose earth was thrown in among the rubble work during building. The door was often no more than a straw mat, as was common in the west of Scotland and in Ireland too at one time.[380] There was no window, though light came in at the 'lum-hole' near the middle of the roof, and there was also a 'reek-hole' at one end of the hut, always stuffed up unless the smoke became intolerable. The fire was in the middle of the floor.[381]

Whereas the lairds had houses built for them, the tenants as a rule built their own. Patrick Fea's Diary gives a vivid picture of building work in Sanday:

1766	10 Oct.	Thatched the Kiln barn and ... loft.
	16 Oct.	Got my House and the Brew House thatched.
	29 Oct.	Thatched my Miln and the last of my Stables and got wood sawn for Couples to the Woman House ... loading Clay for the Gavels of the House.
	30 Oct.	Carting stones all day Heddell made a Couple.
	4 Nov.	Alex.ʳ Heddell all day biging the Kitchen and Cartting Stones with the Oxen.
	6 Nov.	Wrot Mr. Laing for ... 2 trees 16 foot (4.9 m) long.
	7 Nov.	Heddell ... made 2 Couples.
	12 Nov.	Carting stones and sawing that day for the kitchen.
	13 Nov.	Went to Eda and got from John Murray 51 Foot (15.5 m) of old Plank att 1/2 p.ʳ foot allso 53 foot (16.2 m) of the sheathing plank at 1/2.
	15 Nov.	Heddell & Wm. Liddell ... set the Timber of the Kitchen Roof and secured it by bigging about the Couple feet and left it.
	17 Nov.	Carting flags from Spurness and Clay for the Kitchen.
1767	28 Oct.	Begun to repair the stable for my mares ... loading Clay and getting Stones thereto from the old Catlequoy.
	30 Oct.	Got as much wood from Westove as make stals ... and door to the Stable.
	3 Nov.	Got home Stones for laying my Stable.
	6 Nov.	Got the lath put upon the stable ... got the Roof put upon the Stable.
1768	3 March	My men winding Simons to thatch the malt Loft.
	6 Oct.	Thatched the Kiln barn my house and Cross fast the other Roofs.
1768	17 Oct.	Took down the miln it being quite ruinous and James Rowsay in Banks and Henry Murray bth came to big thereon.
	18 Oct.	Biging at the miln and leading some Clay.
	19 Oct.	Biging all day and leading Clay with 4 Horses.
	22 Oct.	Had 4 men working at the flag Quarie all day got 4 Carts home from it and got the stone work of my Miln done att night as also the Krecklines (?) done.
	24 Oct.	Had 3 men in the flag quarie all day and

		carting from it made a house to the Cart for big flags.
	26 Oct.	My masons steethed (laid the foundations of) the Stricks house.
	3 Nov.	Flagged the Miln and thatched it but wanted flags to the Kreel house (?).
1769	24 Oct.	Brakeing stones for a Stable.
	27 Oct.	Had 2 men casting the Steeth of the Stables.
	31 Oct.	The masons began to big att the Stables upon the end of the kitchen, Carting all day Stones from behind the Park.
	10 Nov.	Got the Stonework of my Stables done.
	11 Nov.	Got a part of the Wall flags put on clear'd the masons and gave them 5 Sh. and a firken of Potatoes and ane half Threef of Bent above their wages.
	13 Nov.	Brakeing flags all day Sawing timber for the Stables.
	16 Nov.	Got all my Mangers and Traveses fixt in the East Stable which serves 3 Horses.
	17 Nov.	Got my Eastmost Stable flag'd and rooft.
	24 Nov.	Got the Couples on my other Stable.
1770	8 Nov.	Got all my stable clean'd and fired, and my Mares taken in.
	12 Nov.	Thatched the Stables the Horses all in.
1771	3 Sept.	Kirbister ... agreed with Ed. Moodie to Scleat his house as I did to help myne.
	20 Nov.	Got the Celler in the Closs clay'd and covered with Fiels.
1772	6 Nov.	Got the W^t Stable fully rooft with timber.
	7 Nov.	Put in wood divisions in the W^t Stable and Stal'd some of my horses.
	9 Nov.	Got all the Stables thatched, fired and Clean'd so as they are ready for the horses.
	26 Dec.	The Stable Closs all laid with flags from Halksness.[382]

Patrick Fea had a large farm with several buildings, for servants as well as for stock. Masons were employed occasionally, as well as joiners, but the bulk of the work, including the fetching and carrying of raw materials, was done with the farm's own manpower. Timber was the only material that had to be bought.

A point of interest is early evidence for covering the stonework with some kind of a wash. In the island of Egilsay in the seventeenth century, sand was mixed with lime imported from the Firth of Forth, heaped up until the following year, and then the mixture was used to plaster the houses on the outside.[383] This might have been a form of pointing. On 4 April 1715 David Traill wrote from Kirkwall to his father, asking for 'six or seven meils of lyme to dress the house up the way with . . . if ye have not cashes (baskets) to spaire, I shall send them to you'. By those unable to afford or who did not want to pay for imported lime, cockleshells were burned to make lime for whitewashing houses, in Papa Westray, Walls[384] and elsewhere, just as in the Hebrides. The spread of references over a century suggests that this kind of embellishment was fairly widespread, though the social range of buildings over which it applied is uncertain. Internal limewashing was also done, as when Patrick Fea 'lymed the kitchen so that it is now ready for the Servants'. The inside walls of cot-houses were often plastered with cow-dung.[385]

Lime was also used in better-class buildings. Most of the 300 houses in Kirkwall in the 1780s were said to be built of stone and lime, and slated,[386] but clay and not lime was used in the building of Patrick Fea's outhouses. A namesake of his noted in 1775 that drystone stables were inadequate,[387] but the fact is that even in the poorest houses, like those built against a hillside, earth or clay was used for bonding stones. The subsequent action of the weather picked out all the externally visible earth or clay, making it appear that dry-stone walling was involved. In Holm parish, the yard dykes as well as the farmhouses were of stone and clay. The same was true of the cottages attached to large farms in the early 1800s, though stones and sods could also be used. The farms in Orphir and North Ronaldsay were of stone and clay in the 1840s, sometimes not plastered on the inside; in St Andrews, the walls were rarely built as high as they should for their purpose, and were not rebuilt till falling down.[388]

Even Knox's comment in 1789 about the Kirkwall houses is that of a superficial observer, for not many years later it was noted that the Kirkwall houses were built mainly with clay mortar, a little lime being used on the outside of the wall only. Clearly, this is how David Traill was using his lime in 1715. Therefore, although it is possible to agree in part with the statement, that 'the uncemented masonry of Orkney, whether in the cottages, farmhouses, or these wall (field-dykes), cannot be surpassed', nevertheless the adjective 'uncemented' is hardly tenable. Indeed, the opposite was true. A description of the ordinary houses in St Andrews and Deerness told how the clay slate could be built as easily as bricks. The houses were of one storey, and usually stood in two rows facing each other with a 6 ft (1.8 m) space between. The side walls were about 6 ft (1.8 m), the gables 9 ft. (2.7 m) high. The outside courses were 'lipped' with mortar for about 4 ft (1.2 m), and the centre of each course was closely packed with clay, so that the walls were practically airtight and the houses very warm.[389]

Towards the mid-nineteenth century, however, as agricultural improvements with rotational cropping and proper leases took a firmer hold, so the buildings began to be improved as well. Increasingly, the proprietors became responsible for their erection. First, lairds like Thomas Balfour of Huip in Stronsay put up new steadings for themselves, in his case already by the 1760s, and later on for their tenants as well. By the 1840s, the houses on the larger farms in Stronsay and Eday could be of more than one storey, and were mostly built by the proprietor. In Westray, they were beginning to erect better steadings and houses, and to give 8 to 10-year leases instead of none at all. In Orphir, cottages lately built were much neater than the old ones. In general, it could be said in 1841 that the farmhouses and steadings of the small tenants were more substantial and comfortable than those of most of the small tenantry in other parts of Scotland. Few turf houses were to be seen.[390]

Later in the century, the situation in Shapinsay was that the house was either built by the tenant, who got 'amelioration' at the end of his lease, or by the laird, to whom the tenant then paid interest on the outlay. The tenants in general preferred to build their own, but the plans had to be approved by the laird. In Stronsay, several new cottages had been built, with slated roofs and walls pointed on the outside. At Houseby, a new dwelling house had been built for the tenant, and the steading at Huntown extended.[391]

A large steading with a fixed steam engine made by Clayton & Shuttleworth was put up at Stove in Sanday in the 1860s. On Braeswick townland in the same island, lots of 16 to 20 acres each were made after the abolition of runrig. Tenants then built their own houses, following the instructions that they were to be on the north side of the road facing the sun, of a uniform description, and a specified distance back from the road with a garden plot in front. The days of modern planning had arrived. At Warsetter, Balfour's tenant John McKay, succeeding his father and grandfather, had built a comfortable house and good farm offices. The Earl of Zetland put up a steading at Backaskaill for the tenant John Paul. At West Brough the tenants Jerome and Walter Dennison built a very good dwelling house. In North Ronaldsay, houses were improved by Dr Traill of Woodwick through his factor, Robert Scarth, though neither plastered, nor built with lime. In Westray, the steading at Aikerness was extended by the Earl of Zetland, and Balfour put up a new steading at Trenabie. South of Pierowall, Balfour had erected some very handsome cottages on a number of small 20 to 40-acre farms. T. Traill's father had built a mansion house at Brough some time previously, and there was a recent farm-steading. Gallowhill, Cleat, Clifton and Twoquoy had new steadings, and Fribo a good mansion and steading as well. The large steading at Holland House in Papa Westray was mainly erected by the proprietor, Mr Traill. Carrick in Eday and Westness in Rousay had large steadings with water power. In Wyre, Robert Scarth had also improved the houses.[392]

On the West Mainland, the townland of Ireland had been split into 25 to 100-acre farms, most with new steadings and dwelling houses. The Cairston Estate had good steadings with threshing machinery. Archer Fortescue set up good cottages for his labourers, rent-free, on his Swanbister Estate in Orphir. In Sandwick, tenants' steadings were in general pretty fair, but in Birsay, improvements still lagged, as also in Harray with its concentration of about a hundred small lairds, relics of the udallers, 'proverbially not an improving class'. The same was true of the part of Sandwick owned by about 70 heritors, whose houses and habits were said to be those of the lowest rank of peasantry. It was amongst this udal-derived class of small lairds that the byre-dwellings tended to survive longest. In Evie parish, a large modern steading had been erected at Swannay. In Firth, Robert Scarth bought Binscarth in 1841. He made two new farms of 150 acres each from the waste, and built on each a well-planned slate-roofed steading and four cottage dwellings, each with 10 acres, for labourers. A good house and steading had been built at Quanterness, formerly part of the old Kirkwall common, by Mr Cumming. David Munro's farm of Saverock had a new house and steading with a 6-horse threshing machine. A neat steading was built by Captain Scott at Crantit. Graemeshall in the East Mainland had a substantial steading with a 10 horse-power steam engine. In the South Isles, Carra farm in South Ronaldsay had a good steading.[393]

In general, the building of new steadings reached its zenith in the 1870s, with the laird supplying the wood and slates, and the tenant doing the building. On many smaller farms, the reconstruction of the steading was left to the tenant or owner, and often a new wing was added to an old building at this time.[394] It is the houses and steadings built about 1840–70 that chiefly characterise the farm architecture of Orkney at the present time.

Whilst the farms were undergoing cosmetic treatment, other developments were taking place as well. Kirkwall was growing, and Stromness too, though the houses there were placed irregularly. They were mostly slated with slabs of the local schistose clay. Elsewhere small fishing villages were being developed by the lairds. A site for one was laid out by Holm Sound Bay in 1841. Mr Laing put up the Whitehall fishing station and village in Stronsay.[395]

In 1808, there were said to have been no regular courts of farm offices in Orkney, yet by 1814 there were many substantial, convenient, and even some expensive single and detached farm buildings in several islands. Each large farm had some cottage attached with a garden, grass for a cow, and enough arable for winter provender. At this period labourers and cottagers or cottars were numerous and even supernumerary to farming, because of the demand for helpers in summer. Farms rarely exceeded 40 acres of arable, with a corresponding proportion of waste for grazing. Twenty acres was the average farm size. On large farms, there were workers of three kinds: house-servants, who lived in and were paid in cash; *bollmen* or *bowmen* (Old Scots *boll*, a measure of grain or meal, *c*. 1375) and *cottars* (Old Scots, *c*. 1400), each with a milk-cow and a horse, some having up to 4 cows and 2 horses. Bowmen and cottars were required to shear in harvest and for this got a small piece of land called a 'harvest-fee'. They lived in small houses on the farm. Farmers could remove cottars at will.[396]

The contents of such small farms and houses did not get into the testamentary inventories, though observant travellers help to fill the gap. One farmhouse around 1840 had a small porch to protect the door from the east wind, and a kitchen with deal planks over the rafters to hold nets, lines, and cordage. From the rafters hung bacon, dried ling, cod-fish and smoked geese. Balls of spun wool hung from pegs in the corners, and on the floor was a churn, with cheese and butter-making utensils. There were *collie lamps* (Old Norse *kola*, an open iron lamp) with wicks of split rushes and cakes of tallow for candle making. In the room where the family ate, there were harpoons, fish-spears, a turning-lathe, powder flasks, shot belts and fishing rods, a box-bed, lockers, and a Dutch clock.[397]

The two fullest descriptions, however, date from the twentieth century, and though accurate enough in themselves, they are beginning to have a flavour of antiquarianism. One described the old byre-dwellings in the township of Stenso in Orphir, the other those in the township of Redland in Firth.

The entrance door was of deal boards fixed to the back bars with wooden pegs or 'pins'. These were made with square heads and were set diamond-wise on the outside, so that they made a decorative pattern. The inner ends were wedged to make them secure. Locks were rare, though they did exist, not only in better class houses, but also on the farms, though the latter were of a special kind, made of wood, as in Scandinavia and elsewhere. There were no turning door-handles either. Instead, a wooden latch was operated by a string of tanned hide or skin cured with alum, latterly of binder twine, one end of which was fixed to a thumb-grip. If extra security was wanted, a wooden running bar could be moved into a slot in the frame by means of a 'key', a rod with a crook at one end, pushed through a hole in the door to engage in the notches on top of the bar. The same kind of device may be seen in Slovakian and Hungarian farms at the present day. The door hinges were home-made, of wood, nailed to the jambs with blacksmith-made nails. They could be greased to stop them creaking.

The door, always placed in the but-end near the gable, opened into the *ootbye* or scullery. Above the door and along the gable was the *hallan* (Old Scots *halland*, partition, 1553), consisting of one or two spars 18 in. (46 cm) apart, sometimes wound around with straw ropes, where the hens roosted. Below, calves were often tied, a *polly* (cf. Norwegian dialectal *pyl*, youngster) or tame sheep, a brood sow and her litter separated from the calves by a flagstone, and sometimes the work-ox. Along the side wall two flagstones might be set up, or sometimes an outshot compartment, as a peat-neuk for the day's supply of peat fuel, with a flagstone bink or bench for waterpails, under which two or three brood geese might be sitting on eggs. Alternatively, there was a half-round sae-bink recess in the wall, at a suitable height for putting the sae or water tub onto it easily from the carrying position. The tub could also be left in position, and water poured into it from a stoup or *bummie* (Norwegian *bomme*, box or basket for food) made of hooped staves, about 1 ft (30 cm) diameter at the bottom and 8 in. (20 cm) diameter at the mouth. Two opposite staves were longer than the others, and a round carrying stick went through them. There was also a smaller type with one stave left long for a handle. The sae itself also had protruding staves with holes, and when it was being carried from the well,

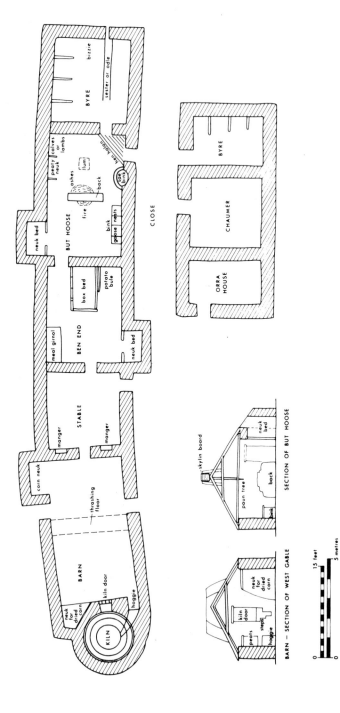

40. An Orkney longhouse, early nineteenth century. After Omond c. 1912, following 14, and Firth (1920) 1974, facing 19. C4077.

usually by women, a long pole went through the holes, and on to the shoulders of the carriers, one in front and one behind, who slung up the 10 gal. (45.5 l) sae between them.

The stone back of the central fire divided the ootbye from the inbye, and the pantree, often a round stick of Highland birch, above the fire held the crook and links or an equivalent made of four or five soot-encrusted folds of straw rope with five or six iron links next the fire. From the couples could be hung mutton or geese to be *reested* (Old Scots *reist*, to smoke-dry or cure, 1508; Norwegian, Danish *riste*, to broil, grill, Icelandic, Norwegian *rist*, gridiron) by the smoke, and pieces of pork and drying fish were fixed to long ropes slung across the house. There was a *brandiron* (cf. Old Scots *brander*, gridiron, Old Norse *brandreið*, grate) of open, gridded construction for baking bannocks, a cast-iron *yetlin* (Old Scots, 1374) or girdle for baking sowan-scones, and three-legged pots varying from 10 gal. (45.5 l) capacity down to small ones for making milk gruel for the children.

The but-end had an outshot neuk-bed, with straw or chaff bedding, as in the box-beds in the ben-end. The largest piece of furniture in the but-end was the *bink* (cf. English *bench*, *bank*), a large slab of blue, smooth stone set on a wooden frame or on two flagstones fixed upright in the ground. It was the equivalent of a modern dresser. Bowls and tins were arranged on it, and pails, pots and cooking utensils lay below. The high straw-backed and hooded seats

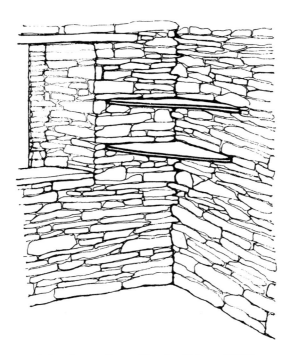

41. Flagstone corner-shelves in a croft near Dounby, Orkney. C5849.

were reserved for the guidman and his wife, whilst the rest of the family used low, round straw stools without backs, or stools, *hassos* (a form of English *hassock*), cut from a clump of coarse grass or rushes. When dug up with a turf spade and dried, this made a neat stool. Straw and bent grass were used to make the spoon-cubbie (Middle Dutch *cubbe*, basket; Danish dialectal *kube*, Norwegian *kupa*, fish-basket) or basket, where the horn spoons were kept. They were made of rams' horns, usually by tinkers, though some households had wooden moulds of their own for horn-spoon making.

Storage space was provided by numerous recesses in the walls. The *aumry* (Old Scots, 15th century; Old French *almarie*, Latin *armarium*) was a pantry or meat-press, about 4 ft (1.2 m) high by 2 ft (61 cm) wide, with three or four stone shelves. The household crockery as well as the food was kept here. Usually it was in the side wall across from the neuk-bed. A young pig or two, and a litter of pups, could also be found in the inbye area, and further recesses at floor level, about 18 in. (46 cm) square, were for brood geese.

The ben-end was entered through the 'cellar door' in the mid-gable. It contained box-beds with hinged or sliding doors, a potato store, a meal girnel

42. Flagstone steps for hens at Appiehouse, Stenness, Orkney. C5841.

43. The sae-bink at Appiehouse, Stenness, Orkney, formerly used for holding the water pail, 1960s.

44. Water carrying in Orkney. Photo. W. Hourston, *c.* 1940. C78L.

45. The plate rack at Appiehouse, Stenness, Orkney, 1960s.

46. Noltland Farm, Westray. There is a two-storey house and one-storey outhouses.
Foundation stones for stacks are heaped up in the cornyard at the back. Per Bryce Wilson.

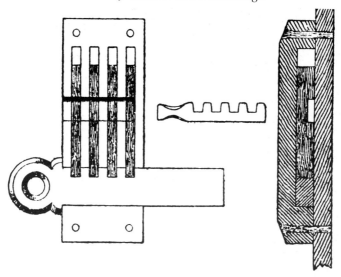

47. A wooden lock from North Ronaldsay, with four tumblers worked by a wooden key. From *PSAS*. 1880. xiv. 157. C5149.

and a clothes press. Sometimes the quern-ledder was placed on the ben side of the mid-gable, and here the bere-meal or burstin', and the malt made from bere, were ground. This was regarded as the best bedroom, and here the master and mistress of the house usually slept. If the family was large, more box-beds could be arranged to form a small closet at the back, which was also used for storing earthenware jars of ale. For this reason it was called the *ale-hurry*.

Few houses had any floor covering or paving over the bare earth. If the soil was damp, stones were placed under the wooden legs of the beds to keep them from rotting. In general, there was neither fireplace nor window in the ben-end except for small skylights, and people were used to working in the half dark. There was plaster on the walls, 'of the coarsest description possible, and decidedly unsanitary, being composed of clay, scrubbs (husks of oats), and cow shaurn (cow dung). The scrubbs acted as binding material to the clay, while the shaurn both gave a smoothness to the compost, and lent to the yellow clay a dull khaki shade'.[398]

18

The Building Trade

ALL of these enterprises provided work for tradesmen. The slating of churches gave work at an early date, for in 1657 an agreement was made with Walter Woolrite or Woolritch, 'slaitter', for repairing the North Kirk in South Ronaldsay. The provision of slates was a community function, for 500 slates were to be produced by different towns – Hoxa 80, Graemsay 100, Herstone 50, South and North Wydwall 90, and so on. For making the roof of the South Kirk wind and watertight, he agreed to find the slates himself. A reference dated 1664 shows that these slates were got at 'Liddell heid'. Between 1665 and 1668, 1200 slates had been supplied for the South Kirk roof. It was agreed with Woolritch and his son Alexander that the slates should be put on and bedded in lime, and the church pointed, before the winter of 1668.[399]

Evidently masons, slaters and joiners were in demand, and could claim good wages. In 1824, however, the do-it-yourself attitude of Orcadians was worrying the Hammermen's Incorporation in Kirkwall, who then revised and agreed rates of prices. The list of rates for slater and mason work gives a good deal of insight into local building techniques.

Slaters

Slating roof with Firth Slate, p. Rood	£0.18. 0.
Ditto, Stromness Slate, p.Rd.	1. 0. 0.
Ditto, Ezdeal Slate, with nails, p.Rood	1.17. 0.
Ditto, ditto, with pins, p.R.	1.10. 0.
Pointing roofs, Firth slate or common, p.Rood	0. 3. 6.
Harling, p.Rd.	0. 3. 6.
Slating Pavilion Corners, p. lenieal foot	0. 0. 6.
Ditto, Flankers, ditto	0. 0. 9.
Ditto, Lead Flankers, ditto	0. 0. 6.
Storm windows, 5 s. each to	0. 7. 6.
Running Skylights, each	0. 2. 6.
Common ditto, each	0. 1. 6.
Hatch Skylights, each	0. 3. 0.
Breaking out Skylights, each	0. 3. 0.
Stripping roof of common Slate, p. rood	0. 3. 6.
Ditto, Ezdeal Slate, p. Rd.	0. 4. 6.

Masons

Standard thickness of walls:— Sidewalls of houses, 2 feet (61 cm); gables, 3 feet (91 cm); above this to be calculated to this standard.

Building houses, 21 feet (6.4 m) high from sole of door to level of sidewall, £1 13s. p. rood of 36 square yards (30.1 sq.m).

Building 16 feet (4.9 m) high, as above, £1 7s. per rood; 12 feet (3.7 m), do., £1 5s.; 7 feet (2.1 m), do., £1 per rood.

Building Dykes – 12 feet (3.7 m) high, 16s. per rood; 8 feet (2.4 m) high, 12 s; 6 feet (1.8 m) high, 10 s.; 4 feet (1.2 m) high, with rag, 8 s. per rood; $3\frac{1}{2}$ feet (1.1 m) high, with rag, 6d. per fathom.

Chimney vents, 5 s. each.

Pinning and harling dykes, 4s. per rood.

Harling houses or walls built with mortar, 3s. 6d. per rood.

Paving with square flags, 5d. per square yard (0.836 sq.m); do. unsquared flags, 3d. per square yard. Causeying, 5d. per square yard.[400]

Tradesmen were, as might be expected, concentrated in the towns. In the 1790s in Kirkwall, there were 22 master wrights with 1 journeyman and 29 apprentices, 7 master masons with 16 journeymen and 6 apprentices, and 6 master slaters with 2 apprentices. In Holm there were carpenters, but no building tradesmen are mentioned. Sandwick and Stromness had 6 joiners and 2 masons, and Stromness village a concentration of 8 joiners and 13 masons. Slaters, oddly, were not included, though the slate quarry in the parish was producing 30,000–40,000 slates per year. Westray had 3 joiners, and Birsay and Harray 11. Orphir had 5 wrights, 6 masons, and a remarkable jack-of-all-trades who combined the functions of kirk-officer, beadle, sexton, cooper, slater, plasterer, boat-beater, gardener, kelper, mason, quarryman, labourer, thatcher, farmer, and father of triplets.[401]

The value of such tradesmen in the community is clearly reflected by their wages. More often than not they were paid by the piece, according to prevailing scales, but on day's wages they averaged double what a day labourer on a farm got. In Cross, Burness and North Ronaldsay, day labourers got 4^d to 6^d, though here they were rarely employed on farms, joiners earned 1/– to 2/– and masons 9^d to 1/3, all without food. In Kirkwall and St Ola, day labourers got 8^d, and joiners and masons 16^d to 18^d a day. The Holm rates were 6^d to 8^d for labourers, 1/– to 1/6 for 'artificers', and in Sandwick and Stromness, 8^d in winter and 10^d to 1/– in summer for labourers, 1/– to 1/8 for joiners, 1/3 to 2/– for masons, and slaters got 17/– to £1.7/– per rood.[402] Rates varied in different areas.

In Shetland there was a similar differential. Labourers got 6^d a day with food in Delting, and masons 10^d to 1/2. In Aithsting and Sandsting, masons got the same, and their servants, 6^d. Wright's wages were 10^d a day. These jobs were not fully specialised, however, for though the parish had 4 masons and many wrights, none earned their bread from these trades alone, but were fishers and farmers besides. In Bressay, Burra and Quarff masons got 15^d to 18^d a day, wrights 16^d. Labourers maintained by the family got 6^d. Amongst the trades-men in the parish were 2 carpenters, 1 joiner, and 1 wheelwright. In North Yell and Fetlar there was 1 carpenter, but, as everywhere else, the people were usually 'their own artificers'. There were two full-time wrights in North-mavine.[403]

19

Living Density

IN comparing Orkney and Shetland, it is instructive to look at the living density in the houses, both in the towns and the landward areas. The information is scattered, but the table that follows gives a clear enough indication of changes that were taking place in the eighteenth and nineteenth centuries.

Samples of Living Densities *c.* 1780–1840

Date	Place	Families	Individuals	Houses	Density p.House	Source
Orkney, towns						
1789–93			1500	300	5	Fea 1775.7,14;
	Kirkwall					Knox 1789. 139;
						OSA.1793.vii.530
1793	Stromness	342	1344	222	6	OSA.1795.xvi.432
1831	Stromness		2236	385	5.8	NSA.1845.xv.29
Orkney, landward						
1787	Crosskirk		581	118	4.9	OSA.1793.vii.461–2,
						469–470
1791	,,		579	115	5	,, ,,
1787	Burness		388	77	5	,, ,,
1791	,,		390	79	4.9	,, ,,
1787	North Ronaldsay		384	61	6.3	,, ,,
1791	,, ,,		420	64	6.6	,, ,,
1787	Ladykirk		803	155	5.2	,, ,,
1795	Sandwick		873	165	5.3	OSA.1795.xvi.432
1795	Stromness		795	184	4.3	,, ,,
1831	Cross	101	541	91	5.9	NSA.1845.xv.93
1831	Burness	81	440	76	5.8	,, ,,
Shetland, landward						
1791	Delting		1338–1561	223	6 or 7	OSA.1791.i.396
1791	Unst		1988	300	6.6	OSA.1793.v.199
1792	Northmavine		1786	290	6.2	OSA.1794.xii.355–6
1831	Sandsting and					
	Aithsting	425	2177	277	7.8	NSA.1845.xv.115–6
1836	Fetlar		859	134	6.4	NSA.1845.xv.26
1836	North Yell		960	150	6.4	NSA.1845.xv.26
1841	Fair Isle	35	232	35	6.6	NSA.1845.xv.96

If these figures are averaged out, even though not adequate for exact statistical analysis, it appears that the average density for Orkney was 5.5 and for Shetland 6.6.

In Orkney, there was apparently little difference between the densities in town and country. The level in the towns may even have fallen for a time at the fallow period in the 1800s between the fading out of the kelp trade, and the growth of agricultural improvements. At all events, the population of Kirkwall had become stationary at 3721 by the 1840s, and house building, 'which in former years went on very briskly, has of late been almost at a stand, and many habitations in the town are at present untenanted'.[404]

The Shetland density no doubt paralleled that of Orkney in earlier times, but by the late eighteenth century the population increase was well established. Many of the houses contained two sets of children, that is a father and his family, and the eldest son and his family.[405] There was a widespread splitting of farms and creation of new, small outsets, and even though these increased the number of dwelling houses, the density did not decrease. This was a direct result of the activities of the Shetland lairds in developing the fishing industry.

Average figures indicate differences between areas, but do almost as much to conceal as to reveal the local situation, for an exceptionally low or high component figure can considerably affect the average. The following table, relating to Fair Isle in 1878, shows that families tended to be even bigger than the average for a generation earlier suggests:

Living Density in Fair Isle, 1878

Farm	Name	Number	Make-up
Vaasetter	James Anderson (farm manager from Shetland)	5	Self, wife, mother-in-law, 2 children
Pund	George Leslie	5	Self, wife, 2 children, servant
The Field	Robert Eunson	9	Self, daughter, son, son's wife, 5 grand-children
*Taing	Jerome Wilson	11	Self, uncle, aunt, wife 7 children
Stonibreck	1. George Stout	8	
	2. George Irvine	5	
Stackhool	1. Alexander Eunson	6	
	2. Widow Stout	6	
	3. William Wilson	5	
*Shirva	1. William Williamson	5	Self, 2 sisters, 2 nephews
	2. Thomas Eunson	9	Self, mother-in-law, sister-in-law, wife, 5 children

Farm	Name	Number	Make-up
Mires	William Williamson	7	
*Briggs	Andrew Wilson	6	Self, sister, wife, 3 children
*Leogh	1. William Wilson	7	
	2. Robert Irvine	3	
	3. Thomas Wilson	7	
*Melville House	Jerome Wilson	10	Self, wife, 2 unmarried children; son, son's wife, 3 children; servant
Gaila	1. Jane Wilson	7	
*	2. Robert Wilson	5	
*	3. Andrew Wilson	8	Self, mother, sister, wife, 4 children
The Haa	William Lawrence (from Dunrossness)	5	
Sculties	William Leslie	4	
*Taft	John Wilson	10	
Hool	Lawrence Irvine	6	
Schoolton	Andrew Stout	3	
Quoy	Laurence Irvine	4	
*Kennaby	Robert Wilson	8	
*Busta	1. Stewart Eunson	9	
*	2. George Stout	7	
*Springfield	Stewart Wilson	8	

This made a total of 30 families, with a total population of 198, averaging 6.6 per unit in accordance with the earlier standard, on figures that ranged between a minimum of 3 and a maximum of 11. There were only six family names in the island. The Wilsons were said to nearly always intermarry with each other, and were all related. The families marked with an asterisk were Wesleyan, the remainder belonged to the Established Church of Scotland.[406]

20

Shetland Houses and Plenishings

EVIDENCE for Shetland is not as full for the earlier periods as it is for Orkney. After the evidence of the Viking sites at Underhoull and Jarlshof, and of the medieval farm at Jarlshof, there is a long gap with little information. Law cases of the early seventeenth century show that fish, cheese, meat, butter and meal were kept in skeos (Norwegian dialectal *skjaa*, drying-house or shed, Icelandic *skjá*, shelter), separate buildings of very open construction, but such goods were also stored in 'selleris' in the houses. Wooden kists also served to store meat, for meat was stolen out of kists in Unst, six 'reistit scheipe' in South Yell, and fish, butter, and socks in Delting.[407]

Because there was a shortage of servants at this period, partly caused by their getting married and taking up house with nothing to live on, it was enacted at a court in Scalloway in 1612 that no one was to take up a house, nor was to set houses or land, if he was not worth 3 score 'gulyeonis' (£72 Scots). If he had less, his house was to be cast down.[408]

In 1633, it was noted that the houses in Shetland were all built of rough unhewn stone, and roofed with divots and straw tied down with straw ropes, and renewed each year about Allhallow tide. Some houses were roofed with deals, which must have come from Norway, and a very few with slates. Some years after this, the number of slated houses was given as four.[409] These would have been the better class houses, and perhaps some of the houses in Scalloway and Lerwick, which contained 100 and 200 to 300 families respectively at this period. Ready framed timber and deals for such houses came from Norway. This makes it clear that in the better class houses a fair amount of timber was used, but the meaning of 'ready framed' is not certain. Probably it means no more than that the roofing timbers were shaped and ready for erection. A difference between the North and South Isles that may have a strong bearing on architectural differences was that the inhabitants of the south parish, Dunrossness, where the land was best, were 'Strangers from *Scotland*, and *Orkney*',[410] who presumably brought some of their own building techniques and forms of farm layout with them.

In the 1680s, the Shetlanders built with broad stones like flagstones, sometimes using little lime or clay or other cement so that the buildings were rather cold. In Lerwick, which had grown in 40 years from three or four families about 1650 to 1660, to about 300 families of merchants, tradesmen, and fishermen, mostly from the north and east coasts of Scotland, most of the houses had two storeys. At the same time, Scalloway had begun to decline, in 1683 having 80 to 100 inhabitants, and in 1695, 90. Limestone was used for building, but not as a fertiliser.[411]

A century later, there were neat farmhouses, built mostly of stone and lime, and thatched, in the neighbourhood of Eshaness, and in Vaila Mr Scott of Melbie had a modern house and gardens.[412] Lerwick had grown to 300 houses, with a population of 903,[413] giving an average living density of 3 to a house, which is considerably less than in Kirkwall and Stromness. Scalloway was going further downhill, with only 31 inhabited houses. One of Lerwick's problems was fuel, since it had been set down on a moor, the whole surface of which had almost been pared bare for firing. All the fuel in the area was used up by the 1830s. In 1801 it was mostly one row of houses close to the shore, with a double row in some parts. The houses, numbered at 200, were only a few feet apart. The street was of bare rock, or of paving stones. The number of inhabitants had crept up to 1400 by 1807, and to 3068 by 1837. The houses were built of breccia quarried above the town, and many had doors and windows ornamented with freestone. They were set somewhat irregularly, generally gable on to the sea.[414]

As a result of fishing developments, the custom had arisen by the early 1800s of the laird building the dwelling house, and letting the tenant see to the outbuildings. The cottages were said to be nearly the same everywhere, with walls imperfectly built of stone and clay, and roofing timbers covered with thin turves and thatched with straw. There were two rooms, with a central fire and a smoke-hole in the larger room. Proper chimneys were beginning to be general by the early 1800s. Though the houses of the proprietors were decent and comfortable, those of the tenants were probably not as good as cottages in the southern parts of Scotland, and the outbuildings were especially poor. The thatch was renewed each year by the tenant in a slovenly fashion. A udaller's house seen about 1840 had a slate roof.[415]

In Sandsting and Aithsting tenants had a choice. Either the house and dykes were built by the laird, or the tenant might do it himself and could then sit rent free for seven years. However, once the laird had put up the house, tenant after tenant had to occupy it as he found it, or repair it, or build afresh himself. Few lairds put up any outbuildings for tenants. The structure was of stone and dry mortar, with the usual roof of turf and straw roped down by straw or heather ropes. Chimneys were rare. In some houses there were two to six small openings that let in light and let out smoke. The window opening could be filled by a bladder or untanned lambskin, freed from its wool and stretched on a frame. In the but-end were to be found a couple of dogs, a cat, a *patty* (cf. Danish *pattegris*, sucking pig, from *patte*, a teat) swine, a calf, and half a dozen *caddy* (pet) (possibly Old Scots *cady*, wanton, 1552) lambs. The dunghill was near the door. In Bressay, many farm cottages had lately been rebuilt on an improved plan. At Uyea Sound in Unst, a number of neat houses had been built by Mr Mouat of Garth with a shop, warehouse, smithy, boat-carpenters, and coopers. On the farms, many tenants had good houses built at the laird's expense.[416]

A certain amount of information relating to Yell and Unst can be got from the Midbrake Papers. A paper dated May 1817 notes that Basil Spence and Thomas Irvine, both proprietors of ruinous houses in the room of Brough, North Yell, on their undivided properties, had people to overlook the houses. Three men said that 'the House presently roofed by Basil Spence together with the Byre newly built by him would Constitute his proportion of the Stones – And That the house formerly possessed by Mr Irvine with the stones of the old Byre together with all loose stones within the Limits of the Houses would be an equivalent for his'.[417] Here is an example of the re-use of stones from old buildings, and an explanation of the paucity of older houses in most parts of Shetland.

On 30 Dec. 1867, Thomas Irvine of Midbrake authorised the establishment of a house by a tenant, Ursula Sutherland, in the following terms:

'I hearby give you permission to build a small dwelling house, under twenty feet (6.1 m) long, upon my Park of Torvhous, on the north side of the Burn below the Brake of Murster, and to enclose a small yard attached to the extent of an English chain in length and breadth, to be possessed by you and your dughters Elizabeth and Joan Anderson and the longest liver of you three; for which permission and accommodation in name of rent you to deliver Annually to Bruce Alex! Sutherland, the tenant on Torvhouse, a pair of men's stout worsted Stockings and 3.ᵈ to me if demanded'.[418] Presumably Ursula Sutherland was a relative of the tenant of Torvhouse, who must have sought the laird's permission to house her and her daughters in this way.

The same source, unfortunately undated, details the specifications for a much grander building, the new manse at Unst. Externally it was 47 ft 9 in. (14.6 m) long by 35 ft (10.7 m). There were two storeys. At ground level was a lobby, 15 ft (4.6 m) by 8 ft (2.4 m), a dining room 17 ft (5.2 m) by 15 ft (4.6 m), a study 13 ft (4 m) by 12½ ft (3.8 m), a bedroom 15½ ft (4.7 m) by 13 ft (4 m), a

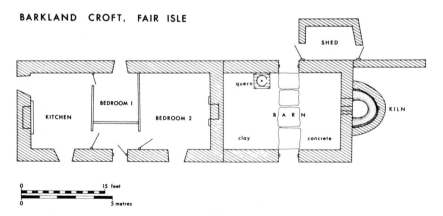

BARKLAND CROFT, FAIR ISLE

48. Barkland Croft, Fair Isle, surveyed in 1962 by A. Fenton and H. Rasmussen. C4076.

kitchen 14 ft (4.3 m) by 13½ ft (4.1 m), a servants' bed-closet 6 ft (1.8 m) by 7 ft (2.1 m), and a pantry 6 ft (1.8 m) by 10 ft (3 m). The upper storey had a lobby 14 ft (4.3 m) by 6 ft (1.8 m), a drawing room 19 ft (5.8 m) by 15 ft (4.6 m), three bedrooms 13 ft (4 m) by 12½ ft (3.8 m), 15 ft (4.6 m) by 13 ft (4 m), and 15½ ft (4.9 m) by 13 ft (4 m), a private closet 6 ft (1.8 m) square and a storeroom 15 ft (4.6 m) by 10 ft (3 m). Around the manse were the farm offices: a barn 20 ft (6.1 m) by 12 ft (3.7 m), a byre 16½ ft (5 m) by 12 ft (3.7 m), a stable 11½ ft (3.5 m) by 12 ft (3.7 m), and a milkhouse, 12 ft (3.7 m) by 8 ft (2.4 m). The last was in itself a status symbol, for in the 1840s there were no proper milkhouses on Shetland farms.[419]

By the 1870s, the pattern that has survived till the present had become fairly well established. The average cottage was about 28 to 30 ft (8.5 to 9 m) long by 8 to 12 ft (2.4 to 3.7 m) wide internally, and was built of rough, unhewn stones, with clay mortar. The gablets were sometimes of turf. The side walls were 4 to 6 ft (1.2 to 1.8 m) in height. The roof had a fairly steep pitch. The house was always pointed inside, and often outside, with the ordinary mortar and lime and sand. The feet of the roofing couples were supported on the middle of the side walls, and did not project over the edge. The covering was the usual one of turf, straw spread vertically, and ropes looped around stones to keep it in place.

Inside there were two rooms. The but-end took up about two thirds of the space, and served as 'kitchen, mess room and general dormitory of the family, and servants if any are kept'. Light came from a window 18 in. (46 cm) to 2 ft (61 cm) square and from two or three smoke-holes in the roof-ridge that also let out the smoke from the central fire. In some cases, the windows were narrow slits, closed with bladders or lambskins more often than with glass. Only the more up-to-date houses had proper chimneys. The floor was of hard clay or earth.

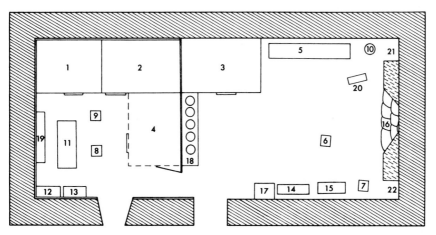

49. Layout of furnishings in a Fetlar house. 1–4 Box-beds (1 for children; 4 as an extra for a large family); 5 Resting chair; 6–9 Chairs; 10 Table; 12–13 Chests; 14 Sea chest; 15 Meal girnel; 16 Hearth; 17 Peat neuk; 18 Stand for buckets etc; 19 Gable chimney; 20 Spinning wheel; 21–22 Presses. From a diagram by J. Laurenson. C5035.

50. A Shetland interior. Baking is being done on a brander, the old man, wearing rivlins, sits in a wooden chair with a wooden hood, and a pig is tethered by one leg on the kitchen floor. From Barnard 1890. The drawing romanticises in the manner of the period. C2318.

The bare stone walls were nearly hidden by numerous chests, supported on beams of wood or slung on ropes from the couples, and by box-beds made like those on board ship. The chests contained not only clothes and valuables, but also the milk and butter of the dairy. There was a resting chair – a long wooden settle – on each side of the fire, a small table, probably a spinning wheel, and a few plain kitchen chairs, as well as pails of water, kegs or jars of *bland* (Old Norse *blanda*, mixture of two fluids, to mix) made from whey, and a churn.

The ben-end was the bedroom of the 'good couple', and served as a drawing room for visitors of special note. Here, a ceiling of lath and plaster or of wood hid the bare rafters, the floor was laid with wood, and there was a proper gable chimney. A window in proportion to the size of the room admitted light, and the walls were well plastered and whitewashed. A few 'neat but plain articles of furniture, together with two or three photographs. or foreign curiosities, tend to remove the impression of wretchedness the appearance of the but-end has produced on the stranger'.[420]

By this date the longhouse as such had more or less disappeared, and the house, barn and byre each had a separate door, though often built in a continuous line. Many houses, however, had a door in the but-end gable opening into the barn, and another called the fodder-door or cuddie-door (origin uncertain; possibly from Old Norse *gátt*, door-opening) in the partition between barn and byre.

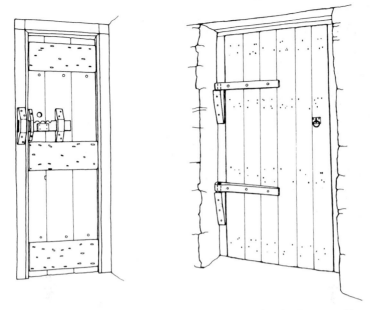

51. Fair Isle examples of wooden door hinges and a wooden door latch operated by inserting a 'key' or finger through the hole in the door. C5363.

The walls of the houses were built on the 'two-skin' principle. The outer and inner faces were built with the best-fitting stones available, and were trussed together at frequent intervals by long stones, *trow-baands* (through-bands) running the full width of the wall, just as in dyke-building. The spaces between the skins were then filled with rubble and dry earth for draught insulation. The inside was pointed with clay, which was sometimes mixed with pony dung as a binding agent, and later on with sand and lime mortar.

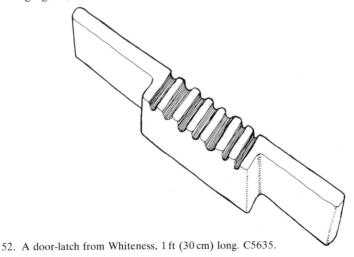

52. A door-latch from Whiteness, 1 ft (30 cm) long. C5635.

The partition between the but- and ben-ends was usually of rough boards. If, as was common, it did not rise higher than the side walls, it was called a *cat-waa* (cat-wall). In smaller houses, the only division was a box-bed placed end on to the back wall; in a larger house, two box-beds could be placed lengthwise front and back, leaving a passage between them.[421]

The *restin-chair* or *muckle-chair* (Fetlar) was usually placed along the wall opposite the hearth-stone on one side of the house. This piece of furniture, standard at one time on farms throughout Scotland and in other countries, was about 6 ft (1.8 m) long by 20 in. (51 cm) broad, with armrests at each end and the back-rest usually closed in up to half its height. The top half of the back was a plain frame, or it could be ornamented by carving or turned pillars. By one wall was a *benk* made by supporting heavy planks of wood on hard turf or stones, at the same height as the restin-chair. The space beneath was used as a store for articles that had to be kept dry. As in Orkney, there were often straw-chairs, with a back, sides, and hood of straw on a framework of wood. The straw was tightly woven to make it draught proof, and the chair was mainly used by the aged and infirm. The dog's place was under the chair.

A set of shelves, the *lem-rack* (Old Scots *lame*, earthenware, *c*. 1500; English *loam*), was often slung from two couples on the front wall of the inbye. Here the

53. Shetland chairs, with and without arms, one latterly used as a commode; and a resting chair. C5806.

54. A wooden 'fleeter' for skimming pots, drawn by T. Irvine, Midbrake. C5930.

family's plates, cups, and bowls were stored. The bottom shelf was boxed in to a depth of about 2 in. (5 cm) and made a container for 'many of the smaller culinary and household requisites, such as the "gruel-tree", "shappin-tree", "fleeter", "horn-geppies", knives and tullies, and also the few home-made "saas" (salves) and remedies for human ills'.

The water-benk was normally along the front wall near the door. It was of wood, about 18 in. (46 cm) high by 2½ ft (76 cm) long. Here stood the *dafficks* (Old Scots *daffok*, tub, vat, 1633 Gaelic *dabhach*) for water carried from the well. In earlier times the container for collecting and storing 'Shetlan'-soda', urine to be used as lye, stood nearest the door and farthest from the fire. It was said to be the only effective rinse for removing fish-oil grease from hand-spun worsted, before it was knitted or woven into woollen goods.

The furniture otherwise was a small table, two or three wooden chairs, and one or two *creepies* or stools. Crofting equipment and material that had to be kept dry was stored in the rafters. The kist lids made convenient shelves for domestic and cooking equipment when not in use, and the roofs of the inbye box-beds were generally littered with an assortment of clothing. On the ootbye floor stood the knocking stone for dehusking bere, the washing tub, kettles, pots, and pails; on the inbye floor were such things as the spinning wheel, reel, cradle, and footwear; on the hearth-stone were the tongs, *essie-brod* (ash board), straw besom, brandiron, kettle, and latterly a teapot. Lighting was by means of a collie lamp burning fish oil in earlier times. Usually a rope called a *collie-rep* was stretched across each room, so that the lamp could be moved to any convenient position in the but-end. The ben-end was in a process of change around 1850. Formerly it had been sparsely furnished, with a box-bed, wooden armchair, meal girnel, bland keg, butter tub, churn, boards for stretching knitted garments, and clean personal and household linen.

When the window tax was repealed about 1851, a small window or skylight was put in, and the chimney moved to the gable, where a 'false chimney' was built to lead out the smoke. In houses where the division was a cat-waa or a box-bed, the partition was now carried up to the roof, and a proper door fitted. Flooring boards were laid over sleepers, and the walls limewashed inside. 'A few articles of rough furniture were added, and this completed a "best-room", where the minister, doctor, factor, lawyer and other special visitors were interviewed or entertained.'[422]

Potatoes were sometimes stored in the corner of the living-room. This corner had the name of *tattie lodie* (Norwegian *lade*, Old Norse *hlaða*, store-house).[423]

Meantime, improvements were going on at the bigger farms in Shetland. By 1874, G. Bruce of Veensgarth on the Scalloway road had built a first-class farmhouse, a substantial steading with a threshing mill attached, and a corn mill three miles away. G H B Hay of Sound and Andrew Umphray of Reawick had also built good new steadings. Umphray's steading included stables, byres, lambhouses, a barn, and water-driven threshing and bruising machinery. David Edmondston could house 40 cattle in his steadings at Ordale on the south of Baltasound. In Unst, the cottar tenant Joseph Monsel had built a house and small shop on the 7 mks of land he rented from Major Hamilton. Peter Smith, foreman of the fish-curing establishment at Westing, rented a farm on Major Cameron's estate, paying £7 a year plus 7 per cent of the outlay of £30 on a new slate roof to the house. This involved raising the side walls to accommodate the ceiled slate roof. The assumed cost of repairing the thatch had been assessed at about 10/–. In some of the cottages put up by Major Cameron, the floor of the best end was made up with boards, whilst the kitchen end had a cover of blue clay said to be equal to asphalt.[424]

Much improving was going on by now at all levels, and this period saw a kind of overall face-lift. The kind of work being undertaken by the estates can be characterised by an Account of Repairs required on Tenant Houses in Papa and probable costs of same, with Lists of Rents 1884:

	Repairs	Rent
John Sinclair Everiegarth £4 – –		
Share Tack in Hurdiback 1 – –		5 ,, ,,
House requires to be pointed with stone and lime at a probable cost of	£1 15 ,,	
Gideon Sinclair Everiegarth		
House requires pointing all over with stone		4 10 ,,
and lime cost about	1 15 ,,	
Robert Hay Everiegarth		
This man dying and has no means		3 7 ,,
will labour none this season but his		
Land can be let just now if the House		
is repaired, House requires new door		
and pointing cost about	2 5 ,,	

	Repairs	Rent

William Humphray North banks
House requires to be pointed all over,   10 ,, ,,
and wall heads covered with cement,
part of new roof cost about   5 ,, ,,

James Scott Hurdiback
House requires entire new roof and   5 14 ,,
some lime cost about   4 10 ,,

John Foubister Hurdiback
This House in very bad order and is   4 ,, ,,
not worth the cost of Lime except some
considerable expences be put upon it,
say altogether equal to 70/– or   4 ,, ,,

James Isbister Hurdiback £5 10/–
Share Tack in Hurdiback   <u>1 – –</u>   6 10 ,,
House requires Door and part of roof   1 5 ,,

William Johnston Olliegarth £3.7/–
Share Tack in Everigarth   <u>1–0.0</u>   4 7 ,,
This man is ground Officer and has no fault
to make.

Laurence Coutts Olliegarth   3 7 ,,
No fault or complaint to make only wants
reduction of Rent.

John Johnston Olliegarth   4 5 ,,
This man is mostly confined to bed but has
a little stock and will be able to pay this
Years Rent. His House is in good order.

Magnus Fraser Biggings £4 – –
Share Tack in Everiegarth <u>1 – –</u>   5 ,, ,,
No complaint to make.

James Fraser Biggings £4 – 12/–
Sh.ʳ Tack in   ,,   <u>1 – 2/–</u>   5 14 ,,
House must have lime and pointing all
over cost about   1 15 ,,

John Humphray Biggings   5 ,, ,,
House must have lime and pointing all
over cost about   1 15 ,,

James Williamson Biggings £4–11/–
Sh.ʳ Tack in Biggings   <u>1– 2/–</u>   5 13 ,,
House requires a little lime about   ,, 10 ,,

	Repairs	Rent
Widow Thomas Georgeson Biggings		4 15 ,,
House requires Door and lime and pointing all over cost about	2 5 ,,	
Bruce Sinclair Biggings £4–10/–		5 15 ,,
Sh.ʳ Tack in Biggings 1– 5/–		
House requires mostly all to be pointed over cost about	1 10 ,,	
Henry Jamieson & Son Biggings		5 ,, ,,
House requires pointing all over cost about	1 15 ,,	
James Isbister Biggings £4 — –		5 5 ,,
Sh.ʳ Tack in ,, 1 –5/–		
Nothing required.		
Gideon Foubister East Biggings		4 10 ,,
House requires Door, and a little repairs to wooden roof cost about	,, 15 ,,	
Fraser Jamieson East Biggings		4 18 ,,
Nothing required.		
John Coutts & Son North House		6 15 ,,
House requires Lime &c. cost about	1 15 ,,	
Peter Fraser East Biggings £3.12/–		
Sh.ʳ Tack in North house 12/–		4 4 ,,
Thomas Ewanson North house		6 5 ,,
House requires mostly new roof and a little Lime probable cost	3 10 ,,	
John Johnson Jun.ʳ North House		2 19 ,,
House requires new door say	,, 10 ,,	
William Scott Jun.ʳ North house £2–4/–		
Share Tack 12/–		2 16 ,,
House requires part of new roof and pointing all round cost about	3 15 ,,	
William Foubister North house		2 4 0
This Tack is vacant and House useless, would recommend its being thrown in with William Scotts land, and thereby save expenses on House if he will take it.		
Thomas M. Adie & Sons Voe		
Booths Beaches &c		13 10 ,,
	40 5 ,,	141 3 ,,

By this time, the day of the money rent had well and truly arrived, and the laird had full responsibility for the upkeep of his tenants' houses. This state of affairs goes back to before 1860, when much fresh building went on with houses 12 ft (3.7 m) wide requiring 10 ft (3 m) couples, with 10 rows of *langbands* or purlins on each side.[425]

In Fetlar, in 1864, a man called Thos. Johnson lived in a small house on the end of Charles Williamson's byre. He had struck Williamson's wife with a spade handle, because of a row that developed when one of Williamson's cows broke loose by night and went into Johnson's house. Johnson rose and retied it, but struck Mrs Williamson when she came in to milk in the morning. Evidently Johnson had to enter his house through the byre, because after this incident Sir Arthur Nicolson ordered the communicating door to be built up and a door taken out leading directly into Johnson's house. This order had already been given in 1862, but Johnson would not allow the man who came to do it.[426]

In 1876, some fishermen from Yell looked at a vacant farm at Aith, but were put off because they would have had to build a byre and barn at their own expense.[427] Tenants were beginning to be much less easily satisfied than in the past. Three years later, a builder looked at the Town of Velzie to see how a house for a tenant could best be provided. More of the existing houses could be made suitable for a dwelling house without taking down the existing walls altogether. The walls of the largest old tenant's house last repaired were in poor condition, not properly founded in some places, clay built, too narrow inside, with no chimneys or windows. The best suggestion was that it should be roofed in for a barn and byre, for 'a tenant now will not put up with the old class of country dwelling houses'.[428]

In 1881, twelve barrels of lime were ordered for repairs to Aith Bank house, and some cement for the roof, on which the slates were cracked and in need of pointing. Both Aith Bank and Still were grey slated. When originally roofed, 'any sort was taken for couples & long bands crooked or straight old or new'. The chimney tops were all adrift. Though wood had come for the repair of the stairs and the loft, local men could not be got to do the repairs because they were at the fishing.[429]

Later in the year, Jas. Hunter and D. Hart got £1.5/– for laying the loft and putting in stairs and windows in Aith Bank house. Jane Laurenson was paid 10/– for eleven pairs of couples, a door and jamb, window and skylight. 840 ft (256 m) of longbands for houses prepared and built at Banks of Aith cost 16/10, at 2/– for a hundred.[430]

By 1886, a new factor had to be reckoned with. This was the Crofters Holdings (Scotland) Act, which gave in the crofting counties, including Shetland, security of tenure, a fixed fair rent, compensation for improvements, and facilities for enlargement of holdings.[431] The initial effect on the crofters was not surprising, and not always appreciated by their superiors:

'I doubt this will be a bad year for getting in rents for whither they could pay or not now with this cursed Crofters Act they are so puffed up with what they see in the papers about Skye that they really think they have no right to pay any rent at all and when I ask for arrears they say they must have something to live on & they have enough to do to live and appear careless about rent, but formerly rent was all their thought if they only could make out their rent – had just to live as best they could.

'*Wm*. Tulloch is taking Cattle from the tenants for Shop goods and serving the youths with Sumons after him urging these young people to take the goods and pay when they could – & he says the Merchant has now a better claim as the proprietor the like never was hear before. This Island is quite diferent from the highlands no living man here has reclaimed any land or improved the holding he is on all was arible land before their great grand fathers perhaps was born & the present tenants now will not labour over the half of their arible because they don't think the native grain good enough its loaf fine Biscuits good flour & Scotch meal – so does these Crofters Com⁵ even reach this length'. And two years later, ink was flowing in the same vein – 'they all want grand houses & will not live in the same sort of houses now as what they did when they yearly paid rent in full'.[432] What could a poor laird or a factor do when his hands were tied? There was little choice but to upgrade the houses, however gradually, and the specifications for repairs to the houses at Still and Aith Bank are typical. The present old roof at Still was to be removed. There were to be new couples and sarking couples well notched and spiked together. Couples and baulks to be of whitewood 5 in. (13 cm) by 2 in. (5 cm), set on wall plates 6 in. (15 cm) by $1\frac{1}{4}$ in. (3.2 cm) at 16 in. (41 cm) apart, and sarking of whitewood $\frac{3}{4}$ in. (2 cm) thick nailed with $2\frac{1}{2}$ cwt (127 kg) nails. The Easdale slates off Grutin roof were to be used as a cover. At Aith Bank, the old grey slate was to be taken off, and couples to be made straight, with new half-couples between each pair. Two roof headed windows were to be put in front of the house, 4 ft 6 in. (1.4 m) by 2 ft 3 in. (69 cm), sunk 2 ft (61 cm) into the wall. A small, lifting skylight, about 12 in. (30 cm) by 9 in. (23 cm), to be put in the roof over the upper closet, with a small opening window in the back wall for light to the back kitchen closet. One of the attics was to be lined with $\frac{5}{8}$ in. (1.6 cm) lining, on the ceiling, sides, and end.[433]

In general, the Shetland cottage or croft house took the form of a but and ben and closet. Sometimes there were extensions, as at Springfield in Fair Isle where what is now an extra bedroom was built as a weaving shed. As with most such places that date from the second half of the nineteenth century, the house is entirely wood-lined. The back-door still has a wooden latch, and the doors leading off the but-end are from a ship called the *Black Watch*, that was wrecked on Fair Isle. The but, ben, and closet have one window each, and the old weaving shed has three windows to give enough light for the work. All are sash windows, 42 in. (1.1 m) by 24 in. (61 cm). There is a chimney in the thickness of the gable, and the hearth, originally open and peat burning, now contains a cast-iron stove. A cross-tree in the chimney supported the crook and links. There was no 'best-room' as such since the family was big, and both the but and the ben were in use all the time.

The dresser stood opposite the fire, with the press at the north wall, and chairs along both walls. The table was in front of the dresser, and was lifted round when needed. At one time there was a box-bed in the home, but latterly bunk-beds were put into the closet to save space. All the kists in the house were home-made by Stewart Wilson or his son Jerome. They also made the beds and chairs, the press and the dresser, and even the straw-backed chairs. The women formerly span wool in the evenings, and later knitted. The men at one time twisted straw ropes or *simmens* to make baskets of various kinds, *kishies*, *budies* and *hovies*. As elsewhere, the older houses were roofed with turf and straw, but now slate roofs predominate. The very new houses or renovated houses have cedar shingles.[434]

In the island of Fetlar, the commonest layout for the older crofts was to have house, barn, and byre in line, each with a separate external door, and also with internal communication. The barn and byre could also be one at either end of the house. Also common was the arrangement of house and byre together in parallel. In this case, a second wall or *burbank* (Old Norse *barð*, brim, edge + Norwegian *bænk*, bench) had to be built to support the roofing couples of the outbuilding. The byre usually had a gable door. On many crofts there was a third house about the size of a barn or smaller. These were horse houses where mares and foals were housed during severe snowstorms. Ponies were considered more valuable than cattle. Where the byre and barn are separate from the house, they may be joined end to end. A pig-sty was also usual, as well as a lambhouse.

A croft house of average size measures about 32 ft (10 m) by 16 ft (4.9 m) externally. The but-end walls were usually plastered with clay, which was given a fresh coat of whitening once or twice a year. Many houses, and especially the ben-ends, were lined with wood, often with salvaged boards lost overboard from the deck cargoes of sailing ships in stormy weather. Lofts were made if wood was available, after the use of a central fire had ended. The kind of loft favoured by fishermen covered the ben-end and extended half across the but, leaving part open so that boat's sails, mast-rigging, lines, and baskets could be easily stowed, along with domestic equipment like meal sieves that had to be kept dry.

The ben-end normally had a wall window. Examples measured 20 in. (50 cm) wide by 26 in. (66 cm) high. The but end had two skylights, about 12 in. (30 cm) by 16 in. (41 cm). Neither the window nor the skylights opened. Water pails, kegs, and wooden dafficks stood on a raised wooden bench before the door outside, though they were taken into the but-end during gales and snowstorms. Ornaments in the houses were exceptional. Any rare shell taken on the fishing lines would be used as an ornament. Hand made models of sailing ships brought home by seafarers were popular. Bookshelves were rare, but on the ben table there might be the Bible and Bunyan's *Pilgrim's Progress*. Pictures on the walls were likely to be of sailing ships. The ben-end served as a 'best room'.

In Fetlar, as elsewhere, croft houses built and roofed by the landlords had walls of rough quarried stone, though the stones might have reasonably square faces if a good vein was struck. At the building site, particular care was taken in laying out good corner and skew stones. The outer and inner wall faces were linked by binders at regular intervals. Gables in particular could split and become dangerous where there were not enough binding stones. The core was filled with a hearting of stone; clay mortar was used in the croft houses. It was quite common, as in a barn built near Sullom Voe in the 1960s, for the upper part of the gable to be of turf, each course being pinned to the one below.[435]

21

Roofing Techniques

IF the wood for the rafters was rough, perhaps driftwood, it was usually trimmed with an adze. An effort was made to make it look reasonably good. Sawn timber was supplied for the rafters and tie-beams of houses built by the proprietors.

Before proceeding to make the couples, a skeleton pair was made out of lighter wood and tried on the walls to get the correct span and height. This was then laid on the ground as a pattern. Each couple cheek was half-checked at the crown, bored with a brace-and-bit or an auger, and fastened by a wooden pin. The point of junction of the rafters was called the *(k)nokkens*.[436] The tie-beams or *twart backs*[437] were also checked and nailed on. The couple feet rested on the wall-head. Once the couples were in place, the laths were nailed on crosswise. Even if the wood had been gathered from the shore or elsewhere, the aim was to have an even thickness so that the turf could lie level.[438] The laths had the collective name of *ovey* (Norwegian dialectal *aavid*, a cross-piece of wood used on a bridge or roof). The main cross-pieces or purlins were the langbands.[439]

Pones (Norwegian dialectal *panna*, roof-tile, Dutch *(dak-) pan*, idem), or thin oval strips of green turf were cut and laid over the roofing timbers. In the seventeenth century the houses in Shetland were said to have been covered with a kind of divot called 'flais'. Such *flaws* (Icelandig *flag*, a spot where turf has been cut, *flaga*, a flake, Swedish *flaga*, thin splinter, Norwegian dialectal *flaga*, to split in pieces) appear to have been frequently torn up by hand from the surface of dry moss land.[440] It was only certain kinds of heathy ground that you could 'rive flaas from, and then it has to be done with a flowing water, then you can rive flaas 10 feet (3.1 m), otherwise you could get them no size at all'.[441] The mark left in the ground by cutting or riving flaas was called a *grüvi* (cf. Norwegian dialectal *grov*, *torvgrov*, idem). Flaws and pones were always used for roofing purposes, never for dyke building.

Pones were cut on the scattald, preferably on shallow, dry, clay ground. At many townships an area of poor grazing ground was set apart to be scalped for pones. They were cut with an ordinary delling-spade, or with a turf spade, either an ordinary moor-spade with a fairly rounded blade or a special type of spade found only in the south Mainland of Shetland and in Fair Isle (Fig. 93).

This has a crossbar handle, a broad, flat shaft made from a plank, and a thin crescent-shaped blade with a short, sharp upward curve at the head. Some were made by Lawrence Brown, blacksmith in Lerwick. Its very localised character suggests that it was developed by some ingenious individual, perhaps not much earlier than about 1900. Its specific purpose was to cut pones, shaped so that they were thicker in the middle than at the side. This allowed smooth overlapping on the roof, like the scales of a fish.[442]

In Fetlar, pones averaged $2\frac{1}{2}$ ft long by 20 in. wide (76×51 cm). If they were cut too large, they were not so easy to handle and were apt to split when being moved. Freshly cut pones were piled up in nines or tens, and left for some days to dry and stiffen up, before being moved on hand barrows to the building site. Pones in Fair Isle measured about $5\frac{1}{2}$ ft by $1\frac{1}{4}$ ft (1.7 m×38 cm), and after they had been cut and the earth shaken off the underside, they were rolled up like wall-paper and carried by having a spade-handle thrust up the middle. The size no doubt depended on the nature of the turf, for in other places they were as small as 15 in. by $5\frac{1}{2}$ in. by $1\frac{1}{4}$ in. thick (38×14×3 cm).[443]

As in slating, *poning* began at the bottom of the roof, but before laying the first course, the workmen put a thin flagstone against the outer side of the roofing couple foot to help to keep it dry and free from rot. Such thin flags, called *ofsahelliks* (Norwegian dialectal *ufs*, eaves, + *hella*, flat stone) or *aisen flags* were not always easy to find and might sometimes be carried some distance. When the pones had been laid on both sides of the roof, coping pones were placed along the roof-ridge. They were larger than the others, and reached down on both sides. Care had to be taken in laying the pones to ensure that the joins of the courses were staggered. To achieve this, the pone was placed in every second tier up and down, making a short and a long in the start of each tier. Wooden *hoose-pins* about 15 in. (38 cm) long could be used to fix the pones.[444] For small outhouses, there was a technique of putting a double layer of pones on the roof, with no covering of thatch. This was known as to *double-pone* or to *yarpone* (Old Norse *jörð*, Norwegian *jörd*, earth, + *pone*).[445] In general, however, straw thatch was the ubiquitous roofing medium.

During the long winter evenings, the menfolk twisted two-strand straw ropes called *links* or *simmens* (Old Scots *siming*, 1616, Old Norse *sima*, straw rope). An expert could make them with little *snud* (Norwegian dialectal *snu(d)*, twisting, Swedish dialectal *snod*, twist in thread) or twist to be turned out of them before they were rolled up into large balls for later use. Straw simmens did not stand severe winter frost well and this meant re-thatching at two-yearly intervals. The coir yarn that came to be used in the later nineteenth century was hardier, and the thatch under it might last up to five years, provided it was of good Shetland oat straw from outfield ground. Most men could thatch, and neighbours helped. The team consisted of three men and a boy. One was on a ladder at the front, one on a ladder at the back, one on the ridge.

First the *linkstones* or *loopstones* that had anchored the ropes were removed, and set along the bottom of the house wall, ready for being lifted up again. Bundles of straw called *hallows* (cf. Norwegian dialectal *halge*, bundle of straw,

55. Straw thatch on a house in Muckle Roe, 1962. The position of the kitchen chimney shows that it is dooked against the gable.

holge, wisp of hay; recorded in Orkney and Caithness, 1567–1623) were thrown up to the man on top, and he placed them along the ridge, counting them to keep a check on the number per side. Then *baets* (Old Scots *beit*, bundle of flax, fifteenth century, Middle English *bete*) or small bunches of drawn straw, *gloy*, were laid along the eaves on both sides at full length. It was drawn out so that all the loose bits of straw had been removed, and the stalks laid parallel, so that it ran the water quite well. The hallows were untied and spread from gable to gable, the first course covering the gloy. The second gable to gable course covered the first. The same was done at the other side, and then the top courses went on. The wooden smoke openings were also covered by doubling straw over a rope and slipping it over, then drawing it in tight to fit the shape of the chimney. The surplus length of straw at the lower end was tucked under the thatching. Two circles of rope were taken round it lower down to hold it secure, with wooden pins to hold them in place.

The last stage was the roping down of the thatch. The two on the ladders hung the link-stones, and the one on top 'cast the links'. In this, the first stage was to make fast one end of the rope to a linkstone. As this was being done, the boy took up position, keeping the rope in his hand to clear any fouls as the ball of simmens uncoiled, so that it could be handed up cleanly to the man on the ridge without snagging the thatch. A bight was then thrown down to go round the

56. Hurdiback, Papa Stour. The house roof was raised and slated in the late nineteenth century, and the outhouses retained their thatch. 1967. 3.37.33.

57. A byre at Mangaster near Sullom Voe, with the thatch held in place by ropes and link-stanes. C5709.

linkstones at the other side. Linking was followed by *fitching* (Old Scots, *c.* 1500, to move slightly to one side or another), which involved roving a length of simmens over and under the links just above the linkstones, from gable to gable. This was to draw down the outer link rope to the level of the under one, so that all the links would lie firmly on the thatch and keep it in place during high winds. For the same reason, 'lang links' were tied across half way between eaves and ridge, until the use of herring nets made them redundant something over a century ago. To finish the roof, the loose, overhanging straw at the eaves was cut and trimmed. In some cases, simmens were spread diagonally over the straw from the ridge to the eaves, about 12 in. (30 cm) apart. This 'gave a diamond effect and prevented the loops or bights of the finishing off simmonds which carried the stones from sinking into the straw'. The thatch on the croft at Stanydale was roped in this way.[446]

A characteristic appearance is given to thatched houses in Shetland, whether one- or two-storey, by the way in which the thatch is tucked in at its outer ends so that the gable skews stand proud. To get this effect, the gables are built fairly thick, so that they have both the skews, and an internal ledge at a lower level, on which the thatch and the ends of the roofing timbers can rest. The latest stage in the roping of thatch was the use of netting wire. Three foot (91 cm) wide rolls were cut into five lengths of 30 ft (9.1 m) which were served together along the 30 ft side. This net was laid over the thatch and the link-stones tied along the lower edge by slings of coir yarn. This worked well.[447]

Though these details relate specifically to Fetlar, they apply throughout Shetland. Thatching with turf overlaid with straw roped with simmens is referred to in the seventeenth century and undoubtedly goes much further back in time. In the 1800s cottages were nearly the same everywhere, with walls of

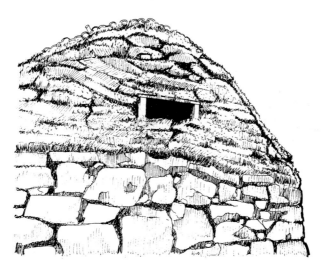

58. The turf gablet of the Mangaster byre, with a wood-framed opening for pushing in driftwood. C5710.

59. The bull's house on a Muckle Roe croft, with a gablet of herring-bone turf, and a roof of turf retained with wooden pins, 1962.

stone and clay, and roofs thatched with pones or flaws, and thatch. Ropes made of heather were more enduring than straw simmens.[448]

In 1963, only two thatched houses remained in Fetlar. Most of the others had roof coverings of black tarred felt, as elsewhere in the Northern Isles. Only better quality buildings had slate roofs, such as the church with seating for 270 put up by the Established Church of Scotland in 1845, the Free Church for 300 built in 1848, the Church of Scotland manse, the Free Church manse built in 1868, and the two-storey houses at Aithbank and Smithfield (built about 1815). The Haa of Funzie already had a felt roof by 1878. In North Yell, there were one-storey farms and cottages with slate roofs at West-a-Firth, South Hall, Kirkabuster, and Heatherdale, the latter a house for Major Cameron's shepherd. Beyan and Windhouse were large, two-storey slated houses. Wind-house had been a mansion house, used by the 1870s as a sheep farm. The Free Church for 300, built in 1848 at the west end of Sellafirth, was, like its manse, slated.[449]

In Mid and South Yell, there were two-storey slated houses at Vatsie, the Haa of Swarister and Gossabrough House, and one-storey slated houses at Newfield, Springfield, and Newhouse, a former farmhouse used as a store. Mr Miles Walker's shepherd's house at the Haa of Aywick had a felt roof.[450]

In 1878 it was said of Fair Isle that the houses were bad, and kept in

60. A roof of flagstones overlain by thatch, near the Loch of Skaill.

indifferent order both outside and in, though some new stone houses with slate roofs were beginning to appear. There was no scarcity of timber, for each house had a large pile beside it from the two or three wrecks that took place every year through storms or fog. The Board of Trade, however, were then contemplating the erection of a lighthouse and fog-warning, and a lifeboat station.[451]

Two years after this survey, in 1880, the croft of Barkland was built. The dwelling house was of the but and ben and closet form, and a barn and kiln were butted on to the end of it. The byre was separate. It introduced a new form of flagstone roofing to the island, explained by the fact that it was built by an Orkney man from Westray, John Arcus, who got two Fair Isle men to carry out the work.[452]

From these samples, it can be seen that in the last quarter of the nineteenth century, the majority of Shetland houses were roofed with thatch, better class and institutional buildings were slated, some smaller houses were slated, especially if they had a link with the new trade of sheep farming, and felt roofs were beginning to appear. Occasionally, turf roofs may still be seen on small outhouses.

ORKNEY

Straw thatch was widely used in Orkney at one time, but the easy access to flagstone had a marked effect on roofing techniques. Cottages were covered nearly every year with a little fresh straw, 'very ill applied', and in such cases the thatch was held in position by stones slung from straw ropes, and laid along or hanging over the eaves. A feature was that the eaves generally had broad flags or slates resting on the side walls to carry off the water that dripped from the thatch, so performing the same function as the drawn straw or gloy of the roofs in Shetland. The ropes could be of heather, and turf also underlay the straw.[453]

Church roofs could be thatched as well, like the old church at Deerness about 1843. People from the different districts in the parish were responsible for thatching it in successive years. The minister of Stenness church required women who violated the Seventh Commandment to wind a specified length of heather simmen for roping down the thatch on the church. The going rate was: 'Bastard bairns ... a simmon clue (ball) apiece.'[454]

Roofing timbers in Orkney houses were of the same A-frame construction as in Shetland. There is no evidence for cruck-frames, with side-members reaching to the floor or well down the walls, taking the weight of the roof instead of the walls. The nearest approximation is the rough, untrimmed 'Highland couple' noted in the farm of Quina near Stromness, the lower end of which rested not on the wall-head, but at a point about 18 in. (46 cm) down the wall. Usually, such couples did rest on the wall-head. The three new 'birks' (birch trees) mentioned in a Stronsay inventory of 1734 may have been for use as couples since other items specified – a large and small 'wombill' or auger, two 'mashes' or mason's hammers, and a small hammer, imply that building was going on.[455] The couple feet on the slightly sloping wall-head were secured there by *aisen*- or *wa'* (wall) *plates*, flagstones fitted at the end of each, and

61. A roof with straw thatch on the upper and flagstones on the lower part, in Papa Westray. Per T. Mackay.

62. A flagstone roof in Papa Westray, with cemented joints, 1920–30. Note wooden gutter and large water barrel. Per T. Mackay.

62a. A flagstone roof in Papa Westray with seamers over the joints, 1920–30. Per T. Mackay.

63. An underlay of simmens to support the turf and thatch, at The Green, Toab, Orkney, 1961.

allowed to project 3 or 4 in. (8–10 cm) over the outside wall. About 3½ ft (1.1 m) up, a lath or *laight* (Norwegian *lekte*, Danish *lægte*) was nailed at each side, and another pair a little way below the ridge.

Once these were in position, a special technique of 'needling the roof' could be adopted as an alternative to wooden sarking. The end of a simmen was fixed to the laight at one side, 'brought over the upper laights, then round the laight on the other side, and over the ridge again', until a web had been formed over the whole roof. For a time the lacework of fresh new yellow straw simmens over the ridge or *main-tree* 'brightened the otherwise sombre colouring of the farmer's abode, but when the all-pervading smoke had done its work of dyeing, and the dampness of the atmosphere had turned the adhering soot into a substance resembling tar, which dropped more or less freely in accordance with changes of the atmosphere, the neat twist of the simmens was no longer recognisable as a thing of beauty. In wet weather liquid soot ran in slow streams down the walls from every cupple foot, while it dropped here and there from the ridge'.[456] Examples of this technique have been recorded in a barn at Estabin (1968) in the parish of Firth, in a byre at The Green, Toab (1961), and in Shetland in a byre at Lingarth, Dunrossness, where turf overlies the ropes. The technique was not recent, for it was common in 1845 in St Andrew's parish where, though a poor quality roofing slate was found in one area, most of the farmhouses were roofed with straw or heather. Simmens of either material 'are

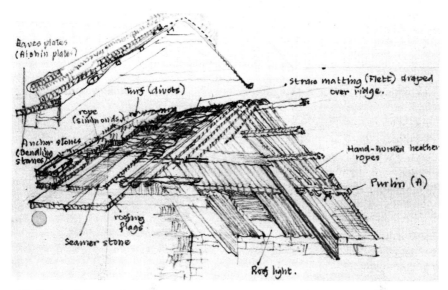

64. Detail of construction with a simmen underlay at Estabin, surveyed 1968. Copyright: Royal Commission on Ancient Monuments, Neg. no. ORD/5/1. Drawn by G. Hay.

65. The same construction, with fewer simmens, on a farm in Dunrossness, Shetland. This may be a sign of Orkney influence. 3.39.18.

passed over the joists from eave to eave, till the whole of the building be once covered. A stratum of loose straw is then interposed between this, and another layer of the same cordage; and these are alternated until a covering be formed, which will hold out the wind and the rain'. It needed repair nearly every year, though this often consisted of nothing more than an additional layer of simmens.[457]

When the 'needling' was complete, thin flagstones were laid along the wall heads with their upper ends resting on the lower laights. The network of simmens and the flags were covered with straw to a depth of nearly a foot (30 cm) and this in turn was held firm against the wind by more simmens looped around stones. These were called in Orkney *bendlin'* stones (Old Norse *bendill*, a band, Norwegian dialectal *bendel*, straw band on a sheaf). Corresponding to the *lang link* of Shetland was the *garbendlin* (probably Old Norse *gjǫrð*, girdle), a term found in North Ronaldsay.[458]

Orkney roofs, therefore, even more than those in Shetland, absorbed vast quantities of simmens, hand-twisted of straw or of heather. Straw was prepared for twisting by being stripped through the fingers to remove the sheaths or *slochs* and was tied in small bundles, of about 4 to 5 in. (10–13 cm) diameter according to a Caithness source,[459] till required for use. If heather was to be used, long thin pieces were plucked out of the hill 'with a flowing tide',[460] or, at any rate, when the new, young heather had finished growing. It was made up into bundles called *nitches* (Old Scots *knech*, a bundle, 1589). Heather was probably more used for simmens than straw in earlier times, since straw was

66. Thatch of thickly placed simmens on an Orkney farm. The skylin' board is visible above the chimney. 1.12.23.

required to fodder the beasts. To twist one nitch was considered a good evening's work.

Whatever material was used, simmens were wound in the same way. The winder sat with the material ready to hand, took a tuft or *taet* (cf. Icelandic *tæta*, a shred, particle), doubled it unequally on itself, and started twisting with his right hand. The separate stalks of the upper strand were twisted with a turn between the fingers to the right, and under the lower strand on the left side. The under strand then became the upper one, and was twisted and turned under as before. Fresh straw or heather was picked up with the right hand and fed in as each strand began to peter out. As the rope formed, it was held between the thumb and two first fingers of the left hand. Loose, protruding ends, left where each tuft had been added, were later trimmed off with a knife. As the simmen grew longer, the end was first gripped under the left armpit, and eventually twisted right round the body. There was often competition to enliven the evening's work. The one who produced the biggest ball in the shortest time was the champion, though the smart ones might try to slip a turfy peat into the centre of the ball when they started winding, to give it more bulk.[461]

For some of the older men, the winding of simmens helped to provide a living in winter-time. They made them into balls of such a size, that when a man laid his chest on top, he would just be able to touch the ground at each side with the tips of his fingers. Such balls were *six-foot clews* in Orkney, and in Shetland *breist clews* or *ell clews*. One that could be held up to the chest with the arms round it and the fingers interlocked was, in Shetland, a *skurt* (Norwegian,

67. A flagstone rooflight, from Orkney. 3.39.11.

Danish *skjød*, lap, bosom, influenced by English *skirt*) *clew*, because it could be held in the bosom. The smallest were called *bighters* in Shetland, because used to tie *bights* or loops.

There was a special way of rolling simmens in Shetland so that they could be withdrawn from the inside of the ball. A wooden pin called a *mid-pin* was used. It was slightly tapered for easy removal. A groove was made on opposite sides from the centre to the thicker end, and a hole bored through the grooves near the end. The end of the simmen was passed through this hole to keep it firm, laid along the groove, and taken a couple of turns round the centre of the pin. Winding was done by rotating the pin so that the simmen was laid in even rows, first from left to right, then from right to left, till the requisite size was obtained. By using a *windie*, a lengthened mid-pin mounted on two small trestles and fitted with a crank-handle, the winding could be done very quickly. An Orkney equivalent was to double the end of a simmen back on itself and take a few turns round the doubled portion, which then acted as a pin. This was probably the technique that gave rise to the idea of a mid-pin.[462]

Flagstones were also widely used in Orkney roofing techniques. In Westray, two kinds of flagstone were found, blue and grey in colour. The blue was harder and more durable, and found by the sea-shore. The softer greystone flags, ranging from half an inch (1.3 cm) to 3 or 4 in. (8–10 cm) in thickness, were also widely used. Several quarries had been opened since the mid 1830s to get roofing flags, but the 'common people' used either blue or grey flags, whichever were most convenient, raising them and putting them on without further

68. The hole for suspending roofing slates is made with a pick.

dressing in the shape in which they got them. The flags could range up to 8 or 10 ft (2.4–3 m) square. In Stromness, stones for houses were quarried near the shore and carried to the town in large boats.[463]

In some cases, flags covered the entire roof. Because of the weight of the stones, the pitch had to be relatively shallow. There were two ways of laying flags. One was to lay them out on the roof and cover the joints or seams with other flags, called *seamers*, which gave an up and down appearance; the other was to set the seamers under the joints, so producing a smooth upper surface. Either way, it was common for the flagstone to be covered with turf, to improve the insulation against wind and cold, and also to protect the flags themselves from frost. They might also be covered with straw thatch.[464] In more recent times, cement has been used to fill the joints on a flagstone roof.

Examples can also be found of roofs that are half-thatched and half-flagged. One is on the older half of the double farm of Gateside, North Ronaldsay, which was standing empty in 1964. Here, heavy flagstones run half-way up the roof, and the remainder is a *tekk-ruif*, thatched roof, with numerous simmens looped around *bendling-stones* in the normal way.[465]

The wall-plates laid on the wall-head to form the eaves were known as *tekkels* (Norwegian dialectal *tekel*, roof, small roof, Old Norse *þækjul*, overhang of a roof, balcony) in Westray. Another name for the eaves was the *odder* (Orkney) or *obder* (Shetland), from Old Norse *ofdyri*, *uppdyri*, a lintel, and referring specially to the lintel or *odder-stane* above the door.[466]

Small windows were also placed in the roof. Glass was an expensive item in

69. Slates are shaped by means of a slate-knife with an off-set blade.

earlier days, and though a laird or merchant was able to order 6 dozen window frames of the largest size and 4 dozen of the smaller sizes from Hamburg, as James Henderson of Gardie in Shetland did in 1770, poorer folk had to make do with a skin, or might simply stuff a light-opening with a bunch of straw or heather if the weather was poor.[467]

Roof lights were usually made by cutting an opening in a flagstone, up to a foot (30 cm) square, but usually less, and filling it with a pane of glass set in with putty. In 1882 a donation was made to the National Museum of Antiquities of Scotland of the 'stone frame of a window, now becoming somewhat of a rarity. I saw it lying on the top of the wall of a ruined homestead, not far from Boddam. ... The house, a but and ben, had no windows made in the walls, and you entered through a roofless byre, also without windows, to get to the door of it. This kind of window is laid resting on top of the wall, sloping up into the bottom of the thatched roof ... Most of the cottages now have small windows in the wall, and often the older stone window frame is still used at the eave, like a skylight ... The opening out in the pavement-like stone is filled up with a small pane of glass'.[468]

22

Sleeping Accommodation

IN Viking houses, there was a raised platform, *pallr*, at either side of the hearth, that provided both sleeping accommodation and seating. In excavated tenth century houses in Iceland such platforms were found to be 1 to 2.25 m wide, and one example at Skallakot in Þjórsárdalur had rows of stones set cross-wise, suggesting a division between sleeping places. No traces of wood remained, but the archaeologists consider that there were wooden-framed beds here, as well as in some eleventh century examples. This seems to have been a special Icelandic development that lasted till the nineteenth century. The base was built up of stones and turf, and as often as not this alone formed the bed space. This kind of dais or platform long survived in the Northern Isles, as did its dual function. It is probably what was meant by the 'broad benches' on which people lay around the central fire of a Shetland house about 1614–18.[469]

A much reduced version of the dais may be seen in the seats of turf for the family that a traveller found around the fire of a blacksmith's house near Vailey Sound in Shetland in 1834. On a grander scale, a small landed proprietor at Burrafirth in Aithsting sat on his 'high seat' at the end of the room, with two rows of servants along each side of the room. The visitor had to pass between them to reach the laird. Later a bed was supplied for him in the ben-end, which also served as the granary. It consisted of straw spread on the floor, with blankets and clean sheets over it. When the same visitor called at a farmer's house at the Hill of Aithsness, Vementry, he passed through the byre into 'a spacious room with a central fire, clay floor, and soot covered walls, with two long forms for the servants of each sex, and a high and separate chair for the mistress of the house'.[470]

Whether or not Viking antecedents can be seen in this kind of arrangement, the fact remains that such ways of seating round the fire may provide an origin for the long wooden bench or settle, the muckle chair or restin' chair, which could double up as a bed when required. Settles of this kind were found throughout Scotland and in much of Europe, as characteristic and essential pieces of kitchen furniture.

Other early types of beds were also found. In a description of a cottar's house in Orkney, it was said that 'parallel to, and about two feet (61 cm) from the horribly damp north wall, a row of flags was set up on edge, fixed in the earthen floor. The trough formed by the damp wall, for back, the damp earth covered with a little straw or heather for bottom, and having the cold flagstones for front, was the bed of the Orkney peasant during the greater part of last century'. It was considered that the introduction of box-beds towards the end of the eighteenth century was one of the greatest improvement that took place in the domestic economy.[471]

Such hollow beds have even older antecedents than the Viking *pallr*, for they are reminiscent of the flagstone-enclosed area on either side of the hearths in the Stone Age huts at Skara Brae. They are also more closely related to the outshot neuk-beds, the fronts of which are generally formed by two upright flagstones. In Orkney the nature of the stone played a strong part in shaping the bed. The lack of beds as fixed features in Shetland no doubt points to the more recent nature of Shetland building, but it is remarkable when it is realised that built-in alcove beds are widely distributed, not only in Orkney, but also in the western half of Scotland, in Ireland, Northern England, Scandinavia, Brittany,

70. The neuk-bed at Langalour, Orkney. 4.9.8.

71. The wooden box-bed at Bewan, North Ronaldsay, 1964.

Belgium, Holland, and North-West Germany.[472] The Orkney neuk-beds have three main forms: the full outshot, as at Mossetter, Nether Benzieclett and Langalour, the half-neuk bed, with a shallow outshot, as at Winksetter, and the unique (for Orkney) style of Kirbister, where the bed is completely within the thickness of the wall.

Kirbister, which was occupied till 1962, shows a series of bed types. The wall-bed was superseded by a box-bed in the kitchen, and this in turn by beds of modern form placed in the bedrooms. Box-beds, however, were by no means confined to kitchens, and often served in the Northern Isles, as elsewhere in Scotland, to divide the ben-end into separate areas, or sometimes to divide the but- and ben-ends from each other. They became increasingly common from the end of the eighteenth century. For adults, they were about 6 ft (1.8 m) long by 4 ft (1.2 m) wide, and for children 5 ft (1.5 m) long. In March 1847, a visitor to a house measuring 14 by 12 ft (4.3×3.7 m) observed in it a single box-bed. He asked where the man and his wife and six children slept at night. The answer was: 'Weel . . . jeust look i' the inside o' the bed, an' ye'll say it's weel planned tae haud eight o' us. The wife and I lie wi' our heeds at the head o' the bed, the two eldest lie with their heads at the foot o' the bed, the peerie (little) t'ing – that is the baby – lies i' his mither's bosom, the ain next the peerie t'ing lies i' mine, and the middle two lie on a shelf in the foot o' the bed, over the heads o' the eldest twa. An' trath I can tell you we are no' cauld gin I close the bed doors'. This bed measured 5 ft 8 in. long by 3 ft 10 in. wide by 4 ft 8 in. high (1.7×1.2×1.4 m).[473]

Box-beds often had sliding doors, sometimes with hearts, clover leaves, or diamonds, carved out as finger-holes. The mattresses in them, as in beds of other kinds, were sometimes stuffed with a kind of seaweed called *marlak* (Norwegian dialectal *marlauk*) in Shetland. This was *Zostera marina*, sought after because it was proof against fleas. Because of their enclosed form, they could be used for bleaching woollen shawls, which were hung up inside and fumed with sulphur.[474]

Though seaweed, straw, or chaff were good enough for tenants' beds, those of higher rank preferred the comfort of feathers. Thomas Awchinleck, commissary of Orkney, had two feather beds, six bed coverings, and 9 pairs of old bed plaids in 1612; Ester Thomsone had in the house of Halcro four feather beds with bolsters, pillows, blankets, sheets, and coverings in 1632; Jannett Loutit, wife of a merchant burgess of Kirkwall, four half-worn feather beds in 1687, with 10 pairs of blankets and 10 pairs of sheets; Marione Yorstane, wife of Magnus Brandie, carpenter burgess of Kirkwall, an old feather bed with a bolster and two 'codds' or pillows in 1680, with 6 pairs of old blankets and two old coverings; Elizabeth Cromartie in Stromness had two bedsteads, and four pairs of bed plaids in 1680. Numerous other examples can be found in the inventories included in the Testaments. Eider ducks were in demand, and there was no shortage of goose feathers, of which 66 cwt 1 qr 22 lbs (3376 kg) were exported from Orkney in 1801–2, 30 cwt 3 qrs 4 lbs (1564 kg) in 1802–3, 74 cwt 2 qrs 26 lbs (3797 kg) in 1804–5, and 90 cwt (4592 kg) in 1805–6.[475]

23

The Hearth

HEARTHS serve more purposes than one. The fire gives warmth and light, cooks the food, gets rid of combustible rubbish and in some instances could dry the grain as well. Peat ash provided manure for field, garden or plantiecrue, either directly, or after use as byre-bedding. The simpler the dwelling, the simpler in form the hearth was likely to be, and the more purposes would it serve. Specialisation of use for cooking and heating increased with sophistication, but specialisation was nothing new, for even in Viking times there could be in the same house a cooking fire, *máleldr*, and a fire for heating the room, *langeldr*. A law of Magnus Lagabøter in Norway stated that three hearths were permissible on a tenant farm – one in the house where the farmer sat and slept, one for cooking, and warming the house-folk, and a third for drying the corn.[476] Probably the central fire, surviving as it mostly did in a longhouse, represents the least specialised of all forms of hearth.

At Jarlshof, the long hearth of the Viking houses had become restricted in size to a squarish shape measuring about 6 ft by 5 ft (1.8×1.5 m) by the late eleventh to early twelfth century. The square form survived, for example at Effirth in Shetland[477] and at Kirbister in Orkney, but squareness was not a marked feature of what Shetlanders called the 'roond fire'. It varied between 4 and 6 ft (1.2 and 1.8 m) in diameter, depending on the width of the house, and was placed at a point a little more than half-way in from the outer door, to allow working space in the ootbye. It was made of stones bedded in the earth floor and clayed over, usually standing about 4 in. (10 cm) proud. An example seen in Foula in 1902 consisted of a flat stone set on a floor of wooden planks.

The stone back standing between the hearth and the door characterised central fires in Orkney, and died out much earlier – if it ever was common – in Shetland. Only one house had a central fire with a back by 1905 in the parish of Tingwall.[478] It could consist of a single low stone, of a flagstone on end, or of a substantial piece of walling like the Kirbister example (see pages 131–33), which could be about 6 ft (1.8 m) broad by 4 or 5 ft (1.2–1.5 m) high by 1½ ft (46 cm) thick, sometimes with a crow-stepped top.[479] A hole about a foot (30 cm) square in some of the backstones allowed the ashes to be pushed through to the ootbye, where they were contained within a circle of wet, sandy peats. These were powdered by the hot ash, and the whole mass was used for bedding in the byre.

Continual scooping up of the ashes left a hollow in the floor, called in Orkney an *assie-pow* (ash-hole),[480] and in Shetland a *leepie* (perhaps Old Scots *lipie*, a basket, measure; cf. Norwegian dialectal *løypa*, mud-hole, heap of pig-swill). This was described as measuring 3 ft (91 cm) deep by 6 ft (1.8 m) long by 4 ft (1.2 m) wide. A mat of straw or rushes with lifting handles, called *rudistag* (Norwegian dialectal *rudda*, *rodda*, woven or plaited holder for carrying hay; second element obscure), was laid in the bottom and the ashes and rubbish of all kind were thrown on to it. When the leepie was full, the contents could be readily lifted out to the midden.[481] Whether leepies of the size described were common is not certain, but they form a parallel to both the Orkney assie-pow and the Caithness lazy-hole, which was a pit for ashes below the fire. In some

72. A Foula interior with a central fire. Coalfish is drying in the heat and smoke above. Photo. H B Curwen, 1902.

places wooden containers, *essie-backets*, were used to carry out ashes, and a home-made riddle could be used to recover combustible pieces.

There were two ways of fixing the crook and links over the central fire. One was to suspend them by a rope or chain from the roof-ridge itself. The second was to fix them to a cross-beam, called the *crook-bauk* (Shetland), *crook-tree* or *pan-tree* (Orkney) that lay across the house from wall-head to wall-head, as at Kirbister.

Smoke from the fire found its way out through a smoke-hole or *liora* that also served to let in light, a fact preserved in a Norse phrase heard in Cunningsburgh, Shetland, in 1774 and in the early twentieth century in Yell, used as a hint to speed a delaying guest on his way:

'Myrk in e Liora, Luce in e Liunga, Tim in e Guest in e Geungna (It's dark in the Chimney, but it's still light thro' the Heath, it's time for the stranger to be gone)'.[482] It would, in fact, be difficult to say whether the emphasis was on letting out smoke or on letting in light at an earlier date, for the word has the same root as Old Norse *ljós*, light.

The liora, recorded by that name in 1774, is the same as the *ljore* or *ljori* of Norway, North Jutland, West Sweden, the Faroe Islands and Iceland. It consisted of a barrel or wooden vent in the roof, up to about 2 ft (61 cm) square and protruding 18 in (45 cm), placed not over the fire, but a little way along from it, and usually bound around with straw ropes. 'Conflicting draughts from the doors sent the strong-smelling peat smoke through every corner of the

73. A central fire in Orkney. Note the box-beds and straw-backed chairs. Photo. T. Kent. C1554.

74. The central fire at Kirbister, Orkney, 1960s. Photo. W. Hourston. C801D.

dwelling, and it may be that it acted as a disinfectant as well as a deodorizer where man and beast were herded together in such limited space'.[483]

In the Northern Isles and Caithness, as in Scandinavia, a board on the end of a pole was thrust through the smoke-hole, and could be shifted from side to side according to the direction of the wind. It was always set to windward. This was the *skylin board* or *skyle* (Norwegian dialectal *skyla*, to hide, shelter; Old Norse

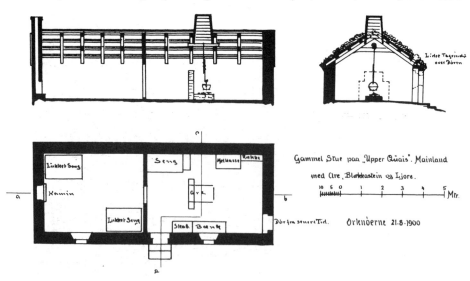

75. An Orkney house with a central fire and back in the kitchen, and a gable chimney in the room end. From Dietrichson and Meyer, 1906. C5810.

skýla, to screen, shelter; Norwegian dialectal *skyle*, *skjul*, a cover over a chimney). In Sandsting and Aithsting a piece of peat or divot, or two pieces of board joined at right angles on the end of a pole, were used in the 1840s.[484] The use of sods on the windward side of the chimney was frequent on low buildings like the peat-houses of Fetlar. The sod was then also called a *skyle* and the process was *to skyle the lum*.[485] In the 1870s in Shetland, though houses on improved estates had chimneys, smoke-holes with skyles on the ends of poles were still more common. The practice of building regular chimneys was becoming more general by the early 1800s and had become fairly common by the 1830s, but their spread was partial and as often as not confined to the ben-end. An example is a house near Stenness on the Mainland of Orkney, surveyed in 1900. Here the kitchen has a central fire with a backstone, and a wood-framed, square, smoke-hole in the roof. The ben-end to the north, however, had a gable fire and chimney. The occupier thought the house had been built about 1830.[486]

This kind of difference in types of fireplace within a single house was widespread in Scotland. It involves separation of functions, for the ben-end fireplace was used mainly for heating, and then for the most part only on special occasions. In their early days there was no doubt an element of prestige in hearths with gable chimneys, and this, as well as an increasing desire to remove smoke from the house, probably speeded the nineteenth century adoption of chimneys of canopy type, called in Shetland *widdie* (wooden) *funnels*, usually made of wood and dooked on to the gable. An alternative was the *faase lum*,

76. The thatched wooden smoke hole or liora at Kirbister, with the skylin' board protruding, *c.* 1960.

77. Interior view of the Kirbister smoke hole and skylin' board, showing the pole by which it can be adjusted and the slots that keep it in position, *c*. 1960.

false chimney, built with stone cheeks against the gable. These were taken to a height of about 3½ ft (1.1 m). A stone lintel was laid across, and a *crook-bauk* or bar for the crook and the links was placed to rest on the lintel, with its rear end driven into the gable wall. Then the stonework was built up to terminate in a square opening, but in many cases the stones were carried only a little way above ceiling height and the smoke was allowed to rise by itself to the chimney.[487] An example of this can be seen at Houbie in Fetlar. Here and in other houses, the stonework of the gable has been shaped in the form of a half-round hollow, which helps to recess the fire somewhat. The common custom of regularly whitewashing the inner face of the fireplace gave a pleasant, light appearance to the kitchen. The use of stone cheeks for the faase lum made it simple to fit presses at each side, and perhaps made free-standing cupboards

78. A wooden canopy chimney at a gable end, in a Shetland croft. 3.43.2.

and kists less essential than in the past. The cross-bar in the chimney for the crook and the links was known as a *rantree-beam*,[488] or a *rammle-back* in Orkney. The latter word was also used in South Ronaldsay for a space up near the roof where odds and ends were stored to keep dry.[489] Norwegian dialectal *randa-tre* also has both these senses. Originally it was of wood, later of iron.

From the central fire with a back, therefore, two lines of evolution are possible. Either the central position could be given up entirely and the fire moved to the gable, or the back could be expanded into a cross-wall forming a mid-gable, as at Appiehouse and elsewhere. Either way, the effect was to produce a gable hearth. In all cases, mid-gables replacing backs have chimneys in their thickness, and appear to be relatively late. The moving of the central fire to an existing gable probably took place earlier.

Such gable hearths were generally set against a backstone, called in Shetland the *biggit back-stane*, that lay against the wall. This was a necessity where the wall was built of turf, as in the seasonally occupied peat-houses of Fetlar. It may be regarded as a carry-over of the central back tradition, or else an equivalent to the heavy iron fire-backs of the castles and mansions of earlier days. Not all gable fires had backstones, however, and an example seen in Foula in 1902 simply had the fire on a flat slab lying close to the gable.

When gable chimneys were built into nineteenth century houses, the wall was relatively weak, and it was common for a second or even a third and fourth lintel to be built into the gable to take the strain off the lower ones. The

79. An internal gable fireplace on a Westray farm, replacing a former stone back. The byre can be seen through the door at the left. Per Mrs Hintjens. C5031.

80. Spaced stones or safers were used as relieving arches for gable hearths, as in this example from Foula. From a photograph, 1959. C5945.

81. A whitewashed gable hearth at Baltasound, Unst, *c*. 1926. Mrs Sandison is knitting. Per Mrs Davidson. C4766.

82. Cast-iron stoves became common in the late nineteenth century. At Estabin, Orkney. 4.10.9.

secondary lintels are known as *safers*, and give a pleasantly symmetrical effect. Large breast-stones, flagstones set into the gable above the hearth, characterise Orkney fires. Even with a gable chimney, however, the fire could still be on a stone at floor level. This position suited peat, but for coal a grate was preferable. In areas of peat scarcity, grates probably appeared earlier than in other places, for Patrick Fea recorded in his Diary on 16 December 1767 that he was at the smiddy making a grate for his wife's room.[490] However, though grates and hobs could easily be inserted, the change in the 1900s was often to cast-iron stoves, such as the Enchantress and the Victoress, both made by Smith & Wellstood. The Victoress had a fire-box at the front and an oven behind, to which there was access from a door at each side of the stove. Such stoves burned peat as readily as coal, and there is no doubt that the ready availability of peat had an influence in retaining floor-level fires for a long time in the Northern Isles.

Fuel for the Fire

24

Cow-dung and Seaweed

THOUGH much of the surface of the Northern Isles is peat-covered, or has been in the past, not every area had enough peat for fuel. Sanday and North Ronaldsay in particular had neither peat nor wood, apart from driftwood. In 1524 it was noted that the only fuel was seaweed and sandy turves that gave little light on the fire. The fuel that gave most light was cattle dung spread on the wall and dried in the sun ('ex stercoribus pecorum in muro sparis et sole arefactis optimus focus est').[491] It was probably these islands to which Dionyse Settle referred in 1577, when he said they were bare of wood, and had to burn turf and 'Cow shardes'.[492] From the sixteenth century, the better off inhabitants of Sanday got their peat from neighbouring islands, but the poorer folk had to rest content with dried cow-dung or tangle. In 1770, the main fuel in Sanday was 'Cow dung baked with Straw and Sea Tangle'. It was considered a job for the

83. Cakes of cow dung heaped up in Papa Westray, 1974. Photo. M. Wright. 18.28.26A.

wives of the cottagers to make fires of seaweed and dung, 'which in Summer's heat they prepare for the Winter's cold'.[493] It was a winter job to gather seaweed for fuel. Meantime the cutting of sods for fuel, a job done by the men, was also going on, so that by the end of the eighteenth century the waste land in North Ronaldsay was very badly cut up, as was much good pasture in Sanday, especially at Elsness. This was a general pattern, for turf or sandy sods were used as back peats on fires everywhere, and were also used to contain hot ashes. The consumption of sods in this way alone, even in areas where good peat was plentiful, must have been enormous. Added to this was a little coal, brought from Newcastle as ballast in the holds of ships that were coming for kelp. By this date, peat from neighbouring islands, especially Eday, was in wider use in all or most of the homes. In the 1790s, the amounts brought in each year were estimated at one or two tons for cottagers, and 30 to 80 or even 100 tons for farmers, at a cost of about 5/– a ton.[494] The difference between the 5/– to 10/– paid by cottagers, and the 150/– to 500/– paid by farmers is a clear index to the width of the social gap, though in fact very few could afford the larger amounts. The majority of the users were at the lower end of the scale, and the situation therefore reflects the sharing of costs through joint activity in cutting and transporting, as well as rising living standards due to the income from kelp. There are no figures to assess the man hours spent in peat-getting each year as a result of the lack of fuel in North Ronaldsay and Sanday, but they must have been considerable, and acceptable mainly because manpower was not scarce at this period.

Nevertheless the use of cow-dung went on. About 1800 the people of these islands were described as 'of a robust and Sanguine Constitution, with florid or ruddy Complexions. This hath been ascribed to their sparing use of fire. Ill provided with fuel they find a substitute for Turf in Straw, Sea-weed and Cow-dung, dried by the heat of the Sun, in the embers of which the inferior sort bake their Barley-Meal Bread or Bannocks, of an excellent flavour'. Indeed almost every particle of horse and cow-dung was made into cakes about 9 in. (23 cm) in diameter and from 1 to 4 in. (2.5 to 10 cm) thick, dried by being stuck against the walls of buildings or laid on the grass. Similarly the tangles of 'red ware, Fucus digitatus' were dried and stacked for fuel, but none of these shifts made a permanent fire possible. It was lit only for cooking in the poorer houses. Tang burned very fast with a hot flame, and the fire had to be stoked frequently. Mothers might have to lie in bed the whole day with their infants, to keep them warm. Hypothermia may have been a common cause of death in older folk. But where possible, the fire was kept in all the time and the last things done before going to bed were to 'rest da fire, kist (chase out) the cat, an' slok (put out) the lamp'.[495]

Throughout the nineteenth century, this fuel of necessity remained in use. It 'emitted an unsavoury reek that tickles the inexperienced nostril. The islanders eat with relish fish that have been smoked with these dried dung-cakes'. It left an odour on the clothes, but so did peat and turf. If thoroughly dried, however, it burned with a clear flame and with no more smell than wood or grass.

Probably the smell would be offensive only if it was burned too green. The bigger tenants were making more regular use of coal from Newcastle and the Firth of Forth by the 1840s – which must have hastened the introduction of grates in their fireplaces – but the poorer folk still had to make do with *coo's scones* and seaweed.[496]

There were different ways of preparing animal dung for fuel. It could be taken out of the byre and spread on grass to dry after having been broken up into pieces 9 or 10 in. (23–25 cm) across. For this only summer dung was used, winter dung being too thick. The scones were made each day, and were turned with the toe during drying, till they were hard enough to be set up in pairs leaning against each other. They were then stored in a dry place till required. The simplest method was to collect the plats of dung from the pasture and carry them home in sacks for drying. Horse dung was treated in the same way. There is a vague tradition in Sanday of an 'elting day at Elsness', when cow-dung was apparently taken and mixed with turfy earth to form a kind of peat. The name would be from the word *elt*, to knead (Old Norse *elta*, Norwegian *elte*, to knead). This was heard by a Kirkwall lady from her mother, who got it from J W Cursiter, the nineteenth century Kirkwall antiquary.[497] More certain is a tradition that the Sanday people spoke of 'the day o' makin' the muck', when the cottars got together to make cakes of dung, using their bare hands.[498] This is more of a community effort than appears from the North Ronaldsay evidence. Thin, almost liquid dung, scattered lightly over the grass as when the cattle were scouring slightly, dried well and was prized as kindling which could be easily set alight with a wisp of straw. Small pieces of it were called *flinterkins*. Straw dung from the midden was often cut off in squares to be dried as fuel. By about 1930, cow-dung was no longer burned in Sanday on the household fire, but it could be used in the washhouse for heating the washing boiler. There was a memory of a woman called Jenno o'Grindyha who was industrious in gathering cow pats, which she dried on top of a flat dyke or on the flagstones in her close.[499] As might be expected, outsiders were not slow to insult the islanders for their use of cow-dung. They would say, for example:

> 'I have been in Egilsay, and I have been in Wyre,
> But I've never been in Sanday where the coo dung's fire'

which is a bowdlerised version of what was said by the people of Stroma in the Pentland Firth: 'The little island o' Sanday, where the coos shit fire'.[500]

The usual names for cakes of dung for fuel in North Ronaldsay and Sanday are coos' scones and bannocks, both from Lowland Scots dialects. An older term may be *kleepo* (Old Norse *kleppr*, Norwegian *klepp*, a lump, as of dough etc), used in Sanday for 'dried "scones" or "plats" of cow-dung used for fuel', as an extension of its usual Orkney meaning of a lump of something soft. Other terms like *pirlins* (North Ronaldsay 1964), horse dung, *lonyo*, a plat of cow-dung and *loyo* (Norwegian *lo*), a lump of excrement,[501] do not refer directly to their use as fuel.

Animal dung as fuel is not a phenomenon unique to Orkney. There is evidence for it in the Western Islands, the East Central Lowlands, and South West Scotland, as well as in Northern England, Ireland, Denmark, Iceland, and farther afield.[502] Its use was dictated by lack of fuel, and this in turn could have had a bad effect on the amount of fertiliser available for the crops, though this was less of a problem where seaweed was readily obtainable. The related over-cutting of grazing areas and rough ground for turf as fuel exemplifies a resource that of necessity had to be misused because of local circumstances.

25

Peat and Turf in Orkney

IT is said that the Norwegian Einar who became an Earl in Orkney got his nickname of Torf-Einar because in the Orkneyinga Saga he is credited with being the first man to find how to cut peat for fuel, at Torfnes (Tarbatness, at the entrance to the Dornoch Firth) in Scotland, because of the scarcity of timber.[503] This sounds like folk etymology, for peat was undoubtedly being cut and burned long before in the Northern Isles, to judge by the amount of peat-ash found in excavated sites of Stone Age date. In this respect the name 'peat' itself may be important. In the Scandinavian and German languages, and in Anglo-Saxon, the word 'turf' is used for both the surface covering and the good, combustible peat underneath. 'Turf' survives in Ireland in the sense of 'peat'. The earliest recorded occurrence of 'peat' in Scotland is in the form of *peta* in a Latin text of about 1200, with *petaria* appearing in 1262. Since *turbaria* also occurs in early documents, 'turbaries' and 'peateries' seem to have been distinguishable from each other. Though the etymology is disputed, it may be the same word as Medieval Latin *petia*, French *pièce*, English *piece*, a bit of something. This is thought to be of Celtic origin, related to Welsh *peth*. If this is so, *peat* could be one of the rare survivals from Pictish,[504] and so could point to the pre-Viking origin of peat-cutting. The peat-spade name, *tusker*, from Old Norse *torfskeri*, shows that the Norsemen were using the word *torf* for peat when they came to Britain.

In 1597, the island of Sanday was exchanging corn with its neighbours for 'Peitts (a kinde of black Mosse, whereof almost all the North-partes of Scotland, make their fyre)'. Eday was the main source of supply of turf as well as peat, the peats being of good quality, and black, so that they got the name of *inkies*.[505] Patrick Fea, the Sanday farmer, gives some idea of the labour involved:

'17 Sept. 1767: Sent Js. Hay and 5 others to kase and bullan what peats I had in the Calf (of Eday).
25 Oct. 1770: Had 50 Horses leading my Peats from Halksness.
26 Oct. 1770: Had 31 Horses leading peats all day.
30 June 1772: Send up my boat ... to bullen the peats and get the Stack Steeth put in order so as to lead peats next week.

10 July 1772: Sent my Passage boat up for Peats with the Cart and oxen to take down from the moss.
16 Nov. 1772: Got the Peat House filled with peats.'[506]

In this, Fea was probably following the arrangement made as far back as 1683 with the proprietor of Eday, based on an agreement for so much per day for as many peats as a man could cast.[507]

North Ronaldsay had a similar arrangement for working peat in the Calf of Eday, which went on till the nineteenth century when thirty young families removed from North Ronaldsay to Eday. They then worked peat for their relations, who only had to load them into their boats and ferry them home. In the 1860s and 1870s the peat trade with Eday reached its peak, after which it rapidly declined. A major reason for the decline may have been the dislike of it by the men who latterly used their herring-boats for peat transport for the work. This was because the boats were newly hauled down just before the herring season, in the first two weeks of July, and there was no proper bedding or sleeping accommodation prepared for the men. They often had to wade three feet (91 cm) deep in water when loading. The boats had to be ballasted with stones carried to them with horse and cart, and these remained on the shores of Eday when the boats were full. However, the first signs of change began in 1873 or 1874, when William Tulloch of Upper Linnay bought 3 tons of coal from an English sloop-rigged vessel that had come with coal for the lighthouse. This was said to be the first croft to use coal. In 1876 a new factor, Benjamin Swanson, became factor of North Ronaldsay. He owned one or two vessels carrying coal, and offered to supply the islanders. After that, coal became the main fuel.[508]

Eday peat was a valuable resource, which in spite of its plenty required to be conserved. Accordingly, the proprietors began to restrict the quantities cut in the 1790s. In particular, they prevented their small tenants, sub-tenants and cottars from making evaporated salt over their house fires, because of the quantity of peats needed, though this was not so much that it could not be carried home in creels of straw on the back. The salt was exchanged for meal in neighbouring islands, quantity for quantity. The tradition of salt making goes back to the 1630s, when a salt-works was set up in the Calf by the Earl of Carrick. Turf as well as peat was used for the salt-pan. There was another salt-pan in Cava, where peat was also plentiful, though it was given up before the end of the eighteenth century.[509]

The local folk got peats free for their household fires, but outsiders paid for them. In about 1845, 209 fathoms of peat were sold from the Holm of Eday, and 257 fathoms from the Green Holm, the price being 6⁹ per fathom when cut and dried. The Eday 'fathom' measured 12 ft (3.7 m) long by 6 ft (1.8 m) wide by 6 ft (1.8 m) high, giving a bulk of 12.2 cubic metres. The amount paid about 1845 was £139.16/–, for a total of 5592 cubic metres of peat.[510] These dry statistics underline better than anything else the enormous amount of peat that the boats from the north isles had been carrying off in the early summer, century after long century, and since the peat cover was being denuded in the same way all over the Northern Isles, it is scarcely to be doubted that the landscape did look different in Viking and Pictish times.

Around the towns where much fuel was needed, peat and turf was used up quickly. The inhabitants of Kirkwall were in frequent strife with sellers of peat, and it was ruled in 1644 that 'all peatts sold or bought within the toune of Kirkwall sall be measured be ane comon gadge of tenn foott (3 m) allwayes ilk foot containing tuelve inches (30 cm)'. It appears too that at this period peat spades or at least their iron blades were valuable items, and liable to be stolen, for it was decreed in the same town in 1629 that 'no smyth nather within the toun nor parochines sall buy ony maid wark sick as kees pleuch irones Tuskardis spaidis nor uther maid wark nor ony thing that has bene maid wark unles the seller find burch (security) for the samen'. This is one of the earliest references to the tusker. In the 1790s, the citizens of Kirkwall were paying 9^d a cart-load and 1^d a horse-load for peat and turf fuel, which had to be carried two or three miles (3–4.8 km). The annual fuel bill for an ordinary family with an income of about £50 a year was £5, nearly a tenth of the whole. A horse-load meant two creels, a cart could hold 18 creelfuls of peat, and 11 cartloads were required per family. Large peat-stacks, therefore, were part of the urban scene. Some coal was also being bought by this time from the Forth, Clyde, and Tyne. Some of Kirkwall's peat supply came from the good mosses in Orphir.[511]

By the end of the eighteenth century, it appears that peat was wearing out in many places. The island of Graemsay got its supplies from Walls or Hoy. Swona got its fuel from Flotta. Burray had a good peat moss, 9 ft (2.7 m) deep, with well regulated cutting, which supplied some of South Ronaldsay's needs. Some farmers in Firth and Stenness sold peat to Kirkwall and Stromness, and others spent much of the summer cutting, drying and leading peat for their landlords. The result was neglect of the farms. It seems that the good peat was sold for gain, and for home use turf was cut from the moors where there was a mixture of peat moss with grit or clay, and burned along with a few peats, with the aim of increasing the quantity of ashes for manure.[512] The mosses in Sandwick had been exhausted, and most of the hills stripped of their greenery. Much of the summer was taken up with preparing fuel and leading peat. Tenants had to provide two days' carriage of peat on horses, as services. Sandwick had to depend on Harray five or six miles (8–9.7 km) away. Only small mosses with an estimated life of 30 to 40 years were left in Stromness, which got most of its peat by sea. In 1792, 30 tons of coal were brought in, at 10/– a ton, and once the duty had been taken off coal, the pattern of using peat on the kitchen fire and coal in the ben-end fire became established. In Westray, there was only one moss belonging to one heritor, who had lately excluded all but his own tenants from using it. Though fuel was scarce for many families, peat could not be got from neighbouring islands. There was a fear of the peat going done, and the use of coal was becoming a necessity. The mosses in Stronsay belonged to the proprietor of Rothesholm, from which the tenants had always got their fuel in exchange for a payment to the Rothesholm tenants in money or in kind. But politics got in the way. The tenants of the Member of Parliament recently appointed, and of his political friends, were forbidden to use the mosses by the proprietor of Rothesholm. The Court of Session supported him, but it was felt that the loss of the source of fuel would lead to depopulation. Harray had very good black peat, almost like coal. When charred, it would work iron well. Orphir sold 100 fathom (183 m) of peat to Kirkwall and Stromness each year, at £1.8/- a fathom, half of it being for rent and the rest for sale. The annual value, therefore, was £140. The fathom, originally a 6 ft cube (1.8 cu metres), had been gradually increased by the landlords to 12 ft (3.7 m) square by 7 ft (2.1 m) high, giving 28.5 cu metres.[513] This is much more than the Eday fathom, and it gave the landlords a great deal more for their rent.

In the nineteenth century, Graemsay with its 180 inhabitants was still scarce of peat and turf for fuel. Eday was supplying its neighbours. Westray was thought to have enough peat to last a century if properly managed. Though the salt-pans in Cava and the Calf of Eday had been discontinued, salt continued to be made by cottagers in small vessels over their house fires in Eday. Much fine pasture had been ruined in Elsness in Sanday by the paring of turf for fuel, such turf being usually cut for compost in other places.[514] By 1841, fuel was fast wearing out in South Ronaldsay and Burray. In St Andrews, peat was carried for distances ranging between a quarter of a mile (0.4 km) and 2 miles (3.2 km). The leading home of the peat took three to four weeks of constant labour, quite apart from the time involved in cutting and drying. A small amount of coal from Newcastle or the Firth of Forth was being burned. Eday was selling peat briskly. The moss of Rothesholm still supplied tenants there, and some neighbouring families, but in general the Stronsay folk had to get Eday peat, at an average cost of £1.5/- per family. Some of the tenants also used a considerable quantity of coal. Peat was plentiful in Birsay and Harray, and free to the inhabitants. A social distinction in Sanday, no doubt reflected in the hearth types, was that the cottars used cow- and horse-dung to stretch out their supplies of Eday peat, whereas the larger tenants used coal. North Ronaldsay was in general worse off, for the bulk of the population could scarcely hope to pay for either peat or coal. In Westray, which at one time also supplied other islands, the mosses had failed, and Eday peat had to be got, at a cost of 2/6 per square fathom. The poorer people used peat only. Though coal was being imported from an earlier period to Kirkwall and Stromness, the Stromness fires still burned peat, either from the local moss, or, in the town, from the islands where better quality peat could be got. The better off families burned coal from Newcastle and Sunderland. Sandwick, having no moss providing coal-peat, had access by use and wont to the extensive mosses in Harray, 6 miles (9.7 km) from the centre of the parish. Peat getting was a lengthy process. The main fuel in Kirkwall was coal, though the poor used peat.[515]

26

The Orkney–Edinburgh Peat Trade

IN the 1840s, some cargoes of peat were sent from Eday to the Firth of Forth,[516] and for some years a considerable trade was carried on from other parts of Orkney too, providing summer work and extra income for the owners of the peat. The privilege of cutting peat for sale was given only to certain houses, and the quantity regulated by the size of rent of the farm or croft in Stenness. This was additional to what was needed for the household. The quantities were measured by the fathom or half-fathom on lands belonging to the Honeymans and Balfours, while Captain Halcro and others measured by tuskers. A tusker of peats was the amount a tuskerman could cut from sunrise to sunset. One astute Orkney man engaged three strong helpers to take turns on the same tusker throughout the day, and so succeeded in cutting double the normal quantity, legally, because only one peat-spade had been involved. This story is told against Captain Halcro, who was a hard landlord. Another name for the amount of peats cut by one man in a day, or 'the labour of one cottar for a day', was *daawurt*, a form of Old Scots *dawerk*, *dawark*, a day's work, *c*. 1420, which survives in other dialects as *darg*. In Evie, the tusker of peats measured 120 yds (109.7 m) by 2½ ft (76 cm) wide by two peat-depths amounting to about 16 in. (41 cm), totalling 40 cubic metres for a day's cutting.[517] Whereas a tusker or daawurt of peat was an amount of wet peat cut in the moss, a fathom was a measure of peat dried and stacked for shipment.

The size of the fathom varied considerably from place to place, as the table shows:

Peat Fathoms

Place	Dimensions	Bulk (cubic metres)	Horse-Loads	Cart-Loads	Source
Eday	12 ft long × 6 ft wide by 6 ft high (3.7 × 1.8×1.8 m)	12.2			NSA. 1845. xv. 1€
Orphir	Originally 6 ft (1.8 m) all round. Now 12×12×7 ft	6.1			OSA. 1797. xix. 4
	(3.7×3.7×2.1 m) high	28.5			,, ,, ,, ,,

Place	Dimensions	Bulk (cubic metres)	Horse-Loads	Cart-Loads	Source
Orphir	8×8×8 ft (2.4×2.4×2.4 m)	14.5 (fathom)			Johnston, 1907–8, I. 245
	8×8×4 ft (2.4×2.4×1.2 m)	7.2 (half-fathom)			,, ,, ,,
Stenness	16×16×16 ft	43.5			Leask, 1907–8, I. 1130
	(4.9×4.9×1.8 m)				
	8×8×4 ft (2.4×2.4×1.2 m)	7.2	42	14 (small) 6 (large)	,, ,, ,, ,,
Coubister, Orphir (incl. Cava)	8×4×5 ft (2.4×1.2×1.5 m) high	4.5			,, ,, ,, ,,
Greenigoe, Orphir	20×10×4 ft (6.1×3×1.2 m)	22.7	84	28	,, ,, ,, ,,
Veness	Idem	22.7			Johnston, 1907–8, I. 145
Flotta	24×12×4 ft (7.3×3.7×1.2 m)	32.6			Leask, 1907–8, I. 13(
Shetland, 1602	20×16×14 ft (6.1×4.9×4.3 m)	126.9			Shetland Rental 162? (in Leask)

The two Stenness measures were known as 'big fadoms' and 'peerie (small) fadoms', the big one, with its commercial emphasis, being bigger than any other measures used within Orkney. The 14.5 cubic metre Orphir fathom was the fathom of 'debt peats', for rent; the 7.2 cubic metre unit was the half fathom. In 1790 one Coubister fathom cost 3/– sterling at Veness and 6/– at Ireland in Sienness, which included the cost of boat transport from Veness to Ireland.[518]

Peats were sold in Ireland in Orkney at 9/– for a small fathom, and landed in Stromness at 12/–. A big fathom, proportionately, was worth £2.14/– or £3.12/– to the tenant. Since most loads sent to Stromness were sold by the small fathom, the sellers had boats of definite capacities, known as fathom or half-fathom boats. The peats were generally carted to the shore by night when it was cool. When landed they were stacked for measurement and shipment. As the stacks were loaded, much overnight replenishment of them went on by night illegally, so that sellers could often dispose of much more than the amount they were allowed to cut. Another way of increasing the output was by taking advantage of the fact that stacks were measured at the bottom without reference to the top. The *steethe* or base, therefore, was exact, but if it was, say, 16 ft (4.9 m) square, then the top might be built out to fully 18 ft (5.5 m) square. Such 'peat smuggling' was relatively easy, since the tenants had unlimited rights to cut peat for their own private use. Besides the shipments to the Forth, peat was also burned in large quantities in Stromness, before coal came into wide use. This meant that over a period of time large tracts of moss were cleared in Stenness, leaving no trace of their former existence.[519]

For a time the Edinburgh market was a valuable one, until coal became lower in price and more plentiful. Peat went even farther afield, however, for in 1893 the *Orkney Herald* reported:

'Ten tons of peats were shipped by the "Fawn" at Rousay on Monday by General Burroughs, and transhipped at Kirkwall yesterday for Australia.' These peats had a long journey, both in time and in space.

27

Peat Cutting in Orkney

WHEREAS the best, black peat or tusker peat was sold, the people themselves in the Stenness area burned the rough, turfy or sandy kinds, which had a
variety of names, such as *steeps* (perhaps cognate with Norwegian dialectal
styva, to pare off (turf)), *yarpha* (Norwegian dialectal *jørve*, Old Norse *jorfi*,
sand, gravel), *bracken-*, *sandy-*, *spade-* or *foggy* (mossy) *peats*, *greenheads*,
flaymeurs. Often too much turf was taken, leaving only a dead, unproductive
white clay. Where a moss was well organised, the top turfy layer, 6 to 18 in.
(15–46 cm) deep, was laid in the base of the peat bank during cutting, leaving a
surface well below the original one that could ultimately be reclaimed. The
removal of this top layer was called *flaying*, and the turf removed as
the flaymeur. Where the top turf was little over 3 in. (8 cm) deep and the

84. Peat cutting in Orkney, *c*. 1900.

undersurface too shallow for proper peat, the two layers were cut together with a *hack-spade*, for which reason it was said to be 'top an' boddam'. The steep was regarded as the best peat for burning, and was often sold.[520]

Flaying was the first operation in preparing a peat bank, when the cutting began in April. This was done with a *hack-spade*, *moor-spade*, or *flaighter*, with a broad blade about 8 in. (20 cm) across and a stout, straight handle about 4 ft (1.2 m) long. A wooden footstep called a *hack* (cf. Norwegian dialectal *hake*, a hook, spade) was fixed in the shaft a little way above the blade. The blade curves slightly forward in a smooth continuation of the thick, curving lower part of the shaft. A tool that could be used in conjunction with it is the *ritting knife*, with a long blade almost at right angles to the shaft, sharpened on the inside and pulled towards the user. It slit the moor a turf's width back from the edge of the bank, lengthwise and crossways, to ease the work of the turf space. The hack-spade could be used by itself to cut shallow, inferior hill peat, but a special

85. An Orkney tusker for peat, and a turf spade at Brettovale, 1960s.

tool was developed in Orkney for this purpose, probably in relatively recent times. It was called the *luggie* (the 'lugged' or eared spade) because of the short right-angled wing at the end of the broad rectangular blade. The luggie was also used for clearing the top turf from a peat bank.[521] Flaying or delling (delving) the bank to open it was the hardest job, a preliminary to cutting, which started about 1 May.

Peat cutting was done with a tusker which had a footstep, and a long wing up to 12 in. (30 cm) long on the blade. The length of the wing established the breadth of the peat. The iron blades of 'tuskardis' were mentioned in 1629 and a Stronsay inventory of 1734 recorded '2 sufficient tuskars',[522] showing that they were things of value. Cutting with the tusker was a man's job, whereas the women had the task of standing at the bottom of the bank, lifting the cut peat off the tusker, and flinging it on to the back of the bank to dry. With practice, they could make the peats land on their ends in tiers. Work began early in the morning, and after two or three hours there was a pause for breakfast from a pail of hot 'milk-gruel'. Dinner might include 'reestid mutton' and perhaps a bowl of brose made of oatmeal and fat skimmed off broth. Usually meat was kept for supper. The last peat of the day to be cut was called the supper-peat, a square block three or four times the ordinary size, taken out and set on end on top of the bank. Peat cutting was a job done by neighbours who helped each other in turn till all had their peats cut. Often six men would turn up with their

86. A ritting knife for scoring the turf to be cleared above peat. At Appiehouse, 1960s.

87. Drying peat in Orkney: 1. the first stage in raising; 2. heaped up in readiness for being taken home; 3. a herring-bone drying method used in bad weather. C5944.

moor-spades and tuskers, and cut the peat in the different ways demanded by its nature. Sandy peats on shallow soil simply could be dug up with a spade, its measurement being reckoned at 't'ree spade mooths'. This scalping of the moorland left great stretches bare and unproductive. Yarpha peat was also a spade-peat, with grass or heather on top, cut in a wedge shape. It was taken from the moor where there was no depth for cutting tusker peats. The grass-topped peats, called *pelloos* (from Norwegian dialectal *pela*, to pare turf with a spade), gave a clear light. Children learning their lessons by the firelight were advised to 'pick apae pelloo, an' pelloo'll low (glow)'.[523] The coal or tusker peats, however, formed the main fuel supply.

THE ORKNEY EXPRESS.

88. A cart load of peat in Orkney. Mr McGee guides the ox. Per J W Paterson, 1960.

After three or four days the peats were *casten oot*, laid out flat on the heather to dry. When dry enough on the upper side they were set up on end to lean against each other in twos or threes. This was *raising* the peats (cf. Faroese *reisa*, idem), and such a group was a raising, or in Birsay a *raiso* (Norwegian *reis*, Faroese *(torv-)reisa*, small stack of peats). When these were nearly dry, they were put into heaps called *roos* (Norwegian dialectal *rua*), *hobbles* (cf. Norwegian *hop*, Danish *hob*, a heap) or *bullins* (Old Norse *bolungr*, pile of logs, firewood). A roo is a small heap, and the diminutive hoblin is used for six or eight peats together. Before the final leading home, these could be made into bigger heaps called *bullins*. The expression 'to kase and bullan' peats, used by Patrick Fea in his Diary on 17 Sept. 1767, indicates that a *kes*, also used of heaps of fish and of seaweed, was also a smaller heap than a bullin.[524]

In good weather the final stage of making large heaps might be omitted, but it was necessary if there had been a wet spell, and in that case the peats were sometimes built into a dyke rather than a circular heap, often with courses of

89. A stack with horizontal peats, near Kirkwall. Per Miss H. Groundwater. C1530.

90. A stack with herring-bone peats, near Kirkwall. Per Miss H. Groundwater. C1530.

peats sloping alternately in herring-bone fashion. There were therefore up to six stages involved: clearing the top turf, casting, spreading, raising, heaping into small piles, and then into large piles or dykes. A major effort was also involved in getting them to a roadside for the final journey home.

When dry, the peats were taken home from the hill in *laids* (Old Scots *lade*, a load, 1375) on horseback or in carts. A laid was the amount one horse could carry, three to four laids being equivalent to a small cart load, and five *laids* to a large one.[525] The final stage was the building of the large stacks by the houses.

28

Peat in Shetland

THERE are few early references to peat in Shetland. In 1603 the parish of Dunrossness was required to lead to 'my Lord's' house at Soundbrughe 24 fathom of peats, 'of Zeitland fadomis'. Six neutral men were appointed to stent the parish for leading the peats. Since the Shetland fathom of that period appears to have contained 126.9 cubic metres, the laird was doing three or four times better out of his tenants than his fellow lairds in Orkney.[526] By 1683 peat was scarce in parts of Dunrossness, and the Skerries were getting peat from Whalsay and other islands. Though peat was plentiful in the Lambhoga peninsula in Fetlar, a lot of time and effort was involved in getting it, and several of the inhabitants found it easier to get supplies by sea from Yell.[527] In Mid and South Yell a tusker was one of the few essential items for a young couple setting up house on an outset. The mosses on the lower hills in Unst were exhausted by the 1790s, especially on the east side, except for the south-east corner of Muness. The hills of Vallafield and Saxavord had to be used, and some, especially the gentry about Baltasound, had to employ 10 to 20 horses for 6 weeks each year. Others brought peat by sea from Yell. Small quantities of Scottish and English coal were burned by the more prosperous inhabitants. In Northmavine, peat cutting was one of the men's jobs, and peat the only fuel. The peats were good in Walls and Sandness, except for Papa Stour where they were very sandy.[528]

In the mid nineteenth century, Sandsting and Aithsting had plenty of peat. In Northmavine there were two or three better class families using coal. All the farmers in Walls had the privilege of cutting peat fuel in the hill-ground, except for those in Papa Stour.[529] The fuel situation in Papa, in fact, had serious effects on the population. Many of the North House tenants had left by 1881, and there was no chance of getting Mainland tenants because of lack of peat. Many people had burned their chairs, and the turf on the hill dykes had been consumed. Alexander Fraser was to be allowed to use an empty house, and could get someone to cut peat for him in Papa Little. In Papa Stour generally peat had been cut for centuries in places where none should have been taken. The stage had come where no soil was left in the scattald. As soon as a little accumulated round a stone it was again taken for fuel. The worst affected places were North House and East Biggins, where the soil was all sand.[530] In Unst, the situation remained much as in the 1790s. Much time and labour was necessary to get peat from the hills of Vallafield and Saxavord, and 8 to 10 horses worked 5 or 6 weeks every summer to get a family's fuel. In the Lerwick area, a deep moss had been used up. In Bressay, Burra and Quarff, some coal was got from trading vessels, though the main fuel was peat.[531]

Since peat was so plentiful, except in a few areas, little thought was given to conserving the supplies. Some very reproving comments were made:

'The number of peats a man throws out in a short time is great, and the havock he makes, by the number of peat-holes he digs, it is truly distressing to notice. For the holes are never made above a few feet wide, that the digger may find no difficulty in throwing out the peats, separate from each other, to dry; and this is generally all on one side of the bank or hole, as the turf taken off the surface of the hole occupies the other side. The digger never goes deeper than the length of two peats, and the surface turf; and as the Shetlanders are not restricted to any particular part of the common, or to any particular length of the bank or hole, they seldom make them long.'[532]

In 1839, Christian Pløyen also noticed that peat cutting was badly managed, and that no care was taken to preserve the top layer of turf.[533] It appears, therefore, that the long, regular cuttings of the present day, with careful replacement of the top turf to make a new surface at the foot of the bank, is a relatively recent phenomenon, coinciding in part with the recommendations of the Crofters' Commission Report of 1884. This said that a township with insufficient peat within its own boundaries should have the right to cut peat on adjacent land occupied by the same proprietor, without payment, but with due provision for the service of the lands on which the privilege was exercised, and the enforcement of proper regulations for preserving the surface. The restriction of the practice of cutting sods for roofing was also recommended. One of the Articles, Regulations, and Conditions of Lease between the proprietor of the lands of Garth and Annsbrae and his tenants was that 'all tenants are bound in future to cast such peats as may be allotted, in a regular manner, and to lay down the turf in neat and regular order without potting, and to the satisfaction of any one duly appointed by the proprietor'.[534]

The Faroe Islands were having similar problems in the late eighteenth century. There was much wastage of peat through bad management, though good householders would take care to place the turf in the bottom of the bank, and leave a drainage channel at the same time. At this period an effort was made to introduce the Shetland tusker, which was able to cut twice as fast as the Faroese spade or *haki* because of the wing on the blade. It seems to have had some influence, since there was a later type of peat-spade, *torvskeri*, in the Faroes, with a short wing but without the foot-step shown in Svabo's illustration.[535] Before electricity largely ended peat cutting in the Faroes, the cultivating spade and peat-spade with a wing were used like the moor-spades and tuskers of the Northern Isles, one to strip the turf and one to cut the peat.

There was little change in Shetland by the twentieth century. Fair Isle had enough peats, though a large area had been scalped. The tusker was used in the heavy bluish type of peat, but in coarser banks the ordinary delling spade was preferred. The peat at Everland in Fetlar was sulphury and unpleasant to burn, so the main supply came from Lambhoga. Whalsay was not too well off for peats, and those at Skaw were the perquisite of the people in the Out Skerries. Even in the 1930s, however, coal was only being used by the laird, the minister, and the factor for Messrs. Hay & Co. The southern part of Dunrossness was supplied with peat from the Ward of Scousburgh, the Hillwell area getting its peat from near the top of Fitful Head. Wire ropes and cages were often the means of getting the peats down from the hills to loading points for vehicles. The men of Havera had a right to take peat from the Hill of Deepdale on the Mainland opposite, before the island was abandoned in 1923. By the 1950s, the Out Skerries no longer cut peat on Whalsay.[536] Now, coal, electricity and other fuels are making the crofts independent, though they must be paid for in cash. In the 1960s, for example, £1500 to £2000 went out of Fetlar each year for coal.

Harvesting the Peat

Peat casting began in May after the township dykes had been repaired, when most of the seed had been sown. The removal of the top turf was known as flaying the muir, or *ripping*. A moor-spade, much smaller than the Orkney type and like a delving spade without a footstep, was used sideways to make one or more slits in the moor parallel to the edge of the bank, or in more recent times a *ripper* like the Orkney ritting knife was used. The slits were about 6 in. (15 cm) deep and up to 2 ft (61 cm) apart, though less was usual. The turf was stripped off along the top of the bank, one man thrusting a moor-spade underneath, and another cutting each turf across with a spade. Sometimes a woman did the latter job. When it was clear, both workers jabbed their spades into the turf, and slung it into the base or *greff* (Norwegian dialectal *grov*, Old Norse *grøf*, a pit), grassy side up. If the greff was damp, the turf was laid carefully to serve as a drying place for the bottom or *third peat*, if the bank happened to be three peats deep. Pride was taken in getting the top surface of the peat as smooth and level as possible when the turf was being removed.

It sometimes happened that a depth of earthy moor still remained above the good peat, and a second layer had to be removed. This was known as *taking a poning*, and the slabs of earthy peat were used for building around stacks of peat left on the moor during the winter. Any wet, oversized, misshapen and *taaie* (cf. Old Norse *tág*, Norwegian dialectal *tag*, root, fibre) peats, full of roots, cut during the cleaning of the bank, were known as *skyumpacks*, *skyumpies* (cf. Danish dialectal *skumpe*, top turf) or sometimes *corner peats* because their shape was good for building up the corners of peat stacks. They were also used to even up sloping ground on which peats were to be dried.

The heaviest job of all was cleaning *undermoss*, when new banks were being opened in an old, deep moss from which two or three depths of peat had already been removed. To get down to the fresh peat, a square garden spade was used. This process was *skooming* (Norwegian dialectal *skum*, Icelandic, Faroese

91. A Shetland tusker at work. No assistant is required. 3.37.27.

skúm, scum) *the bank*, and during such work an old clay pipe or horn spoon left by previous peat casters sometimes came to light.

Work with the tusker could begin when the bank had been opened on top and the outer edges cleaned down. If the peat was tough a foot-step or *heel* might be added to the shaft, and the peats were then *delled* out, as if with a spade, but the normal Shetland tusker does not have this feature. Working with arm power alone was *running the peat*. A leather palm like that used by saddlers was worn on the left hand for protection, if much casting was being done. The thickness of the peat was determined by the width of the tusker blade, and its width by the length of the wing, which is about 7 in. (18 cm) long, and angled slightly downward. The lower part of the tusker shaft was flat to hold the peat as it was being cut and then slung on to the bank for drying. Shetland peat casters are unique in Scotland in not requiring an assistant to take the peat off the spade as they work. The average size of a Shetland peat is about 14 in. (36 cm) long by 7 in. (18 cm) broad by $2\frac{1}{2}$ in. (6 cm) thick. Seven or eight peats were generally cut from the outside to the inside of the bank, a width which was known as the

RITTING

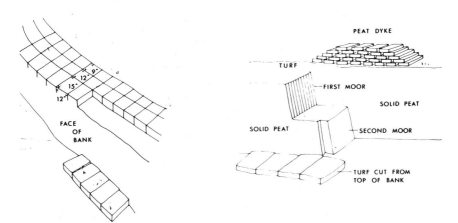

72. Stages of peat-casting in Shetland.

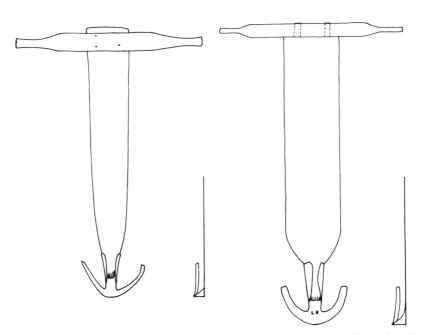

93. A type of turf-spade used in the south of Shetland. The usual moor-spade is more like a delling-spade. C2445.

ootburk, *ootburd* (Old Norse *útburðr*, a bearing out, *útborg*, outworks) or *shoard* (? cf. Norwegian *skorda*, Old Norse *skorða*, a prop). Ootburk, ootburd are also applied to the number of peats cut out of one row of the bank and spread to dry.

Tusker blades were made by the smith in four stages. A blank of mild steel was cut, about 1 ft (30 cm) long by 2 in. (5 cm) wide, with an offset tang at one end. The blank was heated, and the tang bent nearly at right angles, to form the wing. Next the body was beaten out, leaving a constricted neck at the junction of the blade and the socket. At this stage the piece, including the wing, was completely flat. Then the socket flanges were turned back, the wing brought forward at right angles to the blade, and the slight feather at the other side of the blade turned up in a rounded curve. Most blades were made by local smiths, though they could also be bought commercially from spade-making firms like Black of Berwick-on-Tweed.

The moor was three peats deep, or four in well drained conditions. The peats from the first moor were laid at the back of the bank, usually in the form of a dyke with gaps between the individual peats. Those from the next row down, the second moor, were built on the face, and the third moor peats at the bottom of the bank. If there was a fourth moor, a second dyke was built in the greff. Where the first moor was tough and full of roots, the caster often spread them flat in regular lines at the back of the bank, and it was only with the second moor that the dyking started. The laid out peats were known as the *outlay*.[537] The dykes themselves could take three main forms, *kessed*, *stepped up*, and *holed*. Kessed dykes were built of vertical rows of peat, one immediately above the other, each complete row being a kess. Holed dykes had a space between each peat, and in stepped up dykes the peats were built like bricks, end over middle, with no air spaces. The peats always lay at a slight angle to the face of the bank, in the way they fell naturally from the tusker. Often the dykes were completed by setting peats on top at a zig-zag angle, shoulder to shoulder. It was thought that peats were better to be dyked than to be laid out, since the weight helped to squeeze the water out of them. There was, as always, a good deal of rivalry in building good dykes, but though the holed and stepped up dykes looked best, the kessed dyke was more practical, since during raising the whole kess could be rolled out at once by the womenfolk, whereas the peats in the other types of dykes had to be individually handled.

Raising took place after two or three weeks. A good-sized *horse peat* was set on its side, and four peats leaned on their ends against it, two at each side. Another, the *craa* (crow) *peat*, was laid on top at a sloping angle to run the water. In some areas long peats were sometimes laid two by two on top of each other, like headers and stretchers in brickwork. This arrangement was called a *minister*. In two or three weeks more, two to four of the raisings or *races* (cf. Orkney (Birsay) *raiso*) were made into one, a process called *turning the peats*. This might be the final stage before the peats were taken home, but in wet seasons they might first be built into small, round stacks, *roogs* (Norwegian *ruga*, Old Norse *hrúga*, a heap, to heap up), built around with turf peats for protection, and left all winter. Piles of peat were also called *bullins* as in Orkney, or *bols*.

If the moor was properly prepared, a good workman might cast enough in three days to keep a fire going for a year. Nine or ten men working together could easily do this in one day. Until the early 1800s, the day for casting peats was a kind of festival. Thirty or forty men would be invited to cut peats, and in return were well and hospitably entertained by whichever family was having its peat cut. This was done in turn, so that the whole peat-casting season passed with a mixture of hard work and entertainment.[538] Another community activity was the allocation of the peat bank. The people of Noss near Spiggie Loch in Dunrossness gathered at the Mires peats, where the bank was paced out carefully into four equal parts, the cut peats being spread as evenly as possible. Four peats were taken as counters, and the figures I to IV carved in them. The same figures were carved in the four sections of the bank. The peats were laid with the figures down, and someone chose one for each croft.[539]

The transporting or flitting of peats took place about July, by the same methods as in Orkney. In Fetlar the work began at 2 o'clock in the morning, and five to seven laids, each involving a double journey, were carried in a single spell of work. Women acted as *uplayers* at the bank, filling the baskets or kishies ready for transport. To make a kishie hold more, big fibrous peats were set around the edge to extend the rim, and the space within filled with loose clods of peat. At one time, when there were enough people in the island for each household to do its own flitting, nearly all the peats were carried by sea. As the population dropped, sea transport declined in favour of ponies and families started coming together more in work groups. It was only in the early 1900s that flitting with ponies came into fashion in the townships of Tresta and Houbie.

For sea transport, the peats were taken to the loading places in Lambhoga and stacked above them. They were carried on the back down to the boat in big peat kishies with two carrying bands, so that a man going up with an empty kishie would meet his fellow at the half-way mark, turn round, and take the full one on his back. This halved the amount of climbing involved. There were people to fill the kishies at the stacks, and at the boat a *lifter on* passed the emptied out peats to the men loading the boat. The last kishies were set in without being emptied and the extra helpers and the crew sat on them when the boat was under sail. The peats were built carefully at the aft end to prevent people and kishies from falling off. At the Geo of Moowick, where there was a shingly beach, the boats were taken into *noosts* (Norwegian dialectal *naust(r)*, *nøst*, Old Norse *naust*, boat-shed dock), hollows from which the shingle had been shovelled out. Both sides were built up with large, flat stones. The preparation of the noosts each year, before peat flitting began, was hard work, for winter seas had filled them up with stones.

At the home beaches the boat came alongside a wooden *tress* (Old Scots *trest*, c. 1450, Old French *trest*, *trast*, Latin *transtrum*, a cross-beam), or jetty, and the peat flitters had a meal before off-loading. Each family had a place for their

94. Filling kishies at Lambhoga, Fetlar. 2.9.25.

95. Loading the kishies on to the backs of ponies at Lambhoga, Fetlar. 3.44.27.

96. A loaded pony, with large peats in the maishie alone. The horns of the clibber serve as anchors. 1.50.8A.

97. Loaded kishies on the outskirts of Lerwick. The woman wears rivlins. 3.43.9.

roog on the beach, and the peats were taken home from there on pony-back or in carts by those who had them. The last stage was to build the big stacks at the houses. They were rectangular, with rounded corners built up with wedge-shaped skyumpies, and drawn in towards the top, which was often thatched with flat slabs of turf. It was a combined effort, with some workers doing the careful work of building the outer courses, and others filling up the heart. A ladder or *peat-trap* (Old Scots *trap*, flight of steps, *c.* 1540, Dutch *trap*, Middle Dutch *trappe*, step) was used for the higher stages. There was, therefore, much more work involved in sea transport. With ponies, the full kishies had one journey. With boats, they had two journeys on the backs of ponies, and two on the human back. This greater effort, needing more manpower, was responsible for the decline of boat transport, which finally ended in the 1940s. Flitting with ponies was last done in 1956 by Tommy Thomason of Velzie.

In some mosses, peat barrows could be used, either with a flat base and a sloping front-board over the wheel, or with side-frames and a base made of spars with spaces between. Sledges with runners and a body of spar frames were used near Bigton in the South Mainland. Here and there aerial wires were used, for example in parts of Unst, but transport on pony-back or by sea were the chief methods, with carts in a few places, for example on level parts on the estate of John Bruce in Dunrossness where small carts had been introduced for peat,[540] in the days before motorised transport. A combination of methods might be necessary, depending on local circumstances.

29

The Peat Houses of Fetlar

WHEN peat casting was in progress in Fetlar, the men usually travelled to Lambhoga and back each day, but during flitting, workers of both sexes lived in seasonally occupied dwellings, called 'peat-hooses', amongst the peat banks. They are said to have come into fashion about 1860, and before that the only form of shelter was an old sail spread over the flitters. Probably the idea was got from the lodges of equivalent size used by fishermen during the fishing season. The peat houses noted in the 1960s were:

1. The Barn, an old croft at Moowick of which parts were used as peat houses by William Garriock and William Laurence Brown, of Funzie.
2. South Tolgans, 'Johnny Mouat's hoose', still roofed and capable of being used. John Mouat, Houbie.
3. Lower Tolgans. Robert John Jamieson, Baela.
4. Mid Tolgans. William Park.
5. Nort' Hoose o' Tolgans. Andrew Brown, Funzie.
6. Crü o' Helliersness, a croft till 1830, used jointly by Laurence Robertson, Henry Anderson, and Laurence Bain, all of Tresta. Such a shared building was a 'haavers'hoose'.
7. Lower Hoose of Helliersness. Daniel Brown.
8. East Hoose of Helliersness. Robert Scollay, Tresta.
9. Mid Hoose, Helliersness. Thomas Peterson, Tresta.
10. Nort' Hoose, Helliersness. Built for the West Manse minister, the Rev. Jas. A. Campbell, who hired people to flit his peats.
11. Tresta Hoose, Helliersness, used jointly by Davie Anderson, North Dale, and John Robertson, Tansy Knowes.
12. Nort' Hoose, Gilles Field. James Petrie and William Gardner.
13. Hoose o' Heoga Neep. James Coutts, Houbie.

Some of these, when surveyed, had the walls, and to a lesser extent the roofs, still intact (nos. 1, 2, 6, 11). The rest were represented by turf foundations, and most were partially sunk into the side of a peat bank so that the lower course of the walls was of solid peat. The smaller houses had the fire in the corner opposite the door (no. 12), the hearth being made of large stones carefully set to provide a back and prevent the walls from catching fire. The bigger houses had fireplaces in the centre of the gable wall, and the Tresta Hoose even had a

98. The Tresta peat-hoose in Helliersness, Lambhoga, Fetlar, built of stone, wood, turf, and corrugated iron. 1963.

99. The late Willie Garriock and Liza Bruce in the peat-hoose at the Barn, Lambhoga, *c.* 1920–30. Per T. Garriock. 1.48.6.

100. The fire in the Nort Hoose, Gilles Field, Fetlar. The back stones are necessary to protect the turf walls.

'chimney' recessed into a stone-built gable wall. In the Barn and in Johnny Mouat's Hoose, the fireplace was built out into the room, with built-up stone sides whose tops form level binks. The chimneys were wooden canopies nailed to the rafters and pinned to the wall, called *happers* because they resembled the hopper of a mill. In the Barn, this was originally topped by a half barrel. The smaller houses had chimney tops built of turf, and turf could be added on the windward side as required to 'skyle da lum' and improve the draught. An iron back or cross-baak driven into the stonework of the gable or laid across two stones supported the crook and the links for the pot and kettle.

There were benches along the walls, a table, and such crockery as was required. The feature common to all was the plank-covered bed-space that occupied at least half the space at one end of the house. Wooden posts or a burbank of turf supported the planks at a height of about 2 ft (61 cm), the space below acting as a store for equipment. On the first trip to Lambhoga at the start of the flitting, straw was carried in bags to be spread on the planks. Heather could also be used. This was covered with sacking, then a sheet, blankets, and a patchwork quilt made of two sewn together.

Just as the canopy chimneys carried on the obsolescent tradition of widdy-funnels in the main dwelling houses, so also did the form of door reflect earlier traditions. The hinges were of wood, consisting of uprights called *charl-pins* (cf. Old Norse *hjarri*, hinge) on the jambs, and cross-pieces called *harrs* (Old Scots *herre*, 1456, Old Norse *hjarri*, hinge) on the doors. Openings at the ends of the harrs slotted into pins on the uprights, with leather washers to minimise wear. The wooden latch on the inside of the door could be lifted by a length of string

brought through a small hole in the door. The walls also incorporated obsolescent features. The Barn and the Crü of Helliersness had stone walls with turf
gable tops. The Tresta Hoose had one stone gable, and the other walls were
partly of wood, partly of turf. Johnny Mouat's Hoose was of turf. The roofs
were simply made of a ridge-pole, six to nine pairs of couples, overlying
oveyboards, and turf thatch. As a rule an old sail was tied across the roof above
the bed-space to keep off rain when the house was being slept in. Sometimes a
sail laid over the rigging-trees and pegged down at the sides was all the cover a
house would get. The Tresta Hoose and Johnny Mouat's Hoose were roofed
with corrugated iron latterly.

There was a holiday feeling about life in the peat houses. Boys liked to play
pranks by mixing up the pony harness when their elders were asleep, and might
drink milk set outside in bottles in a cold moor-hole to prevent souring. Doors
were blocked so that folk could not get out, and chimney openings blocked to
smoke the inhabitants. Any good-looking girls were sure of visitors, whether
they wanted them or not.

Fires were started with a flint and steel and tinder, but when one was alight,
neighbours would get theirs going by taking a glowing peat in a pair of tongs.
This custom led to a fire in Lambhoga about 1909, between South Tolgans and
the recent dyke that runs from Moowick over Gilles Field to the Klifts, as a
result of which bare patches of ground still remain. A dropped fragment of a
glowing peat set the heather on fire overnight – fortunately near the end of
flitting time so that not much of the peat harvest was lost – and by morning it
was too firmly established to put out. The local press headlined the 'Great Fire
in Fetlar', which lasted till the rain and snow of winter mastered it. Though the
Laird made enquiries about how it started, there was no one who could tell.

Food supplies were easily got by people flitting home with ponies, but those
flitting for the boats stayed for up to a week. A bag of meal, an iron girdle,
potatoes, salt fish, tea, and a fishing rod for catching fresh coalfish from the
rocks, kept them going. Borrowing or exchanging could sometimes be arranged
in an oblique way:

'I might have to affbend (unharness) da mares and geng hame for breid?'
'Na lamb, du needna do dat, we can gi'e dee what'll keep dee gaan ta
Saturday, only we wid like a boil o' fresh piltocks (coalfish) if du can faa
(spare) dat sam.'

When all the peats had been loaded, and the group was ready to leave, the
straw or heather was cleared off the bed-space and piled up outside. More
heather was pulled till there was a good-sized heap, and then a bonfire was
made. This was something the youngsters looked forward to greatly, and the
smoke told the people in the townships that the flitting season was over, and the
flitters would soon be home.[541]

30

Peat Charcoal

IN spite of a suggestion that there was coal in Fetlar and Unst,[542] smiths had to work their iron with peat charcoal in earlier times. This was made from well-dried peat, of medium density, with no intermixture of earth. A *pot* measuring 6 ft (1.8 m) in diameter by 14 in. (36 cm) deep was dug in dry ground, and a layer of peats on their ends was placed in the bottom. About six peats were removed from the centre and burning ones put in their place, but if the wind was strong the space for the fire was opened about 9 in. (23 cm) nearer the lee side. As the first layer of peats was kindled, more peats were gradually applied, irregularly, within the circle, till they were piled in a cone-shaped heap. The heap was allowed to burn for an average of two to two and a half hours in moderate weather. When the whole mass had been completely ignited and the flame had largely ceased, the pile was covered with turf and earth and allowed to cool. The charred peat was used by smiths, and after coal became available, it was often mixed with it, since the mixture was considered better than coal itself.[543]

Peat charcoal could also be prepared indoors. According to a letter written by Thomas Irvine to the Editor of *The Northern Ensign* on 29 March 1873, 'the whole fuel used in Blacksmiths' Smithies in former days in this country was Chared Peat or Peat charcoal, which gave a superior temper to Scythes and other edge-tools. The mode of preparing the Chared Peat was to set on a large fire in the fire-place of the house (not in the Open air) and as the Peats became thoroughly red they were put into an iron Pot or Kettle or a pit dug for the purpose (but the first was preferred) and very closely covered till needed for use'.[544]

There is little doubt that a good deal of peat was used up in the making of charcoal in these treeless islands. In Caithness the crofter or farmer supplied the fuel as well as the iron to the smith. Iron was a valuable commodity, and when the American ship, the *Lincoln*, was wrecked at Skirza Head, her iron bolts were eagerly taken. The name 'coal' was given here to the glowing peat after all the black had been burned away. In some districts, a special peat-bank was cut every year for 'coal' for the smith. Such peats were black and oily, and the 'coals' resembled coke. In the West of Scotland, a stone-lined pit about 2 ft (61 cm) in diameter, with a perforated stone covering, was filled with pre-fired peats to make charcoal for the smiths in Jura.[545] In North Uist smithy charcoal

was made till about 1909–10 in pits 8 ft long by 3 ft wide by 3 ft deep
(2.4 m × 91 cm × 91 cm). This is one of the many essential small industries of
such areas, about which very little information survives. Peat was a surrogate
for wood, in treeless lands, without which the cutting edges of scythes and other
sharp-edged tools could not be properly tempered.

Back Transport, Harness and Straw Working

31

Horses and Ponies

Shetland Ponies

IN Shetland, ponies were kept for riding, or for carrying loads on their backs, but rarely before the present century for pulling carts or ploughs. They were 'Little Nagges', unshod, and 'will clime the rockes and cragges like so manie dogs'. Their hardiness and small size were early recognised. Few exceeded nine hands in height, though the gentry had big riding horses brought from Caithness or Orkney. Like the numerous small horses of Iceland, the majority were never housed, and when wanted for work they had to be rounded up from the common grazings. Unst in particular had many horses, but there were relatively few in Fetlar, where there was not much pasture. The best ones were in Sandsting and Aithsting, and they were also good in Walls and Yell, but the smallest were those in Unst and the northern parts of Yell. Black was thought to be the colour of the hardiest ones, pied horses not so good.[546]

Shetland ponies were called *shelties*, a name which probably developed outside Shetland, because of the trading in horses that went on. It was first recorded in 1633, but must be much older, since already by the 1680s it was possible to speak tautologically of a 'ʒetland shalte'. The simplest derivation is from Norwegian *hiellte*, an adjective describing someone or something from Shetland, as in 'hiellte skiilinge' (Shetland shillings). Hjeltefjorden, the 'Shetland fjord' near Bergen, *hjeltespirer*, 'Shetland spars or planks', and *Jæltebaade*, 'Shetland boats'.[547] If the name was first used within Shetland, it might have been to distinguish the native animals from the 'Norway' mares and horses that are occasionally mentioned, perhaps imported from Scandinavia. A 'Norway' mare was sold in 1731 for £75 Scots, a high price when compared with 4 horses in the same sale that fetched £36 Scots among them. The Rev. John Mill nearly lost a fine horse of the Norway breed in a marsh in 1778. Horses were still being brought in from Norway in the early nineteenth century, and in 1888 Mr Mouat of Garth had a 'valuable Norwegian stallion, and several pretty breeding mares' in Unst.[548]

It was said in the mid-eighteenth century that ponies were kept chiefly for carrying seaweed for manure. The Shetlanders found a means of supplementing their incomes when the Dutch fishermen crowded into Bressay Sound at the time of the Johnsmas Fair, and came ashore to buy stockings, and indulge in racing each other on the backs of little ponies hired for the purpose. Riding seems to have been their major function throughout the year. Though so small that a strong man could lift them 'yet they will carry him and a woman behind him 8 miles forward and as many back'. They had a life span of up to 30 years and could make riding horses for 24 of these, especially if not spoiled by being put to work before 4 years old.[549] The carrying of peat on the backs of mares is not mentioned until later, and this, in conjunction with the Fetlar evidence that peat flitting on pony-back went with a decline in population and the cessation of sea transport, may indicate that there was not such a widespread use of ponies for peat before the late 1700s.

In the 1790s, it was reported from Delting that the innumerable horses were small, and getting smaller, presumably a result of overgrazing. Their hardiness was no doubt due to a process of natural selection, for in winter they were often hard put to it to get enough fodder in the hills, and came down to the shore to eat seaweed. They had generally recovered their full strength by St John's Mass-Day, 24 June, which meant that they were in good heart for the peat flitting period. Unst had 1000 shelties. Sandsting and Aithsting had 800, used for carrying peat and turf and for riding to church. Many were sold each year in Dunrossness to Orkneymen, and to merchants in Lerwick who sent them to Leith, London, Hull, Holland, and elsewhere. They fetched £12 to £36 Scots, or £1 to £3 sterling. The horses of Walls and Sandness were also sold to Orkney men, who came with linen. Fair Isle was supplied with horses from Shetland. Tingwall had a stock of 600 to 700, used for carrying manure from the dunghill, each animal with a person to lead it.[550]

In the 1800s the ponies still went unshod and unattended in herds on the commons, being used seasonally for carrying peat, and measuring 9 to 11 hands high, or an average of 38 in. (97 cm). Many were kept in Sandsting and Aithsting, but little work was done by them. People preferred to carry peat on their own backs, though the ponies would carry turf from the hills for making compost middens. Sales to Orkney had largely died out by mid-century, though they were still exported to Scotland and England. At this time, there was less direct communication between Orkney and Shetland than between Shetland and other parts of Britain. Twenty horses were sold for £50 in 1845 in Mid and South Yell, probably at a May or November sale. The size of the Unst ponies was still decreasing, because the best were exported. Large numbers were kept, however, because each family required eight to ten horses for five or six weeks each summer to get their peat home from the hills.[551] As in Fetlar, the use of ponies for this purpose was dictated by the factor of distance.

About this period, the popularity of Shetland ponies in the outside world helped to bring about an awareness of the need to keep up the breed. Norwegian pony stallions were introduced to Dunrossness, leading to the Sumburgh breed, which ranged in size from 12 to 13.2 hands (1.2 to 1.3 m). A grey Arab stallion was introduced to Fetlar about 1837, giving rise to ponies averaging 11 to 13 hands (1.1 to 1.3 m), said to be 'remarkably handsome, swift, spirited but less tractable than the pure Shetland.' Eventually the prestige breeding of Shetland ponies became an established fact. The *Shetland Pony Stud Book* was published in 1891, and several Shetland pony stud farms were set up, like that of the Marquis of Londonderry in Bressay and Noss, in 1870–99. As a Northumberland pit-owner, he needed a good supply of small ponies to pull the coal wagons in his mines. By keeping his stallions on Noss and his mares on Bressay he was able to control breeding probably for the first time in Shetland. In the twentieth century, studs have also been established abroad.[552]

About 1814, it was estimated or rather guessed that there were ten to twelve thousand horses in Shetland. Department of Agriculture returns from 1870 show a much smaller number:

1870	4851		1910	5742
1880	5395		1920	4587
1890	4803		1930	1952
1900	5898		1936	1649[553]

The increase in the later nineteenth century was probably due to the demand for Shetland ponies in mines and for private purposes; the huge decline in the 1920–30 period reflects changing agricultural needs, with more emphasis on grazing.

HORSES IN ORKNEY

The Orkney pattern was more mixed than in Shetland. The Shetland ponies imported to Orkney were used for carrying seaweed and manure, or for pulling the plough, an activity that was almost totally new to them. The Shetland ponies were mostly kept by small cottagers. From the mid-eighteenth century, however, the majority of the horses came from Caithness, Strathnaver, and Ross-shire. There was a lively trade across the Pentland Firth that took £1200 to £1300 out of the Orkney farmers' purses in the 1770s, prices per horse ranging from £3 to £12.12/– at the Lammas Market in Kirkwall, depending on size and age. One- and two-year old horses were bought and broken in to the plough, and then sold back to Caithness at four to five years old for an equivalent price, or less if they were older.[554]

Orkney farmers did not seem interested in breeding their own horses till later in the eighteenth century. About 1750, nearly 2000 horses were brought in each year. By the 1770s the numbers were declining, till they reached the hundreds around 1800. Part of the prejudice against breeding may have been a dislike of mares, which the farmers would neither keep nor ride, and 'the names they gave them were those of contempt', but though they showed little skill in the matter at first, paying little attention to housing, cleaning, and feeding,[555] they succeeded well enough in the end.

The system of dealing was well developed. In Caithness, the year-old colts, called *staigs* – or *rüls* (Norwegian dialectal *ruvel*, a rough-haired shaggy little creature) in the Northern Isles – were sold about 1770 for 15/– to 30/– each to dealers who exported them to Orkney in August, bringing back in their place cargoes of 4- to 7-year-old garrons. These were sold at fairs for £3 to £5 each as plough horses. By 1812 fewer horses were being reared in Northern Scotland, and prices had risen. Colts cost 50/- to £4, and Orkney garrons fetched £10 to £15 sterling. About 1800, 320 staigs were exported and 80 old horses brought back. By 1812, the number sold to Orkney had fallen to about 250 or 300 a year. The crossing was made from Skarfskerry and Huna in Caithness, in ferry boats, whose usual route was past Stroma to Burwick in South Ronaldsay, thence to the Orkney mainland by way of Watersound and Holmsound. In 1776 one of the boats capsized in the Pentland Firth, with five of a crew, two horse merchants, two women passengers, and 37 horses aboard.[556] Another landing place was Langaber at the Head of Banks in Orphir.

Dealing in horses could be risky, not only because of the wild seas and strong currents of the Pentland Firth, but also because the horses themselves could be wild. One dealer, William Leask of Aglath, died in 1813 from injuries inflicted by a Caithness stallion. The horses were handled in droves, like flocks of sheep, and known horse dealers and others built their peat-stacks in circles to serve as pens when horses were being caught for delivery to purchasers. Orkney men had a test for a horse by pulling its tail. If it backed it was considered good, and a bad one if it went forward. A few horses sold by Orphir farmers to Caithness people at the Kirkwall Lammas market in the 1840s more or less marked the end of this story.[557]

Horses were kept in Orkney in considerable numbers, and were stabled, unlike in Shetland. It was calculated that there were 9000 in Orkney in 1798, and the need for transporting seaweed for kelp was a strong factor in maintaining numbers. Large numbers of horses characterised the Northern Isles, and in areas like North Ronaldsay the common pasture was so overstocked that the dung of the horses was composed half of sand. An estimate for 1805 gave a figure of about 25,000 horses. Much of their work was seasonal, but then they were needed in quantity. The plough too required a team of three or four horses and individual farmers kept a team for each plough they had. This meant nine horses for three ploughs in Birsay, for example.[558] The steelbow goods of the farm of North Strynzie in Stronsay included 19 horses in 1734, each of which had its own name:

1 black horse, 9 year old called Marwick	£19.10/-
1 gray horse called Spanie	£ 7.19/-
1 brown horse called Gorbister	£14.10/-
1 black horse called Wilson, aged 5	£24.10/-
1 brown horse called Baikie	£18. 3. 4
1 brown horse called flettie	£17.13. 4
1 black horse called Yorston, aged 8	£16. 3. 4
1 gray horse, aged 11	£15.18/-
1 black horse called Clouston, aged 7	£23. 0. 1
1 black horse called Luggie	£ 8.18/-

1 horse called Sinclair	£17.13. 5
1 starne red horse, aged 10	£14. 6. 8
1 horse called fidler	£18. 3. 4
1 shaltie	£11. 1. 0
5 old horses	£12.10/–
	£240. 0. 4 Scots[559]

By the end of the eighteenth century, these small horses were beginning to be replaced, at first sporadically, by bigger animals, as improved plough types were adopted, and then generally, as the mid-nineteenth century agricultural improvements went on, and new steadings that included adequate stables were built. Active opposition to the breeding of bigger horses was not unknown, however. In 1808, Mr Draver of Stove in Sanday lost several brood mares when someone ripped them with a sharp instrument by night. In the same year there were two brood mares with two thriving foals in the enclosures of Papa Westray. Mr Spens at Flaws had several good horses, and 'a capital brood mare of the draught kind'. Vestiges of prejudice against new breeds remained for long, and are implicit in the story of George Allan who bought heavy Clydesdales from Aberdeen to reclaim Heathhouse in Stenness. The work was too much for them, and they fell dead in the furrows. He then bought some of the old Orkney breed and succeeded with them.[560]

By the 1840s, Stronsay had 110 large horses, and 189 small ones, no doubt marking a difference between big and small farmers. Cross and Burness had some draught horses 14 to 15 hands (1.4 to 1.5 m) high. In the ploughs, the team of four small horses had been largely replaced by two bigger ones, a change also hastened by a tax on horses applied during the French Wars. Better horses were listed among the main improvements in Sandwick. Native garrons were crossed with Clydesdales and other heavy horses to produce a heavier, stronger breed, standing about 12 to 14½ hands (1.2 to 1.5 m) high, though the effect of crossing them with Clydesdales was to cross them out altogether. Few horses were being imported by this date, and there was a rapid decline in numbers during the period 1830–1860.[561]

HORSES IN THE COMMUNITY

When the horses ran wild in herds on the common grazings, regulations relating to them as part of the community's resources were essential. In 1612 there was made in Shetland an 'act for ryding uther mens horssis and stouing of their taillis', and in 1615, in Orkney as well, another act 'Anent the ryderis of uther menis horss and cutting of the taillis thairof'.[562] Horsehair was a valuable commodity, used to make ropes, fishing lines, bird snares, and in nineteenth-century stables in Orkney, for example at Appiehouse, there were wall recesses for storing it till there was enough to make traces. To *stoo* (Old Norse *stúfr*, stump, *stýfa*, to cut off) or *roo* (Norwegian dialectal *rua*, Icelandic *ryja*, pluck) the tails or manes of other people's horses was punishable by a fine. The illicit riding of ponies, however, left no detectable evidence and was evidently common. Sir Walter Scott observed in *The Pirate* that anyone who wanted a pony caught one, put on a halter or *grimek* (Norwegian *grime*, Faroese *gríma*, halter), rode to his destination and left the pony to find its way home as best it could. No doubt this was a recognised and general convenience, but sometimes such casually appropriated ponies were cruelly treated and ridden to death, and one was cut on the back with a spade 'whereby she is like to perish'.[563]

Legislation was necessary, for the ponies were not ownerless. Though they ran in common herds, they had individual marks of ownership such as the *gatskord* (Norwegian dialectal, Old Norse *gat*, hole + *skor*, notch, incision, Norwegian dialectal *skard*, Old Norse *skarð*, notch), described as a 'mark upon a horse, a circular piece cut out of the centre of the ear and slit to the point'. Cutting or stooing the ears, therefore, was a means of concealing the ownership mark on a stolen horse. The fact that a two-year-old horse was described as unmarked in 1604 implies that this was the exception rather than the rule. Sir Walter Scott noted that there was 'a right of individual property in all these animals, which are branded or tattooed by each owner with his own peculiar mark'. Not only did every pony have an owner, but sometimes also more than one. Just as there were part shares in boats, plantiecrues, cattle, and so on, so also were there half-shares in horses. Teamwork was also required to catch the horses, by driving them into enclosures like the Shetland *hestensgot* (Norwegian *hest*, Old Norse *hestr*, horse, stallion; Norwegian dialectal *hestegard*, Old Norse *hesta garðr*, horse enclosure).[564]

As part of the community organisation, horses had to be hobbled or tethered at certain times of the year to keep them from the crops. An 'Act anent wyld horses' dated 27 June 1617 stated that 'ther sall be na wyld horsis kepit conforme to any Act maid of before and that na man sall put thair horsis without dykis uncloggit in tyme comeing fra the last day of Maij to the tyme the cornes be put in the yeard under the paine of x ls'. The tethering of horses as well as of cattle was still taking place on natural grass in, for example, North Ronaldsay, because of the lack of enclosures, in the late eighteenth century.[565]

32

Transport on Horseback

THE major use of ponies, apart from riding, was for the carriage on their backs of peat and turf, manure, and hay and sheaves of grain. For hay and grain, restrictive devices were used to prevent the ponies from eating them. One was a *kepper* (probably from Scots *kep*, to prevent; but cf. Norwegian dialectal *kipling*, Swedish *kippel*, idem), a short flat piece of wood measuring about 7½ in. wide by 4¾ in. deep (19×12 cm), put between the pony's teeth and held in position by a rope of bent grass or coir yarn passed through holes in the upper corners, and taken over the pony's head. In Orkney, a gag for this purpose was a *kevel* (Norwegian *kjevle*, Old Norse *kefli*, cylindrical piece of wood, Old Norse *kefla*, to gag (a lamb)). 'Eighteen Cavells' were included in an inventory of 1734.[566] An equivalent was the *mesgar* (Norwegian *meis*, basket carried on the back, +? *gjord*, band, girth), *kuivy* (Norwegian dialectal *kuv*, a hump, Icelandic *kúfr*, the contents of a heaped container projecting above its rim), or *huvie* (cf. Norwegian *hov*, *hav*, fish-creel), small openwork baskets of straw used as muzzles.

Whatever load was being carried, the basic harness was the same, consisting of a pad or cover to prevent abrasion of the back, a wooden pack saddle held in position by ropes, and the containers for the loads, paired so that they would balance on either side. The back cover could be a lamb- or sheepskin with the wool still on, as in the Faroe Islands,[567] or was more often a mat of straw with or without a backing of cloth. This *flackie*, *flet* or *flettie* (Old Norse *flaki*, hurdle of wickerwork; Norwegian dialectal *fletta*, Old Norse *flétta*, to plait) was made of parallel bunches of drawn straw, thick enough to fit the circle made by the joined thumb and first finger, and bound by cords or hand-twisted ropes of bent grass or rushes. It was about 3 ft (91 cm) square in Orkney,[568] but measured Shetland examples were smaller. One was 33 in. by 20 in. (84×50 cm), another 31 in. by 20 in. (80×51 cm), reflecting the smaller size of Shetland ponies.

Pack-saddles or *clibbers* (Norwegian dialectal *klyvbar*, Faroese *klibbari*, Old Norse *klyfberi*) can be described as split-saddles, since, unlike the crook-saddles of Western Scotland, they are in two separable halves. They consist of two flat boards whose inner sides lie flat against the horse-pad. On the outside are fixed one or two pairs of upright horns called *nugs* (cf. Norwegian dialectal *knugg*, knot; Old Scots *nog*, pin, 1674), *(k)neebies*, or *neevies* (cf. Norwegian dialectal *knipa*, steep-sided hill-top). On one side the horns are thicker, and contain slots through which the slimmer ones on the opposite side can be passed. They get the names in Fetlar of *muckle* (big)- and *peerie* (small) *neevies*, or *he-* and *she neevies*. The pins of wood or iron that keep them firm are *vernyaggle pins* (Norwegian dialectal *varnagle*, linch-pin, Icelandic *var-nagli*, pin, bung). As a rule the horns have hooked ends to hold the carrying ropes, but in Papa Stour they are plain, like those of the Faroe Islands. In such cases, the ropes went over the farther horn. Probably the style with single horns is the older, since it characterises Shetland and the Faroes and was found in Orkney in the eighteenth century and later.[569] Later Orkney pack-saddles, however, had two pairs of horns.

Ropes called *gointacks* (Old Norse *gagn-tak*, saddle-strap) were knotted through holes in the outer, lower corners of the wooden panels, forming dangling straps across which the *wime-girt* (Scots *wame*, belly + girth, Old Norse *gjǫrð*, saddle girth) or bellyband was fastened. To keep loads from slipping forward, a *tail-girt* was fixed to the saddle and passed under the pony's tail. It had to be well padded to prevent grazing. Breast-bands seem to have been rarely used in the Northern Isles.

The carrying-harness for a horse was completed by a pair of baskets called *cassies* or *kishies* (Norwegian *kjessa*, Icelandic *kassi, kass*, Old Norse *kass*, basket, box), and a pair of open-work nets called *maises* or *maishies* (Norwegian *meis*, Old Norse *meiss*, basket). These were required in great numbers

101. Peat ponies in Orkney, with the bridle of one tied to the tail of the other. From Campbell 1774. C460.

to equip the team of horses, as shown by a Stronsay inventory of 1734 which listed 18 pairs of creels, 18 clibbers, 18 flackies, 20 halters, 7 pairs of meases, 3 old meases, and as much bent as would make 8 pairs more, giving a total of 18 pairs, 30 fathoms (54.9 m) of new hair tethers and 53 fathoms (97 m) of old, and 8 fathoms (14.6 m) of rope.[570] Though most folk made their own gear, there were always specialists like Willie Park at Leagarth who made and sold kishies for 1/6 each, the coir yarn for binding the straw being supplied to him. He was kept in steady work since households might have teams of up to 14 ponies, requiring 28 kishies and if, as sometimes happened, during peat flitting, double sets were used so that one could be ready filled at the bank pending the team's return, then up to 56 kishies were needed. A horse kishie, which was smaller than the one for carrying on the human back, took about 3 hours to make.

To make a kishie, bands of drawn straw, as long as could be got, were laid out in twos, end to end with the thinner ends overlapped to give an even thickness throughout. They were called *hyogs* (Norwegian dialectal, Old Norse *auga*, eye) in Fetlar, though in some parts of Shetland the Scots term *een* (eyes) was used. The bands were doubled over, and the first turn of the rope that bound them together was made along the line of the doubling. This point formed the

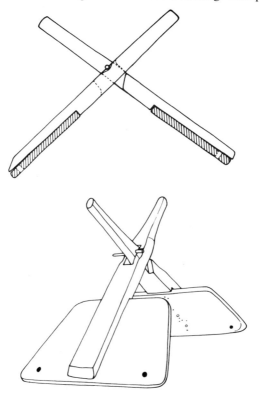

102. A Papa Stour clibber. Elsewhere in Shetland the horns have hooked ends. C225.

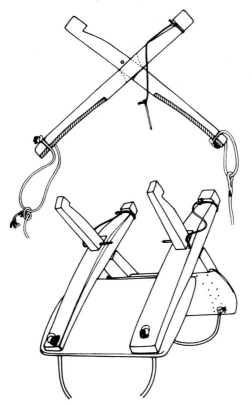

103. An Orkney clibber. Two sets of horns are usual here. C226.

base of the kishie. Binding then proceeded with successive turns or *gengs* (Old English *gang*, going) until the top was reached, but in order to give the sides the necessary rounding, extra hyogs were added, forming a triangular panel at each side. The loose ends of these added bands were trimmed off where they protruded inside the kishie. The rim was made by doubling back the ends of the bands and binding them with a double thickness of rope. This was the only point where a tool was used, a needle of wood or bone about 8 in. (20 cm) long with a $\frac{1}{2}$ in. (1.3 cm) diameter hole at the thick end. With it the rope was pulled through, taken round two bands, pulled tight, passed back between these, taken round two again, and so on. Loose ends were trimmed off once the rim was bound, and finally a carrying band or *fettle* (Norwegian dialectal *fetel*, Old Norse *fetill*, band, strap) was fixed to the bearing-band, which was usually the third geng down from the rim. Another type used on horseback, but less common, was the *rivakishie*, or *reppakishie* (Fetlar), like the kishie but made very open. The first element is from Old Norse *rifa*, to tack together, sew loosely.[571]

The method of making in Orkney was in general similar, with some minor variations. The bottom of the caisie was made rounder, more cup-shaped. A bottom edge was made with a thick, well-bound band of straw, leaving a circular opening that was filled in with a network of bent-grass bands. The rim at the top, called the *fesgar* (cf. Norwegian dialectal *fastgard*, a facing of straw or heather fastened with boards round new or leaky houses), was made by binding on an extra band of straw tightly with bent-grass cords. The carrying-band, made of a three-ply bent-grass cord, was fixed to the rim. As in Shetland, they were used for peat and dung.[572]

In binding the kishie, the cords went over and under in pairs that crossed between each band. One hand held the basket, and the end of one cord was pulled with the other. The teeth had to be used for the second cord, which was fine if the maker had teeth. If not, a wooden hook fixed to a board strapped across the chest could serve the purpose, or an iron hook served with heavy twine and fastened to a belt.

In latter days, the traditional materials, straw, heather, dock, bent grass, local willow and rushes, have been replaced by cane. It is also a sign of the times that

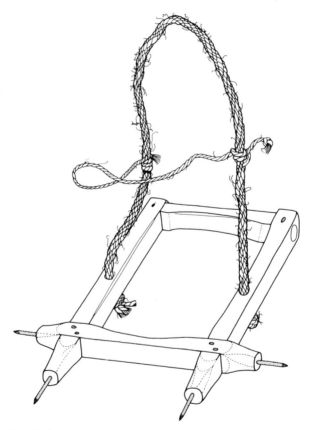

104. Snushacks from Fetlar, put round a foal's head to stop it taking milk from the mare. The headstall is of hand-twisted simmen. C3938.

105. Winding straw simmens, Orkney. 1.38.22.

baskets once made for purely functional purposes are now being made as ornaments to give the fireside a flavour of traditionalism:

'New hand-made Orkney straw caisie for sale; with handles attached; size: 21 ins. high, 17 ins. wide at top, tapering to 11 ins. at bottom; very strong and beautifully made; ideal for holding peats or logs ...'[573]

A feature of the kishie is that neither in the Northern Isles nor in Caithness is there any evidence that it was ever carried with the bearing band across the forehead. This is all the more curious since in the Faroe Islands the wood framed *leypur* is always carried with a brow-band, almost invariably by men, and in the fisher communities of mainland Scotland the use of the brow-band by women is not uncommon, though the shoulder-band is more usual. It is going a little too far to suggest that the Faroese method of carrying with the brow-band was imported from Scotland,[574] since it is not really common in Scotland. The

106. The lengthening simmen was laid around the shoulders. Drawing by W. Mason. Per R. Linklater. 13.8.89.

107. Making a flackie in Fair Isle, *c*. 1920. The teeth and both hands are used to manipulate the bent-grass simmens. Per J A Mann. 1.30.5.

difference in the position of the band may lie in little more than the materials out of which they were made. Though a band of cloth will lie smoothly and comfortably across the brow, a hand-twisted rope of bent grass, or even a length of coir yarn, will dig in painfully, and in these circumstances the rope is best laid 'atween de shooders', between the shoulders.

The making of maishies was one of the most interesting jobs in building up a set of peat-flitting equipment. They were open-work rectangular nets, about 3 ft by 2 ft (91×61 cm), of straw, dried rushes, bent grass, heather or coir yarn. Bundles of rushes made up for maishie making were as big as could be squeezed into the angle between the outstretched thumb and forefinger. They were made to two patterns in Shetland. The first had lengthwise bands arranged in groups of three, the centre band in each group being double, and each group about a hand's breadth apart. The second and commoner form had equal-sized meshes or *eyes*, and dates from at least 1770.[575] Where coir yarn or bent-grass simmens

108. Making a Caisie in Orkney. The two strands of bent-grass simmen criss-cross alternately between each bunch of straw. By courtesy of Orkney County Library.

were being used along with rushes, the lengthwise bands were of rushes, and the cross-bands and edgings of the former materials. The edging was laid double on a rope-twister before being fixed in place, and as this was being done, a third strand, called the *aboot-gaan-störie* or *gurdastörie* (cf. Norwegian dialectal *gyrda*, to put a hoop round a vessel, Norwegian *stor*, Swedish, Danish *stør*, a stake, stave), was added by hand.

In Orkney the maise could have a variant shape. It consisted of two triangular pieces, 4 or 5 ft (1.2 or 1.5 m) wide at the top, and narrow at the lower ends which hung down on either side of the horse when the loop was taken off the horns of the clibber. The wide ends of each triangle were joined by two strong ropes that lay across the back pad, one before and one behind the clibber. In this form especially, the Orkney maise is reminiscent of a type of net, usually in two linked parts, widely used in Europe for carrying hay on the human back. The other Orkney form, more like that of Shetland, was in two separate parts, about 5 ft (1.5 m) long when stretched out, and 3½ to 4 ft (1.1 to 1.2 m) wide at its widest part, narrowing to a loop at each end. It was fixed to the clibber horns, like the Shetland maishie.[576]

The work was begun by hanging a stick with a cord at each end from the kitchen roof. Simmens of double length, four to six in number, were hung over it at equal distances apart. The first eyes were made by twisting five turns with the thumb and forefinger into the top of each double simmen, and then dipping the ends through the twin strands of the first crossband, the halves of the simmen going one at each side of a twist in the crossband to give strength and keep it in place. Work proceeded in this way, always counting say five down and five across to keep the eyes equal, to the bottom. The meshes were about 6 in.

109. In modern days, straw, docken-stalks, bent-grass and heather have been replaced by wickerwork, Orkney. C3022.

(15 cm) square. Then the other border was put on, using a wooden stick to make openings in the ends of the crossbands for it to pass through. The stick was withdrawn at the top, and the border band passed through the loops that were left. The spare ends at the bottom were tucked back, and the aboot-gaan-störie, wound into the border by hand, gripped the loops and tucked – back ends in place. Each corner was drawn out to form a lug for the two carrying bands, the upper and under fettle. The latter was the shorter, and when it was looped round the far side of the pack-saddle, the lower part of the maishie should be on the ground. The longer upper fettle was made for adjustment when being fastened round the horn of the saddle. For peat flitting it was doubled and shortened, but it was kept full length for carrying sheaves. When loading a pony with peat, the long fettle of the maishie was unhooked and laid on the ground. The filled kishie was set into it and the fettle brought back up and hooked on to the horn so that the peats made an even, rounded load against the pony's side. A minimum of two people was needed, because one had to balance the load at one side till the load at the other had been hoisted. The loads were generally turned, that is, the kishies were set in the open maishie in such a way that when the fettle was brought up, the kishie turned upside down. Turned loads could be well topped up. They could also be *set up*, when the kishie lay upright and was not heaped up so much. This method was used with young or aged mares. If the two workers were turning a load and topping it up with extra peats before hoisting, they would shout out the number and quality of peats they were storing, saying, for example, 'Thirty widdy ... twenty blue ... thirty taa-ey ...fifteen mossy', so that the load could be well balanced for the long, steep, uneven peat-road that led from the moss to the houses. For the same reason, kishies were matched in size in pairs, and often a piece of coloured string was tied into the lips of a matching pair. In the latter days of peat flitting, sacks were used, so it mattered less if a load fell off. No kishie was needed for the big, turfy skyumpies. Sheaves and hay[577] were also carried in the maise. To unload, all that was necessary was to unhook the upper fettle, and let the load drop to the ground.

When peat flitting was in progress, the peat roads were alive with people and ponies coming and going. A good pony soon learned the track it had to follow to a particular bank. Generally a 'house-trained' pony rounded up the others and kept them in line, and was ridden by the peat-boy whose job was to lead the ponies back and forth during flitting. One round trip was called a *geng* in Fetlar. The ponies could travel in bunches, or in line ahead, with the halter of one tied to part of the harness of the one in front. This procedure, used especially for longer journeys, was known as *cringan* (cf. Norwegian dialectal *kring*, halter) the ponies. A *cring* was the halter itself, or the line of ponies linked in this way. When standing they were wheeled into a circle, with the head of the first pony tied to the tail of the last, so that they would not go away. The same technique was used in Orkney, but not under this name.[578]

The complete harness of a pack-pony in Shetland was a *bend* (Norwegian dialectal *benda*, to bind, put a band on a load, Old Norse *benda*, to bend), and to put it on was to *bend the horse*. Conversely, to remove it was to *affbend*. For riding, all the paraphernalia were not required, but the clibber was still found useful by women riding to church, for by holding on to its horns they turned it into a kind of side-saddle.[579]

The carrying of baskets in pairs had an effect on the terminology, for in Orkney a single basket for carrying grain to the mill was a *half-lade*, half a load. It was about 3 or 4 ft (91 cm or 1.2 m) long by 18 in. (46 cm) deep. It had sloping corners, with no stiff bottom, and was all of one piece with a handle at each side for lifting it. Because of its function, it had to be fairly tightly woven. When drawn straw had been laid on top of the oats, the two sides were pulled together and laced with rushes made into *floss-bands* (Norwegian dialectal *flos*, *flus*, rind, strip peeled off, *flysja*, to peel). It held about a sack of oats, or 3 bushels. The half-lade differed in shape in different districts. In Evie it was 'shaped like a joiner's bass for carrying tools', in Firth it was like a crab's shell turned upside down. In Orphir each end was covered in like the toe of a slipper, leaving an oval opening in the middle with a stiff rim that was threaded across. The shape was like a little lifeboat. Four people were needed to load the horse with a half-lade, two on each side lifting the baskets by their handles and holding them up whilst the loose narrow end of the maise was lifted and fixed to the saddle.[580]

The basket for carrying meal on horseback was the *meil's caisie*, designed to hold the quantity of one meil (Norwegian *mæle*, a measure equivalent to part of a barrel, Old Norse *mælir*), a measure used in the Northern Isles that varied from place to place and time to time, but was latterly equal to 12 Dutch stones of $17\frac{1}{2}$ lbs, amounting in all to 95 kg. It was tightly woven, with a flat bottom and sides that were rather rounded, like a barrel. It was about 2 ft (61 cm) wide and almost the same depth. The rim was strengthened by two or three extra bands to make it quite stiff, and bands were threaded from one side to the other through openings in the rim, to make a network with a 3 in. (8 cm) mesh. The ends were long to let the network be drawn back in the middle with both hands, so that meal could be filled in. Drawn straw was then laid on top, and the ends of the network pulled tight over the top, and tied.[581]

In the days when grain and meal were Orkney's staple exports, grain was sometimes carried in baskets. Storms shifted the 'cassies' of bere in the *Janet* of Sanday on her way to Norway in 1728. Bere was also shipped in bulk, but was carried to the ship's side in baskets and there weighed on a *pundler* (Old Norse *pundari*, steelyard). Meal was carried in bags containing about 117 lbs (53 kg). In 1716 David Traill wrote to his father to say, 'I shall have out cassies for all your bear that wee take and pockes for all the meall'.[582] The use of caisies for storing grain as well as for transport meant that in Orkney, as in Shetland, many were required. On Patrick Fea's farm in Sanday making caisies, seemingly for grain, was a regular wet-day job in the barn.[583] Because they played a part in the grain trade, their weight was controlled, and in 1615 it was enacted that none were to exceed half a *setten* (Norwegian *settung*, a sixth part of a bushel) in weight, or about half a stone (about 3 kg), that is when empty. They were evidently made to a standard, and seem to have been the sole containers for meal and corn until the seventeenth century, for a writer of 1683 noted that no sacks were used, but only caisies. In South Ronaldsay a barn *kaze* for oats held about a bushel (36 l), and a carrying kaze with a carrying band 1½ to 1¾ bushels (66 to 67 l). Here, the rim was called the *bree-er*, perhaps from Scots *bree*, brow, upper edge of something. The meal pocks that came to be used were made of 'harne', coarse linen cloth.[584] Baskets played an essential role in the economy, therefore, both internally and externally, and enormous quantities of rope and cord were twisted in order to make them, as well as the various elements of the horse-harness.

Baskets and Ropes

33

Domestic Baskets

A range of baskets was made for every conceivable purpose. The name *cubbie* is found mainly in Orkney. There was a winnowing cubbie, a sowing cubbie, a hen's cubbie, in which hens laid their eggs as it hung on the wall, and a spoon cubbie on the kitchen wall for holding the horn spoons, bait and sea cubbies. Less common were the horses' cubbie and kye's cubbie, both used as muzzles, the former put on to keep the horses from eating potatoes in drills that were being earthed up, or growing corn, and the latter when the milk cows were being driven along a path between fields of corn. Whatever the variation in size, the chief difference between them and the caisie was that they were of uniform width for most of their depth, ending in a solidly plaited dome-shaped base. They also had a carrying band, attached to the rim at points about 18 to 20 in. (46–51 cm) apart, long enough to let the forearm pass through and take the weight as the cubbie was slung over the left shoulder. Only beggars carried their cubbies on their backs like a caisie, in which case the fettle had to be longer.[585]

An Orcadian now living in Australia has provided details of cubbie making. There were three different styles. Most common was one made of long, fine straight heather selected smooth and straight, used for carrying turnips from the shed to the byre and for taking in peats from the stack. Twenty to twenty-four taets or tufts of heather were selected, and bound in basket form by means of yarn or 'blackberry heather' which dried as hard as copper wire. This was passed between the taets, over and under, using two lines, till they were all in flat, and the edges were joined together. Then each taet was divided in two to give the size. The heather bands made it open and not too heavy. Then six or seven rows of bindings were put on, and loose ends of heather trimmed off. The rim or fesgar was sewn on with a needle, and the bottom was netted across. The fettle was fixed at points on the taets depending on the breadth of the user's back. The bottom was about 36 to 38 in. (91–97 cm) diameter and the top 66 to 70 in. (1.7–1.8 m). The second style was of drawn straw or gloy, preferably of black oats which were strong and tough. It was used for winnowing. The straw bands were linked by cords of bent grass, cut green in the sand and dried carefully, not burned with the sun to make it brittle. The construction was as for the heather cubbie, but care was taken to avoid getting the straw twisted, and the bottom was made solid in the same style as a straw-backed chair. A metal spike in a wooden handle made openings through which the bent-grass cord was threaded. Winnowing or *windoo* cubbies were carefully looked after, hung up after use, and kept for that purpose, or for carrying seed oats to the sower, or for use as a hopper for sowing. The third variety was the sea cubbie for carrying fish. Long straight heather was used. The taets were pointed one left, the other right, till there were enough for the size required. To make it round, *neuk taets* had to be added. As the binding went on the cubbie was narrowed, so that at the end the shape was that of a jug with a wide, round bottom and a narrow top.[586] Other names for the rim or fesgar of the cubbie were *braid* and *braithin* (Old Norse *bregða*, to braid, bind, Old English *bregdan*, to weave).[587]

The *huvie* was made of straw, mugwort, or dock stalks, used as a fish-creel, or a holder for limpet bait, in which case it was squarer in the bottom than the kishie, and had a carrying band across its mouth. It also had a bee-hive shape for holding salt, and this was probably the form of the 'heave' that hung upon an Orkney wall in 1643.[588]

The *luppie* (Norwegian *laup*, Old Norse *laupr*, small box or basket) was a

110. The straw back of an Orkney chair is made in the same way as a basket. Per Mrs M. Sclater.

111. A bait basket of heather. Orkney. 1.5.6.

small basket frequently used as a measure for meal. Luppies were of various sizes, and so tightly bound that they were almost as firm as wood. They held odds and ends in the kitchen, and could be hung on the wall. A common function in earlier days was carrying oats to the quern or bere to the knocking-stone. They held anything from half a stone to a stone (3–6 kg). They had a steep-sided basin shape, so that they could be turned upside down and used by a child as a stool.[589]

A *toig* or *toyack* (from Norwegian dialectal *taaje*, *taagje*, a basket carried on the back, a creel, especially one made from tree-roots) was a small basket for meal or corn.

A *kilpack* (Norwegian *kylpa*, a pot with a handle) was a small basket of docks or twigs, with a loop for carrying in the hand. It also was the name of a wooden box in which bait was collected.[590]

An Orkney Celebrity.

Annie Harper

112. Baskets were carried with the fettle across the chest. Annie Harper, Orkney, 1894.
1.5.29.

A *skep* was a large straw basket, made to hold about four bushels of corn. It was big enough to be stood in when de-husking kiln-dried bere with the feet.[591]

A *cuddie* (origin uncertain; cf. Norwegian dialectal *kodde*, cushion, Swedish *kudde*, pillow, small bag) was a basket of docks or straw, for holding things like bait, salt and spoons. The limpet cuddie of docks was made to be carried in the hand; the salt cuddie of straw was suitable for hanging on a peg or standing on a shelf.[592]

The *budie* was the kind of basket most used in fishing. It was of straw or docks, and had a bulged shape. A version of it used for taking corn to the mill was carried on the back, but the buddie for fish or bait, carried on the shoulder, was of docks. If a man was going fishing and someone shouted after him, 'mice i' dy cuddie an' cats i' dy budie', this was fatal to the success of the outing.[593] The carrying band was fixed near the top.

ROPES AND ROPE MAKING

For making ropes, natural resources of several kinds were exploited. Shoots of the crowberry heath, *Empetrum nigrum*, made strong ropes for thatching, but this material had become scarce by the 1900s. The fibrous roots of the sea-reed, *Arundo arenaria*, made good loops for hanging caisies over horses' backs.[594] Various wiry grasses from sand dunes, such as the meadow soft-grass, *Holcus lanatus*, lumped together under the name of *punds* (Norwegian dialectal *punt*, Icelandic *pundur*, a kind of bent grass) were used to make tethers and bridle reins. Sheep tethers made from the crested dog's tail grass, *Cynosurus cristatus*, were called *pun tethers*. In making Orkney chairs, punds were twisted into the ends of the bent-grass ropes, because they were thinner, and easier to thread into the needle.[595] Rushes or *floss*, *Juncus effusus*, was in demand and its use was already being controlled by 1623, when an Act of Bailiary prohibited the cutting of bent or pulling of floss before the first of Lammas each year, under the fine of 10/– Scots. It was, like punds, a substitute for the much better quality but scarcer bent grass.[596] Floss was cut in autumn wherever it grew longest in the hills, cleaned of withered stalks and made up into *kirvies* (Norwegian *kjerve*, bundle of sticks or twigs, Old Norse *kerfi*, bundle) or small sheaves which were left to weather for a week or two and then made up into baets of manageable size, which were tied in pairs by plaiting the thin ends together and hung up in the barn till required.[597] Floss made better simmens than straw, though the best were made from bent or from long, thin heather. If straw was being used, Shetland (Tartary) oat straw was preferred, bere straw being much less durable. Straw was normally reserved for simmens used in roping thatch on stacks or the roofs of houses, and in making kishies and back-pads for the pack-saddle. The finest kishies were made of rush simmens, and budies of dock stalks or straw. The maishie was always of rushes in Unst.[598]

Some idea of the time spent on twisting ropes on a big farm, and of the range

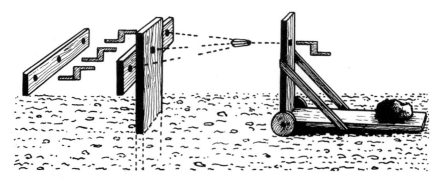

113. An exploded view of the Shetland tuimikins for twisting rope. The fixed element on the left contains three wooden hooks all turned together. The movable part on the right has one hook to twist the three strands into one. A cone-shaped wooden snudder held in the middle lays the strands and evens the tension. C5727.

114. Johnnie and Maggie Anne Mowat making ropes at Houbie, Fetlar, 1963. 2.4.4A.

115. The finger-shaped strand-layer for ropes used at Houbie, Fetlar, 1963. It is here called a key, and may have two or three notches. 2.4.2A.

116. A rope-twister lying on a flagstone stack-foundation at an Orkney farm. The hooks are of metal, with gearing.

117. The movable part is mounted on angle-iron runners.

of materials used and products made, and of their cost, can be got from the Diary of Patrick Fea in Sanday:

21 July 1766:	All day spinning hair in the barn and teasing.
28 August 1766:	To the Lad of Leyland 2 threefs (thraves) for which I received 10 Fathom of Teathers he returned me 2 Sh.
2 September 1766:	To a hair Teather £2.12/–.
6 September 1768:	Had Thos. Swanay pletting bent all day for the house use and he did 20 Threefs.
2 January 1770:	My men making flackies all day.
3 January 1770:	My men making Straw work.
13 March 1770:	My men . . . winding bands for Teathers (apparently of bent).
22 August 1770:	Begun to Spin hair.
28 August 1770:	Had 6 people in my Hay all day and 14 in the bent links. Westove's men had 20 Threefs estimate to 30 Threefs of good bent.
4 September 1770:	Begun to plet bent by 3 men and put it upon the hall.
7 September 1770:	Done with pletting the bent that was on the Shoar and laid 3 rope teathers.
19 October 1770:	Threshing and windeing Simmens in the barn all day.
22 January 1771:	Had a man laying up flackies.
23 January 1771:	3 men makeing Flackies.
11 October 1771:	Gave every one bent to make furniture.
30 September 1771:	Got Rope Teathers for my Shetland Horses they being as yet in Spurness.[599]

On farms of this status, the work could be done by employees, whereas the crofters did it themselves in the evenings. Furthermore, hair and bent grass were the main materials.

Ropes were twisted by hand or by means of rope-twisters. The simplest were *sookans* (Gaelic *sùgan*, hay or straw rope), one-ply ropes of straw or more rarely grass or hay, twisted on the thumb to make a loose rope for a temporary job such as tying straw into bundles. They were also good for *strae-beuts* (straw-boots) or leggings worn in snow. One end went under the instep and over the top of the boot, and the rest was coiled round the top of the boot and up to the knee. The loose end was tucked down under the top row. They were worn by men rather than women, and indeed one woman who wore them in the parish of Firth was ridiculed by her neighbours. The term sookan is not found in Shetland. There, *tuimikins* (diminutive of 'thumb') is sometimes used for a thumb-rope. Simple straw or grass ropes of this nature were also twisted in Orkney on a twister called a *reek* (origin obscure) or *cleek* (Old Scots *cleke*, hook), shaped like a joiner's boring-brace, or like a car starting handle. The Scots name *thra-cruik* or *kraa-cruik* was also used in Orkney.[600]

Two-ply simmens were wound from a range of materials, oat straw, bent grass, heather, rushes, and various grasses. For twisting horsehair, however,

118. Four strands can be twisted together with this frame.

119. The strand-layer is a combination of a grooved cone and a notched wooden square.

and for laying strands of other materials together to make thicker ropes, some kind of mechanical device was used. It was said that a good horse was expected to keep itself in tethers with the hair from its tail and mane, spun in Orkney on a *winchou* (diminutive of 'winch'), a simple home-made device by means of which swine's and cow's hair could also be twisted (having been carded first on wool combs) into single strands which were then twined three together into a rope. Since this rope could not be cut, the necessary length had to be spun at one go. The winchou could not be used safely with an iron stake because of the recoil in the hair rope. An older and more elaborate type of twister was the *tamar-spinnle* (cf. Norwegian dialectal *taumarne*, Old Norse *taume*, genitive plural of *taumr*, rope + 'spindle'), probably the same as the '4 Iron Taum Spindles with all their furniture' referred to in a Stronsay inventory of 1734.[601]

This twister is almost certainly the same as what was called in Shetland the tuimikins, the *spinnles* (spindles), or 'the horse and the mare', consisting of a fixed element, the 'mare', with three or four hooks working against a movable element, the 'horse', with a single hook. When in use, the movable part, mounted on small wheels or skids, was weighted with stones so that it helped to keep tension on the rope being made, whilst still being able to move towards the fixed unit as the rope shortened during twisting. They could be made entirely of wood, even the hooks being formed by pins made to protrude at the ends of the cranks, or simply holes through which the rope ends were tied. Devices of this type were widespread. In the Faroe Islands the very similar *snøristol* has eighteenth century antecedents, and parallels can be found as far off as India. The treble wooden hook was widespread in Sweden. Between the two units, strand-layers or *taps* were employed to lay the strands evenly and help in adjusting the tension of the rope. A common type was cone-shaped, with three lateral grooves along which the strands ran. The Orkney name was *snudder* and in Shetland, *snott* (Norwegian dialectal *snud*, twisting, Swedish dialectal *snod*, a twist in a thread, Old Norse *snuðr*, a turn) or the aphetic form *nitt*. Another form was made in the shape of a wooden hand, with three or more fingers according to the number of strands being twisted. Examples have been seen in Fetlar and in Caithness, and they resemble the Swedish *tvinnstickan*. A strand-layer demonstrated in the 1960s on an Orkney farm near Dounby was a composite, consisting of a grooved cone linked to a square board notched on each side. One unit of this twister had four metal hooks set in a wooden frame like the dashers of a rotary table churn. Whether by accident or tradition, it has a resemblance to four-armed winders found in Sweden.[602] Latterly, such devices were used for twisting coir yarn and binder twine, which replaced hair as a material for tethers and other ropes.

34

Straw Plaiting and
Straw-backed Orkney Chairs

THOUGH the working of straw and other materials for basket making was a domestic craft, part of the everyday round of work, a commercial side also developed in certain specialised areas. In Kirkwall, a straw-plaiting industry, started by a London company, was flourishing by the early 1800s, employing 150 girls who were paid at the rate of 1[d] per yard and could earn 10[d] to 1/6 a day. They worked 30 or 40 to a room. At the same period in Lerwick, the company had 50 girls working in two rooms, at the same wage. This was the first kind of manufacture Lerwick ever had. Split wheat-straw was used first, but being too brittle, unripened and unsplit rye-straw was imported from England and plaited for making into straw hats. By 1814, 1200 to 1400 people, mostly women, were involved in the work in Orkney as compared with 200 in Lerwick.[603]

One of the firms involved in straw plaiting was that of Robert Mainland in Kirkwall. An account book of 1834 lists the debts due from plaiters to the firm, for materials, advances, or provisions. The firm had 1707 people on its books, scattered through Orkney, with the greatest concentration in Kirkwall:

Kirkwall	628	Rousay	111
Egilsay	40	Deerness	148
Rendall and Firth	129	Tankerness	74
Orphir, Birsay and		Holm	54
Harray	61	Gairsay	6
Evie and Costa	122	Westray	30
Shapinsay	108	South Ronaldsay	23
Eday and Fara	78	Wyre	13
Sanday	49	Stromness	33

These workers jointly owed Robert Mainland £1042. 14. 5½. His firm owed the workers £14. 2. 1½.[604]

The industry continued to grow and by 1841 had 2000 girls working full-time and some of the married ones part-time. In Westray, straw plaiting had been general, but 'the very little encouragement now held out has nearly put a stop to this work'. There were a few straw plait manufacturers in Stromness, employing women in the town as well as in the country. Though starting as a 'factory' industry with the women working together, it later became a cottage industry and the plaiting was done at home. Many young girls depended on it completely for their support and were hard hit when the industry, dependent as it was on fashion, went into a decline. In Orphir straw plaiting had been a winter occupation for most of the young women for many years. It was universally done in Shapinsay and in Walls and Flotta. Young girls worked at it in their homes in Firth and Stenness, being employed by Mr Ramsay in Kirkwall and Mr Heddle in Stromness. In Birsay and Harray, straw plaiting replaced flax processing. It had become the main employment of the women, having been introduced in 1807 by Robert Borwick, Kirkwall. The wages were now lower than in the early days of the craft. About 450 women were employed, earning 1/6 to 2/– weekly. Sandwick was a kind of straw-plaiting centre. Here, winter plaiting was complemented by summer work, reaping and preparing the 9 acres of rye that provided the raw material. Thick sowing made the straw long and fine. The stems were cut before the grain ripened, tied near the lower end into small bundles, steeped in boiling water for an hour, spread on the ground to bleach, and carted to the manufacturer's house. Usually only the upper part between the highest joint and the grain was used. It was cut to a suitable length, graded according to fineness, and made into small bundles for distribution to the plaiters. Payment was related to the fineness of the straw and the quality of the plaiting. 6^d a day was the average in 1841. The completed plaits were washed, milled, and passed on to other girls who sewed them into bonnets. The Orkney rye-straw was said to be more durable than Tuscan straw imported from Leghorn, and little inferior in appearance. Women could earn 3^d to 9^d a day. In Kirkwall, as elsewhere, plaiting was entirely a home industry, the straw being handed out by agents.[605] Soon after, however, the industry began to fade out, due to the free importation of better quality foreign rye-straw, and the reduction of duty on foreign straw-plait. By the 1870s, straw plaiting had come to an end in Orkney.[606] In Lerwick, it had already been given up for several years by 1841,[607] and was no longer of importance in St Andrews. The industry continued chiefly in Bedfordshire, Buckinghamshire and Hertfordshire, especially in Luton and Bedfordshire.[608]

The farmer who grew the rye-straw was Mr Watt of Kierfiold. It ripened earlier than other crops, so shearers had the possibility of reaping two harvests in one season. Sowing was in March, at 20 bushels to the acre, and the rye was cut in mid to late July with the sickle. After the small bundles were scalded with boiling water, bleaching lasted for a week, the straw being constantly turned to avoid mildew. The finer top parts of the straw were given to the best plaiters, and poorer ones or beginners might get the coarser lower parts. Plaits were normally named from the number of straws used. The narrowest, with seven straws in its breadth, was called 'sevens', another was 'elevens', and the widest 'thirty-twos'. An average plaiting of the coarsest straw was 20 yds (18.2 m) paid for at 4^d to 6^d a yard (91 cm). Finer work was slower and was worth 1/6 to 2/6 a yard.

The plaiter kept water handy in which to dip the ends of her bundles of straw, and also her fingers, for dampness was needed to keep the straw pliable when working. Before it was handed to the plait-master, the plait was run between rollers to smooth it, and was bleached and cleared of the smell of peat with sulphur-smoke. In its heyday, the industry was worth about £30,000, and employed nearly 7000 women. The main Kirkwall exporters were Messrs. Borwick and Ramsay, who exported to London and Greenock respectively. In Stromness Mr Heddle of Quildon and James Sutherland were the leading plait-masters and exporters.

Just as people gathered together for spinning and weaving, so plaiting also became integrated into the community. Townships often set aside a chaamer for plaiting, so that the work could be done cheerfully in company.[609]

Whereas straw plaiting was an early example of the bringing in of an extraneous industry, a phenomenon that has not been uncommon in the Highlands and Islands, the craft of making straw-backed chairs grew more directly out of the native traditions. Straw stools were of three kinds. The simplest was a low, round stool without a back, that could be easily lifted to and from the fireside. Then came a low-backed stool, with a semicircular back reaching to the sitter's shoulders. Last, largest and least common was the high-backed or 'heided stül' with an arched hood, the equivalent of the easy chair. The seat was made of wood, and the straw back sewn round wooden uprights. The hood was made by gradually contracting the back and sides of the straw work. 'The seat box generally contained a drawer in which the goodman kept the bottle with his supply of snuff, along with the cottage library, often consisting of "Baxter's Saints' Rest", the book of Proverbs, and a few dogeared and soot-stained chap books bought at Lammas Fair.' This is what has come to be known as the Orkney chair, but previously the seat was round, of coiled straw, and the wooden side slips and arms entirely covered with straw and bent-grass simmens. The only wood to be seen was the set of four feet protruding at the bottom. A native of North Ronaldsay is alleged to have invented the wooden seat-box in the first half of the eighteenth century, 'as nailing a few boards together took far less time than working the lower part in straw'.[610]

It is also possible that the 'Home Industries' movement was the inspiration for Orkney chairs with wooden bases. At any rate, D M Kirkness, of 12 and 14 Palace Street, Kirkwall, was making the wooden frames of such chairs from about 1878 and getting crofters and fishermen to make the straw backs in winter or in any spare time. It took a little time for the market to be established, but by 1914 the chairs had a small but fairly good market. In this case, a local craftsman made a marketable speciality by adapting a local product, and harnessing local talent for its production. The business is carried on at the present day by Reynold Eunson, at the same addresss. W. Hay bought the business after D M Kirkness died in 1936, and Mr Eunson took over in 1956, after a break due to the War. In the days of D M Kirkness, Orkney chairs were also being made by William Sinclair, joiner, in Shapinsay, and Charles Loggie and John Sinclair in Rousay.[611]

The Land and its Produce

35

Seaweed Manure

AS a food for plants, seaweed was a valuable resource, 'the very backbone of the old husbandry'. In general, seaweed contains more nitrogen and potassium than animal manure, but much less phosphorus. It is good for sandy soils, which tend to be deficient in potassium. This gave it particular value in the Northern Isles, especially in sandy islands, and Orkney was particularly fortunate in having great stocks of seaweed around her shores. A survey of the littoral zone between high and low water mark in the 1940s showed a potential yield of 38,774 tons, or 21 tons an acre, around Orkney, giving 21.5 per cent of the Scottish total. The sub-littoral resources were estimated at 1,000,000 tons.[612] Orkney was well off, therefore, for manure and kelp.

Because of the value of seaweed for the land, the beaches on which it was cast ashore were well organised from early times. The early sixteenth century

120. Seaweed manure spread on a field in Papa Stour, 1967. 3.39.36.

sources reflect a much older tradition. On 27 April 1509 it was resolved that the community of Toab should not have the right of taking seaweed from the shore at Sabay. The same decision was taken again ten years later, not for the first and probably not for the last time, after John Irvine of Sabay complained about neighbours who took seaweed from his ground and banks of Quhago, without leave or payment. The boundaries between Toab and Sabay were discussed and confirmed, and the people of Toab ordered to take 'nather aird nor stane nor wair nor ony wther thing of the ground of Saba, without leive askit and giwin, and gif thay do nocht, to pay a mark for everie laid or loading vnaskit leive or grantit thairto'.[613]

In 1544, a piece of land was given 'cum privilegio lucrandi *lie wair* marium pro terris stercorandis'. In 1627, it was said of the parts of the parish of Stenness lying far from the sea between the hills that the land was too poor, for lack of seaware and manure, to pay the duty imposed on it by His Majesty's chamberlain. In the inland parish of Harray also, little seaweed was used in the seventeenth century. The ale made there, however, was smoother than that made from barley fertilised with seaweed, for this made it sharp in taste and caused diarrhoea in strangers for the first few weeks. Though the coastal areas got plenty of seaweed manure, the more inland areas were not so well off, for the weight and bulk of seaweed made it hard to carry for any distance either on horseback or on the human back – 'methinks, it is the greatest slavery in the world for the common people, as they do there in winter, to carry this wrack in small vessels made of straw, or cassies, on their backs to their land'. The seaweed was laid in heaps to wait till the time of cultivation, often composted with alternating layers of earth and dung, as also happened in Denmark.[614]

Seaweed had a considerable effect on the economy. Many more horses and servants than were necessary were kept to recover seaweed when the storms drove it ashore. Sandy soil was not cultivated unless seaware was available. Sometimes eighty horse loads in square, ribbed wooden creels, the bottoms of which could be opened, were carried half a mile to a piece of sandy ground that produced only a boll of bere in return. Grain grown on fresh seaweed manure was said to weigh less to the boll than that raised on compost, though a greater quantity was produced per acre. Even in the late nineteenth century, townships like Aikerness were keeping animals beyond the proportion needed for cultivation, because of the labour of the ware shore. Each cottar also kept a horse, and a man from each house had to help at the ware, which was one of the main winter jobs. It was carried in hand-barrows, or in baskets on the back.[615] The question of man and animal power is one of the chief factors that have led to the disuse of seaweed as a manure in more recent times, since there are few horses for getting at places inaccessible to tractors, and there are fewer people on the land.

In Sandwick and Stromness, seaweed was put on to the fields in winter, and also in spring when the compost middens were spread and more fresh seaweed went on, making three manurings in all. In Westray seaweed was applied after oats, immediately before harvest, and during winter when it came ashore. To some extent the manuring pattern was dictated by the weather. If wind and storm drove much ware ashore, it had to be put on fresh, but it made better manure when fermented in heaps. After the oats had been sown in spring, the wared land was ploughed once, and this was called the 'fallow'. Bere land got another ploughing after this, at the time the seed was sown. In the island of Shapinsay, where dung was not much bothered with, seaweed was applied after ploughing, just before the seed was sown. In Kirkwall and St Ola, fresh or rotten ware was used alone or composted with turf, and there was no summer 'fallow' to get rid of weeds. In some areas where seaweed was inaccessible, 'fallowing' consisted of half an acre left lea annually on each farm, ploughed before or after harvest and sown with bere the following year. As a rule, the land was manured before bere, and not oats. Where seaweed was plentiful, it tended to be used alone rather than composted with turf, which involved more time and expense.[616]

In the nineteenth century new crops and new thinking brought some variations in practice in some areas. The use of carts for carrying seaweed increased generally, though already in the 1790s Westray had 40 two-ox carts and Papa Westray 5, for carrying manure. Several oxen were kept for carting seaweed in Cross and Burness. Seaweed carried in carts was being put on the turnip crop in light, sandy soils in Lady parish, and had such a good effect on cabbages that the 'common Scotch grey' could grow to 14 lbs. (6.4 kg) a plant. Even the cropping routine was affected, for it permitted a six-course shift instead of the more usual rotation of three or four. The new husbandry by no means rejected seaweed as a manure, therefore. Indeed there are signs of tighter control of the ware beaches in some areas. The estate factor in North Ronaldsay drew up regulations in the nineteenth century for dividing the ware. Each of the six townships was allocated a part of the beach, which the crofters then had to divide themselves on the basis of rent, acreage, and quality of land, according to the factor's rules. The method was simple. A group comprising half the members of a township made a division by sticking tangles upright in the bank of seaweed, and the other half then chose whichever side they liked. The dividing and choosing roles were reversed each year. This 'pairting o' the ware' was a job for the men.[617]

Different areas had different methods of division, always in proportion to the amount of land held by individuals. At Stenso in Evie all the ware was put in four large heaps or *kests*. Each of those who were carrying seaweed emptied their loads on to each of the heaps in turn, and at the end the heaps were balloted for. Division of the banks of seaweed could also be by lot on the beach itself. The middle of the bank was the best part, because there was most seaweed there and it was less rolled and beaten by the sea. It could happen, however, that one end was near the only point on the beach where ware could be carried up, which saved much labour for the man who drew his lot there.[618]

At the Bay of Ireland in Stenness the landlord 'cut the shores' for kelp, and the tenant got for manure only what the wind blew ashore. In the early 1800s, the ware there had to be divided between two groups known as the *bús* or bigger farms, and the *boons* or small farm units. There were three big farms with a particular order of priority amongst themselves, and six boons. Each unit had so many 'shifts'. The measuring, latterly done by John Smith, of the Hall (one of the *bús*), began at the north edge of the burn of Coldomo 'and proceeded northwards in the following order and measurements:— (1) Aglath, 24 fathoms (43.9 m); (2) the six Boons, 24 fathoms among them, to be sub-divided by them according to the extent of their respective holdings; (3) the Hall, 24 fathoms; (4) the six Boons, 24 fathoms, to be subdivided as in No. 2; (5) Cumminess, 24 fathoms; (6) the six Boons, 24 fathoms, as before. If more ware was needed the measurements were repeated in the same order, until the Hall was reached.' Since a number of places claimed all the ware on certain parts below their houses, these parts were excluded from the measurement. Another complication could arise if the ware came ashore in a lump at one point, leaving some stretches of measured beach bare. This system, reflecting the old runrig division of the land, seems to have survived at least till the sale of the township in lots in 1857.[619]

At Skaill Bay in the parish of Sandwick, certain lands in the townships of Northdyke and Scarwell had customary rights to seaweed proportional to their value. A man from one of these townships *haversed* or divided the ware in two, and a man from the other made the draw. Each division was *thirded*, for each township had three divisions, and each third split according to the number of pennylands claimed by each farmer. After this the seaweed could be piled in 'ware-middens' above the beach. Mr Watt of Breckness claimed the seaweed to the south of the burn below the mill of Skaill as his own, as well as that on a certain point north of the burn. This was known as 'Skaill's ground'.[620]

The name *trip* (Norwegian *trip*, a break or obstruction to be crossed on a path, cf. Old Norse *þrep*, ledge, platform) was given to a pile of stones on a beach marking seaweed divisions. Above the high-water mark, rounded hollow places where each man's seaweed was collected were called *kossels*. The rake for dragging seaweed ashore or spreading it on land was a *klooro* (cf. Nor-wegian dialectal *klora*, Old Norse *klóra*, to claw, scrape).[621]

The gathering and transporting of seaweed was no easy job, and it took up a lot of time in the course of the year. The Diaries of a farmer in the island of Stronsay give some idea of the peak-periods, as well as the number of days worked each month at the seaweed, whether for manure or for kelp, though an allowance has to be made for some irregularity in filling in the Diaries.

A distinction was made between littoral ware and sub-littoral tang, ware being often spread direct, and tang piled up in middens. Ware was further divided into fresh and rotten ware, the latter applied chiefly in March before 'corn', which in Orkney is an abbreviation for 'bere-corn', ie bere or barley. April, May and June were the months for gathering 'kelp-ware' to be burned, and later carted to the store at the pier for shipment in August. There is no suggestion of conflict here between the demands on seaweed for kelp and for manure, but this was past the heyday of kelp burning and in any case seaweed was plentiful. Considerable quantities were involved. Up to nine carts could be

Days Worked per Month on Seaweed

Month	1896	1900	1905	1907	1908	1909	1910	1911	1912	1914	1916	1918
J	1	6	–	1	2	13	10	12	8	4	14	–
F	–	5	3	4	4	5	–	4	3	5	4	–
M	–	4	15	7	5	–	2	9	1	4	1	1
A	–	–	1	1	2	2	1	–	–	–	9	–
M	–	–	–	–	–	–	–	1	–	–	–	–
J	–	1	–	–	–	–	–	–	–	–	2	1
J	–	–	–	–	–	–	–	–	–	–	–	–
A	–	3	–	–	1	5	3	1	6	6	1	–
S	–	–	–	–	–	–	–	–	1	–	1	1
O	–	–	–	–	–	–	5	1	–	–	–	–
N	–	–	1	–	6	1	12	10	–	4	6	8
D	7	–	6	–	3	1	12	3	3	3	1	7

at work at one time, and up to twenty loads a day were specified. Not every year was good. A wet December in 1915 resulted in little ware, only about 60 loads by 1 January 1916. The months with a high incidence of days worked at seaweed mark periods of wind and storm.[622]

The pattern of use in Shetland was less intensive than in Orkney, because the quantity was less. Seaweed was spread fresh if it came at the time of the spring cultivation and sowing, but in autumn and winter it was composted with earth and animal manure, though in general the sources imply that seaweed was a less frequent component of compost middens than in Orkney. Nevertheless, it was an important resource. Land lying back from the coast was of less value, for neither the numerous 'shelties' kept for the job nor the people using their own backs appear to have carried seaweed very far inland. The taking of other people's ware was being punished by fines in 1602, and the old Country Acts included regulations about not cutting tang in another man's ebb. Major T M Cameron of Garth and Annsbrae noted in his evidence to the Crofters Commission in the 1880s that he reserved to himself the rights to all peat-mosses, shell-sand, and seaweed on his property, with power to regulate and divide these amongst his tenants as necessary, according to the amount of land held by each. By the 1930s the system had broken down, and at that period the Board of Trade advertised that seaweed could be taken from any part of the foreshore in Unst without restriction.[623]

Seaweed was used when and where it could be got, often being heaped up in March and April and left to rot before being applied. By the 1840s there may have been some falling off in its use, for the cultivation of bere as a crop was dying out, and seaweed was coming to be regarded as the manure used by cottars. It remains amongst the manures applied on the crofts. In April 1967, a spade-cultivated field was seen with a layer of red-ware from the shore spread over it, before a bere crop. In a neighbouring field was a muck-roog, a dunghill of alternate layers of seaweed and byre manure. This seaweed had been carried from the shore in a kishie on a woman's back. Formerly, when seaweed was more widely used, it was collected in March and piled in roogs or heaps below the banks. When carts came into use, it was piled above the banks since the carts could not go down. Women carried, and the men forked it up into the roogs. This work was done in common, and was followed by the 'pairtin' o' the waar', one pile being allocated to each house. The piles were left for a day or two, then carried to the fields to be built with byre-manure into muck-roogs, which were finished off on top with a layer of broken-up turf.[624]

The Northern Isles were not unique in their use of seaweed. It served as a manure all round the coasts from early times, and survived in some areas, such as Ayrshire, almost till the present day. As a natural resource, it could still have much value if economic working methods could be developed to farm it.[625]

36

Turf and Animal Manure

SINCE townships had to depend on their own resources before the days of artificial fertilisers, the sources of energy directed to the growth of crops were more diverse and treated in more sophisticated ways than are at first apparent. Seaweed shows the simplest cycle of application, apart from manures of limited availability like the marl that was plentiful in seventeenth century Sanday.[626] Though seaweed could be used by itself, however, as often as not it slotted into the wider system by being composted with earth and animal manure. The type and place of the crop also affected the kind of manure and the method of its preparation. Bere on the infield was treated differently from oats on the outfield, and the coming of root crops like potatoes and turnips had a further effect.

121. A mooldie-koose at the North End of Foula, 1958, consisting of turf to be used as byre bedding, kept from being blown away by a stone covering. C3910.

The use of turf and peaty mould had a close association with the houses. The ash from peat and turf fires was husbanded for spreading on the fields directly or more often for use as bedding to soak up liquid in the byres. In Firth and Stenness turf with a mixture of gritty clay was deliberately burned in the house fires to increase the quantity of ashes. Since fire can release substances in the soil in a form that makes them assimilable by growing plants as nutrients, this was a wise move, however empirically the knowledge was gained. Surface turf from the hill-pasture, pared for composting, was called *truck* (cf. Old Scots *trok*, worthless, broken bits and pieces, from French *troque*, barter). It was carried in pony loads from the hill, or sometimes piled just outside the hill dyke in heaps called *mooldie-bings* or *mooldie-kooses*. In the windy conditions of Foula, the mooldie-kooses were formed within a ring of stones and the conical top of the heap covered by a number of flat stones. In some cases, light mossy earth gathered in summer was kept in storehouses for winter use in the byres. Mould was gathered during dry weather, using especially the dry upper surface of peaty hill land where vegetation had not taken root. Seaweed collecting, on the other hand, was more of a winter job. The peeling of turf for manure and bedding did much harm to the common grazings.[627]

This mould could go directly into a compost midden, or into the byre as bedding. A good deal of skill went into the making of byre-manure. Quantities of grass and short heath were cut in the hills in August, carried home when dry, and stacked like hay for use as bedding. From time to time a layer or *sloo* (cf. Norwegian dialectal *sloda*, *sloe*, to trail, drag, Old Norse *slodi*, a drag) of dry mould was spread too, and the sandwich mixture of grass or heath, dung, mould, and ashes could end up 4 or 5 ft (1.2–1.5 m) deep, by which time the heads of the cattle were touching the roof. The black mould was spread regularly, each day, or every few days, and the whole surface levelled off. When the byre was full the contents were carried to a dunghill and the operation was then repeated. Since the cows were housed every night summer and winter, there was never a break in this form of manure production and processing.[628]

The accumulation of manure in the byre was a form of composting of a very necessary kind. Cattle dung contains over three quarters of its own weight in water, and is poorer in soil nutrients than sheep, horse, pig or poultry manure. It is also slow to ferment, and needs the intermixture of liquid absorbent materials to help the process.[629] The setting up of compost middens outside is a logical extension, partly conditioned by the need to empty the byre from time to time. The process of *slooin a midden* was to make a compost of earth, byre-manure and seaweed, usually in that order, with the layers then repeated. Other possibilities were earth, dung, earth and seaweed, rotten seaweed and turf without dung, or cattle dung with ashes and *feal* alternating with mossy turf. Horse dung could also be included.[630] The middens were 'cone-shaped', and often built inside a 10 to 12 ft (3–3.7 m) ring of *feals*. In some areas dung was not much bothered with, for example in Shapinsay, Cross and Burness, and Sanday, where cottars were formerly required to empty the laird's dung-court as a service once a year, and dumped the dung on the beach. This puzzling lack of concern for dung led to the heaping up of piles of rich mould at the old steadings, 'accumulations of the farm manure of many a year, during times when the people were too indolent or too prejudiced to apply it to the soil'. In the days of agricultural improvement in the 1800s, this mould helped greatly in producing turnip and grass crops on sandy soils. Fish or fish offal could also form part of composts in the nineteenth century. The Orkney men netted dogfish and *sillocks*, young coalfish, to be mixed with earth as manure.[631]

On bigger farms manure was carried on horseback. In 1721, six to eight horses were kept by John Traill at Elsness in Sanday for leading muck.[632] Horses remained in common use in this island. Fifty years later Patrick Fea had large numbers to carry manure, as well as ox-drawn carts for heavier loads:

4 April 1766:	Muck't upon 8 Horses upon the Sandy Sheed with new Ware
5 April	: 12 Horses mucking upon the Sandy Sheed
8 April	: Mucking Horse muck upon the Half penny lands
18 April	: Had 16 Horses mucking from the Catle quoy to Inglea, muckt 21 Rigs thereof
11 April 1771:	Begun to dung the potatoe land att Sinomie upon the Oxen Cart
26 April	: Mucking upon 10 Horses and the Cart to the Long land
10 May	: The Cart putting the Sheep Dung upon the Potato ground.[633]

Horses were also used on smaller farms, and Westray and Papa Westray were particularly distinguished in the 1790s by having 45 and 5 two-ox carts respectively for the same purpose. But the carrying of manure to the fields in kishies was commonly done by people, 'on the backs, generally of the poor women'. Women were the alternative to horses for this purpose in South Ronaldsay and Burray. Special kishies were sometimes used for manure. The pair carried by a horse could be of wooden slats, with an openable bottom. The term *happrick* (diminutive of *happer*, hopper) was given in Shetland to a horse kishie joined to its fellow by a band across the back of the horse.[634] Those for human transport had an extra bearing band, which allowed a second carrier to take over at the half-way mark, without lowering the kishie to the ground. Because of the weight, neither horses nor people carried dung for any great distances.

The main differences in manuring techniques lay between the infield and the outfield. The main outfield crop was black oats, and in some areas, such as Sandsting and Aithsting, it was dunged and lightly harrowed after the seed had been sown. As a rule, however, the outfield oats got no manure. In Tingwall in the 1790s, outfield that had been improved by two or three potato crops could bear two crops of oats, followed by a ley year, without manure. In Unst, the outfield was rarely manured, but was dug every second year for black oats. Where manure was used, it was of weaker quality than that applied to the infield. Outfield manure in Sandsting and Aithsting was cow dung, earth, and seaweed if available, laid in alternate layers in small heaps on the land to be manured. When seed-time came, they were dug down and well mixed. After the ground had been delved and sown, the manure was carried in kishies, spread with the hands, and harrowed. The ground dug in one day was sown, manured and harrowed in the evenings. The compost middens were made on the outfield in winter.[635]

The infield crop, bere, was manured regularly. One spot in Sandsting and Aithsting was cropped with bere for forty years on end but elsewhere the ground was rested from time to time. A year was allowed after every two crops in Fair Isle. Bere and oats alternated on the infield, the manure always preceding the bere crop. If manure was plentiful, two crops of bere might be taken before one of oats. In inland districts where seaweed was scarce, each farm laid about half an acre ley each year, ploughing it before or after harvest, and sowing it with bere in the following year. The land got no other rest. Horse and cow dung, with *feal* and *divot*, was the manure used. On the coast, seaweed could be applied in winter, compost in spring, and seaweed again if available. In Stronsay and Eday, the custom was to have half the arable in bere one year, and in oats the next. House dung was put on the bere land before Christmas. Land could be kept in bere for six or seven years, after which it became too rich and spongy, and a crop of oats was taken without manure. All the cultivated land was by the coast and seaweed was the main manure. In Evie, with seaweed, and Rendall, with an earth and dung compost, bere and small grey oats alternated.[636]

If any difference between Orkney and Shetland can be distinguished here, it is that Orkney laid the greater emphasis on seaweed, and compost middens of dung, ashes and earth came second. In Shetland seaweed generally formed part of a compost. In both areas, manuring was mainly before a bere crop. In the early 1800s, lime was rarely used as a fertiliser.[637] By the mid-nineteenth century, there was little change, and the same broad preferences are apparent. Details from Aithsting and Sandsting show that manure for bere was cow dung, earth and seaweed compost, laid on top, and turned under. Dung was seldom put on potato ground, because it was thought to make the tubers softer and more watery, but where used it was laid on stubble and delved under. Here, unusually, the outfield was manured for oats, and potatoes were also grown on the outfield, sometimes being followed by bere. Bere-land manure was always prepared during the previous summer, and allowed to rot for eight to ten months before being delved in. In Fetlar, there were three infield rotations: 1. potatoes, bere with manure laid above, ley, two crops of oats, potatoes; 2. potatoes, oats, bere with manure below, oats, potatoes; 3. potatoes, two crops of oats, bere with manure below, potatoes. In each case, the manure was applied to the bere crop. When bere followed potatoes the ground was not cultivated, but harrowed only before sowing, and the manure spread above it. In the outfield, oats and ley alternated. Things were less evolved in North Yell, where the infield was cropped every year with bere, small grey oats, and potatoes, the latter never manured. In Unst the infield was manured yearly for bere and potatoes.[638]

By the 1870s, where seaweed was plentiful in Orkney, a six-course rotation could be sustained: two crops of oats, turnips and potatoes, bere, first grass, second grass. The seaweed collected in spring and left to rot in heaps for three months or composted, was used as top-dressing on the grass and arable land. Potatoes were manured in Shetland only when grown on the poorest outfield. Where intensive improvements were going on, much manure was used. On the Swanbister Estate, Orphir, Archer Fortescue carried out autumn ploughing after draining reclaimed areas, then spring-ploughed and sowed oats with a new manure, Peruvian guano, of which 200,000 to 300,000 tons a year were being imported into Britain by 1840–50. For the next year's crop of turnips, 20 tons of town dung plus 5 bushels of bone manure were applied per acre. In the first ten years of improvement, 3000 tons of town dung were boated from Stromness to Swanbister, putting to good use a major resource that is now wasted. After turnips, fifteen loads of seaweed were put on to each acre, and ploughed down, before the application of 8 to 12 bolls of lime per acre, as a preliminary to oats and grass seed.[639] The days of modern farming had arrived, and the old kind of energy flow based on indigenous resources was being replaced.

37

The Delling Spade

CULTIVATION by the spade came to be a mark of Shetland farming after the fragmentation of farms and the creation of outsets in the eighteenth and nineteenth centuries, when the smaller scale of the enterprises led to some replacement of the plough by the spade. It was also common in parts of Orkney. The first historical glimpse of the spade appears in the Rental of Burray in Orkney when Adam Alphingstoun was put in symbolic possession of his tack 'be brekin & delving eird' before witnesses. In 1602 a mare was cut on the back with a spade at Gulberwick in Shetland. The *Margaret* of Sanday carried four dozen shovels from Norway in her hold in 1728. Five old shovels, a new one, and a new spade weighing 4 merks were listed in a Stronsay inventory of 1734.[640] However, there is no clear picture of the spade until the late eighteenth century.

At that period, all cultivation was by the spade in Stroma in the Pentland Firth, close to Orkney but administratively part of Caithness. High beds or ridges were made by the men, and crops on them produced greater yields than on ploughed land. In nearby Swona, most of the cultivation was by the spade. In much of Orkney, however, the spade was a mark of social differentiation. In South Ronaldsay, only the poorest dug their ground with the spade, described as a bit of iron about 3 in. (8 cm) broad on the end of a long stick, and in Eday it was the tool used on the small pendicles. It also served as a complement to the plough, which was often followed by three or four people using spades to break the clods.[641]

The Shetland pattern of use was much more intensive. In Foula, all the ground was delved. Some experimentation was going on, perhaps inspired by the lazy-bed method of growing potatoes, for at Gulberwick a new process of sowing oats in beds on peaty land was being practised, with some success. There was a comparable innovation in Bressay. Where the moss was one peat deep near the hills, the peat was dug, and the top sods laid on a fine clay bottom, pressed down, and cropped with grass or corn. If the ground was wet, raised cultivation beds were made, with ditches between. They produced two or three crops without manure. Much land was delved in Unst, even where the plough could have been used, since the splitting of farms had led to a decline in the number of ploughs. The same was true of Mid and South Yell and North-mavine. Fair Isle used the spade only, the 75 acres of arable being split into

122. A Shetland delling spade in use in a potato field. Photo. John K. Wilkie.

small, nearly equal patches. In Aithsting and Sandsting, as in Delting, the spade
was also used to complement the plough, being used to cut and smooth the
furrow before the seed was sown. Most farms, however, had become too small
for the plough, and the 'curious light spade, made for that purpose' replaced it.
Curiously enough, the actual amount of land under cultivation had
increased.[642]

The first evidence for delving by teams of people comes from the relatively
fertile Dunrossness area. Though ploughs were used, 'the ground is chiefly

123. Detail of the Shetland delling spade. Photo. John K. Wilkie.

124. Two delling teams in Fair Isle, *c.* 1920. Per J. Mann.

laboured with spades of a light kind; with these, five or six men and women will turn over as much land in a day as a Scotch plough with eight or ten oxen'. This may have been a generous estimate. Others thought the spade 'so small and ill made, that two or three persons can hardly turn over as much ground as could easily be done by one good hand, with a spade of better form'.[643]

The Shetland delling spade was used at first mainly by men, whilst women and children pulled the light, wooden harrows. The use of the spade to break clods behind the plough was intended to help the operation of the harrows. By 1814, a good nine-tenths of Shetland were cultivated by teams of three or four people using the spade, a situation that continued for some time.[644]

The spade had an iron blade about 6 in. (15 cm) wide by 10 in. (25 cm) long over the socket. The stout wooden handle was 4 ft (1.2 m) long, and a footpeg was fixed about 14 in. (36 cm) up from the lower end.[645] The delving teams rarely exceeded five or six in size. They stood in line shoulder by shoulder, and the one on the left wielding the *fore-spade* set an even pace. Work was done from right to left, and from top to bottom of the rig. The result was that the spits were turned downhill, and over the years there was a gradual erosion of soil on the higher levels and an accumulation of the best earth lower down. Some estates made a regulation that the first row of sods should be carried uphill to fill the void left by digging, but this was seldom seen to, and in any case, as one observer noted sadly, 'new earth was wheeled or carried on to thin parts each year, but this seemed to make little difference'. Each furrow dug was a *geng* (Old English *gang*, a going), and the team of diggers could be called a geng also.[646] The digging depth was 4 to 5 in.(10–13 cm), and a team of three could loosen and turn a clod measuring 1 to 2 ft (30–61 cm) long by 8 to 12 in. (20–30 cm) wide by 4 to 6 in. (10–15 cm) deep, the spades being kept about 6 to 8 in. (15–20 cm) apart.

In digging, the left hand grasped the handle near the top, and the other about the middle. The spade was set firmly into the ground, held so that it slanted a little backwards. Then each digger brought up his or her right foot, and each pressed down on the heel or footpeg in unison, till the iron blades were almost out of sight. The spades 'all worked simultaneously. In this movement the three bent forward and downwards, so that the weight of the spades in their hands caused them to rest the under part of their right forearms on the right leg about mid-way between knee and hip.' The spit that was loosened was lifted a fraction and turned right over, grass-side down. Finally the clod was struck and chopped with the spade-blade to break it up.[647] Poor land might be given a double delving. Observation of delving in Papa Stour in 1967 showed that when the turned clod was being chopped up or *shappired*, the movement followed on smoothly from the turning action, the blade in the meantime being turned through 90° so that the sharp edge cut into the clod. For this reason, spade blades quickly wore to an oval shape. Spade cultivation remained of sufficient importance in the twentieth century that even though many spade blades were made by local smiths, nevertheless the firm of Thomas Black and Sons, Sea View Works, Berwick, found it worth while to produce them for the

125. An Orkney eetch, used in cultivating patches of arable. In the National Museum, Edinburgh. C126.

Shetland market. The blades were jocularly called *muttles*,[648] a name otherwise used by Shetland fishermen for a small knife (Norwegian *mutel*, a small knife).

Some land use terms point to spade cultivation. In making a furrow with a spade, it could happen that some small, triangular pieces of earth were left untouched, and had to be hoed up afterwards. These were *netlebits* (Norwegian dialectal *knatla*, *knitla*, to chop, cut into little bits). Land delved the second time – the second year – after being ley was *attifield* (Old Norse *aptr*, after + *velta*, to turn). However, since the earliest gloss is 'arable ground lying one year lea', it could equally well apply to ploughed land. In Orkney, where the nineteenth century sources are practically silent on spade cultivation, a small patch of arable was a *dello*[649] (Lowland Scots *dell*, to dig).

Shetland was one of the main areas of spade cultivation in Scotland. The late eighteenth and early nineteenth century intensification in its use accompanied a decline in the number of ploughs, the fragmentation of former joint holdings into large numbers of small units, and the development of outsets. The reduced scale of farming made the spade more suitable than the plough, and it was also easier to handle by the women and younger and older folk who had to see to such work when the men were fishing. Nevertheless it is remarkable how work with the spade in teams could reproduce the form of a plough furrow, supporting the conclusion that in the changing economic circumstances of the period, teamwork with the spade was very much a surrogate for ploughing.[650]

38

Plough Cultivation

IT is a curious fact that it is difficult to get back to a point in time when some kind of a plough was not used for cultivating the soil in the Northern Isles. Around prehistoric house sites of Stone Age character, often sited 'in places where the moorland seems to have been uninhabited ever since, except for sporadic iron age squatting',[651] there are sometimes indications of fields marked by stone clearance heaps, which are older than the Shetland name *röni* (Norwegian, Danish, *røn*, *rønne*, Old Norse *hraun*, heap of stones), or *rudge*. To *rudge* (Norwegian dialectal *rydja*, Old Norse *(h)ryðja*, to clear land) was to gather loose stones off a piece of ground and pile them in heaps. Similar clearance heaps have been made or at least added to in relatively recent times. Few, if any, of them were the result of one season's work, but would have been added to, season after season, over a period of time. They may be up to 20 ft (6.1 m) across by 2 ft (61 cm) high.

The early fields may be in groups marked by boundary dykes, as at the Scord of Brouster in Walls, where five or six fields cover about 2¾ acres, an area comparable to the average arable acreage of present-day crofts even in such a fertile island as Fetlar. The fields, which vary from 60 ft to 100 ft (18.3–30.5 m) over their greatest length, are irregular in shape, with curving boundaries formed of drystone dykes. Since the clearance heaps are found both inside and outside the fields, it seems that these field systems with their boundaries are superimposed on previously cultivated areas.[652]

It is likely that the cultivation of these fields was partly done by ploughs. The main evidence takes the form of stone bars with particular kinds of characteristics. The majority are no more than broken tips, showing that the mortality rate was high, but several complete examples have been found. Some have a flattened, oval cross-section, others are rounded and more sharply pointed. The longest so far found measures 3 ft 2½ in. (98 cm) in length and differs from other known examples in having both its ends pointed. On some sites stone bars and broken tips have turned up in considerable quantities. There are, for example, twenty-six from Lower Gruniquoy, Northmavine.[653]

The feature common to all stone bars is the distinctive way in which the tip is worn over an area of about 2½ to 4 in. (6.4–10 cm). The wear fades into the

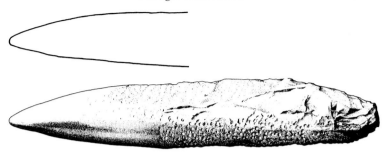

126. A bar-share of stone, with an oval cross-section, 16 in. (41 cm) long. In the National Museum, Edinburgh. AC607. C3975.

marks of pecking or flaking that cover the shank, evidently to give it a better grip in the opening at the rear of the plough-beam in which the stone share was set. The wear is one-sided, and also slopes from front to back, suggesting that the share was held at an angle of 25° to 30° when in use, with a tilt to one side. It can be seen on an example from Unst that when the wear had proceeded so far, the share was turned through 180°. Striations running from front to back over the area of wear make it certain that these stones were pulled forward through the ground in a straight line. These points taken together make it reasonably certain that the stone objects are shares from cultivating implements of a particular type. Further support comes from modern technology, for the iron bar-shares used on horse-ploughs and now on tractor-ploughs have ribs or notches to give them a grip on the frames in which they lie, and the tips wear in a way exactly parallel to the stone shares. They may also be turned when the tip has worn too much to one side. Iron bar shares from the south of England, used in the fourteenth century, have comparable wear marks.[654]

The kind of plough into which the stone shares fitted is evidenced by two finds of wooden plough parts. They came from 6 ft (1.8 m) down in a peat bog at Virdifield in Shetland. They lay one at each side of a straight bar of wood 7 ft 10½ in. (2.4 m) long, and consist of roughly arrow-shaped heads on the end of a shaft. One is 4 ft 0⅘ in. (1.2 m) long, with a head 8$\frac{1}{20}$ in. (20.4 cm) long by 4$\frac{9}{10}$ in.

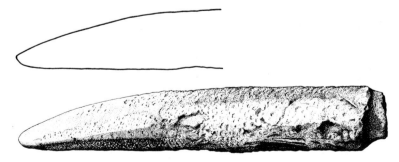

127. A bar-share from Orkney, with a shaped collar at the back, 13.3 in. (34 cm) long. In the National Museum, Edinburgh. AC468. C3977.

(12.5 cm) wide, and the other 4 ft 1$\frac{2}{3}$ in. (1.3 m) long with a head 8$\frac{1}{2}$ in. (21.5 cm) long by 4$\frac{1}{10}$ in. (10.5 cm) wide. These are the combined heads and stilts, similar to examples from south-west Scotland, Ireland, Denmark and elsewhere, of types of ploughs known as 'ards'. In several examples, there are grooves and ridges on the upper surface, marking the place where a wooden bar-share has been gripped in position, as a means of reducing the amount of wear on the ard-head. The Shetland parts, however, have broad, flattened or slightly hollowed areas on top, of such a kind that the flatter of the stone-share types would fit comfortably on to them. They have been so well preserved that each mark of the blade that shaped them by removing flake after flake of wood, can be clearly seen. A comparable ard-head and stilt from Milton Loch in Kirkcud-brightshire has been radio-carbon dated to 350±100 BC. It is likely that the Shetland implements were working at the same period, fitted with their stone shares, and pulled by a pair of oxen fastened by the horns to a yoke like the 4 ft 7 in. (140 cm) long example found in a Shetland peat bog.[655]

The next piece of evidence for ploughs is much later. It takes the form of two quartz pebbles from Jarlshof, each with a highly polished end. Such pebbles have been found in quantities in the Border counties of Scotland and England. Some wooden plough parts from Danish peat bogs contain similar pebbles, thrust into openings in the land-side of the sole as a means of reducing wear. The earliest of the five Danish examples has been radio-carbon dated to AD 1510±100, and all belong to the sixteenth century. These wear-pebbles have convex faces, with parallel striations running across them. Another type with a flat, highly polished face was used on the axles of plough fore-carriages. Axles have been found in Danish bogs with pebbles in position, and similar pebbles have turned up in the Scottish Borders. Wear-pebbles, therefore, point to a medieval type of plough with a long sole and a beam supported on a wheeled fore-carriage. One of the Jarlshof examples was found in the filling of a Viking outhouse which had become ruinous during the thirteenth and four-teenth centuries, and was then used for dumping ashes and rubbish. This pebble is likely to be earlier than the end of the fourteenth century, and is, therefore, the earliest wear-pebble so far identified. Evidently pebbles fell out sometimes and were pushed back into their sockets again, for one of the Jarlshof examples has been worn on two faces.[656] On this evidence, it is likely that at least one example of a medieval plough with a wheeled fore-carriage reached Shetland, but it did not have a long life-span, since the later evidence is exclusively for ploughs of a much simpler type, more likely to be derived from the ards of prehistoric times.

THE DOCUMENTARY EVIDENCE

There is a long gap in time between the archaeological evidence and the documents that first mention ploughs in the early seventeenth century. Plough irons made by a smith, Nicole Thomassoun, were stolen in Delting in 1602, and a complete plough was taken in Whiteness and Weisdale in 1604. Oxen were the draught animals in Dunrossness in 1604. Coulters and socks were mentioned in Harray in 1606 and North Rousay in 1624. In Kirkwall in 1629, no plough irons were to be bought unless the seller could find security for them, presumably in case they had been stolen. At Seatter, Thomas Seatter's plough was led in 1624 by a female servant, Margaret Bimbister.[657]

At this period, therefore, the wooden ploughs were fitted with iron coulters and socks, which were valuable, and were drawn by oxen controlled by an assistant. In the same century, the coulters and socks were described as 'slender and little'. The teams were of four oxen in 'broad band', that is, pulling side by side. One man held the plough, and a helper walked backwards in front of the oxen, controlling them and urging them on. The plough, which had only one stilt, was so light that the ploughman could pick it up and carry it to the other side of the ridge, or home if he so wished. The lightness of the plough was said to be because the beasts had little strength.[658]

Trade was an important factor in promoting a continuous renewal of the influence of Norway on the Northern Isles. In 1652, 'Timber requisite for ploughinge of the ground' was got from Norway in exchange for grain. On 19 May 1728 David Traill instructed James Spence, skipper of the *Margaret* of Sanday, to bring from Bergen '16 dozen good pleugs four dozen skys' and on 4 Sept. he sent from Stronsay to his father in Sanday '12 good pleughs, six skies'. The imported ploughs were probably beams rather than complete ploughs. The Fetlar name *orderous* means a plough beam, though later it was misunderstood and applied to a wooden bar nailed on the front of the beam to take the traces.[659]

Ploughs and plough parts are sometimes mentioned in testamentary inventories. Adam Flawis in South Ronaldsay (died 1601) had an old plough sock; Thomas Garsen in Skabray, Sandwick (died 1612), a 'pleuch and pleuch graith estimet to, £1.10s.'; Hutcheon Sandesone in Kirkbuster, Walls (died 1613) owed Gilbert Yuill, ploughman, his fee of £3 and 'bounteth' of one meill of malt, worth £4.[660] Geill Bras in Linkletter (died 1684) had a plough worth 4/–; Malcom Pease in Lady parish, Sanday (died 1688) had a spade, two forks, a coulter and a sock valued together at £1.10/–; Elizabeth Sclaitter, wife of Stephen Mure in Crussiger in the same parish, had a plough with its graith and three forks valued at £1, and a spade worth 6/8; Magnus Symondsone in St Andrews (died 1678), 'ane old furnished plough' worth 6/8, and a harrow, spade, fork and tusker worth 13/4; Alexr Smith, merchant burgess of Kirkwall (died 1681) had two ploughs and 6 skies.[661] An inventory registered in Kirkwall in 1734 of the steelbow goods, etc. in the lands of North Strynzie belonging to James Fea of Whitehall included 'four ploughs, one of them having all furniture except Culter and Sock whereof three wanting Skys and lives (rear piece of plough) ... Six new ploughs ... Six Coulters and one Sock, and two Culters and four Socks, three lives ...',[662] whilst another dated to 1747–8 showed, for the time and place, a surprising collection of ploughing equipment at Burray. The list is:

'An English plew ... a Coulter, 2 yoakes, and 20 bows for plew oxen with ane

Soam ... and 2 pleugh beams ... 2 pleugh beams, an old "stilted plewgh" wanting Iron ... a wheel pleugh with the box, and Iron axle reach and sheir, wilds and chains of five links, two Scots plewghs for Oxen having Iron Shoding and Sleebands, two Do. Orkney make, one of them new the other wanting the sheir, 2 broken horse plewghs with Iron muzles, a broken horse plew with an Iron reach, a smal Orkney plewgh, iron shod on the earth board, a broken one of the same kind ... 8 plew spades, 9 oxen yoaks, 65 bowes for oxen, 4 horse plew gear, 6 ambles and furniture, 2 how pleughs with Irons and Limbers ... 11 new feathered plewgh socks ... 3 plewgh spades ... 2 plew spades ... a Soam of 23 links, 20 Do. in 3 pairts ... two single horse Swingle trees with a chain of 5 links, and a hook, a Large Iron Coulter ... 2 plew beams ... a new plewgh with ane Iron Sleband and muzle ... two old English plewghs with muzles & Sleebands and one Reach ... 2 new coulters and 2 old ones for English plewghs, 84 links of Soams in different parts, 4 English socks ... 2 old coulters more ... ane Iron muzle for a plew, 5 broken bows and a yoake ... 2 plew gear for 9 horses ... 2 old yoaks for oxen, 4 bowes, with Iron hooks, Slings, ane old plewgh with Sock and muzle ... 3 old English Plewe ... 3 oxen yoaks with two bowes, 2 pair hems with ambels and slings, Six soams for Oxen, 4 whereof has hooks, the other 2 wanting ... 2 muzles ... the Coulter of a Plew with the ring staple & Stock of a yoake.'[663]

This is an astonishing range for an Orkney estate in the first half of the eighteenth century. Ploughs were pulled by both horses and oxen, the latter wearing bow yokes at the centre of which was a staple and a ring or hook, linked by a short length of chain, the sling, to the soam or draught chain by which the plough was pulled, directly or through the medium of swingletrees. The yokes had each two bows, and the oxen appear to have been yoked in pairs, not four abreast as for the one-stilted plough. The types of plough referred to are English ploughs; a wheeled plough with its fore-carriage, presumably also English since such ploughs were not native to Scotland; Scots ploughs, both imported and locally made in Orkney; a smaller plough, probably of similar type, also made in Orkney; a single-stilted plough. The ploughs were of wood, but at least one had its mould-board shod with iron. The iron parts were the share, the coulter, the 'sleeband' or iron band round the coulter mortice in the beam, the muzzle, and parts of the fore-carriage of the wheeled plough.

On this estate, at least, the cultivating implements were as up-to-date as anywhere in Scotland, showing the high standard of farming here, but contrasting sharply with those of the small-scale tenant farmers. In 1757, the one-stilted plough in Orkney had 'plow-irons so clumsy and short, that the furrow is very shallow and unequal, and must often be delved with spades'. Since this source says there were no ox ploughs, horses must have been used in parts of Orkney to pull the one-stilted plough, as appears from drawings on estate plans made around 1770. The team illustrated is of three horses abreast, led by a boy walking backwards in front, with a whip in one hand and the three leading ropes in the other.[664]

The evidence so far has been for teams of oxen in Shetland, and of horses in Orkney. The Shetlanders were said to till with oxen, because their shelties were 'good for nothing in the plough', but cattle were also used in parts of Orkney, for 'they use light Ploughs, drawn by two or by four Horses, or by two Horses and two Cows'.[665] In Shetland the team was mainly of four animals yoked abreast. In Unst, Delting, Aithsting and Sandsting and the Sandwick and Cunningsburgh districts of Dunrossness, oxen are specified. There were teams of four horses, or mixed teams of two horses and two oxen in Unst and four horse teams in the Ness district of Dunrossness.[666] In Dunrossness the use of horses could be attributed to influence from Orkney, but this is less likely in the remote island of Unst. In Orkney, there was a general use of four or three horses yoked abreast, the smaller team being relatively more common in the more fertile areas of the Mainland and South Isles. Teams of three or four horses abreast were used in Stronsay and Eday, Holm, Rousay and Egilsay, Stromness, Evie and Rendall. In Birsay, with 523 horses, teams were of three abreast. Even the biggest farmers here had no more than three one-stilted ploughs, for which nine horses had to be maintained. The total number of ploughs in Birsay was 143. In Harray, 57 ploughs were served by 172 horses. Orphir had 102 ploughs and 380 horses. By the 1790s, however, innovations were appearing. Teams of two horses were mentioned in Stromness, but more common was the arrangement of four horses fastened two by two in line ahead, that coincided with the gradual adoption of the two-stilted plough.[667] A similar innovation was appearing in Caithness at the same date, and its occurrence in Orkney shows the close links between these two areas, evidenced not only by the importation to Orkney of horses, but also of yoking techniques, and of the light two-stilted plough.

Oxen seem to have been more used than horses at an earlier date, as linguistic evidence suggests. In Orkney, the four horses yoked abreast in the team were called the *fur(furrow)-horse* and *fur-scam*, walking on the furrows, and the *volar-scam* and *outend horse*, walking on the unploughed land. *Volar* is from Old Norse *vǫllr*, a field, and *scam* from Old Norse *skammr*, short. The terms represent at least a partial transference from oxen to horses, for scam can be equated with the Shetland *skammjok*, 'the yoke which is borne by the two inside oxen, a shorter yoke in comparison with the longer *utjok* which is borne by the two outside oxen'. An 'outjock ox' was mentioned in Shetland in 1603. The Orkney terminology, though applied to horses, must reflect an old practice in which the draught consisted of an inner pair of oxen linked by a short yoke, and an outer pair, probably placed a little in front of the inner pair, linked by a long yoke. Nevertheless it cannot be assumed that plough-teams consisted entirely of oxen in the Northern Isles before the date of the regular importation of horses from Caithness and Strathnaver, for the mixed situation in Unst has to be taken into account, as well as the fact that already in the late ninth century ploughing with horses was taking place in Norway.[668]

The numerous late eighteenth century sources add a number of details. According to a full account from Aithsting and Sandsting:

'There are 14 ploughs in the parish, 4 oxen in each, who go a-breast. A large yoke is laid on the neck of the two outermost, and a small yoke on the innermost oxen. These yokes are joined by a double rope, to the middle of which is fixed the draught or chain, which is from 24 to 18 feet (7.3–5.5 m) long, from the neck of the oxen to the nose of the plough. The plough is of a very singular construction. A crooked piece of wood, bent (naturally) almost to a right angle, forms the beam; to which is fixed a piece of oak stave, about 7 feet (2.1 m) long, which must be very pliable, and yield to the pressure of the driver's hand, when he would deepen his fur. The coulter stands almost even up and down, and is always too short. A square hole is cut through the lower end of the beam, and the *mercal*, a piece of oak about 22 inches (56 cm) long, introduced, which, at the other end, holds the sock and sky. The furrow is made deep or shallow, by driving a wedge below or above the mercal, on the outside of the beam. There is a stilt on top of the plough; and the man who holds it, walks on the white land at the side of it ... It turns the furrow almost quite round about; and people are employed to cut and smooth it with spades, before the seed is sown.' In Delting, the ploughs were 'made of a small crooked piece of wood, at the end of which is fixed a slender pliable piece of oak, that is fastened to the yokes laid across the necks of the oxen'. In all other descriptions, a draught-rope links the point of the beam to the centre of the ox-yoke. The writer may have made a mistake, but the 7 ft (2.1 m) long wooden bar found with the two ard-heads and stilts from Virdifield should perhaps be borne in mind here. Orkney ploughs at this stage were similar to those of Shetland, but had a small pointed sock, with a smaller coulter. It was said that the mould-strokers did not turn the soil, but rather broke it into pieces, leaving half the surface unturned.[669]

Early illustrations show that single-stilted ploughs around 1800 consisted of a single or composite beam with a loop or ring at the front end to take the draught-rope. The thick, rear end curved downwards, with a mortice near the bottom for a piece of wood, the head of the plough, that held the sock, and on the right side three wooden pegs or mould-strokers that functioned as a kind of mouldboard. An iron coulter with a long shank was fixed in the curve at the back of the beam, so that its tip lay in front of the sock. The sock of an example from Unst illustrated in 1793 is arrow-shaped like the prehistoric ard-heads, but there is no later evidence for this form.[670]

Whereas in Shetland the number of ploughs had decreased by the 1790s, and had been to a great extent replaced by spades, in Orkney the sporadic introduction of two-stilted types did not affect the numbers of one-stilted ploughs, for those mentioned in the parish accounts total almost a thousand. The one-stilted plough was long preferred for cultivating bere crops, and especially for giving the final ploughing just before the seed was sown. It was good for shallow or rocky ground, but less suitable for oatland, which was harder to plough.[671]

Already by the 1770s, Orkney was being affected by the innovation of the two-stilted plough, introduced from the North of Scotland. The social level of its adoption was very different from that of the English and Scottish ploughs imported to Burray at an earlier date. It was said in 1773: 'Of late years there has been introduced into several places of these Isles, a small plow with two handles, called a Highland or Caithness plow by our country people ... (the) handles are placed so much upright, as renders it very hard to manage ... As it is constructed with mold-boards it has the advantage of the Orkney plow, which has only a few sticks (mould-strokers) placed in the room of these.'[672]

This was a lighter version of the heavy old Scotch plough, as found in several parts of mainland Scotland.[673] Its spread in Orkney was not very rapid, nor did it entirely replace the one-stilted plough where it was introduced. Both types worked together for some time, as on Patrick Fea's farm in Sanday when the two-stilted type was tried alongside the native type in 1779: 'My 2 plowghs working as befor and tried the 2 stilted plowghs in the Park, Mr. Campbell at it.' The name suggests that the ploughman was a Scot, perhaps a Highlander. Generally speaking, the two-stilted plough spread more quickly in the more fertile South Isles of Orkney, nearer Mainland Scotland, than in the North Isles.[674] In Sandwick and Stromness a few farmers were using it by the 1790s, particularly in ploughing oat land. In South Ronaldsay and Burray, the two-stilted plough was drawn by four horses yoked in pairs, a new form of team layout that came in with the new plough. In Holm, 'a few two-stilted ploughs in miniature, a faint imitation of the old Scottish plough for tearing out leys, are beginning to be used, but seldom on other occasions'. In St Andrews and Deerness, the one-stilted plough was yielding to 'a wretched imitation of the Scots plough'. In Orphir there were 100 one-stilted ploughs and two 'Highland' ones introduced by Patrick Honeyman in the common Scots form with two stilts. In the North Isles, only in Eday is there a reference to the 'Scotch or two stilted plough', introduced by the tenant James Murray,[675] though he continued to use the one-stilted plough as well.

The two-stilted Scots plough was not unknown in Shetland. In the late 1700s, for example, Sir John Mitchell brought from the South of Scotland a Scots plough with trained oxen, but during the night people came and broke the plough, and hurt the oxen. The Scots plough was 'frequently adopted and laid aside again, by different persons; and on the whole, judged too heavy for our light cattle or horses'. The native plough was praised as light, simple, and cheap, though it was also criticised as dear because it needed a team of four, with four or five people, two or three of whom went behind the plough 'tramping and hacking the peat', and heavy because of its construction, with the share placed 2 in. (5.1 cm) below the coulter and generally extending 2 in. (5.1 cm) before it, and with a distance of 25 ft (7.6 m) between the coulter and the yoke. In 1814, James Small's improved ploughs were still only 'partially introduced' to Orkney, and there were very few in Shetland.[676] They were pulled by a team of two strong horses or two trained oxen. Whereas with the native one-stilted ploughs and the two-stilted Highland ploughs there was a man to control the plough and a helper to control the animals, with the improved type the plough-man himself controlled the team with reins. It was said that the way of plough-ing without a driver was introduced during an early period of the wars with

France,[677] presumably on the assumption that they led to a scarcity of man-power.

By the mid-nineteenth century in Orkney, the one-stilted plough had become a curiosity, largely replaced by the two-stilted plough. In North Ronaldsay, where there had been only one two-stilted plough in 1832, every house had a wooden plough and some an iron one. In Lady parish the team was always of two horses without a driver. Iron ploughs in Stromness parish cost £2.2s., and were coming into use in Orphir, where one-stilted ploughs with three horses survived on some of the smaller farms till the 1820s. They were said to have broken up the ground more completely than the ploughs that replaced them. In Sandwick an iron plough cost £2, a wooden plough £1.10s., and the one-stilted plough had been replaced by the common two-stilted mould-board plough with a pair of horses.[678] In Orkney, the change from the one-stilted to the two-stilted plough, at first the Highland type and increasingly the Lowland Scottish type, progressed through the last decade of the eighteenth century and had become almost complete by the end of the first quarter of the nineteenth century. Traditions have been recorded about the introduction of two-stilted mould-board ploughs with reins. When the first one came to the West Mainland of Orkney: 'The late Hugh Bews, grandfather of the present Mr. James Bews of Yesnaby, was hired as a ploughman on the farm of Skaill to show the West Mainland people how to drive horses in a plough with reins, and also the way to work a cupper or plough with a mould-board. This man's plough had a wooden board, the wood was thought to be warmer for the ground. I have often heard the late William Allan of Eastbigging tell of the vast crowd of people that gathered on the farm of Skaill the first day Hugh Bews yoked his wooden board plough, and to drive the horses from behind with reins, thus doing away with the *pirrin* (from Norwegian dialectal *piren*, weakly, thin), or "ca'ing bairn". Mr. Allan said there was a crowd at the place like a market. William Allan was then a lad of fourteen years old; he was 96 when he died, and that, I think, is about 16 or 17 years ago.'[679] This description takes the mould-board plough back to the early 1800s.

The situation in Shetland was only partially comparable. The Sandsting and Aithsting report noted that there were now no one-stilted ploughs in the parish, and that the type was falling into disuse throughout Shetland. There were, however, only three ploughs altogether. The minister's plough was of Small's make, pulled by two oxen, and the two others, used in Reawick and in Papa Little, were made in Lerwick after a pattern by Morton, ploughwright in Leith Walk, Edinburgh, and each pulled by four ponies. In Dunrossness, ploughs were used at Quendale, Bigton, and Sumburgh, and in Sandwick and Cunningsburgh there were a few ploughs drawn by small horses. In Northmavine there were twelve ploughs pulled by oxen or horses or a combination of each, where there had been twenty-six in the 1790s. It was even suggested that ploughing might disappear altogether in favour of the spade. In Tingwall, Whiteness and Weisdale, the one-stilted plough was still in use, though the two-stilted plough of the Rotherham or Small's type was coming into more general use, pulled by two horses, or helped by two oxen if the horses were small. In Delting the one-stilted ploughs had been replaced by twenty Scotch ploughs. In Unst the old 'Zetland' plough had been completely replaced by the spade.[680]

The pattern reflects a clear social stratification. The few landowners and wealthier farmers used the 'common Scotch plough',[681] whilst the bulk of the people, whose living had come to depend on fishing rather than farming, cultivated their land with the spade. The result as indicated by the cultivating implements was a widening gap between the upper and the lower classes, accompanying a general regression in the practice of agriculture. This was in marked contrast to the situation in Orkney, though from the economic view-point it was balanced in Shetland by the development of the fishing industry.

Effectively, the one-stilted and 'Highland' two-stilted plough had gone from use by or before the mid-nineteenth century, apart from occasional survivals.

In the 1870s the one-stilted plough was still said to be seen here and there in Orkney, drawn by two oxen or an ox and a garron. In Holm parish a horse and bullock yoked together in the plough could be seen on small farms, but the bigger farmers, particularly in the work of reclamation that was then in active progress, used a large or 'Tweeddale' plough with four bullocks or six horses, followed by a smaller 'common' plough. A small farmer could not work up reclaimed soil in this way, and the lack of horsepower also hindered improvement by such people. Some old Orkney wooden ploughs were said to be still in use about Rackwick in Hoy in the 1880s.[682]

In 1864, Arthur Mitchell saw a one-stilted plough working at Cun-ningsburgh, Dunrossness:

'This last I had never seen before; and, so far as I could learn, no one could see it in actual use anywhere in Scotland, except in this particular part of Shetland. Even there, I understood that it was ceasing to be employed in 1864. In a country like ours, where so much mind has been given to the improvement of ploughs, and for the prosperity of which the plough does so much, I felt that

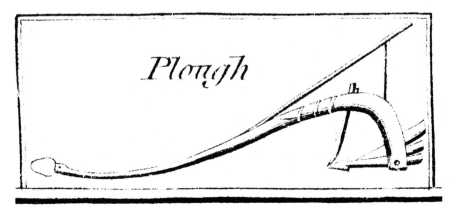

128. A one-stilted plough from Unst. From OSA 1793. v. Frontispiece. C5839.

129. The later form of the one-stilted Shetland plough, with two mould-boards replacing the mould-strokers. In the National Museum, Edinburgh.

130. Two one-stilted Orkney ploughs, *c.* 1890. Per P K I Leith. C1535.

the continual use of this rude implement was remarkable and noteworthy. Accordingly, I purchased the plough.' Unfortunately the plough that was sent to him was a new one made on the pattern of the old one. Only one was said to be still in use in one place in 1874. In general the spade was the main implement, or, on estates like that of A J Grierson at Quendale, iron swing ploughs. Grierson employed two ploughmen at £14 and £20 per annum, plus an allowance of 6½ bolls (910 lbs) oatmeal, 1 Scots pint of sweet milk daily, 4 bolls (48 bushels) of potatoes, a house, peat for the fire, and their grain ground.[683] This rate of payment, though on a par with that of ploughmen in Lowland Scotland, was exceptional in the conditions that prevailed in Shetland.

Ploughing started on Candlemas Day, 2 February, or as soon after that as the weather permitted. By this time all the infield or 'doon land' had been manured with seaweed. Since the horses did little winter work except carrying grain and meal to and from the mill, they were very lively at their first yoking, and 'fled around like birds, and many a golt of a stane flang the man and the ploo aboot'. A yoke, starting about 9 o'clock, lasted five or six hours. When oxen were used, work started much earlier. The first yoking in summer was from half-past four to half-past eight in the morning, followed by a rest and feeding for about five hours, and a second yoking from two till six o'clock. In a season, a plough would turn from 4 to 14 Orkney planks of 40 fathoms each, about 9⅓ acres for an average of 8 planks. In Stronsay and Eday, the estimate for each plough was much greater, 15 acres Scots. The first ploughing was for oatland, which was sown at the end of March and the beginning of April. The bereland was then stirred and harrowed, and sown in late April or May after it had been manured and given the seed furrow.[684]

By the end of the nineteenth century and up until the recent past, the

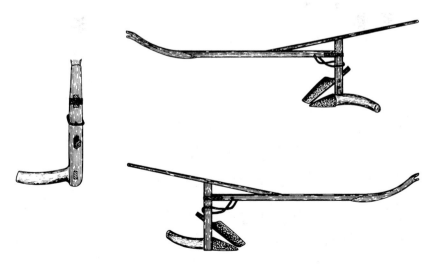

131. Details of a one-stilted plough in Tankerness House Museum. Two mould-strokers are missing.

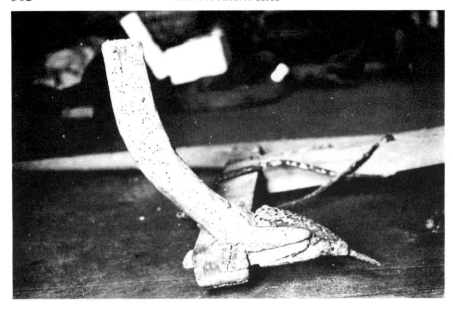

132. Showing the way in which the iron sock is fitted on the front of the ground-wrest and a pin mortised into the head of the plough in Fig. 131.

133. One-stilted Orkney ploughs had short, very broad coulters. In Tankerness House Museum.

standard plough was a light iron type drawn by two horses or ponies, or sometimes two oxen. Traces of older traditions nevertheless remain. Oxen could have someone to lead them, even though they were attached to the plough by means of collars and the ploughman held a pair of reins. A delving spade might be carried on the plough, like a pattle, to clean it, and in one twentieth century photograph of a team of two ponies pulling an iron plough at Fladdabister, just south of Lerwick, the team is not only being led, but the ploughman is walking alongside the plough holding it by one of its two stilts, exactly in the manner of a one-stilted plough. Light, wooden-beamed American ploughs, such as the Oliver 1A, became popular during the twentieth century in Orkney as well as Shetland. They were good in sandy soil and cut a good, big furrow. Six pairs of heavy work-horses competed with iron ploughs at a twentieth century ploughing match in the East Park at Scalloway.[685]

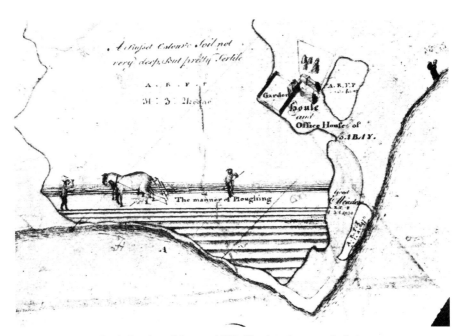

134. The one-stilted plough at Sabay, *c*. 1770. The four horses yoked abreast are controlled by a boy with a whip, walking backwards. From an estate plan by W. Aberdeen. 3.14.4.

Terminology and Construction

Terminology of the One-stilted Plough

Name or Description	Term	Etymology	Source
One-stilted plough	Side plough (O)		OSA 1795. xx. 249
	Stilltie	Stilt = handle	Marwick (1903) 1926. 4
1. Beam	Arr-trees (O)	O.N. *arðr*, plough	Shirreff 1814a. 51
	Orderous (S)	O.N. *arðr*, plough + *áss*, beam	Johnston (1734) 1911 IV. 121
1a. Rear part of beam	Astrees (S)	O.N. *áss*, beam	Jamieson 1825 s.v.
	Stang	O.N. *stǫng*, pole	Marwick (1903) 1936. 8
1b. Front part of beam	Foregill	Fore + probably Norw. dial. *kjøl*, keel, bottom part of plough	,,
2. Stilt	Oure-tree	Sc. *ower*, over, upper	Shirreff 1814a. 51
3. Ground-wrest	Sky	Norw. dial. *skeid*, *skjei*, *skji*, upright part of a plough	Marwick (1728) 1926. II. 135; OSA 1795. VII. 585, *et al.*
	Sproll	Uncertain; perhaps from Eng. to sprawl	Marwick (1903) 1936. 8
4. Mould-strokers	Ear(th)-skies, lug-skies	Probably O.N. *arðr* + *sky*. *Lug* (ear) is due to misunderstanding of the first element	Shirreff 1814a. 51
4a.	Nether-ski	O.N. *niðre*, down	Marwick (1903) 1936. 9
4b.	Millya-ski	O.N. *milli*, between	,,
4c.	Ivverski	O.N. *yfir*, *efri*, upper	,,
	Hirspa or hurspa pin	Perhaps a corrupt form of O.Sc. *hirst*, thin stony ground	,,
5. Share beam, a wooden pin mortised into the plough head to hold the sock	Merkie pin, Markal pin, Mercal	Uncertain; ?Norw. dial. *merg*, *merj*, marrow + *kølv*, piece of wood	OSA 1793. VII. 585; Shirreff 1814a. 51; Marwick (1903) 1936. 8

Name or Description	Term	Etymology	Source
6. Sock or share	Sock	O.Sc. *soc*, 1500	Shirreff 1814a. 52
	Sewch(ar)	Perhaps from Scots *sheuch*, to make a trench	Marwick (1903) 1936. 8
7. Coulter	Idem		
8. Rear-piece of beam	Live, life (O)	Uncertain; perhaps a form of Sc. *luif*, palm of the hand	Marwick (1734) 1922–3. I. 65 Shirreff 1814a. 51
	Sewcher Stang-post or beam	See above	Marwick (1903) 1936. 8
	Head		OSA 1793. VII. 585–6
	Stock		OSA 1793. V. 192–3
	Key		OSA 1794. X. 23
9. Iron Band	Hass spang	O.N., O.Sc. *hals*, neck + Dutch *spang*, buckle	Shirreff 1814a. 51
10. ,, ,,	Throws spang	O.Sc. *thraw*, twist, but really a corrupt form of *hass*	,, ,, 52
	Bridal	= bridle	Marwick (1903) 1936. 10
11. Muzzle	Mou Mull	Sc. *mow*, mouth Norw. *mule*, O.N. *muli*, muzzle	Shirreff 1814a. 51 Jakobsen (1908) 1928 s.v. *mull*
	Kyollks	O.N. *kjálki*, jaw, Sc. *chowk*	Marwick (1903) 1936. 6
12. Angle between stilt and rearpiece	Nic(k) or a(r)se (O)	Specific sense of Eng. *nick*, a notch	Shirreff 1814a. 51
13. Strut between stilt and rearpiece	Steer-pin		Shirreff 1814a. 52
14. Iron staple to take the end of the pattle			

Name or Description	Term	Etymology	Source
15. Plough staff	Pattle or pattle-tree	O.Sc. *patyl*, plough staff, *c.* 1400	Shirreff 1814a. 52
16. Draught-rope	Soam	O.Sc. *soyme*, idem, 1375; O.N. *saumr*, a seam, joining	Shirreff 1814a. 52
	Trauchle soam	Cf. Flemish *tragelen*, *trakelen*, to trudge, walk with difficulty	Marwick (1903) 1936. 6
17. 'Saving Rope'	Savir soam		Marwick (1903) 1936. 7
18. Little crosspiece of wood in the jaws of the plough linked with the *savir soam*	Dotmel	Uncertain; for second element, cf. Norw. *mel*, the bit of a bridle, which the part resembles	Marwick (1903) 1936. 7
19. Strengthener of binder on join between the two parts of the beam	Nobe	Cf. Norw. dial. *nabb*, *nubb*, pin, peg	Marwick (1903) 1936. 8
20. Do., under join	Crobe	Uncertain	,, ,, ,, 8
21. Yoke, to which the swingletrees are fixed (4 ft long–1.2 m)	Master-tree	Eng. *master*	Shirreff 1814a. 51
	Mester ammel	Cf. Dan., Swed. dial. *hammel*, Norw. *humul*, swingletree	Jakobsen (1908) 1928 s.v.
	Ammel tree		,, ,,
	Amble, ammle		Marwick 1929 s.v.
22. Swingletree to which two others are fixed (2½ ft long – 76 cm)	Twa beast tree		Shirreff 1814a. 51
23. Swingletree (20 in. long – 51 cm)	E'e (one) beast tree		Shirreff 1814a. 52

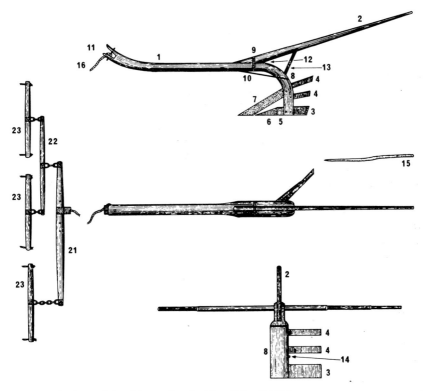

135. Terminology of the Orkney plough. After Shirreff 1814 a..

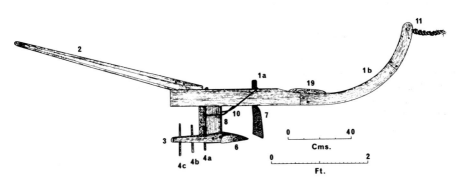

136. The most recent type of one-stilted Orkney plough had mould-strokers resembling harrow-tines.

137. Women occasionally took the plough. Orkney. C79A.

138. Even with a modern iron plough, the furrows may be sorted with a spade, as was usually done with the one-stilted plough. Shetland. Per A. Manson and S. Isbister. 31.19.20.

Details of the construction, terminology, and method of yoking, recorded in the second half of the nineteenth century from James Sabiston of Greeny in Birsay, were put together by George Marwick in the form of a lecture delivered at Dounby in 1903. The draught-rope, measuring about 9 ft (2.7 m) long, was laid double round the draught pin, often the bone of a sheep's foreleg, in the muzzle of the plough. When the plough was in action, the front end of the beam served as a kind of wheel or skid. When turning at the end of the furrow, the ploughman could raise the stilt on his shoulder, and trundle the plough on the *foregill*. A small hole on the underside of the foregill held the rope known as the *savir soam*, which was connected to the main draught-rope as well as to the wooden cross-piece or *dotmel* in the muzzle. If the share came against an obstruction, this device pulled it out of the ground and saved the draught pin from breaking. The foregill and muzzle, from frequent rubbing on the earth, wore out quickly, so that it was logically made as a separate piece. Where it was fixed to the backend of the beam, a wooden spar or *nobe* was used as a strengthener. On heavier ploughs, a similar spar or *crobe* was also fixed underneath. The beam itself had to be twice the length from a man's wrist to his shoulder. The upright *stang-post* at its rear end held the *markal pin* to which the sock was attached. In Shetland the mercal was a piece of oak about 22 in. (56 cm) long.[686] The end of the *sky* or ground wrest was also fixed to the mercal, and the sock was pushed on to both of these parts together. The ground-wrest, in effect, formed an arm of the markal pin. In the plough described by George Marwick, the ground-wrest had three vertical holes in it for three upright pins projecting two, three, and four fingers' breadth below, from front to back respectively. In all other known examples the equivalents are a pair of mould-strokers or a double mould-board. This Orkney variant seems to have been designed to achieve even more of a harrowing action than the others. The stilt was fixed to the top of the beam in such a way that it would come up to the ploughman's haunch bone.[687]

Nine examples of one-stilted ploughs are known to survive in whole or in part, six from Orkney (one in the Stromness Museum, three in the Tankerness House Museum, one in the Glasgow Museum and Art Gallery, and one in the National Museum of Antiquities of Scotland), and three from Shetland (National Museum). Within the range of a broad similarity, several differences can be distinguished. The stilts of the Shetland ploughs form more of a framework. Instead of mould-strokers, there are double mould-boards, a lower one and an upper one set at a slightly different angle, both on the right side of the plough. This form of sophistication could be a response to the introduction of sown grasses, producing a sward that had to be more completely inverted during ploughing. The retention of mould-strokers in Orkney, on the other hand, is due to the retention of the plough for earthing up potatoes or giving the final ploughing before a crop of bere was sown.

The Shetland coulters were fixed in the horizontal part of the beam, and were angled somewhat forward. Those of Orkney were fixed in a slanting opening in the stang-post, and set at such an angle that they were made to 'gripe in on the

139. A small horse and an ox yoked in the plough in Orkney. 19.23.21.

unploughed land'.[688] They were short and broad, with blunt, squarish tips, and because of their shape and angle could function as incipient mould-boards. They helped to make the Orkney one-stilted plough fully capable even of such tasks as earthing up potatoes in drills. The socks of Orkney ploughs are shoe-shaped, simply metal covers for the plough-head. Those of Shetland are feathered, making them more suitable for grassy swards.

140. A long-board plough before an Orkney stackyard. C3212.

An essential piece of equipment was the *pattle* or plough staff. It served to clean surplus earth off the plough, and also acted as a second stilt when the point was placed in an iron staple on the side of the rear-piece. In this way more pressure could be applied to keep the plough deeper in the ground. This job could be done by an assistant, additional to the one who was controlling the animals. The pattle could also be thrown at the animals when they were lazy.[689]

The harness consisted of a *wassie* or collar, 'of twisted oat straw, sometimes covered with coarse woollen cloth, more from a motive to prevent the horses tearing and eating them when ploughing, than as a preservative from the shoulders of the poor animals'. Over this lay the wooden *brechams* or harness to which the *citheropes* or side-ropes, averaging 9 ft (2.8 m) long, were attached. These were supported at either side of the horse by a plaited back-band, and their rear ends were attached to the swingletrees. For a three-horse team there were three single *e'e* (one) *beast trees*, a double one called a *twa beast tree*, and the *master-tree* to which the others were linked. From the centre of the master-tree the main draught rope or *soam* ran back to the muzzle of the plough. A plough rein, or halter made of rope, was a *nap* (origin obscure).[690]

THE SOUTH RONALDSAY BOYS' PLOUGHING MATCH

In South Ronaldsay one of the annual events is the boys' ploughing match in April or late March. Originally it was confined to St Margaret's Hope, but has spread in recent years. In 1957 it was seen for the first time outside South Ronaldsay at the County Show Sports, an occurrence which also made a break with the traditional date. Children aged 5 to 9 are extravagantly dressed as 'horses', and the 'ploughmen' are aged 9 to 14, which is the upper age limit. The

141. An Oliver plough at Ocraquoy, Fladdabister, Shetland, held as if one-stilted, with a man leading the ponies. C4754.

142. Rectangular back-harrows in use in Shetland. 1.38.20.

dressed up, highly ornamented 'horses' are judged in the Cromarty Hall, and the ploughing is then done on the sands, using replica iron ploughs with disproportionately long stilts, made by a local engineer.

The dressing up of the horses now has an unbroken tradition of 70 years, some of the costumes being handed down as heirlooms and sometimes made

143. Harrowing with a horse and two oxen in Papa Westray. Per T. Mackay.

144. Clod-breaking with a flagstone drawn by two oxen. C1552.

145. An ox-drawn stone roller in Orkney. 19.23.10.

even more elaborate from year to year. Alternatively, ornaments are sewn on to an ordinary suit for the occasion. Prizes are given as in normal ploughing matches for harness and decorations, the oldest and youngest ploughman, the youngest horse, the best kept ploughs, the best *feering* (guiding furrow), the best finish, the best ploughed *rig*, the neatest ends.

The origins of the custom are not clear, but in 1956 an old lady of 90 remembered ploughing matches in her childhood, not on the sand but in 'tattie land', when the plough was not a well-made replica, but a cow's hoof fixed on the end of a stick.[691] Even if this custom originated in no more than a boys' game, in emulation of their elders, nevertheless it has gained a vitality of its own in the context of the present.

Clod Breaking, Harrowing and Rolling

The Shetland delling spade was widely used for breaking up clods and smoothing furrows made by the plough. Hoes were also used to some extent. In the parish of Firth In Orkney, it was said that 'the principal cultivator was the *eetch* (adze), which was made in the style of a hoe, but much heavier, and with a deeper blade. It was used to fill backs with instead of ploughing them in, and as there were no rollers to level the ground, the clods were "melled" with the eatch, or with a large wooden mallet made with a long handle'. In Evie, clod-crushing was done by dragging a heavy stone or flagstone across the fields, but nevertheless, 'the ground was well broken up with eatches, which were like big hoes, and were made at the smithy. The hacking with eatches, I am informed, was endless'.[692] The use of hoes in this way seems to be particular to parts of Orkney.

Mells or mallets have a history in Orkney going back at least to 1734, when '7 timber mells' were listed in a Stronsay inventory, along with '3 sufficient harrows and harrowing irons', and '3 harrowbells'. An observer in 1756 noted that the clods had to be reduced by *mells*, and in 1766 Patrick Fea in Sanday 'began to brake fawgh morning and evening with 4 Harrows in Cloan, the men melling thereon'.[693] Harrowing and clod-breaking with mells, therefore, went on together.

Harrows in the Northern Isles were small and light, with only two or three *bulls* or bars in which the teeth were inserted. A very few had four bulls. They were pulled sideways by a 'side-rope' fastened at each end. The two sides were 3 ft (91 cm) long with eight to ten teeth in each, joined by two cross-bars each 18 in. (21 cm) long. In earlier days the teeth were mostly of wood, though some were of iron by the late 1700s. In Tingwall parish, there were harrows with iron teeth on one side and wooden teeth on the other.[694] The teeth were easily lost, so it was the practice to carry a supply of spare teeth to the field. Often a single horse, ox or heifer and one harrow was used in Orkney, with a single driver, but the only difference between these harrows and the back-harrows pulled by men or women was that they were sometimes slightly bigger, though not always. The

146. Tractor-drawn iron rollers in Orkney. Photo: W. Hourston. C79/K.

147. A five-horse grubber at work in Orkney. 1.44.18.

back-harrow was pulled by a rope which ran under the armpits and round the back of the neck. Back-harrowing probably survived sporadically in Shetland longer than anywhere else in Scotland, until within the last decade. In some places, the soil was so light and free that little harrowing was needed.[695]

Rolling of the tilled ground was rare in the Northern Isles, and was seldom or never used by the smaller farmers. A flagstone dragged over the ground both broke the clods and made a smooth surface.[696] By the twentieth century, horse or ox drawn rollers of wood and stone, and eventually iron rollers pulled by tractors, appeared in the islands.

Draught Animals and Transport

39

Oxen

THOUGH early plough parts and a bog find of an ox yoke show that oxen have a long history in the Northern Isles, the documentary sources go back only to the sixteenth century. In 1527 Shetland exported many skins of oxen to Scotland. In 1604 in Dunrossness, an ox was laid in pledge for £8, and an equally good ox had to be given for labouring the ground. This is the earliest documentary record of the link between oxen and ploughing. In 1633 and again in 1733 it was stated that Shetland oxen and cows were bigger than in Orkney, very much the opposite of the later state of affairs, and oxen were specified particularly amongst the products of Unst. The people kept as many oxen and cows as they could feed in winter, the oxen being used for ploughing and the cows producing milk.[697] Horses and sheep fended for themselves in the winter and were not housed.

In Orkney, a Burray inventory of 1747–8 listed:

'2 yoakes, and 20 bows for plew oxen with ane Soam ... two Scots plewghs for Oxen ... two Do. Orkney make ... 9 oxen yoaks, 65 bowes for oxen, ... 5 broken bows and a yoake ... 2 old yoaks for oxen, 4 bowes, with Iron hooks ... 3 oxen yoaks with two bowes ... Six soams for Oxen, 4 whereof has hooks, the other 2 wanting ... the ring staple and Stock of a yoake'. There were listed amongst the stock, 'in the park of Cara Sixteen Oxen and 4 bulls 4 more oxen received from the Tenant in Burra by Jas. McKenzie in exchange for horses, 2 Cowes and 10 Calves, Allso 3 Stalions, 2 horses and one latley bought from Wm. Sinclair in Linklater by Jas. McKenzie, in Glimsholm 3 oxen, in Switha 11 oxen whereof 3 old ones, and in Burra A bull and 10 Cowes. N.B. their was killed of the above Oxen three for the Earls use and another sent to Capt. Couts by the Earls orders'.[698]

Here, on a large estate owned by a Scottish laird, the Earl of Galloway, much of the equipment conformed to the standards of the Scottish mainland. The yokes were bow yokes, and at two bows to a yoke, there were 75 yokes represented in the list, old and new. The yokes had each a central ring or staple furnished with hooks, on to which the hooks of the soam or trace rope were attached. It is not unlikely that some, at least, of the oxen on the estate were imported from the south, and were bigger and stronger than the indigenous ox. On this estate, horses were also used in the plough.

Though oxen formed the mainstay of the Shetland plough-team, this was not so in Orkney. In 1760 a writer, after discussing the one-stilted plough, said that Orkney had no ox ploughs. He had evidently not visited the Burray estate. A few years later, however, it was reported that in Orkney they used light ploughs drawn by two or four horses, or by two horses and two cows. There are hardly any subsequent references to oxen or cattle in the plough in Orkney, apart from Shapinsay, where either four horses or four oxen were used abreast, though they were much used in carts, and for pulling harrows. Where two or three oxen or horses were yoked in the harrows, there was one person to lead each animal.[699]

Whereas in Stronsay and Eday, the Orkney breed of work oxen cost £4, in other places like Evie and Rendall, few or no oxen were used or reared.[700] According to one writer:

'The Ox (*bos taurus*, Lin. Syst.) which is common here, is of a singular breed, altogether distinct from what is seen in the counties nearest us in the south, and probably, like several other of our domestic animals, came originally from the Scandinavian shores. But, from whatever country, or whatever stock they sprung, the cattle of this place, at present, are of a very diminutive size, owing principally to their being reared in too great a number, and, of consequence, half starved in their youth.

'Their colour is black, brown, white, and, in many instances, party coloured, mottled, or brindled; and their shape inelegant, as their heads are low, their backs high, their buttocks thin, their bones prominent; and instead of having large, wide-spreading horns, they have only small ones, that are short and contracted, with their tops bending towards the forehead.

'Notwithstanding these disadvantages in point of shape and appearance, the oxen are strong, hardy, and make excellent workers, provided they be early well-trained to the yoke, and so plentifully fed as to enable them to support their labour. Even on a very moderate quantity of provender, they will perform a surprising quantity of work, in the cart or in the plough; and not for a few seasons only, but for the space of no less than six or seven years. To their capacity for work, they add another excellence, in not being subject to disaster; and they are, at the same time, such rapid feeders, that if put up in the stall, or on good pasture, but for a few months, their beef becomes excellent ... An ox of an ordinary bulk, and of the common country breed, weighs about sixty pounds the quarter'.[701]

When the same writer said that the low country type of plough was in use, drawn by two horses, or two oxen, without a driver, he was referring not to the native oxen, but to the new, improved breeds of the type that some of the gentlemen farmers had started to rear in Kirkwall and St Ola some years earlier. This is amongst the earliest references in the Northern Isles to the new plough type with two draught animals which the ploughman himself controlled with reins, an innovation known in the south of Scotland in the 1750s. Horses remained the chief plough animal in Orkney, and oxen were more usual in the cart.[702] These emphases remained in spite of innovations in equipment and improvements in animals. Nevertheless, there are photographs showing a pair of oxen or a single ox in the one-stilted plough in the 1890s, as well as photographs of the early 1900s showing pairs of oxen pulling an iron plough, or single oxen pulling drill harrows in the turnip field.

In the mid-nineteenth century, Birsay had 137 oxen and Eday 79.[703] Though little information is available about numbers in other areas, it is likely that a good many remained in many places right through the nineteenth century. The last work ox in Orkney died in Flotta in 1950.

The story in Shetland has significant differences. In the early days, Shetland had bigger oxen than Orkney, but this state of affairs was reversed after about 1800. Shetland kept on using oxen four abreast in the plough, in great numbers, and in many districts, with wooden yokes round their necks.[704] The general situation was that:

'When the extent of the farm will admit of a plough, oxen are more generally used than horses; four of either are yoked abreast; a rope is fixed round the horns of the oxen, or the heads of the horses, by which the driver, who walks backwards, pulls them along.

'When any of them do not seem to take a proper share in the draught, the driver endeavours to rouse the exertions of the lazy, by beating the animal in the face'.[705]

In 1814, ploughs drawn by four oxen were in general use, and some of the principal lairds kept four, six, or eight of them on their farms. After the division of the 'rooms' or townships into small farming units from the late eighteenth century, the numbers of ox-drawn ploughs began to decline, and a mixture of horses and oxen began to be employed, or horses alone. Alternatively the spade replaced the plough.[706] The distribution pattern of oxen and horses as draught animals in Shetland had begun to grow uneven. The former general use of oxen was being broken, not necessarily because the areas where the horse was adopted were more advanced, agriculturally speaking, but because of fragmentation of holdings and the reorganisation of the land as a means of subsistence ancillary to fishing. In the mid-ninetenth century, the gentle, active, docile ox was still thought better for draught than the horse.[707] As in Orkney, pairs of oxen remained in use as plough animals into the twentieth century, in places like Fair Isle, but in general, as elsewhere in Scotland, pairs of horses or ponies were the established plough animals by the beginning of the twentieth century.

In earlier days, oxen were yoked in the draught with wooden bow yokes. In Scotland generally the use of wooden ox yokes died out in the late eighteenth and early nineteenth centuries, and oxen began to be harnessed with collars in the same way as horses, the only difference being that the collars were open at the bottom so that they could be dropped straight over the neck. The changeover began to take place in the Northern Isles at the same time, though it is no doubt safe to asume that the large oxen imported to pull the improved types of ploughs were amongst the first to be harnessed with collars. Oxen yoked in the cart in Deerness, for example, had collars by 1798.[708] By the days of photography, all oxen were harnessed in the plough with collars, traces, and swingletrees, and were sometimes controlled by the ploughman using reins, often still with a second person to lead them. A backband of leather, canvas, twisted straw, or rope helped to support the traces. On the animal's face there was a halter of rope, or a bridle consisting of a pair of wooden cheek-pieces, each pierced with two horizontal openings at the ends, and a central vertical opening. From the vertical openings a rope, called the *head-stool*, passed over the head. A *nose-band* linked the front openings in the cheek-pieces, and a *choke-band* the rear openings under the animal's throat. Occasionally there were no cheek-pieces, and instead a light iron bit curved across the ox's nose in the same position as a nose-band. The choke-band and head-stall were then attached to the rings of the bit. When the oxen worked in pairs they were linked by a rope through the nose-band of each halter.

40

Wagons, Sleds and Carts

THE earliest references to wheeled vehicles are from Orkney. In 1721, John Traill of Elsness in Sanday had six oxen for pulling carts.[709] Sir James Stewart of Burray made regular use of carts, and both ox and horse drawn wagons in 1747. His inventory included:

'a pair of cart wheels, and ane old wheel of another cart with a wooden cart axle, ... a large pair of cart wheels Ironshod with the coup of the Cart, ane ox waggon with all its furniture ... a pair of Iron shod cart wheels, a broken iron shood coach wheel ... two large hind wheels of a Coach Iron shod, bushed and ringed ... the Coup, beeam and Shilmers of ane oaxen wean ... the leather furniture of a horse waggen ... 8 new Cart wheel bushes ... the trams and coup of a Horse wain, the Coup of a Corn wain, 2 shod cart wheels, 4 wooden axels, a four wheel Tumbler, 2 wood axels ... the beam of a wain ... the beam of an oxen wean ... 8 bolts for Carts, 2 Iron Slings ... the Hems(?) and Links of a horse cart ... 2 Iron Slings, 2 Iron Shadeings, 2 draw bolts for a Cart ... four brass bushes for Carts ... 3 Iron Lynpins of a Cart ... Two pair of Cart Wheels with the Iron axels and coups ane pair of worn wheels with a wooden axle and Coup ... 7 cart bolts ...'[710]

It can hardly be said, therefore, that wheeled transport was unfamiliar to the Orcadians of the eighteenth century. Wagons, usually drawn by oxen by means of a pole and a wooden yoke, were for heavier loads than carts. The horse-wain, on the other hand, had *trams* or shafts instead of a pole. The term *coup* is known from 1494 in Old Scots in the sense of a small close cart used for carrying manure or earth, and in the inventory appears to refer to the body of the cart or wagon. The bushes, at least four of them brass, make it clear that in most instances the wheels revolved on the axle, but there was also the *tumbler*, whose wheels and axles turned as units. The *shilmers* (Old Scots *shilwing*, 1601), longitudinal side bars, suggest an open-sided construction for one of the ox wagons. There was, therefore, a considerable variety in the equipment for heavy transport, in addition to the coach with two large rear wheels. The quantity of such equipment available and in use at this early date is a corrective to the negative impression given by the rather scanty later records, and also suggests that a developed road system was not an absolute prerequisite for the use of wheeled vehicles. However, it was only the landed proprietors who could

148. Loading a solid-wheeled ox wagon in Orkney. The yoke is by swingletrees and chains. C2948.

149. An ox wagon at Burgar Farm, Quoyness, Hoy, Sept. 1959, with a draught-pole. Per Mrs N. McMillan.

afford vehicles and the animals required for their draught, until well into the nineteenth century. In Shetland, some lairds were using ox-drawn wagons till the early 1800s.[711]

A special type of ox-drawn vehicle was used in the Orkney islands of Hoy, Graemsay, and Flotta till about 1940–50. It was known as a *sled* (Hoy), *coach* or *hurlie* (Graemsay), or *lorry* (Flotta).

The body is a close-sided box with a movable tailboard, as for an ordinary box-cart. The four small wheels ranged in size from 22 in. (56 cm) to 27 in. (69 cm) diameter, and had four stout wooden spokes, or were cut out of the solid, sometimes out of ship's hatches. The wheels had iron *shods* or tyres, and iron bushes that turned around the iron axles, on which they were held by linch pins in the same manner as cart wheels. One wheel, now in the Stromness Museum, was one of four made by the late J. Sinclair, Dean, Graemsay, who, for the wheel, used teak from block ships sunk in Hoy Sound and, for the outer part of the hub, wood from rollers from the bottom of a trawl net. The wheel was rung by J. Park, blacksmith, Stromness. A wagon owned by Hugh Ritch at Ootree, Rackwick, Hoy, did not have a conventional axle. Instead each of the wheels had its own individual short axle, like a barrow wheel, held in a wooden frame beneath the wagon. The axles revolved in their frames, and when these wore too wide through use, leather washers were put in to firm them up. The small wheels produced a low-set vehicle that could be loaded easily with dung, seaweed, turnips, hay, etc., and in Graemsay seaweed was carried in creels from the beach up to where it could be reached by the wagon.[712] To give the body greater depth, additional boards called *shellwings* could be added all round.

150. An ox-drawn cart with shafts, Orkney.

The side ones were usually left in position, held by two wooden uprights slotted through iron brackets, but the front and rear ones could be left off.

The wagons were pulled by a single ox or by a pair. A pair required swingletrees, but a single ox could either have a swingletree, or be hitched straight on to the hooks on the front of the wagon. The trace chain could also be attached to the iron axle. To prevent abrasion of the animal's side, the chains were wrapped around with cloth or sacking. This yoking method involved a problem of braking, for the traces would not keep the wagon from running into the team on downhill slopes. Several methods were employed. A chain fixed to the body of the cart could be slipped into a loop or bolt on a rear wheel to prevent it turning, or an iron shoe could be put under the rear wheels to serve as a drag. Some had a lever – or screw-operated bar and shoe that could be made to press directly on the iron tyre. More simply, a piece of wood could be shoved under a wheel, or the workers could hang on to ropes attached to the back. One Hoy man sometimes put the ox behind the cart when it was going downhill.

The wagons were awkward vehicles, since the front wheels were fixed and could not turn. This led to some experimenting. For example, J. Wilson at Windbreke in Graemsay fixed a single, central wheel in front, made to swivel like the front wheel of a bicycle. A Hoy man, Robert Thomson at Burgar, fitted a turntable and pole on the analogy of the prairie wagons of the United States.

Where a pole was used, as here and at the neighbouring farm of Dale, a cross-pole was used at the front end, as with the pole of a binder or reaper, fastened with straps to the collars of the draught animals. Poles were exceptional, however, and there are no examples with pairs of shafts. Normally the attachment was by traces and swingletrees or *ammles*, and for two animals three swingletrees were required as for the plough. The trace chains were supported at the beasts' sides by backbands of canvas or leather, and held at the ends by the links in the *haims* (Old Scots, 1496, Middle Dutch *hame*) on the collar. In all respects, the oxen were harnessed as for horses. The only real difference was that collars were open at the bottom. Horses in pairs were occasionally used for draught, but were said to be too fast. Mixed teams of a horse paired with an ox, or even a cow, also occurred.

The wagons about which information is available are all of comparatively recent date, built in the 1920s and 1930s. A joiner at Dounby in the mainland of Orkney, A. Tait, took a wagon from Quoyness, Hoy, for repair in 1923, but instead made a new one and kept the old one till it fell to pieces. J. Wilson of Windbreke said that the first wagon of this type in Graemsay was made in the early 1900s, the idea for it having come from Rackwick in Hoy. In view of the early eighteenth century evidence for wagons on the Burray estate, which lay in the South Isles as Graemsay, Hoy and Flotta do, it might be thought that the recent vehicles are direct descendants. Against this a number of points can be raised. The early wagons were drawn by poles, whereas the later ones had none, except for the two that were influenced by the American prairie wagons. The commonest name for the later wagons is sled. The implication is that their origins may lie in runner sledges to which wheels were attached, possibly about or not much before 1900. The manner of harnessing by chains or swingletrees is also reminiscent of sledges, as is the fact that even with wheels, the sleds were difficult to turn. If the sled is a comparatively late adaptation of the sledge, reasons must be sought for its adoption. Local information stressed the handiness of the sled for low loading, and its ability to take heavy loads, up to about a ton. This could also be said of a sledge. A more valid explanation may be that the sled was locally thought to be handier for oxen than the shafted cart. Its use may be related to the kind of draught animals most readily available, and in this connection, J. Wilson of Windbreke stated that it was difficult to transport horses at a time when there was no pier.

A further point is that both sledges and wheeled sledges were found in Orkney, latterly drawn by tractors, for pulling loads of sheaves as well as seaweed and the like. Examples have been noted at Bewan in North Ronaldsay, and near Stromness on the Orkney mainland. One type of sledge in Graemsay differed from the wagon only in having runners rather than wheels. It was approximately the size of the bottom of a cart, made with longitudinal or lateral slats, and without framed sides. In Orphir there was a wheeled sledge , a hermaphroditic form of construction with short, iron-shod runners at the back, and a pair of short, solid block wheels at the front. The floor had longitudinal slats and no sides. In its use of wheels, this vehicle is moving towards the wheeled sled. Another wheeled sledge from the same area has a solid floor, longitudinally boarded, and a shallow framed side of one plank's depth. It appears to have been used for carrying peat.

With this body of evidence, it seems reasonable that the sleds of Hoy, Graemsay and Flotta derive from sledges, to which framed sides have been added to increase the carrying capacity and to take certain kinds of loads, and to which wheels have been added to make it easier for oxen to move heavy loads in soft ground where the runners could sink rather far in. It is probably for this reason that most sled wheels are solid and therefore more suitable than spoked wheels for use on soft, loose ground. In fact, a major use for the sled was in getting peats from the bank to the nearest road, where they could be transferred to wheeled carts. There were few or no made roads where the sled was in use. That there was a need for such sleds under certain circumstances is made clear from the fact that they were used alongside ordinary two-wheeled carts in these islands.[713]

CARTS

As the Burray inventory shows, two-wheeled carts were being used in the early eighteenth century by landed proprietors. The later Orkney evidence can be tabulated:

Source	Parish	Details and Numbers
OSA. 1793. VII. 471, 473	Cross, Burness and North Ronaldsay	Crosskirk – 14 Burness – 8 Ladykirk – 15 North Ronaldsay – 1 } =38, all drawn by oxen
OSA. 1793. VII. 558	Kirkwall and St Ola	Carts in use for some time past
OSA. 1793. v. 409–410	Holm	Small carts coming into use, ox-drawn, with shafts
OSA. 1795. xv. 302	South Ronaldsay and Burray	Few carts
OSA. 1795. XIV. 128	Firth and Stenness	Most farmers in Stenness, and a few in Firth, keep a cart-ox for carrying out manure
OSA. 1795. XVI. 419, 430	Sandwick and Stromness	Sandwick – 11 Stromness – 12 } = 23. None 50 years ago. Drawn by horses or, more often, oxen
OSA. 1795. XVI. 260	Westray	Westray – 45 Papa Westray – 2 } = 47. Drawn by 2 oxen, for carrying manure
OSA. 1795. XIV. 416	Stronsay and Eday	Stronsay – 27 Eday – 5 } = 32. Drawn by 2 oxen
OSA. 1795. xx. 259–260	St Andrews and Deerness	St Andrews – 40. Till 1788, the only carts belonged to the minister, one heritor, and two farmers. Drawn by oxen yoked as for horses
OSA. 1795. XIV. 323	Birsay and Harray	Birsay – 6 Harray – 12 } = 26. Drawn by 1 ox each
NSA. 1845. xv. 95, 99, 109	Cross, Burness and North Ronaldsay	Carts in general use. Oxen kept for carting seaweed North Ronaldsay – only one cart, never used, in 1832. Now general
Ib. 39	Stromness	140 carts
Ib. 26	Orphir	Carts now general
Ib. 60	Sandwick	Carts universal. Cost, £4.4.

Already by the 1790s, ox-drawn carts, of which there were at least 216, were common in Orkney, and amongst their main tasks was the transport of manure and seaweed. Some were drawn by one and some by two oxen, and comparatively few by horses. In the 1800s:

'Small two-wheeled box carts, drawn by two oxen or one horse, are in common use; but some of the gentlemen farmers have them of a larger construction. Not many years ago there were no carts in Orkney; indeed, till some attention is paid to the constructing and repairing of public roads, wheel carriages can never come into general use.'

It is not strictly true that there were no carts in Orkney a few years earlier, but the general emphasis is accurate. The constant and rapid increase in the number of carts in the nineteenth century can be seen from the parts numbered in a 'List of Imports into Orkney coastwise', between 1801–6:

1801 – 900 oak spokes	1804 – 12 dozen oak spokes
33 pairs cart-wheels	53 pairs cart-wheels
1802 – 79 pairs cart-wheels	1805 – 80 pairs cart-wheels
8 carts	2 carts complete[714]
1803 – 42 pairs cart-wheels	
3 carts	

In five years, therefore, there were imported into Orkney thirteen complete carts, 87 dozen spokes representing 87 cartwheels (which normally have 12 spokes each), and 287 pairs of cartwheels – in all, evidence for over 340 carts in five years, some made on the Scottish Mainland, but the majority made up locally with the aid of imported parts.

The Shetland evidence is less copious:

Source	Parish	Details and Numbers
OSA. 1793. VII. 586	Aithsting and Sandsting	Two carts. One put out in a day what 9 people would carry on their backs
OSA. 1793. v. 202	Unst	Only a few carts
Kemp 1801. 20	—	Carts and carriages unknown
Forsyth 1808. v. 127	—	Carts used only by two or three gentlemen
NSA. 1845. xv. 162	—	Carts little used
Ib. 65	Tingwall, Whiteness and Weisdale	Close carts much used

Source	Parish	Details and Numbers
Ib. 58	Delting	13 carts. Only 2 a few years ago
Cowie 1871. 159	—	Small carts drawn by ponies, or more rarely oxen, are becoming common
Evershed 1874. 203, 214	Dunrossness	Small carts introduced for peat on the level parts, on the estate of John Bruce junr; A J Grierson, Quendale, had 4 cart horses and used 'Scotch carts'

Although the reference to 'Scotch carts' shows that Shetland also imported carts from the Scottish mainland, this was in general much later than in Orkney. The contrast between the two areas is pin-pointed clearly.

In the Northern Isles and especially Orkney, the usual team was one ox and latterly one horse between a pair of shafts. The two-ox teams of Stronsay, Westray and Eday did not, apparently, survive the nineteenth century. A Westray septuagenarian, Robert A. Harcus of Rapness, stated in 1961 that his grandmother, well over one hundred years ago, carted with a pair of oxen. He

151. Cart loads of peat at Scapa Flow. 19.23.27.

152. The wooden axle of a small Orkney cart, from the Toab district. In the National Museum. C126.

himself, however, never saw more than one ox (or milk-cow sometimes) harnessed to a cart. However, in Rousay there could still be seen in the 1920s carts with two small spoked wheels hauled by two oxen attached to a pole, according to F. Craigie, and single oxen were also used with similar vehicles fitted with shafts and also with coup-carts.[715]

The small ox- or pony-drawn cart survived well into the twentieth century in some areas, alongside bigger carts drawn by large work horses in others. Though the tables above refer to ox-drawn carts for carrying manure and seaweed, they also carried hay, peats, and any sort of load that was going. The oxen in the shafts were harnessed as for horses, with a collar, a small saddle to take the back chain, and breeching straps. A belly band was not always used. A leading rope was attached to the rings of a curved iron bit, to the side of a rope bridle, or to wooden *branks*. Few or no ox-drawn carts survived the 1940s.

Apart from photographs and references, the only extant evidence of earlier carts takes the form of wooden axles, of which at least two survived through their use as lintels. In 1963 one was still in use as a lintel in a peat-shed on the farm of Mr Gaudie, at Netherskaill, Marwick, in the North Mainland of Orkney, and a second, now in the Stromness Museum, served as a door lintel in the demolished house of Blackhall, in Stenness. A third wooden axle, whose place of origin is unknown, is in the Tankerness House Museum, Kirkwall, and a fourth, very small axle, from the Toab district, is in the National Museum of Antiquities of Scotland. The Tankerness House Museum axle is the crudest of these, and has metal reinforcing plates at the points where the wheel turned. It seems to have been roughly trimmed from a log. The other three are rectangular in section. All have rounded, tapered ends to take the wheels, and all have a pair of bolt-holes for attachment to the cart body. It has not been possible to date any of these with any precision.

Cereal Crops

41

Grain Types and Trade

THE early plough parts found in the Northern Isles, and the stone clearance heaps and dykes, suggest a relatively sophisticated form of tillage in fields at least from the Bronze Age. This is confirmed by impressions of identifiable types of grain on prehistoric pots, as well as by finds of carbonised remains. In Orkney a piece of pottery from a chambered cairn at the Calf of Eday had the impress of a grain of naked barley, *Hordeum distichum*, and another from the cairn at Unston one of hulled barley, *Hordeum hexastichum*.[716] Recent excavations at Skara Brae have confirmed the existence there of barley grains. In Shetland, a house site at Gruting reflecting a neolithic tradition produced 28 lb (12.7 kg) of carbonised barley hermetically sealed under a mass of peat ash, perhaps the result of an accident during drying. This has been radio-carbon dated to 1564 BC±120. Various types of querns for grinding grain were found here and in houses of similar type.[717] Oats began to be grown in Scotland in the course of the Iron Age, and these two crops, oats and barley, remained standard throughout the centuries. The Vikings cultivated both, for about 1117 a man called Thorkel was hurt by falling off a barley-rick in Orkney, and Thord Dragon-skull, servant of Bergfinn in Shetland, was punished by madness for refusing to stop threshing oats in the barn on the eve of St Magnus' and St Lucia's Day.[718] Sixteenth century writers noted that both island groups produced oats and barley in plenty. Hector Boece was particularly struck by the virtue of Orkney ale. Though the people went in for excessive drinking, and made the strongest ale in Albion because they had plenty of barley, 'yit nane of thaim ar sene wod (mad), daft, or drunkin: als (also) they come haill and feir (sound) in thair bodyis to extreme age, but (without) ony use of medcinary, with strang and fair bodyis'. No wheat was grown.[719]

Oats and barley provided both bread and drink, with some seasonal fluctuations, depending on the quantities grown. The summer could be a breadless period if cereal stocks were low, and for this reason the North Ronaldsay folk had barley bread in winter only in 1529, with fish and milk as the summer substitutes. This was a common state of affairs in Shetland, where the cereal crops were seldom adequate, and had to be supplemented by imports from Orkney and Scotland in exchange for fish, milk products, and textiles. In Unst the grain was only enough to maintain the inhabitants for four or five months of the year. As a result the Shetlanders were doubly unfortunate, for drink as well as bread was scarce. Ale was not a common drink, since most of the barley went for making bread, though some Hamburg beer could be got from traders. Barley-bread was much eaten, and appeared better than the oat-bread.[720]

Sanday and Westray in Orkney had a good reputation for barley and oats, Sanday paying to the king 42 chalders of victual, each of 21 bolls. South Ronaldsay produced more grain than any of the other South Isles, and supplied Kirkwall and Stromness. The fields got plenty of manure, and were marked by large clearance heaps.[721] In Shetland, Tingwall had grain to spare in a good season, and supplied Lerwick and Scalloway with meal and malt. The parish of Cross, Burness and North Ronaldsay had a yearly export of 400–500 bolls of bere and 300–500 bolls of oatmeal, in cargoes of 50–60 tons, in the 1790s, and Holm sold its surplus in the form of malt in Kirkwall. Rents and dues were paid in the same form. It was reckoned that about a third of the Orkney crop went in feu-duty, and was mostly carried out of the island.[722]

Much grain was exported from these islands. In March 1700 it was reckoned that the barnyard at Elsness would contain 16 *lasts* of bere, a last containing 24 meils of 30 barrels each. From such barnyards bere and meal were exported, though bargaining was not always easy. David Traill found that a cargo of corn was beginning to heat when he came to Stonehaven three days after leaving Orkney and had to sell the grain in Montrose at 5 merks per boll and the meal at £3 and 1 merk per boll. The merchants paid half the money then, and the remainder was left over till Lammas. In 1705, he sailed from Deersound to Shetland and was stuck for over a month at Levenwick. The bere started to heat, and he tried to cool it on deck but the weather made it difficult. He had to sell about 1800 lispunds of the worst of it at 8/6, and 1200 lispunds of meal at 19/–. Eventually he reached Foysound (Kristiansund) in Norway and got 1 dollar and 3 stivers per barrel for the grain, but only 20 stivers per 'voe' for the meal because Irish meal was going at that rate. Tar and deals were bought for a return cargo. In 1712 Orkney bere was sold in Bergen for 5 merks the barrel and meal at 2 merks 4 stivers the 'voe'. In the same year, James Traill had tried to buy the bere paid as skatt for the 1711 crop in Stronsay and Sanday, but the price asked of 100 merks a chalder was considered too high in relation to current prices in Norway. An effort was made to get cheaper bere on the Orkney Mainland. Trondheim was said to be the best port for sales at the time. The business was well organised. Meal was stored in a lockable meal-house, pending shipment, and appears to have been carried in bags of coarse linen, of which 400 to 500 ells were ordered for packing meal in 1714. There was much anxious discussion of crops in family letters. By 23 March 1700 tilling at Elsness and Marykirk was going well and because the fields had been very well mucked, this gave 'good houps of ane Blised Cropt'. In July 1714, the Elsness crops were bad, though the corn of Housbie was reasonably good considering the great drought there had been.[723]

In September 1717 the crop got a severe shake with a storm of wind and hail. There were also difficulties with tenants, for David Traill wrote: 'I think the kynd dealing the tennants and vassals did meet with from us last year, and how unjustly some of them served us by keeping back the victual deserves kyndly resentment from his Lordship.' In 1728 James Traill wrote to David Traill to say he had sold his North Ronaldsay bere to some merchants in Edinburgh at £76 per chalder, and asked him to make sure the tenants did not dispose of any, 'for I am bound to deliver 18 or 19 chalders, being mr. (master, i.e. proprietor) and superior duety, and the ship will saile about the midle of Apryll to take it in'.[724]

In Norway, grain and meal were sold at Bergen, Arendall, Mandal, Kristiansand, and the Clove, and there were also trading links with Emden in Germany. If prices were low abroad, it could happen – also because of 'the intire penury of money all over this land' – that goods had to be sold at two-thirds of their prime cost and even then over a long period for repayment. A further problem that arose in 1721 was a toll applied by the King of Denmark on bere, meal and malt arriving in Norway. This, on top of the old duty, made it equivalent to a prohibition when the price fell to 3 or 4 merks a barrel. Besides this, when grain was plentiful over the whole of Scotland, and Leith and Fife were overstocked, as happened in 1724, the price of Orkney grain would fall. The same happened in Bergen in 1728, when rye and pease were so cheap that no one would pay much for bere and meal, and David Traill took most of the cargo back with him.[725]

The corn trade, therefore, was made risky by many factors, bad weather at home, stormy seas and delayed journeys that could spoil a cargo, competition at the Norwegian ports, tolls and duties, and even years of plenty that made grain and meal cheap. Yet it must have been worth the risk, for merchant lairds like the Traills persisted with it, and prospered.

Since bere was the grain that was exported, this partly explains the emphasis on bere as the main infield crop, on which the best manure was lavished. Bere was valued more highly than grain in the testamentary inventories. In 1612, for example, a meil of bere cost from £1.6.8 to £3, whilst oats ranged from 13/4 to £2.[726] In the 1680s, the value of oats had risen to about £2, with barley at £3 a meil.[727] Bere also gave a seed-yield ratio of 1:4 as against 1:3 for oats, according to the formula in the Testaments for valuing sown crops that had not been harvested, and though this is a legal formula that in practice must often have been different, nevertheless the differential remains in favour of bere. One spot in Unst, for example, was said to have produced twenty-four fold and in Orkney an acre could produce 6 to 8 or sometimes 10 quarters of bere. In Firth and Stenness, oats yielded 1:3, and bere 1:4 or 5, in Stronsay and Eday it was 1:3 or 4 for oats, and 1:5 or 6 for bere, in Orphir, 1:3 or 4, with no specification of crops, and in Evie and Rendall, 1:3 or 3½ for oats and 1:5 or 6 for bere.[728] Servants also got their wages partly in bolls of bere in the 1700s. Another major reason for bere growing was the fact that the lairds insisted on having a considerable proportion of their rents paid in bere, though oats (from which exportable meal could be made) also played their part. Still in the 1780s bere was a desirable article of export, but it went to Cadiz and Lisbon rather than to

Norway, for feeding mules and asses. Shetland continued to be partly dependent on Orkney for bere and meal too.[729]

Bere was the primary crop in the days before the breakdown of the system of communal farming, though eventually its place was taken by oats. In Shetland its cultivation had almost ceased by the 1840s, though it continues to be grown to some extent in Orkney. An increasing interest in the oat crop in Shetland may be indicated by the cropping of oats in the new lazy-bed technique at Gulberwick.[730]

In the late eighteenth century, information on varieties began to appear. In the advanced parish of Aithsting and Sandsting, barley as well as bere and oats was being grown, and the grain quantities were enough to serve the inhabitants in a good year. Barley with two rows of ears was coming in, as opposed to bere with four or six rows of ears, but was not common, for in 1804 it was said that they had no barley, and sowed *bigg* in May. Bigg was the Norse name (Old Norse *bygg*, Norwegian *byg*) corresponding to Lowland Scots *bere*. In Orkney, a rough kind of black oats, and rough bere, were raised alternately. On farms held by the lairds, the great black oat had been fairly widely introduced, and throve well, but it had not been taken on by the common farmers in the 1770s. The large white oat had been tried, but was not as suitable, because it ripened late, and was apt to shake. In Fetlar, early barley was tried, as well as Polish and Blindsley, but did not ripen well. Some rye and wheat were tried by improvers in Shapinsay.[731]

In most places, the basic crops were bere and black or grey oats, often alternating, but sometimes with bere being grown continuously on one spot for up to fifty years. Oats were sown from mid-March to April, bere in late April to May, with harvesting in September to October. In some areas strict sowing times were observed, as in Sandsting and Aithsting where oats were not planted before 17 April.[732]

The small-scale changes of the late eighteenth century continued into the nineteenth. Bere, *Hordeum vulgare*, still alternated with grey and black oats, *Avena strigosa*, and there was plenty of the 'tall hygrometric oat', *Avena fatua*, oats being sown between 12 February and 20 April and bere between 1 May and 16 June in Orkney.[733] These are modern dates. Those of the eighteenth century were according to the Old Style Julian calendar, with its difference of eleven days. In Shetland, bere with both four and six rows of ears was still grown, the latter being shorter in the head. Barley with two rows of ears was not so good. Wheat and rye had been tried with little success, as well as Angus early oats. Bere was the main infield crop, oats characterised the outfield. Dunrossness was fertile enough to have surplus grain to sell in Lerwick but this was not possible for most other areas. On the average, each cottar required 20 bolls of bere and oatmeal each year.[734]

In the 1840s, oats alternated as before with bere and occasionally barley, though the quantities produced were much greater than in Shetland. Holm and Paplay grew annually 785 bolls of bere and 585 bolls of oats, each of 16 stones Dutch. 170 bolls of bere were payable in kind to the Crown, and some was sold to the distillers in Kirkwall. Part was also sold as malt to the brewers there. Bere was preferred to barley because it ripened earlier, and the black oat to the white because it did not shake so easily in the autumn winds. In St Andrews, bere was sold raw by the *wey* (Old Scots *we(y)*, to weigh, *c.* 1400), a measure for bere equal to 16 stones Dutch or 18½ stones imperial; but when dried, it was then called *melder-corn* and sold by the meil, equal to nearly 11¼ stones Dutch or 14¼ Imperial. These quantities of raw and dried grain were of equivalent value, about 14/– to £1 stg. Oats were sold similarly, but weighed out at about a fourth less than bere, the price being from 8/– to 16/–. Both oats and bere were often sold unthreshed, at prices varying according to the demand for fodder. In Stronsay, the average annual product was 4214 bolls of bere, 570 of white oats, and 5232 of black oats, all at 6 bushels to the boll. Eday produced 1611 bolls of bere, 785 of white oats, and 1445 of black. In Cross and Burness, bere averaged about 44 lb (20 kg) to the bushel, and oats 25 to 28 lb (11–13 kg). 1500 bolls of bere and 1200 of the small grey or black oats were grown per annum. In good years, Orphir could send about 240 bolls of meal and grain to Kirkwall and Stromness, and the tenants of large farms could even export these commodities to Leith. The situation could be reversed in bad years, however,[735] but normally there was a balance for export, as shown by the custom-house accounts:

Year	Bere (Quarters)	Oats (Quarters)	Oatmeal (Bolls)
1790	2880	–	315
1795	4970	–	1552
1800	2430	–	667
1805	2934	–	80
1810	272	–	–
1815	4399	–	952
1820	4710	197	2219[736]

Evidently an increase in the oat crop was beginning in the 1820s, and by the 1840s, as agricultural improvements went on, oats became the main crop in some parts, though bere was still not far behind. In the period 1849–68, for example, David Petrie, on his farm of Graemeshall in Holm, averaged 19 stacks of oats, 15 of bere, and 4 of barley per annum. By the 1870s, bere was often an alternative to oats in the rotations, and new varieties were in use. Sandy, early Angus, and potato oats were sown between 1 April and 1 May in Shapinsay, with black Murkle oats, a Caithness variety, on poorer soils. A sowing of 4 to 5 bushels an acre gave an average return of 24 to 30 bushels at a weight of 38 to 44 lb (17–20 kg) to the bushel. Three or four bushels were sown to the acre. Victoria bere was easily shaken, so less popular. Orkney bere weighed out at 48 to 52 lb (22–24 kg) a bushel, an average advance of 8 lb (4 kg) per bushel on the yields of earlier days. Barley was little grown anywhere in Orkney. Fenton wheat was grown at Balfour home farm by Mr Calder. In the 1920s, stacks of bere were still to be seen in the stackyards of Orkney, though the proportion in relation to oats was small.[737]

42

Plucking, and Shearing with the Sickle

THE oats and bere were sown one-handed from a basket held on the chest with the carrying band round the back of the neck. This was the prevailing method as long as cultivation was in small rigs and patches. The time for sowing had to be judged by the rising temperature of the soil, to test which it was said of Birsay parish that old men would seat themselves naked on mother-earth to see if the mould could be trusted with the bere-seed. Where grain was scarce, as could happen in Shetland, the sowing of barley seed had to wait till supplies came from Orkney. The crops then grew, wind and weather permitting, till the time for harvest in September or October. Sometimes the corn was allowed to become dead ripe first.[738]

In some cases, where the straw was short and as much length as possible was required for thatching, corn was plucked by hand and not shorn[739] but corn *heuks* were the usual harvesting implements. In most of Scotland, the heuks had toothed blades. A Shetland version, however, had a rounded form with a smooth blade.[740] Not all the heuks were locally made, some being imported from Leith and from Hamburg. All appear to have been small: 'The shearer who cuts two thraves of the thickest corn in a day, is hard wrought'. Whatever their source, the sickles were not the ordinary toothed kind, but a 'sort of broad, blunt hooks, that take much time in sharpening'. The imported ones were probably used on the bigger farms, and of the toothed type. In 1803–4, six dozen sickles were imported to Orkney. Sickles made in Sandsting and Aithsting were so small that 35 to 40 cuts were required before the hand was filled with corn. The method of cutting rye in small handfuls was known in later times as *neave-shearing* (from Scots *nieve*, fist). They survived for long, being in common use in the 1870s in Orkney even alongside the horse-drawn reaper, which by that time was in use on medium-sized holdings.[741]

SHEARING WITH THE SICKLE

Shearing with the sickle was usually a team job. On 4 September 1728, David Traill in Stronsay sent to his father four good *hooks* or shearers, and one *bandster* to tie the sheaves they cut. On 26 September 1766, Patrick Fea had 10 hooks shearing in Inglea in Sanday in addition to his own. Cottars, bollmen and *oncas* (scilicet, 'on call') who were required to shear in harvest were formerly paid for this form of tenant-service by getting a piece of land called a 'harvest-fee'.[742] The swathe cut was known as the *shore* (from 'shear'), *race* (probably from Norwegian *reis*, a small stack, as of peats, with reference to the stooked sheaves) or *cut*. Shearers generally worked in groups of two, three or more together on a ridge, the total width cut being the *oon* (Norwegian dialectal *one*, strip of woodland, or of a field to be cut, Swedish dialectal *ân(e)*, swathe, strip cut by one shearer). A group of three shearing with hooks was also called an *oon*. The word is known in Shetland and survives there in place names such as Onn, Ons, Wons.[743] At big farms the system was more formalised and the shearers cut four rigs abreast, three hooks in each rig, making a group of twelve shearers which was completed by two people binding and two making bands. This approximates to the *bandwin* system of shearing, often with groups of seasonal migrant workers from the Highlands or from Ireland, that prevailed in parts of Eastern and Southern Scotland.[744] On some places, for example at Aikerness, there were usually two men and one woman to each rig, and rivalry often led to competing to see who could shear the most. The oats in the furrows and in thin poor land were often plucked by hand. In the second half of the nineteenth century, the bigger smooth-edged sickle began to replace the toothed sickle that had formerly been general, in Shetland as well as in Orkney. It usually had a leather strap on the handle, through which the hand was passed, a loop being taken over the thumb to press or tighten the leather band for a firmer grip.[745] This was quite different in size and shape from the small smooth-bladed, half-round sickle that had been in use at an earlier date.

Two methods of shearing were in vogue: 'In one the oats were parted and gathered together by the left hand and cut by pulling the hook in short sweeps to you. In back hand cutting the hook was swung backwards and slashed forward like a scythe, the cut oats being gathered up on the arm, and when as much as could be conveniently lifted was cut, it was, with the help of the hook encircling it, lifted and turned over the arm on the band. Back hand cutting could not be done with a toothed hook.' To cut with a hook wielded like a scythe was called to *hack* (cf. Norwegian *hakka*, to cut, but possibly Scots), and this was done when the crop was so short that it could not easily be held in the left hand. A small stone used to sharpen the point of a hook was a *glaan* (Norwegian dialectal *glan*, glow in the sky, *glana*, to gleam, shine), originally a fisherman's tabu-name for a whetstone. Fine quality sandstone was necessary, of the kind found around the Loch of the Virigens in Redland.[746]

The need to get the ripe crop cut and stooked quickly meant that many more people were needed at this most intensive period of the farming year. On smaller places all the grown-up members of the family went to the rig, and on bigger farms extra hands were hired in addition to the family and servants. It was a time of group participation in work that was hard, but made pleasant by its communal nature. Even the food provided was better than the everyday fare, and workers looked forward to the *hoosavel* (Norwegian *hus*, house + Old Norse *vǫllr*, field), originally meaning the homefield but extended to the food or refreshment brought to the harvesters. There were also celebrations at the end of harvest. The workers got a specially thick spread of butter on their bread, which went by the name of the *'heuk butter* or *aff-shearing'*.[747]

When the last rig was done the custom was for the neighbours who were helping each other in the township to *cast da heuks*. This was done by one person taking all the sickles by their points, and tossing them all together over his shoulder, at the same time repeating:

> 'Whaar 'ill I in winter dwell,
> Whaar 'ill I in voar (spring) dell,
> Whaar 'ill I in simmer fare,
> Whaar 'ill I in hairst shaer (shear)?'

The direction in which each person's hook pointed was thought to give the answer to these questions. If one stuck in the ground, however, this meant that its owner was unlikely to live long. A very old custom, that survived for at least a century after the Reformation, was that on one day in harvest 'the vulgar abstain from work, because of an ancient and foolish tradition that if they do their work, the ridges will bleed'.[748]

43

The Scythe and Harvesting Machinery

THE scythe has a long tradition in the Northern Isles, but before the nineteenth century its function was to mow grass or hay. It was called a *beyoo* (origin obscure) in Orkney, and a *pawnee* (from *pawn*, to mow, of uncertain origin) or *sye* in Shetland. It had a short stubby blade 'not a span long', varying from 12 to 15 in. (30.5–38 cm) in length, with a long, straight haft and a single handle. The mower stood nearly upright. The top of the haft rested on the bend of his arm, the left hand held the handle, and the right hand grasped the haft. Old men liked to have the blades tempered in a peat-fire, which they thought gave a sweeter edge.[749] A swathe cut with a scythe was a *bout* (Scots) or *skare* (Norwegian *skår*, Old Norse *skári*, id.), and a sweep of the scythe in mowing was a swap (Old Scots *swapp*, to leap suddenly).

Some time before 1888, the Scottish type of scythe with a Y-shaped handle began to be used in Orkney for cutting grain. The Leasks of Flaws, and the Manse, and Dale, in the township of Georth, were said to have been the first to use it for this. These Scottish scythes often had a cradle attachment in Orkney, or a simple grass-hook made of a curved piece of wire in the same position. No scythes seen in Shetland had cradles. Scythes were imported in considerable quantities: 12 dozen in 1802 to 1803 and 6 dozen in 1803 to 1804,[750] for example, and sold through the ironmongers and local shops, usually as separate handles and blades. The mounting of the two parts together was done by the smith who heated the heel in his forge and bent it till the blade could lie at an angle that suited the user. For a time scythes took over from the sickle. The grandfather of W. Irvine at Links in Papa Westray was an expert scythesman who used nothing else to cut his crops and his hay. He could keep two people lifting and tying sheaves, and his skilful action meant that the blade did not require frequent sharpening. He retired in 1948. The custom of giving heuk-butter after cutting continued, but it was renamed *scy-butter*. Reaping machines began to make their way into the islands in the 1890s, at first sporadically, and then increasingly from about 1910. Even so, scythes remained in use for clearing roads to give access for reapers and later binders, and for cutting outlying patches and crops in damp areas. The sickle was last used in Papa Westray by W. Burgar at Edgeriggs, in the 1920s.[751]

Farmers' diaries can often give a graphic, even if laconic, impression of the work to be done in harvest, mostly in late August to October. In 1890, Mr Tait of Work, St. Ola, put up 34 stacks after 16 days of cutting, some up to 10½ hrs., and 7 days of leading. He opened roads with the scythe and cut with a reaper. In 1896, though he had two reapers, there could still be up to six scythes and nineteen hands at work on some days. On 29 October, the 'Hands all enter-

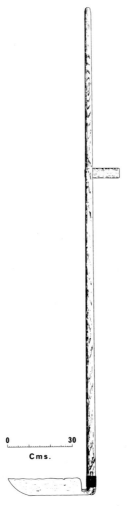

153. A Shetland scythe. In the National Museum.

tained to tea & paid.' In 1914 he was sorting binders at Scarpaquoy and at Odness, and was using one himself, as well as a back-delivery reaper. A binder shed had been erected on the farm. The scythe remained in use as part of the set of harvesting equipment. The harvest of 1923 at Ingsay, a very bad one, was detailed as follows:

154. Scything bere at Easthouses, Eday, 1940s. Right to left: Mary Jane Robertson, John William Tulloch (scyther), Wilhemina Tulloch, John Tulloch, Billy Robertson (scyther). Per J. Miller. 19.23.14.

September 15   Took in green oats
      17, 18, 19   Took in green oats and grass
      20   Cut green oats
      24   Opened out bere
      27   Yoked reaper 9.45, rain 10.30
      28   Cutting bere
      29   Finished cutting bere. Cutting green oats
October   4   Opening Staviger
      6   Opening out Grassway field
      8   Cutting with scythe in Grassway – ground very wet
      9   Opening Meadow
      10   Opening with scythe, Brecks and Swartland
      11   Start harvest. Yoked binder at 3.30 p.m. in Quoys
      12   Finished Quoys, start Brecks with binder, found it very soft, binder sticking a lot
      13   Cutting in Meadow with reaper
      Memo: Never remember such a bad harvest so far
      15   Cutting in Meadow all day till 4 o'clock when amble broke, also yoke on pole
      16   Cutting in Meadow, finished Meadow 5 p.m. Took in 2 loads sheaves for cattle
      17   Cutting Brecks, binder, all day
      18   Cutting Brecks, binder. Light crop; opening out Staviger
      19   Finished Brecks 3.30, started Staviger
      20   Binder, Staviger. Tried to load bere, but wind too strong
      22   Binder, Staviger all day. Heavy crop

23 Finished Staviger, opened out Swartlands
24 Cutting with scythe, then reaper, Grassway
26 Binder at Swartland
27 Cut with 3 scythes till 10 a.m. 2 men from Swannay helping
     us never saw so much wet everything flooded. The like never
     seen before by any one, crops all flat & ground so wet that a
     horse can hardly go through it even on dry land
29 Finished Grassway except a wee lying bit at bottom. 2 men
     from Swannay and Maggie Bruce helping us p.m.
30 Setting up sheaves a.m. Binder in Swartland p.m.
31 Swartland, binder, all day
November 1   ,,   ,,   , finished
          2 Finished cutting a wee bit in Grassway
          3 Put in binder and reaper.[752]

155. Jerrie Stout of Busta, Fair Isle, sharpening his scythe, 1962. 1.29.19.

156. A cradle scythe in Orkney, near Stromness, *c*. 1960. C3892.

157. Oxen bending their heads to the reaper draught in Orkney. C5752.

158. A horse-drawn back-delivery reaper in Orkney. 28.8.27A.

159. Harvesting with tractor-binder in Orkney. Photo: W. Hourston. C80K.

With reapers and binders, there appears to have been a period of hesitant adoption, followed by a quick spread partly due to emulation. In Papa Westray, for example, reapers appeared about 1890–1900. One of the first was a two horse Albion made by Harrison McGregor, with a 5 ft (1.5 m) cut. The cost was about £5 in 1900. A one-horse McCormick side-delivery reaper came to Cott about 1912–13, followed later by a one-horse side-delivery Deering and eventually by a tractor-operated one. Whitehow got a back-delivery Albion about 1916. A one-horse self-delivery Princess reaper made by MacDonald Bros. of Portsoy in Banffshire came to Hinsobrae in the 1920s. Midhouse got a one-horse McCormick reaper about 1920, and a two-horse one in 1939. In Firth parish, a back-delivery McCormick came to Lighthouse in 1902, followed later by a back-delivery Walter A. Wood reaper. The first reaper was shared with a neighbour from 1902 till 1908.

An Albion binder came to Mayback about 1920–30, then a Deering. An Albion, then about the only kind of binder available, was got at Whitehow in 1947, following the purchase of a Ferguson Brown tractor in 1945. Another Albion, and a Ferguson tractor, reached Links in 1948. The McCormick with a 5 ft (1.5 m) cut that came to Midhouse in 1950 was bought from a South Ronaldsay farmer who had advertised it in the *Orcadian*. A Ferguson petrol tractor was bought in the same year. Cott got an Albion in 1913–14, and later a Deering. The first binder at Lighthouse in Firth, got in 1942, was a Hornsby, shared with a neighbour. The general effect of the introduction of tractors in Westray in the 1940s and 1950s was a reduction in and then complete replacement of horsepower. Manpower requirements were also reduced, so that the conjoint farms of Links, Hooking and Hinsobrae, extending to 72 acres, could

160. A Massey Ferguson combine speeds the Orkney harvest. Photo. W. Hourston. C80F.

work with four people less. Binders were welcomed by the local people because they saved work at a time when there were fewer people to do it.

The final development, the introduction of combine harvesters, is still in progress. Hugh Louttit at Bigging in Rendall parish got a Massey Ferguson in 1950. The first combine came to Papa Westray only in 1973. It should be emphasised, however, that the adoption of harvesting machinery and of tractors proceeded more rapidly in other parts of Orkney, and indeed the first 'tractors' to pull binders were Ford cars with spade-lugged wheels added to the rear, probably old reaper wheels. Some were converted to paraffin burning for the purpose.[753]

The rate of change in Shetland was slower. The sickle may still be seen in very occasional use, and scythes more often, where the arable is in small patches. The sickle was last used about 1900 in Fair Isle, and then only for cutting bere. A reaper came to the same island about 1950, but was not used until it could be tried behind a Ferguson tractor that was got in 1961 at Vaasetter. A Massey Harris No. 6 binder came to Fair Isle in 1967, and a power-driven McCormick International binder in 1974.[754] The introduction of harvesting machinery on the bigger farms in Shetland ran parallel to its introduction elsewhere.

44

Sheaves, Stooks and Stacks

SHEAVES of bere cut with the sickle were made large, and tied loosely near the top. This was called *gating* (Old Scots *gait*, sheaf), as in Scotland, and the resulting sheaf was set up by itself, with the base spread out, a process known as 'breaking' the sheaf, also done with sheaves of hay being kept for grass seed. The sheaves were bigger and rounder than those later set together in pairs in stooks, and the ends were made square so that they should stand easily. The band for the sheaf was often pulled out by the root, except when the crop was long enough, when it was cut. When being tied round the rather large sheaf, 'the band is drawn nearer the crop end than the root, and when the ends are pulled and crossed, they are then twisted and turned with dexterity so as to rest against the sheaf, but the ends thus twisted are not turned within the band'. When the

161. Sickle-cut sheaves set up upright, 1774. From Low 1774, facing p. *l.* C136G.20.

sheaf was set up on end, the root end of the band was set on the lee-side, and the corn end given a press towards the lee-side too. This helped to keep it upright, and it was left for five or six days before being screwed. An extension of this seems to be a method noted in Foula of setting up sheaves, not in groups of pairs leaning against each other as for conventional stooks, but in circular groups of five or six. The method is probably old. It appears to be used in illustrations of partly reaped fields near the church at Stenness and the Earl's Palace at Birsay in late eighteenth century Orkney.[755]

In the days of communal farming, the sheaves from the patches of grain on the runrig fields had their individual marks of ownership, so that they could be sorted out after a gale or identified if stolen. The mark was made by tying the sheaf band in a special way, which partly explains why the bandster was usually a responsible male. The custom is old. In 1595, the Bailie Court of Stenness investigated an alleged theft of five sheaves from another man's rig, but it turned out to be unintentional, because both men's sheaves were 'off ane band and nocht na differance betwixt bayth the bandis', surely a confusing circumstance. In 1615 Alister Watsone of Grimnes in South Ronaldsay was accused of stealing sixteen sheaves with other men's bands, and they were found in his *scroo* (Norwegian dialectal *skruv*, Old Norse *skrúf*, corn-stack, hay-cock). In 1923 after a gale in North Ronaldsay, it allowed sheaves belonging to different households to be identified, for 'Verracott had the knot and crook, and North Manse the scythe band and soo's tail'. The custom long outlasted the end of the runrig system, especially on small crofts standing close together, in Papa Westray, and elsewhere. At one time also, old women or orphans were set as watchers, called *mullyos*, to see that one farmer did not make or take bands out of his neighbour's rig, or cut up all the furrow corn at harvest-time. Their name came from the fact that they got the gleanings in payment.[756]

When shearing was finished, the gleaners set to work, picking up stalks of grain called *rips* (Old Scots *rip*, handful of unthreshed grain), and gathering them into small bundles called *mullyos* or *mullyecks* (origin uncertain: cf. Swedish dialectal *möljo*, heap, mass, *mullor*, corn-droppings), or *singloos* (Old Scots *single*, 1508). In Orkney these bunches were hung on ropes in the house to be ground on the quern for making the dish called burstin.[757] In Shetland the first meal of the season was ground from such *mülicks*. After they had dried in the house, the grain was rubbed out by hand, dried in a kettle over the fire, and ground on the quern. From this came the first very welcome new bread of the season. Sometimes the mullyecks were gathered by the children and young folk of each household, and made into burstin for the harvest celebration known in Dunrossness and elsewhere as the *affwinnin*, *affwinnin-day* or *affwinnin-feast*. Gleaning, therefore, also had a role in the community functioning. The end of shearing was also marked in Aithsting by a dish called the *affsharin mil gruel*, that is the milk gruel, or porridge made with milk instead of water, eaten when shearing was over.[758]

Sheaves dried individually or in stooks were built into scroos or in Orkney

162. Stooks and stacks at Moan, Finstown, Orkney. Per Mrs M. Sclater.

desses (Old Norse *des*, haystack) in the field, pending later stacking, or were carried home on the human back, on horseback, in carts or on sledges, the horses being muzzled with a basketwork kuivy or fitted with a wooden gag, a kevel or kepper.[759] Scroos could have temporary foundations of straw or some other material, but more permanent foundations were also possible, for in a 1747 inventory, three pieces of beams from ships' decks were listed as *screw-steeths* (*scroo* + *steethe*, foundation). Scroos varied in size, containing a couple

163. Back burdens of sheaves being stacked in Shetland. Photo. J D Rattar. C1641.

of cartloads of sheaves, or from 24 to 48 sheaves, that is one or two *thraves*, or a thrave and a half,[760] depending on the size of the sheaves. To make a scroo, 'first, set one sheaf upright. Then lean one at this on the north side. Then another on the south side. Then two sheaves leaned at this on the east side. Then two sheaves leaned on the west side. This formed the steethe of seven sheaves. Then a sheaf with tail end spread on the north side. Then another so on the south side. Then two so spread on the east side. This made six sheaves so spread. Then a second tier in the same away atop of the other. This completed the *kripple*'. This term, probably cognate with Norwegian dialectal *kreppa*, to squeeze, press together, seems to relate to certain sheaves in the scroo. The description here mentions seven steethe sheaves, but another source lists 5 'steethe sheaves', 4 'steethe quarters', 8 'double quarters', 3 'kribble', 3 'double kribble', and 2 'top sheaves'. This made a total of 25, one more than a thrave.[761] In Orphir the scroos held a threave, and the two last sheaves were put across each other and 'so tied together by portions of themselves, that they are not apt to fall even when the wind is high'. In good weather they stood for a week before being stacked. Such an interim stage was a mark of a rainy climate. In preparation for building a scroo, sheaves were gathered in a circle round the site, and handed to the builder by an assistant, often a woman. The finished scroo, topped by two sheaves spread out to run the rain, was 7 to 8 ft (2.1–2.4 m) high. In Fair Isle mullyecks gleaned from the rigs and tied in bundles called *kippocks* (Norwegian *kippe*, Old Norse *kippa*, bundle) were thrown into the middle of the scroo as it was being built.[762]

164. Round scroos of grain and rectangular hay desses at the Biggins, Papa Stour, 1967. C3891.

In Shetland a scroo is a small stack either in the field or in the stackyard. In Foula, the scroos are sometimes made with a layer of hay between each gang of sheaves, to help drying and to discourage mice. Some crofters had tried putting flagstones between the gangs to keep mice out with the pressure, but this did not work. Scroos were here thatched with sheaves of *rør* (Norwegian *rør*, Old Norse *reyr*), the common reed, *Arundo*. In a place like Foula, where gales are frequent and sudden *flans* (Old Scots *flan*, a blast, *c.* 1475; cf. Icelandic *flana*, to rush blindly, *flan*, a rush) of wind come hurtling down from the great cliff-top of the Kaim, scroos have to be anchored very securely. Three methods are used: to hang stones around on the ends of simmens, though the vibration of the wind could shake them loose; to tie the simmens to wooden stakes; to knock in four posts with two crossplanks fixed to lie north-east, north-west, south-west, south-east. The scroo was built on top, and roped to the planks. Stones could be piled on the ends of the planks for more stability.[763]

In Orkney the equivalent of a scroo was sometimes a *dess*, which could be

165. A kepper, fitted into a pony's mouth to stop it eating grain, when it was carrying sheaves on its back. Made by J. Laurenson, Fetlar, of bent-grass simmens and wood. In the National Museum. C394.

166. Setting up small field-stacks or desses in Orkney. 3.43.3.

167. Stack foundations at a Westray farm. There is a circular, roofed horse-walk for driving the threshing mill behind the barn to the right. 18.28.30A.

168. Orkney stacks, similar in shape to those of North-East Scotland, and roped down with thick, straw simmens. Per Bryce Wilson.

169. Forking from a rubber-tyred cart drawn by a tractor, in Orkney. Photo. W. Hourston. C78F.

larger than a scroo and smaller than a stack. Though the word is used in Shetland, it always refers there to a haystack with a rectangular base. There has therefore been a development of sense in Orkney, where the form of the dess is circular. In this sense it goes back at least to 1767, when Patrick Fea wrote: 'was oblidg'd to take in a Diss of Otts ... as I could not cast a Stack'.[764]

Another Orkney name for a stack on to which a small top had been built as an overnight protection, was *whum, home,* or *whummle* (Norwegian dialectal *kvelm, kvalm,* truss of hay, Swedish *valm,* small haycock). Usually the name applies to the top itself, but in Stronsay it is the whole stack. Mr Tait 'took in and threshed a home' on 11 October 1899, '4 homes of white (wheat) from Nelliespark' on 4 October 1900, and 'headed up a home' on 12 October 1914.[765]

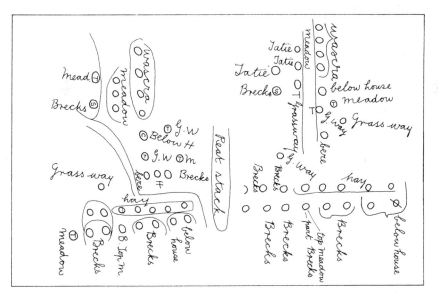

170. W. Tait's diagram, in his Diary for 1927, of the stacks in his cornyard. C4971.

Within the cornyard dykes, the upkeeping of which was a responsibility imposed by the community on the individual,[766] the Shetlanders built their small stack, as often as not called scroos like those in the field, and the Orcadians put up their bigger stacks, or *rucks* (Norwegian *ruka,* heap, stack, Old Norse *hraukr,* heap, but probably in Orkney through Scots). Already by 1814 Orkney rucks were said to be very well built, in the shape of 'the lower frustum of a cone inverted, with a cone placed on the top of it'. The heads were small, so they required little covering to protect them from the weather, though the number of simmens sometimes put on was a covering in itself. This comment was probably a little too complacent, for fifty years later an agricultural writer was saying that the shape of stacks had improved, though on small holdings they still shaped them to slope from bottom to top, so that a good deal of thatch was needed.[767] Many corn-yards contained well built stack foundations, especially where flagstone made the job of building easy, and on these bases were built the stacks of grain which swelled out from the base to overhanging eaves before being finished off at the top. In 1874 the eaves' diameter was given as 6 to 8 ft (1.8–2.4 m), with an apex rounded like an egg, and secured with simmens placed close together over the crown, and fastened below the eaves or *easin* (Old Scots *eisin*, eaves, 1553). Little thatch was needed. It is significant that a good deal of the terminology of stacks in Orkney is due to influence from Scotland, and in particular the North-East. Easins is one example. Another is *etherin* (Middle English *edder*, to plait), a name used in the North-East shoulder of Scotland for an oval or shuttle-shaped ball of straw rope about 10 to 11 in. (25–28 cm) long, used for lacing across vertical ropes on a stack, so that a network appearance was produced. This term as well as the oval ball to which it refers are found occasionally in Orkney. The grandfather of an informant who had lived in Firth parish came from Aberdeenshire, like several others in the 1850s, and etherins remained in use amongst his descendants, as well as the thrawcrook with which they were twisted. Other informants confirm this background.[768]

In parts of Orkney, the last sheaf of harvest was put up in the rafters of the barn and given to a mare and foal on New Year's morning. This was still happening in the 1920s.[769] This may also be due to North-East influence, for in general, though there was some laughter over the last sheaf, and efforts made to avoid cutting it, the main emphasis was on getting the grain into the yard. Young men would almost reach the stage of using their fists to avoid bringing in the last load. The competition was furious as leading got down to the last few loads, and a figure in the shape of a female dog, called the *bikko* (Old Norse *bikkja*, bitch), was put on the cornyard gate to greet the last comer. Those in the yard barked at him in derision when he arrived. The mistress gave him a 'piece' to eat, after which everyone would throw clods at him. The last one in might also be splashed with cold water. In Whalsay, the last one in with his sheaves was called 'dirt-a-slap'.[770] There is a trace of a similar custom in Shetland, where even a young boy barely able to carry one sheaf would struggle to avoid being last. But if he was, he might get a piece of a flour bannock or of an oatmeal *brünie* well spread with fresh butter as a consolation. In North Yell, the last back burden was stopped at the yard gate and could not go farther till the bearer had eaten a piece of buttered bread. This load was called the *hoidinfer* (origin uncertain).[771] In Orkney, a sheaf was made into the shape of a dog by the workers on a farm that had finished leading its crop before its neighbour, and slyly put in a prominent place about the neighbour's steading, or presented to him at his door in the morning.[772] This is evidently a later version, adapted for an individual farming rather than a runrig system.

In Shetland the leading home of the crop was known as *herding* (Old Norse *hirða*, to gather in hay), and when it was all into the stackyard it was *gorhirded* (Old Norse *garðr*, yard + Old Norse *hirða*). At this time the *herdin' bannock* was eaten. In Dunrossness a celebration at this time was called the *inpittins* ('putting in'). The Orkney equivalent for the harvest home was the *muckle supper*, when 'the pig or a sheep was killed, puddings were made, fowls roasted, and ale brewed'.[773] But this was not a regular point of conspicuous consumption.

45

Threshing

THRESHING BY HAND: LASHING

A method of threshing sheaves for a temporary or small-scale purpose or for keeping the straw as whole and unbroken as possible for thatching roofs or making straw articles, was by splitting them into bunches and lashing the heads against a hard or toothed surface. Another common reason was to half-thresh a sheaf for foddering animals, usually horses, a practice known in Orkney as to *aaber* (Norwegian *avberja*, long or threshed straw, Swedish dialectal *abärja*, to thresh by lashing) and to *nizz* (Norwegian *knys(j)a*, *knusa*, to crush, beat, pound). Some grain was left on, and the half-threshed sheaf was then called an *abir*, an *abir-tait* (cf. Icelandic *tæta*, shred, particle), or *nizz-meat*.[774]

Devices for lashing were both fixed and movable. In Shetland the *hog's back* was a block of wood about 2½ ft (76 cm) long, mounted at a convenient height on a trestle, with protruding nails on top. A ladder with some of its rungs studded with nails could serve the same purpose. Threshing was done by splitting the sheaf into handfuls and striking each handful on the block or rung, at the same time dragging it back through the nails to clear the grain more effectively.[775]

In Shetland, a wooden threshing frame with three, formerly five, wooden cross-bars studded with iron staples was photographed at Houll, North Roe, in 1930. A more sophisticated corn-beater at Busta, Fair Isle was still in use in 1962. It stood 51 in. (126 cm) high and was 26 in. (64 cm) wide. The sloping front part contained five iron cross-bars made from old cart-wheel rings. Lashing was done against these cross-bars, and the grain was collected on a canvas sheet, nailed to two wooden side-pieces, laid on the barn-floor below.

In some instances, lashing gave rise to a special building feature in the barns, in the form of a stone built to protrude about 6 in. (15 cm) from the inner wall at a convenient height (about 1 m above the floor), as in the old barn at Dalsetter in the South Mainland of Shetland, and at Appiehouse, Stenness, Orkney. Lashing was done on this *shackin-stane* or *gloy-stane*. They were complementary to the flail, not a substitute for it, and were situated – sometimes in each of the side walls of the barn – a little way above the ends of the threshing floor. The name gloy-stane comes from *gloy* (Middle Dutch *gleye*, *gluye*, Old French *glui,* (bundle of) straw, Old Scots *gloy*, 1513), a word used in Shetland,

Orkney, and Caithness for cleaned, unbroken straw used for various domestic purposes, kept till needed in little sheaves 4 to 5 in. (10–12 cm) in diameter. The best kind of straw was that of black oats, the longest straws being selected and made into a bunch for lashing.[776]

The Flail

Until the arrival and spread of threshing machinery, the flail was the main threshing implement. The flail itself consisted of three parts, a wooden handle, a souple or beater of wood, rope, or rolled sealskin, and a joining band. The different ways in which the two units are linked by the band is what gives flails their regional characteristics. In some cases, flails of a formerly widespread

171. Johnie Mouat with his flail, at Houbie, Fetlar, 1963. 2.5.15A.

172. Flail-threshing in Orkney. By courtesy of the Orkney County Library. C5751.

173. A wooden frame with cross pieces made from cart-wheel rings, used for threshing by lashing, at Busta, Fair Isle, 1962. 1.28.16.

type have come to survive only in certain areas. This applies to a type of flail now confined to Orkney, in which the joining band is retained by cross-pegs at the ends of the souple and handstaff. In the 1840s it appears to have been fairly common in South Scotland,[777] but subsequently died out there. The type has been described in detail:

'We will suppose that you and I take a turn at the old mode of threshing. We take for a beginning two sheaves from the corner of the barn, and lay them down on the clay floor, the long way of the sheaf extending across the barn. We take a flail off the pin stuck in the wall, on which they are hanging, and note that it consists of two rounded sticks of hard wood joined together by a thong of hide, or sheep skin, or in olden times, strong bent cord. The thicker and shorter staff, measuring slightly over two feet (61 cm) long, and about two inches (5 cm) in diameter, is the threshing stick or soople. The other, nearly 3½ feet (107 cm) long and about 1½ inches (4 cm) in diameter at the hinged end, and slightly less where we hold it, is the hand staff. In the upper end of the hand staff is a round hole and a little from the end of the soople, a hard wood pin is driven through a hole in it and projects a short distance at each side. The broad thong of hide has a loop hole in each end. After passing the thong of hide, which has first been steeped in water to make it pliable, through the hole in the hand staff, each end is put on the pin of the soople and firmly bound above and below the pin by narrow thongs of hide tied round and round to prevent the ends coming off the pins. In some cases, instead of a hole in the hand staff, a pin was put through it like the soople, and the thong taken through the loop of the thong on the soople, passed over the pins on the hand staff and secured as before; or thongs of equal length were placed one on each side over the holding pins. If the hood or hinge is not secure we may "fell" one another, hence our careful examination.' Two to three inches (5–8 cm) were allowed between the heads of the souple and the hand-staff, which was usually of hazel.[778]

Even in such a small area as Orkney, there could be several variations. Omond referred to three ways of fastening the hood in the extract above, and was aware that there could be many more. His material related to the parish of Evie. He also noted for Sandwick that there 'the hood was made from a piece of hide, the ends of which were tied together firmly, forming an oval of sufficient length to slip the one end over the pin and under on the soople, and the other end of the loop over and under the pin of handstaff, the part between being then seized tightly round and round so that the loop could not come over the pin'.[779] As shown by surviving flails, this fixing method was also done with twine.

There was also a group of flails with either a hole or a groove on the head of the souple as well as of the handstaff. In Orkney, such a groove was called a *knepp* (Old Norse *kneppa*, to join together).[780]

In Shetland, the characteristic flail is the hole-flail, with a long handstaff, a short thick souple, and a long joining band or *flail-tow*. Two examples recorded in the island of Papa Stour in 1967, one recorded in Fetlar in 1963, and another from Shetland preserved in the Göteborgs Historiska Museum, Sweden, have the following measurements:

	Handstaff	Souple	Joining band
Length. 1.	3 ft 4 in. (102 cm)	1 ft 9½ in. (55 cm)	1 ft 7½ in. (50 cm)
2.	3 ft (91 cm)	1 ft 6 in. (46 cm)	2 ft (61 cm)
3.	2 ft 10 in. (86 cm)	1 ft 7 in. (49 cm)	10 in. (25 cm)
4.	108 cm	58 cm	29 cm

	Handstaff	Souple
Diameter. 1.	1¼ in. (3 cm)	2 in. (5 cm)
2.	1¼ in. (3 cm)	2¼ in. (5.7 cm)
3.	–	–
4.	–	6.5 cm

The flail from Papa Stour, no. 2 above, had a well worn, knotty souple, evidently a piece of driftwood, and a joining band of plaited binder-twine. One islander, a woman, who had made a joining band of coir yarn, was rather ashamed of using this inferior material. According to Peter Scott of the Ark, the longer the flail-tow, the harder the blow that could be given to the grain. The flail staff was so handled that the souple did not rise above the head, but was always circling in front of the body. December in particular was the month for threshing with the flail.

All the examples of this type seen on the crofts have joining bands or *sooplibands* of rope, also known as *thongs*, *tedders*, *ties* or *fasties*, though thongs of leather or sheepskin were also used. The handstaff or flailtree, also called the *maister*, is always of wood, but the souple could be of rolled seal-hide as well as of wood. The seal-hide was cured and rolled up until its diameter was about 2 in. (5 cm), and then it was bound over its entire length. This was said to be preferable to wood, which could bruise the grain.[781] In some cases, in Orkney and the Hebrides, as well as in Shetland, the souple was of rope. Examples noted in 1962 at Troswick in the South Mainland of Shetland had a souple of rope wound round with rubber, 24 in. (61 cm) long by 1¾ in. (4.5 cm) diameter, and a handstaff of wood, 37 in. (94 cm) long by 1¼ in. (3 cm). The handstaff had a grooved end holding a rope ring that intermeshed with a second ring fixed to the end of the souple. In the second example the souple was of tarred rope served with tarred cord, with a loop of sheepskin at the end. The total length was 30 in. (76 cm). The handstaff, 43 in. (109 cm) long, had a hole at the end, containing a ring of rope that linked with a second ring fixed to the loop at the end of the souple. These flails are much more substantial than the small ones described above, a fact that may reflect the superior productivity of the South Mainland of Shetland.

In Fair Isle two flail types were noted. The first was a hole-flail, with a heavy souple and a rather short handstaff, said to be because it was used in a barn with rather low rafters. It was used by W. Stout at North Leogh. He normally worked with another thresher, and his habit was to deal with only two sheaves at a time. They were first threshed with the bands on, then turned and threshed again. Then the bands were taken off, and the grain from the bands was stripped off with the fingers. The threshed grain was stored in a barrel; and in due course the grain itself was beaten with the flail to remove the husks. This was the process of *hummelin'* (Old Scots *hummill*, awnless, 1475).[782] At Busta J. Stout had a small flail of the same kind, made to teach his son the art of flail threshing. At Quoy, there was a flail with a relatively short wooden souple with a hole for a joining band of rope, the ends of which were lashed over a groove on the head of the handstaff.

A variant, presumably made on a one-off basis, and not traditional, is a flail photographed on a Shetland croft in the early 1930s. This had a hole in the handstaff, a joining band of rope, and a souple made of a length of chain. This would have been used for threshing bere rather than the more easily bruised oats.

The South Mainland of Shetland and Fair Isle are more open to influences from Orkney and Scotland than other parts of Shetland. This can be seen in various ways, for example in features of buildings and in corn-drying kilns, and the same seems to apply to flails, although the Orkney form with a cross-peg has not been recorded in Shetland. This in turn may emphasise the late arrival of that type in Orkney itself. The hole-flail with a short souple and a joining band whose length is more or less equivalent to that of the souple characterises the more northerly parts of Shetland and the small islands, and may represent an older flail type that might once have been found in Orkney as well, though no trace of it survives. There is no means of guessing at the flail types represented by entries in early inventories, such as the '5 threshing flails' in the new barn at the House of Burray in 1747, or the 7 souples and 8 flails in a 1734 inventory from Stronsay, though the fact that flails and souples are mentioned may indicate that they were more substantial than the small, simple hole-flails used by the poorer folk whose goods never gained enough status to make them worth inventorising. Evidently direct influence from Norway can also be postulated, to judge by the order for various wooden items including souples that John Traill of Elsness in Sanday gave to his son David on 6 August 1728.[783] Probably the holes or grooves were made after their arrival, however.

In the outlying parts of Orkney, flails with grooved handstaffs and souples may still be seen, like one with a sheepskin joining band or *höd* observed on the farm of Gateside, North Ronaldsay.[784] There was a similar one at the farm of Dennis Hill, with a joining band of rope tightly lashed around along its length to keep it in position.

The Shetland hole-flails have holes in both the souple and the handstaff, and share the general Scottish habit of having to be rotated in the hand. The same applies to hole-flails in the more northerly coastal areas of Norway, and in the South-West, especially Rogaland, the handstaff often has a groove instead of a hole, as in Fair Isle. The hole-flail relates to poorer arable areas, often with a pastoral nature, and is distributed in Northern Scandinavia and Finland, the Alpine areas, the North-West Iberian coast, the Cevennes, North-East Poland, the East Baltic, and the north and west of Britain.[785] These are the main European relict area, and it can therefore be suggested that hole-flails are older than flail types in more advanced areas. It may be assumed that such flails once occurred in Orkney too, since they are common in Shetland, and are known in the Hebrides. They were also known in Caithness, where, according to oral information noted in 1968, holes were bored in the souple and handstaff with a hot iron, and the joining bands or *joinin's* were of sheepskin thongs, put in cold water for a day or two to soften before being attached. The local woods supplied branches for making the flails.[786]

TECHNIQUES OF FLAIL THRESHING

Threshing was a clean operation, requiring a clean threshing floor of wood or of clay. At Everland farm, in Fetlar, Shetland, wooden hatches were set into part of the barn floor. Here the grain was hummeled or dehusked with the flail, and threshing could also be done. The Fetlar name for such a threshing floor is *barrow*. This must be related to the verb *berry*, to thresh with the flail (Norwegian *bara*, to strike heavily on, Old Norse *berja*, to beat). In the small barns of such farms, flailing on the wooden or clay threshing floors was usually done by two men working together.[787]

Clay threshing-floors were specially made in the barns. On 20 and 21 October 1766 Patrick Fea in Sanday drove 28 horse loads of clay to the barn and had 'got my Threshing barn floors finished and fitt for threshing'. In early twentieth century plans of Orkney farmhouses,[788] the threshing floor is shown as a narrow strip of clay lying to one side of the opposite doors of the barn, but not between them, for this was the winnowing area. It was said that cleanliness was scrupulously observed in the barns. Root ends and coarser parts of straw were laid at the door, and on these the farmer wiped his boots every time he went into the barn.

There are relatively few accounts of flail threshing techniques, but enough exist to provide a fairly clear picture. George Stout of Field in Fair Isle related in 1962 that when the grain had been harvested, a stack containing 4 to 5 threaves (i.e. 96 to 120 sheaves) was taken into the barn to be threshed with flails. The sheaves were laid two one way and two the other, with their beards meeting. One side of the sheaf was threshed, then the other. When most of the corn was cut, the band was removed, opened out, and thrown down to be threshed. Sometimes the chaff stayed on and would not come off. Generally two men worked together, and would thresh 20 to 30 sheaves, depending on the number of animals to be fed. The straw was thrown to the side till there was enough to serve for one day or for two as the case might be, and was then made up into bundles called *winlins* (Old Scots *windle*, to bundle brushwood, 1536; Middle Dutch *windelen*, to swathe). The corn was piled in a heap or *bing* until there was enough for winnowing. After the straw and chaff from the threshed sheaves had been removed, the grain was put on the floor by itself and hummeled or dehusked with the flail.[789]

A bigger-scale method was described by another Shetland informant. Several sheaves were laid in a circle, ears inward, on the swept barn floor. Up to five threshers stood around, and the leader struck, followed by the rest clockwise in turn. After about 15 minutes there was a pause for the straw to be turned over and given a few strokes with the flail to finish off. The straw was then removed to a corner, except for what was left as a bed for fresh sheaves. After threshing, all the straw was taken up and shaken to remove the grain, which was stored in barrels, boxes, tubs and anything else available till it was taken out for winnowing. It was said that threshing was always done at the time of the growing moon to make sure that the grain used as seed would be productive.[790]

In Orkney, a detailed account was written about 1912, as if teaching the art of flailing:

'As a beginner finds it easier to thresh with the right foot extended and the right hand furthest up on the hand staff, you will go to the west side of the clay floor opposite to me and having the oats ends of the sheaves pointing towards your left side. You then swing the soople by moving the hand staff to your left, and raising it till the soople swings above and behind your head and comes down with a whack on the head of the sheaf, not your own head, and not the supple backs (rafters), but to make the oats dance off the straw on the floor. I, on the other side, with left foot extended, and left hand furtherest up on the hand staff swing the flail in the same manner, but, though I am on the opposite side the soople swings round in the same direction as yours – or the sooples in both cases travel towards the top end of the sheaves thus avoiding collisions in the air.

'To start, we do not give the full stroke, but raise the hand staff just sufficiently to turn the soople over, over hand and not over head, threshing, and so we give turn about tap, tap, tap, tap, till we get the time about rhythm, and then muscle and sinew must be used till we make the rafters ring and the chaff fly from the threshing floor. When we have finished one side of the sheaves we turn them upside down and thresh the side that was under. Then we pull off the bands, strip the heads on the hand staff, and if gloy is needed lay them in a corner, if not we throw them down on the sheaves and thresh again. Now turn the straw with the hand staves and finish threshing by giving a sliding movement at the down stroke to the soople, edging the straw away to the side.' When two people were threshing, four sheaves were laid in pairs, heads together. Careful threshers did not draw the threshed straw away with their flails, but at the end threshed it by lashing it in bunches against the handstaff to make sure no oats were left.[791]

According to another account, the sheaf was unbound and laid with the stubble end against the wall. After some minutes of threshing the sheaf was turned with the handstaff of the flail and a quick twist of the right foot, for threshing on the other side. After three turnings, the grain was well threshed off. A sickle was kept at hand to cut off the root ends of the bands, because in earlier days the sheaves were made thicker, and the crops were shorter. The straw was shaken up and flung loosely into a corner, the grain being heaped at the side of the floor.

'When two men were engaged in wielding the flail, they stood facing each other with the threshing floor and sheaf between and in front of them, and with alternate strokes they beat off the grain. On large farms several men were at work at the same time, and it was indeed a pleasing sight to watch them as they whirled aloft the soople of the flail before bringing it down with steady beat on the sheaf. As they bent and swayed with each stroke they went through a regular series of attitudes which displayed their manly physique to advantage ... After each day's supply of straw had been threshed, one of the barn hands swept the oats together into a heap and *bussed* it. This process he performed by getting down on his knees and raking out the broken straw with his hands, the oats passing between his outspread fingers. Then he gave the handfuls of oats a quick jerk forward, and sent the grain about two feet (61 cm) ahead, leaving the broken straws behind'.[792] The Shetland name for this process of *bussing* (Norwegian *bos*, *bus*, straw for bedding, small pieces) was to *hand trist*, the second element of which derives from Old Norse *þrysta*, to squeeze, press.

THRESHING MACHINERY

Threshing-mills, of which the first fully successful example was patented in 1786, reached Orkney in the 1820s. Sanday had two by 1823, there was one at Huip in Stronsay, and one in Papa Westray. In Cross parish, there were two wind-mills and two water-mills on the land of J. Balfour of Trenabie, and in Burness, a wind-mill and a water-mill on the land of T. Traill of Westove in 1845.[793] The water-mills were probably for grinding meal. In 1857–8, David Petrie, factor and farmer of Graemeshall in Holm, recorded in his diary the arrival of a threshing-machine:

1857, 24 Nov:	3 Carts at Kirkwall for wheels of thrashing machine	
5 Dec:	Carts at Jas. Tait's St. Andrews for wood of The Mill	
1858, 2 Jan:	Carting material forming the walk for horses driving the Thrashing Mill	
6 Jan:	Carting gravel for do.	
9 Jan:	Filling and painting cover of Thrashing Mill	
13 Jan:	1st thrashing on Mill	
14 Jan:	Thrashed 1 stack Oats on mill, 2 hours	
3 Feb:	Thrashed 1 Oat stack, less than 2 hours.[794]	

By the 1870s there were both horse- and water-driven mills. Most farms on the Mainland of Orkney had threshing-mills of two or four horse-power, the gearings being made by firms like Harper & Co., Aberdeen. Mr Balfour at Holland had a fixed steam engine for threshing, like James Scarth at Scar House. The one at Messrs. Irving's and Hourston's farm of Stove in Sanday was a Clayton and Shuttleworth model. At Trenabie, water power for Mr Balfour's threshing machine came from a dam filled by the sea. Water power was also used at Carrick in Eday and at Westness in Rousay. The 300-acre farm of Saverock in the West Mainland had a 6-horse threshing machine. John Walker of Maryfield in Bressay had the only steam threshing-mill in Shetland. G. Bruce had a threshing-mill at Veensgarth, as had Andrew Umphrey at Reawick, and A J Grierson at Quendale.[795]

174. A horse-walk at the Bu', Burray, for three pairs of horses, *c*. 1908. From Mr Kennedy. Per Bryce Wilson. 28.8.31A.

In Stronsay, Mr Tait's mill was driven by horses that walked round and round on a circular mill-course built up of stones that had to be renewed from time to time. By the 1920s, the horses had been replaced by a 5 horse-power oil engine. Mill-courses in the Northern Isles were normally uncovered, with a few exceptions such as the roofed-in ones at Carson in Stromness and Saverock in St Ola. The horses were harnessed to the outer ends of long poles through which they transferred their energy by means of gearing, as they walked around, to the mill inside the barn. Two to four was the average number of horses, yoked in pairs, though the number could be as high as eight. It was said of an eight-horse mill in Sanday that the mechanism was so heavy that it took some time to get up to speed. There was the same problem in reverse for stopping the mill, and a sheaf would be jammed into the mill and held firmly, to act as a brake. The horses had to go steadily to let the mill work efficiently, and as a rule one of the younger folk would drive them. If the horses got out of hand the mill would be damaged, and when this happened at a mill in Gairsay the threshing drum went through the roof. John Spence of Beaquoy in Birsay fitted up seventeen horse mills between 1885–95.[796]

Mills operated by hand-power are said to have begun to appear in Orkney about the 1850s. Two hands turned cranks to rotate the drum, as a rule, and others fed in the sheaves and cleared the straw. They were adopted by small farmers who could not afford bigger-scale threshing machinery, and were instrumental in ending the use of the flail. Many were made locally, and others were got from outside, like the hand and pedal operated wooden threshers made by Shearer of Turriff in Aberdeenshire, and the cast-iron 'Tiny' Threshing Machine made by G. Murray & Co., Engineers, Banff Foundry. Sometimes

175. A pedal and handle operated hand-threshing mill, made by Shearer Bros., Turriff Aberdeenshire, on a farm near Stromness, Orkney. C3643.

176. A barn-mill at Kirbister Farm, converted to water-power from being a hand-mill, 1950s.

they were adapted to wind and water power, or could even be driven by a second-hand car engine.[797]

Wind-mills usually had six triangular sails, any number from two to six being set, depending on the force of the wind. The sails were set to the wind and held in place by guy ropes. To stop the mill, the sails were turned edge to wind and the sails taken off. There was no governor, and if the wind rose, sheaves had to be fed in more quickly to keep the mill-speed down. Wind-mills of this kind were used till the 1940s in Papa Westray, when both they and hand-mills came to be replaced by engines such as the $3\frac{1}{2}$ h.p. Lister introduced to Hinsobrae in 1928.[798] A South Ronaldsay variation had four rectangular sails covered with canvas, the amount of which could be varied to suit the wind conditions. These sails were not otherwise adjustable and were fixed to work between south and south-east.

Water-power is relatively scarce in Orkney. For this reason, barns containing mills turned by water wheels were built at odd angles to the steading or even at some distance away. Alternatively, power from a wheel on a water-course was transferred to the mill by pulleys on posts, but this involved loss of power in relation to distance. Two hundred yards (183 m) was about the limit.[799]

46

Grain Storage and Winnowing

GRAIN was at one time commonly stored in straw baskets, 'cassies', and transported in them as well. There were no sacks for keeping grain. The straw containers were made bigger or smaller, for setting in the barn or carrying on the backs of people or of horses. In the Orkney barns there could be *corn neuks*, outshots in which corn was stored, some measuring 5 ft (1.5 m) long by 3 ft 6 in. (1.1 m) deep by 5 ft (1.5 m) high at the front, reducing to 3 ft (91 cm) at the back. The corn neuk was sometimes in the side wall, but more often at the right hand side of the kiln entrance at the end of the barn. An Orkney name for such a recess, or for a receptacle for holding grain, was *ray* (Old Norse *rá*, corner). A method of grain storage, also known in Caithness, South-West Scotland, and Ireland, involved heaping the grain outside after it had been threshed, and

177. Winnowing grain at Delting, Shetland, May 1961. Photo. A J Cluness.

178. Winnowing riddles at Daybreak, Papa Westray, 1974. Photo. M. Wright. 18.28.29.

thatching it around so that it looked like a big bee-skep.[800] According to a description of 1814:

'In defect of a granary, thrashed grain is preserved in a simple manner in the open air in these islands. It is stacked on a circular foundation of straw, about a foot (30.48 cm) thick, and surrounded with strong straw ropes, here called simmons. The pile is carried up perpendicular, or gently expanding for several feet, say five feet (1.5 m) high. Straw, drawn into thatch, is placed in a vertical position around the heap, from four to six inches (10–15 cm) thick, and surrounded with the ropes. The pile is gradually contracted to an apex, after it has expanded, perhaps more than two feet (61 cm) in diameter, from the foundation. Forty Linlithgow bolls are sometimes preserved in one of these piles, here called beaks or screws. It is necessary that the pile be placed on dry ground, that the covering be attended to, and any parts wasted by the weather or vermin carefully repaired.'[801] Grain could keep for up to a year in this way.

Such outdoor straw-rope granaries were a response to two factors. The first was the small size of the outbuildings, which restricted facilities for indoor storage. The second was the grain trade itself, which in Orkney as well as in Caithness led to the production of surplus grain that had to be stored pending shipment, preferably at a time when prices were good. It is possible that the occurrence of such granaries on small farms in Orkney is a later reflection of a system that developed as a result of trading in grain.[802]

Barns in the Northern Isles, as elsewhere, usually had two doors opposite each other, or a door with a wall opening across from it, so that a winnowing draught could be got. Sometimes, as at Barkland in Fair Isle, there was a row of flagstones between the doors to give a clean floor for the purpose. There was an art in creating the right kind of draught in the barn. If the wind was too strong, a mat or flackie was put in the doorway to moderate it. Such a wind was called a *tirso* wind, because the mat was made of *tirsos* (origin uncertain), the marsh ragwort *Senecio jacobea* or the common dock, *Rumex obtusifolius*.[803] If the wind was blowing on to the gable, at right angles to the required direction, it could be diverted through the barn by placing a wooden door or the like at an angle outside one door, which was known as skyling the wind, and another at the other door angled to keep the wind out. This produced an unsteady draught called in Orkney a *kinlit* (kindled) wind. In some barns, the doors were made in two halves, so that the upper section could be closed if the wind was too strong. It was only if the door was in one piece that the opening would have to be partly filled with bunches or windlings of straw or a loosely plaited flackie. The lower part of the lee door was always kept shut during winnowing to keep the chaff from blowing outside, the upper half being left open to let the dust escape.[804]

179. A corn byke in Caithness, 1905. From Dunbar 1931–2, LXVI, 136. Similar ones were made in Orkney.

Flackies served not only as doors, but also as ground-sheets on which the corn was winnowed, whether the work was being done inside or outside the barn. They also made covers for straw bins or baskets used for storing grain. A Shetland name for such a winnowing-sheet was *flackie-corn*.[805]

To clean the grain, the barnman took a winnowing basket or *windoo-cubbie* under his left arm, sometimes with the band of it round his neck, or in Shetland a *budie* or small barrel, and let the grain trickle out gradually, catching it in his right hand and tossing it upwards with his outspread fingers. The heavier grain fell straight down and the lighter stuff blew to one side, when it could be readily separated. The heap of good corn was then picked up in handfuls and sifted through the fingers till the chaff was completely cleared. Nevertheless, many bad and light grains, and the seeds of weeds, remained.[806] This process was the same whether the work was done in the barn or on a piece of ground that caught the wind outside. Near the meal mill at Ireland in Stenness, 'dere waas whit dey ca'ad da Millbrae api' da heich grund, an' dat waas da piece whar maist o' da aits waas winood. Da aits fell api' whit dey caad a flaitie made o' strae like da back o' a ald back steul, an' da caff jeust bleu awa'.[807]

Winnowing through the fingers was seen in Orkney in 1757. In North Ronaldsay in 1793, seed oats were treated in this way, but bere seed was put through a riddle to clear the awns. '2 sufficient riddles' were mentioned in a Stronsay inventory of 1734, and examples noted in recent times are both round and square. By 1805, though fanners were known on the Mainland of Scotland, winnowing still continued to be done between doors in Orkney.[808]

Winnowing could be done for seed, or after kiln-drying and hummeling to prepare the grain for grinding. The hummeling process was often done by trampling and rubbing the bere, warm from the kiln, with the feet in a straw basket or *skeb* (Old Norse *skeppa*, basket, bushel; Old Scots *skepe*, c. 1400).[809] This was a job young folk liked to do. A spade-blade could also be used. At Troswick in Dunrossness John Leslie was using a half-barrel as a container in 1962, and hummeling was done with a wooden *chappin-tree* (Old Scots *chap*, to strike, c. 1568), a spar of wood with a cross-bar handle, and short metal blades set at right angles into the working end. Such a container was a *rubbin'-tub*. Some device of this kind was probably indicated when Patrick Fea noted in his Diary for November 1771 that there were '2 helping with the Corn humler'. Five years earlier he mentioned hummeling two kilns of bere in order to 'cassie' it, or put it in baskets. The other major way of hummeling dried grain was by spreading it on the threshing floor in the barn and beating it with the flail. This was especially necessary because the small oat, like bere or barley, had long awns which had to be cleared off before the grain could be taken to the mill. To get rid of the dust or *ting-vangs* (origin unknown), the grain was again winnowed.[810]

In addition to winnowing by hand and riddling, a method of cleaning corn before grinding was by shaking it with a twirling motion in a circular *wecht* (Old Scots, c. 1568), a wooden hoop two to three feet (61–91 cm) in diameter, with a base of skin. The effect was to gather broken bits of straw and weed seeds at one side so that they could be picked off and thrown away. This refuse was called *röd* (cf. Norwegian dialectal *ryd*, refuse, Old Norse *ryðja*, to clear) or *floss* (Norwegian dialectal *flos*, *flus*, rind, scale, peeled off strip). A Shetland name is *dumba* (Norwegian dialectal *dumba*, dust, chaff, Old Norse *dumba*, cloud of dust, especially from threshing corn). To clean grain by removing the husks and awns was to *snod* (Old Scots *snod*, smooth, even) it, and the awns themselves were called *shos* (origin uncertain) or *skeggs* (Norwegian *skjegg*, Old Norse *skegg*, beard, awns).[811]

47

Corn Drying and Corn Kilns

THE need for drying grain arises for three main reasons. In some areas, where the summer is short and moist, a crop may never ripen properly, and the grain for the next year's seed has itself to be dried. This was necessary in the Faroe Islands.[812] Secondly, since man does not for preference live by bread alone, kilns are required for drying malt, for stopping the germination in the seed once it has started, as part of the process of making ale. Kilns in Orkney remained in use for this purpose long after the practice of drying the year's crop in them had ceased. The primary reason, however, is to prepare the grain for grinding. It is not easy to grind soft grain. In an experiment carried out with a rotary Roman quern, a pound of roasted wheat was ground into flour in a few minutes, putting it through the quern twice. A pound of undried wheat took nearly three quarters of an hour to grind, and had to be put through eight or nine times.[813] Drying allowed the kernels to granulate easily, so that good meal could be made.

There were various ways of drying grain on a small scale, of such a kind that they left no trace in the archaeological record. The chief of these is pot drying, especially in connection with the preparation of the dish known as burstin, probably because the grains or *mettins* (cf. Shetland Norse *met*, Norwegian dialectal *mata*, to swell in the ears) burst during roasting. For this, grain was dried over the fire in a round-bottomed pot in which it was turned with the hand or a flat piece of wood, a *turnin' brod*, until hard and brittle, parched to the point of roasting and of a crisp, brown colour. An obsolete Shetland word, *to loom* (cf. Swedish dialectal *lumma*, to warm, Norwegian *lum*, warm), was applied to pot drying. It was then ground in a hand-mill or knocking stone, mixed with buttermilk, and eaten without further cooking, or baked into thick cakes. An alternative was to put the grain into a container of straw or some other material, and to roll heated stones into it. This was done in St Kilda and no doubt elsewhere in the West as well as in Shetland and Orkney. In 1643, an Orkney witch was found drying corn to the devil by means of a hot stove on a 'flakkit' (*flackie*) in the firehouse or kitchen of a farm. The fire-crackled stones often found at archaeological investigations may not be pot-boilers, as commonly suggested, but corn-driers. In Orkney a *hellio* (Norwegian, Old Norse *hella*, flat stone) was a stone with a rim of clay around it, used in parching corn.[814] The second element is the same as in the Faroese *munnhella*, literally

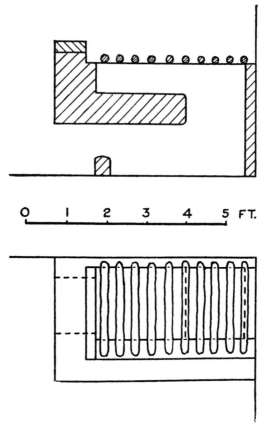

180. Plan and section of a four-sided kiln, with a baffle to keep sparks off the drying floor. From Scott 1951. Vol. 25, 199. C5753.

'mouth-stone', the hearth in which the fire of the Faroese type of kiln burned. How the parching was done in the hellio is not stated, but the use of hot stones is likely.

KILN DRYING

Stone-built kilns can be rectangular in form, circular or semi-circular. The former type appears to be the older and is now restricted in its distribution to the smaller farms of the northern parts of Shetland. Unlike corn kilns in the rest of Scotland, which normally stood some distance from the houses, those of the Northern Isles are characteristically placed inside or on the end of the barn. Circular ones form the end piece in long houses and in barns that are free-standing.

The four-sided kiln was built into the corner of the barn, so that two of its sides were formed by the side and gable walls. None are now known to be in

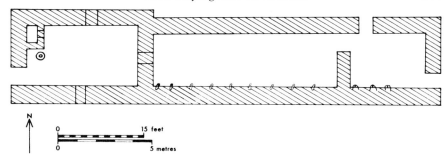

181. A four-sided kiln with a knocking-stone alongside at Smithfield, Fetlar. Surveyed by A. Fenton, 1963. C5847.

use. Obsolete examples have been noted at Effirth, Stanydale, Northbray Croft, and Northmavine Croft, all on the Shetland Mainland.[815] There is another, still in a fair state of preservation, in the barn built in 1815 at Smithfield in the island of Fetlar. It is of clay-bound stone, the walls ten inches (25 cm) thick, with an eight-inch (20 cm) square fire-hole or *kiln-huggie* in the short side, in which the fire of hard, dry pieces of peat was lit. The top of the wall is stepped to form a retaining shelf for the wooden cross-bars or *kiln-trees* set across the top, spaced out regularly with a few inches between each. The kiln sticks were laid from front to back, more rarely from side to side, the ends nearest the back or side wall of the barn being supported in each case on a transverse bar of wood. A vent or chimney was fixed at the back, against the wall of the barn, to draw off the smoke and prevent it from tasting the grain, and also to bring the heat more evenly over to the back of the kiln. The bed on which the grain was laid to dry was made of drawn straw, and spread two or three inches (5–8 cm) deep over the cross-bars, at right angles to them. Perforated metal sheets were sometimes tried but were not liked since there was a tendency for the bottom corn to be heat-blackened or *scuttered*. Sacking was also laid on top of the straw bed, so that grain should not be lost. Three sizes of flat, thin stone lay by the fire-hole, to be set on edge as required to regulate the draught when the fire was lit. About half a barrel of grain could be dried at a time, which compares with the half to one barrel that Faroese kilns could deal with in the late eighteenth century. The risk of fire was considerable and someone had to be there to ensure that the straw did not catch alight, and to turn the grain, either with the hand or a flat wooden board. When drying was complete, the grain was scooped off, sometimes with a plate, and put into a wooden tub or straw basket, a skeb.[816]

Though lacking at Smithfield, many of the four-sided kilns had a flat stone placed as a baffle at the top of the inside of the fire-hole to shield the inflammable drying-floor, and to catch any grain that trickled through the straw bed. This feature is called the *kilpinstane*, a name that, like the element *kiln* itself, exists in a large number of forms varying chiefly through palatalisation of the first letter and subsequent interchange of *ky* and *hy*. This interchange matches similar variations in Norwegian dialects,[817] and the fronting of *ky-* to *ch-* in the form *chylpin-stane* also happens in Faroese. *Kiln* occurs only in English and in Swedish, Norwegian and Danish, and may have reached the Scandinavian languages from English. At any rate, the variations suggest that kiln and its derivative kilpinstane (kiln+?pend+stone) were in use in the Northern Isles early enough to participate in a range of sound changes characterising Norse-derived dialects possibly, therefore, before the end of the fifteenth century.

Four-sided kilns were small. The one in Fetlar was 4 ft by 3 ft (122×91 cm), one in Papa Stour about 4 ft (122 cm) square, and another unlocalised was 6 ft by 3 ft (183×91 cm). The remains of a kiln in the barn at Hamna Voe measured 6 ft by 3 ft 4 in. (1.8×1.1 m).[818] The height in general was little more than 2 ft (61 cm).

Some writers have called the four-sided kiln the 'North Shetland' type. The

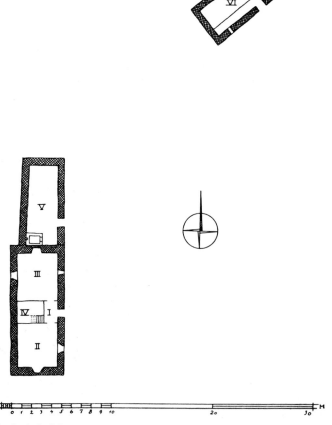

182. A sinnie, in building v, at Northmavine Croft, Shetland. From Roussell 1934. 63.

term is misleading since the present distribution appears merely to reflect a survival pattern. A four-sided kiln formerly existed in the corner of the barn at Appiehouse in Orkney, and in the Viking settlement at Freswick in Caithness that lasted until the late thirteenth century, a building presumed to be a barn contained a four-sided structure measuring 9 ft (2.7 m) in length from the intake of the vent to the rear of the chamber, and expanding from 14 in. (36 cm) at the vent to 3 ft 3 in. (99 cm) at the inner end.[819] According to the excavator, the rounding of the corner in which it was placed, both internally and externally, showed that it had formed part of the original building. The width had been reduced at one side by a lining of stones, no doubt intended to carry the drying floor. Peat ash covered the floor of the flue to a depth of several inches.

This broader distributional pattern is also supported by the terminology. The Shetland names for the four-sided kiln, *sonn*, *soin*, and the diminutive *sinnie*, appear to be related to Gaelic *sòrn*, a kiln or its flue or fireplace, and also to a hearth. The Caithness *sornie*, 'the flue or hot air channel leading from the fireplace to the underside of the drying platform of a kiln, and, by extension, the fireplace itself',[820] is a diminutive based directly on Gaelic. The Gaelic word is the origin of Faroese *sodnur*, the fire-place of a kiln, for the *-rn-* combination is generally pronounced *-dn-* in Faroese. Associated compounds are *sodnhûs*, kilnhouse, *sodnkjeer*, a separate room in a house where corn is dried, and *sodnspølur*, the laths of the drying floor. Nevertheless built structures for drying grain were apparently not very common in the Faroes. Corn kilns are first mentioned there in 1669, but only under the Danish name *kiolne*, kiln.[821] This does not, however, affect the existence of *sodnur* as a borrowing from Celtic, and further corroboration comes from the Icelandic equivalent, *sofnhus*, with its drying area, the *sofn*, floored with spars, the *sofnraftar* or *sofnspelir* on which straw was spread as a bed for the grain. Such kilns remained in use in Iceland for drying a kind of rye till the 1890s, and have been recorded from the second half of the eighteenth century. A small rectangular building excavated at the farm of Bergþórsvoll, which probably belonged to Njál who died in 1011, has been tentatively identified as a drying house.[822]

The Faroese kiln may be in an outhouse specially built of earth and stone for the purpose, though it is more commonly at the end of a byre or barn. A partition of stones and clay, built from wall to wall about 4 ft (122 cm) high, has in the middle a 2 ft (61 cm) wide aperture covered with a flat lintel stone, in which the fire is lit. Spars of wood laid from the top of the partition to the gable bear the straw drying-floor. Whether in a separate building or not, the Faroese kiln is always four-sided and therefore parallels the Shetland *sinnie* and the twelfth–thirteenth century Freswick kiln. Indeed it may also be built, as in Shetland, in the angle between the side and gable wall.[823]

In West Norway (Sogn) the name *þorn*, applied in a probate inventory of 1314 to a building, is represented in modern Norwegian by *tonn*, *torn*, a floor of wooden slats on which malt was dried. This has been associated with another West Norwegian (Trøndelag) name, *sonn*, though it is more likely to belong to the group of words like *tarre*, *terre*, applied to drying. It is generally accepted that *sonn* is a borrowing from Irish or Gaelic *sòrn*, probably in the Viking period, and it is conceivable that the Shetland forms came by way of Norway.[824] At any rate, there is here a cultural element and a set of regionally variant names that demonstrate a degree of unity in the Scandinavian and Celtic countries.

THE CIRCULAR KILN

In Orkney and the more fertile parts of Shetland, especially the South Mainland, a circular or semi-circular type of kiln was in general use, built against the gable wall of a barn or forming an extension to it, with access from within the barn. Many survive, though not in use. One of the last to be active was at Troswick in South Shetland. Internally, the bowl of the kiln is egg-shaped, with an open top that could be closed by a wooden cover, a turf, or sometimes a large thin flagstone. About a third of the way up, a ledge supported the beam and spars of the drying floor, the far end of the beam being recessed into the back wall just below the level of the ledge so that the spars or *kiln-sticks*, when laid from beam to ledge at alternate sides, formed a level platform for the drawn straw, or, on larger farms, a horsehair mat. The ledge, and sometimes the arrangement of spars laid on it, was called the *hemlins* in Orkney.[825] This may be related to *hemmel*, used in Northern England and South-East Scotland for a rack in a cattle court for holding fodder, and if so the word is an example of indirect influence (cf. Norwegian dialectal *hjelm*, a slatted room) reaching Orkney by way of the Scottish dialects. It could also, however, be related to Swedish dialectal *hammel*, a little bar or beam, with transference of sense to the stone ledge that supported the beam.

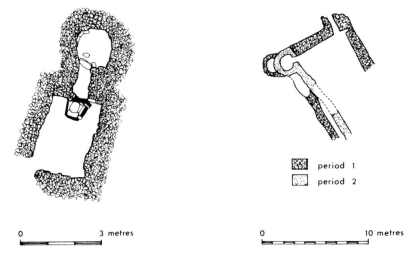

period 1
period 2

0   3 metres

0   10 metres

183. Round kilns, right: at the medieval farm at Jarlshof. Shetland, fourteenth century. After Hamilton 1956. 191–2; left: at Gröf i Oræfum, Iceland, 1340. After Gestsson 1959. 32.

The central beam is the *kiln-ace* (Norwegian *ås*, Old Norse *áss*, pole, rafter) in Orkney and *kiln-simmer* (Scots *summer*, Old French *somier*, a beam, joist) in Shetland. This beam, like the kiln-sticks, had to be as free from tar and resin as possible to lessen the fire risk. In the island of North Ronaldsay the sloping part of the inside walls of the kiln is called the *tramins*. The application may originally have been to the ledge for the cross-beams since the word derives from Scots *tram*, a beam, shaft. This argues for Scots rather than Norse influence, especially since the type of kiln to which *tramins* was applied is a nineteenth century innovation, built on the analogy of the kilns attached to commercial mills. Most parishes in Orkney had such combined mills and kilns by or soon after 1850, and this in turn had an effect on the form of farm kilns.[826]

The layout of the arrangements for heating and access varies according to the size of the kiln. The simplest is the type commonly found in, for example, Fair Isle, where the existing farms date back to the 1870 to 1880 re-organisation. Here, the semi-circular kiln is against the end wall of the barn. Two openings in the gable wall lead into the bowl of the kiln, an upper and larger one serving as the kiln door, providing access to the drying floor at a height of 4 to 5 ft (122–152 cm), and immediately below it, at floor level, a smaller one, in the mouth of which the fire of peats was lit. The heat had to travel no farther than through the combined thickness of the gable wall and the stonework of the bowl. Between the two wall openings was a recess that served as a footstep for access to the kiln floor.

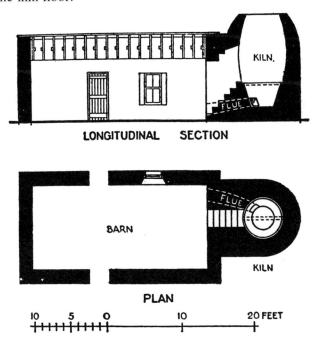

184. The kiln at Exnaboe, Shetland. Copyright: Royal Commission on Ancient Monuments, from the *Orkney and Shetland Inventory*, 1946. T.56. C5754.

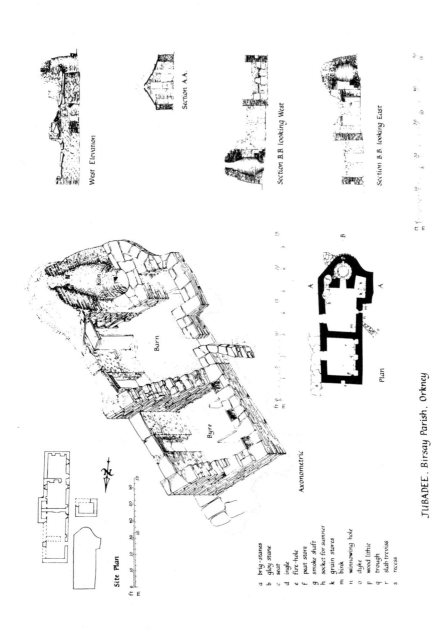

West Elevation

Section A.A.

Section B.B looking West

Section B.B looking East

Kiln

Barn

Byre

Axonometric

Site Plan

Plan

a brig-stanes
b gloy stane
c seat
d ingle
e fire-hole
f peat store
g smoke shaft
h socket for summer
k grain stores
m bink
n winnowing hole
o dyke
p wood lithic
q trough
r slab treviss
s recess

JUBADEE. Birsay Parish, Orkney

185. The kiln at Jubadee, Birsay, Orkney, surveyed 1968. Copyright: Royal Commission on Ancient Monuments, Neg. no. ORD/2/1.

The kiln entrance had no door, but when in use a flackie was hung over the opening so that the draught would be directed through the fire-hole and flue. Too strong a draught was undesirable.

The Fair Isle and Dunrossness name for the fire-hole is *kiln-sluggie*, but elsewhere it is *hoggie, kiln-hoggie*. These forms with other minor variants derive from *kiln +logie*, known in Old Scots from the sixteenth century apparently as an adaptation of Gaelic *logan, lagan*, a hollow or pit. In Orkney, Caithness, and Fair Isle the names *ingle, ingle-hole* and *kiln-ingle* were also used.[827]

Ingle, ultimately from Gaelic *aingeal*, fire, is known in Scots from the early sixteenth century. Though, like *sinnie, ingle* and *kiln-hoggie* (with its variants), they exemplify Gaelic influence on the terminology of kilns in the Northern Isles, they are more likely to have got there through Lowland Scots than as a result of direct contact.

The larger kilns of Orkney and the South Mainland of Shetland stood 12 to 15 ft (3.7–4.6 m) high, often overtopping the roof ridge of the barn by 2 to 3 ft (61–91 cm) with walls up to or over 3 ft (91 cm) thick. Internally, the bowl was about 4 ft (1.2 m) in diameter at ground level, expanding to 8 ft (2.4 m) at the level of the ledge, at which point the kiln wall was about 3 ft (91 cm) thick. Above this the wall was thinner, reduced by the width of the ledge, i.e. about

186. The kiln at Jubadee, from the South-East, 1968. Copyright: Royal Commission on Ancient Monuments.

4 in. (10 cm). Externally the kiln walls were perpendicular up to at least the height of the side walls of the barn, where they started to slope inwards in the form of a dome, leaving an opening at the top 2 to 4 ft (61–122 cm) in diameter. In some districts of Orkney the top was finished off by courses of sods to a depth of about 2 ft (61 cm).[828] As indicated by Patrick Fea's comment in his Diary on 23 October, 1766 – 'Clay'd the Kiln without' – clay mortar could be used for binding and pointing the stonework to insulate against loss of heat. There is usually a considerable thickness of stonework between the barn and the bowl of the kiln, and the kiln-door and drying floor is often reached by a short flight of three or four steps. The entrance to the drying floors of bigger kilns could be closed by a wooden door, but in general they were quite small, about 3 ft by 2 ft (91×61 cm), and could be easily closed by a straw mat or one or two bunches of straw. The flue does not run directly through the wall but curves round at ground level so as to bring the heat in from the side, the length of the flue minimising the fire risk. This arrangement of the flue is also usual for kilns on the Scottish Mainland and in the Western Isles.[829]

The peat store for small kilns was outside the barn, as at Barkland in Fair Isle, but the larger kiln-barns had internal wall recesses or outshots for the storage of peats and sometimes for grain. The mouth of the fire-hole was within easy reach of a person seated in the peat recess at its left-hand side. In some barns the peat store was in a wall recess situated right above the fire-hole itself. In more sophisticated kilns, the dried grain could be shovelled into a *shoe* or passage about 15 in. (38 cm) square, which slanted down to a recess at the opposite side of the kiln from the peat recess and fire-hole. At a kiln in Birsay, an outshot on the right-hand side is divided in two by a flagstone to provide stores for peat and grain, and at Winksetter there are four recesses, two for grain, one for malt, and one for peat.[830]

It is likely that the round type of kiln was introduced to Shetland from Orkney, where the trade in grain and oatmeal made them necessities of economic life. Nevertheless, the earliest dated one is to be found in Shetland, at the medieval farmstead that replaced the Viking settlement at Jarlshof. Excavation showed a round kiln in the corner of the barn, protruding like a corner turret. Within its foundations a later one had been built, oval in shape, measuring 3 ft 9 in. by 4 ft 6 in. (114×137 cm) with a flue at ground level.[831] The older kiln has been dated to the fourteenth or fifteenth century. On the farm of Conglabist, said to be the oldest in North Ronaldsay, and at Fladdabister in Shetland, the kilns are similarly placed in the corner.[832]

In this connection, a unique and, for such an area, unexpected piece of dating evidence came to light in south-east Iceland during investigations of the ruins of the farm of Gröf i Oræfum. Behind the back gable of the north-west end of the house there was a kiln-house, consisting of a square building with one entrance, to one gable of which a corn kiln of oval form (1.8 m × 1 m) was linked. Heat was conveyed from a hearth on the floor straight through the back gable and kiln wall into the bowl, below the drying floor. The ashes in the hearth suggested that the fuel was birch, not peat.[833]

187. A square kiln of twentieth century date at Symblasetter in the South Mainland of Shetland. 3.39.8.

188. A rectangular kiln with a square wooden chimney, formerly thatched around with straw ropes, at Ancum, North Ronaldsay, 1964.

189. The door of the Ancum kiln, inside John Tulloch's barn, 1964.

The farm was overwhelmed by a volcanic eruption in AD 1362, and there is here a circular kiln of fourteenth century date, comparable in form to those of Orkney whether it was for drying grain or not. If this means that direct influence from Orkney can be postulated, the beginnings of the round kiln in Orkney can be pushed back to at least the fourteenth century. This date is supported by that of the kiln at Jarlshof, which must in all likelihood owe something to the Orkney tradition. Exnaboe in Dunrossness also has a free standing kiln and barn,[834] very like the one at Gröf, though on a bigger scale.

A development of late nineteenth and twentieth century date is observable in, for example, the Dunrossness area (Symblasetter), in North Ronaldsay (Ancum), and at Curcabreck in Sandwick. Here there are square or rectangular kilns built on to the end of the barn in the same manner as the round kilns, owing nothing to the old four-sided type, but influenced by the kilns attached to meal-mills. Indeed, the square form at Curcabreck conceals an internal circular bowl below the level of the drying floor, above which it is squared off again. At

Ancum in North Ronaldsay the kiln is rectangular, splaying out at each corner from ground level up to drying floor level to its full width and length. In this instance the floor has two stout bearing beams to support the kiln-sticks. Externally, this kiln resembles a small house built longwise on to the end of the barn, with its roof standing at a higher level than that of the barn. A wide wooden chimney, formerly bound round with straw rope, protrudes from the middle of the roof ridge.

The amount of grain that could be dried at a time varied according to the size of the kiln. In 1634, David Mowat of Banks in Birsay put 6 meils of oats on to his kiln to dry. Patrick Fea dried seven barrels of bere in his kiln on 10 January 1766, though he does not say if this was at one drying.[835] It is likely to have been two, since the one described later with an 8 ft (2.4 m) diameter floor could hold about four sacks of oats spread to a depth of 3 in. (7.6 cm). This amount could be dried in six to eight hours, depending on the draught and heat. The draught could be altered by adjusting the opening of the barn door or doors. The same straw bed could be used at least twice, though seven or eight times were possible. If the floor took fire, the whole could be thrown into the bowl by pulling out the main beam, in the hope of smothering the flames. After an hour or two of drying, the steam had almost stopped rising from the oats, and it was carefully turned in handfuls so that as little as possible should trickle through the straw. Before taking off the oats, a few bones were sometimes burned in the fire, with the idea that this gave the meal a pleasant flavour. Bones from recently cooked meat, with plenty of marrow, were thought best.[836]

As with four-sided kilns, the fire-risk and the need to maintain a steady heat involved constant attendance. The cold draughts could lead to a severe cold after five or six hours at the job. Whereas in the Faroe Islands work at the kiln was formerly a woman's job, this was not so in the Northern Isles. One kiln-man generally saw to the work there, though in the evening one or two friends might gather in the barn to exchange news and gossip, and children would play in the shadows of the barn. At Hallowe'en, however, the kiln took on a special significance for young unmarried women. In Foula, for example, as elsewhere in Shetland, three or four young women would go to the kiln to 'wind the clew'. This involved letting the end of a clew or ball of wool down the kiln-chimney and saying, 'Wha hauds my clew-end (who holds the end of my ball of wool)?' The voice that answered would be the voice of the girl's future husband, or his name could be given. The same custom could take place in a mill, and *castin' the clew* might be done by men as well as women.[837]

In Foula, a piece of knitting in progress had to be finished before Christmas, otherwise the saying was that 'it'll be lying in the kiln-mouth'.

48

Grinding the Grain

QUERNS AND HAND-MILLS

GRAIN has been ground in the Northern Isles since Stone Age times. A dish-quern lay in the house at the Ness of Gruting where barley dated to 1564 BC ± 120 was found. Saddle-querns and grain-rubbers came from a building at Stanydale. Over thirty parts of broken trough-querns were found at the Berrie Hoose in Whalsay. Trough-querns were used in the Bronze Age at Jarlshof. They took the form of stone blocks containing hollow depressions. One example was 2 ft (61 cm) long by 1¼ ft (38 cm) wide, with an oval rubbing area 15 in. long by 11 in. wide by 4 in. deep (38×28×10 cm). This was the standard quern type in the Bronze Age village, and though known in Denmark and the West Baltic lands from the Middle Neolithic period, is rare elsewhere in Britain, and so gives evidence for pre-Viking contact with Scandinavia. Saddle-querns made of sandstone also remained into the period of the Iron Age settlement.[838] The grain was ground in them by means of stone rubbers which were probably held in two hands by the operator, who stood or knelt by the closed end of the quern. It was a painstaking process, scarcely suitable for the mass-production of meal.

Rotary querns or hand-mills reached the country only a short time, if at all, before the Romans arrived. They were in two parts, with the upper part rotating on the fixed lower part. This was a great advance in both speed and efficiency on trough- and saddle-querns, though the old and the new types evidently remained in use alongside each other for some considerable time. There is little doubt that the first rotary querns had a high novelty value, for the Iron Age people at Jarlshof made miniature versions 1¾ in. (4.4 cm) across, as did their Viking successors.[839]

Rotary querns survived in use into the twentieth century in both Orkney and Shetland. Documentary sources begin to tell of them in the seventeenth century. In 1624, the witch Marable Couper prevented Margaret Mowat of Banks in Birsay from grinding bere on the querns (the word being used in the plural), 'and the thing that was ground was lyk dirt'. At the same period there were few mills save hand-mills in Shetland. The grain was not dehusked before grinding as a rule, but the dehusking of bere in round hollows in knocking stones did take place, then as later.[840]

In Orkney, where the tenants were expected to have their grain ground on the estate water-mills, attempts were made to enforce regulations against the private use of querns from at least 1699, when David Traill sent to his father, John Traill of Elsness, a copy of 'the act for taking away the quearnes'.[841] Even earlier, in August 1625, the Sheriff of Orkney agreed to a request by William Sinclair of Tolhoip, heritor of Sabay mill and tacksman of its sucken, that the heritors, feuars, farmers, tenants and tacksmen of lands in St Andrews parish should have their querns taken from them and kept at the mill as long as it was working. This was to prevent them from avoiding their dues as feudal suckeners of the mill by grinding their own grain. Similar decrees were made in 1664, 1694 and 1695 anent the mills of Cairstane, Sanday, and Firth.[842] In 1687, George Sinclair, tacksman of the mill at Deerness, was complaining that the parishioners were not having their corn ground at the mill, but by their own querns. The miller asked for a warrant from the Bailie Court to have the querns broken, and the bailie ordered all querns to be handed over to the miller, or broken, or else the people had to compound with the miller for the multures they should pay.[843] Querns remained in use nevertheless, especially for grinding malt, and could do a lot of work in a day. 'It must be kept continually going, which those accustomed to it, do equally well with both hands, keeping it going with one and feeding it with the other, and thus they continue for a long while together, notwithstanding of the severity of the labour.' The enforcement could only have been partial or regional, however, for a 1723 Inventory from Stronsay mentioned a quern pick weighing 6 merks, and another from the same island in 1734 a pick of the same weight, two mill picks, a knocking stone and mell, and an old quern.[844] Since the horizontal water-mills of Shetland were private, no such problems about querns seem to have existed there, and hand-mills and water-mills existed happily side by side. Every man had his own in Aithsting and Sandsting, and in the 1840s there were fifty water-mills there, and querns without number.[845]

Because querns were things of value, they often appear in the Testamentary Inventories. A quern and quern house were valued at 15/– in Kirkwall in 1687, and another at £1.4/– in 1681. In 1678 an old quern in St Andrews was valued at 6/8. Two old querns and a quern house in Kirkwall in 1681 were worth £1.2/–.[846] In these cases, a quern house is not a special building, but housing for a quern, that is the platform on which it stood.

The hand-mill consisted of two circular stones, about 21 in. (53 cm) each in diameter and 3 in. (8 cm) thick. The top stone had a round, central opening about 4 in. (10 cm) in diameter, through which the grain went to be ground. The bed-stone was fixed to a platform of wood or of stone, and the top stone was turned by a wooden handle $1\frac{3}{8}$ in. (3.5 cm) in diameter, fixed in a hole set about $2\frac{1}{2}$ in. (6.4 cm) in from the edge. A tube of wood or of iron about 2 in. (5 cm) in diameter was fixed in a hole in the centre of the bed-stone as a bush, through which was passed a wooden pin or spindle, 8 in. (20 cm) long by $\frac{1}{2}$ in. (1.3 cm) in diameter at the upper and $1\frac{1}{4}$ in. (3.2 cm) at the lower end, movable up and down through the platform. It could be raised and lowered by a bar of wood on which it rested. One end of the bar was fixed to the wall or to the back of the platform. It was an elastic flat piece of pine about 3 in. (8 cm) broad by 2 in. (5 cm) thick by 2½ ft (76 cm) long, and the lower end of the spindle rested in a hollow in it, about 15 in. (38 cm) out from the wall. A cord tied to the front end of the bar was taken through a hole in the front of the platform and round a wooden pin called a *lighter-pin* which, when turned, lengthened or shortened the cord, so raising and lowering the bar, called the *lightening tree*, and with it the top stone. The upper end of the spindle lay in a hollow in a piece of oak called the *soil* or *sile* (Norwegian dialectal *sigle*, Swedish dialectal *segel*, *sil*) that lay across the eye of the top stone. The meal sprang out all round the circumference of the stones as grinding proceeded, hence the need for the quern to sit on a clean platform or sometimes in a flat basket called a *buivy* (origin uncertain), wider at the mouth than at the bottom. A cloth was normally spread over the *quern-bink* to catch the meal. Some of the quern-binks or ledders, as at Winksetter, Clowigar, and Linnyeth in Harray, were big enough to have held two querns.[847]

Orkney querns were of similar dimensions to those of Shetland, though sometimes a little thinner, 2 to 2½ in. (5–6.4 cm) across. The bottom stone was picked with a quern pick into rough grooves that radiated from the centre to the outer edge. These helped to hold the grain against the turn of the stone and

190. Thomas Gray using a knocking stone and mell at Griciegarth in Foula, Shetland, 1902. Photo. H B Curwen.

191. John Gray, the Burns, Foula, facing a mill-stone, 1902. Photo. H B Curwen.

192. A quern with a partly shaped eye at Clumly, Shetland.

made better and quicker grinding. If the stones were not picked, the meal would clog, and the friction of turning produced circular grooves. The top stone was slightly hollowed underneath to fit the convexity of the lower stone, and was also picked. The 3 in. (8 cm) to 4½ in. (11 cm) diameter eye usually had a raised rim round its edge. Diametrically opposite notches about 1½ in. long by ½ in. deep (4×1.3 cm) at the underside of the eye held the wooden *sile* in place. At right angles to these were two wide, shallow grooves, running a few inches in on the stone to let the grain spread out from the eye to get a grip of the grinding stone. The stones used in Orkney were called 'Sholtie stones', that is 'Shetland' stones, marking the place from which they came. They were of mixed schist, 'hard, flaky, and with pearly glistening scales showing on the surface'. There was often no platform with a device for adjusting the top stone. Instead, the top stone and sile could be lifted, and one or two thin leather washers added to the top of the iron or wooden spindle. This left more space between the stones, and the meal could be ground more coarsely. This was necessary for oatmeal and malt. No washers were needed for beremeal or burstin, however, since these were ground much more finely. The operator turned the mill clockwise with one hand and fed grain in from the other hand, letting a little at a time trickle from his closed fist. Slow feeding produced finer meal. Too much at a time lifted the top stone and made coarser meal. The main difference between querns was the way in which adjustments were made. The centre spindle could pass through the sile, or the sile could rest on the spindle and turn with it. It could be

193. A hand-mill on a wooden stand at the Biggins, Papa Stour, 1967. 3.35.12.

raised by tapping from below. The use of a lightening-tree in a frame permitted easy adjustment.[848]   Oatmeal could not be properly ground in a quern, since good meal could only be made if the grains had been dehusked first, and this could not be readily done on a quern. For *shilling* (Old Scots *schele*, to husk, 1473) oats, the stones had to be set to run $\frac{1}{4}$ in. (0.6 cm) apart all round, but the position of the turning handle near an outside edge made the pressure irregular and uneven. Big grains, *grots* (groats) were often left amongst the meal and had to be sifted out. Querns, therefore, were more suitable for grinding bere. The meal itself was usually sifted twice, once through a coarse or *grof* (Old Scots *grof*, 1551; Middle Dutch *grof*, rough, coarse) sieve, and once through a finer sieve. The *sids* (Old Scots *sid*, 1686, a form of 'seed') of oatmeal were set aside for making sowens, and bere sids steeped in water made a good drink for calving cows. Sieves were of sheepskin stretched on a frame about 18 in. (46 cm) wide by 3 in. (8 cm) deep, with holes pierced by a hot wire.[849]

MALT, BURSTIN AND KNOCKIT CORN

Querns survived long because they served two domestic functions, hence the frequent appearance of special quern-binks or quern-ledders with flagstone bases in Orkney houses. These were used to grind malt and to grind burstin. Every farmer was his own maltster.

Orkney's reputation for good ale is supported by the evidence of the Testamentary Inventories. In 1613, Jon Wedock in Kirkwall had a brewing vat worth £4.[850] Quantities of malt are frequently included. Jon Elphingstoune of Lopness had two vats worth £6, brewing vessels worth £6, with other vessels and a quern worth £4 in 1685. Malcom Peace in Sanday had a quern and a puncheon worth £1.6.8 in 1688. A brewing kettle belonging to Mr Thomas McKenzie, minister of Shapinsay, was valued at £40. Jannett Loutit, widow of a merchant burgess in Kirkwall, had a brewing vat with all the brewing vessels, such as puncheons, barrels, cogs, tubs, worth £4, and an old brewing kettle worth £10, in 1687. Magnus Symondsone in St Andrews had a little old brewing vat worth 12/– in 1678. Alexr. Smith, merchant burgess of Kirkwall, had brewing vessels worth £9 as well as an old meal *ring* or sieve worth 4/–, in 1681.[851] A sufficient vat and two masking shovels, for stirring and turning malt, were mentioned in a Stronsay inventory of 1734.[852]

For malt-making, the bere was not hummeled too hard. It was put to steep in a barrel or large tub for about 48 hours, often from Saturday afternoon till Monday forenoon. The water was drained through a tap and the bere left to *sipe* or drip till evening. The grain was then spread on a barn floor, preferably of earth, at first in a fairly deep heap of two or three feet (61–91 cm) or more since it was 'black cold' with the cold water. It lay like this overnight and in the morning it was turned with a shovel to put the outside to the centre and the centre to the outside. The procedure was repeated at night, the heap being thinned to prevent over-heating. The aim was to get it to blood heat, tested by shoving the hand into the pile. Turning and thinning went on night and morning till it lay about 6 in. (15 cm) deep, and the bere began to *cheep* (Old Scots *chip*, fifteenth century) or germinate. Turning still went on twice a day, till two, three, or up to five rootlets showed, and the shoot had grown about half way along the grain or *puckle* (Old Scots *pickill*, 1552). At this point the 'coming' or growing had to be stopped by thinning to cool the heap, and by trampling with the feet, up and down in straight lines. Alternatively the grain could be heaped and two or three people rubbed it by shuffling round it, twisting their toes and heels alternately in a half circle as they moved gradually in towards the centre. Sometimes a broom was stuck in the heap and as work proceeded the handle lost its support and toppled. The one it struck would be the first of the company to get married. After tramping, the grain was again heaped up in a cone-shaped pile and covered with some straw and a *flaikie* to induce heat and more fermentation. The grain showed renewed signs of budding and a strong, liquorous smell came off it. At this stage it was said to be in 'sweet heap' or 'sweet bed'. Some people liked to give the grain a good heat in sweet bed, others kept it no warmer than the hand. It could be rubbed again before being taken in sacks to the kiln for drying, after which it was winnowed to clear the 'comings' or sprouts, and ground in the quern. Grinding was done in small quantities for immediate use, about half a stone to a stone at a time, the rest being stored in a dry place for future use. Old men said it took three weeks to make malt right.[853]

The day before brewing, all the utensils and containers were washed and aired. For a brewing of a hundredweight of crushed malt, two fills of a boiler of water were needed for the first masking. The first pot, when boiled, was emptied into the barrel and a sack put over to retain the heat till the second pot boiled, when it was time for masking. The vat had been prepared in the meantime by taking a handful of oat straw and spreading it across the tap opening in the bottom. A half-moon shaped stone was laid over it to keep it in place, the straight side lying on the bottom and the curve against the round of the vat, lying at an angle of about 45°. Masking proceeded by using alternately a pailful of water from the boiler and a pailful from the first pot, that had cooled down a little. If boiling water were put on the malt it would coagulate, and no liquid could be drawn off. Malt and water were put into the vat time about. A *masking pin* or *-sheul* was used to stir up and mix the malt and water. It also served to indicate the strength of the mixture. When the pin was pushed down to the bottom of the vat, it would fall slowly to one side if there was too much liquid. When the pin would stand erect, a cap would be put on top of it, and if it then fell to the side, more malt still was required. The pin had to stay upright, but if the mixture was too thick it was liable to stick. When the right strength was got, the pin was withdrawn, laid across the top, and the whole covered with a thick cloth or meal sack.

The vat then stood for two hours, and meantime the water was boiled again for the second and third maskings. The wort was drawn off the vat into a pail, and would run a clear amber if all was well. The first pail, which often contained some sediment or *groot* (Norwegian *grut*), was usually tipped back in so that it could come clear through the straw filter. The wort was put into the empty boiler as it was drawn off. In bulk it was about half the amount of liquid put in, the other half having been absorbed by the dry, crushed malt. At this stage the second water was put on the malt, using about half as much as for the first masking, and the wort was taken to the boil. About half a pound of hops was broken and put into the first wort. It had to be watched closely because it would rise like milk. This was prevented by taking a big mug and taking some liquid out and pouring it in again. Some could be emptied into a pail, if necessary. In a few moments it would stop rising and settle into a steady boil, which lasted for two hours. It was then emptied into the wort barrel. The second water was drawn off the malt for boiling, and the third water put on the malt. The second wort, when boiled for two hours, was mixed with the first. The third, called *plink* (cf. Norwegian dialectal *bleng*, buttermilk thinned down with water), was kept by itself, and was sometimes made up a little when boiling by putting in it a cotton bag filled with crushed malt.

When the wort had cooled to lukewarm, some was put to *barm* (Old Scots *barm*, yeast). Barm taken from weak wort or ale could not at first barm strong wort. It worked best when each brew would manufacture its own barm. Barm increased as it was used and barm off weak ale could work itself up till it would 'cut' the stronger stuff. If the first barming was not properly 'cut', the ale would taste too sweet, but it could be put on the barm again with some fresh hops, and would then come all right.

When pouring the wort, it was strained into the wort barrel through part of an oat-sheaf laid over a riddle, to keep back the hops. These were put back and boiled in the second water.[854]

It was chiefly for drying malt that farm kilns survived into this present century, and querns for grinding it. The other major use of the quern was in preparing burstin, after the grain had been well toasted and browned in an iron pot over glowing peat embers, or earlier by having hot stones rolled amongst it. Any grains that got burnt were called *ministers*, and were discarded because they left a sharp taste. After hummeling and winnowing, the burstin was ground on the quern and sifted. In some cases it was coarsely ground and mixed with sour milk or butter milk for immediate eating,[855] but it could also be ground very fine. It was always made in spring, for summer use, and served either as a main meal, or, when stirred with milk into *louts* (perhaps an adaptation of Norwegian *lut*, lye, from the resemblance to the curd-like appearance of the soap-lye), used as a cooling sequel to the dinner. If not thoroughly mixed with the milk, the fine burstin formed little, dry lumps which could burst when swallowed, leading to violent coughing and sneezing. Thick, round scones called *burstin' brunies* (cf. Norwegian *bryne*, slice of bread or cake) were sometimes also made in Shetland. A traveller noted in his diary on Sunday 29 July 1832: 'Rose late; hot bursten broonies for breakfast'[856] – surely a good way to start the day.

The method of drying grain to the point of parching, grinding, and eating with milk is probably a very old way of converting cereals into food. Bere or a mixture of bere and oats was used, and in earlier times wild oats were stripped when ripening, about Lammas, to be made into burstin.[857] This was a kind of food-gathering exercise.

Thickening for broth or soup was made by drying a few handfuls of well-dressed bere and putting them into the knocking stone with a little warm water to be dehusked with a mallet. The husks were floated off by steeping in water, and the grain left round and whole, an earlier equivalent of milled pearl barley. A great quantity of husks was left in the bere, and when the broth was boiled these rose to the top. A band of straw was placed round the mouth of the pot, in which the husks partly stuck. At the proper moment it was whisked across the mouth of the pot and so skimmed off most of the husks. The process was called *pufflan* (origin uncertain) *the pot*.[858] This 'knockit corn' could also be mixed with boiled kail or cabbage to make a substantial meal. In Orkney, knocking stones of red sandstone came from Eday, and whinstone ones from the mill-stone quarry at Yesnaby.[859]

WATER AND WIND-MILLS

The harnessing of water-power for driving mill wheels was one of the great technological advances in the history of the processing of cereals for food. This appears to have happened in the Mediterranean area during the first century BC, giving rise to the horizontal mill, so called because the water-wheel turned horizontally. It was linked to the stones without intermediate gearing. The vertical mill with a vertically turning wheel and gearing to speed up the turning rate of the stones dates from about the same period.[860]

The horizontal mill may have reached Ireland by the third century AD, to judge by documentary sources which themselves date to the seventh century AD. Recently the timbers of a mill found in County Derry have been dated by a technique of tree-ring chronology to the mid-eighth century AD[861]. When it reached the Northern Isles is not known, but it is distributed in Britain in Shetland, Orkney, Caithness and Sutherland, the Outer Hebrides, Mull, the Kintyre peninsula, and probably Galloway, the Isle of Man, and Ireland. The distribution is affected by geography and climate. Horizontal water-mills always lie near small streams in hilly or at least sloping terrain. They are not set directly on the streams but are connected by means of a millrace and sluice gate, and where the stream is meagre or the fall slight a dam or system of dams is usually required to build up the necessary head of water. It was common for such mills to be workable mainly in the winter time when there was sufficient rainfall to fill the streams and the dams. There were exceptions, such as the mill in Rousay, that 'goeth ordinarily all the Summer over, which is rare in these Isles'.[862] It must, of course, be remembered that vertical mills were often also seasonal in their use. For example, the John o' Groat mill in Caithness and the Boardhouse mill in Orkney both work only in the winter seasons now, when grain is available for grinding. The question of grain supplies, therefore, must also be considered in relation to the working season of mills, whether vertical or horizontal. Where the terrain is more flat, with rivers rather than streams, the bigger vertical mill fits more naturally into the geography and economy.

Lord Sinclair's two early Rentals, of 1492 and 1502–3, show that mills were well known then in Orkney. They are mentioned at Scapa, Holm and Firth, and there were others at Papdale, Sabay, and elsewhere.[863] Whether they were horizontal or vertical mills is not certain, but the likelihood is that both types were present. Mills on udal estates had *suckens* (Old Norse *sókn*, parish, jurisdiction), districts in which a mill had the monopoly of the multures. This appears to be similar to the feudal form of astriction to a particular mill. However, as shown by a declaration made before the Sheriff in 1542–3 regarding William Irvine's rights in the mill of Sabay, the parishioners appear not to have been absolutely constrained to use that mill. Nevertheless it was the only one in the whole parish and so the people had to pay their multures to Sabay.[864] This was almost certainly a vertical mill, for a horizontal mill could scarcely have served such a large district.

Evidence for horizontal or 'click' mills relates to three mills that stood on the Burn of Corrigall in Harray. An action was brought in 1496 by William of Corgill against Magnus of Corston, who had built a mill below him that prevented the passing of fish in spawning time. This mill had to be demolished and Magnus got a place for another elsewhere. The blocking of the burn must have been due to the periodic diversion of the water of the burn into a lade. William himself had a mill at the head of the spawning area, so it was not disturbed. He was also, however, at loggerheads with another neighbour, who had a mill lower down. This also affected the fishing, and William closed his sluices whenever this neighbour attempted to grind. An amicable solution was reached, one man getting his water as required, the other being allowed to fish in his neighbour's stretch. Horizontal mills must be involved here, since no one could have been allowed to interfere with the water of a district mill, and these were evidently private.[865]

In 1575, Lord Robert Stewart took from the udal mills the suckens 'whilke were observit of befor inviolate',[866] and gave them to a miller, or leased them to a large proprietor. Mills of this period have been traced in the records. There were two in Harray, the mill of Conyear (also called the mill of Rusland or the mill of Harray), and the mill in the urisland of Grimeston. Stenness had the bishopric mill of Stenness and the udal mill of Ireland, and Firth the mills of Firth and Burness. Birsay had three bishopric mills at Boardhouse, Kirbister and Seatter, and one at Sabiston. Evie had three, the mills of Evie, Woodwick and Costa. There were four in Rendall, the mills of Isbister and Tingwall, and those of the Bu or Hall of Rendall and of Gairsay. Sandwick appears to have had three, at Skaill, Tenston and Rango. Stromness parish had two mills, at Cairston and Voy, and Orphir three, at Kirbister, the Bu, and Clestrain. St Ola had the mills of Scapa (or Lingrow) and of Papdale, and for a short time there was one at Wideford. The mill of Sabay was in the East Mainland, as was the mill of Holm. This makes a total of 28 on the Mainland of Orkney around the year 1600. To this total must be added the island mills. There were five in South

Ronaldsay at Cara, Sandwick, Windwick, Brough and Widewall. Hoy and Walls had the mills of Hoy, Osmondwall and Ryssay. Gairsay had one. In Rousay there were mills at Banks or Frotoft, Sourin and Scockness. The Sanday mills were at Boloquoy, Cleat, Bea, the Bull of Brugh, Stousater in Burness, Westair (also called Rusness or Sellibister), and Newark or Langtes. In Papa Westray there was the mill of Hooking, and Stronsay also had a mill in 1614. Eday had a loch and a mill in 1683.[867] There were, therefore, at least 50 mills, probably of the vertical type, in Orkney, as well as an unknown but probably not very high number of horizontal mills. To these, the people were astricted or 'mill-sookened', and were not only obliged to have their grain ground in them, but had also to take a share in the maintenance of the mill fabric and roof. When the mill of Bea in Sanday needed thatching, this intimation is said to have been made at the Cross Kirk:

> 'Ye sookaners o' the Mill o' Bae
> Come tae her the morn wi' simmons an' strae'.

The Elsness mills in Sanday, which were themselves suckened to the Mill of Bea, were producing 17 meils of meal a year in about 1721, measured on the malt pundler.[868]

Patrick Fea's Diary gives a lively picture of grain processing in Sanday:

1766.	3 Jan.	Cleaning my Ingled (kiln dried) Otts which was of Raw Otts 75 gave of clean Ingled Otts 57 bar^s. (i.e. there was a wastage of 18 barrels).
	10 Jan.	Put 7 bar' bear upon the Kiln and dry'd it.
	6 Feb.	Got some bear put to Kilnbarn for drying.
	12 Feb.	Got all the seed Otts out of the barn being there so long for want of wind to dress it.
	17 Feb.	Set my Miln to work to grind bear meal got 4 cassies ground that day.
	18 Feb.	Grinding all day got 4 cassies ground ... at night hard frost by which one arm of the Miln Wheel was broke.
	20 Feb.	Robt. Miller att Stove putting new Arms to the utter Miln Wheel.
	26 Nov.	Sheeling 4 Cassies of Otts the first 4 Cassies being in Meal broke my Axle.
	1 Dec.	Robt. Miller at Stove makeing an axle tree to the Miln.
	15 Dec.	Humbled the 2 Kilns of bear in order to Cassie it.
	17 Dec.	Got another Kiln dryed and humbled it, & the other 2 in order to sheel the dam being fuller Sheeld the 3 Kilns Otts and ground the meal att night.
	22 Dec.	Got my Miln draught and Dam helped & ground the Cassie of Sheeling & 9 Cassies of bear.

1767.	4 Feb.	The mill grinding till the Tyde stopt her.
	6 Feb.	Sifteing meal in the loft.
	27 June	The boat returned (from Quendale) with the Horses and Miln Stones.
1768.	30 Dec.	Paid Richard Spence 12 sh Sterling for makeing the utter wheel to the Miln & put it up to the Couples of the Miln to dry till Tarr'd.
1773.	12 Jan.	Got the Bear meal girnells lifted and put upon the North side of the Loft.
1796.	12 June	Had 2 men at the Windmill Shiling 3 Sacks of Bear for fine meal and got home being ground.[869]

Fea's mill, therefore, had an 'outer' wheel, tarred for protection, with a set of arms or planks to catch the water. These were evidently easily damaged. The mill was near enough the sea to be affected by the tide. It was used for grinding oats and bere, and the top stone could be lifted for sheeling oats. Bere was being sheeled on a wind-mill by the end of the century. In each case the fine grinding into meal followed the sheeling. There appears to have been a build-up of dried grain, pending a grinding session.

Since Orkney is poor in water-courses, wind-mills were relatively common. Besides this Sanday example, there were two in Holm by the 1790s, and one in Westray.[870] They seem to have been of particular merit for grinding bere, for the two put up in South Ronaldsay shortly before 1795 ground bere only and were paid with the sixteenth part of the produce. The wind-mill in Papa Westray is said to have been put up in the early years of the nineteenth century. The earliest source appears to be a deed of partnership dated May 1763 for a wind-mill to be erected before 1 October 1763 on the Outer Holm of Stromness, to grind 'malt and oats, bear or barley into meal ... and to make hulled barley'. This was a commercial enterprise sponsored by Robert Honeyman of Graemsay, who made an agreement with Robert Gordon to put up the mill for £110 sterling and to provide a miller at a wage of £10 sterling a year. Honeyman was to supply a house and kailyard for the miller.[871]

In the 1790s in Orkney, therefore, mills were numerous, and driven by both wind and water. Holm had two corn-mills besides a wind-mill. In South Ronaldsay and Burray groups of six people could be seen with six horses carrying 3 bolls of bere to the mill. Sandwick and Stromness had eight water-mills, and a mill-stone quarry, sited on the west coast of Sandwick, producing ten mill-stones a year priced at 2/– per inch of thickness at the eye. Westray had three water-mills and a wind-mill, and Papa Westray one water-mill.[872]

At Stenness, there was an old mill, demolished in the early 1900s. It had a thatched roof, and a vertical wheel turning at the gable end. Bailie William Smith, as tenant, paid a rent in the eighteenth century of 5 meils of oatmeal, £10 Scots yearly with £20 every three years, and one mill-swine worth £2 Scots. He also purchased the mills of Swannay and Seatter in Birsay, demonstrating that mills were profitable investments.[873]

In the 1840s, Holm and Paplay had one water-mill to which the tenants were astricted, paying in multure a twelfth part of oats ground, and a sixteenth of bere. This mill had no kiln attached to it, but every farmhouse and manse had its own. Evie had a meal-mill at the Loch of Swannay. In St Andrews there were two small horizontal mills. In Sandwick, the Lochs of Skaill and Clumlie turned mills. There were two wind-mills and two water-mills in Cross, and one of each in Burness. The fact that milling was not a full-time job appears from the list of occupations in the parish. Of the two millers specified, one was also a smith and the other a carpenter. There was a good mill by the Loch of Kirbister in Orphir. By the 1870s, Orkney was in general well supplied with meal-mills. There was an excellent one on the Cairston estate, and at Scar House, James Scarth had introduced a steam-engine to drive his mill. By this date no water-power was being used in Sanday, and only one of the wind-mills survived.[874]

Because of the early importance of vertical mills, Orkney had relatively few of the horizontal variety. In about 1822–4, one was built at Millbrig, Birsay, north-east of Dounby, by John Spence, replacing an older mill which had become ruinous. It was used by the Spences until 1877 and by Nicol Folster for some years after that. It was photographed in 1909 and a drawing made of it some time before 1911.[875] In the 1920s a road contractor, Robert Adamson, found that the stones in the burn that fed it could be quarried easily and cheaply, so he quarried the burn right up to the mill, and a deluge of rain completed the destruction of the mill's water supply. Because of its uniqueness in Orkney, it was repaired by the Orkney Archaeological Society and offered to the then Office of Works in 1932. Since then, it has been a Guardianship Monument. A piped supply of water has been engineered so that the mill can operate for short periods.[876]

This mill measures 15 ft by 7 ft by 5 ft high (4.6×2.1×1.5 m). It has the unusual feature of having two rows of paddles, one above the other, on the water-wheel, each paddle measuring 7 by 12 in. (18×30.5 cm), and fixed to the drum or *tirl* (cf. Faroese *tyril*, Icelandic *þyrill*, milk-whisk, Norwegian dialectal *turul*, *tverel*, plunger of a churn), which is 2 ft high by 1 ft wide (61×30.5 cm). Inside, there is a wooden hopper called the *head*, supported by beams protruding from the gable and one side wall. Slung below the hopper is a wooden shoe, by which the *shelling* (grain to be *sheeled*) is directed into the eye of the top stone or *rinner* (runner). A *clapper* or wooden tongue hangs from the hopper frame and is struck by a knob of wood fixed on top of the rinner, so that it clicks at each revolution, whence the name 'click mill'. The rate of feed can be regulated by raising or lowering the front of the shoe by means of a cord attached to a *maitin'* ('meating' or feeding) *pin* set in the upright of the hopper frame. The resulting vibration makes the grain trickle into the shoe. The bottom end of the upright rests on the wooden framework, the *crubs* (Norwegian *krubba*, crib, feeding trough), surrounding the stones. Ground oatmeal is discharged through a spout or chute into a *bing* (Norwegian *binge*, corn chest, Swedish dialectal *binge*, a heap, 1513) or box sunk in the floor. There is only one small roof light above the hopper. The mill was said to grind about a bushel an hour.[877] There was another horizontal mill, the mill of Skelday, a little below this one.

Across from the single door is a wall opening, the winnowing hole. The story was told that on one winter evening when the miller was hard at work, some boys made *tam-o'-reekies*, smoke-guns consisting of hollow kail stocks filled with bog-hay and a live coal, and blew smoke through the winnowing hole till the miller came out half-suffocated shouting, 'Boys! boys! this'll no do'.[878]

The paucity of horizontal mills in Orkney is more than made up for by the large number in Shetland. When Sir Walter Scott visited Shetland in 1814 as a Commissioner of Northern Lights, he estimated them at 500, a figure that has been accepted but not yet checked. He later made the Scottish factor in *The Pirate*, Triptolemus Yellowley, say:

'Can a man ... or even a beast, look at that thing there, which they have the impudence to call a corn-mill, without trembling to think that corn should be entrusted to such a miserable molendinary? The wretches are obliged to have at least fifty in each parish, each trundling away upon its paltry millstone, under the thatch of a roof no bigger than a bee-skep.'[879]

The earliest illustration of a Shetland horizontal mill dates to 1774. It differs from the Orkney example in having a different kind of clapper, simply a piece of wood fixed to the hopper by a string. It caused vibrations by rattling on top of the stone. The hopper was presumably slung by ropes from the mill couples, as

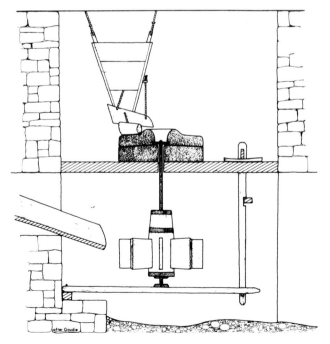

194. The elements of a horizontal water-mill in Shetland. After Goudie 1904. 260. C1199.

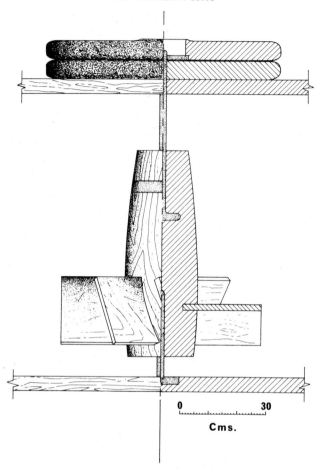

195. Construction of a vertical mill wheel. The spindle does not pass right through, but is in two pieces, the upper one with a right-angled bend to grip within its wooden casing. The feathers are angled to catch the full rush of the water. Left: half elevation; right: half section. From Bixter, Shetland. Original in the Royal Scottish Museum.

was usual in Shetland. In addition, the tirl has only a single flight of feathers.[880] In Unst, tirls were about 4 ft (1.2 m) long, with twelve small wooden feathers or *awes*, on which the water fell from the chute at an angle of 40° to 45°. An iron spindle in the top end of the tirl linked with the top stone of the mill, and an iron pivot at the base turned on a hollowed plate of iron. The stones were 30 to 36 in. (76–91 cm) in diameter, the same as the diameter of the tirl and its feathers. They were made of the local micaceous schist, called *grüt* (Norwegian dialectal *grjot*, *grøt*, species of stone, Old Norse *grjót*, rough stones). Most of the mill-stones used in the South Mainland of Shetland, for example, came 'at the expense of laborious transport and much inconvenience' from the island of Colsay.[881] Such mills could belong to individuals, or they might serve about six

196. The interior of the Dounby mill, drawn by G. Ellison, *c*. 1911. 4.13.23.

families. Five or six families would co-operate in the building, the only material to be bought being the iron for the sile, also known as the *ground-sile* or *ground-keeng*, the plate on which the lower end of the spindle revolved. The women often saw to the grinding, and as they sat by the stones they would have a peat or two burning on the floor, and a pot of tea going.[882]

The mills varied in size from 12 to 17 ft (3.7 to 5.2 m) or more, by 10 to 12 ft wide (3 to 3.7 m), with walls 4 to 5 ft high (1.2 to 1.5 m) by 2 ft thick (61 cm), and gables 6 to 8 ft (1.8 to 2.4 m) high. The water-wheel turned in the *under-hoose*, below the mill, and the spindle with its iron plate rested on a *sole-tree* or *under-balk*, of which the inner end was fixed by a wooden pin to a bolster. At the other end was an upright bar that penetrated the floor of the mill, where it was held in place by a cross-bar that could be raised or lowered by a wedge known as a *swird* (sword). This device was the lichtenin' tree. It may not be as old in the Northern Isles as the mills themselves are, for some mills had no sole-tree, but only a pivot stove with a hollow on top. A Faroese mill at Kvívík, for example, had an iron cup on the base of the tirl, which turned on a fixed spike. There was no means of raising the top stone.[883]

The *upper hoose* was the body of the mill, with a single door sometimes set in the gable wall, the stones, and the *luder* (Norwegian *lur*, plank under a hand-mill, Old Norse *lúðr*, floor around millstone where meal accumulates) or platform where the stones turned. In one corner there could be a small peat fire, as in one of the Clumlie mills, but this is exceptional. Lower down the same burn is a mill that was still used in 1967 by the farmer at Troswick, who also had

197. The lower mills on the burn of Gilsetter, Fair Isle, early twentieth century. Photo. G.W.W. 3.42.34.

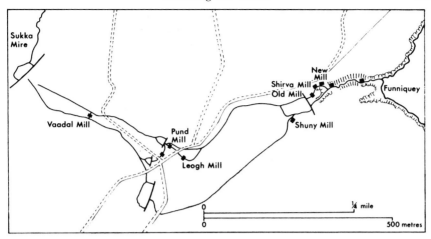

198. The mills and dams on the burn of Gilsetter, Fair Isle. C5842.

a working corn-drying kiln. Here the floor is flagged and cemented, and formed into a channel 6 in. (15 cm) deep around the mill-stone. The beremeal could be swept along it and readily scooped up. The hopper is supported by two wooden arms hooked into the rear gable wall, and supported by wires up to the rafters at the front. This mill had fallen out of use in the past, but was restored by Gilbert Goudie out of his antiquarian interest some time before 1904. It is the lowest of eight horizontal mills that once existed on the burn that flows out of the Loch of Clumlie. Two of them have a stone about $1\frac{1}{2}$ ft wide by 9 in. to 1 ft deep (46×23 to 30 cm) protruding from the gable wall alongside the door, to help in getting loads on and off the back. Some of these mills were individually owned, others were worked by groups of neighbours.

A dam and lade are invariable features of horizontal mills, to accumulate a head of water, with a sluice-gate or *kluse* (Old Scots *clouse*, 1493) or *mill-brod* (broad) by which the water could be turned on and off, and sometimes a *by-board* to divert the main stream into the lade or dam. There could be a second sluice at the point where the lade entered the wooden trough or flume that directed the water on to the wheel. Sluices were of wooden boards sliding in grooves, which allowed control of the amount of water that passed through.

The *troch* (trough) could be 10 to 12 ft (3 to 3.7 m) long by 12 to 14 in. (30 to 36 cm) wide at the top, 6 to 7 in. (15 to 18 cm) wide at the base, and 12 to 14 in. (30 to 36 cm) deep. It sloped at an angle of about 40°, giving a fall of 3 to 4 ft (91 to 122 cm), sometimes narrowing at the point where the water debouched on to the paddles. Trochs were substantially made, and some of the Irish examples were cut from solid blocks of oak.[884]

The feathers of the wheel were set at an angle to get the full force of the falling water. They varied in number, though twelve was common, and were quite flat, averaging 9 in. high by $9\frac{1}{2}$ in. wide (23 by 24 cm), though originally they may have been more scoop-shaped like the paddles of similar mills in the

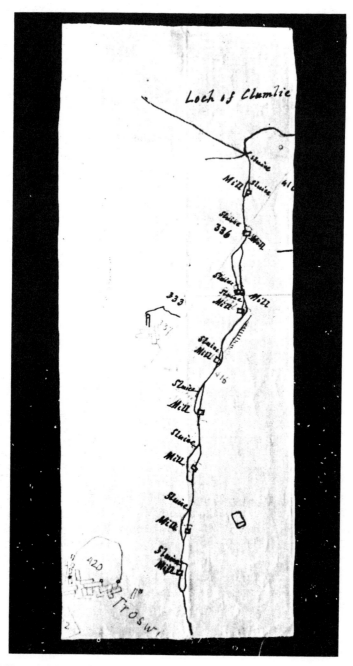

199. Mills and sluices at Clumlie, noted by G. Goudie, late nineteenth century or early twentieth century. In the Public Library, Lerwick. 3.43.7.

200. The interior of the Boardhouse Mill, driven by a vertical water-wheel. One of the last to be operating in Orkney. 4.11.21.

201. Scooping up grain with a power-operated shovel on the smoky kiln floor at Boardhouse Mill. It is pulled by a wire driven from the water wheel. 4.11.23.

West of Scotland and in Ireland. Faroese mills also had flat paddles, however. The tirl into which they were fixed averaged 1 ft 9 in. (53 cm) high by 7 in. (18 cm) in diameter at the top and 9 in. (23 cm) in diameter at the bottom. The length of 4 ft mentioned for the Unst tirl in 1793 probably includes the spindle, though tirls of equivalent length could be found in Faroese mills. The spindle could be up to 4 ft (1.2 m) long and had to be rectangular in section if the tirl was to grip it. An alternative that saved iron was to let the spindle into the top of the tirl, and to include a right-angled bend that gave the necessary grip. The gudgeon pin was then inserted separately at the bottom, as in an example from Bixter in Shetland, dating from about 1870. The spindle passed through an opening in the firmly fixed bed stone of the mill, blocked by a plug of wood or cork known as the *grotti* (Norwegian dialectal *grotte*, Icelandic *grótti*, idem). In Shetland, the grooves in the underside of the top stone, that held the sile into which the top of the spindle fitted, got the name of *lith* (Old Norse *hlið*, gap, gate, space).[885] In Orkney the floor area where the stones lay was sometimes called the *hirst* (Old Scots *hirst*, *c*. 1420), evidently a borrowing from the Scottish dialects. One mill examined in 1913 on the Burn of Clumlie had stones placed in position in 1868. The turning speed was found to be 50 to 60 r.p.m. and the output 0.6 to 0.75 bushels an hour.[886]

In the late eighteenth and nineteenth centuries, horizontal water-mills became very common in Shetland, one of the few exceptions being the Quendale Mill, built in the mid-nineteenth century by Andrew Grierson. It had an overshot wheel. It had a great influence on the locality and far around, in particular for grinding oats. Bere was usually kept for the horizontal mills.[887] In the island of Papa Stour, covering about 6 square miles, twenty-four mills and mill-sites have been noted. On the Burn of Gilsetter in Fair Isle there have been nine mills, with a system of dams to feed them. One stream in Sandness had five mills, one of them with only eight paddles on the wheel.[888]

However, horizontal mills may not have been so common before the eighteenth century. In the Faroe Islands, only nine were known in about 1781. Of these, three were in Tórshavn and two were owned by priests. One writer 'wished that such mills were more common, especially in the farming townships, since the terrain is suitable in most places, and a lot of time and expense could be saved'. By the end of the century the numbers had begun to increase, and twenty were reported by about 1798. The wheels had eight paddles and a turning rate of about 100 r.p.m.[889] This increase appears to have taken place in Shetland too, though at an earlier date and on a bigger scale. In Orkney, by contrast, the number of vertical mills and the system of astriction combined to eliminate horizontal mills.

Such mills are now things of the past, though there was a brief reflowering during the First World War, when supplies of flour were scarce. One example in Fetlar was built then by Daniel Williamson, Everland, and Andrew Brown, Banks o' Funzie. The same is true of Fair Isle, where the last mill in use was worked during the First World War. Curiously enough, it was the development of herring drifters that really brought the regime of the water-mill to an end in

202. A wind-mill in North Ronaldsay, Orkney. Drawn by T S Peace. 1.4.15A.

203. The remains of the North Ronaldsay wind-mill, and the later vertical water-mill beside it, 1964. 2/47.

Shetland, for they started taking corn to the big mills like those in Kirkwall, where it was ground easily and with no loss of time to the crofters. The ready availability of flour from the Canadian prairies from the second half of the nineteenth century also played its part in bringing the long era of horizontal mills to an end. How long that era was cannot be said exactly, but the terminology shows links with Scandinavia only in relation to those parts that are the same as in hand-mills. The conversion of hand-mills to water-power may, in the light of the pre-Viking Irish evidence, have a non-Scandinavian source.

Root Crops and Gardening

49

Turnips

TURNIPS were already known in late seventeenth century Orkney as a garden crop, and in mid-eighteenth century Shetland they appeared in gentlemen's gardens,[890] but they were far from common and there is no clear indication of their more extensive use until the second half of the eighteenth century. Even then they were still only grown, along with carrots and parsnips, in gardens in parts of Shetland, such as Delting, though in Dunrossness turnips and carrots were abundant and in Fetlar turnip, radish, and cresses grew well.[891] In Orkney too they remained a garden crop. They were grown in Cross, Burness and North Ronaldsay, in Shapinsay, in St Andrews and Deerness, where they throve well but were seldom used, and in the gardens of Birsay, along with onions, leeks, garlic, parsnips and carrots. In Sandwick and Stromness only one resident heritor, William Watt, was growing turnips and in Westray no green crops like hay and turnips were grown.[892]

In the early nineteenth century, Burray was growing good turnips, as well as carrots, peas and onions, and the drill cultivation of turnips had begun. This is the first clear evidence for field cultivation. In the following year one traveller noted that turnips had lately been introduced by a few. Still in 1814, however, the cultivation of turnips was 'by no means so much attended to in Orkney as its importance well merits, especially as a considerable part of the soil is so eminently calculated for producing full crops of that beneficial, and even almost indispensable esculent'.[893] Various recommendations were made on dealing with the crop. Drilled turnips were to be preferred to broadcast turnips, since it was more easily possible to clean the ground, and plants would be bigger. Ploughing of turnip land should take place soon after Christmas, so that it should be as dry as possible during winter. A second ploughing should be given after the spring corn had been sown, and the land harrowed fine to preserve the sap for the vegetation of annual weeds. When these had grown, the land was to be ploughed again, harrowed, and picked free of weeds. These operations had to be continued at suitable intervals till the first week of May, when the *ruta baga* seed should be sown. Field yellow and white globe turnip had to be sown from early to mid-June.

When cleaned and well pulverised, the land should be ploughed in drills or 'one bout ridgelets', between which manure was spread by women, boys or girls. The drills were split by the plough to cover the manure, and the roller and drilling machine followed, planting the seeds. Sowing should be phased so that the plants did not all come ready for hoeing at one time. Horse- and hand-hoeing should take place as soon as the first rough leaves were big enough to 'cover as much space as a Spanish dollar'.

Drills should be 27 to 30 in. (69–76 cm) apart, and the plants hand-hoed at 10 to 12 in. (25–30 cm) apart. Ruta baga plants, and the drills for them, could be a little closer. A scuffler or drill-harrow, run between the drills, cut away weeds to within $1\frac{1}{2}$ to 2 in. (4–5 cm) of the turnip plants to make hand-hoeing easier. Two or three weeks after, the scuffler or a small plough, drawn by one horse, should again be used, and a second hand-hoeing was advisable.

It was suggested that since the hills of Hoy, Rousay, Eday, and parts of the Mainland were more adapted for sheep than for black cattle, part of the turnip crop would be good for the sheep flocks in spring, particularly the breeding ewes and hogs. Normally, however, the crop was intended for cattle feed in winter.

Turnips were seldom frost-bitten in Orkney, and careful storage was less necessary than on the Scottish Mainland. They should be pulled by women, loaded into carts, and taken to a dry spot of ground. The storage pits were about six feet (1.8 m) wide and as long as required, with a triangular shape, and covered with straw thatch. The fact that this sermon was preached is significant of the fact that Orkney had not as yet really started on the course of agricultural improvement that has led to its present prosperity. The main facts then were that 'in 1808 Captain Sutherland had 15 acres of excellent turnip in Burray, and had about the same quantity in culture annually. There were also many smaller fields in different parts of the country equally good, and some even better'.[894]

By the 1840s the situation had changed. In Holm and Paplay, 65 acres of turnip were sown, and 2 to 3 tons of turnip seed were being exported annually to Edinburgh and elsewhere. Turnips were still rare in St Andrews. In Stronsay and Eday they were grown on the bigger farms, the Stronsay total being $59\frac{1}{4}$ acres and Eday 36, as also on the principal farms of Westray. In Cross and Burness turnips and sown grasses were included in some rotations. In Lady turnips, manured with horse- or cow-dung, were grown in drills, and rotted sea-ware was a good fertiliser in light, sandy soil. Turnip husbandry was reckoned along with better horses and better implements as one of the main improvements in Sandwick.[895]

In Shetland at the same period the situation was slower to develop. Field turnips were becoming more general, and did well in Sandsting and Aithsting, and in the Tingwall area, where red and green tops, and Swedish turnips were included in improved rotations, usually with a sequence of turnips and potatoes, big barley with grass seeds, hay, pasture, and finally oats. Yellow turnips were preferred to Swedes. They were grown in Northmavine. In Fetlar, a small udaller called Jerom Johnson, who had improved his kailyard into a garden about 1820, was growing turnips in it as well as flowers, onions, pease, carrots, and tobacco. He is said to have been the first to introduce field turnips to Fetlar. Another Fetlar farmer, George Lyle, had enclosed 2 to 3 acres and was growing Scots oats and barley, field and garden turnips, cabbage, greens and pease. There were also a few turnips in Walls and Unst. In Bressay, the proprietor brought in a grieve from Berwickshire, who latterly took on a small farm himself and grew good grain, turnips, rye-grass and clover.[896]

The main subsequent developments took place in Orkney, where people like David Petrie experimented on the Graemeshall estate with varieties such as purple top, yellow bullock, Skirving's purple top, Aberdeen improved, Crooksveld, Drummond Extra Improved, etc., in the 1860s, especially when the introduction of Peruvian guano as a manure was beginning to make big changes in the nature of fertilisers. He grew turnips not only as winter feed, but also to produce seed for his own use and for export. The seeded plants were cut, and threshed by being shaken out on a big canvas sheet. The average dates for sowing the seed lay between 31 May and 26 June.[897] Turnips had become standard features of the rotation, forming part of one shift each year, usually along with potatoes and sometimes mangolds. The thinning of the turnips was usually a job for women and boys. The steady increase in the turnip acreage was regarded as one of the great improvements.[898] The 1200-acre farm of Houseby in Stronsay grew 130 to 150 acres of turnips each year, about an eighth of the total acreage. When Archer Fortescue bought the Swanbister Estate at Orphir in 1845, no turnips at all were grown. He used turnips heavily manured with 20 tons of town dung and 5 bushels of bone manure per acre, as one of the crops in carrying through his massive reclamation programme. James R. Pollexfen's father was an early improver on the Cairston Estate by the Bridge of Waith and was dealing in turnip seed at an early date. By contrast, the 16 acres of turnips grown by A J Grierson at Quendale in the South Mainland of Shetland was small-scale stuff.[899]

Turnips as a common field crop, with all the associated organisation and tools date essentially from the mid-nineteenth century in the Northern Isles. The extent to which women and young folk were used in some of the processes, such as hand-hoeing, may be in part traditional, in part a result of the local economy. For example, in Fair Isle and other areas where a good part of the economy depends on lobster fishing or some other kind of fishing, and the men are away or are otherwise occupied when the crop needs singling, this task fell to the women. Much of the equipment comes from the south, though the great variety of one-horse seed sowing machines, mostly for one drill, and mostly made of wood, indicates a certain amount of regional adaptation. The metal seed boxes were all imported and bought from local merchants, but the wood work may often be that of a local joiner. A seed box in the form of a tall, tapering, four-sided wooden spout was characteristic. All-metal, one-drill seeders were being purchased quite recently from English firms. Bigger farms could afford the same kinds of equipment as on the Scottish Mainland, and the one-drill seeders are normally found on the crofts. Where a crofter has a double-drill seeder, it is likely to have been bought second-hand and brought, for example, from Mainland Scotland.

Not only the equipment, but also the names connected with turnip cultivation come from the south and are generally Scottish or more particularly North-East Scottish terms, since this area had a fair influence on the agricultural development of Orkney and to a lesser extent Shetland from the mid-nineteenth century onwards. This is indicated by the terminology: *neep* (Old Scots, *c*. 1470), the general word for turnip; *neep-cutter*, a turnip-slicer; *neep-grund*, ground prepared for cropping with turnips (in Shetland from 1900); *neep-lan(d)*, ground from which a turnip crop had been taken; *neep-lantern*, a turnip hollowed out, with the shape of a face cut in it, and a candle placed inside, usually carried by children at Hallowe'en, in part reminiscent of the custom of setting a turnip lantern on another man's midden at the New Year in Fjend County, Denmark;[900] *neep-muck*, manure for putting on turnip ground; *neep-saaer* (sower), a turnip-sowing machine; *neep-seed*, turnip seed (in Shetland from 1890); *neep-shawin*, the removal of turnip shaws with a special knife.[901] Few or none of these terms have been recorded in the Northern Isles before about 1890.

Work with turnips is not light. In 1923, for example, W S Tait of Ingsay specified 143 loads of turnips carted between 5 January and the end of April, and in addition unspecified numbers of loads were brought in on nineteen days, using up to three carts. In May, the work of opening drills started, followed by dunging and sowing manure, closing the drills, sowing Swedes, and rolling. The yellow turnips were sown in June. All this used a total of eighteen days. The types sown were Magnum Bonum, Northern King, Webster, Bangholm, Yellow Challenger, Centenary Yellow, Lordhall, Smith's Prize, Tipperary, Superlative, Aberdeen Golden Top Yellow, Model Golden, and Sittyton. In July and August, twenty-one days were taken up with scarifying and scuffling the drills, and singling. Carting began again on 25 October, and from then till the end of the year thirty-eight loads were mentioned and carting took place on eleven days besides. In all a hundred days were taken up with turnip work, or 29 per cent of the whole year.[902] It is little wonder that in Orkney, as elsewhere, the turnip acreage has dropped sharply in recent years, from 5331 acres in 1959 to 1481 acres in 1969, and in Shetland from 597 to 381 acres in the same period. The grazing acreage has increased in proportion.[903]

50

The Potato

THE introduction and spread of the potato was a matter of considerable importance in areas where the bere and oat crops were barely enough to last through the season, and where the mainstay of the daily diet had to be dairy products, cabbage and kail, and fish caught at the shore.

Potatoes had reached the Northern Isles by the 1750s, first as a newcomer to the crops in the gardens of big houses, but soon afterwards being cultivated as a field crop. In 1774, fields of potatoes were noted in South Ronaldsay, Orkney, and in Aithsting and Sandsting, and South Delting, Shetland, where the people were said to live for several months of the year on potatoes and fish. Unst also had plenty of potatoes, and in Foula, where they had been recently introduced, they were a means of saving meal.[904]

Patrick Fea in Sanday was never far behind when it came to new crops:

1767.	7 March:	Had 18 Horse mucking upon the Potatoe ground and planted that day 1 Firken in 2 beds.
	23 October:	Takeing up some of my Potatoes got up 8 bar.s and put to the loft.
	24 October:	Took up the last of my Potatoes ... I have in all this year 22 bar.s
	23 December:	My men in the Ware ... began to form beds for the planting of Potatoes.
1768.	25 February:	Planted the most of 2 beds with Potatoes had 12 horses dunging upon it being the 3rd day and 5 beds dunged.
	30 March:	Planting Potatoe and dunging 2 headrigs for more planting.
	25 April:	Done with planting my Potatoes and planted in all the 10 beds 2½ bars.s[905]

On the assumption that Fea had the same number of beds in both years, there was a yield of 22 barrels on the 2½ barrels planted, i.e. a seed/yield ratio of 1:8.8 Potatoes thrived in the sandy soil of Sanday and North Ronaldsay, and sold in 1773 at 8^d to 10^d per setten or 2 stones.[906] By the 1790s practically every farm grew a few potatoes, though rarely in sufficient quantities for anything more than domestic use, except in such parishes as Tingwall, where potatoes were grown and sold in the towns of Lerwick and Scalloway, and to visiting boats.[907]

To begin with, lazy-bed cultivation was practised in old pasture or outfield land, with animal dung or seaweed as a manure. The lazy-bed technique was widely recommended in the agricultural writings of the period as a means of reclaiming waste land, but was not suitable for the growth of potatoes on any scale, and in Lowland Scotland it did not last long. It was soon discontinued in the Northern Isles as well, though surviving sporadically in areas like Yell, and Lady parish in Orkney where it was said that after a potato crop on lazy beds, oats or bere could be grown without the use of further manure.[908]

By the 1790s, potatoes were being grown on the infield soil and were incorporated in rotational sequences. In Tingwall, the rotation, or rather alternation, was bere, oats, potatoes, and bere again, sown without further ploughing. Bere and potatoes came to be the main infield crops. They were not entirely confined to the infield, however, and in Sandsting and Aithsting only half the crop of potatoes required for family use was grown there, the remainder being grown in the outfield.[909]

At first there was a tendency to plant the tubers too close together for horse-hoeing or cleaning by means of the plough. They were set in one furrow, and covered with the sod cut from the next. In previously dug ground, they might simply be dibbled in. Planting took place about mid-April. In Sandsting and Aithsting, where about a quarter of the arable was under potatoes by the 1840s, before the shoots appeared above ground, the top weeds were turned up with the hoe or spade, a process known as 'shovelling the potatoes'. After a few days when the weeds had withered, a double draught of the wooden harrows was given. In June, the crop was hoed, usually twice, and in July the potatoes were earthed up or *happit*, when the stems were about 6 in. (15 cm) high. October was the time for digging or *ripping* (English 'rip', to tear) the potatoes with the delving spade.[910]

Information on yields is scanty. The produce in Sandwick and Stromness was estimated at 60 barrels per acre at 1/6d. a barrel in the 1790s. Here, potatoes had become the principal food. None had been grown there about 1750, but now each farm grew a patch, amounting to about a quarter acre per plough. This gave 56 acres, producing 3360 barrels, worth £252. In 1845 Stronsay and Eday produced 6034 barrels at 2/3d. each, worth £678.16. 6d., and Mid and South Yell 900 tons at £1.5.9d a ton, worth £1125. At this rate, the potato crop was second in value to the year's bere and oat crop (£2300), and well in advance of any other source of income.[911]

Potatoes were of much value for nutrition towards the beginning of harvest, by which time the last year's stocks of grain were running low, and bread was scarce. They made an excellent accompaniment to the small fish caught by fishing from the rocks on the shore, and it is likely that quite a large part of the season's potato crop was often eaten straight from the ground in this way. With increased amounts of potatoes, however, the question of winter storage arose, and it is in this sphere that new features began to appear in and around the farm buildings.

In Tingwall, stored potatoes were protected from frost by piling them in three feet (91 cm) deep pits in the barnyard, covering them with earth, and then building a stack of corn over them. To these, names like *tattie-hock* (*tattie*, potato+*hock*, from Scots *howk*, to dig), and *krubbie* (Norwegian *krubba*, crib, feeding trough)[912] were applied. They were also simply called *tattie-holes*, and as such were in use in Papa Stour until comparatively recently, though not covered by a stack of grain but by turves.

204. The half-underground tattie-hoose at the Biggins, Papa Stour, 1967. 3.37.31.

Alternatively a *tattie-hoose* could be built, partially underground. One type was described as circular with turf walls and wooden rafters, thatched over with turf. The space inside could be split by wooden boards into storage sections. There was a hatch in the roof and another at the base, said to be partly intended for ventilation, and partly for filling and emptying.[913] Another type was rectangular, built back into a slope in the ground, and roofed with wooden rafters and straw thatch like an actual small house. Two examples were noted in Papa Stour in 1967, a disused one in the kailyard at North Banks, and one in use just behind the house at Biggins. The North Banks tattie-hoose measured 12 ft long by 7 ft wide (3.7×2.1 m), with a central door in the downhill gable measuring no more than 1 ft 8 in. wide by 2 ft 1 in. deep (51×64 cm). The walls were partly of the natural earth, and partly of stone, with gablets of turf. In order to provide internal supports for the ends of the sets of roofing couples, pillars of flat, oval beach stones had been built up, in decreasing order of size from bottom to top, making a pleasing building feature. At Biggins the door is in the downhill gable, and high enough to get through without too much difficulty. When examined, this tattie-hoose was still full of potatoes and the door was blocked up by turf. The potatoes were taken in through the door here, but at North Banks they must have been emptied in through the uphill gablet, which, being of turf, could easily be removed and replaced. According to the local people, the circular tattie-holes gave better protection against frost than the tattie-houses.

Inside storage was another possibility. A boarded corner in the living-room of a house for preserving potatoes from frost was called a *tattie-cro* (Norwegian *kro*, *kraa*, Old Norse *krá*, nook, corner), *lodie* or *tattie-lodie* (Norwegian *lade*, barn, Old Norse *hlaða*, store-house)[914] and at the present day there are barns with low wooden partitions behind which potatoes are stored.

In Shetland, potato growing has remained essentially a matter for supplying domestic needs, and this is in general true of Orkney as well, but already by the mid-nineteenth century some of the more enterprising farmers there were developing their markets. David Petrie of the farm of Holm, for instance, shipped 27 tons of potatoes to the Isle of Man in 1851, and in winter 1854–5 at least 73 tons were sent south to London and Leith, an amount representing about 10 acres under crop. He was growing a number of varieties, Common Orkney Red, Blue Kidney, Prince Regent, Rocks, all now obsolete.[915]

By the mid-nineteenth century, too, the crop had become such a standard one that it formed part of the wages given to farm-servants in kind, with meal and milk, alongside their money wage.[916] This element in their wages remained as a perquisite into the twentieth century.

On W S Tait's farm at Ingsay, work with potatoes began on 4 April 1923 and ended on 29 October. This involved nineteen days' work, 5 per cent of the farming year. The activities included lifting from pits, grubbing, scuffling and hoeing, sorting and riddling, lifting from the drills, and pitting in earth covered pits. Sutton's Abundance and Arran Chief were the types mentioned in 1923. In 1925, half a ton of Kerr's Pink, costing 6/– a hundredweight, were taken home and planted. In 1928, Boxers and Duke of York were added to the list, and in 1939, Golden Wonders and Kepplestone Kidneys. A digger drawn by a pair of horses was first mentioned in 1936.[917]

Potatoes were eaten in all sorts of ways, sometimes alone with milk or butter and salt, but usually in combination with something else, especially fish, or more rarely salt or dried pork, beef or mutton. Until a generation ago, many people ate them for three meals a day, including breakfast. In Orkney practice, breakfast potatoes were boiled in their skins, and were then strained, peeled, and put back in the pot over the fire. Oatmeal and salt were sprinkled on, and they were mashed and supped out of the pot, accompanied by sweet-milk or buttermilk. For dinner, they were again boiled in their skins, and were emptied into a large basin or tipped on to the middle of the table. The family gathered round, and each took a potato and peeled it, using neither fork nor spoon, before dipping it in a bowl of melted fat or butter to add more taste to it. Dried dogfish, boiled or roasted on an iron girdle, went well with potatoes. As a follow-up came thick butter-milk and oatmeal or sometimes sour clotted sweet-milk and burstin. For supper, pared potatoes were mashed with turnips, sprinkled with salt and pepper, and eaten with bere bannocks. This dish was sometimes called *clapshot*. An alternative for supper was to roast the potatoes in the embers of the peat fire. They could be scooped out of their charred skins or, when the skins were brown and crisp, mashed with butter – skins and all.[918]

51

Gardening

PLANTIECRUES and kailyards served as gardens for most of the small farms, but the lairds and bigger tenant farmers had good gardens and were evidently keen to experiment. By 1693, cabbage, carrots, parsnips, *crummocks* or the plant skirret (Old Scots, 1693, Gaelic *crumag*) and artichokes were being grown in Shetland gardens. Patrick Fea in Sanday was planting leeks, onions, carrots, parsnips, beets, lettuce, spinach, curled kail and savoys in 1769. Beans and peas also did well.[919] This kind of range was no doubt fairly typical. What is much more unexpected, however, is the range that Thomas Irvine of Midbrake covered. On 9 August 1820, he planted in his garden four red, four white and four blackcurrant bushes, four gooseberry bushes, four firs, eight larches, an ivy plant which appeared to thrive until the peacock destroyed it, four Scottish thistles and a cluster of creepers, all got from the nursery of Mr Dickson Senior of Shakespeare Square, Edinburgh, on the morning of 27 July, and transported by Irvine in his sloop, the *Lord Fife*. In November he took eight thorn bushes, properly wild roses, from the north side of Helgigill, where he also found some honeysuckle, and planted them at home. He also pruned and trimmed an alder and a willow and planted the slips. In February 1821, he laid out a border for a thorn hedge, and put six plants in. One of the thorns from Helgigill blossomed in Autumn 1823. Walks were also laid out. In March, he got from Dickson three white and three red Antwerp raspberry bushes, eight green and four 'stript or varigated' hollies, 6 rose and 6 large Carolina strawberries. Straw was laid by way of experiment under the roots of some of the strawberries. More thorns and honeysuckle were got from Helgigill in April. Thorn seemed to fascinate him, for he planted in a wooden box three rows of seed, the first taken from the pods on bushes brought from Helgigill, picked about Christmas and hung up to dry in linen bags since then, the second picked two years before from bushes at Helgigill and the third from fresh ripened pods from the same place. All failed. Thrift was used for edging some of the walks. On the north side, 240 cabbage plants went in, and turnip seed got from Dalsetter, which by 28 July had mostly run to seed. Radishes and lettuce were planted between the rows of raspberries. Carrot and parsnip seed from Lerwick and from Leith did well.

In May scarlet runners and speckled kidney beans went in, but failed to spring. He also put in alder seed, Norway spruce fir and Scots fir, and others in pots in the garden. Chilly winds and severe droughts killed them. Four hundred more cabbage plants were planted, as well as mustard, using both Scots and Shetland seed, and cauliflower seed. 28 June was a day of triumph: 'I took up the first dish of Radishes from the Garden they were of the proper size and tasted very good, but for want of regular watering during the long continued dry weather & northerly wind they were not so sappy & mild as they otherwise would have been. The winds had continued to blow from the North, North East, & North West points for *10 weeks*!' In July Globe Turnips and Swedes were sown.

At this point he got masons to erect a new wall on the north, east, and south sides of the garden, a total length of 235 ft (71.6 m), put up in 13 days. On the north and east sides the foundations were 3 ft (91 cm) wide and the wall narrowed to 18 in. (46 cm) on top. The south side wall was 2 ft (61 cm) wide at the bottom and 15 in. (38 cm) wide at the top. The wall was 4 ft (1.2 m) high, and cost in all £26 (1/1¼ per fathom).[920]

Irvine's experience is characteristic. In such islands, gardening is possible, but the climate and in particular the wind make it at best a difficult and uncertain pursuit.

52

Hay and Grass

THE importance of grazing as a conditioning factor in the form and expansion of settlement cannot be doubted. Early writers comment frequently on the abundance of pasture and cattle. It was noted in 1521 that Orkney butter, seasoned with salt, sold very cheaply in Scotl nd. Cattle, sheep, and goats in the Northern Isles produced plenty of milk, cheese and butter. The grass of Fair Isle was short but good, giving good milk and butter.[921]

Grazing was of different kinds. The hills produced rough pasturage consisting largely of *lubba* (origin uncertain; cf. Icelandic *lubbi*, shaggy), the leaves of heath-rush and other small rushes and sedges, and coarse boggy vegetation. In the valleys the meadow ground grew grass which, when cut at Lammas, made good hay. Unst in particular was noted for grazing oxen, kine and sheep. Small islands and nesses always had good natural grass, making the sheep fat on Colsay and on Sheep's Craig in Fair Isle. Holm near St Ninian's Isle, Crossholm, the Ness of Cumliewick, Mousa, Papa Little, the Isle of Nibon in Northmavine, and Weather-holm in Unst all pastured sheep, and Colsay, the Ness of Cumliewick, Mousa and Weatherholm carried cattle as well. In Orkney, the Horse of Copinsay grazed twenty sheep, and there was good grazing at Glumholm, Swina and the Calf of Flotta, in the Holm of Scockness in Rousay, and elsewhere. The value of the meadows in Shetland is shown by the fact that they were enclosed by dykes.[922]

Generally speaking, however, the lack of enclosures meant that there were no sown grasses, and in South Ronaldsay, horses and cattle were tethered on natural grass. Around Stromness, there were 30 arable spots, and no fewer than 2116 grass grounds, in the infield, outfield and meadow. Bog-hay was plentiful in Orphir, and Bressay, Burra and Quarff had some large meadows yielding hay. In Burra hay was cut only when wet, and left for two or three weeks till it had been rained on.[923]

By 1806 some attempts were being made to grow rye-grass and Dutch clover, for example at Aikerness and Burray in Orkney. In 1845 Holm and Paplay had 829 acres of grass and was actually exporting rye-grass seed to southern seedsmen. St Andrews, a less improved parish, had little hay. In parts of Cross and Burness, sown grass as well as turnips was being included in the rotations. The Shetland pattern remained little changed. Hay from the natural meadows often became malted instead of remaining simply as dried grass, and coarse hay known as *tekk* ('thatch'), consisting of heaths and rushes, was cut in the scattald for use as bedding. Bog-hay was cut about Lammas and dried, though it was often much wasted before being stacked, from the prevalent idea that it would heat and rot if the juices were not washed out first. The instrument used to cut it was the straight-handled scythe. Like the sickles, scythes were also made in Sandsting and Aithsting. Natural rye-grass here got the name of *acre-a-bunk* (Old Norse *akr*, field + Norwegian *bunke*, a species of grass, especially *Deschampsia caespitosa*), and natural clover was *smora* (Norwegian dialectal *smæra*, clover, usually *Trifolium repens*). Meadow hay in Mid and South Yell was valued at £150 and in Northmavine at £100. Unst had about 2000 acres of meadow and grassland, producing good natural hay and pasture for milk cows, and in the fertile parish of Tingwall grass and hay formed part of improved rotations, consisting usually of turnips and potatoes, bere with grass, seeds, hay, pasture, and then oats.[924]

Once cut with the scythe, hay was treated in various ways. In Fetlar, on small patches, no further tools were required. Almost immediately after cutting, the hay was lifted by hand, well shaken to aerate it, and piled in very small heaps. Later these small heaps were combined into bigger, but still fairly small, *coles* (origin uncertain, perhaps Old French *coillir*, to gather), still using the hands alone. In some cases, after the hay had been cut and spread out to dry, it was raked into long strips to keep it from drying too quickly and losing its food value. This was called to *queerve* (Norwegian dialectal *kverva*, Old Norse *hverfa*, to turn something) the hay.[925] A 'botle (Old French *botel*, small bundle) rake' was made by Ed. Maxwell for Patrick Fea in Sanday in 1774,[926] presumably for raking hay into bundles. To put hay, or corn, into small cocks was to *skrivle* (cf. Norwegian dialectal *skryva*, Old Norse *skrýfa*, from *skrúf*, corn-stack), and the cock itself a *screevelin*.[927] The general, rather idealised, pattern of activity on Orkney farms was that the workers were divided into groups of three, two to carry and build the cocks, and one to rake, each group taking on a certain number of ridges, or of swathes if the wind was in an awkward direction. Small cocks were first made, with little taper except at the top, and after two dry days made into larger ones, 6 or 7 ft (1.8–2.1 m) high by 4 ft (1.2 m) in diameter. A few days later they could be put into 'tramp ricks' containing 50 to 100 stones of hay, the cocks being carried by hand or dragged by a horse to the building spot. Though this may have happened on bigger farms, the more usual method was to cut the grass, let it dry a little in the swathe, and put it into small cocks which were later piled into medium-sized pikes, in which they might be left for several weeks.[928] Where hay patches lay in intermingled ownership, there was often nothing to show boundaries except the different lie of the cut hay where one mower had finished his work and another had begun.[929]

In Orkney, hay stacks were often large and circular, as on the Mainland of Scotland. The older form, still to be seen in Shetland, was smaller, with a rectangular base. This could be called a *gilt* (Norwegian dialectal *gylta*, sow, Old Norse *gylta*, *gyltr*, young sow), especially in Orkney and Caithness, and in Shetland it was 'a longish heap of mown heather and coarse grass piled up in a ridge for drying in the out-field', for use as thatching and bedding. More usual in Shetland, however, was the word *dess*. Mown heather for thatching was also set up in desses, having been first dried in small oblong piles called *riggins* (Old Scots *rigging*, roof-ridge, 1507).[930]

Before the introduction of rye-grass and sown grasses, the main source of hay was bog-hay, cut from the meadows along the burn banks, in late July and early August, beginning in the lower lying parts and working upwards. The time of mowing the hay was said to be a time of rejoicing in Orkney, with some kind of celebration on 'mawin'-day',[931] but in general, until the nineteenth century, hay seems to have played a relatively small part in the economy of these islands.

Cattle and Milk Products

53

Cattle

EARLY writers commented on the good store of cattle that the pasture of the Northern Isles could support. In winter, conditions were less kind. The available fodder was limited, hay had to be rationed, and before the days of turnips, cattle came through the winter in a very weakened state. If all was well, it was reckoned, in the mid-nineteenth century, that if a tenant kept three to six cows in the summer on 10 to 12 acres, he should be able to fodder seven to ten cattle of all ages in winter. In Aithsting and Sandsting the tenant of 3 merks of land could keep four to six cows and overwinter twelve to fifteen head of cattle. These are probably optimal figures, however, for in Dunrossness only one cow was allotted to each merkland.[932] During periods of dearth such as occurred in 1759, 1766, 1770, 1772–4, 1778, 1781–6, 1801–7, 1811–13, it is significant that the sales of the hides and other parts of cattle that had died in the spring were very high. The phrases *apo* (upon) *liftin*, *at the liftin*, *in liftin* speak for themselves. It was applied to a beast so weakened that it was unable to get to its feet in spring, from February to May. This was partly due to the keeping of more cattle than could be supported.[933] In such circumstances, all available fodder resources were utilised, including heather and a kind of seaweed called *mooi* (Norwegian *mo(e)*, fine sandy soil, Old Norse *mòr*, a sandy plain) found on muddy, sandy stretches of foreshore. Both fresh-cut and boiled seaweed could be given sparingly to cattle in spring. *Hinniewaar* (honey + ware), *Alaria esculenta*, was one of the kinds of seaweed parboiled and fed to the cows with its juice, along with kail runts split up and any other edible domestic material, and even boiled fish.[934] Under normal circumstances a small *hallow* or *wap* (Old Scots *wap*, to wrap, c. 1400) of straw was given between two cows, night and morning, and the same at noon if they were kept in the byre by bad weather. Cows in calf got in addition cabbage or potatoes chopped up and mixed with bere-chaff or coarse *sids*, or some meadow hay in lieu. An aspect of this regime was that young *queys* might be up to five or six years old before calving.[935]

As a rule the young cattle went onto the scattald at the end of May or the beginning of June, with unlimited freedom of grazing. The milk cows pastured on the township grass till mid-day in summer, when they were milked and put to the hill. In the evening, they were brought back, left to feed for a few hours, and put in the byre overnight. After November the young cattle came in from the hill and were tied up, 'set to the band', in the byre for the winter.[936]

In 1808 it was estimated that Shetland had about 30,000 milk cows, 1000 oxen, and 10,000 young cattle, a ratio which by no means squares with the figures given for 1845. In fact, an estimate made about 1814 amounted only to 15,000 of all ages. The cows were small, weighing at most 2 to 3 cwt when fat.[937]

In Orkney, the cattle were very similar to those of Caithness. Improvements were being made before 1808 by individuals like Captain Sutherland of Burray, who was concentrating on the Dunrobin breed from Caithness. Crosses with native cows did well. Mr Baikie's farm in Egilsay, Cliffdale in Shapinsay, and Melsetter in Hoy all had good cattle, but these were all isolated examples. Cattle for droving sold well and by the 1830s Scottish farmers were buying both Orkney and Shetland cattle in spring, feeding them in summer, and selling them in autumn in the English market as part of the droving trade. In Orphir sixty to seventy head of black cattle were sold to Caithness farmers each year in early summer.[938] The small Shetland cow, with long narrow horns and short legs, produced sweet and tender beef.[939] Orkney cattle, however, got little praise. They were also small and at one time had been smaller than those in Shetland. In 1814 they were described as being of various colours, though black was common, with low heads, high backs, thin buttocks, and horns that were 'short and contracted, with their tops bending towards the forehead'. Overstocking was one of the factors in keeping the quality low.[940]

The colours of the Northern Isles cattle were white, black, brown or red and generally not uniform. A *grimet* (Norwegian *grimet*, Faroese *grimatur*) cow had a white face with dark spots or stripes.[941] A *lenget* (cf. Old Norse *(bak-) lengja*, a stripe along the back of cattle) cow or horse had a stripe across the back, or black and white stripes or markings over the back. If it was *ridyid* (from Old Scots *rigge*, back, 1375; cf. Old Norse *hryggr*), it had a different coloured stripe down its back, often running from the back of the ears to the tip of the tail. In Birsay, this stripe was always white. Such a stripe was a *rig* in Shetland, giving rise to the cow name *Rigga*.[942] If the cow was *sholmit* (Norwegian dialectal *hjelmutt*, Icelandic *hjálmóttr*, from Old Norse *hjálmr*, helmet), its face was white and it might get the pet name *Sholma*. If it was *vandit* (cf. Old Norse *vǫndr*, wand, stripe in cloth, Faroese *vond*, weaving or pattern of cloth), it was usually of a brown or dun colour with black stripes, zebra-like.[943]

It was only much later in time that cow names became personal rather than descriptive, as in W S Tait's Diaries in the 1920s:

1923.	19 March:	Put cow Elsie to Finstown got price £17.
	9 April:	Float here today for Polly cow sold to J. T. Flett.
	15 April:	Shiela cow calved.
	19 July:	Topsie cow calved.
	19 Sept:	Nanyie cow calved in Meadow all right.
		B.P. (black polled) heifer.
1937.	1 Nov:	Queen heifer calved a bull calf.[944]

In the days of runrig farming, the cows were housed every night, being

205. A veggel or dook for fastening cattle in the byre, at Kennaby, Fair Isle, 1962. With such a fixing, the rope usually went round the cow's horns. C5634.

206. Triangular partitions in a byre, Fetlar, 1963. C5713.

bedded with dry earth and turf or heather until the composted muck was deep enough to bring their heads near the roof. In summer they grazed outside near the houses on the tether, or in the charge of a herd. All other cattle were turned on to the hills and moors. In 1633 Catrein Miller in Orkney had a son herding the cows and stock of Johne Broune, and in November 1700 Magnus Craigie's wife was herding her cows at the back of a barn,[945] that is, at a period of the year when the arable fields would have been open to all grazing stock. The grazing at the back of the barn was probably privately held. Tethering was often on strips of pasture within the township called *messagates*, from Old Norse *messa*, mass, Communion service + *gata*, way, path, since these were paths through corn-fields, originally leading to the church. In some instances, a cow or ox might be grazed for the six summer months, at a cost of 6/– to 8/–, the owner providing a tether. In 1576, Olaw in Heliness, Fetlar, had permission to pasture his cattle on the tether on his neighbour's grass,[946] and the custom is no doubt old.

Cows in the Northern Isles were usually fastened in the byre or on the tether with the rope round their horns. If they had no horns, which was rare, a loop was made in the tether, a *neck-band*, to fasten them by the neck, or else a rope-halter called a *grimek* was put on. This kind of fastening, however, and its name, usually apply to horses. When the rope was round the horns, there was less danger of a cow getting a hind foot caught in the rope if it was rubbing its neck. To prevent abrasion, a bit of soft cloth was put round the roots of the horns.[947] For outside tethering, a wooden stake was knocked into the ground, wood being preferred because there was so much spring in a hair tether that an iron stake was considered dangerous. Hair tethers were unpleasant to handle in

207. The byre partitions at Busta, Fair Isle. The cows are fastened to an iron rod. 1962. C5714.

208. A lithie for fastening cows in an Orkney byre. C5844.

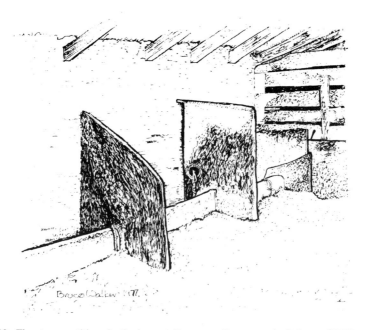

209. Flagstone partitions in the byre at Pow, near Stromness in Orkney. C5708.

wet weather. Through the stake went a rope with a knotted end, and part way along the rope was a swivel or *swill*, a 3 or 4 in. (8–10 cm) length of wood with a hole in each end, which kept the rope from unravelling, especially if it was newly made. The halter itself consisted of two wooden cheek-pieces, linked with ropes above and below the muzzle. Another rope went through holes in the centre of the cheek-pieces, and round the animal's head. Wooden *branks* (Old Scots *brankis*, 1548) can still be seen on tethered beasts, and iron ones may also be found. In Harray, Orkney, a hitch of the tether taken over an animal's ear to prevent it pulling out its stake was a *fang* (Old Norse *fang*, a gripping).[948] A hitch was also taken over the cow's ear when flitting it. For unruly animals, a special form of restraint was the 'bultin' klug' or *klüre* (Old Scots *clour*, bump, swelling, *c.* 1500–12), a clog of wood or shaped piece of stone slung between the horns so that when the cow tossed its head to 'bolt' someone, the clog struck and quietened it. Some older examples in stone are attractively decorated.

210. Flitting cattle in a small boat, Orkney. C79E.

The lack of fencing could lead to a conflict between the handling of stock and the cropping of the fields. The result in the second half of the nineteenth century was a widespread increase in the tethering of cattle, as well as horses, sheep and pigs, on a scale never seen before, with collars, chains 6 to 7 yds (5.5–6.4 m) long, and iron pegs replacing the old hair tethers and wooden pegs. Though time consuming, tethering is no doubt the best possible form of

211. Hoisting cattle into the boat for transport from Orkney to the Scottish Mainland. Per the Orkney Association, Edinburgh. C2221.

212. A cow tethered by the Low Road, Bay of Firth, Orkney. Per Mrs M. Sclater.

controlled grazing. The method, observed on the unfenced strips in North Ronaldsay in 1964, was to move the stake about half the length of the tether at regular intervals, resulting in a series of overlapping circles.[949] This action, as in Shetland, was 'flitting the coo'.

In the hungry days of winter and spring when little milk could be got, the cattle could be bled once or twice. The blood was boiled, thickened with oatmeal, poured into containers and eaten with a little milk. Some cattle were slaughtered in autumn and the meat preserved for winter use as *vivda* (Norwegian dialectal *vovde*, fleshy part of limb, leg-muscle, Old Norse *vǫðvi*, muscle), cured and dried in the open-air without the use of salt, and often kept in open stone huts or skeos or in a cave into which the tide flowed.[950] This method of conservation was on the way out by the 1770s, and in any case far more of the beef was salted and exported than was eaten at home.[951] Country folk brought their cattle to the three-day Lammas fair in Kirkwall for slaughter and in Shetland they were sold to Lerwick merchants, killed, and sent packed in salt to Leith. Cattle, and sheep, were the main source of income before the commercial development of fishing, and though the stock numbers remained about the same after that, the gain was less because they were spread over a greatly increased number of families.[952]

In the course of the nineteenth century, it became common for neighbours in a township to club together to buy a cow at the Hallowmas market, and to slaughter, cut up, salt and divide it between them for winter use.[953] As a rule, however, the amount of salt beef available to the ordinary farming folk was strictly limited, and eaten mainly on special occasions. It was boiled and eaten with potatoes and turnips, after they came on the scene, and cabbage, but the more wasteful method of roasting was rare, except on outstanding occasions such as the Yule dinner.[954]

Parallel to and preceding the sale of cattle on the hoof was the sale of salt beef, hides, and the skins of calves as well as neats' tongues.[955] In the early years of the nineteenth century the following amounts were quoted:

Year	Salted Hides	Barrels of Beef	Calf Skins	Cows and Oxen, live
1801–2	363	150	250 dozen	–
1802–3	22	–	153 dozen	233
1803–4	722	64	172 dozen	473
1804–5	906	67	224 dozen	–
1805–6	636	78	171 dozen	87

To this can be added $8\frac{1}{2}$ cwt of cow and ox hair in 1803 to 1804, and 7 cwt in 1805 to 1806.[956] Over the five-year period, hides totalled 2649 and calf skins 11,640, or 4.4 calf skins for every hide. There was, therefore, a regular slaughtering of calves, and many probably died in their first few weeks.

It goes without saying that the cows and calves were very much part of the household. If they fell ill, the standard of living fell, and cures of various kinds were tried, like the young shore-crab, the *mettly-crab*, given as a medicine to a cow that had lost her appetite. This must be an old cure, for the name is

213. A cheese-vat at Appiehouse, Stenness, Orkney. Stones of increasing weight are put on during pressing.

214. A spring-loaded Don cheese-press, a type that came in about the period of the Second World War. Orkney.

215. Cheeses made with the Don press, with a 'hangman' cheese in the cloth alongside. Orkney.

216. Open-air milking by Bobby Coutts, in Fetlar. 4.50.1A.

apparently from Old Norse *matleiði*, loathing of food, loss of appetite, Norwegian dialectal *matlei(d)*, off one's food. When someone took a cow to the bull, he was given on his return a piece of buttered bread, a *klino* (Old Norse *klína*, to smear, Norwegian *kline*, to spread upon), formerly made from the 'rue' or the seeds of weeds such as corn-spurrey. If the cow was about to calve, an Eday woman would say it was 'at the point o' tinsal' (cf. Norwegian dialectal *tynnsla*, a becoming thin).[957]

People called or spoke to their animals as they would to their children. A coaxing call in Shetland to a cow at milking or to a calf was 'shüta! shüta!' (Norwegian dialectal *søta*, sweet one, used as a coaxing term, Danish *søde*, sweet). A pet- or call-name for a calf, heifer or cow was 'kussie! kussie!', or in Orkney *kussack* (Norwegian dialectal *kusse*, *kussa*, calf, Old Norse *kus*, *kus*!, call to a cow, *kussa*, a cow, *kussi*, calf, bullock). Orkney call words to calves were *peed* from *peedie*, a variant of *peerie*, small, and 'sook! sook!' or 'sucko! sucko!' (from 'suck').[958]

Cheese

Cows were milked three times a day about 1800, and gave good milk in small quantities, about two or three quarts at a time. In the 1840s in Aithsting and Sandsting, the amounts were 5 quarts in the morning, 3 at mid-day, and 5 again in the evening,[959] a very marked improvement. By that date little or no cheese was made in Shetland. In 1633, however, good cheese was made and earlier records exist of cheese being kept in and sometimes stolen from skeos.[960] At the same period Orkney had 'great plentie of milk, cheese, and butter'.[961] Whereas in Shetland cheese-making disappeared entirely, in recent years Orkney cheese has gained a high reputation and is marketed throughout Britain. Significantly, Shetland lies outside the sphere of influence of the North of Scotland Milk Marketing Board. Orkney cheese is made in creameries, as well as on individual farms for home use or limited local sale. In Kirkwall shops it is possible to buy both polythene-packed, firmly pressed, commercially produced Orkney cheese and unpacked farm cheeses, less well pressed so that the individual pieces of curd are still visible, but with a freshness of flavour that the factory product cannot reproduce.[962]

About the period of the Second World War, a patent spring-loaded cheese-press, the Don Cheese Press, came into fashion, but previously the curds were wrapped in cheese-cloth and placed in a wooden cheese-vat or cog perforated with holes. The wooden lid was put on, and pressing was done by laying stones on top, the weight being increased gradually. The degree of pressing, as a result, was relatively slight.[963]

Though Orkney's reputation for cheese is relatively new, nevertheless a number of kinds were made on the farms. Cream cheese was made entirely from thick cream by heating and the addition of rennet. It was very rich and was made in small quantities at a time, since its keeping qualities were negligible. A commonly made type was skim-milk cheese, made with the milk left after the cream had been skimmed off. It was considered a little tough even when eaten at the green stage, after pressing but before drying. Some makers added yellow dye, and some mixed butter into the curd before it was put into the cheese-press, to make it look and taste richer and freer. Buttermilk cheese was also rather hard and indigestible, and butter could also be mixed into it. As it matured the flavour mellowed and the cheese became riper and more crumbly. Sweet-milk cheese was made from whole milk. When the pot was lifted off the fire the leathery curds, taken straight from the whey, were sometimes eaten and were known as 'squeaky' cheese because of the noise made when chewed. It was also good when eaten green, and after it had dried hard.[964]

Rennet was usually made from the stomach of a recently born calf. This was called *kyessel* (Norwegian *kjæse*, rennet, *kjøsel*, cheese made of new-calved cow's milk) in Orkney. A common Orkney alternative was made from a pig's

217. A plunge-churn used by Mrs H. Stout, Busta, Fair Isle, 1963. There was no lid. 1.29.23.

stomach, and this was said to give a bitter flavour. A vegetable alternative, known in Shetland, was *yirnin' girse*, the butterwort, *Pinguicula vulgaris*, whose leaves were put in the milk to curdle it.[965]

Cheese played a part in Orkney wedding ceremonies. The *hansel* (Old Scots *hand(d)sel*, 1375) was a present of 'a bit of each kind of cake at the wedding and cheese, and was wrapped up in paper as it was usually taken home'. It was distributed by the *hansel-wife*, generally the bride's mother, from a large sieve or tray.[966]

BUTTER

Throughout the ages, butter was the main product made from the milk of the cows of Orkney and Shetland. At one time butter paid over half the land rents, a factor which may itself have left little milk spare for cheese-making. A distinction was made between 'meat and grease butter'. The better quality meat butter was kept for home consumption, and the poorer grease butter used to pay the rent. This was assembled from the tenants and exported. In 1729, James Traill wrote to David Traill about 'packing the butter of Northronaldsey and sending it into toune'. Much of it went to Edinburgh, where it was sold as 'Orkney' butter, but the farmers took little trouble over keeping it clean. Little wonder that as early as 1521, Orkney butter, seasoned with salt, sold very cheaply in Scotland. It was churned as it came from the cow, unstrained and full of hair, and sold for smearing sheep and greasing coach wheels.[967] The process of collecting, packing and transporting can be seen from Patrick Fea's Diaries in Sanday:

1766.	2 April:	Sent 9 half barrels butter and a Firkin to the Sloop at Calf Sound marked PF & B.
	19 November:	Received the Butter of the Ground and packt it.
1767.	22 January:	My Boat came for me with ... 7 half barels grease butter.[968]

As long as butter was an element in rents paid in kind, there was no great incentive to upgrade its quality, and there was probably no general improvement till the influence of the Colleges of Agriculture, founded about the time of the First World War, began to make itself felt. As recently as 1959, butter that was full of red cow-hairs was got at a croft on one small island in Shetland, no doubt reflecting the kind and nature of the butter that was usual at an earlier period in time. Butter also served as a cash-equivalent, for in 1576 Magnus Leslie of Ayth in Bressay had a reested swine for which he paid two lispunds of butter. He also had in his house four lispunds of butter 'ryndit with hinnie', covered with a skin of honey, and two cogs and four lispunds of salt butter.[969]

For making butter, the milk was left to stand in the churn for two or three days till it thickened naturally, when it was known as *soor* (sour) milk or *run* (Old Scots *yirne*, to curdle, *c*. 1500) *milk* in Shetland, and *louts* in Orkney. With four or more cows, churning would be done once a day. When the butter was about to come, or if it would not come easily, some red-hot *kirnin* (churning)-*stones* were thrown in with the tongs to help the separating process. When this happened, the butter floated to the top, but a side effect was that part of the curd was incorporated with the butter, giving a white and yellow spotted appearance. The Shetland name for such heated stones was *kleebies* (Norwegian *klebber*, *klybberg*, soapstone).[970] It is possible that the functional need for dropping heated stones into the churn has led to the special form the upright churn has in the Northern Isles, wider at the top than at the bottom, and usually lacking a lid. This was called a *plout-kirn* (*plout*, an onomatopoeic word to indicate the sound + Old Scots *kyrn*, 1478),[971] operated by a plunger known as the *kirnstaff*, *plouter*, or *kirnkorses* (churn + cross). The head was cross-shaped, or could be a disc of wood with round holes cut in it. In winter, the churn was set near the fire and turned from time to time, to help the butter to come. Working the plunger was no easy job. It was lifted with a half-turn to near the top, without splashing, and thrust down again with a half-turning motion. The modern equivalent of the heated stones was a kettleful of boiling water, poured round the sides of the churn down into the milk. When the butter had gathered, it was lifted on the kirnstaff into an earthenware milk basin and washed several times in cold water to get all the milk out, otherwise it would turn sour quickly in spite of being salted and sugared. Then it had to be *haired*, by passing a knife through it several times until all the hairs had been removed on the edge. The salt and sugar were blended in thoroughly before the butter was shaped with butter-pats and weighed. It is said that butter will not stay good when packed into a large jar, unless the butter is all made from one churning. To overcome this, so that summer butter would keep for the winter, a layer of sugar was put into the jar between each churning[972] just as honey was used in the sixteenth century.

Though cleanliness with churns and milk pails is now the order of the day, in eighteenth century North Ronaldsay they were never washed, from the notion that if this was done the cows would give less milk, and of poorer quality. Some thought that when they threw out the water from washing they were also throwing out the profit of their cattle.[973] Since cleanliness and temperature are critical factors in butter making, it is little wonder that the butter failed to gather in the churn on many occasions, leading to loss of temper and accusations of witchcraft in this delicate domestic area. There were women like Anie Tailzeour in Orkney who knew how to do things:

'Tak thrie hairis of (from) the kowis taill, thrie of hir memberis, and thrie of hir papis, and gang thryse woderwardis about the kow, and straik hir in the left syd, and cast the hair in the kirne, and say thryse, "Cum butter, cum", and sua thei sould haue the haill proffeit of that flock, quhair that kow was' (1624). To regain the profit, Marion Richart's formula in 1633 was to go to the sea, count nine waves, let one of the nine go back again and take three handfuls of water from the next, put it in a stoup, and carry it home to put in the churn.[974] All this supernatural psychology no doubt had little effect on the butter itself.

In churning, small butter particles are left floating on top of the buttermilk.

These were called *flowins* (from 'flow') in Orkney. Before butter pats came to be used, the butter was slapped and worked with a stick called a *klash-tree* (Old Scots *clasch*, strike noisily, *c.* 1500). Milking and butter-making utensils are mentioned in eighteenth century inventories. A Stronsay inventory of 1734 included a kirn and an old milk jar with iron lugs.[975] The contents of the two milkhouses at the House of Burray in 1747 include a range of churn types, few of which were found on tenant farms till much later. In the 'upper' milkhouse, there was:

'A table & shelfs, a wide mouthed dutch Jarr, a firken with greese butter, a little hand Churn, a basket for holding delph plates, a wooden balk, with 2 broads (i.e. a weighing beam with two pans), a wooden bowle, 2 milk Syers, 3 mouse traps, ane oaken pint kan & ane earthen stoveing pan.'

The 'old' milkhouse contained:

'A smal Copper Ketle, a Barrell and half barrell both empty 2 large brass pans, & 2 smal ones with bowls, two Spitt Churns & a standard, a Smaller hand Churn, 2 barm Kans, a Large Cheese Sae, a yetling (iron) Pott, 7 Cheese fatts, ane Iron Skimer for oill, a Plout Churn, a smaller one, 4 butter Kitts, a Sowen Kitt, 2 litle noraway Kitts with covers a three leged bumick (wooden vessel, probably from Norwegian *bomme*, box or basket for holding food) with a cover, 4 whey tubs & 6 greese Tubs, 5 old Kans, 4 wanded hampers, a wooden Cheese Squezer, 7 lugged buckets, 3 noraway Saes, 2 milking pales, a Jar Gantrees, ane Oaken barrel, two Do. more 5 Cutts (?) of Good Iron, 8 butter ankers, and another cheese fatt.'[976]

Evidently both cheese and butter were being made on a fair scale, with eight cheese vats and a wooden press, and at least six churns of different types in the milkhouses. Apart from the upright churns of two sizes, it is not certain what the others were like in appearance, though the 'spit' churns may have revolved on a spit or axle. As often happens, such inventories show a state of development that is otherwise unsuspected. In Scotland in general, it was in the second half of the eighteenth century that patent barrel churns and box churns were replacing plunge-churns, and estate owners in the Northern Isles were following the Mainland trend. Nevertheless, the plunge-churn still does active service on many crofts, and here and there, perhaps a trace of old ideas lingers on, when a housewife will not let the churn be taken outside.

OTHER MILK PRODUCTS

The range of products from milk was by no means finished with butter and cheese. The buttermilk itself was of much importance. It was called *blatho* in Orkney, and *bleddik* (Gaelic *blàthach*, in Old Scots from *c.* 1500) or *gyola* (Norwegian dialectal *kjore*, curdled milk, *kjøra*, a cheesy sediment in whey) in Shetland. When boiled or processed by having heated stones dropped into it, a white, cheese-like substance called *hard milk* in Fair Isle separated from the serum. It could be supped with sweet milk, or hung up in a cloth and left to drip for a time, making a kind of soft cheese. The serum was put into oak puncheons in summer time and stored for winter use as the drink known as bland. In 1604 Magnus Wischert in Shetland was accused in the Sheriff Court of damaging 'ane barrell bland'. It was a universal drink, a substitute for ale or beer, for which grain could not always be spared. When it reached a fermenting, sparkling stage it was fit to drink, but beyond that it became flat and vinegary, though its quality could be maintained by regularly adding fresh serum. Poorer people drank it warm from the churn, whilst the better off matured it in casks in skeos. For lifting the buttermilk out of the churn to boil it in a pot, *kirn kaps* (Old Scots *cap*, Norwegian *kopp*, Old Norse *koppr*, cup, bowl) or bowls, traditionally imported from Norway, were used. Bland was the drink that fishermen normally took with them when they went to sea in their open boats. It also served to augment the feed given to calves in the byre. They were not allowed to suck the cows, but were first given her milk, and then a drink of bland.[977]

The use of hard-milk or kirn-milk separated from buttermilk in Fair Isle and elsewhere is paralleled by *hung-milk*, made from full milk coagulated by the heat of the weather, and hung up in a linen bag till the whey had dripped from it. The result was a kind of unpressed cream cheese.[978]

Coagulated or soured milk was popular. A Shetland variety was called *strubba* (cf. Norwegian dialectal *stroppen*, half brooded, of an egg, Old Norse *stropi*, the thickening contents of a fertile egg), milk that had first coagulated and then been whipped up to a thick consistency. It could be eaten with rhubarb or pudding. Sweet-milk could be curdled by the addition of sour-milk or buttermilk, followed by heating. In Shetland this was to *ost* (Norwegian dialectal, Icelandic *ysta*, to cause milk to curdle, Swedish dialectal *ust(e)-mjölk*, Icelandic *ystingr*, curdled milk) the milk, and the product was *ost-milk* or *eusteen*. Even sherry or any acid 'comforting' liquid could be used to induce curdling. A special Shetland dish was *clocks* (cf. Norwegian *kleksa*, soft lump or mass), a preparation of new milk boiled for hours until it became thick, brown and clotted. Gallons of milk could produce only a moderately sized dish of clocks, which 'not even its exceeding goodness can justify for being a most absurd waste of good milk'. The thick milk of *beest* (Old Scots *beist*, 1596) from a newly calved cow was also cooked or baked to make a kind of soft, cheesy dish, regarded as a great delicacy.[979]

Sheep and Textiles

54

Native Sheep and New Breeds

THE keeping of sheep in the Northern Isles dates back to the Stone Age. At Skara Brae in Orkney, finds of sheep bones were numerous, some large and some small, indicating rams and ewes of a breed not unlike the Soay sheep. The same is true of the bones from Bronze Age Jarlshof in Shetland. When the Vikings arrived they found numerous sheep in the Northern Isles and brought some with them as well. Wool combs with one row of teeth from Viking graves, as at Westness, Orkney, suggest that the long fibres were combed straight, but the short, fine fibres were probably not combed out as in later worsted manufacture.[980]

The value of sheep lay in meat and wool, not only for domestic use, but in the sixteenth century for the payment of teinds or tithes. David Trumble, the Kirk Officer of South Ronaldsay, had the task of collecting the small teinds which included wool and lambs, and for salary got 'ane meill of malt and ane auld casting of claithis yeirlie, or ellis the awaill (value) thereof, ane lamb & ane fleische of woll'. He and Alex. Sudderland were to ride and stent (assess for dues) the lambs and receive the wool teind on St Colm's Day, and were to receive the lambs on St James's Day or before. Wethers were also paid as part of the rent. Teind wool was reckoned as about a merk for every seven sheep.[981]

Orkney ewes were said in the sixteenth century and later (one writer following the other) to give two or three lambs at a time, and even up to four, no doubt a tribute to the good grazing, but not necessarily according with reality. Later sources suggest that two was the norm.

The sheep were left to graze unherded on the hills and nesses and holms, and as a result, the mortality rate could sometimes be very high. In 1832, Thomas Irvine of Midbrake in Yell noted that of the sheep on the Holm, 'the Ravens had killed 5 Lambs. This is the 3rd season that they have done so since the Eagle lefte off building his nest in the Holm'.[982] In the bad winter of 1784, 4506 sheep were lost in Delting, as well as 427 black cattle.[983] Other factors also affected numbers. In Shetland the fragmentation of holdings due to fishing needs was said to mean that few tenants could afford to buy sheep, and had to take them on *steelbow* (from *steel*, the metal, implying something fixed, rigid, + *bow*, undivided farm or principal farmhouse), a form of land-tenancy according to which the tenant got stock, growing grain, implements, etc. on the condition that the equivalent in quality and quantity should be returned at the end of the lease. The combination with *bow*, corresponding to *bu*, may suggest that the practice came to the Northern Isles from Scandinavia. Equivalent terms are found in other languages: German *stählen* or *eisern Vieh*, French *cheptel de fer*, late Latin *pecora ferrea*, implying a possible derivation from an early Germanic custom. It could be a reflection of a way in which udal estates were held firmly together, and was known as much in Orkney as in Shetland. The North Strynzie inventory of 1734, for example, is 'of the Steilbow goods, seed, and Servants bolls'. As a method of control and exploitation of tenants it was open to abuse, surviving till as recently as 1874 in Shetland, and in the conditions prevailing there in the second half of the eighteenth century it could well have led to some reduction in sheep numbers. However, the requirement that rents and tithes should be partly paid in lambs made the keeping of some sheep obligatory, though the numbers were again conditioned by the need to sell off stock to afford the necessaries of existence.[984] Wool had to be got too, for clothing, and for making knitted goods for sale.

In Orkney, sheep numbers were also falling by the 1790s. Those in Firth and Stenness had been reduced by a tenth since about 1770. Twins were said to be common. There were 135 Orkney sheep in Walls and Flotta, where formerly there had been about 2000, though 315 Tweedsmuir sheep and 21 rams were replacing them. Between 1788 and 1794, seventy-one Highlanders cleared from Strathnaver in Sutherland brought a considerable stock of sheep with them to this parish, as well as horses, cows and goats. By the 1840s further changes were taking place. Eday had 300 Cheviots and 180 Highland sheep besides 920 native sheep. In Burness, the Orkney sheep, much reduced in numbers, grazed on the tether in the summer. Merinos were introduced at Stove in 1808 by Malcolm Laing of Papdale and, when crossed with Cheviots, did well. Orkney ewes were also crossed with Merinos. Archer Fortescue introduced Cheviots to Orphir. In Kirkwall and St Ola, sheep numbers had dwindled.[985]

By the 1840s in Shetland, crossing was also taking place. The sheep-stock of Fetlar was said to be more mixed than that of North Yell. In Aithsting and Sandsting, the native breed was beginning to be crossed with black- and white-faced rams. The rams were put to the ewes at the beginning of December. The weaker lambs were housed till about Whitsun, and some people built small lambhouses to keep lambs in at night. They were fed night and morning with hay or cabbage, or coarse *sids* and cut potatoes. More often the lambs stayed around the dwelling-house fire. Already by 1814, however, Mr Gifford of Busta had a mixture of Northumberland muggs and the black-face, with a dash of the Cheviot breed, all crossing with the native Shetland ewes and these crosses mingling with each other again.[986]

By the 1870s in Shetland, the old pattern of community existence was being further affected by the clearance of former settlement areas to make grazing grounds for the new commercial breeds of sheep. These were enclosed by substantial sheep-dykes on the Galloway pattern. Clearances were going on in the northern half of Fetlar from the 1850s, and in some of the eastern valleys of Bressay and at Noss, where settlements were removed to make way for sheep-walks. Clearances started in Delting soon after 1768. It is no surprise that sheep-farmers were very unpopular amongst the fishermen-farmers. The average holding on the small tenant farms was thirty to forty, of which sometimes only three or four were ewes. When kept within dykes, a form of shackling was used, involving the tying of a fore and hind leg loosely together, to prevent jumping. On the big sheep farms, however, stocks were considerable. G. Bruce in the valley of Dale, Tingwall, with some of the best grass in the valley, on old arable, had 600 Cheviot, 600 black-face, and Leicester rams. He had ploughed 200 acres in Veensgarth, to be laid down as permanent pasture for 300 ewes. John Walker, agent for Major Cameron, had introduced extensive sheep-farming at Noss, with 300 Cheviot ewes there, and more Cheviots on three other farms in Delting and Yell. A further five farms there ran 3000 black-face. David Edmondston kept 400 black-faced ewes on farms belonging to Thomas Edmondston of Buness in the north of Unst, including 1500 acres of good heather and township ground at Hermaness on the Burrafirth Farm, where there had formerly been a fishing station. David Shepherd, an 'energetic Scotch farmer', had the only sheep farm in Whalsay, at Symbister.[987]

Orkney was not affected by clearances for sheep-farming in the same way as Shetland. Laing, who introduced Merinos from Tweeddale to Eday and Sanday in 1808, had by 1813 260 pure Merinos, about 620 Merino–Cheviot crosses, about 27 South Downs, and their crosses with Merinos, and the rest were Merino–Orkney crosses. This experiment was finally abandoned. About 1844, some half-bred sheep were imported from Caithness to Orkney, and following that Cheviots and Leicesters, mostly rams, were brought in and bred from. These breeds, and crosses with each other or the Orkney sheep, had become usual by the 1870s. Balfour Castle home farm had Leicester rams. Messrs. Irving and Hourston, the joint tenants of Colonel Balfour at Stove in Sanday, had 1050 acres, of which 640 were arable, and the rest sheep-pasture. They had 90 cattle and 700 sheep. At Swanbister in Orphir, Archer Fortescue surface drained all his hill ground and ran 640 breeding ewes and 150 ewe hogs.[988] The general effect was that the standards of the tenants' stock were also raised, and sheep husbandry became much better integrated into the general farming system than it did in Shetland.

Sheep Handling in Recent Times: A Fetlar Example

With larger crofts and more space, many crofters are running a number of the heavier breeds like the Suffolk, but these need good grazing and do not thrive on the hill. Cheviots are numerous in Fetlar, and the native breed, brought in from other isles, is crossed with them, though the hardiness of the native breed has to be maintained. The real Shetland tup was described as an odd-looking specimen, with large horns and a kind of small mane, and a beard like a

218. A pair of lambs tethered in Foula. Per A. Holbourn. C5104.

billy-goat, called a *waderlock* (Old Scots *widderlok*, *c*. 1460, the lock of hair in a horse's mane grasped by the rider when mounting).

Where flocks are relatively small, the crofters know each ewe by sight, and know when the older ones are due to cast their lambs. Whereas in earlier days sheep were kept more for their wool, now breeding is also of importance. Ewe lambs are kept each year for breeding from, the selection being made from lambs out of good ewes. These gimmer lambs replace the old ewes that are laid off, and they may be outwintered or housed in a 'lambie-hoose' fitted with hay-racks, a trough, and water-pot. Lambhouses, now found widely in Shetland, reflect the increased interest in breed quality of the last few generations. Small hog lambs may also be kept for marketing next season. Housed lambs are run out on nearby grazing by day, and are rounded up and put into the lambhouse overnight. Housed or pet lambs are *allie* (Old Norse *ala*, to feed, rear) lambs in Shetland and caddy lambs in Orkney (as well as in Shetland).

The lambing season began in the latter part of April and May and was a busy time for those who had to go some distance to the lambing pens. Good weather and a good show of spring grass made a lot of difference, and in case of bad conditions, an empty house could give blessed shelter. The work was easier if the croft had enough people to take turn about at the lambing, but a single man had to be alert day and night. Too long a gap between rounds could result in hanging cases, lambs dead with only their heads showing. Lambs left by their mothers for the first time could be attacked by ravens or black-backed gulls. Some losses occurred even in favourable circumstances and if a good milking ewe lost her lamb, the skin was flayed off and put on a lamb belonging to a ewe that had twins. The ewe was then, ideally, penned up in a stall with the lamb till she took it on. Young sheep were not as good as older ones for this, and a good deal of patience was needed.

The lambs were marked when they were about a month old. Ear clips and tattoo marks are now used, though the time-honoured custom of cutting lug marks remains. Each crofter had a particular mark which belonged to the croft. If anyone wanted to make an alteration or adopt a new one, the request was submitted to the Grazings Committee for approval and entered in their Register. The basic stock of Fetlar marks is:

1. A rift or rit
2. A shear or shuil
3. The tap aff
4. Three lappid or three tappid
5. Half awa before
6. Half awa behint
7. A crook
8. A bit oot behint
9. A strae draw
10. A witter
11. Cross cut behint
12. Cross cut afore
13. Twa bits awa before
14. A rit and a hole
15. A shuil an' a hole
16. A heel (= whole ear) an' a hole
17. A heel
18. A stoo (obsolete because severe: half the ear or more was cut off)

For quick spotting in crowded punds, many crofters also put a paint mark on the back or rump, each one using a different colour. Another custom was to put coloured tyle on the bellies of the tups during the rutting season, December. This left a mark on the ewes that had been served, so that the sequence of lambing could be noted. This is no longer done, since wool brokers complained about discoloured wool and cut the price of tup-marked wool.

Shetland sheep will run longer than the larger breeds. Some have lived to over twenty, but Cheviots are pretty well run out at eleven. When a sheep reaches eighteen months to two years old, depending on size, feeding and condition, it casts its lamb teeth and begins to grow its set of eight teeth which, by the age of five, are fully developed and the sheep becomes 'full mouthed'. Old sheep due for casting are kept apart from the tups and are kept on better grazing to fatten for the next season's market.

Till quite recently, the casts were used as a source of food, and salt-dried or reested mutton was popular, but now fresh butcher meat or tinned meat are

219. Sheep-dipping at Lower Rumin, Rackwick, Hoy, using a portable wooden dipping tank. Andrew Bremner (with sheep) and James Sutherland. 1.26.9.

more common. The cast-iron three-legged pot is no longer regularly full of kail and *mutton-bru* (Old Scots *bro*, broth; Old French *breu*, soup) or broth as it used to be. From early times, mutton has been salted and dried in skeos, when it was known as *blown meat*, and it was one of the products used in barter with the Hanseatic traders for linen, muslin, beer, brandy and bread. Salted mutton was also an Orkney product.[989] In the nineteenth century, mutton was the only kind of fresh meat, with pork occasionally, that the cottars had.[990] The men did their own butchering, and many can still do it. Most districts have experts who are asked to help their neighbours, payment being as often as not in tobacco or a dram. Formerly most of the entrails, the *faa* (Norwegian dialectal, Old Norse *fall*, carcase of a slaughtered animal, usually implying the previous removal of the entrails), were used for making puddings and sausages, but now only the liver and some fat is kept. The lungs were called lights, as in English. Two fleshy growths on top of the heart, cut off and not used for cooking, were 'deaf lugs'. The kidneys were *neirs* (Old Scots *nere*, *c.* 1400; Norwegian dialectal *nyra*, Old Norse *nyra*), the stomach was the *bag* (cf. Old Norse *baggi*, purse), and the lean flesh inside and at the back part constituted the *collops* (Old Scots, *c.* 1508). The large intestine was the *sparl* (Faroese, Old Norse *sperðill*) *pudding*, used to make sausages containing chopped meat, fat, spice, etc. The name 'Sparl' was applied to the inhabitants of Delting, from their fondness for a 'sort of sausage made of lean and fat meat, chopped up and dried with salt in a sheep's intestine'.[991] The small intestines, chitterlings, were 'strae (straw) drawn', pulled through a loop to thin them, and when dried were used as wheel-bands on spinning wheels. The large intestine was also called the *lang lungie* (Icelandic, Faroese *langi*, the long(gut)), and the caecum the *short lungie*.[992] The small bead-like lumps of dark flesh found in the fat of sheep or pigs were *clyres* (Middle Dutch *cliere*, a gland, probably through Old Scots). The skins

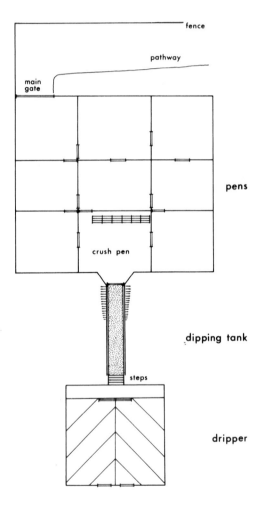

220. Plan of a modern pen, dipping tank and dripper in Fetlar. From a sketch by J. Laurenson. C5943.

could be used for making meal-sieves and fishing buoys[993] and in more recent times there has been a demand for cured skins for bedroom mats.

In former days there were punds at Funzie and Hestaness, and Dennel's Pund in Lambhoga. Those now used are at Everland, and one at Cuningsgard, serving Funzie, Houll and Baelagord. A dipper erected shortly before 1965 serves Aith, Aithness, Houbie, Tresta, Northdale, Leagarth, Baela and all the other crofts farther west on the island. The dipping of sheep was a practice that began in the islands soon after 1900. At first the dipping facilities were rather makeshift, and home-made tanks were used, that the sheep were lifted bodily into and out of. Often an old boat was used to hold the liquid, like the fowerern at Cuningsgard, with a door cut in its side for entry. Wooden tanks were also made, and set at the exit to a raised pen through which the sheep had to pass. If no water supply was laid on, the tank had to be filled by buckets, the people forming a chain from a nearby loch or burn. They were later replaced by concrete tanks and dripping pens which let the liquid run back, and avoided waste. Public sheep dippings were organised in Fetlar by the Grazings Committee who ordered the dip and rendered the accounts to the shareholders. Nowadays the dip is supplied in drums with instructions about the quantity of dip to water. A man checks with a marked stick to see if enough water has gone into the tank, the dip is poured in and stirred, and it is ready. Formerly dip came in 3 gal buckets and was of a fairly stiff consistency. Water had to be boiled in a large iron kettle, an easy job in summer but difficult in bad weather and wind, to reduce the dip, which was scooped out of the bucket with a sharp-edged piece of wood. Big-scale proprietors used big cauldrons on built-up stone fireplaces. Dippings took place in early spring and in midsummer, though new types of dip have now made once a year sufficient. On the day set by the Committee, the sheep were driven from the hill, care being taken to round up all of them, especially with the one annual dipping. Two members of the Committee saw to filling the tank and measuring out the dip. At the modern dipper at Setter Pund, there are separate pens for the different flocks, but otherwise they were all driven together. One man stood by the tank to see that each sheep passing through was fully submerged. Another plunged the sheep and called out the name of the owner to the tally man, who marked a '1' on a square of cardboard for each name called out. Several hands attended in the pen nearest the tank, and had the next sheep ready when the plunger had cleared the one in hand. Not everyone was a good plunger. It was necessary to have command of the ewe, which should be lifted by the tail and pushed head down into the tank. If she dropped on her belly she would splash the liquid. Black-faces were easier to handle because of their horns. After emerging from the tank the sheep stayed in the dripper till much of the dip had dripped from their fleece. When the dip got low, the tank was filled again, and during this lull the workers lit cigarettes and sweets would be passed round by the women-folk.

The dipping time for sheep and lambs was about 20 July. The driving date for clipping year-olds and *eild* (dry) sheep was the end of June. Milk ewes were clipped in July, since early clipping could reduce the milk flow to lambs through cold. At one time sheep's milk was made into butter and cheese, but this practice appears to have been rare and was not known by the 1760s.[994] When marking the lambs, at clipping time, the general rule is to cut a piece off the tails. Present-day buyers insist on this for ewe lambs, since large tails – not a problem with native sheep – have resulted in ewes failing to have lambs. The tails are now clipped down at the time when tups are run to the ewes.

Castration, now done at a punding with rubber rings, was formerly done with a knife. A Shetland sheep owner in the early nineteenth century invariably gelded all his finest fleeced ram lambs, so that they would not stray in the tupping season and be picked up by thieves, which was common. The only chance a fine fleeced ram lamb had of being left in the scattald was if it was a *riglin* (Old Scots, 1563), with only one testicle in its scrotum and the other undescended. though this served to propagate one defect, just as the gelding of good ram lambs prevented propagation of good fleece qualities. An anorchous ram, neither of whose testicles had descended, was a *whilin* (perhaps a variant of Norwegian dialectal *tvilling*, twin, twin animals being sometimes sterile).[995]

The other public drives of importance are to administer fluke drench, which is given in each of the winter months to prevent liver fluke. This has saved many animals and has helped to improve the flocks. Apart from this, sheep are subject to various diseases. Braxy or *vinster* (Norwegian dialectal *vinster*, the fourth stomach of a ruminant) was a sure killer for lambs. It is inflammation of the stomach brought on by eating frosty grass, October being the worst month for it. Now it can be countered by an injection, but the old cure was for shepherds to carry a bottle or so of salt water. On a frosty morning they would round up the flock into pens and administer a dose to each, the idea being that it would melt any frost in the stomach. The eating of seaweed also helped.[996] Another ailment, sleepy sickness or 'stomach staggers', really milk fever, also now cured by injection, was formerly treated by blowing air into the udder. Quite often a thin straw was used, though it was no easy task to get it inserted in the nipples. Other diseases were the rot or green-sickness, sturdy, water or *kwerkapus* (Norwegian dialectal *kverka*, to choke, *kverk*, throat, Old Norse *kverkr*, throat + Old Norse *puss*, bag), a dropsical swelling below the throat, also called *bolga* (Icelandic *bólga*, swelling), blindness, and the scab.[997]

Scab was introduced to the South Mainland of Shetland about 1779, reducing the stocks south of Mavis Grind by two-thirds. Mr Dickson, who had a flock of 800 sheep there, found that the application of Norway tar in autumn and winter when scab appeared, and bathing the sheep well in tobacco water after clipping, was the best remedy. In the days before dipping, there was little that could be done to stop the spread of infectious diseases, particularly when the sheep of different owners ran in common. *Shell sickness*, thought at one time to be equivalent to *water* or dropsy, is a thickening of the larger intestines into small white lumps resembling shells. Liver-fluke or sheep-rot is *mu*, *mu-(or moor-)sickness*, or *hert* (heart)-*mu* (probably Norwegian dialectal *mø(d)a*, to weary, weariness, Old Norse *mœða*, to weary, distress) in Shetland.[998] An

221. Rooing or plucking Shetland sheep. Photo. J D Rattar. 3.43.19A.

222. Clipping sheep in Orkney. Photo. W. Hourston. C78E.

epidemic disease of an undefined nature was called *faar* (Norwegian dialectal *faar*, illness, *farang*, epidemic, Old Norse *fár*, dangerous illness).

Though the substance of this section deals with Fetlar, much of it can be generalised to other areas of the Northern Isles.[999]

WOOL AND WOOL PRODUCTS

Wool was a desirable commodity, and misappropriation was made easy by the special nature of the wool, which could be plucked or *rooed* (Norwegian *rua*, Icelandic *ruja*) with the fingers. The sheep were neither clipped with shears, nor washed. In Shetland in 1612, the illegal rooing of sheep was widespread, and to make sure that regulations were observed, rooing was made a public occasion, and the identification marks on wool sold, as also on hides and skins, were to be shown to the bailie. Such controls lasted a long time, and even in the nineteenth and twentieth centuries, estates were regulating the place where rooing should take place and the time when it should be done, the announcement sometimes being made by the beadle at the church door about the first of June.[1000] Part of the reason for this was that sheep ran in common, so that equity could only be observed if the work of rooing was done jointly, each man picking out his sheep according to their identification marks.

By the same token, dogs were also under official control. The native sheep were not herded in docile flocks, but ran wild and had to be caught with specially trained *had* (Old Scots *hald*, grasp, 1375) *dogs*, which ran down and held the sheep individually. For this reason, it was made illegal to go through a neighbour's scattald with a sheepdog at night, or at other times without reliable witnesses, and sheepdogs were only to be kept by approved persons. This was to prevent people with dogs from taking and rooing sheep belonging to others, for the wool was not easily identifiable once it had been removed from the marked animal. When rooing day came, the parish bailiff and the lawrightmen, his assessors, and the owners of the sheep all came together, and the trained dogs caught the sheep that were pointed out to them. At this period, rooing was about the beginning of May. Sheeps' Craig in Fair Isle was an exception, for there the feeding was so good and the sheep so fat that they fell of their own accord on being chased once round the rock by a man. If they did not, they were not fat enough for slaughter.[1001]

Even with the native sheep, plucking was not the exclusive way of fleecing. In Walls in Orkney they were sometimes sheared in the 1760s, but more often, as elsewhere, the wool was cut off with a sharp knife. Rooing was still the main method, however, and the use of blades may have been because fleecing took place a little early, before the new wool or *lith* (Old Norse *hlið*, gap, space) had lifted properly from the base of the staple. At the present day little shearing is done in some areas, such as Foula, though it gives a greater weight of wool. There, the most common way is to use a knife to help to remove the fleece, though less wool is got than by rooing or shearing.[1002]

Rooing allowed this short, fine wool to be got unmixed with hair, hence the

223. Sheep in Fetlar, two of them with wooden checks to keep them from breaking out, 1963.

224. Sheep waiting to be shipped from Orkney to the Scottish Mainland. Photo. W. Hourston. C78J.

high reputation of knitted goods from these islands. When the sheep had been caught by dogs for plucking, their feet were usually tied together to make them lie quietly. The work was normally done in punds or crues into which the sheep were driven for fleecing, the marking of lambs, and the castrating of rams, or for the butcher. Each neighbourhood had its special pund just as each had its special scattald where the sheep of the 'scat-brithers' pastured together. Anyone whose sheep pastured a good bit away or in another parish was an 'out-scat holder'. If stray sheep were found, and kept a year, they could then be sold, half the profit going to the parish poor, and half to the finder.[1003]

Sheeps' fleeces in Orkney did not usually weigh over 3 lbs Amsterdam weight, and were for the most part mixed with hair. A merk of good wool, about $1\frac{1}{2}$ lbs, was the average. Orkney sheep, which were very short-tailed, and had horns, had coarser wool than the Shetland breed, coloured grey, dark tawny, black, and white.[1004] Shetland sheep were also small-tailed, and gave only about 1 to $1\frac{1}{2}$ lb of wool and 20 to 24 lb of mutton. In colour they were white, black, grey, *katmogit* (Old Norse *kǫttr*, cat + Shetland *moget*, having the belly of a certain colour, different from that of the body, Norwegian *mage*, Old Norse *magi*, stomach), used of an animal with a light-coloured body and darker belly and legs, reddish-brown or *moorit* (Norwegian dialectal *moraud*, Old Norse *mórauðr*, reddish, yellow-brown, of sheep or wool), black and white, *shaela* (Norwegian *hela*, hoar-frost) or a silvery grey, greyish-brown or bluish-grey colour, or piebald. White-wooled sheep were rare. Fleeces in Bressay, Burra and Quarff weighed out at 1 to 3 lb.[1005] A writer of the 1870s noted that Orkney fleeces were seldom over $1\frac{1}{2}$ to 2 lb. The Orkney sheep themselves weighed about 4 to 6 lb a quarter. They had very short bodies and legs, long necks, 3 in. (8 cm) tails, and white or grey faces. Only a few had horns.[1006]

As early as 1724 the entrepreneurial enterprise of the Traills in Orkney was encouraging them to build a waulk mill, for previously the cloth was not good and had been thickened or waulked only with the hands. The waulk mill was probably intended for flax rather than wool, however. The main form of wool processing remained on a small domestic scale, as an easy source of additional income and as a basis for barter with the merchants who set up their booths in the islands each summer. The Hollanders bought many stockings in both Shetland and Orkney in the 1600s. Knitted gloves were added to fine stockings in the 1700s, and in 1767 the list of exports from Shetland including 50,000 pairs of stockings at 6d per pair, worth £1,250, and rugs and fine stockings, worth £400, and linen, meal and malt were being bartered in Shetland by the people of Holm in Orkney for fish, wool, and coarse stockings.[1007] The Irish fishing fleet lying at Deerness in summer traded for gloves and stockings,[1008] so the Orcadians either kept the coarse Shetland stockings for themselves and sold their fine ones, or else resold the Shetland produce. There was already appearing a greater emphasis on knitting in Shetland than in Orkney, with more diversification of products, for the Shetlanders were also making night-caps and rugs, sometimes used to cover beds, though apt to gather dust. They seem to have been peculiar to Shetland. They were of different coloured worsteds sewn

225. Mrs Robert Jamieson of Sloag, Foula, 1902. Photo. H B Curwen.

on to a very coarse ground, of various patterns some of which were in imitation of carpets. They cost from 16/– or 18/– to £2.2/–, whilst the coarse stockings that formed a very big article of trade fetched 6d to 8d a pair in 1774. Lerwick was the centre of the trade. 'Single stockings' were exported from North-mavine. The colours of the wool came from native dyes. A reddish-purple dye, corcolit, was got from rock scurfs, *Lich. tartareus*, ground to a powder and soaked in urine for several days. It was made up into balls of 1½ lb, ready for use. The worsted was boiled in it as long as was necessary to get the depth of colour required. A yellowish brown was got from Old Man, *Lich. saxatilis*, and yellow from heath. These dyes were being produced in Foula. As yet there is no indication that Fair Isle had any special claim to fame in respect of native dyes. Rugs or woollen bed covers were being made in Lerwick itself in the 1790s.[1009]

In Orkney some of the country folk who brought goods to the Lammas Fair for sale to merchants from Moray and elsewhere evidently had looms, for they

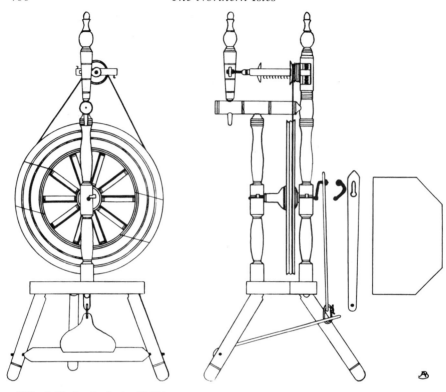

226. A Shetland spinnie. C1624.

made blankets as well as stockings and caps. Fine worsted stockings and coarse woollen goods were traded with the Dutch and Danish herring busses, and there was also a 'petty commerce' with Edinburgh, Newcastle, London, Norway, Hamburg, Spain and Portugal.[1010] The world was wide for these little islands. The sale of garters from Shetland[1011] indicates the existence of a garter loom, possibly of a type that survived in Fair Isle into the twentieth century. In 1791 both women and children worked on stocking making in Shetland with wires, getting 4d a pair, rather less than in 1774. Blankets and coarse cloth were also made in Shetland, but mainly for home use. It was the stockings, gloves, mitts, night-caps and garters that were sold or bartered in Lerwick.[1012] By the 1790s knitted goods were ceasing to be listed amongst the exports of Orkney though in some areas such as Sandwick and Stromness woollen stuffs and cloths were made for home use, and knitted stockings were sold to sailors at 1/6 to 5/– a pair.[1013] Stockings continued to be widely made in Shetland, and wool spun on household spinning wheels. The lower classes wore the coarse, home-made cloth, and tanned sheepskins served as oilskins for the fishermen. Scottish or English cloths were becoming more frequent, however, for Sunday clothes.[1014] In Birsay and Harray there were no fewer than 58 weavers, most of whom handled linen, and only a few wool. Here the old men and women still wore black clothes of coarse undyed *vadmell* or *wadmal* (Old Scots *vedmell*, 1506; Norwegian *vadmål*, Old Norse *vaðmál*, from *vad*, cloth + *mál*, measure), formerly woven on an upright loom, the *upgastang* (up + go + Old Scots *stang*, pole, 1508; Old Norse *stǫng*), but on Sundays the young men went in for south country clothes with cotton waistcoats, and corduroy breeches, and some had cotton or thread stockings. They wore hats instead of bonnets, and buckles had become universal on their shoes. The women, for Sunday or holiday wear, had calicoes and calamancoes or neat stuffs, with grey or brown or scarlet cloaks, and some scarlet plaids. Shoes and stockings had almost ceased to be home-made.[1015]

About 1800 in Shetland, the women knitted stockings and mittens when they were not working in the fields, selling the stockings at 4d to 5d a pair, or fine ones at up to 30/– or 40/–. The clothes commonly worn by the poorer folk were of wool. Flannel was made of soft sheep's wool. The fishermen wore dressed sheepskin, wool side in, with large boots tanned and made by themselves. Fair Isle men in a boat wore a night-cap on their head, a flannel coat and breeches, and no shoes or stockings. For church they had linen shirts, scarlet cloth or fancy cotton vests, corduroy breeches, and coats of English cloth, and the women wore printed cotton gowns, and red plaids or cloaks. It was said that vanity characterised the Shetlander, and avarice the Orkneyman. Comment was also made later on the Shetland passion for dress. The women and girls of Quendale in Shetland wore scarlet petticoats of wadmal in 1842.[1016]

By 1808, much of the Orkney wool was used at home in the form of blankets, coarse cloth, and stockings, especially in the country. In the towns, most folk had come to wear English cloth. In the 1840s, most of the cloth in Westray was from their own sheep, dyed if it was to be worn. Woollen cloth was chiefly made for blankets. In Northmavine and in Walls, Shetland, everyday dress and blankets were home-made, and Sunday dress of Scotch or English cloth. The produce of stockings and gloves was valued at £60. In Bressay, Burra and Quarff, the manufacture of Shetland hosiery was 'carried on by the industrious', though not in as great quantities as formerly. The same was said of Unst, where the women produced stockings and gloves highly prized for their softness and beauty of texture. Though the demand had gone down, much was still sold. Stockings fetched 1/– to 10/– a pair, the very finest £2; gloves from 1/– to 10/– and even up to 15/– a pair. Wadmal, dyed blue, black or red, constituted the bulk of the daily wear of men and women. The spinning of native wool was done straight from the sheep, without washing.[1017]

The growth of the Shetland woollen trade as an organised cottage industry has its origins in 1790, when the recently formed Highland and Agricultural Society of Scotland appointed a Committee to consider the subject. At this period an estimate of 100,000 sheep was made[1018] and since in 1814 the estimate was for about 70–80,000 a small decline in numbers seems to be realistic, though a rapid growth, with different emphasis, ensued later in the nineteenth century:

227. Carding and spinning in Shetland. Photo. J D Rattar. 3.43.21.

228. A horizontal wheel and a hank-winder in Orkney. By courtesy of the Orkney County Library.

Source	Year	No.
Shirreff 1814b. 62	1814	70,000–80,000
Department of	1870	80,631
Agricultural	1880	78,284
Returns (in	1890	98,300
O'Dell 1939. 98)	1900	110,037
	1910	153,014
	1920	140,150
	1930	160,876
	1936	168,209

Shetland wool became a matter of prestige in Edinburgh, and this in turn boosted the hosiery industry in Shetland. By 1797 its annual value was estimated at £17,000. About 1870, a fashion started for weaving Shetland cloth in its natural colours, whereas dyeing had been the norm previously. This was done as a cottage industry, merchants supplying the raw materials and buying back the finished goods, so that the weavers were entirely bound to them. As long as this truck system was in vogue, there were two prices, one the price for cash, and one the price for credit for material delivered, whether woven cloth or hosiery. Credit was usually paid in goods, at equivalents often well below the true value of the commodities, and the producers finished up in a state of perpetual debt. The system of barter was logical, for hosiery had long been used as a form of currency, but the growth of a prestige market opened the eyes of merchants to the possibility of commercial profit, particularly after the knitting of fine woollen shawls and later on of veils and other fancy goods led to a large demand from about 1845 onwards. Goods given in lieu consisted usually of tea, soap, or fine clothes, and some cash might be given or more often a 'line' or credit note, which could itself be sold at a lower value to another when the knitter ran short of meal and other provisions. The possible range of abuses is obvious and resulted in the Truck Acts which followed an inquiry by the Truck Commissioners in Shetland in 1872.[1019]

Knitting did not maintain a consistent impetus from the 1790s onwards. At first its value dropped to an income of only £5000 in 1809, and it was only with the appearance of finer, more specialised items in the 1840s that the cash flow increased. By the 1870–80s, £10,000 to £12,000 a year was being brought in, and specialisation was appearing in different areas. Soft underclothing was made in Northmavine, stockings in Nesting, haps and socks in Walls and Sandsting, fancy coloured gloves in Whiteness and Weisdale, shawls and veils in Lerwick, tweed in Northmavine, Delting and Lunnasting. By 1911, Shetland hosiery, including Fair Isle hosiery which had now become a thing in itself, and Shetland rugs, brought in £30,390, even though this was a relatively poor year.[1020] The industry has subsequently gone from strength to strength, drawing on the innate skill of Shetland knitters and the inherent qualities of the wool of Shetland sheep.

229. Parts for spinning wheels were made on turning lathes like this one in Foula, 1902. Photo. H B Curwen.

Work was done communally whenever possible, and this led to the development of the function known as a *cairdin*, when a family had wool ready for carding by hand, which was easy to do with Shetland wool. A group of women would be invited for tea in the afternoon, then carding and talking went on till about 11 o'clock in the evening, when supper-time came. At this point young men would arrive and dancing went on till the small hours of the morning. Mechanisation of this and other processes had begun by 1914, however, for example in the plant of Messrs. Thomas M. Adie & Sons, at Voe in Delting.[1021]

Fair Isle hosiery probably represents the most direct link with the old knitting industry in its much more widespread form, and sticks to hand-carding, hand-spinning, and dyeing with vegetable dyes. It also preserves designs that have otherwise vanished, though they are part of a wider European tradition. In 1914 the Fair Isle women were knitting mainly night-caps, Tam o' Shanters and men's jerseys, and only subsequently has a greater degree of sophistication developed.[1022]

NORTH RONALDSAY SHEEP

North Ronaldsay, the most northerly of the Orkney island group, has a breed of sheep that is discussed almost as much in print as the sheep of St Kilda. A 5 to

230. A garter loom, drawn in a house in Birsay, *c.* 1911, by G. Ellison. 4.13.19.

231. The remains of a garter loom at Barkland, Fair Isle. 1.28.2.

6 ft (1.5–1.8 m) high dyke built right round the 12-mile perimeter of the island, corresponding to the hill dyke of other areas, keeps the sheep clear of the township's arable and grass, and seaweed is their chief source of food. In summer they feed most on seaweed laid bare at low ebb, and in winter much food is driven ashore by the storms, so that they are at their prime during Christmas and the New Year. In other parts of Orkney, sheep ate seaweed on occasions, but in North Ronaldsay it constitutes their main diet and it is said there that sheep fed solely on seaweed thrive better than those fed on grass.

The building and maintenance of the dyke has involved much community effort, and both the dyke and the system of sheep husbandry it represents is practically the sole remnant today of the old communal system of agriculture in Orkney.[1023]

232. Weaving in Fair Isle, Shetland. Per J. Tweedie. 30.17.28.

Under favourable conditions, the sheep might live for up to ten years or more, having different names applied to it according to its sex and age. A last year's lamb is a *hog* (in Old Scots from 1306), a two-year-old female a *gimmero* (Old Scots from fifteenth century; Old Norse *gymbr*, ewe-lamb, Swedish dialectal *gimmer*, *gemmer*, a sheep that has not yet borne lambs, Norwegian dialectal *gimber*, young sheep), and older females are simply *yowes* (ewes). Two- or three-year old males are described as being 'under the second oo (wool)', or 'under the third oo'.

In Orkney generally, sheep of this type, which had disappeared almost everywhere except in North Ronaldsay by the mid-nineteenth century, were known as 'bussie broos' (bushy brows), or as *keery* or *keero* sheep, a word apparently derived from Gaelic *caora*, a sheep, *ciora*, a pet sheep, and found in Caithness in the form *cairie* or *kairie*, a small breed of sheep with wool of mixed colours, presumably similar to the old Orkney type. The occurrence of the name on both sides of the Pentland Firth certainly implies traffic across it, and

233. Preparing the warp in Fair Isle. Per J. Tweedie. 30.17.25.

the importation of half-bred sheep from Caithness into Orkney is known from about 1840,[1024] though there is no evidence that the word is much older than this in Orkney.

The number of sheep in North Ronaldsay is something over 2000. In the 1790s there were 1900, in 1883, 2000,[1025] and in the 1902 *Native Sheep Regulations* a total of 2302, made up of 2122 to tenants, 65 to non-tenants, 10 each to the official Sheep-men, and 15 to the Registrar. The numbers have remained fairly stable over the last two centuries. The regulations are no longer being strictly enforced, and no attempt has been made to check the scores for a number of years past.

The sheep are free to wander round most of the foreshore except for the part cut off by dykes, called *furvos* (origin obscure), carried out to the head of steep drops at Doo Geo and Roof Geo, about 200 yards (183 m) apart, marking off a section of foreshore reserved for the Holland Farm sheep. In general, however, the sheep tend to stick to their own part of the beach, which is known as their

234. Warping the threads in Fair Isle. Per J. Tweedie. 30.17.26.

clowgang (Old Norse *klaufa gangr*, tramp of cattle, from *klaufa*, cloven footed animal, + *gangr*, a walking; cf. Faroese *gonga*, flock of sheep that graze together), a word elsewhere applied to the pasture-land or sheep-walk of a township, or to a township's group of sheep, which kept by themselves in moving from one area of pasture to another. In 1623, the *clowgang* was equated with the commonty.[1026]

The three periods of activity, apart from lambing, were during the pundin's when the sheep were driven into the pounds situated at nine points along the surrounding dyke. These were the Inglasgoe pund, the Snatan pund, the Hangie pund, Irestaing pund, Backness pund, Geo-o'-Rue pund, Bridesness pund, Stromness pund and Twingness pund. When pundin was due to begin, a recognised signal, such as a straw cubbie, or a sackful of straw at the end of a pole, was put up for each district. This was known as a *waft*, and on its appearance the personnel gathered at the shore.

In other parts of Orkney the signal was a *beulding pin*, a piece of wood about 8 in. long, $1\frac{1}{2}$ in. broad, and $\frac{1}{2}$ in. thick ($20 \times 4 \times 1.3$ cm), with a hole in one end to which a string was fastened, sent from house to house as a reminder that the *beulding* (Old Norse *ból*, pen for cattle or sheep, *bøla*, to pen cattle for the night) or poinding was about to begin.[1027] Dogs were not much used to drive the sheep. Instead, the time of a flood tide was chosen so that the space between the water and the sheep-dyke was as narrow as possible, and the drivers came behind the sheep, rattling tin cans together and making a great deal of noise, the faster ones keeping right up on the tails of the sheep to give them no time to think and break back. Once the sheep were in the pund, the opening was built up quickly with stones.

The Hogmanay or New Year pundin took place at the Dennis Head pund, to select sheep for killing, generally three or four to a house. Killing or butchin' took place as a rule when the sheep were five or six years old. The meat is dark in colour, with a characteristic flavour. They were worked most economically when five fleeces were taken off them before killing, though they were more tasty for eating at three or four. Fewer sheep are now being eaten.

The pundin for shearing was in late June–July, sometimes into August, depending on when the tides were suitable. The bigger sheep were clipped at the end of June, and the smaller ones left until the new wool or lith had developed between the old fleece and the skin, usually not until they were over a year old. Until the lith developed, shearing was difficult, giving rise to a saying 'to clip hard at the aal' oo'' (old wool) in relation to a task that could not be accomplished without effort. The word rooin' is here used by a transference of sense for clipping with the shears or a pair of scissors, indicating a change at some time in the method of removing fleeces. The wool itself is of good quality, but low in quantity, for a fleece weighs only 2–3 lb, with a wastage of almost 50 per cent in scouring.[1028]

The pundin for scoring, i.e. for keeping a tally of the number of sheep, was in February. The score was kept by the laird's factor. Two sheep men were appointed by each township district, of which there are six – Busta, Nesstun,

Hollandstun, Linklettun, Ancumstun (locally always called Eboy) and Eastin' or East-North Yards. As the sheep were driven through the gate of the pund, the two sheep men shouted out the names of the owners, as indicated by the sheep marks, and the clerk ticked them off in his score-book.

The North Ronaldsay Native Sheep Regulations of 1902 gives the score for each of the seventy-one crofts and farms at that date. Since then, however, many units have fallen empty, as indicated by an asterisk in the Table below. The 1902 Regulations are a revise of those of 1839 and 1873, on the enforcement of which 'considerable difficulty and inconvenience' had arisen, and result from a discussion between a deputation of tenants and the Proprietor, W H Traill, at Holland House, on 30 October 1902, when it was agreed that in the future, as in the past, tenants alone should have the privilege of keeping sheep on the shores of the island, except for the portion permanently allocated to Holland Farm. The numbers of sheep were reapportioned as follows:

1902 APPORTIONMENT

Holland	60	Claypows	30	Nether Linay	50
Howar	60	Scotsha'	25	Westness	60
Cruesbreck	60	Phisligar	27	*Nether Breck	10
Kirbest	60	Greenspot	25	Senness	25
*Bridesness	25	Greenspot	25	Lochend	25
*Greenwall	50	*South Gravity	20	*Midhouse	20
Greenwall	20	*North Gravity	30	*Conglabist	25
*Howatoft	30	Sangar	30	Quoybanks	25
Cursetter	20	North Manse	30	Sandback	25
Cavan	20	Verracott	30	Scottigar	25
*Nessmuir	20	Purtabreck	40	Rue	25
*Viggay	25	Waterhouse	30	Vincoin	25
*Breckan	20	Milldam	20	Dennis Hill	25
Treb	20	*Cauldhame	30	*Grind	25
*Stenabreck	25	*Sugarhouse	10	*Sholtisquoy	25
Southness	25	Roadside	25	*Westhouse	25
*North Ness	25	Barrenha'	30	Garso	25
*Newbigging	45	Holm	30	*Garso	25
Gerbo	20	Ancum	40	*Bewan	20
*Gateside	25	Upper Cott	40	*Seaside	20
*Gateside	20	Upper Linnay	50	*Parkhouse	20
Peckhole	60	Burray	25	Neven	20
*Hooking	60	*Brigg	25	Antabreck	40
*The Mills	15	*Longar	45		

2122

* Farms empty 1965.

Parts of the 1902 Regulations have been published previously,[1029] but the whole document is reproduced here since it gives a clear picture of the community organisation in relation to the system of sheep husbandry and maintenance of the sheep dyke.

North Ronaldsay Native Sheep Regulations

1902

REGULATION FIRST. One Sheep Mark only shall be held and marked on, by each of the Tenants Aforementioned, and no other persons whatever shall have the right to keep Sheep on the shores of the island except on production of written consent from the Proprietor to do so.

SECOND. Each Tenant shall, on or before the first day of February next, record his Sheep Mark in the Sheep Book, and receive extract of such record from David Knight, who is hereby appointed Registrar.

THIRD. Whatever Hoggs found in Spring 1903, or in any year following, when the Sheep are numbered, marked with any mark not recorded as above, shall be forfeited and sold by the Sheepmen, the proceeds to be handed over to the 'Nursing Fund'.

FOURTH. The Sheep shall be allowed free passage round the whole shores of the Island, except between 'Doo Geo' and 'Roof Geo', or natural bridge.

FIFTH. The Tenants shall be bound, whenever called upon by the Sheepmen, to repair and keep up the whole outside dykes, and they shall be obliged to do so in proportion to the number of Sheep they have the right of keeping.

SIXTH. Any Tenant refusing or delaying to build up his share of the dykes when called upon, the Sheepmen are hereby authorized to execute the necessary work at his expense, four pence per hour per man being the rate fixed for such work; and if the Tenant refuses to pay, his Sheep shall be forfeited and sold by the Sheepmen to defray the cost, and the balance, if any, handed over to the 'Nursing Fund'.

SEVENTH. Any Tenant who shall forego and wholly give up his right of keeping Sheep now and in all time coming, and shall subscribe a minute in the Sheep Book to that effect, shall be freed and relieved from the burden of keeping up any part of the outside dykes, and be at liberty to use all legal means for his defence against their encroachments, and to make the whole Tenants, conjunctly and severally, liable for damages sustained.

EIGHTH. No Native Sheep shall be allowed inside the dykes except the ewes during the lambing season and any such Sheep or Lambs which are kept inside the dykes, if found straying loose at any time, shall be forfeited and sold, and the proceeds paid into the 'Nursing Fund'.

NINTH. The Sheep shall be numbered in the month of February of each year, and the Sheep found over the number allowed to be kept by the Tenants respectively shall be forfeited, and such forfeiture shall be taken out of the Hoggs, and out of the older Sheep only when the number of Hoggs do not cover the surplus. Any Sheep so forfeited shall be sold by the Sheepmen, and the proceeds given to the 'Nursing Fund'.

TENTH. A man from every house shall attend at each poind on the public appointed poind-days and if ruled otherwise, or in any other place, it must be done in the presence of one of the Sheepmen. Any Tenant infringing the Regulation shall be fined the sum of five shillings such sum to be paid to the 'Nursing Fund'.

ELEVENTH. No Sheep shall be killed in the Island without first being shown to one of the Sheepmen.

TWELFTH. No Lambs shall be taken from the Ewes until they first have been marked; and after being marked, they must remain with the Ewes for four and twenty hours.

THIRTEENTH. No dogs shall be allowed in the nesses for two and a half months, beginning on the fifth of April and ending thirtieth June, and no straying dogs at any other time. Any dogs doing damage shall be shot by the Sheepmen of the township where found.

FOURTEENTH. No binding or shackling of Sheep shall be allowed in any of the nesses, but the owners shall make their dykes above sheep-leaping height, according to the several divisions authorized and apportioned by the number of their Sheep.

FIFTEENTH. Two Sheepmen from each of the five townships, and one from Hollandstoun, shall be elected by the districts respectively to carry out and enforce the foregoing Regulations, strictly honestly, and without fear or favour. The first election of Sheepmen shall take place on the sixteenth day of December 1902, and the next election on the second TUESDAY of November 1907, and so on, every five years thereafter on the second Tuesday of the month of November.

SIXTEENTH. Each of the duly appointed Sheepmen shall be allowed to keep ten Sheep over and above his allotted number as a remuneration for his trouble, but shall not be bound to uphold dykes for more than his statutory number as appearing against his name. The outgoing Sheepmen to have twenty-four months from the date of the election of new Sheepmen in which to get rid of their extra ten Sheep.

SEVENTEENTH. New Sheepmen are to be sworn in before a Magistrate or a Justice of the Peace.

EIGHTEENTH. The Sheepmen in portioning off the dykes that each house has to maintain, are not to take into consideration the dykes round Planticruives or Enclosures outside the Sheep Dyke – these are to be maintained by the Tenants themselves.

NINETEENTH. All disputes regarding dykes and Sheep that the Sheepmen cannot settle may be referred to the Proprietor, or, in his absence, to his Factor, whose decision will be final. The Registrar, for his services, shall be allowed to keep fifteen Sheep without being called upon to keep up any share of the dykes.

It was unanimously agreed that the following Non Tenants shall have the privilege of keeping Sheep to the Numbers appearing against their names, provided always that they strictly adhere to the foregoing regulations along with the Tenants; but the Proprietor reserves the right to disallow this privilege at any time, with power to him to grant a similar privilege to any other person he may think fit.

Names of the Non Tenants allowed to keep Sheep and the Numbers.

W. Tulloch. Upperbreck	10
Sibella Tulloch. do	10
Thos. Tulloch. Cruesbreck	10
Peter Swanney. Nessmuir	10
John Tulloch. Longar. Now at Rue	15
Janet Tulloch. do	10
	65

All previous rules are hereby cancelled.

(Sgd.) William H. Traill,
Proprietor.

THE LUG MARKS OF NORTH RONALDSAY SHEEP

The ten basic sheep marks of the various crofts and farms are the *axe* and *stair axe*, the *drawn hemling* and *stooed hemling*, the *bit* and *thumb bit*, the *shear*, the *piece off*, the *rip* and the *crook*. An eleventh, the *scart*,[1030] is now obsolete. These are the major marks, visible to the eye at a reasonable distance. In addition, most owners have a hole or small bit or two so arranged that if the ear was damaged it would still be possible to determine ownership.

Many more combinations of these marks are possible, and would have been necessary in the days of higher population. The number of inhabitants has declined so much, and so many crofts have fallen empty and their land and stock been taken over by the next of kin or heirs of the deceased, that many have gone out of use.

LIST OF SHEEP MARKS, 1934

(Compiled by Willie Swanney, North Manse, and collated with a list by John Muir, Roadside. Marks on the left ear are given first, the sheep being seen face on).

1. Bewan.   Thumb bit behind, three rips (stooed).
2. Rue   (a) Shear, three rips.
         (b) Stair Xs behind, hemlin before and hole.
3. Vincoin.   Axe behind, piece down off.
4. Scottigar.   Stooed hemlin behind, thumb bit behind.
5. Sholtisquoy.   Axe behind, crook behind.
6. Sennes.   Thumb bit before, stooed hemlin before.
7. Lochend.   Rip, stooed hemlin before.
8. Garso.   (a) Stooed hemlin behind, thumb bit before.
            (b) Rip, crook behind.
9. Seaside.   Piece down off and bit behind, cross bits.
10. Sandback.   Rip, axe.
11. Dennis Hill.   X before and bit behind, hemlins before and behind.
12. Grind.   Shear, axe behind.
13. Quoybanks.   Hemlin before, piece down off and bit behind.
14. Midhouse   Two bits behind, rip.
15. Neven.   Three rips, shear and bit behind.
16. Parkhouse.   Four bits, three rips.
17. Nether Breck.   Axe, four bits (J.M.).
18. Westness.   X behind and bit before, three rips.
19. Nether Linay.   Stooed hemlin before, thumb bit before.
20. Brigg.   X behind, on both ears.
21. Upper Linay.   Piece off and bit behind, X behind and hole.
22. Cott.   Stooed hemlin before, thumb bit behind.
23. Longar.   Hemlin before and hole, stair Xs before.
24. Ancum.   Hemlin before and bit behind, on both ears.
25. Burray.   Hemlins, shear.
26. North Manse.   Piece off and bit behind, three rips.
27. Verracott.   Piece off and bit behind, stooed rip.
28. Antabreck.   Shear and bit behind, crook behind and bit before. This mark was started in 1933.
29. Purtabreck.   Bit before, bit off the top and four bits.

30. Sangar. Shear, piece down off.
31. North Gravity. Piece off and bit behind, two bits behind.
32. South Gravity. Shear, rip.
33. Greenspot. (a) Three rips, X behind.
                (b) Rip, crook behind.
34. Waterhouse. Stooed rip and cross bits, cross bits.
35. Milldam. Three rips, piece off and bit behind.
36. Phisligar. Shear, X before and hole.
37. Barrenha'. X behind, hemlins.
38. Scotsha'. Piece off, shear.
39. Holm. Hemlins, X behind.
40. Cauldhouse. Cross bits, stooed rip and cross bits.
41. Hooking. Shear, hemlins.
42. Stenabreck. No entry. Empty from the 1920s.
43. Bridesness. Thumb bit behind, stooed hemlin before.
44. North Ness. Piece off and bit before, on both ears.
45. South Ness. Three rips, hemlins.
46. Newbigging. Hemlin before and hole, on both ears.
47. Gerbo. Piece down off, X before.
48. Peckhole. (a) Crook behind and bit before, shear.
             (b) Piece down off and bit behind, on both ears.
49. Claypows. Hemlins, X before.
50. Nessmuir. X before and hole, shear.
51. Gateside. (a) Two bits before, rip.
             (b) Thumb bit before, stooed hemlin behind.
52. Viggay. Three rips, on both ears.
53. Breckan. Two bits behind, shear (J.M.).
54. Cavan. X behind, shear.
55. Cursiter. Axe, two holes (J.M.).
56. Howatoft. Thumb bit behind, stooed hemlin behind.
57. Kirbest. Three rips, four bits.
58. Cruesbreck. X before, piece off and hole.
59. Greenwall. (a) Three stooed rips, thumb bit behind.
              (b) Two bits behind and a hole, shear.
60. Howar. Thumb bit before, three stooed rips.
61. Nouster. Three rips, X before and bit behind.
62. Twingas or Twingness. Hemlin before, two stair axes behind (J.M.).
63. Lurand. Hemlins, three rips.
64. Holland. Stooed hemlin behind on both ears.
65. Mrs. Traill. X before and bit behind, three rips.
66. Treb. Rip, two bits behind.
67. Roadside. Piece off and cross bits, hemlins.

Six croft names, Greenwall, Greenspot, Garso, Gateside, Rue and Peckhole are entered twice. The first three are separate crofts, as was Gateside until a few years ago. Gateside is, in fact, one building, comprising two dwelling houses end to end, built as a unit. The occupiers of these crofts were originally close relations and Greenspot and Gateside are examples of crofts being divided between two sons. This took place well over a hundred years ago.[1031]

Mrs Traill, in number 65, was the wife of the proprietor. Like the Lady of Elsness in Sanday, she ran a flock of sheep on her own mark.

IDENTIFICATION MARKS ON ANIMALS

'All their Sheep are marked on the ears or Nose, every man that hath Sheep, hath his own whereby his Sheep are distinguished from others; and its strange to consider how so many different marks could be invented as are found cut in so little room.' In Orkney, as in Shetland, the ears were 'cut into a thousand different forms, to mark out the persons to whom they belong'.[1032] Identification marks were not confined to sheep, being also used on cattle and horses. In 1602 there were court cases in Shetland about the marking of year-old stirks. Two years later a man was fined for marking a 'quoyak' of his own one day after the appointed date, and the selling of an unmarked cow was judged to be theft. Marks were also used in the seventeenth century as safe-guards against dealing in stolen animals, for no flesh could be sold till the bailie had seen the beast and its mark and had noted the original owner's name.[1033] The apparent strictness of the system argues that there was a need for strictness.

The main emphasis, however, was on marking sheep, and to a lesser extent horses, for when these ran unherded, theft and confusion of ownership were easy. Cattle were more closely tied to the house and the need for marking was less. Their domestic integration is indicated by the number of calls to cattle (see page 438), but calls to sheep are limited to lambs, 'kiddie! kiddie!', *caddie*, *kiddo* and *tiddo*, all of similar origin. No calls to horses have been noted, except in Orkney *tur-tur*, to frighten one off. The pigs that rooted around the doors and in the kitchen were addressed as 'geesie! geesie' or 'geese-geese' (Norwegian dialectal *gis*, Swedish dialectal *giss*, call-word to swine), *koots* or *kutch* (both forms of the Shetland call to a calf, *kussie*), *pad*, *paddy*, *paddo*, *patty*, *patsie* or *poot*. Geese also had their call, *toots*, and hens *tikkie*,[1034] probably from the sound they make. Names and calls are not visible to the eye, however, and the creatures that ran in common outside the township dykes had to have their individual owners' marks.

In some instances, sheep, horses and cattle were on the same mark, in others, there were differences. In 1828, general marks for sheep, horses and cattle were specified for Andrew Manson in Oxnasetter, Eshaness, who had 'the Right ear a piece of the Top and two rifts the Left ear half away behind', and Margaret Jamieson in Lochend, who had 'Right Ear a piece of the Top and a piece out before, left ear a piece of the Top and half behind'. In 1845, Simon Robertson of Ollaberry's mark for cattle and sheep was 'a piece off each side of both ears and a hole on the right ear'.[1035] In 1860, George Bain, Cullivoe, Yell had a mark, 'Right Lug Rifted & a Bit on each side – the Left Lug the same,

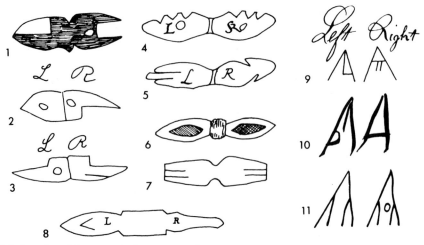

235. Samples of sheep marks from manuscript sources:

    1 Jas. Moar Jun[r]. Gloup Mark viz Right Lug Midled — (illegible).

    2 George Moar Gloup 1 mark viz the Right Lug half behind and a hol on it the Left lug knead and a hol on it and no more.

    3 And[w]. Manson in Kirkabister 1 mark viz the Right Lug half before and a Rift behind, the Left Lug half befor and a holl in it and no more.

    4 Alex[r]. Fordyce, Unst. — (illegible).

    5 And[w]. Fordyce Montulie — a crook before and a crook behind on the right and the left two rifts or three laps.

    1–5 from General List of All the Cattle Marks of North Yell.

    6 Johnson, Samuel – The heart of both Lugs cut out leaving the sides and top standing. June 16th 1856.

    7 Nesbit, William. Kongnaseter. The top off Both Lugs and two rifts in the cut of each. May 11th 1869.

    8 David Moar, Busta. May 21st 1883 — (illegible).

    6–8 from Register of Marks.

    9 Andrew Manson Oxnasetter His mark on Horses, sheep, and Cattle is the Right Ear an piece of the Top and tow (two) rifts the Left ear half away behind. 23 October 1828.

  10 Magnus Williamson in Mangaster his Mark on Horses Sheep and Cattle the right ear off at the Root. the left ear a rift and a bit out behind. 28 Jany 1825.

  11 Simon Robertson of Ollabery his mark on Cattle and Sheep is a piece off each side of both ears and a hole on the right ear. 6 May 1845.

    9–11 from The Marks, or Characters, on the People of Northmavine's Cattle.

Given to him by his aunt ... who brought it from Fetlar where it had been used as a horse mark'. Marks, therefore, belonged to families earlier on, and became attached to the individual crofts and farms later. Marks could also be sold, like the sheep mark sold by Miss B B Irvine of Midbrake to Lodwick Danielson of Lingarth, Yell, in 1872. In 1851, James Clark in Yell had as a horse mark, half behind and two bits before on the right lug, and half before on the left. His sheep mark was slightly different, however, being half behind and a rift before on the right and half before on the left.[1036]

Some control of the numbers of marks came from the fact that they related to scattalds or clowgangs belonging to particular neighbourhoods. The same marks could be repeated in a different area, so that overall, a relatively small number of marks in a variety of combinations was sufficient.

In 1299, an Ordinance known as Soid Brevet, 'the note or letter about sheep', was promulgated by King Haakon in relation to the Faroe Islands, and since a copy was sent to Mr Sifvort, Provincial Judge of 'Hetland',[1037] it is likely that it was intended to cover Shetland as well. In 1637 when it was re-enacted by King Christian iv of Denmark, no mention of Shetland was made. Nine points were made:

1. *To know Sheep*. We have been informed of a bad custom that hath been in the land more than it should, about sheep; neither ought we to have suffered it so, but rather let every one be contented with his own, as it belongeth to him, according to Law. Now it is so, that if two men or more have sheep in one close (field or pasture) and both will kill their sheep, each taketh what he can get that is not marked, with dogs or otherwise, whether it be lamb or old sheep and whether it belong to him or no. Now of this it seemeth unto us and other good men, that it ought not to be so; and that nothing unlawful be begun in the Land, we therefore make this Ordinance thereupon. That if any will take out his lambs and old sheep that are not marked, he must produce two impartial witnesses that they are his sheep, and that they know their dam; if he wants such witnesses, let him be as owing nothing therein.

2. *Taking away another mans Sheep*. Now if any man goeth into another mans field or close, and drives away his sheep to his damage, so that it be worth half a mark, he must answer the full price to him that owneth the close, as he is able, and to the King half a mark of silver, and restore the sheep as good as they were, and if a man accuseth another that he hath been in his field or close and done him damage, let him pay the damage if there be witnesses, according to the Sentence of lawful Judges, or deny it by lawful Oath, which 6 understanding men shall declare good; and let those to whom the sheep and close belongeth be warned and summoned three days before to the common pound, that is the enclosure wherein they use to drive their sheep; Let him that doth not appear lose his cause and be fin'd to the King two ortes of silver. Now let every man know that if any own close and sheep together, they must not have more dogs than honest men will judge fit; and if no dogs are agreed upon, let them be for their equal advantage.

3. *Of putting off Sheep that feed unlawfully*. Item, if the fields are situated together, and two men have each their Close or fields, and Sheep goe from the ones close into the others, being wont thereunto, and going therein always; and he that owneth the close will not suffer it, but speaks about it, he that owneth the sheep must take them out, and carry them all into his own close; but if the same sheep run into the same close a second and third time, those sheep shall belong no more to him that owneth them; except he that owneth the close will let out the field, whereupon the Sheep feed for a Gilder; but if he will take no

hire, he that owneth the sheep, take them out at his conveniencie within the space of twelve months; but if he that owneth the sheep will not proffer any hire, nor sell the half flock to him that owneth the close, let him forfeit his flock; which men should drive into the pound where they feed and each hold the pound open according as he hath part in the sheep. If it be done otherwise, let them be fined 3 Ortes of silver to the King, and damage paid to him that receiveth damage, according to the Law. If men are together in a common pound (that is the inclosure wherein they drive sheep together) let each one mark his lambs according as the dam belongeth to him, and look how many there be that have two lambs; and if there be any strange sheep in that pound, the shepherds must take notice how many have lambs, and mark the lambs of every one as many have lambs and are not gelded; but if any mark sheep false, let him have his sheep that owneth it, when it is well known, or the equivalent; for he forfeits nothing that marketh amiss in the same pound.

4. *Of wild Sheep.* If men own wild sheep together in one close, and some will make their sheep tame, and others will not; let them chuse that will have their sheep tame, and bid a price to the rest, that will pay for them both, and let him rule his sheep that owneth tame sheep, and if there cometh wild amongst them, let him hinder it, and not let wild sheep come amongst the tame; but if he slips wild sheep amongst the other tame ones, let him therefore undergo the Law, and, pay the Adversaries fine according to Law, and 3 Ortes of silver to the King, and then let every one make tame his sheep, which are left in the close.

5. *If any goeth alone in another mans close.* If any man goeth in a close without sending word or warning him that hath Sheep in the same Close and marks the Sheep or Lambs of any, putting his mark upon them that were not marked before, without telling the owner of it, he hath marked in secret. Therefore let him pay to him that owneth according to sentence, and to the King 3 Ortes of Silver, if it be worth Ortes, but if it be less, let him be declared a dishonest man. Further more, if he marketh Sheep that were marked before and puts his mark upon the mark of him that owneth them, then he is a thief.

6. *Of Dogs.* If any man taketh along with him in the Fields or Closes any Dog that bites other mens Sheep, let him give the owner as good Sheep again; but if he biteth oftener, let him pay as if he had killed it; but if the Dogs that are consented to indamage any Sheep, let the man whom the Dog followeth give as good Sheep again, and have afterwards a good care of his Dog. They are pernicious Dogs that bite Sheep more than once, and some go out of themselves to kill Sheep. There ought to be as many Sheep in a Close as there hath been formerly, except one can see that the Close can feed more; then let as many be put in as will be agreed upon, and no more in each Field, neither Sheep nor Kine than one knoweth to be just, and keep them in ones own Close and not in another mans, or answer for it according to Law.

7. *Of Interdiction concerning Sheep.* If a man lets his Sheep Feed or grow in another mans Close or Field, and will not cease, though he that owneth the Close will not suffer it; the owner must make interdiction thereupon. Whereof the first forbidding must be from St. Olaus week till St. Andrews day; and if the

Sheep be not then taken out of forfeiture, the proprietary thereof shall have a third part in the said Sheep.

The second interdiction is from St. Andrews day till Lent; if the sheep be not then taken out of forfeiture, the proprietary of the Close is then to have two parts in the said Sheep. The third interdiction is from Lent to St. Olaus week; if the Sheep be not then taken out of forfeiture, let the proprietary of the Close keep all the Sheep, except there have been great distress so that he could not take out his Sheep, though he would, yet in that case the proprietary of the Close shall be paid for it. That Sheep is Close fast where she brings a Lamb, and continueth the Winter over.

8. *How one must goe into a Close.* If the Closes or Fields are lying together, and the ones Sheep go into the others Close, let him that will go to divide the Fields, warn the other to meet him, or go together with him, following so together; if the one will not come or go, let him that warned him, go into his own close, and not in the others; but if he goeth to divide Fields, and in anothers Close, let him answer the other in Law for it, as if he had not warned him. But if he hath not given him warnings and goeth never-the-less, let him answer in Law the other that was at home since he doeth him wrong, and pay all the damage that is done that day, or by reason of his going, as also the adversaries Mulct, and 3 Ortes of silver to the King.

9. *How to tame Sheep.* If any have a Close or Field together wherein are wild Sheep, and some will make the Sheep tame, and others will not, let them chuse that will tame the Sheep, and will bargain for his Cattle, and not they that will pay for them both, or let those that will not make tame bear all the damage that can come thereof, except there hath been great calamity.[1038]

These early regulations contain much that is paralleled in the Country Acts and other enactments on the Northern Isles. They stress the need for identification marks and also demonstrate their practical necessity within the organisation of a community. But it is human to err and rules that give protection may themselves create offenders. Much of the information available on identification marks is due to transgressions of the law. In 1576, Henrie Spence in Yell had a servant who went to the *cruive* to mark his master's lambs, and got into trouble by marking one of the vicar's sheep by mistake.[1039] In 1602, a young boy called William Henderson marked a 'lamb of Erasmus Mansonis at his awin hand by (without) the knowledge of his nychbouris'. The owner got to know immediately and it was judged to be not exactly theft, yet for a first fault he was fined 4 marks to the king, the lamb was marked to be given to the king, and he had to give Erasmus a lamb of equivalent value. An appeal failed. In the same year Nicole Seter was fined for marking a neighbour's lamb, not knowing if it was his or not. In 1603, Andrew Stewart in Futabrughe mis-marked a lamb of James Johnson accidentally, and returned it immediately. In 1604, a lamb mis-marked by its owners, Olaw Manisoun and Magnus Jhonsoun, was ordered 'to be inbrocht to my lordis hous as escheit'. An honest man, Nicole Manisoun, marked another man's lamb and left another of the same hue in its place, having thought the first was his own. Some six-year-old hogs going unmarked in the hills of Northhouse were required to be brought to the lawthing. One Nicole in Papa Little and Nicole Manisoun had only one mark between them, and the *fold* or *foud* (Danish *foged*, Icelandic *fogeti*, Middle Low German *voget*, overseer, bailiff), originally an official of the Norwegian crown who presided at local Things or local councils and collected taxes, and later equivalent to the bailie, was ordained to make each of them have a 'kenning mark' different from the others'.[1040]

The earliest known document on lug marks is a manuscript preserved in the Kirkwall Free Library, entitled an *Act anent Sheep-marks within the Bishoprick of Orkney*, dated 1683. According to this, at a head court in Kirkwall, the Sheriff, Sir Alexander McKenzie, considered the complaints that had arisen because many families made use of several distinct marks, and many individuals of more marks than one, 'and thence aryses great prejudices contentiones sclanders and animosities amongst many in the country by the many several distinct and diversified sheip marks to mismark ther neighbours sheip and lambes and by the variousness of the said sheip marks some pairt or toacken or other cannot bot in some measure resemble ther neighbours sheip marks which is the ground of the many complaints and contentions in the country as said is'. Accordingly, the Sheriff, with the unanimous consent of the gentlemen present ordained 'all and sundry famillies within the said bishoprick to betack themselves to and make use of one Stock mark for ther sheip and dischairges (forbids) them to make use of any by mark or aithken so vulgarlie termed to ther children or freinds in ther famillie butt such as shall be approven of by the baillie of the parochine and marked with the said stock mark in the said baillie court books and warrands to be taken out be them from the said baillie for the saids by marks and aithkens'.

The same rule was also to apply to single persons. Infringement meant confiscation of the stock of sheep, a fine of £40 Scots (£3.5 sterling), and imprisonment. A five-year period of grace was allowed for getting stock properly marked, beginning with the following season's lambs (the Court was held on 12 January). These instructions were to be made known by the bailies at meetings summoned in the various bailiaries throughout the islands before 6 May following, so that no one would be able to plead ignorance as an excuse. Bailies who refrained from taking action were themselves to be punished.

This suggests that in the seventeenth century in Orkney generally there was a confusion similar to that in North Ronaldsay in the nineteenth century, which the local 1902 Regulations were designed to correct. The problem was constantly recurring, as a result of the splitting and amalgamation of families through inheritance, marriage, etc., and a multiplicity of marks left the way open for what one court book entry described as 'the abhominable cryme of thift', hence the restrictions on going with a sheepdog through a neighbouring scattald or commonty between the hours of sunset and sunrise, without giving previous notice of this intention.[1041]

Manuscripts in the Kirkwall Free Library throw light on eighteenth century local procedure on sheep husbandry and the ownership and transfer of marks. The earliest records the purchase of eight score ewes, lambs, and hogs by David Traill of Midgarth in Stronsay in 1719, at 19s. Scots (1s. 7d. sterling) per head. They were delivered to him before three witnesses, and he promised to pay within a certain period.

In 1720, there is an *Extract of Ane Act of Court of ane Sheep-mark in favour of David Traill of Migrath*, recording a meeting at St. Peter's Kirk, Stronsay. It states that:

'The ilk (same) day there was A Court holden by James ffea of Whitehal, Baillie, anent good Neighbourhood – Compeired David Trail of Migarth and gave in the Sheip mark as follows, The right Lugge cut off and an Ax behind the left Luge and ane hole under The Misness off which sheepmark as above was Intimate to the hail Inhabitants then present and no Objections made Why the said Mark should not be Sustained. Therefore the Baillie did Homologate and Confirm the said sheep mark to the said David Trail of Migarth in all time coming and Does heirby warrand the said David Trail of Migarth to mark his sheep there on as his proper Sheep mark in al time coming after the date heirof.'

In the island of Sanday in 1733, there is a disposition of a mark in the following terms:

'I Olipher Scott Lawfull Sone to Umquhile Thomas Scott Sometime Takes-man in Scare in Burness Parish in Sanday in Orkney. and fforasmuch as ther is ane Sheep Mark belonging to me by Right and propertie as recorded, quhich is ane clow in the Right Lugg with two Crooks: ane Hembling before in the Left and a Cruck behind with ane button on the Nose, which I be tener heirof doth freely dispone, Sell and Overgive my right Title propertie and pretentions to and in favours of Lawrens Calder Servtor to the Lady of Elsness ...'

This was done in the presence of four witnesses.

In the same island, another disposition was made by George Traill of Hobister to his daughter Sibilla Traill in June 1744, of 'a sheep mark belonging to me upon the pasturage of Sellibister, Being a piece off the Right Lug and a hole in said Lug, Three Lapps on the left Lug and a button on the nose, which Sheep mark formerly pertained to the deceased John Scott tenant in Cleatt in Lady parish and Island of Sanday, and was Comprized from him by two Lawright men, and allowed in part payment for what he was resting me for his said Labouring of Cleatt, as per his Accompt in my Compt book for Cropt 1740, Together also with three Sheep and two Ewes I have precently on said mark with powers to the said Sibilla Traill ... to mark thereon the use and dispose thereof at their pleasure in time coming. In witness whereof these presents are written by James Traill my Son and Subscribed by me att Eastburgh in Sanday ... Together with ffreedome of pasture for the sheep on said Geo: Traills mark, either in Sellibister or upon the ffidges'.

A third Sanday manuscript, dated 1737, records the mark of Patrick Traill of Elsness, 'a Clow and a Cross bitt in The Lefft Lug; And Ripp with a pice cutt down of the Right with a Button on the nose which is Insert in the Court Book in Lady Parioch on the said Elsness name in anno 1633'.

Amongst the remaining manuscripts are on-the-spot recordings of sheep belonging to different tenants in 1731–2, using the technique of upright strokes joined by a cross-stroke whenever the tally of uprights came to four; lists of the numbers of sheep on various grazings in the 1720–1730s, sorted by types (wethers, ewes, hogs) and colours (white, grey, black, tawny), and by ownership (the children's, a sister's, the farm grieve's); and a list of the lug marks of sheep, as follows:

An Acompt of the marks of the – Ouskeray Blonging to the famalay of Elsness, 2 June 1730.

On the Shear mark	39
More on the shear mark	59
On the axe mark	14
At the Clay Bought	14
On the mark of houal (Houll)	12
On the Houalis marke	11
On the heamlin marke	7
More	5
On the thrie Lape marke	2
More	4
On the ripe marke	4
More	4

In May of the same year, the Elsness family had the following numbers of sheep on the Holm of Midgarth:

On the Shear marke	210
On the axe marke	34
On the marke of howall	11
On the Stouake marke	10
On the Ripe marke	4
Marked on the Sheare mark – Of Lambes	72
Marked on the Axe marke	4
On the marke of howell	4
On the hemlin marke	4
On the Ripe marke	4

The family, therefore, had a total of 532 sheep on these two grazings, identified by seven lug marks.

All the Sanday lug marks are known in North Ronaldsay except that the 'thrie lape mark' of Sanday is now known in North Ronaldsay as 'two rips'. The modern North Ronaldsay mark, 'a piece down off' is an abbreviated form of 'a pice cutt down of', as in Patrick Traill's mark of 1737.

This eighteenth century evidence shows community activity in relation to the administration in the legal documentation of marks, the intimation of new or changed marks to the whole inhabitants, who were thereby made witnesses, the transfer of marks in the same way as pieces of property from one person to another (generally a relation), and the taking of a mark by two Lawrightmen or district officials (see Donaldson 1954. iv for details of these officers) in part payment of a debt, presumably since a man without a sheep mark had no legal right to keep sheep. The marking of sheep has remained a function of communal activity through the centuries. It is still done at the present day, but publicity is organised in a different way, hence announcements such as the following in a Shetland newspaper:

'I wish to use the following mark on my sheep: Right ear middle in, left ear two holes. Would anyone having any objections to this mark in the island of Yell, please contact me at the following address. David D. Hughson, Bugarth, Mid Yell.'[1042]

Though the medium is different, the effect is the same.

IDENTIFICATION MARKS ON OTHER PARTS OF THE BODY

In considering identification marks in general, it is necessary to bear in mind the repeated official efforts that have been made to simplify a system that tended to become recurrently confused, and to make it foolproof. The cumulative result has been to sweep away a variety of marks and combinations of marks, in particular marks (excluding keel) made on parts of the body other than the ears.

Sometimes a patch of cloth about three in. (8 cm) square was sewn on to the wool of the hip, a white patch on a black sheep, or black or grey on a white sheep. This was called a *clout* or *euchkin*.[1043] *Clout*, a Scots word, meaning a piece of cloth, patch, rag, was first recorded in the sheep mark of W. Nicholson of Orphir on the Mainland of Orkney in 1827: 'Right lug off, sheer mark a bit behind in left lug and tail off and a clout affore.'[1044] *Euchkin*, a variant of aithken, was equated with 'by-mark' in the Act of 1683 (see p. 480).

Marks made by attaching a piece of cloth or thread to some part of the body, or to the ear, were also used in Shetland, where the names *dram*, *laget*, and *kadel* were applied, and they have been recorded in the west of Scotland in the island of Arran in Bute, where thin strips of cloth, or thread, of various colours, were said to have been thrust through the external membrane of the skin. An early Shetland source refers to a sheep 'lugmerkit with ane peice clayth'.[1045]

In North Ronaldsay a little patch of cloth or a piece of wool of a different colour from that of the sheep was sometimes attached when the sheep were clipped in the summer to distinguish those that were to be slaughtered in winter. More commonly, however, a tuft of wool was left unclipped, for the same reason.

The nose of the sheep could be marked by slits, causing deformation of one or the other nostril. Such a slit was called a *rip*, *skirt*, *nos-skerd*, *nos-skerdin* or *teen*.[1046] Examples are:

Robert Langskeal, Blomore, Holm, for June 1750:
A prick mark in the left lug, a hole in the right lug, a bit before and a skirt in the right nostril.[1047]

Magy Gray, Tweenbreaks, Orphir, for 1827:
Three laps in right lug and left lug and tail off and rip in the nose.
Another Orphir mark of 1827, used by Harry Gray, Boull, was:
Crop in both lugs, a hole in right and the mid nose out.[1048]

There is also a seventeenth century mark used by Magnus Symondsone in the parish of St Andrews on the mainland of Orkney:

Ane black ew with a mark and helme before the left lug behind upon the right lugg and the midd nose out and the tail of (f).[1049]

Here, the 'mid nose out' must refer to a cut or notch in the septum, and is, therefore, a translation of the Norse word *misness* (Old Norse *misnesi*), of similar meaning, in the 1720 document (see page 481). Skirt corresponds to the second element in the Shetland words *nos-skerd (in)* and *gatskord*, the latter a combination of a hole and a slit in the ear. *Teen* is not otherwise recorded or paralleled, and may be a misprint or misreading.

Marks elsewhere on the face were the *button* and the *wool* or *oo*. The *button* was made by pinching up the skin on both sides of the nose till it stood out like a pea, then tying it round with a length of thread. It is mentioned in a Sanday document of 1733 and is remembered, though no longer used, in North Ronaldsay. The wool was made by cutting the flesh to the bone, and twisting it so that it rose like a wart or mole. The face was then described as *oowed*.[1050] This mark was used in 1813 by Isabella Langskaill, of Ingastock in Holm: 'Three laps in left lug, a bit behind, a bit behind in right lug and a wool on the face'.[1051]

Marwick has taken the past participial form *ood* to be substantive, though also giving the term *'oo ipo the face'*, and has erroneously suggested a derivation from Old Norse *hutt* or *hott*, the rounded top of an object.[1052] Oo, however, is the Lowland Scots vocalised form of 'wool', though it might, of course, derive from Old Norse *ull*, but again with Scots vocalisation.

Finally, a sheep could be marked by removal of the tail. Examples of marks involving the 'tail off' have been given above. A record from Skaill, dated November 1755, involves the transfer of a mark from Robert Graham of Breckness to Margaret Hourston, daughter of Alexander Hourston in Banziclete, in which part of the tail was removed: 'A bitt before on the right lugg and a rift on the left lugg, and a bitt of (f) the taile'.[1053]

TERMINOLOGY OF MARKS

(O = Orkney;   S = Shetland;   N = Northern Isles)

Afbreg(d), *Obregd* (S). To alter a sheep's lug marks: an additional differentiating mark in a sheep's ear, made for example when a flock changes hands.[1054] In 1829, sheep belonging to the mother of Thomas Irvine of Mid-

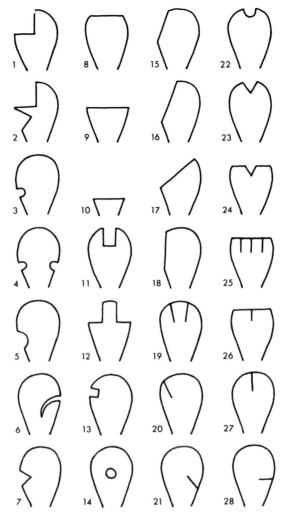

236. The range of sheep marks in the Northern Isles. C5929.

1 Axe. half, half (taken) up.
2. Stair axe.
3 Bit.
4 Cross bits, gong bits.
5 Thumb bit.
6 Crook (North Ronaldsay).
7 Crook (Nesting).
8 Crop off, bit off, kuivy,
    piece off, stoo.
9 Half off.
10 Aff at the root.
11 Middle, cut out of the middle.
12 Middle standing.
13 Witter (Nesting).
14 Hole.

15 Feather, piece taken (or drawn)
    up, side taken up.
16 Hemlin, drawn hemlin.
17 Stooed hemlin.
18 Strae draw.
19 Lap (three laps), three rips, two
    rifts, two rits, rit and three laps.
20 Fidder.
21 Hingin widder or fidder.
22 Scart.
23 Shear. shuil.
24 Skirt.
25 Four lops in the stump(1742).
26 Stooed rip, rit in the stoo.
27 Rip, rift, rit, rit and two laps.
28 Slit.

brake, out with Margaret Fraser, had an 'obregt' consisting of 'a slit behind the left Ear & a string in the left Ear, the House mark (without the hole) on both Ears'.[1055] From ?Old Norse *á*, to, additional, + Icelandic, Faroese *bragð*, Norwegian dialectal *bragd*, sheep mark.

Aff at the root (S).   Whole ear off.[1056] (Nesting).

Afmark (S).   An altered sheep mark,[1057] an 'off mark'.

Aithken, euchkin (O).   Old Norse auðkenni, einkenni, einkunn, a cattle mark, *einkynna*, to brand or mark sheep or cattle on the ears.[1058]

Anchor mark (O).   Used by Wilm. Gray, Croval, Orphir, in 1827, said to be formed of two triangular pieces cut out near the tip at opposite sides, making a shape like the fluke of an anchor. Compare Icelandic *laufað*. Two crooks opposite each other could produce this effect (mark of Andrew Fordyce, Montulie, North Yell).[1059]

Axe, ex (O).   Compare Ayrshire *aux bit*, a V-shaped nick behind, Kirkcudbrightshire *fore axe nip*. It corresponds to Shetland *half oot* or *-away*. Icelandic *blaðstýft*, and Faroese *hálvt frá horni* or *hálvt frá hálsi*.[1060]

> *Stair Axe* (O).   Combination of an *axe* and an angular notch, giving the appearance of steps of a stair. The *stair* does not appear separately now, but in 1742, John Johnston, merchant in Stromness, had a mark: 'the Top of (off) the Left Lug and fouer Lops in the Stump and two Staiers in ech side of the right Lug'. Compare Icelandic *stig, vagl, vaglskora* or *vaglskorið*.[1061]

Bit (N).   A small half-round notch in the side of the ear, or sometimes a V-shaped nick. Also in Shetland, a *bit oot, biddie* (Foula – V-shaped nick). Compare the V-shaped Icelandic *biti*, Faroese *bragð*. *Bits* could occur in multiples, as in the mark of Jas. Hunter, Yell: 'Right Lug Three bits behind and Two before, Left Lug half before'.[1062]

> *Cross bits.*   Two bits, opposite each other in one ear. Compare Icelandic *gagnbita*, Faroese *tvíbragdað*.[1063]
>
> *Gong bits.*   Similar to *cross bits*. Icelandic *gagnbitað*,[1064] Old Norse *gagn*, opposite.
>
> *Thumb bit.*   Used in North Ronaldsay for a large *bit*.
>
> *Square bit.*   Used at Mangaster, Sullom. Compare Icelandic *lögg*.[1065]

Button.   A nose mark, made by pinching the skin till it stood up like a pea or button, then tying it round with thread.[1066]

Cleep (S).   In Foula, a V-shaped nick in the tip of the ear, like a small *shear*. Probably from English *clip*, a cut.

Clout (O).   A patch of cloth sewn on to the wool of the hip as a mark.[1067]

Crook (N).   'A larger piece taken out of the middle of the lug', or 'a semicircular notch in one side of the ear'. A 'crook or bit' were equated in the mark of Janet Davidson, Kongnaseter, Yell in the early 1800s.[1068]

Crop off (O).   The end of the ear cut off straight.[1069]

Cut (S).   Equivalent to a *rift* or *rip*: also occurs laterally.

> *Cut out of the middle*, or *out of the middle* (S).   A notch taken out of the top of the ear.[1070] See *middle*.

Dram (S). An added piece of wool, cloth or thread fixed to the ear of a sheep or the tail of a horse.[1071] Cf. Norwegian *dram(b)*, show, Icelandic *drambr*, a lump, knot.

Drawn up (S). Having a diagonal slice cut off the side of the ear.[1072]

Eurnaskep (S). A mark to distinguish animals belonging to two families. In one case, 'both ears are cut half through from point to middle *behind*, and in the other *in front*'.[1073] (Old Norse *øyrnaskap*, 'ear-form', cf. *eyrna-mark*, ear mark).

Feather, fedder, fidder. Also *widder, witter* (S). A thin slice off one or usually both sides of the ear, a slanting cut, especially from the upper edge of the ear. James Anderson, Kirkabister, Yell, had in 1860: 'Right Lug Feathered behind, a rift before, Left Lug Stued'.[1074]

> *Hingin' widder* (or *fidder*) (S). A slanting cut from halfway down the ear up towards the tip, the opposite of *fidder*. Icelandic *hangfjöður, hanga*.

The original sense appears to be that of a slanting cut, cf. Icelandic *fjöður*, Faroese *fjeårar*,[1075] with later confusion from English 'feather', construed as to trim or slice the sides of the ears.

Gatskord (S). 'A slanting cut from the top of the ear along the edge, usually with a hole in the centre', 'a hole in the middle of the ear, and a slit from the middle of the hole upward and out at the top.' Also used of a mark on a horse.[1076] Norwegian dialectal, Old Norse *gat*, hole, + *skor*, notch, incision, Norwegian dialectal *skard*, Old Norse *skarð*, id.

Half (S). Half the top of the ear removed, with a right-angled cut. Similar to *Axe*.

> *Half taken up*, or *half up*, a slice off the side of the tip.
> *Half aff*, the upper half of the ear off.
> *Half stued*, probably the same as *axe, half.*[1077]

Hemlin (O). A semi-circular piece taken out of the side of the ear; a slice off the ear. From Norwegian *helming*, Old Norse *helmingr*, a half part. Cf. 'a helmin before and one behind on the left lug, a hole in the right and a bit before, and a skirt in the right nose'.

> *Drawn hemlin.* A slice off the ear. Compare Shetland *strae draw*, Icelandic *hálftaf*. Two *hemlins* or *drawn hemlins* on an ear correspond to Shetland *feather*.
> *Fore helman* (O). Mentioned in *The Orcadian* 15 June 1939, but not described.
> *Stooed hemlin.* Not noted outside North Ronaldsay. It corresponds to Icelandic *stýfður-helmingur*, but the *stoo* (see below) and *hemlin*, appearing as two cuts in Iceland, are here amalgamated into one.[1078]

Hole (N). A hole in the ear, general.

> *Heart hole*, the whole heart or centre of the ear cut out as in the mark of Marble Anderson, Kellister, Yell, 1835: 'Right Lug Rifted, Left Lug a Heart hole', and of Samuel Johnson, 1856: 'the heart of both Lugs cut out leaving the Sides and top standing'.[1079]

Kadel (S). A coloured thread through the ear or a string round the neck.[1080] Old Norse *kaðall*, rope.

Knee (S).   A slanting, obtuse-angled cut in the side of the ear; also as a verb. John Johnston of Midfield, Yell, had 'the Right Lugg half knee'd behind' in 1802. Anne Moar's sheep in Yell had a hole in the left ear, which was also 'half kneed before' in 1838. In 1837, the left lugs of sheep belonging to James Danielson, Cullivoe, Yell, were 'knaed around'.[1081]

Kolled (S).   Having the top of the ear slightly rounded.[1082] From Old Norse *kollr*, Faroese *kollur*, top, head.

Kuivy (O).   The tip cut off,[1083] a Westray name. Norwegian dialectal *kuv*, rounded top, *kuva*, to dock.

Laget (S).   A strip of cloth or piece of wool tied to a horse's mane or tail or to a sheep's ear, horn or fleece.[1084] Norwegian dialectal *lagde*, Old Norse *lagðr*, tuft of wool.

Lap, lop (O).   Made by cutting the ear longitudinally to make flaps, usually three in number, as in 'Andw. Taylor, Schigibist, 3 laps in right lug and a shear mark in left'.[1085] Old Scots *lap(e)*, flap, 1438; cf. Norwegian *lapp*, patch. Compare *rip*.

Middle (S).   A rectangular cut from the top to the middle of the ear. Compare Icelandic *mið-hlutað*, Faroese *midt ûr hajlun*.[1086]

This mark goes back to the seventeenth century, for Thomas Irvine of Midbrake's house mark was 'both lugs Middled a hole and a bit before on the Right Lug', the original record of it being 'dated 16 hundred and odds' and kept amongst the title deeds in a little oak charter chest. The mark was lodged with the Sheriff Court at Lerwick in 1804 or 1805 in the course of a process about sheep.[1087]

> *Tap middle*, a narrow V-shaped slit in the top of the ear.
> *Middle standing* (S).   A part (=*axe*) cut off at each side of the tip leaving the middle part: 'Left Lug Middle standing.' Compare the Icelandic *heilhamrad* and Faroese *heâmars merkji*. This mark is called *axelmärk* in Sweden, which suggests a possible link with the *axe*.[1088]

Minister's mark (S).   Both ears cut off.[1089]

Misness, mid nose out (O).   A cut or notch in the septum. Old Norse *misnesi*, septum, of which *mid nose out*[1090] is a rough translation.

Nos-sker(din) (S).   A cut in the nostril. Irvine of Midbrake's 'halvers sheep' with Betty Bruce Fraser had 'the House Mark without the hole & the left nostril Nosescor'd'. Old Norse *nos*, nose + Norwegian dialectal *skjerda*, cut, slit, or more likely English *nose* + *score*, to mark, scratch, cf. 'Rt. nose scored'.[1091]

Oo, wool (O).   Similar to *button*, formerly made by cutting the face to the bone and twisting the flesh so that it rose like a wart or mole.[1092] Old Scots *oull*, wool, 1447.

Piece (N).   A small nick cut out of the ear near the base, = *piece before, piece behind*. Cf. *bit*.

> *Piece off*, the tip of the ear cut off.
> *Piece taken (or drawn) up*, a slice off the side of the tip.
> *Piece taken (or drawn) up on both sides*, a slice off each side of the tip.
> Compare Icelandic *hvatt*, Faroese *hvatt*.

Piece out of the middle at the top, = cut out of the middle.

    Square piece out. A mark used at Mangaster, Sullom, was a 'peice of top and square peice out behind' in the right.[1093] Compare *square bit*.

Prick mark (O). A 'prick mark in the left lug' was one of the marks of Robert Langskeal, Holm, in 1767.[1094] Perhaps a V-shaped notch.

Pundlar mark (O). Used by Wilm. Gray, Croval, Orphir, in 1827.[1095]

Rift (N). A narrow slit in the ear, similar to *rip*. Old Scots *rift*, cleft, *c*. 1420. It could be at various points, even low down at the root.

Rip (O). As for *rift*. In North Ronaldsay, though a single slit in the top of the ear is a *rip*, two slits are now called *three rips*, whereas in Shetland this is *two rifts*, and similarly in Iceland, *tvírifað í heilt*. In the early 1800s, a mark belonging to Willm. Spence, Brakon, in Yell, had the 'Left Lug three rifted or four toped', clearly equating the two expressions. The Orkney name *lap* or *lop* has been replaced in North Ronaldsay by *rip*. The term *two rips* was recorded in 1910. The single slit is *heil-rifað* in Icelandic, *rivað heilt* in Faroese. From English *rip*, to tear.

    Stooed rip. A rip made after the ear has been *stooed*, by cutting the tip across. Compare Icelandic *stúfrifað*, Faroese *rivað stúv*, *rivan stÿgv*.[1096]

Rit (N). As for *rift*, *rip*, the slit also sometimes in the nostrils.[1097] From Old Scots *ritt*, to rut, 1683.

Scart (O). A semi-circular cut which removed the tip of the ear.[1098] Old Scots *skart*, to scratch, *c*. 1400, but see *skert*.

Shear (N). A V-shaped notch in the tip of the ear. Compare Icelandic, Faroese *sÿlt*. From English *shear*, to cut. The interchangeability of *shear* and *shuil* is shown by an entry for Andrew Anderson, Busta, Yell: 'Right Lug Sheered (Shuled) & a Hole, Left Lug a Bit before and a Bit behind.'[1099]

    Clow-sheer (O). A mark like a cleft in a hoof.[1100] From Old Scots *cluif*; Old Norse *klauf*, Norwegian *klauv*, a hoof + *shear*.

Shuil (S). 'A slit by which the ear is separated into two lobes,' a V-shaped notch. Similar to a *shear*, and now partly replaced by *shear* in Shetland. A mark belonging to Andrew Moar, Cullivoe, Yell, dated 1761, was 'the Right Lugg Shulled with a Rift on each side of the lug. Cut downward, the left lugg shulled with a Rift on each side of the lugg Cut downward and a holl on said lugg'. Probably from Norwegian dialectal *sula*, a cleft, Faroese, Icelandic *sÿlt*, a sheep mark of this form,[1101] but conflated phonologically with Scots *shuil*, Old Scots *schule*, *c*. 1400, shovel.

Side taken up (S). A slice off the side of the tip.

    Both sides taken up, a slice off each side of the tip.[1102]

Skert, skirt (O). Made by cutting off the ear-tip and notching the cut-edge or by making a similar kind of cut in the nostril.[1103] Cf. Old Norse *skarð*, cut notch, Norwegian derivatives *skjerding*, a sheep mark of this shape, *skjerda*, a cut, slice. See *scart*.

Slit (S). A cut in from the side of the ear, straight in or slanting. Compare Icelandic *bragð*, *hnífsbragð*.[1104]

Stoo (N). To cut off the ears or tail as an ownership mark, the tip of the ear cut off. Old Scots *stow*, to crop the ears; Old Norse *stýfa*, to cut off, *stúfr*, a stump. Compare Icelandic *stýft*, Faroese *stývt*, *stújvt*. Swedish (Öland) *styft*. See also *stooed hemlin*, *stooed rip*.

Stook, stouake (O). Diminutive form of *stoo*.[1105]

Straedraw (S). A thin slice cut off along the full length of the ear. Peter John Williamsons's halvers mark with Mr Pole in Cullivoe in 1852 was the 'Right Ear Straw-drawn before and a bit out behind – Left Ear a Bit out of each side'. Bruce Moar of Lingarth had as a mark in 1866: 'Rt. Lug Strawdrawn before & a bit behind – Left Lug Strawdrawn behind and bit before.'[1106]

String (S). A thread tied to the ear: 'a slit behind the left Ear & a String in the left Ear'.[1107]

Teen (O). A slit in the nostril, making one nostril bigger than the other.[1108] Origin obscure, perhaps a mistake for *teer*, a tear, rent.

Thread. Similar to *string*: 'a Thread in each ear & 2 rifts behind the right Ear'.[1109]

Top (S). In the Yell phrase 'three tops', 'four toped', equivalent to a *lap*.[1110]

Top or *tap off* (N). The tip of the ear cut off, as in the 1839 mark of William Nesbit, Kongnaseter, Yell: 'the top off Both Lugs and two rifts in the cut of each'.[1111]

55

The Linen Trade in Orkney

IN 1770, a Company of Linen Manufacturers in Zetland was established. The linen-bleaching enterprise was at Catfirth Voe. It collapsed in 1776, and little further attempt was made to grow flax in Shetland. Shetland people were said not to be inclined to spinning.[1112] This was no doubt an attempt by the promulgators of the Company to participate in a trade that in Orkney was evidently prosperous. There, flax was being grown in the seventeenth century, and the spinning of linen yarn was described as the only industry in 1760. Near Grimbister Holm was a linen manufacture for weaving and bleaching, and a house for drying.[1113] The growing of flax for linen was encouraged in Holm by the proprietor, who brought home flax-seed, lint-wheels and reels, these also being given annually by the Society for the Encouragement of Arts, Manufactures, etc. to those unable to buy them. Cloth was accepted in lieu of land rent, and some linen was sold in Shetland for money or for barter. A little flax was being grown in Aithsting and Sandsting at this period. Country folk brought coarse and fine linen to the Lammas Fair in Kirkwall and both linen yarn and cloth were exported, and though there were not the same great numbers employed in spinning as there had been formerly, nevertheless a great deal of flax was being grown and made into linen.[1114]

The 1790s pattern shows that there were weavers in Cross, Burness and North Ronaldsay earning 6[d] to 1/– or 1/3 a day, or else being paid by the yard. Kirkwall was exporting linen yarn and coarse linen cloth, and importing flax, since the home production evidently exceeded the supply. The manufacture of linen started in 1747 and had flourished. The work was done as a home industry, material being given out from shops for weaving. There were in the town 53 master weavers, 8 journeymen, and 14 apprentices. In Holm, flax had been grown since the 1690s, in big enough quantities to supply domestic needs, and also to sell on the East coast of England each year. For some years before 1787, about 20,000 yds (18,288 m) had been made and bleached yearly. The grist, that is the size or thickness of the yarn, was usually 900–1200, though some had exceeded 1800. There was no lint mill in the parish, but the flax was processed with breaks, switches, and coarse heckles. Some linen yarn was spun, if not woven, in Fair Isle. A lack of flax was complained of in Firth and Stenness. There were 33 weavers and 3 flax-dressers in Sandwick and Stromness, where the spinning of linen yarn was, with stocking knitting, a main manufacture.

Much linen and yarn was exported. Westray had 23 weavers. In Shapinsay, 'tolerable flax' had formerly been grown. The spinning of tow and linen yarn for sale was a job for the women. Birsay and Harray had 40 to 50 weavers, mostly producing linen. The women either spun the lint or bought bags of it for making into linen, using an 800 reed, for sale in Edinburgh, Newcastle and Shetland, at 11^d per yard (91 cm). In Orphir there were 6 weavers and linen yarn was produced.[1115]

In 1805, 20,000 yds (18,288 m) of linen a year was being woven for the English market in Deerness. Flax was grown by one of the main proprietors in Sandwick and he was planning to erect a flax mill. By this period, the spinning of linen yarn and the weaving of linen had almost completely replaced wool processing, so widening the difference between Orkney and Shetland in the field of textile production. Linen working suited the local cirumstances of Orkney and had improved the economic state of many Orcadians. For the first 15 or 20 years after its establishment in 1747, it was in the hands of one or only a few individuals, and flourished, producing 25,000 spindles of linen yarn each year. There followed a decline when some others sought to enter the market by importing flax, employing people to dress it, and giving it out to spin among the women. The spinners, seeing the competition amongst their employers, took the chance to boost their wages, but the quality of production fell at the same time. The market reputation of Orkney linen suffered, but much was still spun and sold in Edinburgh, Glasgow and Newcastle, and bought by travelling merchants from Moray and Inverness who came to the Lammas fair, and exchanged goods for it. There was still enough left over for the annual production, about 1795, of 30,000 yds (27,432 m) of coarse cloth for home use.

After a spell of uncertainty, the quality picked up again, stimulated partly by a company of thread manufacturers in Montrose. One Orkney merchant who established a link with them about 1800 introduced the two-handed wheel, as well as a woman to teach its use. Those who learned to use it got a free wheel and reel. Two hundred girls were quickly trained, and could earn about 6^d a day, a fact which made it difficult for people who needed servants to hire them. In 1799, 50,000 yds (45,720 m) of linen were stamped, some yarn was bartered, 50,000 spindles of it were sold and 50,000 more sent to the thread manufactory. A flax mill had also been erected.[1116]

Imports and exports in 1814 show that the importance of linen was being maintained:

Imports	Dressed Flax (cwt)	Undressed Flax (cwt)	Total (cwt)
1801–2	154	244	398
1802–3			230
1803–4	490	215½	705½
1804–5	151½	320	471½
1805–6	526	297	823

Exports (yds)	Linen Cloth (yds)	Yarn (spindles)
1801–2	57,320	37,130
1802–3	46,900	46,640
1803–4	36,100	39,450
1804–5	47,847	26,110
1805–6	37,144	17,310

In 1801–2, wooden machinery for a lint mill was also brought in. By 1814, the growing of flax had been largely abandoned in Orkney, partly because it was a crop that was very exhausting to the soil, and only certain deep, alluvial soils could bear it.[1117]

By the 1840s, the linen industry had largely ceased in Birsay and Harray, only a very few looms remaining. In Tingwall, flax and hemp grew well, but people did not know how to manage it when pulled.[1118] From the second decade of the nineteenth century, linen working was increasingly replaced by straw-plaiting, which was easier to do. In both cases, however, these activities provided a great deal of work for the women, and added an element to the family income which must have had its inevitable effect on living standards in Orkney.

Pigs, Rabbits and Geese

56

Pigs

THOUGH now rare in Shetland, pigs were formerly common there. Regulations were being made in the sixteenth century against the uncontrolled rootings of swine and used by Laurence Bruce of Cultamalindie to exact general fines. In most parishes, three dollars were taken, but in Dunrossness, where the folk claimed that they had no grice, the fine was three dollars a man. At this period there was a widespread slaughtering of swine to avoid fines, which must have reduced the stock considerably. In the early nineteenth century, however, a great many were bred there, of the same type as in Orkney but not as numerous, and they were still doing much damage in the corn-lands and meadows in winter after the crops were off. In summer they ranged the commons, grubbing up tormentil roots and other food for themselves. They were of medium size, black or dark red, brown, dirty white and tawny in colour, with short arched backs and flat bodies, covered with long stiff bristles over a fleece of coarse wool. Ropes could be made of this, and the seller of a pig might bargain to have the hair returned, so that he could make ropes to tie up boats, and to tether animals, and for fowling on the cliffs. They had strong, erect ears and strong noses. They fattened quickly if reasonably fed, and produced meat that was preferred to that of any other animal. In spring, fresh or salted pork made a good addition to the diet of every class. They made 'delicious Hamms'.[1119]

Some were tethered by one front leg in the kitchen, where they acted as living refuse disposal units, others had low stalls with stone partitions between them, where the *galts* or *gaats* (Old Norse *galti*, *gǫltr*), young pigs or castrated boars, could be fattened up. Pig-styes were often built on the common grazings. A sheep stolen in Rousay was put 'in ane Swyne sty in the hill' in 1700. These styes or little huts on the commons were to keep the swine from the corn. A century later, when the land had been improved, pigs were housed in styes in winter. Those in the island of Hoy were of turf, with two stones at the entrance between which the pigs could go to rub themselves. The pigs went to the hill about 15 April. They could be marked for identification like other animals, for in 1604 'ane sow quhilk was markit fra Olaw Smyth' was taken out of the Hill of Hildeso.[1120]

If a sow was in season, it was *roing* (cf. Old Norse *ræða*, to be in heat, of a sow, *raði*, a boar). A sow with young was a *sielack* (perhaps from a diminutive form of Old Norse *sýr*, a sow, but compare Gaelic *sìolag*), and the last pig in a litter, generally the smallest, a *water-droger* (Old Norse *vatn drugari*, 'water-carrier'). A young pig was a *paalie* (origin uncertain; cf. *palie*, used of a stunted young animal, especially a lamb) and a male pig for breeding a *bearie* (probably from *boar*) or *runnie* (Norwegian dialectal *rone*, Old Norse *runi*, boar).[1121] A young pig or grice was given to the owner of a boar as pay for service.

Early records are scanty. In the 1790s Aithsting and Sandsting had many swine, not ringed, in Unst hogs were numerous, and Walls and Sandness had vast numbers running wild. More precise figures come from Orkney. Crosskirk had 81 swine, Burness 36, Ladykirk 18 and North Ronaldsay 2. There were vast numbers of the small, ugly, high-backed, coarse-bristled swine in Kirkwall and St Ola, no doubt helping to feed the hungry in the town. In Firth and Stenness they were numerous. Sandwick and Stromness had 250 each, Westray 417, Rousay and Egilsay several, Stronsay 300 and Eday 100, selling at 10/– each, St Andrews and Deerness 500, which did much damage to the fields, Walls and Flotta 133, Orphir 435 and Evie and Rendall 400–500, unringed, most of which were sold.[1122] This was the foundation for an export trade from Orkney which in 1801–2 include 2 barrels of pork and 128 pork hams, in 1802–3 80 pork hams, in 1803–4 6 barrels of pork and 3 cwt of pork hams, in 1804–5 33 barrels of pork, and 12 cwt and 32 dozen pork hams, and in 1805–6 5 barrels of pork and 1 hogshead and 20 cwt of pork hams. This export had been going on since at least the seventeenth century. A relatively small amount was killed for home consumption. 17 December was known as Sow Day in part of Sandwick, when a sow was killed from the herd of swine.[1123]

In the 1840s, Shetland tenants could run as much poultry and as many geese and swine as they liked. The breed was unchanged. In Sandsting and Aithsting, every family kept at least one, and many two, which were fed and killed about Candlemas for their own use. Several families also kept herds, left to fend for themselves on the hills in summer, eating roots and earth-worms, an occasional bird's nest, and sometimes young lambs or weak sheep. Even here they were scavengers. Breed improvement had come about by means of swine brought in by some of the Greenland ships. A 15-day-old native swine was worth 1/– to 1/3, but one of improved type was 1/3 to 1/8. A full-grown, fattened native swine, one- to two-years-old, cost 8/– to 10/–, the new ones £1 to £1.10/–. Fresh pork sold at 2d a pound. A young swine was a *runnie* or a *grice* (Old Scots *grys(e)*, c. 1390; Norwegian *gris*, a pig(let), Old Norse *griss*, young pig), and one that ran around the fireside a *patty*. In Mid and South Yell, the produce in 1841 included 250 swine killed, at 10/– each.[1124]

In Orkney, the native swine had become almost extinct in St Andrews parish by the 1840s, but Stronsay had 310 worth 5/– a head, and Eday 223. In Cross and Burness, the Neapolitan, the Berkshire and other improved breeds of swine had been introduced, and many were exported alive each year to Aberdeen and Peterhead. Nevertheless, in the second half of the nineteenth century the pig numbers fell continually in both Orkney and Shetland. By 1936, the Department of Agriculture returns specified only 94 pigs in Shetland, Orkney having 2767 at the same period. By 1969, Orkney had only 381 breeding pigs, and they were not even mentioned for Shetland.[1125] In Orkney they were a useful means of converting the whey from the creameries into hard cash.

The entrails of pigs, like those of cattle and sheep, were widely used for making sausage-like puddings, stuffed with meal and suet. They are still used occasionally for this purpose, even though home-slaughtering no longer takes place. On a visit to Orkney in 1968, on a cold October day, I came upon a man and two women washing pig's puddings in a stream where it ran into the sea near the farm of South Ettit in Rendall. The pig had been killed in the Kirkwall slaughter-house and the entrails had been retrieved for making mealy puddings. They had not kept the stomach, which at one time would have been used for making a haggis. There were several feet of intestines in a bucket, which were cut into 2 ft (61 cm) lengths and washed in the cold running water. Surplus fat was detached by stripping the entrails through the hand. They were then turned outsides in and the process repeated. The cleaned lengths of intestine were soaked in salt water for three days before being stuffed with a mixture of meal, suet, onions, etc., and tied off into a string of separate puddings. They could be stored in oatmeal until required for eating, and were very tasty when boiled and roasted. The skin coverings could be eaten as well. Puddings of this kind contained no meat, whereas when the stomach was used to make a haggis, it was stuffed with the chopped up heart and liver as well as with oatmeal and other ingredients. The head and feet of pigs and cattle were boiled to make potted meat, i.e. brawn.[1126]

The curing of pork was as in other areas. A nineteenth century Shetland recipe involved a mixture of salt, brown sugar and saltpetre dissolved in water, and flavoured with cloves, ginger and cinnamon. The injunction was to 'mix all well together and rub thoroughly on the meat and pack down closely into an oak cask, filling up the holes or spaces between the lumps of meat with clean hard stones, and cover with a cloth. Let it stand for 6 weeks, then take up and wash the pieces and hang up to smoke for 12 weeks or more'. Such a combination of curing and smoking must have given very long-lasting qualities to Shetland pork.[1127]

PIGS IN FETLAR

The old native breed of pigs died out about the 1920s, and thereafter pigs coming to the island were mainly bought at the Aberdeen stock markets. Piglets were shipped in large crates, each piglet being numbered for identification by its purchaser. Large numbers of pigs were shipped to Shetland in general during the Second World War. They were kept in 6 ft (1.8 m) square styes, with earthen floors and straw-thatched or later wooden roofs. A small stone court alongside let the pig outside. There was straw bedding on one side of the sty.

The piglets did well on sow's milk, but when weaned time and patience were necessary to teach them to take milk out of a bowl or saucepan. As they got to the finishing-off stage, they were put on extra feeding for several weeks before being slaughtered. Formerly oats were used, boiled in a large iron pot with potatoes, or mixed with raw cut potatoes. Oats could also be fed raw. It was thought that oats helped to make the bacon more streaky and wholesome.

Formerly, summer was the worst time for pigs. They had then to be content with fish offal, half-raw dogfish, boiled dockens in buttermilk, cabbage blades and chickweed. When tethered on ground that the crofters did not want rutted up, rings were put in the pigs' snouts. This kept them from burrowing for grubs and *grice murricks* (diminutive of Old Norse *mura*, Norwegian dialectal *mura*, *grisemure*), 'blue girse' or silver weed, *Potentilla anserina*,[1128] which has a small, hard, edible root bulb. After the potatoes were lifted the pigs were tethered on the ground, and the rings snipped off. A round ring with the ends of the wire twisted together was used on young pigs. Older ones had a double ring, consisting of a wire whose points were thrust through the snout and then each bent back and twisted round the main strand of wire. Any good-sized pigs were also tethered on land to be sown with corn in the spring, and did a good job of turning up the soil. The tether was put on one foreleg for a while, then changed to the other to prevent rubbing. More recently, piglets bought from the markets for fattening have been fed on pig-meal and other products, and powders are available to prevent swine-fever.

Pigs used to be kept overyear to be slaughtered at fifteen to eighteen months' old, as a rule in November. There was a superstition that if this was not done at the time of a full or filling moon, the flesh would run away into fat. Every household kept at least two pigs, one for slaughter, and one coming on. A house with, say, a woman and a girl in it would be content with a *patty grice* or young pig of about 80 lb, but a well-fattened one would weigh 180 to 200 lb.

About 1940, each island was supplied with a humane killer, a pistol that discharged a fairly large bolt into the pig's brain, and this was put in the charge of a qualified man who lent it free when required. When the pig dropped on the straw placed near it, it was then bled with the usual butcher-knife or *tully* (Norwegian dialectal *tolekniv*, Old Norse *tálguknifr*, carving knife). Following the older method, a start was made early in the morning of the short November day. All requirements were at hand, a good fire going, and plenty of wood and blue peats lying ready. Often the pig was taken into the kitchen and laid on a small, strong wooden table about 20 in. (51 cm) high, facing the light. Before this it had been tripped up on its side, and the four legs tied and braced tightly together, and the jaws tied with coir yarn which does not slip easily, or with a simmen twisted out of Shetland oats. Despite the tied snout, the pig could still make plenty of noise. The pig was then stuck with the knife at a point $1\frac{1}{2}$ in. (3.8 cm) in front of the breast-bone. The blade went straight in. A good butcher did not like a broad-pointed knife, preferring to see a neat 'stickie-hole'.

The blood was usually collected in a tub as it drained through this opening. When near the end, and it was judged that all the red blood had run out, the tub was removed and a smaller vessel put in its place to catch the bitter 'black blood' or heart blood, the last to come away. This was not kept for use. Half a cup of salt was put into the tub of red blood and it was stirred briskly with a stick to keep it from clotting. Its purpose was to make black puddings, when it was thinned with lukewarm water and mixed with oatmeal, pepper and salt. Bleeding could take up to fifteen minutes. It was thought that fat pigs bled more quickly. At this point the butcher and his helpers had a smoke and a dram.

The pig was plotted with boiling water so that the bristles could be scraped off. About 9 gallons of water were needed, and all the black iron family pots were kept going over big fires. There were always willing helpers at this job, for a bit of fresh pork was a certain reward. The water was lifted with a large enamel can with a handle on the side, called a 'shappin can', because when the contents were emptied over the skin, the bottom was used to give several *chaps* or knocks as if to force the scalding water into the pores of the skin. The cans used to be stocked by ironmongers, and held about half a gallon. The bristles were scraped off with the butcher-knife or some other sharp knife, worked against the lie. The bristles in the mane or crest of male pigs, called *grice birse*, were plucked for use by shoemakers in hand-sewing leather. Plotting was done by taking an inner door of the house or a barn door and laying one end on the killing table and the other end on a large tub, at a slope so that the water would run into the tub. The pig was laid on the door, head towards the tub, and the belly was scraped, followed by each of the sides. A cotton rag was plugged into the stickie-hole to keep water from oozing in. Helpers not engaged in scraping or plotting kept the door clean by wiping it down into the tub.

The next stage was opening and cleaning. First the feet and the head were taken off. A piece of thin hempen rope was passed through a slit in the lower lip, and the head hung out to drip on a pin of wood or iron on the outside wall, till any liquid or blood had drained out or dried. The entrails were removed by first cutting the *muggie-lep* (Norwegian *mage*, Old Norse *magi*, stomach + Norwegian dialectal *lepp*, strip, flap, Old Norse *leppr*, little piece or bit), the part that covers the bowels. This part was also salted, but was inferior in quality to the rest of the flesh. The intestine or *striffen* (from Early Middle English *striffen*, thin skin, membrane, perhaps from Old Irish *srebann*, Gaelic *streabhon*, membrane) fat was removed and the entrails put into large budies or close-made fish or herring baskets. On the following day, the womenfolk, regardless of weather, took the 'puddings' to a burn to wash them out. One woman cleared the intestines of fat and cut them into suitable lengths. This process was 'redding up the puddings'. Almost every part of the entrails was kept. Any intestines too small for making mealy puddings were salted with the other parts, and used for tripe-soup. The two heart-valves or 'deaf lugs' were cut off and disposed of, as were the male breeding organs and the internal breeding organs of sows. The names of the internal parts were the same as for sheep (see pages 451–52).

The pig was then laid on a table, covered with a cotton sheet or meal bags, and left to be cut up on the following day, salting taking place about 30 hours after killing. Cutting up was nearly always done in the kitchen, the butcher giving a hand and getting as his pay a four-rib side piece. The cut flesh was laid on the table in the order in which it would be packed into the curing barrel. The first cut was right down the back, on each side of the spine or *rig* (Old Scots *rigge*, back, *c*. 1420; Old Norse *hryggr*), a stretched cord being used to guide the knife, and the saw followed these lines, separating the ribs from the spine. The carcase was then in two halves, and the $4\frac{1}{2}$ in. (11 cm) broad 'rig-piece' was cut into 8 in. (20 cm) lengths for salting.

In former times, some of the older pigs, especially boars and galts, were skinned or flenched, and the cured and dried hides were in demand for making skin-shoes or *rivlins* (Old Scots *reveling*, *c*. 1420; Old Norse *hriflingr*). Though thinner than cow- or horse-hide, it lasted just as well.

The head was cut into three parts. The first cut was horizontal, in line with the mouth, and the lower or cheek half was called the 'shocks' (Old Scots *chouk*, *c*. 1470; Norwegian *kjake*, cheek, Old Norse *kjálki* jaw-bone). The top part, the 'heid', was sawn into two halves down the middle, and the brains or *harns* (Old Scots *harnis*, 1375; Old Norse *hjarni*, brain) removed. The snout was the *trunie* (Norwegian dialectal *tryne*, Old Norse *trýni*). The shocks needed plenty of salt, and were packed well to the bottom of the curing barrel. A reested pig's head, with a flavour of peat-smoke, was one of the best relished parts of a pig. One section was enough to make a large-sized family pot of kail (broth). It was said that some of the strongest fishermen took such a heavy diet of 'grice heid an' kail' that they could go the clock round before another serving.

The old form of curing pork was dry-curing, in which both men and women helped. A start was made with the hams or hindquarters. Some butchers put a deep cut down the centre of the ham and filled it with salt, but others disapproved of this because if the liquid was not fully dried out, it would ferment and ruin the meat. To be safe, each ham was sawn into two pieces. If the salt was too dry, it had to be moistened slightly before being rubbed into the flesh. It was found once in the Houbie district, when too dry salt was used, on removing the flesh after its usual month, that it had gone sour because the salt had taken so long to melt down. For dry-salting, a basin of salt was kept at hand, and rubbed in carefully. The hams and shoulders were packed first into the tub, and a liberal quantity of salt sprinkled over the layer. This was done for each successive layer, and the barrel of flesh was kept in the house. The 'bludie ribs' lay next to the shoulders, then four 'side pieces', and the 'sweet-cut' next the hams. Salt was the only ingredient in dry-curing. No sugar was used in Fetlar.

Wet-curing began with the importing from southern markets of pigs that put on much more weight than the hard-grown native breed. As a precautionary measure, the new method of curing in brine was adopted. Brine was prepared in buckets filled with water, often sea-water. Salt was stirred in bit by bit till the brine was solid enough to float a potato on top. When the flesh was laid in the brine a stone was laid on top to keep it from rising, and the barrel closed with a wooden lid covered by a meal bag of jute or cotton. Curing was from four to six weeks, and then, on a dry day, the flesh was taken out and strung up on pins against the walls to dry. There were nails, pins and pegs in the inbye-ends of all the houses, where both fish and flesh were cured in the heat and smoke of the

237. Stalls for pigs in the house at Midhouse, Harray, Orkney. C5712.

peat-fires. Young pigs were cured in large tubs, large ones in full-sized barrels. This was the 'saatin (salting) tub or barrel'.

Nearly every part of the pig was used for food. Kidney or *neir* fat, much superior to the other intestinal fat, was in part cut up as an ingredient in white puddings, and in part rendered and stored in earthenware jars. This *swine same* (Old Scots *sayme*, fat, *c*. 1425; Old French *saim(e)*, lard) was not used for cooking, but as grease for tools, and as a remedy for burns and scalds it was thought superior to *geese-creesh* (grease). The other intestinal fat was rendered in the same way. The refuse that floated to the top was scooped off with a wooden spoon. The kidneys were fried and eaten the day after butchering.

The liver was double cooked, being first boiled and lightly peeled, and then sliced and fried in fat. It was not a choice article of food, however, being rather hard and bitter. The heart was never used fresh, but always salted, and ultimately used for soup like the other entrails. One of the favourite meals was the collops, bits of lean meat taken off when the cuts were being shaped. The part cut near the hams was the 'sweet-collops', and this, fried with the kidneys, was much looked forward to.

238. Slaughtering a pig in Papa Westray, early 1930s. Right: David Groat, Quoys; left: Donald Mackay. Photo. John D. Mackay. Per T. Mackay. 19.24.11A.

The lungs or *lights* are now thrown away or put into a hole in the midden. The old folks, however, were less wasteful. Most commonly, the lights were used for soup-making, after having been in salt with the pork. They would be cut up and each person would help himself, but though eatable, they were only just. Alternatively, they were cooked fresh, boiled for an hour in water, with salt. However, the lungs had an ill reputation for disease, so in order to let any possible defects boil out, an inch or so of the windpipe was kept above water, tied with a string to the lid. It was thought that any bad germs would be forced out through this opening. Brains were eaten, but not very much. More often the dog got them. When cooked, they were fried and stirred around into a mince-like consistency, and meal was sometimes added.

The pig's feet were well scalded, and laid at the bottom of the pickling tub under the hams. They were popular for making a tasty pot of soup. Two bones

The Northern Isles

239. Cleaning pig's entrails for making mealy puddings at South Ettit, Rendall, Orkney, in the 1960s. 4.10.10.

in each leg, about $2\frac{3}{4}$ in. (7 cm) long, were generally claimed by the children to make a toy called a *snorie bane*, so called from the snoring noise it made when rotated quickly by means of a twisted cord fastened round it.

When the intestines had been cleaned, one end was tied, and the other end blown into and tied off. This made air-filled balloons or 'blown puddings' which were hung up to dry, to be filled with more substance later. The sparl, leading to the rear end, was considered among the best. Black or 'bluidy' puddings were made by mixing blood diluted with lukewarm water with meal, pepper and salt in a basin. Filling was done with a spoon or with the fingers, and an expert did not overfill, for an air-space should be left when the ends were tied off. The puddings were boiled, put in a basin, and were ready for the table next day, when they were sliced into rounds and fried in fat. White-pudding making was similar, with a greater range of ingredients. Some people like a filling half of flour and half of meal, and in addition there were currants, raisins, sugar, salt and pepper, cinnamon and fat. When the black or white puddings were boiling, they were looked at now and again to see if they were distended by air. If so, they would be pricked, to prevent bursting.

The stomach, or bag, was washed in running water, turned inside out, and put into hot water so that the stomach coating could be scraped off. This process was called *leeping the bag* (Old Scots *lepe*, parboil, in 1513; cf. Old Norse *hleypa*, to curdle (milk), as by heating, Norwegian dialectal *løypa*, to half-roast food). It was stuffed after cleaning and scraping, and a little more boiling.

Sometimes sausages of a kind were made by filling a pudding with finely cut pork. After a few days it was boiled and sliced for eating. This was a sparl. When a pan of fat pork had been fried and a lot of fat left over, oatmeal was stirred into the fat and spice added. The result was a filling meal called *hoonska* (origin obscure). This term also applies to a blood pudding made of ox-blood and oatmeal, and to a mixture of ox-blood, cabbage and oatmeal boiled together.[1129] The flesh itself, smoke-dried above the fire, was always popular. This was *reested pork*.[1130]

57

Rabbits

ONE of the many points that distinguish Orkney from Shetland is the presence of rabbits in such large numbers that they played a considerable part in the economy. In the seventeenth century and later rabbits were plentiful in Burray, and North Ronaldsay and Sanday had rich warrens, full of rabbits. Rabbit skins were listed amongst the products of Orkney.[1131] They were also valued in Shetland, however, for it was decreed in 1604 in Whiteness and Weisdale that no rabbits were to be shot or netted in anyone's links without permission. Though preyed on by hawks, eagles, dogs, cats and otters, not to mention man, they increased prodigiously, feeding on corn and grass, and even on seaweed and roots in bad weather. Their burrowing could have a bad effect on sandy areas, making them liable to wind-erosion. Most were brown, with the belly a shade or two lighter in colour.[1132]

They were found in most of the Orkney islands. Burray had a particularly extensive warren, whose inhabitants did well on the 12 to 20 acres of turnips Captain Sutherland planted in 1808. He found, however, that rabbit bites did not make the turnips rot, and so he established an amicable modus vivendi between himself, the rabbits and the cattle for whom the roots were destined. Patrick Fea of Sanday was in the business too, and his Diary records:

2 Feb. 1767: Sold my Rabit Skins to Jo. Murray att 4 Sh. 3 per doz.
7 Mar. 1768: Put on board Browgh's sloop a Cassie of Rabit Skins in which were 55 Do. and 6 Skins with 3 Calf Skins above them.[1133]

In 1792, 36,000 rabbit skins were sold from Stromness. In 1801 to 1802, Orkney exported 9076 rabbit skins, in 1802 to 1803 621, in 1803 to 1804 13,848, in 1804 to 1805 13,842, and in 1805 to 1806 9744.[1134]

In the 1840s, the athletic minister of Stronsay and Eday calculated that there were 3200 and 1630 rabbits respectively in these islands. It was said of Burness that rabbit skins and kelp had formerly provided most of the farm profits. By 1874 the warren at Keirfiold in Sandwick had been taken in and improved.[1135] The dividing of the commons, and their breaking in for cultivation, brought this long-standing trade to an end.

58

Geese

BY the mid-eighteenth century quantities of salt geese were being exported from Orkney, as well as goose feathers. Sandwick and Stromness were exporting both salted and smoked geese in the 1790s. In 1792 4424 lb of goose feathers were exported from Stromness, as well as 240 smoked geese and 10 barrels of salted geese. Exports in 1801 to 1802 were 66 cwt 1 qr 22 lb of feathers, and 57,000 goose quills, in 1802 to 1803 30 cwt 3 qrs 4 lb of feathers and 39,000 quills, in 1803 to 1804, 64 cwt 1 qr 18 lb of feathers and 37,700 quills, in 1804 to 1805 74 cwt 2 qrs 26 lb of feathers, 82,700 quills, and 9 boxes of goose hams, and in 1805 to 1806 90 cwt of feathers, and 101,000 quills.[1136] It is because of this aspect of the economy that so many of the older farmhouses in Orkney have goose-nests built into the kitchen walls, at ground level, and brood geese and ganders frequently figure in the testamentary inventories. A visitor saw a bare-headed, shoeless boy herding a flock of geese in Stenness in 1842. In Lady parish, it was once the custom for groups of men to go to the big houses on

240. Taking geese to the market. From Barnard 1890. C1509.

New Year's morning to wake the family by singing the New Year's song. In return, they were entertained with ale and bread, and got a smoked goose or a piece of beef. In the 1870s large quantities were still reared on moorland, though this was becoming a thing of the past as a result of the division of commons and their subsequent reclamation.[1137]

Geese were also kept in Shetland by several individuals. At critical times and places, hens had their feet *smocked* (cf. Icelandic *smokka*, to put on an article of clothing, Norwegian *smokk*, finger-stall), tied or sewn up with cloth rags, to keep them from scratching in newly sown ground, and geese were fitted with a kind of clog or patten. To tie the toes of geese together to keep them from straying far was in Orkney to *kromo* the geese (Norwegian *krumma*, hand, Old Norse *krumma*, paw).[1138] After the crops were in, geese were allowed into the townland like all the other creatures. As with pigs, there were little huts, *geese-hooses*, for the geese in the scattald. Some of these were to be seen at Aikerness in Orkney, the geese being penned in them each night and let out in the morning. Enclosures for penning geese were known in Shetland as *styags* (possibly a diminutive of English *sty*, but cf. Old Norse *stí*, Old Swedish *stighia*, Swedish dialectal *stig*, *styo*).[1139] In later times in Fetlar it was a custom that geese were driven into the barn every Saturday, and one was picked out and killed for the Sunday dinner. This regularity of consumption was modern, however. The earlier style was to kill geese in October, clean, quarter and salt them, and hang them up to cure in the peat-smoke. When a goose was killed and eaten fresh, the blood was saved, and mixed with oatmeal and fat to make the stuffing.[1140]

Though geese were hard on the corn-crops, if they got the chance, and consumed a lot of grass, nevertheless a lot of care was taken of them. No doubt identification marks were cut in the webs of their feet, as happened, for example, in Denmark, but much of the knowledge of keeping geese in the townships has gone. It can only be guessed at, on the analogy of information from other areas, such as Denmark, and Sweden.[1141]

The Shore and the Sea

59

Wild Fowl

AS a source of both food and profit, wild fowl and their eggs and feathers were of value in parts of Orkney and Shetland. Fowling rights were amongst the feudal appurtenances listed in an Orkney charter of 1587, in keeping with Hector Boece's comment in 1527 that 'copious wild fowl' were amongst Orkney's resources. Sea fowl were a common food, and rewards were given for the heads and eggs of birds of prey like crows and eagles.[1142]

In 1633, Westray was said to be rich in wild fowl, and both sea- and fresh-water fowl were included amongst the winter food of the Shetlanders. Sea fowl were taken with 'grins' (a metathetic form of Old Scots *gyrne*, *girn*, a noose, snare), slipped over the heads of the birds when they were sleeping. At the east and west ends of the Mainland of Orkney, and especially in the island of Copinsay, many feathers were got by taking sea fowl on the cliffs. A man was let down with a strong rope about his middle, and he threw down the birds he caught to a boat waiting below. Plovers, doves, swans, ducks and geese were amongst the wild fowl to be had.[1143]

About 40 miles west was Suleskerry and an island called Stack, and the Clett, where a boat or two went about Lammas to get *solan geese* (Old Scots *soland*, 1450, from Old Norse *súla*, gannet + ? Old Norse *ond*, duck) or gannets, and *skarts* (Old Scots *scarth*, 1450), cormorants or shags. Feathers were amongst the goods sold or bartered to the Dutch fishers, who came in at Levenwick, and in Fair Isle they were the chief commodity, sold to a Hamburg merchant who had his booth at the South Harbour. Some gannets and shags were being shot in Shetland after the Second World War, for sale in London.[1144]

Writing pens, probably of goose quills for the most part, down and feathers, were amongst the Orkney exports of 1693. Birds of various kinds were taken on the rock ledges, *toists* or *teisties* (Norwegian dialectal *teiste*, Faroese *teisti*, Old Norse *þeisti*), the black guillemot, *lyers* (Norwegian *lira*, Old Norse *líri*; Faroese *líri* refers to a nestling shearwater) or Manx shearwaters, both fat and delicious, the latter 'so *very fat*, that you would take it to be *wholly fat*', kittiwakes and gulls. The shearwaters were roasted on spits, complete with guts, and sprinkled with ginger and vinegar. Men in a boat went under the rocks with a large net having two long ropes at the outer corners. This was pulled up by men on the cliffs till it covered the places where the birds sat, and when the men in the boat made a noise with a rattle, the startled birds flew into the net

241. Gathering eggs on the Orkney cliffs, early twentieth century. Per R. Linklater. C3837.

and were caught. The net was then let down into the boat and the prey seized. Other fowlers went down the rocks on ropes held by colleagues, or fixed to stakes, to take as many young birds as they could carry.[1145] This particular form of collapsible net for the mass capture of birds on cliffs, worked from a boat without having an exactly fixed site, does not appear to have direct parallels elsewhere, though nets that could be raised and lowered on poles, set at points where ducks and the like usually flew, were widespread.[1146]

The sea fowl eaten in winter in Shetland were probably salted and smoked, whilst those eaten in summer were fresh. The down and feathers were a useful source of gain. Fowl and eggs were said to be the main support of the people of Foula. Poorer folk had to use netting or snaring devices, but the gentlemen who could afford to indulge in fowling for pleasure killed sea fowl with small shot from boats. Business was also combined with pleasure, however, and men would also go down the cliffs on ropes for eggs and birds for the proprietors, who had the rocks divided amongst them in proportion to their land-holding.[1147] The impression is given by these early sources that more meat was eaten then than in later times, beef, mutton and pork as well as the flesh of sea- and fresh-water fowl, with their eggs in due season. The eggs of sea fowl from a Holm near St Ninian's Isle were considered very good when boiled hard and eaten with vinegar. Even fresh eggs could be kept for several months without preservatives of any kind, and could have been available for winter food.[1148] In Dunrossness, lochs with duck, teal and swan provided good shooting. The

242. Fowling in Orkney using a cradle between the mainland and a stack. Per Bryce Wilson.

243. Gathering the eggs. From *The Captain*. Per Bryce Wilson. C5952.

people of Fair Isle got much profit from feathers, 'but they buy them dear, with their hazard always, and sometimes the loss of their lives, for they Nest in high Rocks, more than a 100 Fathom depth from the Surface of the Earth, as many Fathoms high from the Sea, they go down in Ropes to catch them, and sometimes in stead of catching the prey, they sometime catch a slip and are either crushed on the Rocks or drowned in the depth'. A rope and cradle had been fixed across to the Holm of Noss, giving risky access to the Holm's wealth in sea fowl,[1149] but this was no more dangerous-seeming than climbing down a rope fixed to a stake hammered into the soil at the edge of the cliff. For egg collecting a basket was fixed to the climber's side.[1150] In Hoy, fowlers would use ropes of straw if hair ones were not available. Ropes of swines' hair were preferred because they did not cut as easily on the rocks into which people set their feet when they were lowering a boy on a rope. He used a stick in awkward places to avoid friction with the rocks. The reward was in feathers at 8d to 9d a pound. The climbers were known as *rockmen*. The best climbers in Shetland were said to be in Foula. They used wooden stakes or even knives thrust into the ground to support their climbing ropes, and evidently took pleasure in the excitement of the climb. Two climbing ropes seen in Shetland were each 24 fathoms (44 m) long and covered with salted cow hides to protect them.[1151]

Climbing with ropes was evidently the major fowling method, but there were others too. On the rocks of the Pentland Firth, 'they take a Line, upon the end of which they fasten some Fish-Hooks, above the hooks there is also a Pock fastened, and so from the top of the rock they let down the Line thus furnished with Pocks and hooks, striking the heads of the young Fowls in their Nests with the Pock, upon which the Fowls do gape and cry; as if it were their Dame coming with meat to them, and so lifting the Line they let the hooks fall into their mouths, which taking hold of the Fowls, they become their prey'. This was

244. Hauling up a basket of eggs. From *The Captain*. Per Bryce Wilson. C5949.

245. Two baskets of eggs taken by William Foubister (between the baskets) on the Copinsay cliffs, in the 1910s. Per R. Linklater. C394.

246. A rockman using a hooked stick to get himself round awkward corners, in Shetland. From Barnard 1890. xxv. C1510.

on the Caithness side, but in later times there was a parallel technique at Gloup in Yell, where *scories* (Norwegian *skåre*, Old Norse *skári*) or young gulls, and kittiwakes, were caught by letting lines down the cliffs, and jerking the hooks into the young birds. The flesh tasted strong and fishy. In the district of North Ireland in Orkney, the *horie-goose* (origin unknown) or brent-goose, *Branta bernicla*, was caught by poles and nets at low tide, perhaps of the same form as nets much used in the northern districts of Fenno-Scandia, set on poles to protrude above the water.[1152]

Another method was the use of horse-hair girns or snares. According to a Fetlar informant, these were made in latter days by means of a light spindle or *dipsie* often made of a herring-net cork with a notched piece of wood fixed in it. A single strand of horsehair was doubled and hooked on to the spindle, and this was spun to the right with the thumb and forefinger to put in the twist. Powdered resin was put on the fingers to grip the hair, which for preference should come from a horse rather than a mare. The loop was made by taking the end of the twisted hair through the eye made by slipping the noose off the spindle.[1153]

Feathers continued to be a source of profit through the eighteenth and into the nineteenth century. In 1809, exports of feathers from Shetland had a value of £50. Ropes continued to be used, in Walls and Flotta for catching the shearwater, and the men of Walls and Sandness in Shetland maintained their reputation as expert fowlers.[1154] Whereas fowlers in St Kilda and the Faroe Islands worked together, in Shetland they worked individually.[1155] In Stronsay, the young *scarf* (Norwegian *skarv*, Old Norse *skarf*; Faroese *skarvur* means a shag, never a cormorant[1156]), or cormorant, *Phalacrocorax carbo*, was thought good to eat, if first buried for twenty-four hours in the earth to make it more tender and less fishy-tasted. Soup was also made of it. Scarfs continued to be eaten, and are said to have been widely used during the Second World War and after. Latterly they were skinned and hung up for a while, though some people wrapped them in a cloth and buried them in the earth for a week. They were then parboiled in several waters, the water being poured away each time. The bones were picked out, and the flesh put in a stew-pan with butter, plenty of onions and pepper, and sometimes a little minced pork or ham. The scarf, perhaps for this reason, was the seabird that was hunted longest. It was a winter job. A fine, dark night and a smooth sea were necessary for going into the caves where the birds were to be found. A candle lantern or a collie lamp was taken in the boat, and lit in the cave. When a noise was made by shouting or beating the oars on the gunwale, the hollow cave redoubling the echo, the scared birds flew on to the light. If the cave was high enough, a sail was hung up on a mast and set taut so that the birds might strike it and be stunned. The men stood up in the boat and struck down the approaching birds with a bat-shaped piece of wood. In Fetlar practice, twelve hours under the earth took away the fishy taste.[1157]

It was said that great numbers of scarfs could sometimes be caught when they were asleep on the rocks, but first the one or two birds that acted as sentinels had to be quieted. The leader of the expedition crept slowly and carefully along, till within a short distance of the bird. He dipped a worsted glove into the sea, and gently threw water on the face of the guard. This seemed to reassure the bird, which would put its head under its wing and fall asleep, for the last time. Its neck was then broken and the other birds could be taken at leisure. The fowler's great enemy, however, was the gull, which was apt to give warning of his approach.[1158]

In the nineteenth century, there were three main fowling methods on the cliffs and in the geos of Westray and Papa Westray. One was to enter a cave or geo with boats. If it was a geo, two men stood at the top of the rocks on each side at the end next the sea, and two more on the rocks or in boats at the water's edge below. The four men held ropes fixed to the corners of the net. When a sharp stroke was made with a stick on a thin, flat board, the birds dropped from their nesting places and flew seawards into the net. The net must have had a bag-shape, since the birds 'lodged in the tunnel at its extremity'. If a cave was being worked, the net had to be drawn across the mouth of it, the two men holding it above dangling from ropes if there was no place to stand. Alternatively, it might be stretched up on two long poles held by people in the boats. The method is parallel to the seventeenth century form of cliff-netting, adapted to suit particular conditions. Seventy score of *auks* (Swedish *alka*, Danish *alke*, Old Norse *alka* or *álka*; Faroese *álka*, razorbill) or common guillemots, *Alca troile*, were caught in one day by this method in a Papa Westray geo, and the feathers of auks caught there by one boat in two days were sold for £9.18/–.[1159]

A second method was by means of a noose of hair on the end of a long flexible pole. The user was suspended on the cliff by several ropes, and one hung downwards to the bottom of the rock. By means of these he could be moved in any direction to get at birds. When he had caught enough, he sent them up in a rope lowered for the purpose. The birds generally sat quietly till the noose was slipped over their heads. This technique was known in Shetland as *to kilp*, and the rod was a *kilpin-stick* (Norwegian *kylpa*, to fish with a rod, Icelandic *kilpr*, loop of whalebone used as a bucket handle).[1160] This device was formerly used in Foula for taking puffins. In Fair Isle, guillemots were taken with horsehair snares. The noose could be pulled tight by means of a line that ran up the rod to the fowler's hand. Female *lungies* (Norwegian dialectal *langve*, *lomvi*, Old Norse *langvé*) or guillemots, *Uria aalge*, let themselves be taken peaceably, but males were more difficult and often had to be snared by the foot. Several hundred might be caught this way in a day.[1161]

The third Westray method was to catch the birds in the air by means of a net with three sides each 3 ft (91 cm) long, forming an equilateral triangle. A long, light rod was fixed to the two pieces of hoop forming one of the angles of the mouth of the net. The user stood out of sight behind a rock, and held the rod with the net dangling. Near him were live or dead birds set up as decoys. When a bird came sweeping along the precipice, he reared the net in its path so that it flew into it and was caught. This worked only in a strong gale. One man had been known to take about 300 birds, mostly auks, in a single day. The name for this technique was *swappin* (Old Scots *swapp*, to jerk, leap, 1375).[1162]

CLIFF SCENE

247. Swapping for auks in Orkney. 11.11.26A.

For the *tammie* or *tammie-norie*, the puffin, *Fratercula arctica*, which nested in burrows under stones at the tops of cliffs and high rocks, the method employed was to thrust a stick with a hook on the end into the burrow, and drag the bird out by force. In Unst, this was the annual ploy. The same method was used in the Faroe Islands, the hook being called a *lundakrókur*, in Iceland and in Norway. In Foula, the hooked stick was called a *croakie* (probably from *crook*, a hook) and it is said that it sometimes brought up strings of puffins clinging to each other. Puffins were also taken out by hand, but though the Faroese might do this by letting the bird bite their hand and so draw it out, Shetlanders were more circumspect and wore a double glove like the Norwegian fowlers.[1163]

Eggs were not much taken for sale in Shetland, but served as food for 'multitudes of the inhabitants', the method of collecting being 'so very hazardous, as to satisfy one of the extremity to which the poor people are driven for want of food'. For taking eggs, the rockman could carry a hoop net, which allowed him to stretch to eggs he could not otherwise reach on ledges. When he had filled his basket by means of the net, he climbed back up the rope and went on to harvest another section of the cliff.[1164] In more recent times, the eggs of the puffin, fulmar, kittiwake and eider duck were taken for domestic use.[1165]

The eider duck, *Somateria mollissima*, or *dunter* (Norwegian *dynta*, to move with a bobbing motion; Scots *dunt*, to bump, beat) was treated almost like a domestic fowl. She was tame enough to let herself be lifted from her nest, and each time eggs were taken she would pull more down and lay again, so providing a double reward. The male also provided down, for nest-building, and the game could go on till the birds were partly denuded. In eighteenth century Iceland, down and eggs were taken only twice, though in the Western Islands the same custom prevailed as in the Northern Isles. By the time the duck had pulled from her breast a second and even a third supply of down for a nest, she was exhausted, and then the drake would provide his differently coloured

248. A team of auk-swappers in Westray, with their net. Per Bryce Wilson.

down. By the 1900s the taking of eggs and down once only was normal.[1166] Half a pound was got on an average from one female in a season, the produce being greater in a rainy spell. Light and warm clothing could also be made out of prepared eider duck skins. The eggs of the black and common guillemot, however, were taken for sale.

In the island of Copinsay, part of the parish of Deerness, guillemot eggs were gathered regularly till the end of the nineteenth century, with a short-term revival of interest shortly before the 1914–18 War. Sometimes a device called a *snatcher* was used to get them. It was about 10 in. (25 cm) long by 5 in. (13 cm) wide, and could be closed over the egg by means of strings running through two eyes. A simpler parallel in Foula, for getting at awkwardly placed eggs, was a spoon on the end of an old fishing rod.[1167] The expression for fowling on the Copinsay cliffs was 'running the Lee', which is a 200 ft (61 m) high cliff, and the sections where the work could be done were called *races* (probably a special usage of English *race*), each with its name – Window Race, Pulpit Race, Corner Race, Mussater Race, Doonheelan Race, Poolie's Race. Organised *lee-ing* went on into the second half of the nineteenth century. A Deerness man called David Wards had a great reputation on the cliff. He used a rope fixed to a stake, the other end of the rope going round his waist, and the rope ran over a wooden device called a *clibber* or *clipper*, set at the edge of the cliff to prevent the abrasion of the rope. This is the same word as the word for a wooden pack-saddle. The fowler apparently also sat on the clipper at the end of the ropes.[1168] Wards wore on his feet strips of sacking wound over his socks, and carried a basket for eggs on his back.

The taking of eggs was done in two stages. On the first day all the eggs were destroyed – at least in the latter days of the practice – and a few days later, when a second run was made, it was certain that all the eggs gathered would be fresh. Teamwork was normal. Sometimes the rope, of heavy manilla, was let out by four to eight men at the top of the cliff, precise signals being used for lifting and lowering the rope holding the rockman. The normal length of rope was 200 ft (61 m). A watchman was stationed some distance off, where he could see the climber and give guidance to those on top. Care was especially necessary when the rope passed over a rocky overhang, for enough rope was needed to let the rockman swing inwards and land safely on a ledge. Wards would untie the rope and lay down the basket on a suitable ledge, to let him get more freedom to move about. When ready to come up, he signalled, and a man at the top, tethered to a rope, would bend forward to get the full basket off his back. The last organised egg-collecting took place shortly before the First World War, when the sons of Robert Foubister, farmer in Copinsay, went down the cliff. Running the Lee was done every five days for a season of six weeks. The auks' eggs were boiled, fried, scrambled or poached, one or two to a meal depending on size. They tasted stronger than a hen's egg and had a darker yolk. When sold, they went to R. Garden's shop in Kirkwall, being picked up as a rule by his horse-drawn travelling shop. The price given in 1900 was about 3/– a dozen, and 580 dozen were sold. The last selling of eggs took place in 1914. The cliff

rights went with the farm. The average crop of eggs was a few puffin and
fulmar eggs in June, about 10 dozen kittiwake eggs in June, about 6 dozen eider
duck eggs in June to July, 540 to 630 dozen guillemots' or auks' eggs in June to
July, and over 100 dozen seagulls' eggs. Kittiwake eggs were gathered in a hat
held in the hand, those of seagulls in a bucket, but the main crop of guillemots'
eggs went into a cubbie or basket on the back, in quantities of about 20 dozen at
a time.[1169]

Birds were also taken for food. According to an old man from Deerness,
'there's nothing as good as a pot of kail with an auk in it'. Scarfs were eaten in
Copinsay too, being carried home on a rope round the shoulders, and either
buried for several days or hung by the feet to let the blood run to the head,
before being boiled.[1170]

In Westray, many people took their living out of the crags until the 1890s,
after which period fowling was carried on only to add variety to the diet. In
1837, a visitor observed that 32 score young gulls had been killed on the Holm
of Papa Westray. They were salted, and the best of their feathers taken for
sale.[1171] Young birds were taken, after they were fully fledged, as well as old
birds and eggs. Eggs were taken from 1 June onwards. The nest was cleared out
completely, and put in a bag or creel, or under a man's cap. Sometimes a man
lay at the top of the cliff and pushed the eggs with a long wand into a string bag
fixed to the end of a wand held by another. Young birds were caught on the
nest, old ones in the air by means of a rod with a net on the end. Swappin was
usually done by a group of men and boys at the top of the crags, but if the need
was great a man might go himself with only his wife to manage the rope. Some
of the women could work the swap net. There are stories of men swapping sixty
to seventy birds in an evening, filling a hundredweight sack in an hour, and
catching eighty-six birds in two hours with the big net. The men could get lice
off the birds, that dug into the skin. In the Faroe Islands, poor people might be
described as *lúsaskarvur*, the lice among the shag's feathers.[1172] John Drever
and William Mackay, North Via, were probably the last to go auk swapping in
Papa Westray. They did it from a boat, in the 1920s. At one time a group of
eight men shared a big net hung in a geo, the birds being collected by a small
boat below. Sometimes the birds were shot.

Westray shares with the Faroe Islands a linguistic distinction between the
shag and the cormorant. In both areas the shag is a *scarf* or *skarvur*, and the
cormorant, *Phalacrocorax carbo*, a *hibling* or *hiplingur*.[1173] The scarfs were
taken by night as they slept, and auks in the evenings. The birds were carried
home complete, in a creel or sack on the back, or in a boat, and dried and
plucked. The main but not the only time for scarfs was September. It is told of a
Westray man that when landed from a boat at Red Ness, he caught the watchman scarf and then ran along the ledges, catching ninety-six sleeping scarfs in
all, wringing their necks and lowering them to the boat below. Auks were
caught by an experienced fowler called a *pooltie* (origin uncertain, but probably
a special usage of *pult*, a short, stout person), who was lowered on a rope to run
along the ledges catching auks. The men above hauled up the creels as the

pooltie filled them. It was on Fool Craig (Old Norse *fugl*, bird) that the last great auk known to have lived in the British Isles was shot about 1813.[1174]

There are no records of egg sales in Westray. The eggs were eaten at home, and the birds were taken mainly for food and feathers. Twelve auks produced 1 lb of feathers, and a man could pluck five birds in an hour. The feathers were used to stuff mattresses and pillows for home use and for sale, at 6 lb of feathers or seventy-two birds to a pillow, and 60 lb or 720 birds to a mattress. Feathers were stored in sacks in a dry place, and individuals sold them in the Kirkwall market. At one time a Westray merchant shipped a ton of feathers to London, but they did not keep.

Birds were mostly eaten fresh after being singed and plucked. Auks were in best condition in July, when they were most oily. The commonest way of preparing them was by parboiling and frying in butter, with shallots. Some people said they tasted like beef, some better than beef, others that they were a bit like liver, possibly because the meat was rather dark. Some people salted them slightly. Eider ducks were also shot and salted, one man saying that he ate all the livers and hardly tasted the meat. The heart and gizzard were also eaten. The women baked *fatty-cutties* with the fat from eider ducks. *Cuttie* (cf. Gaelic *cutach*) is the name normally given to the black guillemot, *Cepphus grylle*. Young kittiwakes fried in butter were regarded as a delicacy, and tasted like chickens. The feet of the solan geese were used in the Faroe Islands.[1175]

Murderers consisting of a lead with hooks attached were let down to catch young birds, the device being like the fishing tackle with the same name. For eggs, a pole with a claw on the end, that could be closed over the egg, was also used.[1176]

It need scarcely be said that fowling was dangerous, though accidents do not appear to have been common. When Scott visited Fair Isle in 1814, a 'fine boy of fourteen' had dropped from the cliff two weeks before into a roaring surf, but a writer on Foula said in 1863 that not one life had been lost there at fowling in the nineteenth century, and only two that he could hear of in the eighteenth.[1177]

Some further details about fowling methods come from nineteenth century Shetland. Cormorants could be caught in great numbers by going in a boat with a fire under the cliffs by night. The birds flew to the fire and could be clubbed as they approached.[1178] Small birds that came in winter, the 'snaa fowl', snow buntings and twites, could be caught in corn-yards by a number of horsehair nooses fixed to a 'snaa fowl brod' (board), of which an example is known from Fair Isle.[1179] A similar idea is known from Fetlar, where a hoop of wood or iron was fitted with criss-cross cords to which horsehair nooses were tied. Oats and chaff were scattered on the snow, and the girn set on top. Pigeons or starlings hopping around for grains got their legs or necks trapped. An alternative used by the young lads was the 'trappa-door'. This was simply a door set on edge in the snow, supported by a stick. Grain and chaff was scattered beside it, and when the birds started eating in numbers, the stick was jerked away by means of a cord. Several birds could be caught beneath the falling door.[1180] A way of catching swans at one time was to shoot them, using a horse as a decoy. They fed

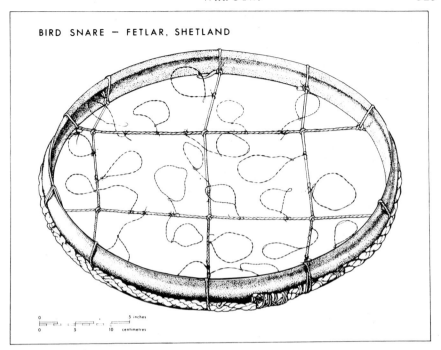

BIRD SNARE — FETLAR, SHETLAND

249. A girn with horsehair nooses for catching small land-birds in snow. Made by J. Laurenson, Fetlar, 1960s. C1267.

in the middle of the lochs by day, but in the evening came nearer the banks, feeding on insects. The fowler led his horse along the bank, keeping it between the swans and himself, till within shooting range. In calm weather they could also be taken easily because they could not get airborne without a breeze of wind. Tame ones were marked on the feet.[1181]

For a long time the taking of birds and eggs was an essential part of the economy in certain areas, of both domestic and commercial importance, until changing conditions and legislation such as the Sea Birds Preservation Act of 1869 and the Wild Birds Preservation Act of 1880 and 1881 brought the systematic practice to an end.

60

Seals and Otters

AMONGST the resources of the sea-shore were seals, caught for their skins and fat, and sometimes for their flesh. People were prepared to go 40 miles to Sule-skerry for the skins and fat of seals, sometimes a dangerous trip when many men could be lost, but 200 to 300 seals might be taken with the use of clubs. This outing took place once a year.[1182]

They were caught in different ways. In 1603, it was ordained that no 'selchie netis' were to set on my Lord's holms without leave. They were knocked down with clubs, and shot with muskets, on the skerries of Hoy and Walls, of North Ronaldsay, Eday, Westray and Wyre, the Pentland Skerries, and Little Holm in Yell Sound. Nets were set up before high water around the haunts of the seals on the Skerries, with the upper edge at such a height that the seals could swim over. When the tide fell sufficiently and enough of the net was clear, a sudden alarm was given which drove the seals into the net and entangled them. The nets were generally set at night. Netting was practised in North Ronaldsay and young seals were clubbed. The netting of seals in high summer is documented from 1537 in Åland, as well as in Iceland and Norway.[1183]

Shooting with a gun was the main method of killing, however. This required skill, for if the bullet did not go through its brain, the seal would escape. A seal-hunter's equipment consisted of a gun, a waterglass, a *clam* (cf. Norwegian *klemme*, to grasp with the claws, *klamme*, fetter, clamp), a stout rod 12 to 20 ft (3.7–6.1 m) long with a ling hook firmly lashed to the end. This was needed in case the seal sank. The waterglass, simply a wooden box with a pane of glass in the bottom, allowed under-surface viewing, and was generally used with a coat or cloth over the head. The clam itself had jaws 2 to 3 ft (61–91 cm) wide when open, with two lines, one for lowering and one for closing the jaws over the dead seal. The laird of Burness in Shetland used a very thick-barrelled fowling piece for seal-hunting, deadly up to 60 to 80 yds (55–73 m). He hunted from a 17 ft (5.2 m) keel boat, with a crew of four, going off for up to a week at a time and staying at the houses of brother lairds. He could get a catch of 40 or 50 seals at one outing. A good dog could be trained for retrieving in seal-hunting.[1184]

Seal-skins were amongst the exports of Orkney from at least the seventeenth century. In 1801 to 1802, 12 seal-skins were mentioned, 373 in 1802 to 1803, 14 in 1803 to 1804, and 48 in 1805 to 1806.[1185] The skins were used at home and away for various purposes. Some of the Orcadians, especially country people, wore seal-skin shoes, tied around the feet with string, or leather thongs, without being sewn, or calf-skin. The hair side was worn on the outside. Skins were also made into slippers, and covers for trunks and saddles.[1186] The people of Burrafirth in Unst sold the skins of seals they caught, and salted the meat for eating at Lent. Olaus Magnus noted in Sweden in 1555 that seal-flesh was regarded as fish by the church in Sweden, though eventually the eating of seal-meat on fast days was forbidden in Norway. Later in time the eating of seal-flesh went down in the world, and was confined to poorer people, the flesh being salted and hung in the chimneys to be smoked.[1187] At one time, hunting must have been very intensive, for by 1683 it was said that their number was diminishing. Oil was also a product of the seal, used in the Northern Isles, as in Norway, for light.[1188] Seal-oil was also fed to cattle in recent times. They did not take to it easily at first, but would take any amount once they got the taste. It put a beautiful sheen on their coats. The oil was also good for harness. A good-sized seal gave about 5 gallons.[1189] Seal-oil was also used in spinning.

In the sea-language of fishermen, a seal was a *round-heid*, but the more general name was *selch* or *selchie* (Old Scots *selich*, twelfth century), applied to the common seal, *Phoca vitulina*. Natives of North Ronaldsay got the nickname, *selkies*, perhaps because of the longer survival there of the eating of seal-meat.[1190] This seal also got the name of *tang-fish*, *tangie* or *tongie* (Norwegian, Faroese, Old Norse *þang*, seaweed). The large grey seal that frequented the open sea, probably *Halichoerus grypus*, was the *haaf-fish* (Norwegian *hav*, Old Norse *haf*, sea ocean). By synecdoche, seals were also called *hides* in Orkney, and the same name was given to the people of North Ronaldsay.[1191] This may be associated with the Orkney belief that seals could discard their skins and return to their original human state from time to time. Such beliefs are easy to understand when the eerie and very human *bogling* (probably from *bogle*, ghost) call of the North Ronaldsay seals echoes in the darkness from behind the sheep-dyke in the ears of the solitary walker. Traditions about seals in human form are legion.[1192]

OTTERS

Otter-skins were also being exported from Orkney in the seventeenth century and later. In 1805–6, nine were exported. In Shetland they were said to be so plentiful, 'and even so familiar, that in cold Winter Nights they will come into Peoples Houses, and lie down by the Fire like a Dog.' They were rarely shot, but knocked down with sticks. Their skins were saleable, and their fat produced some oil. The skin of a winter-killed otter, with plenty of fur, fetched about 10/– sterling in the early 1800s. The name for it in sea-language was *dratsie* (cf. Norwegian dialectal *dratla*, Icelandic *drattast*, to trudge, plod, Old Norse *dratta*, to walk heavily and slowly).[1193]

Otters were commonly caught in stone traps, *otter-hooses*. Traces of these are still to be seen, built above ground across the otters' tracks, about 2 ft high by 2 ft wide by 9 ft long (61×61×274 cm), and roofed with fairly heavy, flat

250. An otter-house in Shetland. 3.25.20.

stones. At one end was a flat stone on its edge, with a small hole in it to admit the light. The other end was closed by a door sliding up and down in grooves, made of old black oak or similar wood because the otter was too wary if white wood was used. It was raised and kept up by a black string, the end of which was taken down through an opening between the roofing slabs, and along one side of the inside wall. A stone on the floor, well into the far end, was placed on another to pivot, and the end of the string gripped between these. The otter displaced the stone and released the string, the door fell, and it was caught. It made for the stone with the light-opening, without turning, and gnawed at the hole until captured. This was done by shooting, or by letting a loop of rope down through the roof stones and poking the otter with a stick till it got its head into the noose, when it was hanged. A trap noted in Havera in the 1950s was shaped like a bee-skep, with its entrance to the seaward side.[1194]

The skin of the otter, when dressed, was glossy and beautiful, like the finest sealskin. The spread of firearms greatly reduced the number of otters. A fisherman in the Skerries shot a great many, and sold the skins to hawkers in Lerwick, at 5/– to 7/6 each. Elegant vests could be made of their skin.[1195]

61

Sillock, Piltock and Dogfish

THROUGHOUT the centuries, coalfish have been fished from the shores, as a main source of both food and oil for the ordinary folk of the Northern Isles. At different stages in its existence, the coalfish, *Gadus virens*, had different names. In its first year it was a *sillock* (cf. Swedish dialectal *sil*, the young of fish). At the next stage, about the second year, it was a *piltock* (extended sense of Old Norse *pilt*, young lad, boy). In Orkney, as widely on the east coast of Scotland, a coalfish in its second year was a *podlie* (Old Scots *podlo*, 1525). The name *cuithe*, *cuddy* or *coothin* (Norwegian dialectal *kôd*, fry, especially of the coalfish, Modern Icelandic *kôd*, the young of plaice) is given to the coalfish in Orkney, from its first to its third year. The generic name *gray-fish* was also given to coalfish in their second or third year in the Northern Isles. After that, it is a full grown *saithe* (Old Scots *seath*, 1632; Old Norse *seiðr*, Norwegian, Danish, *seid*, *sei*).

From the early 1600s at least, sillock were caught in quantity for the oil from their livers,[1196] which were boiled in a pot half full of water. The oil that rose to the surface was skimmed off and put into stone jars for future use. The livers were washed in fresh water and left to drain through straw before being boiled. In Orkney this was called *breathing* (Old Norse *brœða*, Swedish dialectal *bräda*, to melt) the livers. The oil was lifted off with an iron spoon bent to suit the purpose, or with a shell fixed on the end of a stick. The livers could be rolled in oatmeal and eaten when all the oil had been removed, but such *crappened* (cf. Dutch *kroppen*, Middle Dutch *croppen*, Middle Low German *kroppen*, to stuff the crop) livers were not easy to digest.[1197] Probably some of the oil paid by Shetlanders as part of the King's rents, and sent south for soap making, was from this source. In 1652 alone, over 502 barrels of oil were paid as part of the rent in Shetland.[1198] Livers could also be made into pies and broiled on the coals. In the late eighteenth century, the poorer tenants were selling oil from these small fish caught in the voes at 30/– to 50/– a barrel. Three hundred barrels were exported to Hamburg and Dublin in 1790. Up to 2000 barrels of oil had been got from sillock livers in a seven-month period, though in the early 1800s the quantity had been reduced to about 300 barrels a year. Orkney exports in 1801 to 1802 amounted to 10 gal, in 1802 to 1803, 38 barrels, in 1803 to 1804, 6 barrels, in 1804 to 1805, 10 barrels, and in 1805 to 1806, 63 barrels.[1199]

Coalfish were also important as food. They must be regarded as a hunger-food, filling the gap when other sources failed, for the poor often had to live on them for many weeks at a time, sometimes beating them small in lieu of bread. The almost exclusive living on fish by the poorer classes was thought to be the cause of scurvy, which was prevalent.[1200]

In the 1770s in Orkney, coalfish were widely caught around Flotta and Switha by boats from the South Isles, from May onwards. Dogfish, which drove the coalfish off, were also valued for food and oil. The nine families on Swona depended on coalfish and dogfish as well as on their crops, drying the fish in skeos. Fish cured in this way were tougher than those dried over a fire. Fish and oil were the only produce of this island. In Sanday, the lower classes lived on fish, salted and hung in the chimneys to smoke.[1201]

In the scale of commercial values, coalfish came at the bottom. Shetland fishers got 1d for saithe in the 1780s, whereas cod, tusk and ling sold at 2d to 6d. Many saithe were caught in the Sumburgh Roost, from boats of Norway build containing three or four men. Two rowed, one sat at the stem, and one at the head, with floating lines thrown out on the tide side. The hooks were baited with the whitest part of the belly of the coalfish, cut to the size of a herring. The men rowed on the edge of the broken water, and when the tide had run, used a technique of dragging for coalfish by putting a lead or sinker of $1\frac{1}{2}$ lb on the line, letting it run 20 fathoms (36.6 m) deep, and then hauling it up quickly.[1202]

Rod fishing, especially for coalfish, was also carried out extensively from small boats inshore. Either the boat was anchored in smooth water between the shore and the tidal current, or it was rowed very quickly, *andooed* (Norwegian, Faroese *andøva*, Old Norse *andœfa*), against wind and tide, by one of its two or three occupants, to hold it in position. The name *eela* (Norwegian dialectal *ila*, Norwegian *ile*, Old Norse *ili*, a stone used as an anchor) was applied to this kind of fishing. Fishing in this way became rare because of the use of the fly, but it could parallel closely the craig-fishing technique with limpet-bait, *soe* (Norwegian dialectal *så(d)*, Old Norse *sað*, seed, sowing, Norwegian *så*, Old Norse *sá*, to sow), the boats being anchored at the chosen spot by means of a rope and stone called an *eelasteen*, *faas drave*, or *fastie*. The period for this type of fishing for piltocks, using limpet-bait but no flies, was April and May.

The fisherman took with him a good supply of half-boiled limpets 'which he chewed to an oily pulp before spitting them out in a rapid series of blobs on the sea immediately around the boat. As the oily "vam" (cf. Norwegian dialectal *vam*, mishap, used figuratively) spread, sillaks were attracted to the area and as soon as the lust grew, the fisherman no longer had to bait his hook but just kept "soing" and taking the fish aboard on a bare hook'.[1203] The oarsman or in Caithness *annosman*[1204] sat on the fore-taft, and one or two men sat aft with rods and flies on the stem-taft, which was often lifted on to the quarters. Rods a foot or so longer than for craig fishing were preferred. In favourable conditions, large catches of sillock and piltock could be taken. The flies were worked over the stem, and allowed to stream out to the combined length of rod and line. Four to six hooks were common. The flies, however, did not float on the surface, but were submerged, since it was the usual practice to hold the points of the rods under water. Poke nets could also be worked from such boats.

Summer and autumn fishing for piltock differed in that the rods and tackle used in autumn were stronger. According to one account, the fishers, each with two rods, trawled their lines astern. The slightly flattened haft of the rod rested along the thigh from the joint to the knee. When one line was being unhooked, the other had to be left, otherwise there was a risk of entanglement. In this way up to 900 piltock could be drawn in three hours, which in August could weigh 150 to 160 lb.[1205]

A North Ronaldsay account tells how cuithe-fishing was done from yoles. The men chewed limpets and spat the mixture out around their own line. As for the line, 'we snudded hid wursels. Thoo wud snud a short lent o' horse hair atween the tick tome aun the fish, aun then snud a straight long hair, aboot eighteen inches long. A loop was put on it where there wus a lead – at the ither end wus the hook. There was a thin sheet o' lead (lead-luss) tae sink thee tome – on the loop o' the snud. The tome tapered tae the end. Thoo hid a stock o' snuds aun hooks in thee bannet, aun a stock o' lead-lusses in thee pooch. Thoo crushed the lead togither in thee teeth. Hid tuk ane tae seeven lusses tae sink thee tome rapidly tae the bothom; hid wus hanked in peedie hanks in thee left haund, aun the rest in the right, and flung oot straight as an arrow, keepan the wand snog . . .'

The cuithes were much caught about Hallowmas. They were eaten fresh, or split, salted, and dried over the smoke, or soured before being eaten. The Eday people, in an island well supplied with peat, had a good chance of drying cuithes in quantity, strung across the house to get the benefit of the open fires. Cuithes were also hung around the houses, where they dried as hard as wood, and gave off a kind of phosphorescence.[1206]

As with any type of fishing, the texture of the sea-bed was important, and in the case of sillock and piltock the best grounds were those with a tangly bottom, in and around areas of sunken rocks called *baas*. This was a very common term in place names. For example, in Fetlar, the best eela grounds, listed from east to west round the island, are Artie's Baa, Berg Baas, Rab's Baas, Gambla Hel-licks, da Hivda, da Skukkies, da Baas o' Holm, Klunger, da Finnie Baas, Oot an Eeast, Hestaness, Bight o' Skamro, Baas o' Urie, Hairy's Knuckles, Bight o' Mailand, Brennick Bas, Bight o' Selligeos, Mouth of Moowick, Hoga Baas, Silvie Baa, Heogs Baa, Scarfa Skerry, Soders Baa, Bight of Combs Geo, Aid Skerries. Even where the word baa is not used, some other name referring to rocks is usually present. At such places, the coalfish were often found in dense shoals, and when tightly packed were said to be *steaded* (Norwegian *støde*, fishing ground, *støda*, crowded mass).[1207]

In the 1790s, the place of the coalfish in the subsistence pattern was prom-inent. In Delting, each householder with a small farm could feed his family from the produce for three-quarters of the year, if the sillock and piltock fishing did not fail. Sillocks also eked out the grain stocks in the parish of Lerwick and in Northmavine. In Unst, the poorer folk got food and oil from the 'small gray fish', caught from the rocks. In Bressay, fishing for sillock was a winter job.[1208] In Cross, Burness and North Ronaldsay, 'cuths', said to be called 'podleys' on the south coast, were caught, but no fish or oil was sold. In Holm, fishing took place during summer and harvest. Each individual had a seat or share in a fishing boat, the catches being for home and family use. In Firth, some sillocks were caught in November. In Stromness harbour, where the poke-net was much used, sillocks were caught in quantities from September to March, yielding a lot of oil. In Westray there was no one who earned a living entirely by fishing, which was only done to supplement the family food supply. The men caught 'cooths' or 'grey fish', and young cuiths which were called *tibricks* (perhaps a variant, with transferred sense, of Gaelic *dubhb(h)reac*, black trout). Dogfish were also taken for their oil. Similarly in Shapinsay the men fished for sillocks 'for their daily support', and in St Andrews and Deerness the country people caught coalfish, as well as some cod, skate, haddock, halibut, dogfish and a few ling. Sillocks were numerous around the shores of Birsay, and dogfish, caught on handlines, were sold to neighbouring parishes at 6d a dozen. They were best in June, July, August. The oil from the livers sold at 10d a pint. Dogfish were also caught on hand lines off the Orphir coast between mid-June and the end of August. The oil was extracted from the livers, and the flesh cured and smoked. If the dogfishing failed, oil was very scarce. At other seasons the main fish taken were 'keiths' or sillocks which were smoked, and constituted a major element in the food of the inhabitants. There were twenty-four boats in the parish, each crewed by four or five men, but the emphasis on kelp making as a major commercial activity hindered further development of the fishery.[1209]

Nineteenth century sources bring out further details. In Orphir, sillocks were caught all the year round, dogfish only in the summer. The latter, known as 'piked dogfish', were dried and cured as food for the poor, and lamp oil was made from their livers. In July–August, dogfish were widely caught in Orkney with hand-lines, for oil and food, the bodies being dried and stored unsalted for the winter. Sillocks were also caught closer inshore, and the oil from their livers was used by the local people. It got rancid quickly, however. Thornbacks, locally called skates, were also a food of the poor. Like the dogfish, they were dried without salt – which was expensive because of the salt-tax – and could be seen 'hanging about the chimneys of the meaner cottages'. In Shetland, the house gables were hung with hundreds of piltock, strung on spits and exposed to dry without salt. Fish so dried in the sun and wind were called *scrae-fish* (Old Scots *scrafish* 1561; Old Norse *skreið*, shoal of fish, *skǫrð*, *skreið*, dried fish).[1210]

The late eighteenth-century pattern at this level of subsistence had not yet greatly changed. Work specialisation was still rare. In Holm and Paplay, for example, every householder, whether tenant or cottar, had a share in a fishing boat though none was a full-time fisher. It was essentially a community of small farmers who fished for home supplies, not for any commercial reason, and if they were not farming or fishing they might be acting as shoemaker, tailor, smith or carpenter. Fishing, at least as a trade, was seen as incompatible with improved farming. The local development of the herring fishery, however, had some effect on the older order, for where, as in South Ronaldsay and Burray, the people had fished sillocks and podlies for wind-drying and sold them by thousands, catching other fish for their own families, now the time spent in herring fishing was reducing the time spent in laying in stores for their domestic needs. Nets were used to take up fish in the bays, a practice known as 'sillock-sweeping'.[1211]

In the North Isles of Orkney, conditions were more closely analogous to those of Shetland, and around Stronsay and Eday, the main fishing, using both bait and fly, was still for sillock or cuith, which provided food for three-quarters of the year. In Cross and Burness, coalfish were caught on the fly from the rocks or from the stern of a small boat. In Westray, dogfish and coalfish were caught for oil and for home consumption. Sillocks and cuiths caught on the Orphir shores in winter provided good food, as also in Walls and Flotta.[1212]

In Shetland at the same period, saithe were the most widely spread fish around the shores, and the young coalfish were 'really the staff of life to the inhabitants', largely taking the place of bread during the four years of scarcity preceding 1840. Mussel scalps in Sandsting and Aithsting provided bait for small fishing. Sillocks in the first year grew to about 6 in. (15 cm), and piltocks in the second year to 10 or 12 in. (25–30 cm) long. A second year fish was a *bilya piltock* (probably Faroese, Icelandic *beli*, Old Norse *belgr*, belly, but cf. Swedish dialectal *bäll, bell*, Danish dialectal *bælle*, little boy), and one of three years a *steven piltock* (cf. Norwegian dialectal *styving*, half-grown halibut, young lad). The Fair Islanders concentrated on saithe, having given up the fishing for ling and tusk at a distance from the land. About 40 tons of dried saithe were transported to the Leith market each year, and the oil was also a gain. Coalfish were caught in quantity in Delting for home use, as food and for oil.[1213]

Both sillock and piltock were of very great importance in the domestic economy, with the possibility of income from the oil. They were not exploited commercially, and fishing for them remained a prerogative of the ordinary folk of the Northern Isles. Dogfish, *Squalus acanthias*, served a similar purpose, but in Orkney rather than Shetland. Commercially speaking, dogfish are regarded as a nuisance on Shetland grounds, feeding greedily on fish and other organisms. The name is *hoe* (Norwegian *haa*, Old Norse *hár*, dogfish, shark), with the derivatives *koly-ho* (perhaps from *collie*, a lamp using fish oil), the lesser dogfish, *Scyllium canicula, hodry* (*hoe* + Norwegian *drøi*, big, bulky), a very large kind of dogfish, *hokel* or *hokillin* (cf. Norwegian *haakall, haakjerring*, Old Norse *hákerl, hákerling*), a large kind of dogfish, and *hoketling* (Faroese *hákelling*), a young dogfish. Hoe was also used as a nickname for the inhabitants of Birsay in Orkney. It is only in relatively recent times, since the late 1950s, that dogfish have been caught for commercial sale around the Northern Isles.[1214]

251. A piltock-wand and docken-budie carried by Peter Scott, The Ark, Papa Stour, 1967.
3.38.9.

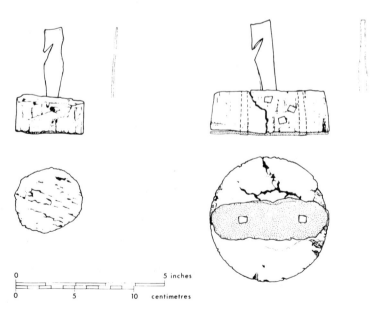

252. Dipsies for twisting horsehair bird snares (left) and fishing tomes (right), made by J.
Laurenson, Fetlar. C1265.

CRAIG FISHING

In coastal areas, particularly where land resources are limited, fishing from the rocks has been common from earliest times. Amongst the poorer people it has often been an absolute necessity. The craig-fishings were 'to the ancient dweller of our islands what the fishing boat is to the modern fisherman'. Proprietary rights were claimed in them and up till about the mid-nineteenth century it appears that 'sanguinary encounters' to defend these rights were not unknown.[1215]

Craigseats were well known and much frequented places, especially when the population was at its height in the early nineteenth century. Throughout the Northern Isles, wherever the rocks were suitable, they could be found. The name given to them was *craig sitting*, *craigasoad*, or *craigstane*. The men who fished from them were *craigers*, and the phrase applied to fishing for coalfish with a rod was 'to go to the craigs'. *Craig* and the compounds noted here are Scots in origin, but another term, *bersit* or *bergset*, goes back beyond that, for it is compounded of two Norse words, *berg*, a rock, and *sæti*, a seat.[1216] The terminology, therefore, not only points to long continuity of use, but also to historical change.

Craig fishing with rods is still practised, more for pleasure than from necessity, in order to get fresh fish or to lay in a stock to be dried and salted for winter. At present, as in earlier times, the fish chiefly caught are coalfish, especially in their younger stages. When they reach the later 'saithe' stage of development they are more often caught offshore. The *pollack*, *Gadus pollachius*, or *lure* (Norwegian *lyr*, Old Norse *lýrr*), resembling the coalfish but of an inferior flavour, was also caught, and occasionally mackerel. Craig fishing was a job for the men, but boys also took to it early as noted in Shetland in 1633 with reference to 'young Sheaths (saithe), called by the Inhabitants Pelltacks, which in fair Weather come so near the Shore, that Men, yea Children, from the Rocks with fishing Rods, caught them in abundance'. The writer, an Orkney laird, knew the young coalfish by the name 'podlines'.[1217]

Fishing from the rocks of the shore can be done with a rod and line of fixed length, a length of cord and a float, or a circular net. The fishing rod or *wand* as used in Shetland was home-made, of two or sometimes three lengths of wood, with an average length of about 11 ft (3.4 m) if bamboo was available, but if made of a slip of Norway pine a length of 8 or 9 ft (2.4–2.7 m) was more usual. The wooden parts were scarfed together, and served with twine over the joints to give strength and flexibility. Like an angler's rod, it tapered from the main part or *limb* towards the point, which was known as the *tap* or *mull* (Norwegian *mule*, Old Norse *múli*, muzzle, snout). There was no reel, and the line was of fixed length, so adjusted that when the fish was lifted from the water it swung in convenient to the fisher's hand. The line was secured to the point of the rod with a whipping of yarn, called the *mulin* (from *mull*),[1218] and an extra length was brought back down the body of the rod, through a ring, to be fastened approximately half-way down. In Fetlar, the name *undertome* (Old Scots *toume*, 1670;

Norwegian dialectal *taum*, fishing line, Old Norse *taumr*, string, cord) was given
to this extra piece. The cast or tome was made of horsehair, twisted by hand as
for fowling snares. In course of time, horsehair lines were replaced by fine
hempen cord with a short length of gut to which the hook was attached, leading
to the disuse of the old horsehair tome and single hook, and to their replacement by the 'sillock and piltock flee' (young coalfish fly). The fly consisted of a
number of 9 in. (23 cm) lengths of gut knotted on to each other seriatim, in such
a way that a two-inch (5 cm) length of each, called the *bid*, was left dangling.
The lure, usually a tuft of white hair known as the *buskin* (Old Scots *busk*, to
array, 1375; Old Norse *búask*, prepare oneself) from cow, dog, cat, hoe-tail or
man, was attached to the end of the bid along with the hook, and the whole unit
was fixed to the line by a short length of cord. Three to six flies were common,
set about a foot (30 cm) apart. The hooks were often bent pins or small hooks
with the barbs pinched down, since barbs were a nuisance in getting the fish off.
The multiple hooks greatly increased the catching power. In 1721, 2000 small
'Celacoks' (sillock hooks), and bundles of tome lines, were included in the
cargo of the *Margret* from Hamburg, and a Queensferry boat that came to
Shetland from Hamburg in 1734 carried a bundle of 'Tomalyn' (tome line)
suitable for piltock and sillock fishing.[1219]

An essential adjunct to craig fishing was limpet bait. A limpet-knife, in Fair
Isle called an *ebb-pick*, often the broken blade of a kitchen knife fitted in a
wooden handle, was used to lever limpets off the rocks, and they were collected
in a straw and bent grass limpet cuddie, or a small wooden box. They were
parboiled, and taken by the craiger to his craig-seat, as dusk was falling. The
limpet bait was attached to the hook, or mashed to serve as ground bait. The
first step was to prepare the mashed bait, or soe, and as a rule this was done in
cup-shaped hollows near the craig-seats, some of them natural, others arti-
ficially formed. These hollows have been the subject of learned antiquarian
discussion from time to time, but their purpose is clear. A letter that sums the
matter up in a convincingly practical manner appeared in the *Shetland Times*
for 17 January 1885:

> Sir, – My investigation into the cup-holes has been confined to the sea-board, and chiefly
> those places frequented for rod fishing. With this limitation, I proceed to say what I have found.
> First, I have not found cup-holes on the shores of quiet voes, but on rocks exposed to the open
> sea, and consequently to the tides. On some places a small mussel grows visible at half-tide; at
> other places these mussels – locally called pills – are not to be found. I have never found these
> cup-holes but in the neighbourhood of these mussels. In some places I have found one hole only,
> in other places two, and frequently three. Where there are three, one is larger than the other
> two. All are of the same depth – about six inches or so, and no doubt made by human hand.
> Second – their apparent use. If they have had a mysterious use, I must leave that for others to
> discover. Fishing from rocks exposed to the tides the fish won't stay. A lure called 'soe' is needed
> to bring the fish, and this has to be repeated every now and then. The best lure known is these
> small mussels pounded into a jelly. This can be done with a handy stone and smooth bed, but this
> process is often inconvenient. You have to bring the stone each time, as you find the sea has
> washed away the one you brought before. Then a clean surface is rare, and the least weed on the
> rock spoils the lure. On the other hand, the hole is clean, and no stone is needed. A pounding
> stick, or even the butt-end of a fishing rod answers well. Third – the process. On a rock where six

or eight may have sat down to fish, two boys are told off to prepare this lure. A small quantity is put into the little holes, and when well pounded put into the centre big hole, and so on until the big hole is full. This commonly serves while the fishing lasts for the time being. The men of former times were practical, if anything; they spared no pains or tact to secure success, and these cup-holes, whatever other end they secured, were the things wanted to successful fishing. My impression is that no high end was intended by the cup-hole makers. – Yours, etc. A.

When the lure of mashed limpets was doing its work and the first fish appeared, the craiger would take limpets between his teeth and chew them to the correct degree of softness before putting them on the hook. An expert was said to be able to bait the hook by slipping it into the chewed limpet gripped between his front teeth, but lesser men took the bait between their fingers first. The 'sillock and piltock flee', however, did away with the need to use chewed limpets as bait.

For successful craig fishing, an offshore wind was required. The wind on the fisherman's back and a smooth sea with a good *lioom* (Norwegian dialectal *lømme, ljome*, Old Norse *ljómi*, shining, radiance, *ljóma*, to gleam) from the oil in the belly of the limpets helped to bring the fish *at*, but in the fall of the year the young sillocks were often close into a good craig seat, and little bait was necessary. In Orkney the oily patch made by throwing or spitting out limpet bait was called a *glee* (Norwegian dialectal *gly*, soft, loose slime on fish, *glya*, slime, transparent mass, Old Norse *gljá*, to glisten), *ligny, linyo* (Norwegian dialectal *lygna*, from Old Norse *logn*, calm), *uthy* (origin uncertain; cf. Norwegian dialectal *udu, vudu, ida*, Old Norse *iða*, eddy), and the bait itself was *furto* (origin uncertain; perhaps related to *frush*, spit out, from Norwegian dialectal *frøsa, frusa*, Icelandic *frussa*, to spurt, sputter. Cf. Shetland Norn *furso*, id.), *raa-saithe* or *saithe* (*raw* + *sæd*, Old Norse *sæði*, seed). When the men chewed limpets and 'spat out furto', it caused an oily smooth patch. 'Nowadays, people are usually too "nice" to chew the *furto*, and chop it up instead with a stone on the rocks.'[1220]

If the wind was not suitable on one part of the coast, the geography of the islands often made it possible to cross to the other side of the land to get the wind on the back. When the fisherman left the seat the stone pounder was taken out of the soe-hole and laid for safety in a hollow above high-water mark, so that it should not be washed away by breakers.

A skilful angler could handle two rods at a time. Whilst one was lifted to take off the fish, the other was gripped between his knees. The practice of holding a 'wand' in each hand was also known in the early 1800s[1221] and when the fish began to 'set in' or shoal in the voes in the winter time, lying in a dense swarm, all with their heads in one direction,[1222] fish could be hauled out up to the limit of the fisherman's speed. The fish were put into a basket of straw and bent grass, or of docken-stalks and bent grass. It was the custom with older fishermen to empty out the catch and count it, whether it was large or small. The same was done at the eela. Counting has only been discontinued in recent years. When he came home, the craiger would say how many score he had got.

The prevalence of craig fishing in earlier times and its close integration with

253. A sillock-poke in Shetland. From Barnard 1890. xvii. C1514.

the life of the ordinary folk is shown by the beliefs and lore associated with it. For example, scum or froth on the limpet brew was reckoned a good sign for fishing, as was a number of birds sitting on the craig seat. According to a Westray man, 'If we were going to the fishing, and had half boiled the limpets before we went, and if that was upset after it was boiled, there was no use going to the fishing, for no a living bone would we get.'[1223] Seals were not regarded favourably around the fishing places. If a fisherman had left anything behind, he would not go back into the house to get it, but would shout outside for someone to bring it to him. He was also careful to avoid women when going to the fishing, but if he met one by chance, he spat three times when she had passed. On the other hand there was no superstition about women if they came laden with provisions and tobacco to the fishing lodges where the men involved in line-fishing had been leading a bachelor life.

An alternative to the fishing-wand, much used by older men on the craig seats, was known in Fetlar as a *steepa-dorro* (probably from *steep*, soak + Norwegian, Old Norse *dorg*, trailing fishing line). It consisted of a length of heavy cord several fathoms long. At one point a cork float was attached, and from it hung a length of about 6 ft (1.8 m) of line, at the end of which was a hook with a fairly large limpet as bait. The shore end was anchored to a stone on the craig seat, and the flat and tackle were thrown out as far as required. Agitation of the float showed when a fish had taken the bait, and the tackle was then

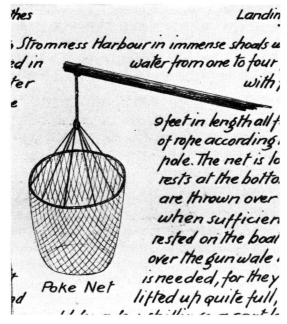

254. An Orkney poke-net, drawn by G. Ellison, *c*. 1911. 4.13.15.

255. Lifting a poke-net in Kirkwall harbour. Detail from a postcard photograph lent by P. Burr, per Miss H. Munro. C5565.

pulled in. Fish caught in this way were chiefly rock cod, large piltocks, and small tusk or cod, which lived a little farther off the rocks than the young coalfish. There can be little doubt that this device was used from Norse times or even earlier as an alternative or complement to the rod with which fish were taken much closer in.

A third method of fishing from the craig seats was by means of poke-nets, or 'sillock-pocks'. These were not as widespread in use as fishing rods, because they were more expensive and time consuming to make, and the range of craig seats from which they could be worked was more limited. A poke-net required an easily accessible cleft or *geo*, with room to work. They were 'made in the form of a parachute or umbrella suspended from the top of a long pole, and thereby let down into the sea'. The diameter of the net was commonly 5 to 6 ft (1.5–1.8 m) in Shetland, or sometimes up to 6 or 10 ft (1.8–3 m), but in Orkney it ranged up to 8 to 10 ft(2.4–3 m).[1224] According to James Laurenson in Fetlar, the mouth spread was $3\frac{1}{2}$ to 4 ft (1.1–1.2 m). The light iron hoop was suspended from three or four stays gathered together and tied to the end of the pole, which was 6 to 8 ft (1.8–2.4 m) long, by which the net was raised and lowered. The ring was of iron to give rigidity and weight, for when in action the net was sunk beneath the surface. The bag was of cord, and tapered towards the bottom. The pock was used in water not over one to two fathoms (1.8–3.6 m) deep. To sink the bag to the required depth in the sea, a stone was put in as ballast. As bait, salt herring could be put in the bag, but additionally or instead pounded limpets, sometimes mixed with mashed potatoes, were thrown into and over the body of the net as ground bait to attract the young coalfish. This could create a kind of frenzied excitement in the fish that brought them swarming together, when they could be caught in huge numbers, by lifting the net through the swarm, emptying it, and getting it back into the water again as quickly as possible. A five-foot (1.5 m) net could scoop up about a bushel to half a hundredweight of fish at a time in such conditions and twenty or thirty barrels could be filled quickly.[1225]

The usual technique was to keep the net sunk for three or four minutes after spreading the bait, and then to raise it. This the operator did 'by a peculiar process. Planting the hinder end of the pole on the rock, he sits across it, grasping it higher up with both hands. His fulcrum thus established, he slowly falls backward, the weight of his body acting as counterpoise, and the pole moves towards the perpendicular, hoisting the dripping net, from which water pours in a thousand streamlets, while some thirty or forty hapless victims flounce and tumble in the meshes they cannot escape from'.[1226]

As spring advanced, the sillocks drew off to deeper water, and dispersed, though still keeping near the coast, mostly near the rocks and tideways. It was said that after three drinks of the May flood, that is on 2 May, they became piltocks. In summer they grew quickly, got fat and improved in flavour, with flesh of a grey colour.[1227]

In Orkney, Stromness harbour provided a safe and convenient place for a more commercial use of the poke-net. Sillocks were caught there with a poke-net, in water one to four fathoms (1.8–7.3 m) deep. The net consisted of an iron hoop 10 ft (3.5 m) in diameter with a net of $\frac{1}{2}$ in. (1.2 cm) square mesh about 6 ft (1.8 m) long, all fastened together at one point, to a single rope whose length could vary depending on the depth of water. The net was lowered on a stout pole from the stem of a yawl in the harbour, and was generally allowed to rest on the bottom. A bait of mashed crabs was thrown out, and the net was hauled as soon as the sillocks had gathered. This usually took place in November. In frosty weather when the fish were plentiful, no bait might be needed. The fish were sold for a few shillings a cartload for manure in the fields, or were kept in large floating boxes for bait for the long-lines of the trawlers that went to the fishing banks of North Faroe, Iceland, and elsewhere.[1228] This practice was on a bigger scale than the more domestic poke-net fishing of Shetland, or of the Caithness island of Stroma in the Pentland Firth.

The closest analogy to the poke-net in the Northern Isles is the hoop-net for fishing lobsters (see page 544). In other parts of Europe, where such 'dip-nets' are used, the shape is often square rather than round.[1229] The evolution of poke-nets in the Northern Isles may be more influenced by lobster hoop-nets and hand-nets, for their use seems to accompany changing living standards and an increasing commercialisation of fishing.

After a summer night's fishing, a score or so of piltocks were beheaded, gutted, and plunged into boiling water with an extra handful of salt. As for potatoes, sea-water was always used. Five minutes was enough to boil them, and they were served with a cupful of the water in which they were boiled poured over them. They were also good when eaten cold, when they had a 'peculiar oysterish flavour'. Soup made of piltocks was liked. Many were hung up for a few days, sun-dried and then boiled or brandered over the coals. Others were washed and steeped in salt water, then dried above the hut fire and stored for later use.[1230] The catching of sillocks was sometimes organised on a community basis. When shoals came into the Bay of Firth in Orkney, notice was sent to the neighbouring parishes that there were sillocks at the 'Head o' Firt'. There, they were caught in large nets and swept to the shore, where a train of carts was waiting. Beside the kailyard of Thickbigging two peat stacks were built side by side, about $2\frac{1}{2}$ ft (76 cm) apart at the bottom, and this space was often filled half way up with sillocks in readiness for buyers. When the carts laden with fish got home, all hands helped to 'dight' or clean the fish. Gills and guts were thrown away, and livers put in a vessel. After being washed, the fish were left overnight in salt and water, and then put on spits. Either the spits were thrust through the mouths, or the fish were hung over them in pairs by the tails. Thin straw ropes were stretched across the house at intervals in such a way that the spits could be supported between them, above the fire, till they were so dry that they snapped across between the fingers. A quicker way was to dry them on a straw bed in the kiln, using a moderate heat. Either way, they were called 'melder' sillocks, using the term normally applied to dried oats, and stored in a basket or sack till required for use. Then they were soaked in warm water till the skins could be removed, and were boiled for eating with potatoes and dippings. For a snack between meals, the skin could be peeled off dry and the fish eaten raw. Fresh sillocks were often dipped in oatmeal and fried. When fried or baked on the coals without being cleaned, they were called *moogildins* (origin uncertain, perhaps Old Norse *magi*, stomach + *kýla*, to stuff, cram the belly). The same name was given if the fish was also roasted with extra livers stuffed inside. If the tails of the fish turned up during the cooking process, it was thought to be a sign that more were to come. A late-night meal of dried sillock and black potatoes boiled, with a glass of milk, forms a pleasant gastronomic memory of a visit to Fetlar in 1963.[1231]

62

Shellfish and Lobsters

OYSTERS had some importance in Orkney already by the sixteenth century, and were being included in items in Earl Patrick's Rental of 1595. They could be so large that they had to be cut in two or three before eating. They were got by cutting them with a knife from among the rocks, or by the use of drags. Those got in Deersound were cooked by being pierced with iron spits. Some large oysters were got in Walls in the 1770s. In the 1790s there was an oyster scalp in Bressay and some oysters could be got in St Andrews. In the 1800s there were oysters in the Bays of Firth and Deersound. They were gathered at low water on ledges in the Bay of Firth, with a pair of long tongs. By the second half of the nineteenth century, however, the celebrated Orkney oysters had become very scarce, though the Bay of Firth Oyster Fishery continued until after 1911.[1232]

The *dreg* (Old Scots, c. 1508) was mentioned in the seventeenth century, and a type described two centuries later, with reference to Shetland, had ten teeth, presumably in the form of a rake. When pulled behind a boat, the dreg was attached by a *dreg-tow* or rope. Dredging was largely for bait. For this purpose the large horse-mussel, *Modiolus modiolus*, was sought after, and in particular, cod were fond of it. This mussel was called a *yam* in Orkney and a *yoag* in Shetland. The origin of both words is uncertain, but the Scandinavian equivalents are Old Norse *aða*, Faroese *øða*, Norwegian *odskjil*, *ovskjel*. In Foula, the compounds *jognakessi* and *jognakoddi* (a kishie or cuddie for yoags) incorporate a genitive plural form, as does the Foula place-name Jognapøl, a small creek where the mussels were gathered for bait at low water. Mussels were dredged from beds or *scaups* (Old Scots *skalp*, 1536) by a towed *dreg*, or by a *mussel-draig* in the form of a rake with hooked teeth, or gathered by hand in the *mussel-ebb*, the beds exposed at ebb-tide. Their primary use was for bait.[1233]

The cockle, *Cardium edule*, was common, and was also gathered with rakes on the sandy shores at low water. In spring and summer so many were got 'as to make an article of food, which is considered pleasantly delicate, as well as nourishing'. Some were sold by the country people, and some very large ones were found around Flotta.[1234] A common use of cockleshells was for lime in lime plaster, after they had been burned in a kiln.[1235] The name *buckie* (Old Scots, c. 1500) was given, as elsewhere in Scotland, to the whelk or any mollusc of the genus *Buccinum*. The *wilk* (Old Scots, 1500) was usually the smaller periwinkle, *Littorina littorea*. A powder made by drying wilks and their shells and grinding them together was known as a cure for the yellow jaundice.[1236] That the wilk was used as a hunger-food in times of scarcity is made abundantly clear by the Shetland saying, 'to gang i' da wylk ebb', meaning to be reduced to poverty. Wilk was used as a nickname for the people in the island of Veira in Orkney.[1237] The limpet (Old Scots *lempet, c.* 1568), a mollusc of the genus *Patella*, was the main bait for craig fishing knocked from rocks in the limpet-ebb with a *limpet-pick* or small chisel, and parboiled. Like many other resources of the shore, they often formed part of the food of the poor, and in 1762, a complaint was made that the burning of seaweed for kelp had left the limpet-bearing rocks unprotected by ware-blades, so that the limpets fell off in the heat of the sun and the poor were deprived of their sustenance. Harra Ebb was traditionally a portion of the foreshore allotted to Harray folk in famine years to get limpets and other shells. The natives of Stronsay were nicknamed 'limpets'. The razor-clam, *Solen*, or *spoot*, so called because it spouts or squirts liquid when disturbed, was also eaten. When fried or stewed in milk, it was regarded as a delicacy.[1238]

The crab, *Cancer pagurus*, which got the general Scottish name of *partan* (Old Scots, *c.* 1420), was common on the rocky shores and was caught by hand or drawn from its hiding place with a hook, in fine weather. Though of good quality, there was no special market for crabs in the 1880s. They were eaten at home, or sold to gentlemen's families. With the development in recent times of freezing plant, it has become possible to market the crab in a way never before possible in both Shetland and Orkney.[1239]

The lobster, *Homarus vulgaris*, was plentiful around places like Flotta in the eighteenth century, being caught in small nets baited with any kind of garbage, and hauled up in them. By the 1790s, Sandwick and Stromness had two lobster boats, whose catches were sold to London smacks, and Orkney as a whole had about 60 lobster boats, with two men in each. Lobster fishing was on the increase. The boats had a 12 ft (3.7 m) keel, and cost about £6. Fifteen smacks were working to and from London.[1240] In Shetland, the Northumberland Company for the Improvement and Extension of Fisheries had had three or four boats there for some years, served by four six-oared boats apiece, but lobster fishing had been unsuccessful. There was also the London Company, which the people of Walls helped to keep supplied with lobsters. Eday had several lobster boats, and some of the small farmers of South Ronaldsay spent a few months each year fishing lobsters. A few hands had started lobster fishing in Westray in the early 1800s. They were taken in water 2 to 6 fathoms (3.7–11 m) deep, during the night or in dull weather if by day. They were not then caught in creels, but in nets fixed to $2\frac{1}{2}$ ft (76 cm) diameter iron hoops, with lead sinkers, baited with fish, flesh or any kind of garbage. When caught, their claws were bound with twine to prevent them damaging each other, and they were put into large floating chests to await shipment to London, alive, in thousands weekly, in the wells of fishing smacks.[1241]

Under the English company, lobster fishing was expanding at this period and

256. A boat loaded with creels in Orkney. Photo. W. Hourston.

257. A lobster kist for keeping lobsters alive in the sea, in Papa Westray. The *Wolverine* in the background was the only lobster boat in the island in 1974. Photo. M. Wright. 18.28.35.

by 1808 about 100 boats with 10 men in each were engaged in the trade. By 1833, they were yielding about £2000 a year. In 1841, 2900 lobsters were caught in Stronsay, worth 3d each, and Eday had 19 lobster boats each employing two men. Cross and Burness had 14 lobster boats. Some Stromness boats went lobster fishing each summer in May and June, and between about 1829 and 1841, an average of 11,622 lobsters went annually to the London market in Gravesend smacks that called twice a week during the season. On the Orphir coast and around the shore of Cava, small-scale lobster fishing had gone on for some time. For a few years before 1841, only one boat and two men had been employed. They took their catch to Stromness once a week for shipment, storing the lobsters in floating chests in the Bay of Houton.[1242] By 1834, about 100,000 lobsters were being exported annually. The trade was lucrative, and added a welcome element to the income of the small farmers who chiefly practised it. By the 1880s, however, because of carelessness in observing the close time, and by taking under-sized fish, the annual quantity taken was on the decline. The movement of lobsters south to London continued, however, by passenger train and eventually by air, with a continuing increase in the value of shellfish after the war, and the development of local fish-processing plants. In both Shetland and Orkney, the expansion of shell-fishing has put the main emphasis on the lobster, though this has carried with it an increase in the catching of crabs.[1243]

Now lobsters and crabs are caught with fleets of creels, each with a rectangular base, a bow-shaped top, and one or two openings, depending on size. Such creels began to come into use in the Northern Isles, as elsewhere in Scotland, in the first decade of the nineteenth century. Three English smacks supplied Shetland fishermen with 'trap-baskets' in 1808.[1244] Before then, and for long after, the hoop-net was used. In North Ronaldsay, it was described as an iron hoop about the size of a bicycle-wheel, with three or four equally spaced ropes coming together into one that was held up by a buoy. This prevented the lobster from lying on top of the rope and being jerked off when the ring was lifted. The net was fixed below it, and two strings, the *mid-band*, were stretched across the hoop to hold the bait. Sometimes there were two bands set at right angles. The boats went out on clear, still nights, when visibility in the water was reasonable, for the lobster had to be seen as it took the bait. They might also go by day if conditions were suitable. They had to make absolutely no noise above the fishing grounds. The rings were let down to rest on the ocean bed, and when a lobster came at the bait, they had to be raised absolutely vertically, and as quickly as possible, otherwise the fish would escape. This meant that the men had to be in constant attendance. Creels, on the other hand, could be shot and left to do their own work, but it was not till the second half of the nineteenth century that creels reached North Ronaldsay, under the influence of the east coast of Scotland.[1245] Hoop-nets no doubt survived long around North Ronaldsay and places like the Pentland Skerries because of the strong tides and currents, and it is no accident that North Ronaldsay creels are smaller and more strongly made than in most other parts of Orkney.

63

Whales and Whaling

THE type of whale that was common in the waters of the Northern Isles, as of the Faroe Islands, was the *ca'in* whale (from Scots *ca'*, to drive) or blackfish, *Globiocephala melaena*. Whale oil was listed amongst the products of Shetland in the sixteenth century.[1246] Since the technique of catching ca'in whales was to drive them ashore, they may be regarded as a product of both sea and shore, in whose slaughter people of all kinds took part.

The division of the profit was strictly regulated, as in the Faroe Islands. When a school of whales was stranded, the bailie of the parish had to be notified. His job was to check the numbers for the admiral, representing the Crown, who then held a court there, and the judge heard the evidence about the number of whales, and where and how driven ashore. Judgement being made according to law and the country practice, the admiral then divided the catch into three equal parts, one to himself, one to those who caught the whales, and one to the proprietor of the ground on which they were driven ashore. Two honest men were judicially sworn to arrange the division. The minister or vicar claimed and usually got the teinds, and the bailie claimed the heads, and got them if the admiral considered that he had done his duty well.[1247]

One of the reasons why the admiral should hold court was that according to Scots law, whales above a certain size belonged to the king and were 'royal fish'. The size was defined as one that could not be drawn from the water to the nearest point of land on a wain with six oxen. The court decided this question, and also protected the people against the illegal carrying off of the whale by the admiral. Disputes were frequent between the three interests. In 1739 the Earl of Morton, who was invested with the rights of Admiralty, made an agreement with about twenty Shetland heritors to ease the fixing and appreciating of the shares of the different claimants. The record in the Stewart Court Books of Shetland stated that the agreement should remain in force during the period of the Earl's right of Admiralty, and assumed his right to 'all whales and pellochs (the *pellock* or porpoise, *Phocaena phocaena*, Old Scots *peloka*, 1331, origin unknown), as well great as small, of whatever kind or denomination.' On this basis the principles of division were to be:

'*Primo*. Of all whales or pellochs, not under one (1.8 m), nor exceeding four fathoms (7.3 m) in length, driven on shore and secured within the islands of

Zetland, the persons actually employed in saving and securing them, are immediately to have one third part delivered over to them, without any diminution whatsoever, at the sight of the baillie of the bounds where they are driven onshore. And the proprietor or proprietors of the ground where such whales are driven or run onshore, to share the other two third parts, delivered to them upon giving receipt and obligation to the baillie to be accountable to the earl, or his order, for one of the said two third parts, at the rate of ten shillings Sterling for each pelloch.

'*Secundo*. Of any whale fish exceeding four fathoms (7.3 m) long, the heritor or heritors of the ground where the same is driven or run on shore, shall have the sole management or disposal of having the same made in oyle, upon giving proper security to the baillie to account to the same and the earl, or his order, upon oath, by equal divisions, for two thirds of the oyle, and paying them, respectively, fifteen shillings Sterling for each barrel there – the heritors having all the charge upon the subject'.

This was not in accordance with the law of Scotland, and was without consultation with the tenants. Since porpoises could sometimes be shot with fowling pieces, and could be lifted into a boat by an individual, the Earl might as well have claimed a share of every fish that produced oil. Evidently he was taking advantage of the fact that porpoise fishing was already organised to some extent. In 1734, Fetlar had four 'pellick' boats, each of which paid a teind of three cans of oil or £1.4/– Scots (2/– stg).[1248] This, however, did not condone the Earl's action in relation to small whales, but his power here was cancelled with the abolition of heritable jurisdictions in 1747, when he received £7200 stg in indemnification for his losses. In 1766, he sold his legal rights in Shetland to Sir Laurence Dundas, who still kept on insisting on his third part of the whales caught.

Continual resistance to this alleged right was kept up by the tenants. A catch of 23 whales at Sellavoe in Sandsting in 1784 was claimed in the name of the admiral and sold. Though an appeal went to Lord Dundas, and though he ordered that the salvers should get their claim, they are said never to have got their share. The admiral's right was to royal whales only, according to the law. The heritors continued to claim a share of small whales on the basis of the 1739 agreement with the Earl of Morton, and also as proprietors of the shores on which the whales were killed, and because their claim conformed to the 'use and wont' of the country. They also included the claim as part of the bargain made with tenants on setting a twelve months' lease. The first point became invalid, if ever legal, in 1747. The second was doubtful, for much of the beach above high-water mark was reckoned 'public or royal', a fact on which was founded the privilege of drying and curing fish in Shetland. The asseveration of the heritors that the slaughtering of whales and boiling of blubber injured their kelp shores and land was scarcely tenable since the hurt, if any, fell on the tenant using the relevant piece of land. The use and wont claim was hard to substantiate, except in relation to teinds and the bailie's share for superintending division. It was set aside in 1803, when Mr Robert Ross of Sound, with 70 or 80 men, drove 40 whales ashore on land belonging to Mr Scott of Scalloway. The owner was indemnified for possible damage to kelp, and then the proceeds were divided equally amongst those who had caught the whales. The plea of custom, put forward in this instance on behalf of both the heritor and the admiral, was here successfully resisted. If, however, a claim to a third formed part of a lease, it was legally binding.[1249]

A test came in the period 1805–8 with the 'Uyea Whale Case'. In 1805, the tenants of the Isle of Uyea helped by men from the Unst side drove 190 whales ashore in February, 120 more a few months later, and 50 more on the same spot in 1806, near a booth belonging to Thomas Mouat. He claimed a third share for himself and a third for the Crown. The Uyea men, however, claimed the whole and threatened violence to anyone who interfered. An Edinburgh lawyer, Thomas Small, persuaded the fishermen to take the case to the Court of Session. They thought they had won a victory, but the owner of Uyea threatened to evict the four families there, making the island into a sheepwalk. Eventually most of the men accepted Mouat's offer of a half-share, and those who held out for the whole lost their case when it came up for appeal in 1808. Three of the four Uyea tenants apologised to their laird and were allowed to remain, but the fourth made no concessions and had to leave. In agreements then made, the tenants bound themselves to give the laird a half-share of all whales. The Crown's claim was conveniently forgotten.[1250]

In 1886, the Crofters Holdings Act became law. Its effects were deep and widespread, giving tenants a secure base from which they could now bargain. Tenants had long been arguing against the laird's right to claim a share of whales killed below low-water mark, which was outside their property. With the removal of the threat of eviction, tenants were in a better position to stand up for themselves. They had a chance when, on 14 September 1888, over 300 whales were driven ashore at Hoswick. They fetched £450 at auction, and the two landowners involved claimed their usual share of one third. The men refused. The case was tried in Lerwick, where Sheriff MacKenzie ruled that the landowners had no right to a share. A further appeal to the Court of Session in Edinburgh resulted in the ruling that all proceeds should go to the captors alone.[1251] The Hoswick Whale Case, reported in detail in *The Shetland News* in 1889 and 1890, marked the end of a long course of legal history.

From the eighteenth century, references to the catching of whales are numerous. Some were caught in Unst in the 1790s. Whales killed in the 1820s on the sands of Hamnavoe in Yell were up to 22 ft (6.7 m) long. In colour they were a shining black, often with white or grey about the belly. The head was round, short and thick, the under-jaw being 3 or 4 in. (8–10 cm) shorter than the upper. They had small eyes, and teeth averaging 1 in. (2.5 cm) long, and 24 in number. A blow-hole near the neck allowed them to spout water and air. At a whale drive in Hamnavoe, the boats herded the school from a distance of about 50 yds (46 m), the men shouting and dropping large stones to keep the whales on course. No harpooning took place in deep water, for they would then

258. Whales captured at Weisdale, Shetland, 8 February 1903. By permission of Shetland Library and Museum..

immediately make for the open sea. As soon as they were stranded, the slaughter began, and continued, till 'the sun set upon a bay that seemed one sheet of blood'. Some of the folk then went home for a rest, others worked on to separate the blubber and prepare it for rendering. A good whale produced about a barrel of oil.[1252]

In Hoy, Orkney, one traveller observed six or seven young women going to cut rushes for lamp wicks, to be fuelled by oil from stranded whales.[1253] A shoal of 50 small whales ran aground on Rothesholm in Stronsay in November 1834, and yielded about £100 of oil. Early in 1841, 287 whales that came ashore on the west side of Eday yielded a return of £398. In Cross and Burness, whale hunting was regarded as the most exciting of all forms of fishing. Shoals ranging from 50 to 500 in number, with whales 5 to 25 ft (1.5–7.6 m) long, 'got occasionally embayed; and upon this happening, all boats are launched, all hands active, every tool which can be converted into a weapon of offence to the strangers, from the roasting-spit of the principal tenant, to the ware (seaweed)-fork of the cottar, is put into requisition. The shoal is surrounded, driven like a flock of timid sheep to shallow water on a sandy shore, and then the attack is made in earnest. The boats push in, stabbing and wounding in all directions. The tails of the wounded fish lash the sea, which is dyed red with their blood, sometimes dashing a boat to pieces. The whales in dying emit shrill and plaintive cries, accompanied with loud snorting, and a humming noise easily mistaken at a distance for fifes and drums.' This description closely parallels the procedure in the Faroe Islands, where the whole operation of driving the whales to recognised beaches, and of killing them and dividing the produce, was highly organised. There was a similar procedure in Denmark, with regulations going back to the sixteenth century. As late as the 1840s, shoals of a thousand or more were seen around Shetland each summer, and those caught provided flesh for food, oil for light, skin for leather, and offal for manure. The lairds here also exacted a share of the produce of stranded whales.[1254]

Whale hunts still took place in Orkney in the 1860s. A visitor to Stronsay saw a school driven into Mill Bay. Folk from far and near assembled to kill them on the shore with harpoons, three-pronged graips, and hayforks. Women took part as well. The boat crews beat pitchers, rattled rowlocks, and shouted, as they surrounded the school in a crescent shape. A skiff that shot from the shore in front of the whales disturbed them so that they turned and got away, though the boats followed and eventually got them ashore at Rothesholm Bay, 'the best whale-trap I know in Orkney'.[1255] Sixty were slain at Sourin, Rousay, in 1861, and sold for £260. Three hundred were caught in the 1870s in Linga Sand, Stronsay. It was noted that they always ran up wind, if possible, and that if the leader was once ashore, the rest followed easily. They could be easily killed with a rifle bullet in the throat. A dyke at Grainbank Farm, Wideford Hill, was composed of the skulls of ca'in whales driven into Kirkwall Bay. In August 1879, 108 whales caught in Catfirth Voe fetched £88, blubber prices being then low. In March 1884, 154 killed in Weisdale Voe were auctioned for nearly £300. It is an indication of the excitement of the hunt and perhaps also of the (alleged) avariciousness of the Orcadian that when a Westray farmer, about to make a coffin for his newly dead wife, heard the call, 'Whales in the bay!', he set off immediately. First he took care to leave two of his men working on the coffin, for that was two men fewer for sharing the produce. The laird who was to make the division was surprised to see him at such a time, and the farmer explained: 'I could na afford to lose baith wife and whales on the same day.'[1256]

Ironically, the Hoswick Whale Case marked the last appearance of a shoal of whales of such a size, though several smaller ones have been noted. The last organised hunt, involving 100 whales, may have been at Weisdale Voe on 7 February 1903. A *caa* of whales came in at Reawick in 1928, and some attempt was made to catch a small school that came into Stromness harbour in the 1930s, without success.[1257]

Schools of ca'in whales tended to be larger in Shetland than in Orkney, but not as large as in the Faroes. The largest school recorded in Shetland, totalling 1540 whales, came into Quendale Bay on 22 September 1845. Though the Faroese eat whale meat regularly, the people of the Northern Isles seem to have avoided it, unless forced to eat it in time of famine, as in Northmavine in 1740. Generally, however, the bodies were left to rot on the beaches, and only lairds like Mr Hay and Mr Bruce in Shetland thought to use the carcases for manure on the land.[1258]

This kind of whaling was a domestic exercise of a sporadic nature, depending on the chance occurrence of schools. More important in terms of individual income in hard cash was Arctic whaling. Whalers heading for Greenland and the Davis Straits picked up men in Shetland and Orkney. Each whaler might want twenty to twenty-five men. In 1816, 34 whaling ships were recorded at Stromness, of which 25 came from Hull. Fifty men from Stromness alone were at the Straits in 1821. Agents amongst the Stromness merchants acted as recruiters. Whaling came to an end through over-use of the resources, the giant Greenland whale being more or less wiped out, and whalers were seen less and less often till they vanished at last in their turn, a few years before the First World War.[1259]

In Shetland, the pattern was slightly different. Whereas Orkney men began to be employed mainly after a revival of British whaling in the 1760s, in Shetland large-scale recruiting for men was going on from the middle years of the eighteenth century. Between 50 and 90 vessels a year were coming between 1755–75, increasing from 1784–93, with as many as 253 in 1788. Nevertheless recruitment was opposed by the lairds. The French Wars brought a temporary slackening in whaling activity, but from 1793–1813 half to a third of the adult male population saw service in the navy. Between 1803–8 up to a third of the men were at sea in any one year. Whaling revived in the early 1800s, and because of the bad effect of this and employment in the navy, some lairds resorted to fining men for going to the whaling. Nevertheless, in 1808, 600 Shetlanders were employed on whalers from Hull, Dundee and Peterhead, getting an estimated £7000 or an average of £11.13.4 per man on their discharge at Lerwick. There were 1400 Shetlanders aboard about 70 whalers in 1825. Wages of £2 a month or £12 for a season in the 1790s had risen to £24 a season a century later.[1260]

The whaling season was often extended by skippers who wanted to get as much catching time as possible, with the result that boats were lost in stormy weather going or coming, and were sometimes trapped in the ice. Some were lucky, like the *Truelove* of Hull, which made 72 whaling trips. Others, like the *Jane* and *Viewforth* in 1836, and the *Diana* in 1867, escaped from the ice only after months of suffering. After the decline of the Greenland whaling in the 1860s, sealing provided a partial alternative there. In 1874, there were still 600–700 Shetlanders on whalers. In 1888 only 7 whalers came to Lerwick to complete their crews, and by 1907 this outlet was finished. Dundee jute manufacturers had to look elsewhere for their whale and seal oil.[1261]

Another phase of whaling began then. Following the invention of the Svend Foyn explosive harpoon in the 1860s and its wide adoption in the 1880s by the Norwegian whalers, the whales on Norway's coast were almost extinguished and whaling there was banned in 1904. However, Norwegian companies, with British government agreement, established whaling stations in Shetland, two at Ronas Voe in 1903, others at Collafirth and Olnafirth in 1904. These provided local employment though there was much opposition, especially from herring fishers. Whale grease on the beaches was a bad nuisance for three years, until

259. A whale at Olna Whaling Station, Shetland. Photo. R H Ramsay. Per Mrs Begg.

machinery was installed that could extract all of the oil, steam the flesh and bones, scorch them dry in kilns and powder them for fertiliser. Anti-whaling demonstrations were held, and the Shetland County Council made a direct appeal to the Prime Minister in 1908. By this period, all vessels were working and 326 men were employed ashore. A catch of 651 whales gave oil, whalebone, cattle food and other products worth £63,000. Shore processing went on till the 1920s.

Messrs. Leask and Sandison acted for the *Scotia* of Dundee, which sailed for Greenland in 1911, taking nine Shetlanders aboard to complete a complement of forty-two. One of the men described how the Greenland whale was never found in open water, but in openings among the pack ice, making the risk of being frozen in all the greater if a whaler stayed late in the season. Seals and some polar bears were taken as well. It was in general a lazy life unless there were fish about or unless the boat was on the move. Thirteen whaling ships caught 599 whales worth £61,500 in 1914. By 1928, over-exploitation had brought this lucrative industry to an end.[1262]

The final phase was the development of whaling in the Antarctic by Christian Salvesen & Co. of Leith, who established a base in the Falkland Islands in 1908 and at Leith Harbour in South Georgia in 1909. Numerous Shetlanders were employed, reaching a total of 200 between 1945 and 1963, bringing in about £200,000 a year in wages. By 1963 this southern stock of whales was also being worked to extinction and Antarctic whaling from British ports became uneconomic, and ceased.[1263] The harvest of whales will not grow again quickly.

64

Fishing Boats from Norway

SHORTAGE of wood in the Northern Isles, especially in Shetland, meant that the needs in timber had to be met by imports. For many centuries Norway provided a ready source not only of raw material, but also of shaped products, including boats. The latter were of the small, open, clinker-built variety that survives in Shetland under the name of the Ness yole (Old Scots *yoll*, 1584; Dutch *jol*, Middle Low German *jolle*) or the now practically obsolete Fair Isle yole, the broad timbers from the Norwegian forests permitting a small number of strakes. A thousand years of trade and intercourse have left their mark on the form, building techniques, and terminology of Shetland boats, all the more since trade relations continued till the second half of the nineteenth century.

Iron clinker nails found at Jarlshof give proof of the clinker building technique, but tell nothing of the actual size of the boats. Four outline drawings on slate of boats or parts of boats found at Jarlshof show vessels with a sail and steering rudder near the stern. There is a considerable gap in time between this ninth or tenth century archaeological evidence and the documentary sources of the early sixteenth century, apart from details in the Orkneyinga Saga. However, timber was being imported from Norway to Iceland from the reign of Harald Fairhair, so it is at least likely that Shetland also participated. In 1186, King Sverre made a speech in Bergen in which he specially welcomed the traders from Orkney, Shetland, the Faroes, and Iceland,[1264] and the popularity of Bergen as a rendezvous for traders from Shetland is attested by the name *Hjeltefjorden* (Shetland Fjord) that leads into Bergen from the north.

One ship from Shetland is known to have visited Bergen in 1519, and two in 1521. The customs accounts for 1566–7 referring to Sunnhordland mention seven Shetland ships loading cargoes of timber and boats. Out of a total of 35 boats, 17 went to Shetland, whilst 12 went to Orkney, 4 to Kirkcaldy and 2 to Leith. Amongst the timber products were *hjeltespirer,* i.e. 'Shetland spars or planks', of which 700 went to Shetland and 1500 to Leith. Export of this product to Shetland must have been common, before it could have acquired this regional name. Between May 1577 and May 1578, records show that four small Shetland ships came to Sunnhordland and returned with cargoes of timber and boats. They came from Voisgjerdt (probably Voesgarth in Unst), Velle (?Vaila), Kirkebosted (?Kirkabister) and Fedeluer (Fetlar). Some of these boats were small, for in 1582 it was said that the Shetlanders 'fish in small vessels of two Oars which they buy off the Norwegians'. However, since yoles normally have two or three pairs of oars, it has been suggested that this early reference is simply an observer's view of a boat being held in position by a pair of oars during line fishing. With the 'little cock-boats, bought from the Norway men that make them', the people fished for themselves, salting or wind-drying the fish, and paying their rent with the money from its sale. Some attempt was made by Lord Robert Stewart to control the trade, for in 1575 he ordained that no one was to bring home boats to Shetland, nor sell them, without his permission, and he sought to establish a specified price for them.[1265]

Between 1597 and 1627, 126 ships from Shetland and Orkney visited Sunnhordland, out of a total of 847 foreign vessels, making 14.9 pcr cent. In 1577, 9 ships from Scotland and the Orkneys loaded timber in Os, twenty miles south of Bergen, one of the ships also buying some boats. In 1610, Scottish and Shetland ships loaded 46 boats in Os. All the trade in timber and boats was carried on by the consumers, not by the Norwegians.[1266]

Contemporary information about boats in the Northern Isles is scanty, but there were boats of different sizes for different purposes, for ferrying and communications as well as for fishing. The people of Burra, for example, were required by regulations of 1603 and 1604 to keep a boat on the east side of the isle for their Lord's service, and each last of land had to serve equally or else the commons had to furnish a boat amongst themselves. It was forbidden to move merchandise in boats by night. If the Lord or his deputy were resident in the country, the boats from the west side of Burra had to stay on the east side for their service, summer or winter. At other times, the rates for serving strangers and passengers were laid down as 'ilk four earing boit to Meawick or Skalloway for one flitting one half mark and ilk sax earing ten Schillingis'. The commons of Burra were required to provide a ferry boat for transport themselves. There were, therefore, at this time, boats with 6 oars, 4 oars, and perhaps one pair of oars, used either for fishing or for ferrying. The four-oared ones were *fowererns* (cf. Icelandic *feræringur*, Norwegian dialectal *færing*), a name first recorded in 1561 in Orkney. The word *haerenger*[1267] for a boat with four oars and a 15 or 16 ft (4.6–4.9 m) keel is probably for 'Hardanger boat'.

In 1633 the people of Unst had a bark for trading with Norway, bringing back ships, barks and boats of all kinds. These included 'Norway Yoals' that held two or three men each. These small boats were said to be about the same size as 'Gravesend oars'. At the time of the Protectorate in 1652 it was stated in the Proposals for Orkney and Shetland that 'our shyre in all times bygone has had Comerce and tradinge with Norrway for importing of boates for our fishinge'.[1268]

Trading was carried out between the two island groups by open boats, capable of carrying 60 meils of victual. Several sailed from Orkney to Shetland each year, laden with corn, meat and malt. If all the grain had been used for food it could happen that the spring sowing of barley seed was delayed till fresh supplies arrived. At this time, Orkney was said to get much of its money from Shetland.[1269] Since 24 meils of bere were equivalent to 30 barrels, a boat of 60 meils may have been of a capacity equivalent to about 75 barrels of grain. The specification for such a boat has been preserved. It was built in 1662 by Thomas Baikie, Kirkwall, for two Stronsay men, and was 'ane great Boat of and about the burdein of thriescore twelve meills, of threttie foots of Keill with sex stroak of oack round about with thrie oaken balks and sex iron bolts with sex knee heads upon the said balk(s) with twa masts twa raes (yards) and sex oares with ane hung back rudder of oack and helme conforme with ane pump and roan (channel in pump-taft) and pompstafe. And that her fluir (floor) bands be no wider betwixt than ane foot and also obleiss him to cause build the said boat of ane sufficient mowld with ane foirsuite (covered in forecastle) till the foirbalk sufficientlie pickit and maid water-tight ...' Such a boat had a 30 foot keel, a capacity of 6 to 7 tons, six heavy strakes for strength below the gunwale on each side, two masts, and sails and rigging. It was only partly decked.[1270] The price was £160 Scots along with two meils of malt and two good sheep. Such boats were big enough to trade with Norway.

The main areas of Norway from which boats were exported were Os, Tysnes, Fusa, Strandvik and Samnanger. Tysnes specialised in building boats for export to Shetland and according to a manuscript dated 12 June 1714 in the Royal Library, Copenhagen, the boats being exported from Godøysund in Tysnes were 'only clinked together with a few nails and before being taken on board the ship they were numbered and marked and then taken apart again and when the ships arrive at their place of destination, they are discharged and put together again in accordance with the before mentioned numbers and marks – thus a small ship's hold can carry 70, 80, 100 even 120 boats'. Mostly it was ships from Shetland and Orkney that came to Godøysund for loads of timber

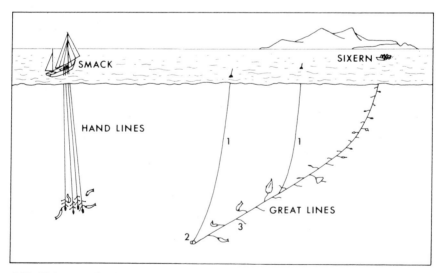

260. Right, greatline fishing from a sixern. The buoy-ropes are marked 1. Left, hand-line fishing. After Goodlad 1971. 108.

261. Ness yoles in the South Harbour, Fair Isle, 1962. There is an old Fair Isle yole in one of the nousts at the head of the beach. Photo. H. Rasmussen. C5939.

and boats. In 1733, Gifford gave orders to John Harrower to go from Hamburg to Norway with his ship, the *Mary* of Yorry, to purchase '30 four oared yoals and all their apartinant. Less or more of them as your Sloup can contain, but no six oard Boats'. He had to 'take non but Good large four oard Boats and tell the Bouers youll tak non but Such as are Good and Suffitient, for if you take not Care they will Impose upon you and Give you Insuffitient yoals, which will be useless to me'. He was permitted to take enough spirits with him from Hamburg 'to Give the Norraway Bowers in Drams which they most have when they Bring the boats which they Take down and let them be all Right marked'. This refers to the practice of dismantling made-up boats for easy shipment. In 1744, Gifford of Busta's ship *Sibella* took back from Norway eight unassembled six-oared boats and twenty four-oared boats, and between 1755 and 1757, seventy-five boats a year were exported from Bergen to Scotland and the Northern Isles.[1271]

262. A sixern in Fetlar, originally from Papa Stour. 1963.

263. Fishing sixerns at Fethaland, Northmavine in the 1890s. Photograph J D. Rattar. By permission of Shetland Library and Museum.

In 1750, cod and ling fishing was carried on from small '*Norway* boats' with
four oars. Fishing by this time was being done for the lairds at whose booths the
fish were salted for export in November, though by 1774 changes had taken
place in Orkney, for at Walls cod fishing had been given up and the 'Fish house'
on the Aire was ruinous. In Shetland on the other hand there was no falling off.
There were to be found small Norway boats in which two or three men each
with a pair of short paddles could row or sail. Alongside these were the bigger
sixerns (Norwegian dialectal *seks(æ)ring*, Old Norse *sexæringr*, first occurring
in Orkney in 1566), the boat on which the haaf fishing was based, having in
Northmavine an 18 ft (5.5 m) keel, a 6 ft (1.8 m) beam, 6 oars and a sail, and
costing £6 sterling. Northmavine was one of the best of the fishing places in
Shetland and had at this time about 100 boats fishing from the beginning of
June till the second week of August, with 6 men in each. By this period, the
sixern was well established in Shetland, alongside the small yoles. It is evident
from Gifford's instruction of 1733 that Norwegian six-oared boats were known
and, by implication, imported, though on this occasion he did not want any. The
sixern undoubtedly originated in Norway, and in the 1780s 'the boats, which is
the greatest expense, the fishers have also from their masters; they are all
Norway built, and brought from a place called *Geau-Sound* (Godøysund),
because their form is preferred by the Shetlanders, though they are exposed to
the greatest danger in these slender machines'.[1272]

As long as unassembled boats were being imported, the Shetlanders must
have been re-assembling them and making all watertight and seaworthy. This is
an incipient form of boat building. It is likely that at least small boats were being
built locally, and old or damaged ones had to be repaired in Orkney as well as in
Shetland. Patrick Fea in Sanday, for example, had his own built:

1770.	2 June:	Went to Savill and got wood for a Keel, Stern and Stem to my Boat.
	13 June:	Thos. Spence putting in the Stomack pieces the Boat being on the Stocks upon Tewsday sawing Deals all day with 2 men.
	14 June:	Thos. Spence put up the first Stroke to the Boat.
	15 June:	Thos. Spence putting up the Second Stroke.
	22 June:	Th. Spence done with the first 7 Stroaks of my Boat and begun to dress floor Timbers for her.
	3 July:	Thos. Spence putting the 9 Stroke about my Boat.
	5 July:	Thos. Spence had 11 Strokes upon my big Boat.
	9 July:	Got some Timbers for my Boat from Wm. Grot for which must give him bent (grass).
	27 July:	Thos. put the beems in the boat and kneeheads.
	28 July:	Sent Jo Hay to Eda in order to make bolts for the boat and long nails (probably because peat charcoal could be got there).
	31 July:	Att the Smidie and got the last of my Ironwork made for my boat.

> 1 Aug: Sent to Savill for 15 pynts of Tar.
> 1771. 11 July: Cut out a mainsail and foresail for my boat and made a Colt rope(?)
> 1773. 8 July: Sent a yoal to Eda for peats and a tree to be a gaff for my Boat.
> 12 July: The carpenter made the gaff and boltsprit to the Boat.[1273]

There is an element of innovation in the 'modern' fore and aft rig described here.

Though boat builders were sometimes employed, like those from Stromness who made boats for people in Birsay and Harray in the 1790s, nevertheless boat building remained a relatively unspecialised craft. In Cross and Burness, even the craftsmen, including boat builders, who came nearest to being specialised, 'always shear in harvest and go out to some of the fisheries in summer'. This was thought to be unfavourable to both skill and profit, but diversity of employment was essential for earning a sufficient livelihood.[1274]

Still in 1836–40 the boat builders in Tysnes were making some larger boats 'under the name of *Jæltebaade*, "Shetland boats", in the manner that all the boats' materials (keels, frames, planking, etc) are made ready for clinking, the different parts are numbered and transported to Bergen' for further export. As recently as 1856–60, about thirty 'Jæltebaade' were being exported each year.[1275]

These latter-day exports appear to have been larger boats, more akin to the sixern than the yole, as might be expected from the changed nature of the market they had to serve. However, about the beginning of the nineteenth century much more native Shetland boat building was taking place in response to the more commercial approach to fishing. During 1806–14 the English blockade of Norway cut off supplies of boats and wood at a crucial period, enforcing the local construction of boats from 'sawn boards' or deals.[1276] These were apparently not as well liked as the Norwegian models, but there must have been an overlap period when both locally and Norwegian made boats were in use, lasting until the 1860s when further changes in the fishing industry began to make haaf fishing out of date.

In historical times the sixern is a late development, dating from the middle of the eighteenth century. The nineteenth century 'jæltebaade' were bigger than the centuries-old yole, undoubtedly made in response to the changed requirements in fishing. Local Shetlanders had centuries of experience in re-erecting and repairing yoles, and of fishing and working in them. At a time of timber shortage it was natural that Shetlanders should build more boats locally, both the yole and the sixern. The Norwegian 'jæltebaade' were probably different mainly in the number of strakes, just as Norwegian built yoles had five strakes between keel and gunwale whereas locally built ones had six.

The yole, once general all over Shetland, became mainly confined to the South Mainland and Fair Isle, hence the distinguishing names Ness yole and Fair Isle yole. Of the Ness yole, it is said that 'as she is certainly one of the most ancient boat types surviving around the coasts of Great Britain today, she must also surely be one of the most conservative craft afloat. Not only are her proportions constant, she must also conform within inches to a certain standard measurement which must have been laid down in remote antiquity'. This measurement was 15 ft (4.6 m) between the scarves or *skairs* (Norwegian dialectal *skar*, scarf-joint, Icelandic *skara*, to clinch a boat's planks) of the keel, 21½ ft (6.6 m) over the stems, 5½ ft (1.7 m) in midships beam and 21 in. (53 cm) inside depth. 'Add a foot to this overall measurement, or subtract a foot, and men of Dunrossness will tell you that, though she is still probably a good boat she is no longer a yoal.' The Fair Isle yole, described by Tudor in 1880, is more extreme than this, no doubt as a result of gradual adaptation to the local conditions of 'furious tideways' where saithe flourished. It was long and narrow, measuring 16 ft (4.9 m) over the keel, and 22¾ ft (6.9 m) overall, with a 6 ft (1.8 m) beam. The depth at stem head was 3 ft 3 in. (99 cm), at stern post 3 ft 1 in. (94 cm) and amidships 1 ft 9 in. (53 cm). Tudor's stern and stem head depths have been amended from 2 ft 3 in. (69 cm) and 2 ft 1 in. (64 cm).[1277]

Ness yoles have three thwarts, and are propelled by three pairs of oars pulled by three men who might sit on plaited-straw mats laid over the thwarts. The mast is stepped through the midship thwart and the sail is a square sail, set 'flying', that is outside the rigging, with two or three rows of reef points. 'Such a sail has tremendous lifting power, and a deep-laden yoal will lift her bow a hand's breadth to the upward pull of her sail.' Even in the 1950s the fishermen of Whalsay claimed that such a rig could not be surpassed for a small undecked fishing vessel.[1278]

Suppleness and speed were two characteristics of the yole. Her clinker-built frame made a light shell, and when she was standing on the beach, it was possible by shaking her stem to make the other horn oscillate back and fore at least 6 in. (15 cm). The speed requirements, based on man-power alone until recent days, involved a high length-to-beam ratio, and a shallow draught. The dimensions of Ness and Fair Isle yoles appear to represent an optimum in length-to-beam and depth-ratios for local conditions.

The sixern had an 18 ft (5.5 m) keel and a sail with 28 yds (25.6 m) of canvas in Delting, and cost £104.9/–. It could last six years (though good boats might last up to 50 years), and go 10 to 15 leagues out with its crew of six. Dunrossness in the 1790s had three boat types: a larger and a smaller boat with six oars, and four-oared boats. There were about 200 in the parish in all. Six-oared boats in Lerwick were of two or three tons burden, and numbered 36 in Sandsting and Aithsting. In Unst there were 78 boats, many of which were assembled there from boards brought ready shaped from Norway. They had keels of 15½ to 18½ ft (4.7–5.6 m) and six oars. Bressay had 26 large fishing boats, Quarff 5, and Burra, Havera and Papa 28 smaller boats. In Northmavine, there were fishing stations at Hamnavoe for 12 to 15 boats, at Ronas Voe for 4 to 5, at Uyea for 14, at Sandvoe for 5, and at Fethaland for about 60. Boat building was one of the men's accomplishments. Fair Isle had 14 boats, with two or three men in each. In Walls and Sandness, fishing sloops that came in summer were served by

4 six-oared boats apiece. The Northumberland Company for the Improvement and Extension of Fisheries had had 3 or 4 boats there for some years past, for taking cod, tusk, and ling. By 1798 they seemed to be giving up. Foula had 16 boats at Ham in summer, of which 11 came from Walls. Overall, the parish had 42 six-oared boats with 6 men in each, and 16 four-oared boats with 3 or 4 men.[1279]

At the same period in Orkney, there were 144 fishermen and 18 fishing boats in Birsay and Harray. Boat carpenters were hired from Stromness and paid by the piece, at 2/– per foot (30 cm) of keel. The boats worked from four summer stations and had keels of 16 to $17\frac{1}{2}$ ft (4.9–5.3 m). Rousay had 24 boats, Egilsay 12, Wyre 6 and Eynhallow 2. There were 80 boats in Shapinsay, mostly for fishing or for carrying the island's rents and feu-duties paid in kind to Kirkwall. Major Balfour, like a Viking of old, had 20 boats, 8 vessels, 4 brigs and 4 sloops, requiring 50 sailors to man them. There was a good harbour at Elwick. When fishing was good in Walls and Flotta, 12 boats went to sea with 6 men in each, otherwise only about 6 boats went out. Orphir had 24 boats with 4 or 5 men in each. In Evie and Rendall, though there were 30 boats of $1\frac{1}{2}$ to 2 tons burden, mostly with four and a very few with six oars, there were nevertheless no merely professional fishers. In 1806, Orphir had 24 boats, each with a crew of four or five, engaged in dog fishing.[1280]

In nineteenth century Shetland, boats fishing for cod, ling and tusk measured 16 to 19 ft (4.9–5.8 m) long. The largest were used on the west side of the islands and were 6 ft (1.8 m) wide and $4\frac{1}{2}$ ft (1.4 m) deep. The best boats for fishing were considered to be those with a 30 ft (9.1 m) keel, a width of 10 ft (3 m) and a depth of 5 ft (1.5 m), with a deck and lug-sails, but this was not what the ordinary fishermen had to use. Bressay had about 12 boats of 18 to 20 ft (5.5–6.1 m) keel for haaf fishing.[1281] Boats were still being imported from Norway in the form of boards, and were 'of a class not in use in any other part of the kingdom'. Import duties on timber were making it expensive to get boats in this way. In Northmavine, the boats that had carried on the ling fishing successfully for many years were becoming reduced in number because of the scarcity of fish, low prices, and the great expense of fishing. Formerly the boats based on the various fishing-stations could fish near the shore and get fish in plenty. Now the boats had to sail or pull 40 or 50 miles out to reach a fishing-ground, staying out two or three nights if the weather was fine.[1282] Distance increased the danger of accident. In Fetlar, as elsewhere, the spirit of the fishermen had been considerably damped by the catastrophe of 1832, when the wind blew lumps out of feal dykes and many men were drowned. It had been the custom for each tenant in Fetlar to keep up a sixth of a boat for ling fishing, furnishing lines and other materials himself, and giving the fish to the landlord or tacksman at a certain rate. Latterly, economics had an effect on the work organisation, and the fish-curers had begun to give boats and lines free to the fishermen, but they got a reduced price for the fish. The older situation still prevailed in North Yell. The ling fishing boats in Fetlar have been listed as follows:

Date	No. of Boats	Keel Length	Beam	Crew per Boat	Crew Total	Catch in Cwts
1834	2	19 ft 6 in. (5.9 m)	7 ft (2.1 m)	6	12	90
	5	19 ft (5.8 m)	7 ft 6 in. (2.3 m)	6	30	230
	4	19 ft (5.8 m)	7 ft (2.1 m)	6	24⎱	276
	3	18 ft (5.5 m)	6 ft 6 in. (2 m)	6	18⎰	
	3	13 ft (4 m)	5 ft 6 in. (1.7 m)	4	12	75
	17				**96**	**671**
1835	2	19 ft 6 in. (5.9 m)	7 ft (2.1 m)	6	12	90
	6	19 ft (5.8 m)	7 ft 6 in. (2.3 m)	6	36	329
	5	19 ft (5.8 m)	7 ft (2.1 m)	6	30⎱	297
	2	18 ft (5.5 m)	6 ft 6 in. (2 m)	6	12⎰	
	4	13 ft (4 m)	5 ft 6 in. (1.7 m)	4	16	54
	19				**106**	**770**

The figures for North Yell were:

Date	No. of Boats	Keel Length	Beam	Crew per Boat	Crew Total	Catch in Cwts
1834	8	19 ft (5.8 m) and 20 ft (6.1 m)	7 ft 6 in. (2.3 m)	6	48	550
	2	19 ft (5.8 m)	7 ft 4 in. (2.2 m)	6	12	68
	1	19 ft 6 in. (5.9 m)	6 ft 6 in. (2 m)	6	6	34
	1	18 ft 6 in. (5.6 m)	6 ft (1.8 m)	6	6	14
	6	19 ft (5.8 m)	7 ft (2.1 m)	6	36⎱	572
	2	18 ft (5.5 m)	6 ft (1.8 m)	5	10⎰	
	1	19 ft 8 in. (6 m)	6 ft 10 in. (2.1 m)	6	6⎱	53
	1	17 ft (5.2 m)	6 ft 4 in. (1.9 m)	6	6⎰	
	3	18 ft 6 in. (5.6 m)	6 ft 6 in. (2 m)	6	18	70
	25				**148**	**1361**
1835	8	19 ft (5.8 m) and 20 ft (6.1 m)	7 ft 6 in. (2.3 m)	6	48	595
	3	19 ft (5.8 m)	7 ft 4 in. (2.2 m)	6	18	160
	1	19 ft 6 in. (5.9 m)	6 ft 6 in. (2 m)	6	6	40
	1	18 ft 6 in. (5.6 m)	6 ft (1.8 m)	6	6	13
	6	19 ft (5.8 m)	7 ft (2.1 m)	6	36⎱	609
	2	18 ft (5.5 m)	6 ft (1.8 m)	5	10⎰	
	1	19 ft 8 in. (6 m)	6 ft 10 in. (2.1 m)	6	6	$47\frac{1}{2}$
	3	18 ft 6 in. (5.6 m)	6 ft 6 in. (2 m)	6	18	$94\frac{1}{2}$
	25				**148**	**1559** [1283]

Bressay had 13 ling fishing boats, of 18 to 20 ft (5.5–6.1 m) keel, Quarff 4 and Burra 10, of 15 ft (4.6 m) keel. There were generally six men sharing in each, and a haaf boat could be hired for the season for £2.8/–. A man hired to complete a crew would be paid between £1.10/– and £3. Noss was used as a station by the Quarff fishers, who, like the Bressay folk, might be at sea and sometimes out of sight of land for one or two nights. The Burra folk went only a mile off, set their lines in the evening, and drew them on their return the next morning. In Unst, the boats were described as larger than in former days, having 18 to 22 ft (5.5–6.7 m) keels and six of a crew. They were owned by the men or hired out to them by the lairds or any others for whom they fished. Only a few boats went to the ling fishing from Lerwick. In Sandsting and Aithsting, ling fishing was carried on in boats of 18 ft (5.5 m) keel, with six of a crew. In 1841, there were 8 boats where there had been 36 twenty-five years before. They fished from Papa Stour, which was nearer the grounds.[1284] Sixerns did not evolve in Orkney, though mid-nineteenth century references to boats were numerous enough, and there was no question of organised fishing for ling as in Shetland.

65

Yoles and Sixerns:
Construction and Terminology

THE sixern and the later sixern derivatives marked the end of the long link
with Norway, though carrying in their genes the lines of their Norwegian
ancestors. In 1633, fishing for ling and cod was entirely done in yoles rowed two
or three leagues out by two or four men according to size, and fish were very
plentiful. By 1680, however, the fishing seemed to have fallen off, 'not-

264. Boats at Ham Voe, Foula. Photo. H B Curwen 1902. C6031.

265. Boat-building in Fair Isle. 1.26.12.

266. Boat-building in Fair Isle. 1.40.23.

withstanding that greater pains is taken by ye Fishers now than ever before, who with small Norway Yoells (two or three men in each of them) will adventure to the far Sea, and oft times endure hard weather'. All the same nearly every trade and employment in Shetland was in some way connected with the sea. The men fished for themselves, or for sale, had shares in boats for fishing, worked their arable and had grazing for cattle. A few followed no other trade but fishing. For Shetlanders, it was a serious matter if anything prevented fishing, such as the smallpox which about 1680 reduced the number of families in Fair Isle to a point where the fishing boats could scarcely be managed.[1285] As yet, however, though trading with merchants gave a shape and form of organisation, fishing remained largely a domestic enterprise. As long as the fish clustered around the coasts there was little problem, but when they moved to deeper water, perhaps because of temperature changes, the yoles were less suitable for the longer journeys that had to be made. It was a long time, however, before adaptations were made, and the yole was still universal in 1750. The big Northmavine boats of 1774 may represent the beginnings of the sixern, though it cannot be certain whether they were imported or locally made. Six-oared boats like those brought from Norway by the *Sibella*, in 1744, or the one for which Messrs. James and George Irvine of Midbrake paid £4 to Andrew Irvine, Lerwick, on 14 May 1791 may have been yoles rather than sixerns. This is confirmed by a list of Shetland boats made in 1767, when there were 290 with a crew of six, 100 with a crew of five, 60 with a crew of four, and 150 crewed by two old men and two boys. The bigger ones had 16 to 19 ft (4.9–5.8 m) keels, those on the west side being largest with a 6 ft (1.8 m) beam and a depth of 4½ ft (1.4 m). They could go 5 to 12 leagues out, leaving at mid-day on one day and returning between 3 and 6 p.m. on the next. Since 48 per cent of the boats listed here had a crew of six, it is unlikely that so many could have been sixerns at this early date, though the haaf fishing rhythm is already evident. In 1814 the

267. North Ronaldsay skiffs, used for lobstering etc. 1960s.

Northmavine boats had an 18 ft (5.2 m) keel and a 6 ft (1.8 m) beam, with six oars and a lug sail, still 'much the same as a Norway yawl'.[1286]

Positive evidence that the Norway yoles were being adapted by Shetlanders comes from a Sketch of a Plan for enlarging and improving the Scale of Ling fishing on the coast of Zetland, dated 1814. Here it was said that the present six-oared boats were admirably adapted to the habits of a Shetland fisherman and the scale of his means. They had been gradually improving over centuries and now 'through the unaided exertions of the native carpenters' had reached a high peak of excellence, though there was still room for improvement in the rigging and fishing tackle. They had 17, 18 or 20 ft (5.2, 5.5, 6.1 m) keels and were completely open, a fact that limited their scope when it came to quantity of produce and all-weather fishing. For this reason it was considered that such boats might be attached to vessels big enough to provide shelter and accommodation. Sloops of 20 to 35 tons were too small, as had already been proved, but the ideal might be a vessel of 110 tons, suitable for foreign trade, accompanied by 4 boats of 16 ft (4.9 m) keel, each with 5 packies of lines containing 16 bughts and 3 buoys.[1287]

Attempts made with sloops were, as it turned out, not very successful, chiefly because of the difficulty of handling the supporting boats in bad weather, but the concept shows the lines along which people's minds were running. Expansion then, however, was limited by the nature of the human resources and the scale of operations it could sustain. More people could manage more boats, as the lairds realised, and this led them to fragment existing agricultural holdings and create outsets, but fewer people could not easily manage bigger boats, for they could not then be drawn up on the beaches. Some growth in numbers did occur, for whereas in 1767 there had been 290 six-oared boats, in 1814 there were 500, with a manpower of 3000, each making up to 32 fishing trips during the eight-week season.[1288]

In the 1790s, there seem to have been two classes of haaf boat, a lighter one with a keel of 17 to 18 ft or more (5.2–5.5 m) and a deeper, heavier one that was a step towards the new pattern. Such boats had oars 10 to 14 ft (3–4.3 m) long. The rudder was seldom used in any weather along with the oars. They also had a mast about 18 ft (5.5 m) long and a square sail about 15½ ft (4.5 m) deep by 12 ft (3.7 m) broad at the top and 14 ft (4.3 m) broad at the bottom.[1289] A 'representative sixern of the old time' dating from 1817, the *Haaf Fish*, built for Thomas Edmondston, had an 18 ft (5.2 m) keel, and measured 28 ft (8.5 m) over the stems, with a beam of 6 ft 8 in. (2 m) and an inside depth amidships of 27 in. (68 cm). The proportions are not so different from those of a large Ness yole. Though sixerns became fuller and deeper, their overall length remained fairly constant for a long time, partly because of the need to haul them up on beaches, though by the 1840s keels had stretched to 19 to 20 ft (5.8–6.1 m) and by 1874 to 22 ft (6.7 m) at the biggest fishing-stations.[1290] In the 1890s and early 1900s an even larger class came in, with keels of 23 to 24 ft (7–7.3 m). An example surviving in Fetlar, but made in Papa Stour, and latterly used as a flit-boat, had a 21 ft (6.4 m) keel, and several of the best of the Fetlar sixerns had 22 ft (6.7 m) keels. These bigger-sized boats, with higher freeboard, fared better than their smaller predecessors in bad storms like those of 1832 and 1881. All this time the yole kept on being used too, being built of light, tough timbers specially picked in the inland woods of Norway, and shaped for boats in pieces 8 to 14 ft (2.4–4.2 m) in length by half an inch to the quite heavy three quarters (1.3–1.9 cm) in thickness. These were expensive, having to pay the same duty as bigger deals, and the practice of importing ceased about the mid-nineteenth century though yoles have continued to be built ever since. Sixerns and yoles or fowererns worked in a complementary way to each other, for when the sixerns were laid up at the end of the haaf fishing term in August, the fowererns were then fitted out for hand-line fishing.[1291]

Though the lodges were got ready in May, work on preparing the boats and lines began in April. The timbers were coated with Stockholm or fir tar, as well as the buoys, whether made of kegs, sheepskin or dogskin.[1292] The oars were examined, as were the *rooths* (Old Scots *routh*, rowing, *c.* 1420; Old Norse *róðr*, rowing), that part of the gunwale with a clamp of hard-wood or iron where the oar worked, and the *cabes* (Norwegian *keip*, Old Norse *keipr*, rowlock) or upright pegs set in the rooths, against which the oars worked. A fastening, usually of cow's hide, passed through the rooth and was adjusted to the correct length round the oar. This was the *humliband* (Norwegian *hamleband*, Old Norse *hamla*, *hǫmluband*) or *shangie* (origin uncertain).[1293] As a protection against friction, the underpart of the oar and the side that worked against the cabe could be shielded by covers of thin hardwood called *slates* or *sclates* (Old Scots *sclate*, a slate, 1456).[1294] The loom of the oar was square, and it could not be feathered. In sea-language the oar was a *rem* or *remmack* (origin uncertain; cf. Norwegian dialectal, Old Norse *reim*, strap, band, Swedish dialectal *räimu*, narrow board, Low German *remme*, strake, *reme*, punting-pole or tiller), and the handgrip was the *nave* (Old Scots *nave*, fist, 1375; Old Norse *hnefi*, fist, *hnefa*, to clasp with the fist).[1295]

The sixern and yole had several names for different parts. In Unst, the planks next the keel were the *boddam* (bottom) *runners*, next came the *hassings* (Norwegian dialectal, Old Norse *hals*, forepart of a boat next the stem), divided into *fore* and *aft hassings*, the parts that curved towards stem and stern.[1296] The *swills*, *suls* or *sulbørds* (cf. Old Norse *sólborð*, *sólbyrði*, gunwale) came next and the *reebing* (Norwegian dialectal *rip*, strip, sheer strake of a boat) or top strake. It is not possible to be precise about the names of all the strakes, nor are these names confined to one strake only, partly because the number of strakes varies, and the boats imported from Norway, to which the names were originally given, had fewer strakes than Shetland products.[1297] The *rimwale* (cf. Faroese *rim*, top strake, + *wāle*, gunwale) was a board running round the gunwale, variously described as the gunwale strake, a board nailed on top of the gunwale, or the inside wale.[1298] A fitment in the gunwale was the *vaity-kabe* (Norwegian dialectal *vad*, Old Norse *vaðr*, fishing line + *cabe*), or *waith-horn* (Norwegian *vadhorn*, Old Norse, Faroese *vaðhorn*), an upright piece of wood, or originally horn, with a notch in the top, in which the fishing-line could run when being cast or hauled. In Orkney, a small plate of wood with a groove in it, nailed to the gunwale to protect the wood and ease the hauling of the line, was a *tomboy* (*tome* + Norwegian dialectal *bøye*, *bøygjel*, a cleft stick on which a fishing-line is wound).[1299] In the bottom strake was the *nile-hole* for draining water from the bilge, plugged by the *nile* (Norwegian dialectal *nygla*, Old Norse *negla*, bilge-plug, Norwegian dialectal *nygla*, to plug a nile-hole, *nyglehol*, nile-hole). Under the timbers were limber-holes or openings called *rossholes* (cf. Norwegian dialectal *ræsehol*, hollow in a drainage channel, *rås*, hollow for water) or *draabellies* (English *draw*, to drain off water, + *belly*), that allowed the water to run freely along the keel, so that the boat could be baled from one point.[1300]

The boats were clinker-built, each strake overlapping the one below, with a strip of tarred cloth between the overlaps. Rivets known as *seams* or *seam-nails* (Norwegian *søm*, Old Norse *saumr*, seam in sowing, nail) were driven through at points along a groove or *sem-fer(d)* (Old Norse *saumför*, rivet in boat's plank run along the edge of the plank to guide the builder, and clinched against a metal washer called a *ruive*. A short metal tool with a round hole at one end, known as a *seam-kløv* (seam + Old Norse *klauf*, Norwegian *klov*, cloven hoof, *klove*, a cleft stick, kind of pincers), was used to drive the washers on the rivets. In 1730 Gifford of Busta commissioned the master of a sloop to get him '2 firkins seam and roove' from Leith and an Orkney inventory of 1747 listed 'seem and ruve for boats'. Boat building, therefore, was in full swing at this period. The nails that fastened the bottom boards to the keel were *grund-sems* (ground + *seam*).[1301]

The men sat on *thafts* or *tafts* (Old Scots *thoft*, 1513, Old Norse *þopta*) with their feet on the loose flooring-boards, the *tilfers* (Norwegian *tilfar*, id., Old Norse *þilfar*, deck of a ship). Each thwart had its name. Nearest the stern was the *eft* (aft) *taft*, and next came the *skair-taft*, so called because at this point the strakes had originally been scarfed or skaired instead of being bent. It was usually occupied by the linesman, and was seldom rowed from.[1302] There followed the *midship taft*, and the *fore taft* was nearest the stem. The low seat in the stern occupied by the helmsman was sometimes called the *stamron* or *stammereen* (Norwegian dialectal *stamn*, prow or stem of a boat + *rong*, stem seat, Old Norse *stafn*, id., + *rǫng*, knee-timber), but as a rule the fore and aft bands half up the boats, supports for the bow and stem, were the stammereens.[1303] The thwarts rested on the *wairin* (Dutch, Flemish *wegering*, *wijgering*), or in Orkney also *stringer*,[1304] a strip of wood nailed to the ribs below the gunwale, and the cross-beams below the thwarts that fastened the ribs firmly were *hadabands* (Scots *haud*, hold + *band*). The *kannie* (cf. Icelandic *kani*, beak of a boat) was 'a yoke-shaped piece of wood between the stammereen and the stern', and the *hinnie-spot* (origin uncertain. Cf. Faroese *ennispónur*, id., Old Norse *ennispænir*, prow-ornament) was a three-cornered piece of wood linking gunwales and stern.[1305] A small fitted timber at the bow or stern of a boat was in Orkney a *hurry-timber* (from *hurrack*). A bar of wood across the floor of the boat to press against with the feet when rowing was a *fitspar* or *feetspur*, or *paal* (cf. nautical English *pawl*, bar to lock a capstan or winch, French, Dutch *pal*, Latin *palus*, stake). In Fair Isle there was the *fit stap* (foot step), a wooden band half way up the inside of the boat in the owse-room, serving both as a foot-grip when rowing, and as a support for the fish board used to keep fish out of this area.[1306] All parts of a boat were removable, to lighten it for hauling up.

Knee-timbers were *cragacks* (cf. Norwegian dialectal *kragg*, stunted, crooked tree), and the knee-shaped piece of wood fixed to the end of a keel to secure it to the stern or stem was in Orkney a *haavie* (Norwegian dialectal *hav*, handle, bent-up part of sledge runner) or *mullack* (diminutive from Norwegian *mule*, Old Norse *muli*, snout, muzzle).[1307]

In Orkney the groove cut in the stern, keel and stem for the boards to fit into was the *chack* (check) or *huidins* (from *hood*).[1308] Since the boats were constantly being hauled up and down beeches, often over wooden or whalebone runners or *linns* (Norwegian dialectal *lunn*, Old Norse *hlunnr*), there was much wear and tear on the keel and a covering of wood or metal, the *keel-draught* or *dright* (*keel* + English *draught*, probably originally Norwegian dialectal, Old Norse *drag*, the iron rim under keel), was fitted. Similarly, there could be a wooden strap or *bilge-kod* (Old Scots *cod*, cushion, pillow, *c.* 1420, Old Norse *koddi*) to protect the timbers of such shallow-keeled boats when they were being hauled up on their side. It was also said to stop rolling and could help in checking leeway. The fore and after parts of a false keel, protecting the stem and stern, were *drawils* (Norwegian *draghals* from Old Norse *drag*, iron rim on keel + *háls*, part of bow of boat). The track on the beach up which the boats were hauled to the noost or scooped-out stance, sometimes a shed, for a boat, was called a *red* (origin uncertain).[1309]

The mast was the *stang* or *stong* (Old Scots *stang*, a pole, 1508; Old Norse *stǫng*). The sail or *skeg* (Faroese *skeki*, rag, Icelandic *skiki*, strip of cloth) could be raised and lowered on it by means of a ring- or yoke-shaped *rakki* (Norwegian dialectal *rakke*, Old Norse *rakki*), or traveller, fixed to the mast by a rope known as the *rakkiband*. It could be made of a cow's horn or of a piece of hardwood,[1310] and by means of it the yard or *rae* (Old Scots *ra*, yardarm, 1494; Middle Dutch *ra(e)*, Old Norse *rá*) was attached to the front of the mast. This form of wooden traveller was also called a *parly*, from nautical English *parrel*, in Orkney. The halyards were *tows* (Old Scots *tow*, a rope, 1470; Dutch *touw*, Middle Low German *touwe*) and the crew member who managed the sails and halyards was the *towman* or *towsman*. The single halyards were fixed to the yard between the arms of the rakki and passed through a sheave at the head of the mast. 'They were always endless, and attached to a large cleat on the after side of the mast at a convenient height, the fall leading up again to the yard.' The *head tow* was a rope from the mast to the fore ring. Forward in the gunwales were *tack bores*, holes through which the tack rope was *roved* from the outside, with *tack nails* placed a foot (30 cm) aft of the bores for securing the tack rope. The *strood bores* were set amidships on either side for securing the shrouds from the outside, and the sheets were roved through *sheet bores* or *sheet cleeks*, holes or rings, set aft. The sail had a row of holes along the edge in line with the reef points, by means of which the sail could be partially reduced when the necessity for reefing was in doubt. In Fair Isle such holes were 'cloufs or kluves', but elsewhere in Shetland the name was *smitin* (Old Scots *smyt*, 1494, rope attached to one of the lower corners of a sail, Dutch *smijt*, Low German *smite*, Norwegian *smit*).[1311]

With three or four qualified boat builders and plenty of helpers, a Fair Isle yole could be built in three or four days. For all the skill and knowledge that went into it, it could be done on the spot without a special workshop, leaving no trace of the place of building afterwards. This was also true of the work of itinerant builders in Norway who made boats to order with materials supplied by their clients.[1312]

66

Haaf Fishing

HAAF fishing (Norwegian *hav,* Old Norse *haf*, sea, ocean) for cod, ling and tusk in waters up to or over 40 miles out became organised into an industry by the breed of merchant lairds that evolved in the eighteenth century, in part following the imposition of a Government tax on foreign salt in 1712, and the offer of a bounty on all fish cured by British salt and British merchants. The trade was taken out of the hands of Dutch and Hansa traders and curers, and tenants came to rely more and more on the lairds, whether they wanted to or not, during the ensuing vacuum period when the older regular traders vanished.[1313] Thomas Gifford of Busta, Chamberlain of the Earldom, Steward Depute and Admiral Depute of the County, a Commissioner of Supply and largest proprietor in Shetland, an extensive fishcurer and prominent merchant, put the matter clearly: 'its not unknown to any of you that the fishing Trade is the principal Means providence has ordained for the support of the paroch of Northmavine without which ye could neither subsist your families nor pay the land rent and other publick burdens'. Yet the tenants, for whom he was acting as middleman for providence, were not necessarily grateful for the money and effort he had put out on developing the trade at Hillswick and for his support of the poor in whose hands much of his stock was sunk: 'Yet if ther was 20 small traders seting up in the paroch having each of them but 2 or 3 barrels of salt and some watters and Tobacco the fishers will sell ther fish to them befor me at that same price I give them and even my own tenants that stand bound by ther tacks under a failzie to the contrary are not ashamed to act such a knaveish and dishonest part.' This did not mean that his tenants had fishing tenures in the later sense of the expression, though he did bind himself to supply all the necessary equipment in return for receiving all their white fish at the booth of Hillswick at all seasons of the year, at the common price. 'And for Encureging the white fishers, there shall not one barrel of herring be taken from any man within the said paroch that is not a white fisher to me or hath some concern therein and that none may be induced to leave the white fishing to follow the Herring, ther shall not a herring be received from any fisher in Northmaven befor the last of Jully so, as every man may have equall chance for the herring and no disturbance made in the White Fishing.'[1314] Clearly, the new discipline was being shaped, and an Act of George I in 1727, authorising a bounty on all Scottish cured fish, gave an official incentive.

268. Fishermen's lodges at Stenness, Shetland, late nineteenth century. The lodges are roofed with turf. There are fishing wands and lines by the doors. 3.43.4.

Gifford's Letter Books give details about the expansion and shaping of the white fishing industry. Salt for curing was being imported, along with large quantities of ground lines, tome lines, ling and haddock hooks, hemp linen for boat sails, and much else, from Bergen, Hamburg, Amsterdam and elsewhere. The '3 or 400 lbs of Iron Ketles' ordered from Amsterdam in 1733 were no doubt to be used by the fishermen in their boats and lodges, which may indicate that the kind of fishing organisation involving stations where the men lived for the season in small, stone-built lodges, had already begun, though the fact that Busta ordered thirty four-oared boats from Norway in 1733, 'but no six oard Boats', showed that the industry was still domestic and related more to inshore and middle distance than to deep-sea fishing, though the ground was being prepared for rapid growth in the second half of the century, aided by the opening up of new trade outlets in Spain. Italy, Holland, Flanders and England were also customers for the dried stock-fish produced in Norway as well as in Shetland. Markets included Hamburg, Barcelona, Bilbao, Leghorn, Genoa, Bremen and Verden.[1315]

By 1774, every marketable fish caught by every island boat went to the laird in Foula, as in Sandness and elsewhere. Low prices were given, and the men, who depended on the laird for supplies and equipment, were always in debt. There was a fishing station at Papa Stour, 'formerly' much frequented and by implication not so much by this date. At Ronas Voe were several seasonal huts built by fishermen for summer use. Uyea and Fethaland also had fishing stations. Eighty-five boats fished from Stenness, and a few boats belonging to one man fished from Hamnavoe. Here the fish were split differently from elsewhere in Shetland, since they were intended for the Irish market. Only the three upper joints of the back-bone were cut out, whereas one half was pulled out elsewhere. Funzie, in Fetlar, had a fishing station with a few boats. North-mavine, one of the best stations, had five fishing beaches from which a hundred boats worked between the beginning of June and the second week in August. Thirty or forty of these boats came from neighbouring isles, but belonged to heritors with land in the parish. About 50,000 ling were caught each year. These boats, sixerns of 18 ft (5.5 m) keel, carried 120 *bughts* (Norwegian, Danish *bugt*: known from 1602 in Walls) of lines each 55 fathoms (100.6 m) long with hooks set at 4 fm (7.3 m) intervals. This made a total length of line of 6600 fm (12,070 m) and 1600 hooks, the whole costing £10 stg. This and a haddock line for catching bait made the cost of fitting out a boat £18 stg.[1316]

In the 1790s, prices to fishers were 4^{d} to 6^{d} for the largest size of marketable ling, and 2^{d} to 3^{d} for the tusk, a fish of the cod family resembling a ling, but shorter. Cod measuring 18 in. (55 cm) from the nape of the neck to the last joint of the tail brought 3^{d}. Not all the fishing was for the lairds. Some adventurers from the south had been coming for several years with vessels of 60 to 70 tons. They purchased local boats and hired fishermen by the month or by the season, each vessel requiring three boats with five men in each over the six-week season from 1 June onwards. The boats got a bottle of gin and some biscuit during fishing.[1317]

For haaf fishing, the buoys were of anker kegs with upright poles to which a vane or bundle of heather was attached. There were 20 to 25 score hooks on each line, set up to 3½ fm (6.4 m) apart on the attached *snuids* (Old Scots *sned*, 1565; Old English *snod*). To secure the lines, the fishers made a line tub of 'a parcel of barrel hoops crossing them with rope yarns, or old lines in the form of a net'. The lines laid on this were untied at 50 fathom (91 m) lengths or boughts. When coiled, they were also tied on top with yarn to keep them from slipping or falling out. Night was the time for ling and tusk fishing, the lines being laid across the tide to keep the hooks from being forced together. A man called Cobb was said to have introduced the idea of suspending the hooks and bait from corks. This kept the bait off the ground and made it look alive, more tempting to the fish.[1318]

As the lines were hauled and fish came up, they were hoisted over the gunwale by means of a *huif* (Norwegian dialectal *hov*, pot-hook),[1319] *hug-giestaff* (Norwegian *hugg*, Old Norse *hǫgg*, stroke, blow + *staff*), *clep* (Norwegian *klepp*, gaff), *pickie*, *pick(ie)-hook* (cf. Norwegian *pikka*, to tap), a wooden stick about a foot (30 cm) long with a stout hook at the end, often marked with the initials of its owner. Care was taken to get the gaff into the head or gills and not into the body, since that place would not take salt. The throats of the fish were cut, using the knife called a *skune*, *skunie* (origin unclear; cf. Gaelic *sgian*, knife) or *tully*, sharpened by a whetstone called a *glaan* or *gloanie*, and they were thrown down to bleed, before being gutted and headed. The livers were thrown into a cask. The tongues, cheeks and *sounds*

(Old Scots 1530; Norwegian *sund*) or swimming bladders were kept and fetched a guinea a firkin. The sounds could be sold to an isinglass factory in London.[1320]

Sources of the 1790s contain a good deal of information about the haaf fishing and its effects on the land. The Delting boats carried 120 ground lines worth 26/– each, 8 ground lines for buoy ropes worth 20/– each, 4 buoys worth 20/– each, and 4 haddock lines and hooks worth £24. Lines might last up to four years. The six-man crew needed 15 lispunds of meal and 12 pints of spirits to see them through the season, and brought their own butter, milk and other provisions to the fishing stations. The fish were delivered to the lairds at 42/– a quintal or hundredweight. At the main stations, each boat could catch about 800 ling, amounting to 100 quintals, so that the income per boat was 4200/– or £35 per man in the season. The ling, cod, tusk and oil together brought in about £237, expenses were £235.16/–, and the profit that remained was £2.16/– for the whole boat. Each tenant had to fit out a share of the boat in proportion to the extent and value of his land. East-side fishing was less prosperous than on the west. As far as the lairds were concerned, however, the average profit made on fish cured for export to Spain, Hamburg and Ireland amounted to £10 stg. per sixern. In Delting, the demands of fishing had led to the cultivation by fishermen families of some spots on the coast of Meikle Roe since about 1750, and Little Roe, Brother Isle and Fishholm were only occupied for the sake of the fisheries. The corn they grew was usually blasted by the salt driven on the wind. In general, farms had been split to accommodate more men, and the encouragement of early marriage left few bachelors. There were no leases. Since every man between 18 and 70 was fishing from 1 June to 14 August, 'everything in the farming line must consequently go to wreck'. Even in Dunrossness, one of the most fertile parishes, fishing was the basis of the economy. Nearly all the cod, ling, tusk and saithe caught were sent to Hamburg or Leith. In Lerwick, as elsewhere, farms had to be cultivated by the spade rather than the plough because the men were fishing at the time of cultivation.[1321] In Sandsting and Aithsting, tenants got holdings, whether outsets or divisions of formerly larger units, conditionally on taking a one-sixth share in a boat, and delivering the wet fish to the laird or his tacksman at 3/6 stg. per quintal, and oil at 10^d to 1/– a can. Men who worked on the land were employed for only three-quarters of the year at £15 to £18 Scots, leaving them free for the ling fishing in summer. This paralleled the effect of kelp working in Orkney. The men got £12 to £24 Scots, and boys who worked on the beaches £6 to £10 Scots. Yet in spite of the intensity of the fishing, with men fishing for the lairds or in some cases going to the stations at Walls and Northmavine and fishing for fees, its organisation was so recent that the first master of a boat to the haaf was still alive in 1793, and people remembered when there was not one six-oared boat. Unst also had fishing tenancies, the rent being paid in fish. The boats carried 30 to 60 ground lines according to size, each of 55 fathoms (101 m) with 18 to 20 hooks on half-fathom (91 cm) lines. The smaller boats caught about 300 ling, the larger ones 500 to 600 in a season. Piltock bait was used. In

Bressay, Burra and Quarff the spade had largely replaced the plough because of fragmentation of holdings and the requirement to fish for the lairds. Leases were few. Off the Burra coast, lines set in the evening were drawn in the morning.[1322] In Northmavine there was a large fish-drying beach at St Magnus Bay, Hillswick, with warehouses and cellars for salt and fish. Other stations were Stenness, Hamnavoe, Ronas Voe, Uyea, Sandvoe, Fethaland and Burravoe. Uyea had no beach, so the fish landed there were carried to Fethaland. Boys learned fishing early, and helped at the fishing stations, along with old men. The skippers had to be ready at the station in the first week of June. Each boat carried 100 to 120 lines, 50 fm (91 m) long, each with 10 hooks set 5 fm (9 m) apart on 4 ft (1.2 m) cords. The set lines extended over 6000 fm (10,973 m) or 6½ miles. Four haddock lines were carried for catching bait, and haddock, piltock, halibut, cod, tusk or ling were used roughly in that order of preference for baiting. Sail was set about 10 a.m. to 2 p.m., and the boats reached the fishing grounds about 6 to 7 p.m., 10 to 40 miles out, after which the lines were baited and set. For stores, the boats carried half an anker of bland, a cake of bread for each man, and a bottle of Geneva. These cakes of bread were sea brunies of oatmeal. Meal carried in a bag for emergencies was kneaded, if it should be necessary, in the ouskerry along with some water, and the lumps were eaten. They were known as *dungels* (Norwegian dialectal *dunge*, heap, pile) on the west side of Shetland and the North Isles as *crüles* (Danish *krølle*, Norwegian *krull*, a curl, Norwegian *kryl*, a hump). In Nesting the main part of everyday subsistence derived from catching piltock and sillock, whilst the 'great fisheries' for cod, ling and tusk were done for the lairds. If this failed, the folk became a burden on the lairds. In Papa Stour, convenient houses had recently been erected by the proprietor near the curing beaches, to deal with the ling that was caught 30 to 50 miles off at the haaf. The only leases were verbal, the condition being that the tenant had to fish for the laird. Here, too, farms had been split to accommodate more fishers. In Tingwall, most of the inhabitants fished for ling, working from stations 10, 20 and 30 miles off.[1323]

For the same period in Orkney, this kind of fishing is hardly mentioned. The cod and ling fisheries in Sandwick and Stromness were only a league off. The boats, costing £7, carried great lines of 1000 fm (1829 m) each with 20 score hooks, worth £4, or small lines with 300 hooks, worth £1. Six-man boats were used in Walls and Flotta.[1324] The enterprise, however, had a domestic character. Orkney's economic outlets lay in directions other than haaf fishing.

By 1800, the lairds had fully taken over the functions carried out in earlier times by the booths of foreign traders. They supplied their tenants with boats, lines, fish-hooks and other fishing gear at a certain rate, as well as meal, tea, sugar, spirits, tobacco and sometimes English cloth. The men, working from the bachelor lodges of stone and turf at the fishing stations, often absorbed their own profit and more in these goods and fell into debt. If a line was lost, the cost of replacement was heavy in relation to earnings. Furthermore, since fishing was done at the time of cultivation, farming suffered since women and children were not as efficient as men, and grain could often be scarce. In such a case, the laird supplied grain to his tenants, who fell even more deeply into debt. Little of the Government bounty of 3/– per cwt of fish exported was passed back to the fishermen,[1325] except indirectly through the support a benevolent laird could give his tenants in hard times. In fact the laird had to support his men, for without them he could get no profit from fishing, but this did not prevent the regulation of prices for provisions sold and fish bought so that debt was perpetual, and the men remained bound. There were, however, small merchants moving around the islands who traded clandestinely, usually at night, with the bonded fishermen, giving them better prices for their fish. Efforts by the lairds to combat this led to three forms of tenure arrangement. One was where the tenant paid a low rent and gave the laird preference as a buyer of his produce. A second involved a higher rent paid in money or produce, and the right to fish and sell freely. A third was where the selling of fish to the laird, usually at a relatively low price, was a condition of tenure, and a high rent had to be paid as well. This happened mainly in Aithsting and Sandsting, Weisdale and Tingwall. The first arrangement was the most common, though by the mid-nineteenth century increasing competition from merchants had encouraged most lairds to grant tenancies on a free-fishing basis, in payment for cash. Amongst those who allowed tenants a free market in fish from about 1778 were Bruce of Sumburgh, and Lord Dundas, through his tacksman.[1326]

In the early 1800s, the regular fishing season stretched from about 20 to 25 May till 12 August. The men who had to work from stations often came home only at the week-end with a week's supply of fish. Those who lived at home could more easily combine farming with fishing. The boats still came from Norway and varied in size according to the distance of the fishing grounds, the larger ones having up to seven of a crew. Sometimes the laird had two or more shares in the boat, and hired men to fill the places. The skipper could also have two shares. West-side boats carried up to 120 bughts of lines, a stretch of nearly 7 miles, but elsewhere the number seldom exceeded 50.[1327]

Assembly at the stations in May made a busy scene. Each lodge had to be re-roofed with timbers, and turf cut to cover them. For food the men brought mainly oatmeal, for they could catch their own fish, and the factors supplied them with spirits. The first job was to get a supply of bait, haddock or saithe for choice. Then all set off about the same time, between 10 a.m. and 2 p.m., for the fishing ground, often kemping to see who would get there first, 'with no other means of support than a small quantity of bread hastily baked, a few gallons of water, and a slender stock of spirits'. Following a general practice, each boat took its first turn in a sunwise direction as it set off.[1328] Each boat took on board its own moorings, usually a large stone with a stout rope or chain round it, when it put to sea. The mooring-stone had its particular berth in the boat. Quite often, boats going to the distant or 'fram' haaf went in pairs, the second boat being called the *ranksman*. At the ground, the lines or *tows* were baited and set, usually with no more than three buoys. In sea-language this was to *lay de mar* (Old Norse *marr*, Norwegian *mar*, sea, ocean). Six- or seven-score ling were considered a good, average haul, along with tusk and cod, since 6 to 10 wet ling amounted to a hundredweight. Halibut, skate or other fish remained the property of the fishers.[1329]

A set of 20 bughts, each consisting of 45 to 50 fm (82.3–91 m) of tows, was called a *packie* (diminutive of 'pack'), and the set of packies carried on a boat was its *fleet of tows*. The fishing depth for ling varied from 50 to 100 fm (91–182 m). One man cut the haddock or piltock bait, two baited and set the lines over the starboard side or *lineburd*, and the others rowed. The port side was the *bakburd*. Attached to the first buoy was the *damp* (cf. Norwegian, Swedish, Low German *tamp*) or end of the buoy rope, and to this the end of the greatline, called the *sambord* (Old Norse *sam-*, together + ? *burðr*, a bearing or bringing or ? *band*, binding).[1330] Sinkers called *cappie-stones* (Norwegian *kopp*, *koppul*, small round stone, Old Norse *köppu-stein*, boulder) or *steeths* were used to anchor the lines firmly, with smaller sinkers called *bighters* at 120 fm (219 m) intervals along the line. This took about four hours and then the men rested, tiding the lines for a couple of hours, and had their food. Hauling was started by lifting the buoy-rope. One man hauled, wearing a hauling mitten or *dag* (cf. English *dag*, a rag), a second took the fish off the hooks and threw them into the stern compartment or *shot* (probably from Low German *schot*, a board for closing an opening), and a third gutted them and threw the livers and heads into the middle of the boat. The last haul of fish before returning was not gutted.[1331]

The shot or *run* was the biggest of the six compartments in a boat, the others being, from stem to stern, the fore-head, fore-room, mid-room, oust-room, and hurrack or kannie (terms also applied to the yoke of wood at this point), marked off from each other by the thwarts and the gratings, *fiska brods* or *fiska-feals* (Norwegian *fiska*, Old Norse *fiskr*, fish + Norwegian *fjel*, Old Norse *fjöl*, board),[1332] beneath them, with the mast trunk between the fore- and mid-rooms. Most of the ballast was in the fore-room, as well as the peat fuel, the large three-legged iron fire-kettle in which the fire was lit, and the pot. Provisions and utensils were kept here in a tarpaulin-covered sea-chest. Water containers lay forward in the head, and the sail, kept in the bows when not in use, formed the bed and blankets for the men at sea. With the canvas over them, the men would *dwall ower* (Norwegian *dvale*, lethargy, *dval*, sudden cessation of wind, *dvala*, to abait; Icelandic *dvali*, short rest). There were besides 6 miles of line with 5000 hooks, buoys, sinkers, rope, boathooks, oars, oilskins and other supplies including, perhaps, a *luder-horn* (Old Norse *luðr*, trumpet), a bullock's horn used for signalling in fog. Luder-horns usually came from Highland cattle, and were bought from the old Lerwick merchant curers. Some were better than others in carrying strength, those with thin sides being considered best. Before use the horn was dipped under water to wet the inside, which made it easier to sound. It was used especially when lying to the lines to answer fog signals from passing vessels to guard against being run down. There was a system of signals which the crews understood among themselves. In case of fog also, the bow-tow holding the end of the greatline to the horn of the boat was tied with a slip-knot and a buoy bent and placed near at hand so that the knot could be quickly slipped and the buoy thrown overboard if a vessel came too near. The oars were also shipped and dipped under the tafts, ready for instant action.[1333]

The shooting and hauling of the lines was done from the mid-room in fine weather. Hauling six miles of line was no light job. First the buoy was taken on board, then the anchor line and the sinker and then the line with its hooks. At this point the boat commenced pulling in the direction of the line with one or more pairs of oars, according to the weather. Following the custom that avoided mentioning the fish directly, the first one that appeared near the surface was called 'light i da lum', the second 'white inunder', the third 'white inunder white', the fourth 'wheeda' (Norwegian, Danish *hvide*, white, Old Norse *hvíta*, feminine of *hvítr*, the white one), and then 'white inunder wheeda' or 'wheeda-hint (behind)-da-wheeda'. In Fetlar, the expressions were 'hyda' or 'shu comes hersel' for the first one, 'hyda inunder hyda' for the second, and 'hyde inunder' if a line of fish was seen.[1334] The cod and ling, averaging 30 to 40 lb each, often swallowed bait and hook together and the hooks were extracted with a notched stick, the *kavl-* or *kavlin-tree* (Swedish *kavle*, short piece of wood, Old Norse *kefli*, piece cut off, cylinder). For this reason the space where the work was done could also be called the *kavel*. Halibut of up to 2 cwt and huge skate were hard to deal with and it might need all hands to get them aboard, using the gaffs, but when laid on top of a full run of fish they formed a cover over which the sea could pass without washing out some of the smaller fish.[1335]

Next came the *owse-*, *oust-* or *ouster-room* (Norwegian dialectal, Old Norse *ausa*, to bale, Old Norse *austrrúm*, baling compartment), in which the baling scoop, the *ouskerry* (Norwegian dialectal *auskjer*, Old Norse *ausker*, *austker*, *austr-ker*, scoop, ladle for baling), also called a *kap* (Scots *caup*) in Fair Isle,[1336] was used. Behind this area was the shot. The fish that went into it acted as ballast and the stone ballast, up to a ton of beach stones, could be thrown overboard. Quartzy or white-veined stones in the ballast were unlucky. A broad plank was kept handy for fitting in here as a fore and aft shifting board, to hold the catch stable in rough weather. The *hurrack* (Middle English *hurrock*, fourteenth century) or *kannie* was the stern compartment in which the helmsman stood when the boat was under sail. Here, too, was the compass or *diacle* (Old Scots 1488, probably from *dial*) with the pump close to it. In Orkney even some small boats had pumps by 1747.[1337] Few pieces of equipment can ever have been used to the limits of their functional capacity in the same way as such a fishing boat.

On returning from the haaf, the fish were unloaded, and the lines spread out to dry. Some mended the tows, others fished for or gathered fresh bait, and food for the next day's trip was also prepared.[1338] Sleep was a precious commodity, and over half the floor space in the lodges was taken up by a bed, just as in the peat-houses of Fetlar. Apart from the lodges, a building to be found at most stations was the *böd*, measuring about 30 by 15 ft (9×4.6 m), erected by the curer above the beach. It was a store for dried fish, salt, tar and other stock-in-trade.

In winter and spring the men caught ling on hand-lines, and these were allowed them, though if they were in debt to the laird the tenant was expected to sell him any surplus. Ling caught then were 'winter fish', which were split and laid in salt till the end of spring, when they were taken out of the brine, and washed and dried for exportation. This activity characterised Unst, Fetlar, Burra, Northmavine and Dunrossness.[1339]

Overall, about 1809, a total of at least 459 boats were fishing, crewed by 2754 men who set 483 lines. According to costings worked out then, the average profit per boat was £10.16/–, giving £1.12/– to each man, though he also had some of the fish as food and generally sold a fair amount clandestinely. Lairds paid about 4/– per cwt of wet fish, whereas free fishers could get 6/– to 6/6. Because fish in drying lost three-fifths of their weight, $2\frac{1}{2}$ cwt of wet fish made 1 cwt of dry, which sold at about 18/6 per cwt. Since the cost was 10/– for the fish plus 3/6 for curing costs, the profit per cwt to the laird was 5/–. Some of the lairds employed sloops to accompany the boats, to accommodate the men and let them spend the full week at sea. Each sloop had three to five boats. Though the system worked well in good conditions, stormy weather brought its own difficulties.[1340]

The processing of fish on the beaches was a well-organised affair. The landed fish, already gutted and headed, were passed over by weight to the factor before processing began. Then a *splitter* with a large knife opened the fish from head to tail and took out half the backbone next the head. He passed it to the *washer*, who cleared all the blood particles with a heather- or feather-brush and sea-

269. Fish drying on rocks in Foula, 1902. Photo. H B Curwen.

water. Finally the *salter* placed the fish in the vat, skin-side up, between layers of salt, with heavy stones on top to keep the fish in the pickle.

For salting and curing, vats were carefully made of full-length Bergen double deals, with covers of the same material. A tarpaulin was laid over them in case of rain to keep the pickle pure. The boards 'must be dove-tailed together, laid face to face, and chintzed with white oakum as in ship building', care being taken not to let tar get onto the inside. The corners and bottom were strengthened with metal, and a tap fixed to draw off the foul pickle. The vats were placed on a gentle slope, to help to run off the pickle, and for easier cleaning by scrubbing with brooms and hot water. In filling the vat, a thin sprinkle of salt was laid on the bottom, then a layer of fish laid out without being folded over, and so on in alternate layers, with more salt being used in the higher layers since the curing time was shorter. Too much salt, however, would cause salt burning.[1341] After some days the fish were taken out, washed and brushed from shoulder to tail, following the lie of the scales, and heaped in small *clamps* to let the water drain. The next stage was to spread them skin-side down on a beach of round pebbles, for exposure to the sun, care being taken to guard them from rain. They were spread and clamped in turn in piles of increasing size, until dry, when they were built into a large stack called a *steeple* (Old Scots *steple*, to pile up in a stack, 1642; Dutch *stapel*, heap, *stapelvisch*, half-cured fish). To keep the pressure equal, the steeple was again taken down and rebuilt so that the uppermost fish got their turn at the bottom. The end of the drying or *pining*

270. Fish drying on a pebbly beach near Lerwick. 3.43.2.

271. Stacking and curing cod at the Holms, Orkney, 1912. Photo. G. Ellison. C5942.

(English 'pine', to shrink) process was marked by the appearance on the fish of a white bloom or efflorescence. The whole process ran from early June till mid-September. The fish were then stored tightly and covered with mats in a dry fish-cellar lined with wood, or shipped off to market.[1342]

Nothing was wasted at the station. When the gutting and splitting were done, the heads, livers, roes or *rans* (Old Scots *roun*, 1536, originally from Old Norse *hrogn*, roe) and the bone cut out were divided and carried home in kishies by the women, or on pony back if a long journey was involved.[1343]

At a more domestic level, cod caught in the voes were made into stock-fish by being wind-dried in skeos. The stealing of fish from a skeo was first noted in 1602 and the islands must have been dotted with them at one time, each skeo standing in its own atmosphere, each a proper distance from the other, and placed to catch the wind. Since no salt was used in curing it, there was no restriction on the sale of such fish to any market that could be found, mostly the shipping.[1344]

By the mid-nineteenth century the general procedure had changed little. There was discussion about continuing the fishing for a couple of months after August, when cod and ling drew near the shore and herring bait was plentiful. At the same time, the practice of starting the fishing season earlier had been discouraged to avoid interfering with the spawning ling, and so to conserve stocks. Under a free-fishing system where the lairds had less supervision of the curing beaches, it was considered that the work was less carefully done and their reputation reduced in the market. The kind of boat in use was described as 'the old Norway model improved . . . one of the finest combinations for rowing and sailing, and when not over-masted, (as it always is) and under skilful and intrepid management, is as safe as an open boat can well be'.[1345] In Aithsting and Sandsting, only 8 boats of 18 ft (5.5 m) keel were fishing out of Papa Stour, though there had been 36 in the 1820s. They were based on lodges that were put in order eight to ten days before the start of fishing. Wood and turf for them were carried to the island, and the roofs were removed at the end of the season. Permission was given for the lodges to be built on unenclosed or uncultivated land not more than 100 yds (91 m) above high-water mark. On a Monday morning, a 900 fm (823 m) haddock line was set for bait. The sixerns left about 10 a.m. and got to the grounds 45 to 50 miles away about 6 p.m. They each carried a fleet of 6 packies of lines, at 16 bughts to the packie, and 960 hooks to the fleet. For every fleet there were 4 buoy ropes, 90 to 100 fm (165–183 m) long, and sheepskin buoys with 16 lb kappies or *bolta stones* (probably from *ballisten*, a round sea-worn stone, from Old Norse *bǫllr*, ball), and a 2 lb stone sinker or *bighter* (Dutch *bocht*, Danish, Swedish *bugt*, a loop, from being tied on to a loop on the line). Cutting up the bait was to *snee* (Norwegian dialectal *sni(da)*, Old Norse *snída*, to cut) it. One man did this, two baited alternate hooks, and the others rowed. With the lines set, the boat lay for three or four hours by the last buoy before hauling began, with one man hauling, one using the gaff and removing and *snooding* the hooks, that is wrapping the tome round them to keep the line from ravelling, a third gutting and heading, and the other three andooing or *shoughing* (cognate with English 'shove') the boat, stern foremost. Eight-score ling were reckoned a good haul, giving 16 cwt at 5/–, or £4 in all. It was rare for more than two trips to be made to the haaf each week, but in good weather the lines might be baited and set a second time before the home journey.

Back on Papa Stour, one man went to the lodge to get the fire going whilst the others landed the fish and saw to their weighing. The further processing was not the concern of the fishermen. Only one proprietor in the parish was letting his land on a fishing tenure by this time. His tenants manned seven boats, and the laird held one of the six shares in each boat, putting in a *feedman* (hired man) whose pay was 2 lispunds of meal and £2 stg. Provisions per man for the season were 2 lispunds of meal, 2 ankers of potatoes, a pork ham or a smoke-dried sheep, and half a lispund of dried bere, which they knocked in a knocking stone they carried with them, to make broth. Little spirits were used because of the high duty, so they drank water or had a small cask of bland. At Johnsmas, 24 June Old Style or 1 May New Style, they always had a holiday, and when they left the lodges at Lammas they assembled for a parting cup and a toast, 'Lord! open the mouth of the grey fish, and haud thy hand about the corn'. This thought for the returns from both sea and land surely characterised fishermen-farmers. The farewell celebration was the fishermen's *foy* (Middle Dutch *foye*, *voye*, from Latin *via*, journey). After it, the lodges were unroofed and the boats loaded for the return journey. In later days, the foy was soon after 21 August when the haaf fishing had ended for the season. The crew gathered at the skipper's house for drams, tobacco, tea and biscuits bought from the curer when accounts had been squared at his shop. 'The boys and lasses of the township were not far away when the "foy" was on. They were sure to get some "overs" from the feasts. In fact, it was part of the festivities to hand out to the youngsters. Any old woman in the township who may have spoken a "guid hansel wird" was sure to get her share of the overplush.'[1346]

In Fair Isle, the haaf fishing had been given up, and the men concentrated on saithe. On the Shetland Mainland in Dunrossness, Bruce of Sumburgh's tenants were still curing their own fish and delivering them to him at a fixed rate. Because of this his lands fetched high rents in relation to lairds who took the fish green from their tenants. Fishing remained the main summer job in Northmavine, though the haaf boats had been reduced in numbers through the scarcity and low price of fish, and the expense of fishing. The stations at Stenness, Hamnavoe, Uyea and Fethaland were active. The town of Scalloway was increasing in size because of the fishing and its good harbour. There was no requirement for the tenants in Tingwall, Whiteness and Weisdale to fish for the lairds or sell their fish to them. They could do as they pleased. The men of Delting went to the stations in Northmavine and Papa Stour each year for the haaf fishing. The effect of fish-curer merchants could be seen in Fetlar from the fact that they were providing the men with boats and lines free, and taking their fish at a reduced price. Formerly, as still in North Yell, the men kept up the boats and lines themselves, and passed on their fish to the laird or tacksman. The fishermen of Quarff used Noss as a fishing station, along with men from other parishes, paying a few shillings for the use of the lodges. Bressay folk worked from their own homes, and Burra fishers, because of the closeness of the grounds, could set their lines at night and return to haul them in the morning. They got 6/6 a cwt for wet ling, and 4/6 for cod and tusk, earning £4 to £5 a season on the average. In Unst, young men were more interested in the Greenland or the haaf fishing than in working on the land, in spite of disasters like the 1832 gale, when five boats from this parish were lost. The bigger boats now used carried 60 to 100 ground lines each 42 fm (77 m) long, with hooks on 3 ft (91 cm) lines fixed 5 fm (9 m) apart. Boats and lines were either provided by the fishers, or hired out to them by lairds or merchants who bought the fish green and cured it for the market. They could get 5 to 6/– or even 7/– a cwt. Only a few boats fished for ling from Lerwick.[1347]

By the mid-nineteenth century, change was beginning to be evident. The sixern was growing bigger, though the need to draw it up on the beach made a limit beyond which it could not go. Herring fishing with nets could not be readily carried out from sixerns, because of their small size and relatively low load-carrying capacity. The herring fishing was a prime reason for making the sixern obsolete. The disaster of 1832, when 105 men were lost, gave the sixern a check, though for a short time only. Some half-decked boats were introduced soon after, and after the loss of 58 men in a second disaster in 1881, when many decked boats caught in the summer gale survived, the use of the open sixern as the vehicle for commercial ling fishing virtually came to an end, and a number of writers began to indulge in defamation of its seaworthy character.[1348] Haaf fishing came to an end, therefore, after a life of over a century and a quarter, not through any doubts about the sixern's seaworthiness, but rather through changing economic and social circumstances, marked on the one hand by new kinds of fishing, including steam trawling on ling grounds, and on the other by measures following the Truck Commission Report of 1872 that broke the grip of the lairds over their fishermen-farmer tenants. But the spread of free-fishing by the 1840s shows that change was well on the way even then. The official end came about 1900, a number of sixerns having been fishing the inner grounds till then for the merchant curers.

67

Handline Fishing, Tackle, Bait and Meiths

FOR craig fishing, limpet was the main bait, as also in haddock fishing, though much more was needed for this job. Haddock was caught for bait in ling fishing, but when this finally petered out about 1900, haddock fishing largely replaced it amongst the crofters. Fowererns were generally used, or 12 to 13 ft (3.7–4 m) keel boats with a four-man crew. This was winter fishing, and to venture up to 5 miles out in such small boats was not without danger. It took some time to set and haul four lines in the short days and long hours of darkness of a Shetland winter. Gathering bait for the haaf lines was often a two-stage affair. First piltock was caught with rod and line, or mussels and limpets were gathered at the ebb. These were used on the haddock lines to get haddock bait for the great fish.[1349]

The haddock line consisted of four bughts each of 60 fm (110 m). The tomes, each with its hook, were mounted on the *bauk* (cf. Norse *bakka*, fishing line with many hooks) at 3 ft (91 cm) intervals. The hook was attached to a length of two-ply hair tome as this was not so easily bitten off by the fish. The tome was about 2½ ft (76 cm) long overall. Spindles and whorls known as tome spinners in Shetland, sometimes consisting of a circle of peat with a notched stick inserted, were used to twist the horsehair, in the same way as for fowling snares.[1350] A spinning-wheel could also be used. The twisted horsehair lines were called *imps* or *himps* (Old Scots *imp*, a cutting, *c*. 1500, to graft, *c*. 1470) as elsewhere on the east coast of Scotland, or *bids* (Old Norse *bit*, bite, *biti*, small piece). A length of spun horsehair line could be doubled on itself and when the ends were released, the halves twisted together to make a line of double thickness. Another way was to work two tome spinners together, each rotating on its own axis, and one circling round the other.[1351]

The four bughts, one per man, had 480 hooks. The baited lines were stowed in a wooden *scull* (origin uncertain; cf. Old French *escu(e)lle*, dish) or *line box*, deep at one end and shallow at the other. Ropes taken through holes in the sides kept the lines firmly in position when the boxes were being carried to the beaches. Limpet bait was used, but mussels were preferred, where they could be got, and some were even imported from the south. The lines were set in the same way as in haaf fishing, with buoys and sinkers at each end.

The bait could vary considerably in type, especially when the need for it was pressing and anything was used that could be got. A bit of white cloth smeared with swine's fat sometimes did well, especially for a *hocken* (Norwegian dialectal *hæken*, greedy, Old Norse *hakka*, to eat ravenously) fish, a cod or ling that was *in purta* (Old Scots *powerte*, 1375, Scots *puirtith*, poverty), thin and hungry. If other bait was scarce, one of the crew would cut up or snee the first fish caught, whether mackerel, herring, or some other kind of fish. The squid, *Sepia officinalis*, called the *amok* (origin uncertain), was a favourite, partly because it was tough and stood firmly on the hook. The old fishermen preferred squids when they had been for some hours in a fish's stomach, for this gave a better colour and made them more fishy. Any tusk or ling with a squid in its stomach would spew it up when landed in the boat.[1352] Sometimes if large packs of dogfish were around, the fishing was spoiled because they took the bait, and a partial answer to this problem was sour eel, which dogfish did not like, though ling and cod took it eagerly. Lines for eel, similar to those used on the haaf for ling, were set in the late evening close along the shore, baited with piltock, and were hauled in the morning. Since they were widely used for bait, the catches were sometimes light. Eels were hung in the barn till sour, and their smell was certainly not calculated to help any young lad who was in his first season on the sixerns. The conger eel or *sleekie* (from *sleek*, sly, smooth), found in deep, dark inshore water overshadowed by high cliffs, was prized as bait for ling and halibut. Eel flesh was not eaten, but the skin made a good gun cover and the oil was kept as a remedy for sprains and rheumatism. If conger eels were taken on board, they were killed, because they were bad for fouling the lines as they wriggled through the boat. To dispatch them they were taken inboard over the gunwale belly up, and given a heavy stroke on the navel with the back of the huggiestaff.[1353]

Getting bait for the haaf lines with over 1000 ling hooks was a big job, especially when several hauls were made during the trip. If bait ran out the haddock lines were set over sandy ground. Both craig- and eela-fishing were sources of piltock bait. Herring could also be got from the herring boats that shared the grounds in later times. Ling fishermen, however, did not much like the appearance of herring shoals, since they tended to be followed by dogfish.

The tide was an important factor in line fishing. The boats were carried with flowing water and the ebb-tide, and different tides suited different fishing areas. Some Fetlar ling seats fished well with either tide. Most kinds of fish took best when the tide was moving most strongly and least well in the slack between tides. Tides, therefore, were of much importance and every movement was observed carefully and added to the tale of experience. The same was true of weather conditions. After a severe storm with big breakers, there was little point in trying the inshore grounds for the fish would have moved to deep water. Loud thunder was thought to affect fish by putting them off feeding for a few days.[1354]

The range of different names for fish, at different stages of growth, is a further indication of the close, detailed interest taken in this most essential means of subsistence and basis of commerce. Coalfish had several names (see page 527). A young ling, *Molva molva*, was an *ollick* (diminutive form of

Norwegian *aal*, eel, or strap), when 3½ ft (1.1 m) long it was a 'grown ollick' and when larger than that a *kirsen* (Norwegian dialectal *kirsten*, Christian, decent) ollick. When fully grown it was a ling. A small tusk, *Brosmius vulgaris*, was a *brismac* (Old Norse *brosma*, a fish of the cod kind), and the name *tusk* is from Norwegian *to(r)sk*, Old Norse *þo(r)skr*. An undersized lean or old cod was a *ruggie* (cf. Shetland Norn *rag*, Norwegian dialectal *rak*, an emaciated or miserable creature, Icelandic *hrak*, something worthless), a name also applied as a nickname to the people of North Sanday in Orkney.[1355] Usually a cod, *Gadus morrhua*, was a *keelin* (Old Scots *ke(i)ling*, 1380; cf. Old Norse *keila*, large cod, a word possibly of Celtic origin; Gaelic *cilean*).

Handline fishing continued after the sixerns had been cleaned out, drawn up to their winter noost, and secured, generally bottom up, for the winter months. Then the smaller boats were rigged out, and fowererns with five or six of a crew went to the ling seats, with water to drink and two 'sea brunies' apiece, round oatmeal cakes fired on a gridiron, to eat. They would sail or row, depending on the wind. As in earlier days, men from different townships preferred their own grounds. In Fetlar, Houbie and Tresta men went to the west grounds, the men of Aith fished the mid-grounds, and those of Funzie the east grounds.

Several of the ling seats were small patches of hard ground on a sandy bottom, not easy to find with a strong bearing tide running and in poor visibility. The best ling seat on the Fetlar ground was 'Aids deep', lying 7 miles off in 80 fm (146 m) of water. Such inshore grounds were called *seats* (Norwegian dialectal *seta*, fishing-ground), *klaks* or *klakaskurs* (Norwegian *klak(k)*, small heap, (sand)bank in the sea, Icelandic *klakkr*, upstanding rock + Norwegian, Old Norse *skor*, hollow, chasm, or Old Norse *skǫr*, edge, boundary). *Skur* was a name given to the boundary between two inshore fishing grounds.[1356] Between the seats and the offshore grounds were areas called *raids* or *raiths* (origin uncertain; cf. Old Scots *reid*, 1561, Dutch *ree(de)*, roadstead, anchorage), or *lyings* which, in the old form of domestic fishing, were allocated to the crews of individual boats, the fishing area being identified with reference to landmarks known as *meiths* (Old Norse *mið*, a fishing bank marked by prominences) or *hands*. Up till the mid-nineteenth century it was considered almost an act of theft, or at least of aggression, if a crew set their lines on another man's raid, even if he was ashore at the time. In Fetlar the far grounds were also called the *shutten*, perhaps from the fact that when the skipper was satisfied that the right spot had been reached, he would say 'All right boys, shoot', and the bow-speet would be dropped overboard. The distant or fram haaf was also termed the 'ocean', where fishermen worked with the highest points of the land trembling on the brink of the horizon. Less remote was the 'in-haaf'. In general, the inshore grounds, the in-haaf, extended about 7 miles out, the middle fishing grounds 15 to 20, and the deep-sea grounds or fram-haaf 30 to 50 miles out. Another name for the deep-sea grounds was *leegins* (perhaps from Old Norse, Norwegian dialectal, Faroese *lega*, a lying-place, where boats can anchor). It was the development of the sixern that allowed these grounds to be exploited from the mid-eighteenth century onwards. Because they were too far out for meiths to be easily used, the dry-card compass or diacle came into use and was common by the 1880s.[1357] Small boats of 8 ft (2.4 m) keel or over were used for the inner hards, fowererns for fishing farther off, and then sixerns for the farthest grounds.

For inshore and middle-distance fishing the positions of the ling seats and other productive fishing spots were got by lining up two meiths or bearings from opposite directions. The Fetlar ling seats, beginning at the east seats and working round, are:

Seat	*Meiths*
Stranda Sands	W: da Haa door o' Hollo (at Hestaness)
	E: Hosta and da Tind in line
Mü	W: da Laydie o' Sunkre at Snap Point
	E: Brunnes Knowes at Strandbrough Ness
Da Lig	W: Scord of Grunisgeo over Snappa Skerry
	E: da Lig Hill at Strandbrough Ness
Aid's Deep	W: Scord of Grunisgeo over Snappa Skerry
	E: Vallafield hard up at the Outer Brough
Vaardens	W: Bigholm at Snap Point
	E: Toe of Unst at Hosta
Akkles	W: Hyler of Aith at Lequolk
	E: Toe of Unst at Hosta
Easter Sedick	W: Mid Yell Voe over Horn of Ramsness
	E: Da Yiggle o' Hools Geo at da Fura Stacks
Da Villa	W: Scord o' Aywick over Horn of Ramsness
	E: Mid Büd at Clayie Tonga
Halloween Skur	W: Kristian's Hoose over da Kest
	E: Knowe o' Sutisen at Lequolk
Waster Sedick	W: Mid Yell Voe over Horn of Ramsness
	E: Da Knowe o' Rufrapund at da auld Sheep Pund
Sooth	W: Ronas Hill at da Muskie o' Burravoe
	E: Knowe (or Brugga) o' Rufrapund over Jacob's Hoose
Waster Deeps	W: West Sheek o' Blo Geo at Hoga
	E: Soond a Fura Skerry open
Easter Ruad	W: Taings of Sheniberg and Helersness in line
	E: Kristian's Hoose at Hoga
Waster Ruad	W: Brug o' Bastavoe at Horn o' Ramsness
	E: Brugga o' Stakkaberg at Hoga
Sandy Böd Sedick	W: Houll o' Basta at Foreland
	E: Tolga Scord over da Run Geo

Da Wrak	W:	Tower of Brough (Kirn) at Foreland
	E:	Skerry o' Quoda i da Maamy Soond
Da Skurrens	W:	Scord o' Aywick at Horn o' Ramsness
	E:	Hooses of Velzie at Breest o' Bigholm
Seah or Se-a	W:	Taings of Helersness and Sheniberg in line
	E:	Heog Stack at Hoga
In On	W:	Selligeos at Hiplin Stack
	E:	Da Muckle Hylden at da Hoga

Aid's Deep, Sooth, and Waster Deeps were the best of these, in that order. In earlier days the meiths were kept secret from neighbouring fishermen, and if a strange boat approached, the local boat would move off or run down bare hooks to mislead the visitor. No boat would ask another for bait, nor would anyone give another a bearing.[1358]

272. George Stout (Fieldie) of Field, Fair Isle, with two reels or dorros below his arm. 1.28.11.

Fishing for ling on these seats was done with a *speet* (Old Scots *spete*, spit) or *bow-speet*, sometimes called a *pap*, a bow-shaped rod thrust through a sinker, from each end of which dangled a line and hook. In recent times the bow has been of iron, but formerly whalebone was used, for the word *skog* (Norwegian dialectal *skåk*, swingletree or tracebar of a cart or carriage) is defined, from 1838, as the 'cord of a fishing line consisting of a rod of whalebone with a cord and hooks attached to each end'.[1359] If fishing was good, the linesmen usually got a pair and four men would soon make a good catch. The boat moved with the tide and had to be pulled back to the tide side of the seat before the speets were shot again, this operation being called *takkin'* (taking) *on*. While the lines were running to the bottom, seeking the fish far below, the men smoked or cut bait, and the younger ones took a surreptitious bite of a brunie, for skippers thought it a sign of softness if their men wanted food and drink too soon.

Before the bow-speet with its metal hooks became general, the old tackle, surviving up to about the beginning of the nineteenth century, had wooden

273. John Georgeson of the Haa, Papa Stour, with a V-shaped reel and line, and a sprule with ollick or cod-hooks (the haddock sprule is lighter, with smaller hooks), 1967. 3.35.32.

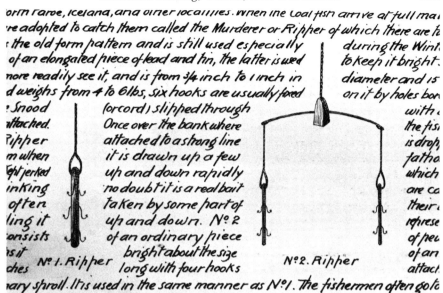

274. Types of murderers or rippers used in Orkney. Drawn by G. Ellison, *c.* 1911. 4.13.16.

275. A catch made by Charlie Thomason with a murderer off Fetlar, Shetland. 1.50.30.

hooks called *snaara-pins* (Norwegian dialectal *snar*, a twist, Old Norse *snara*, to twist, make a turn), about 3½ in. (9 cm) long. The pins were sharp at both ends, with a notch in the middle where the *tome* was fixed, and a slack at one end, where a loop-fashioned half-hitch was passed around, by which the hook with the bait on was kept in a hanging position up and down along the end of the line. By the slightest touch this half-hitch slipped off, and the pin stuck across the mouth of the fish,[1360] usually across the gullet or in the gills. The snaara-pin was held firm by a sinker and fixed to the tome or skog at an angle by a woollen thread, sometimes called a *fursin* (Norwegian dialectal *forsyn(d)*) making it easier to swallow end on. Bait was tied to the pin by the same kind of coarse thread, also called *vaav* or *vaaving* (Norwegian dialectal *vav*, wrapping, strip of binding). The pin, sometimes known as a *varnagel*,[1361] could be of bone, but this material splintered and broke more easily than wood if caught in a rocky cleft when fishing on a hard bottom. With the snaara-pin the tome was about a fathom (1.8 m) long, but later, with the bow-speet, it was shorter and had a swivel fitted, to turn out the twist caused by the movement of fish being hauled in deep water. Terminologically, the Orkney equivalent of the speet is the *sproll* (probably cognate with English *sprawl*), a word also known down the east coast of Scotland. In 1891 it was said to have been a new invention in Orkney, enabling the fisher to use two hooks on one handline. A piece of line plaited with three strands and used in cod-fishing instead of a sproll was a *fortam* (Norwegian dialectal *fortaum*, snood of a fishing line) in Hoy and a *forehandline* in Westray.[1362]

The speet began to be ousted about the 1940s in Shetland by the *murderer*, a cylinder of lead 5 or 6 in. (13–15 cm) long through which three holes were bored, the middle one at right angles to the other two. Six hooks were fitted to short lengths of hemp or nylon cord passed through the holes. A shorter length of lead could have two holes and four hooks. Though it could fish better than the bow-speet, the main defect was that if a large fish took the top hooks, which hung along the lead, they were often hooked only lightly in the skin of the lip and could break away. Also, since the hooks dangled in grapnel fashion, the murderer could catch easily on an uneven bottom.[1363] The equivalent in Orkney and in North-East Scotland was a *ripper*. Examples are known of the use of two four-hook rippers on the arms of a sproll.

A fish widely caught for use as bait was the mackerel. For this, and other fish, the tackle was a *dorro* (Norwegian, Old Norse *dorg*, trailing fishing line) or, in Orkney, *darro*. The name was used both for the line and for the wooden frame, rectangular or V-shaped, on which the lines were wound. The reel was also called a *soolack* (Norwegian dialectal *sula*, Faroese *súla*, a forked wooden implement on which a line is wound). The rectangular form, which is probably later in date, was called a *grind* (Norwegian, Old Norse *grind*, gate). A Stronsay name for the V-shaped reel was *pricks*, and in Deerness *studdle* (Old Norse *stuðill*, a prop).[1364] Dorros made by the old fishermen were of considerable length, with up to 30 hooks. The gut was plaited or hand-spun into a three-strand tackle, with a short length or bid at every join, on to which the hook and

276. Line tubs in a boat in the South Harbour, Fair Isle. This type of tub is unique to the island. 1962.

277. Baiting haddock lines in Fair Isle. Per Miss M. Wilson. 1.38.24.

278. Casting lots for a haul of fish in Birsay, Orkney. Photo. T. Kent. Per P K I Leith. C3941.

lure was served. White hair was formerly used for 'buskin', and later when dyed yarn became readily available a strand or two, preferably of bright red, was put on with the hair. Another form of lure was 'hoe fins', the tail or back fin of a dogfish, left under an ebb-stone till the skin had rotted off, leaving a thin fibre-like substance that was bright and shiny. The feathery part of a goose quill was also used, and the exotic taste of the mackerel made it take a bit of chamois leather cut into a wing-shape in preference to anything else. Tide waters were best for mackerel. At one time they were cured quite a lot for food, but latterly salt curing has ceased and now they are only eaten when fried fresh.[1365]

Handlines were kept in constant motion up and down as the boat was rowed gently forward, a process called in Shetland to *ross* (cf. Faroese *ræsa*, to run a line to the sea bottom and then pull it up a few fathoms) and in Orkney to *taft* (origin uncertain: perhaps related to *thaft*). To *rick* or in Orkney *rake* (Norwegian *rykk(e)*, Old Norse *rykkja*, *rykkr*, tug, jerk) was to catch a fish by jerking up the hook, hence the name *rikker* or *rikki* for a fish-spear, often a spar of wood with a hook on the end.[1366]

Sinkers for handlines were formerly made of soapstone, later of lead, and the fishermen may still speak of 'handline stane' or 'lead stane', commemorating the earlier material. The name *kavi* (Norwegian dialectal *kava*, Old Norse *kafa*, to dive under water) could also be given. Small, boat-shaped sinkers were made by running lead into wooden moulds, which could be used dozens of times. A hollowed out peat could serve, but it had to be absolutely dry or the molten lead would fly, and it could only be used once. In Orkney, a sinker could be called a *baldos* (origin uncertain; cf. Shetland *bolta-stane*), *lead-luss* or *lussy* (probably Norwegian dialectal *flis*, splinter, *flysja*, to slice, split).[1367]

68

Cod Fishing

THE cod has been a fish of much value for food from early times. Cod and ling were the main fish represented by the numerous fish-bones in the Bronze Age levels at Jarlshof, and in the Viking middens there were bones of the cod, saithe, and ling. The skull of one cod was 12 in. (30 cm) long. 'Gilt killing' (Old Norse *gildr*, Norwegian, Swedish *gild*, Swedish *gill*), cod of full value, were paid as part of the South Ronaldsay boat teinds in 1584, and no doubt cod was one of the kinds of fish that, in wind- and sun-dried form, made up the riches of Shetland in the 1520s and 1570s. In 1594 fishermen from Fife were required to pay various fees to Earl Patrick. Every greatline boat, with its 'land lyar', a small boat for going ashore, was to pay as teind fifty marketable ling each year, and a barrel of fine Scottish salt for leave to dry fish within the flood mark. A dozen cod and a dozen skate were taken for leave to dry fish above the flood mark. When the greatline boats went to the cod handlines, each was to pay a hundred cod a year. Boats that came with their 'land lyar' especially for the cod handlines paid a hundred cod a year, with a barrel of fine Scottish salt for leave to dry fish below the flood mark, and two dozen cod for land leave.[1368] Hand-line boats, therefore, were more heavily taxed than the greatline boats.

Other sources also refer to greatlines in the sixteenth century. In 1567, and 1579, greatline boats were listed in the Edinburgh Testaments and greatlines in 1576, 1577, 1584 and 1590.[1369] In 1576, Bruce of Cultmalindie took from each of certain boats from Burray, Gulberwick, Quarff and Trondra, fishing at Havera, one cod and one ling, and a further cod and ling was taken when these boats came to their merchants in Scalloway. In Fetlar, where 'thair haill sustentatiounis and lyvis fude (specialie in the tyme of winter, quhen thai dar not travell to far seis in fisching, for storms of weder upon their small scaffis) consists on thair fisching within the bayis and soundis adjacent', and where people had fished freely with 'small lyne, gritlyne, or hand lyne', now winter-fishing was forbidden and several fishermen had been fined. Greatlines were for ling, turbot and skate as well as for cod, and these sources show that longlining was known around the Scottish coasts over a century before its alleged invention by a Møre farmer in Norway in 1680. Handlining was done in winter, when the use of long-lines of greatlines was impossible.[1370] They were complementary techniques.

Cod fishing was being given up in Orkney by the 1770s, a fact which points to changing economic emphases there, and the nineteenth century development of cod fishing around Orkney came from outside. Late eighteenth century sources say little about fishing in Orkney. Indirectly, fishing provided income for young Orcadians, many of whom engaged for five years at a time with the Hudson's Bay Company, or enlisted with the Iceland or Greenland fishermen for three or four months each year. The fashion of getting Orkney men for the Northern fisheries and the Hudson's Bay Co. appears to have grown after about 1741–3, leading to a decrease in population in some parishes. In 1798, about 1000 men had gone for these reasons from St Andrews and Deerness parish. There was much emigration from Birsay too. Before the 1740s, labour had been supplied more from England, Ireland and Shetland. This sea outlet for the young men had an effect on the land as well, for a careful man with five years' savings from a spell with the Hudson's Bay Company could outbid local farmers for rents. Though this gave them a foothold on the farming ladder that they might otherwise not have got easily, it also led to some over-renting of the land.[1371]

The Hudson's Bay Company started as a fur trading enterprise in 1670. By 1704, Orkney men were already being employed by it, though it was left to the ships' captains to find men. Expansion of the Company between 1772 and 1799 increased the labour force in Canada from 181 to 529, and in 1791 a Stromness merchant, David Geddes, was appointed agent with responsibility for recruiting labour, advancing wages, and meeting bills. This regularising of the system ensured a steady labour supply, and led to the emigration, much of it temporary, about which the writers of the First Statistical Account complained in the 1790s. The Company liked Orcadians because 'they were free of the taint of rebellion in favour of the exiled Stuarts, no recruits being forthcoming for that cause even when Stromness and Kirkwall was briefly in Jacobite hands in 1746; they were very poor and hence starting wages, rising with each re-enlistment, of £6 a year for labourers and of £15 to £20 for craftsmen and sailors seemed princely; they were accustomed to great hardship and thus could endure the rigours of the Arctic'.[1372]

By the 1790s, Orcadians comprised three-quarters of the employees of the Company in Canada, the majority being manual workers. The main competitor to the Company was the merchant navy, and the navy itself during times of war. During the War of the American Revolution, 1200 of a peak complement of 99,831 navy men, or 1.2 per cent, were from Orkney, many of them press-ganged into service. This reduced the numbers of men available to the Hudson's Bay Company. The supply was also affected by economic conditions at home, for the early nineteenth century development of herring fishing on inshore grounds encouraged men to stay at home. Gradually the link with Orkney weakened. In 1821, the Company amalgamated with its Canadian rival, the North West Company, and there followed a much more regular enrolment of Canadian workers. Though Stromness remained a gathering point for Scottish recruits, these were no longer Orcadians only, and when the *Prince Arthur* and the *Prince of Wales* called in 1860, they picked up a mixed bag of men from the Hebrides and the Highlands as well as Shetland and

Orkney. For much of the nineteenth and part of the eighteenth century, therefore, the young men of Orkney had an opportunity for relatively lucrative employment that was for the most part denied to the haaf fishers of Shetland, and they could use the money to gain a firm foothold on the land afterwards.

Just as an outside body, the Hudson's Bay Company, played a role here, so also did another, the Thames Company (London) in the development of Orkney cod fishing. It was said to have started in the Burray area in 1817, and by the early 1840s, 11 sloops were involved there. During 1840–42, 18 sloops had been fishing for cod, each curing over 380 tons. Cod was fetching 10/– a cwt. In Stronsay and Eday, it began in 1828 with the use of small sloops, for the most part decked. Cross and Burness had 15 boats and sloops on cod and herring by 1841, and eleven of Shapinsay's 50 herring boats worked at cod fishing during the season. The quantity caught, cured and dried in the North Isles of Orkney during 1840 was:

Area	Tons	Area	Tons
Westray	120	North Ronaldsay	10
Eday	109	Cross and Burness, Sanday	14
Stronsay	30	Lady Parish	6
Shapinsay	65	Rousay and adjacent isles	90
			444

This total, sold by the fishermen themselves, gave £5400. In Walls and Flotta, Pentland Firth cod were so prized that a number of well-smacks were fishing there for the London market.[1373] This meant, however, that the need for a shore establishment with curing facilities was eliminated, and that local involvement and income was minimal.

According to a North Ronaldsay writer, cod fishing was of various kinds, though the main fishing was in sloops with big crews. Fishing was done in the slack of the tide, and the boat sailed against the tide, lying at the job for up to a week. The heads and livers were kept, and the cod were taken to a curer on Westray. The cod took salt just as well when they had lain a few days. There was also a curer for a few years in North Ronaldsay. Fishing was from Beltane (mid May) till the end of June, 6 or 7 weeks in summer, and 6 to 7 tons was an average catch, rising to 10 tons in a good year. Yole fishing for codling, with 2 or 3 men in a crew, took place at the same time, though not so far out. The codling were also sold. Codling fishing also went on at the saithe fishing time, and in fact nearly replaced saithe fishing entirely. All this was with handlines. But after 1890–2, all the big boats became sloop-rigged. Scots fishers with boats bigger than yoles, using longlines, came on the scene. With their 12 miles of line they could fill a boat at one haul, and could also get bigger fish than the local men got on their handlines, for all their skill which was already noted in the early 1600s when North Ronaldsay was said to be the chief fishing place in Orkney, and was acknowledged by the west-coast fishermen of Scotland, who would say the only good fishers in Orkney were 'Arcach Eilean Ringansey', the Orcadians of North Ronaldsay.[1374]

In Shetland, cod fishing was carried on from sloops of 18 to 40 tons burden. By the 1840s, Sandsting and Aithsting had 8, giving a total tonnage of 224. Each had a crew of 9 to 12 men, who hired the sloop for the season, from Whitsunday to Lammas, the cost being half of all the fish caught to the owner, and the oil from the livers. The owner was bound to keep the sloop seaworthy, and also cured all the fish, the men paying 2/– stg. per cwt for their half. This amount was deducted when accounts were settled at the end of the season. It was understood that the sloop owner was to have preference, on equal terms, to the purchase of the men's share of fish and oil. In some cases a few men purchased a small sloop in partnership and fished with her, taking on extra hands as required either as sharesmen or for a fee. Sometimes they got a half share and half fee. The gear required for the sloop was two lines of about 100 fm (183 m), a lead of 3 or 4 lb, with a *scob* (Old Scots *skob*, thatching rod, 1536, Gaelic *sgolb*, splinter, thin stick), a bent iron rod 2½ ft (76 cm) long passed through the upper end of the lead, with a tome and hook at each end baited with a large mussel or yoag. This tackle was the equivalent of the bow-speet or sproll. Since 1600 to 2200 mussels were needed for bait each week, the supply was of much importance and people who dredged bait got from 4d to 6d per 100, the expense being divided between the owners and the men.[1375]

This need for bait explains the importance of the mussel scalps, such as the three within Bressay Sound. Here the people of Lerwick had had the exclusive practice of dredging mussels for generations as bait for haddocks and small cod which they fished from small boats with handlines in summer and longlines in winter. When kept at their domestic level, demand did not exceed supply, but from about 1811 three Lerwick merchants, Messrs. J. Hay, T. Ogilvy and G. Angus, had been employing boats to dredge mussels for the supply of cod fishing boats. Not only did they largely destroy the scalp, but also, since they took the hauls ashore for cleaning, young mussels and spawn were not returned to the sea to build a new generation. Mussels were also essential to the ordinary folk who needed them for haddock fishing, which formed the basis of their subsistence. A petition having been presented, the Vice-Admiral Depute put an interdict on dredging till the matter could be fully investigated.[1376]

The average catch in a season was 5 to 18 tons, depending on the size of the sloop, and the price had been stationary at £10 a ton for some years before 1840. The men took home fish-heads and small fish for the weekly supply of their families. For their own supply in the sloops they had 8 lb of oatmeal baked into oatcakes weekly with two-thirds of a barrel of potatoes and a supply of smoked pork or mutton for the season, and as much fresh fish as they chose to eat. Before sailing, the men were bound to bend the rigging and sails, and ballast the sloop. After fishing, they unrigged and dried the ropes and sails, heaved the ballast, cleared the vessel and drew her up, secure for the winter. The fish livers were then melted into oil and the produce divided between owner and men.[1377]

By 1841, cod fishing had been almost given up in Northmavine, where it had been a complete failure for some years. In Walls, much cod was caught by old men and boys using smaller boats than those for the haaf, no doubt taking advantage of the period after August when cod draw nearer the shore. In Bressay, young men from nearly every family had 'run eagerly to Lerwick' in February and March to engage in the Greenland and Straits' fisheries, and in recent years in the cod fishing, leaving much of the burden of agricultural labour on the women. Haaf fishing therefore was not solely responsible for this situation. Cod fishing to the west and south of Bressay, beginning about Whitsun, was carried on from small sloops of 15 to 20 tons. The parish itself had 6 sloops, and seventy local men engaged in it in 1840. Eight or ten men were partners in a sloop and boys – who needed less pay – were sometimes hired to make up the complement, getting £2 a season, or 1/6 per ton of fish. An average season's catch was 4 to 10 tons. In general the sloops were decked, ranging up to 40 tons, and handlining for cod, using shellfish bait, was usually done in the south and south-west sides of the Shetland coast.[1378]

Good cod fishing grounds were sometimes jealously guarded, with an eye to conservation of stocks. One such was the Codling Hole, lying between Weatherholm, Foraness and Collafirth Ness, and used by the Swinister and Collafirth men. Regulations were drawn up on 17 Feb. 1841 by the fishermen themselves:

1st. That evray Boat intending to Sett Lines are to be there about Son Sett.

2nd. that they sett their Lines stright.

3rd. that in Setting there Lines they are to keep a Equel distance from each other and give Everey man a Equel share Everey one in his Turn accordin to the plan showin if 2 boats heas the Inside this night they are to take the out side next night and regularey in there turn.

4th. that no man are to hale his Lines in the night time or alone non are to be seen there on any pretence whatever of fishing in the night time the Lines are all to remain un Haled til brod daylight that it be known that Everey Boat heas arived.

5th. that no day Halls are to be mead in within the Primeses of the Codlin Hole.

6th. that no man or men are to go there to Fish on Monday Morning becaus wi think som may Incroch on Sabath Night.

7th. That no man gos there to fish from this ded (date) with cod Lines until the Midel of March say the 15 day New stile.

8th. In Testomoney there off to adopt and keep the same regulatones wi all subscribe our Names as honest men and wi all subscribe to do all in our power to apprehend aney one there transgresing the nowsinded (signed) regulatons.

9th. It is considered that the owner or Comander of Each boat is sufisant to Sind.

Seventeen men signed from Swinister and seven from Collafirth.[1379]

Cod fishing, which slotted as an extra source of income into the economy of Orkney, had a more prominent part to play in Shetland where it changed the pattern of fishing activity and the form of the relationships between tenant, laird, sea and land that characterised haaf fishing. The seasonal rhythm of activity was also affected in relation to both fishing and farming. The capital built up by lairds and merchants from haaf fishing allowed investment in decked boats until the cod fishery became 'the most heavily capitalised branch of fishing, employing the largest vessels on the most distant grounds ever to have been operated by Shetlanders'. With such specialisation there went an increasing degree of divergence between activities on the sea and on the land.[1380]

Handlining for cod did not begin until about 1800, partly because the main cod grounds were farther out than the traditional ling grounds, and partly because haaf fishing with great lines for the demersal ling and tusk on the bottom could not be combined with handlining for the pelagic cod at higher levels. Though sixerns brought these grounds within reach, the size of the boat was too limited for cod fishing on any scale. The discovery of a prolific cod bank south-west of Shetland, in 1788 and again in 1817, called the 'Regent's Fishing Bank' or later the 'Home Cod Grounds' was a strong contributory factor in establishing this home industry on a commercial base. The Napoleonic Wars, which kept the Dutch doggers off the banks, may have allowed cod stocks to build up. At any rate, a few vessels of 6 to 35 tons burden with 6 to 8 of a crew started the cod fishing around Foula and Fair Isle, using handlines baited with two or three hooks. By 1819 there were 24 vessels fishing for cod, employing 200 men. Their 342 tons of dried cod fetched £12 a ton, of which £3 was a Government bounty, whereas tusk and ling were fetching £22 a ton.[1381]

Because of the bounty, detailed statistics were kept by the skippers and the weekly fishing pattern can be established. The sloop *Jameses*, a Scottish vessel of 32 tons burden, with a group of three Lerwick owners who employed a skipper and ten of a crew to fish for them, caught cod as follows in 1820, using mussels and sometimes buckies as bait:

Date	Place	Distance (Miles)	Depth (Fathoms)	No. of Cod
May 6	Papa Westray	25	45	148
13	Foula	20	50	8
20	,,	25	45	456
27	,,	30	40–50	332
June 3	North Ronaldsay	12	48	132
10	Foula	20	50	120
17	Papa Westray	12	38–45	625
24	Papa Westray	16	45	1110
July 1	Foula	25	40–50	609
8	,,	30	40–55	1295
15	,,	30	40–50	1306
22	,,	18	55–60	410
August 5	,,	18	50–60	651

Total 7202[1382]

Cod had darker flesh and a less pleasant taste after salting, hence the lower price paid in the salt fish markets abroad. An additional bounty in 1820 of £3 per registered ton for vessels of over 20 tons pushed the numbers of vessels up to 80 by 1829, when the bounty ceased, though the Shore Curing Books suggest a smaller rise from 14 boats in 1821 to 37 in 1829. At the same time, the number of curers rose from 9 to 22, and the fish caught from 80,671 to 213,452. The first sloop to be registered in 1820 in the islands under Act I, George IV, c 103, 'An Act for the Encouragement and Improvement of the British White Fisheries', was the *Ann*, built in Shields. She was flush-decked, square-sterned, and measured 39 ft 3 in. (12 m) overall by 11 ft 3 in. (3.4 m) beam and had 6 ft 3 in. (1.9 m) depth of hold.[1383]

By 1820, cod fishing was being intensified through larger boats that allowed sea trips of 7 to 10 days, involving accommodation for the first stages of preservation in the hold, with the fish cleaned and packed with salt in layers. The range extended till by the 1870s areas as far off as the Davis Straits and the North Cape of Norway had been explored for cod by sloops or slightly larger sailing smacks, with the Faroe Islands as the main centre of operations. The abolition of the bounty, which led to some decline in cod fishing around Shetland, was part of the pressure that led to the Faroes in the search for more productive grounds, first in the 1830s, and then in the late 1840s, with Icelandic grounds being reached in the 1850s. Between 1840 and 1849, several vessels fished up the Davis Straits on the Disko Bank, and along the Greenland coast, probably because many Shetlanders were already familiar with these waters through whaling. The optimum years for the Faroe smack fishing came between 1860–80.[1384]

In 1872 the Faroese themselves took up cod fishing from smacks, following the initiative of Shetland and other parts of Britain, by purchasing old vessels in Britain. Governor Pløyen and three Faroese colleagues travelled in Shetland in 1839 to study fishing methods and eventually the Faroese began to try things out for themselves. After the firm establishment of the smack fisheries about 1900, the number of vessels quickly rose to over 100. Spring fishing was off the Faroes, and summer fishing off Iceland. The Greenland fisheries started after 1925. Shetland cod fishing is said to have started on the Faroe Banks about 1810 and ended in 1906 with the sloop, the *William Martin*, which had a Faroese skipper and crew. Several Faroese fished in Shetland ships and learned the details of the work of handline fishing, as done by Shetlanders, in intimate detail. The Shetland fishers frequently came into the Faroese fjords for mussel bait, the getting of which was a continual problem, and either gathered them themselves or bought them. In Sørvagur the Shetland name for them, *wulks*, is still remembered. At one point a Danish law prohibited the Faroese from selling bait to Shetlanders, which had the effect of stimulating mussel dredging on Shetland scalps, as at Bixter and Trondra. When the sloop *Fox*, of 38 tons, was purchased in 1872, an old Shetland skipper told an acquaintance from Tórshavn that the year 1873 would never be forgotten by Shetlanders, for they lost their good fortune when the Faroese got fishing vessels. Faroese fishing took a little time to build up, but it is scarcely surprising that the Shetland technique and knowledge helped them greatly.[1385]

Cod fishing was a considerable employer of manpower in Shetland. By 1860, over 1000 men were regularly sailing in smacks, about a third of the island's total of fishermen. For distant grounds, crews were of 12 to 15 men, who were generally younger than those forming the crews of 8 to 10 men in sloops fishing on the home banks. Cod also led to a relocation of the focus of fishing activity, for sloops could not be hauled up on beaches like haaf boats, fowererns and small boats, with Scalloway, Voe, Skeld and Reawick as notable growth points.[1386]

Line fishing began to decline towards the end of the nineteenth century, and distant waters became less and less fished by Shetlanders in this way, partly because the main effort was being concentrated on drift-netting for herring. The banks were also being swept clear of cod by steam trawling by the 1880s, and on the Faroese banks local competition was growing stronger. Crews were also becoming harder to find, since the young men were being attracted by the iron sailing ships and new steamers of the merchant navy from about the 1890s. Herring fishing also had much attraction for the men, for they did not have to be away for long periods. Larger boats from the Scottish Mainland were also taking up the long-line fishing from Shetland and many of the bank smacks found that longlining was of more profit than handlining. These and other factors combined were making it necessary by 1904 for smack crews to be completed in the Faroes, and by 1906 the last smack owned in Shetland sailed for the Faroes with an all-Faroese crew, and by 1908 had followed her sisters into Faroese hands. Old links died slowly, for as late as 1912 two Faroese smacks were captained by Shetlanders.[1387]

69

King Herring

IN spite of the wealth of herring in the seas around the Northern Isles, this fish was chiefly exploited by other nations, in particular the Hollanders whose activities reached a peak in the seventeenth century, when up to 20,000 Dutch seamen were coming each year. The main effect on the Northern Isles at this period was through the marketing outlet this provided for local produce, and also through the duties, including teinds, that the Dutch and all foreigners had to pay for herring and white fish caught around the coasts. For Stronsay, frequented in 1619 by 20 to 30 sail of the Dutch fleet, the teinds produced an average of £800 Scots per annum.[1388] Besides the Hollanders, there were also French, Belgian, English and Scottish fishermen. The ordinary folk benefited by selling their produce, and the lairds by collecting dues and letting buildings as shops to the men from Holland, Bremen, Hamburg and so on who came to get fish and sold liquors, wheaten-bread, linen and muslin. These booths were numerous, and fetched rents of about 20 'dollars' a year, when only 40 or 60 'dollars' was enough to build one.[1389]

Following the wars of the late seventeenth century, Dutch fishing declined significantly and was not revived in the same way. However, the intense concentration on cod, ling and tusk, using boats and equipment of a nature that matched the available manpower and harbour or beach facilities, meant that little direct interest was shown in herring for some time. Thomas Gifford of Busta, never a sluggard in economic matters, was thinking very positively about herring already in 1718. He wrote a Memorial in which he alluded to the great profits made by the Dutch, and pointed out that the Dutch did not start fishing, according to their law, before 14 June Old Style. Gifford thought that herring caught before then would, therefore, fetch a good price in Hamburg, and 'seeing our people in Scotland are not aquanted with fishing after the maner of the Dutch, by shooting and hailing ther nets out of the ship without the help of any boat, nether having nor useing ships for that purpose, I propose for ane experiment that a good cliver sailing ship, of about 30 last burden (about 60 tons), might be sent over here, in the month of Aprill, with the nesesary provision under writen, and I should find here 2 or 3 good, light fishing boats that could goe into the deep sea wher the Dutchmen comenly fisheth, man'd with people of this contrie who understand that business, they having the ship along with them for ther protection in case of blowing weather, and what herrings they could pack then aboard the ship and once a week rune in to ane harbor and have them repackt ready for exportation and the debentors secured'. For this he wanted 30 lasts of herring casks, 10 of them filled with Spanish salt, 20 herring nets about 12 to 14 fm (22–26 m) long by 6 fm (11 m) deep, 90 small kegs for buoys, 150 lb of buoy-ropes, 12 herring gutting knives, 12 herring creels, a cooper and his kit for dressing barrels, and 20 bolls of meal for food to the fishermen. Evidently, everything would have to be done from scratch. There is, however, no evidence that this economically shrewd plan was ever put into effect.[1390] The Dutch method of salting and barrelling herring was being done locally by 1750, however, but the bulk of the activity remained in Dutch hands. Some herring were being caught in the Bay of Scalpa in 1726. In the 1780s there were still 600 to 700 Dutch herring busses on the east coast of Shetland, each bus being of 50 to 70 tons, and having a fleet of 50 nets, 50 fathoms long by $7\frac{1}{2}$ fathoms (91 × 14 m) deep, with a crew of fourteen. The fish were barrelled straight away, so that knowledge of coopering was essential, and along with the busses were 'jaggers' for carrying herring caught between 24 June and 15 July to Holland, Hamburg and Bremen.[1391] Dutch fishing with busses around Shetland had virtually ceased by the 1830s.

In the 1790s, some local herring fishing was being done. In Delting, herring caught in the voes in August to December were sold to the lairds at 5 to 6/– a barrel of 800 to 1000 herrings, and this pattern of domestic herring fishing outside the haaf fishing season was probably general. In 1801 it was still only on a small scale. By the 1830s, partly under the influence of cod fishing, herring fishing was on the increase in Orkney. A total of 724 herring boats was catching about 42,073 barrels a year, sold to curers at 10/– per cran or barrel. In 1823, 34,000 barrels of herring fetched £17,000, more than twice the £7280 got for 560 tons of cod at £13 a ton. The numbers of herring boats greatly exceeded the 18 sloops that were catching cod, however. At the same time there was some decline in Shetland from the 1834 peak when 50,000 barrels were taken. The pattern of herring fishing was actually complementary to cod fishing, for it began in August after the cod had ended.[1392] This helped to stretch the fishing season, and speeded on the process of specialisation.

In 1838, South Ronaldsay had 245 herring boats. Most of the small crofts had had their rents doubled, in the hope that they would be paid from fishing profits. The people spent much time on herring fishing, and less than formerly in laying in stores for their families' provender, a situation exacerbated by the fact that bad weather could prevent fishing during winter. It was said that hundreds had married in the hope of getting £3.12/– of wages from herring fishing. The crew of every boat got a bottle of whisky. In St Andrews, herring was the only large-scale commercial enterprise. Curing started only in 1833, and the station was only getting into its stride. Fishermen in the parish, however, had been delivering their fish to be cured at other stations for several years before. In Stronsay, Mr David Drever, farmer at Huip, began herring fishing in 1814, and soon after, Mr Laing of Papdale, working with a London company, 'afforded such encouragement, that the harbour of Papa Sound,

279. Herring drifters at Stronsay, between the wars. Per Bryce Wilson.

admirably fitted for this purpose, and in the vicinity of the finest fishing-ground, soon became the great resort of boats from the North Isles, and indeed from all Orkney'. A commodious village for fishermen, and a pier for curing and loading fish, were built. Herring fishing started in late July and lasted for 6 or 8 weeks, being carried on by about 400 boats manned mostly by four and sometimes by five men. Papa Sound was a lively place, for anchored in it were 25 to 30 sloops and brigs, the majority from south-west Scotland, attending on the fishing. Besides coopers, several hundred women were employed to clean and salt the fish. 'Numbers of persons also resort to the station to traffic with the curers and fishers, while visitors come to witness the busy scene, so that the fishing-season is a memorable part of the year in the parish of Stronsay'. Since 1837, some individuals had tried to establish a herring fishing station at Stromness, without outstanding success, but they were persisting. In Orphir there were 9 herring boats by 1841, each crewed by 4 men. They worked around Stronsay in late July, and moved two weeks later to South Ronaldsay where they stayed for about a month, or until the herring shoals left. Vessels from Rothesay and Ireland came to receive the barrelled herrings, the price being 9 to 12/– per cran or barrel. An average season's catch was 55 crans, giving a return of £33. When the first excitement for catching herring was in the air in the early 1820s, a completely rigged herring boat with a set of nets cost £90, roughly three times the seasonal return (not counting wages, repairs, etc.). By the 1840s, the price had fallen to £70. However, 'this fishing has been found to be a precarious concern, and less lucrative than was expected'. The 50 herring boats in Shapinsay averaged 60 crans a season, at 10/– per cran. The herring caught by men from Walls and Flotta were not cured on the island, but at whatever station was most likely to provide a sure purchase,[1393] a form of flexibility that was a new phenomenon. The characteristics of the Orkney herring fishing, therefore, are those of individual, relatively small-scale enterprise, allied to flexibility in outlets at curing stations, though these were showing signs of becoming increasingly concentrated. A concentration of labour during the season, much of it female, was also needed.

In Shetland, the Sheriff-Substitute, Mr Duncan, is said to have established the herring fishing in the early 1820s. In the early stages, the lateness of the season, from mid-August to mid-October, made fishing dangerous for small boats in stormy seas. Though the Government early gave bounties for fishing and curing herring, restrictions were at the same time applied on the outfit of the herring fishing vessels. The problems were such that till well through the first half of the nineteenth century, no attempt was made to set a herring-net in the dead water in the voes. In Aithsting and Sandsting, James Garrick of Reawick was amongst the first to start, using second-hand boats from Wick in Caithness, each carrying about 20 nets. He did well, catching about 700 barrels in 1840. If the boat and nets belonged to the fishermen he got 6/6 a cran; if they were provided, the owner kept half the catch and paid the men 2/6 a cran for their half. The tenants of Mr Bruce of Sumburgh began a herring-fishing enterprise under his patronage, partly in Dunrossness but more in the parishes of Sandwick and Cunningsburgh where a number of large boats had been fitted out at great expense. Mr Bruce's presence at Sand Lodge, near the stations, gave great encouragement. Each year three or four brigs or sloops came to Levenwick Bay from Rothesay to take the herrings as they were caught at a stipulated price per cran. Mr Bruce of Bigton had started on a similar enterprise with his tenants. In Northmavine, though herring fishing had been tried, there had been little success, perhaps because the boats were not of the proper size and construction, and the nets not of the right dimensions and depths. In Tingwall, Whiteness and Weisdale, herring fishing had been carried on actively for some years, the men getting 7/– a cran. One boat took 297 crans in one season, and in 1835, over 15,000 barrels were shipped from Scalloway alone. The fishing had not been so good during 1838–41. In Delting, 528 barrels of herring were cured in 1840. Fetlar was considered to be one of the most commodious stations for herring fishing in Shetland, with fish coming into the bays from late June or early July, until mid-October. The bays were often fished by boats from other parishes, which might land their fish there because of bad weather, selling them to any curer who would take them, at the price he offered. There were curing stations at Urie, Strand and Aithbank. In North Yell, there were two, at Cullivoe and Beyan. The herring boats had 18 to 21 ft (5.5–6 m) keels, with crews of four or five. Twenty-one were fishing in 1834, and 25 in 1835 in Fetlar, and in North Yell 32 and 38. Nets varied in size from 32 yds (29 m) long by twelve-score meshes deep to 50 yds (46 m) long by fifteen-score meshes deep. Between 1834–41, however, herring fishing had fallen off, 'many of the small adventurers have been ruined, while those of great capital have suffered much'. In Walls the recently introduced herring fishing started after the ling fishing season ended in August. The same was true in Bressay, the fishing being carried on by men who also took part in the cod and ling fishing. Ling fishing boats were used as well as larger ones specially prepared for the purpose. In 1840, Bressay boats got 1528 crans, and Quarff boats 390 crans. About 30 women and children were employed in Bressay in the season. Burra men had not yet started herring fishing. In Unst, herring was beginning to be seen as a potential source of great additional wealth. The lairds furnished nets, hired them to the fishermen, or gave them as an advance on the price of fish caught. Casks and salt were provided, and the lairds undertook the expense of curing and marketing the herrings. Since there was much competition, the fishermen were sure of getting the highest price that could be afforded. The 840 barrels of fish cured in 1831 were worth £504. In Nesting, Mr Bruce had 14 to 16 herring boats and Mr Hunter about 7. Mr Bruce averaged 20,000 barrels a year. In Lerwick, herring fishing was done in the same manner as on the coast of Scotland, in larger boats than had been in previous use. The catch for all of Shetland in 1834 was 50,000 barrels, though a decline followed. In 1839, 174 boats, mostly from the parish, landed fish in or near Lerwick, but the catch was only 4872 barrels, leading to severe losses in both fishermen and curers. So much capital had been invested, however, that it could not easily be withdrawn, and efforts to expand were still being made. Messrs. Hay and Ogilvy, for example, were in the process of establishing a herring net factory.[1394]

For this period, therefore, the situation was very much as in Orkney, though the closeness of the link between laird and tenant in Shetland remained a marked feature.

The fact that herring fishing was slow to develop was not the fault of the Government. In 1750 the Society of the Free British Fishing, established the year before, sent two busses to Shetland, seeking to rival the Dutch, and by 1753 there were 38 British busses in Shetland waters. The main effort of the Society, however, was concentrated on the west coast. This was not an indigenous development in Shetland, for there was little or no direct local participation. Meantime, vessels from the Continent continued to fish around Shetland. In 1784 there were 166 vessels from 7 Dutch ports, 44 Prussian, 29 from Denmark, 7 from France, and 13 from Flanders.[1395] The area remained as much an international cross-roads as ever.

A bounty of £3 per ton offered in 1808 had little result, chiefly because it applied to vessels of 60 to 100 tons and Shetlanders were not geared to this scale of operation. In 1809 only one Shetland vessel claimed the bounty. The point was clear. If a herring fishery was to be properly developed locally, Shetland had to act as a shore-base for stores and for processing, and the ships should be of a size to fit the local circumstances.[1396] Meantime, however, an atmosphere of interest was being created, and when the nature of the bounty changed in the 1820s, being offered as a 2/- bonus on each barrel of herring cured and 2/8 on each barrel exported, lairds and merchants, singly or in partnerships, were quick to start investing in somewhat bigger half-decked and later decked vessels, at first bought second-hand from Scotland and later built by Hay and Ogilvie in Lerwick. Profits built up from the haaf and the cod fishing were no doubt applied in this year, making a sequential chain of development, and the scale of equipment and operations was right for local conditions. The returns were considerable in the 1830s. A catch of 10,000 crans in 1830, at $3\frac{1}{2}$ cwt to the cran, rose to 36,000 in 1833, but the initial upsurge was checked by a disastrous storm in 1840, and the collapse of the

280. Kippering in Shetland. From left to right: Joy Slater, Agnes Halcrow, Bertha Umphray, Celie Sinclair, Teenie Christie, Nellie Watt. From the Scalloway and District SWRI *Village History*, 1966.

281. Loaded with barrels of herring, Stronsay. 28.8.14.

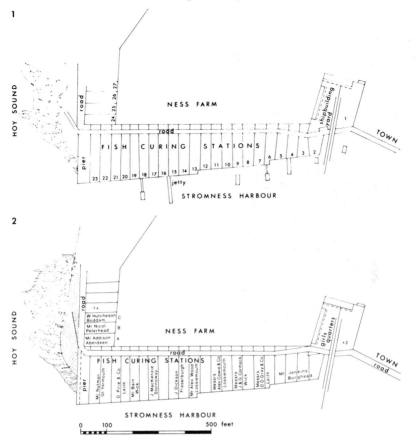

282. Lay-out of the fish-curing stations at Stromness Harbour, with the names of the curers. Per Bryce Wilson. C5011.

fishermen's bank in Lerwick in 1842. This removed the possibility of getting credit for equipment from many crews, and the boats could not be maintained. It took 30 years for the industry to pick up again after the initial but temporary boom, when Hay and Ogilvie, the largest fishing company in Lerwick, owned or financed 100 boats, each of them costing £60, and each fleet of nets being worth £120.[1397]

In 1851, there were only 12 herring stations in Shetland, operating on catches still made from small boats, mainly sixerns, since the bigger ones were too costly. Four years later the number had risen to 18, but the industry remained secondary to the ling and cod fisheries, and was widely dispersed through the islands. A dramatic change came in the 1870s. In 1874, 1100 barrels of herring were cured ashore in Shetland, and 50 boats were fishing. In 1881, the totals were 59,586 barrels and 276 vessels, and by 1884, 300,117 barrels and 932 vessels.[1398] The general excitement can be seen from the reaction in the islands. At first efforts were made to continue along the old lines,

283. Herring gutters from Nairn etc. by their quarters in Lerwick, *c.* 1910. Per Miss M. Bochel. C5746.

284. The inside of the herring gutters' quarters, with wooden bunks, a brick fireplace, and wallpaper on the wall.

with numbers of dispersed land bases. In Fetlar, herring stations were established by 1858. A Memorandum of Agreement between Sir Arthur Nicolson and Messieurs Hay & Co., Merchants, Lerwick, included the following points:

1.   A three-year lease of the herring station, booth and piers of Urie for £5, and the herring station at Aith for 2^d per cran for all herrings cured there, or 6^d per cran if a pier was erected. On such erection that plus the farm of Aith Bank would cost £6 per annum.

2.   Hay was to buy the herring caught by Sir Arthur's fishermen tenants, at not less than 8/– a cran, plus small bounties and an allowance for spirit during fishing. Hay was to supply fishing materials where necessary.

3.   Sir Arthur was to take no responsibility for his fishermen, but was merely to indicate his approval of the transaction, and withdraw his restriction on their fishing for other people without his consent.

4.   The price of the herrings should, after deducting the advances or part advances to the fishermen, at the option of Sir Arthur, be paid to him on account of the fishermen, or any of them or to themselves, at his option.[1399]

Here can be seen the change in primary responsibility from laird to merchant, though the old form of work organisation endured.

In Papa Stour conditions were becoming difficult by 1881. For lack of fuel, tenants were leaving, especially from the now totally deserted area of North House, and they could not be replaced by Mainland families. Because the men were busy fishing every day possible from mid-March till the end of September, they found it difficult to get peat supplies from Papa Little, this being possible only in fine settled weather. The scarcity of people meant that a Papa man with a boat had to make up the crew from Sandness, 'because the Papa men were unfit for the work and exposure in one of these Boats – they work Long Lines for Ling and Cod from middle of March till June – and Herring fishing from June till end of September – the rest of the Papa Men still go in Small Boats according to their ability'. It was thought they would do better using bigger boats, though a boat with nets and lines cost about £400. 'We would help them as far as was prudent to establish a summer herring curing on the Island ... If something is not done by which the young men can earn money on the Island like their neighbours on the Mainland the Island will soon be depopulated and it will not do for a Grazing Island. Indeed even on the Mainland since these large Boats were introduced there is a tendency to congregate together into fishing villages as in the south.'[1400]

The future was beginning to shape itself, even in such a small island as Papa Stour, where the mixture of benevolent self-interest as expressed in the factor's letters led to fairly quick action. There was also a spirit of excitement to spur things on – 'a great stir now with the Shetland men bringing big boats from Scotland and Orkney for the ling and herring fishing. The Scotch curers trying to catch and engage any station they can get hold of'.[1401] The sea was peppered thickly with boats fishing. As a North Ronaldsay man put it, 'I mind the beginning o' the Shetland fishing wi' the Scots boats. A whole line o' scores o' boats could be seen fae here – a line fae Kinnaird Head tae Fair Isle ootside o' Nort' Ronaldsay.'[1402] Only four years later, in 1885, a herring curing station was constructed in Papa Stour. Its detailed cost is as follows:

1 July 1885. Materials etc. for Pier

	£	s	d	£	s	d
To freight iron frame pier from Glasgow per rail				1	16	10
Telegrams about frame etc.					5	6
Freight and shipping charges on Iron and Wood per 'Sea Mew' Leith to Shetland				8	3	0
Paid P. & W. McLellan for Iron frame work				120	0	0
Wood for Pier supplied by J. M. Adie & Sons, viz:						
140 stringer wood	7	0	0			
115 ft (35 m) do. @ 7d	3	7	1			
40 ft (12 m) Planks @ 6d	1	0	0			
2064 Battens @ 3d	25	16	0	37	3	1
Hire of 'Sea Mew' and Crew erecting iron frame work 4 days at 25/–	5	0	0			
Ditto for 'Lady Nightingale' 23 days at 20/–	23	0	0			
Paid crew of Boat 'Welcome Home' for use of Boat	1	0	0			
Paid Labourers for Work erecting Pier	7	10	9	36	10	9
46 lbs Rope for securing frame @ 6d				1	3	0
Use of Warps, Chains, Blocks & Tools				5	4	0
John Brown's account Work and Materials for Pier				52	10	2

Stores

	£	s	d	£	s	d
To 420 feet (128 m) Stringers @ 7d	12	5	0			
2340 feet (713 m) Battens @ 3d	29	5	0			
1910 feet (582 m) Coupling	24	5	0			
220 yards (201 m) Lining	13	15	0			
280 yards (256 m) Felt	11	13	4			
900 Bricks @ 7/6	3	7	6			
160 yards (146 m) Stringers @ 7½d	5	0	0			
600 yards (548 m) Runners @ 1½d	3	15	0			
600 yards (548 m) Flooring @ 1/8	50	16	8			
275 feet (84 m) Sacking @ 1/1	14	17	11			
1800 feet (549 m) Lining @ 1/1	9	15	0			
Tar for Roof	1	1	0	179	16	5
Mitchell Georgeson's Account work at Pier and Stores				62	16	6
Mr. Birnie's Account levelling and metalling station				50	0	0
				£555	9	3

According to the Account of P. & W. MacLellan, Iron and Steel Merchants, 129 Trongate, Glasgow, to Messrs. J. M. Adie & Sons, Voe, dated 29 May 1885, the pier specifications were:

'An Iron Pier 20 ft (6.1 m) long by 8 ft (2.4 m) wide formed of rolled H beam piles 8 in. by 6 in. (20×15 cm) by 34 lb per foot, cross beams 5 in. by $4\frac{1}{2}$ in. (13×11 cm) by 22 lb per foot, and T iron horizontal and diagonal ties 5 in. by 5 in. by $\frac{5}{8}$ in. (13×13×2 cm). All as per tracing and estimate delivered in Glasgow ... £120 net.' This material was forwarded to Leith for shipment to Shetland. A further account for metal posts, stays, bolts, etc., for £52.10.2, came from John Brown, Smith, Freefield Iron Works, Lerwick. The joiner work, including window nails, hinges, building found, brick 'stalks', etc. in the erection of the stores and pier, cost £62.16.6.[1403]

Curing stations like this sprang up all over the islands. However, though Shetlanders played a great part in herring fishing and found a hitherto undreamt of means of accumulating capital and reinvesting, whether they were lairds or merchants or fishermen, nevertheless it was not for them a self-contained activity, but a part of the 'great seasonal migration of activity' around the British coasts. It was a time when fisher lassies from the Scottish fishing towns might move as gutters to Lerwick and to Yarmouth as the boats followed the shoals. Generally speaking the form of development in Shetland was due to the initiative of outsiders, particularly from the North-East of Scotland, who introduced the larger scale of herring fishing they had been practising at home, as a logical follow-up to their earlier success with longlining. Bigger-scale catching also needed a highly organised shore handling and marketing system, and in this immigrant Scots played a great part. It paid them to do so, for in the record year of 1905, half the entire Scottish catch was landed at Shetland. From 1783 vessels crewed by 12,500 men, 645,000 crans worth £576,000 were landed, and 1,024,044 barrels were cured. The Shetland contribution was 300 boats manned by 2000 fishermen.[1404]

In the twentieth century, the form of the marketing organisation and the auction system of sales, replacing contracts between vessels and curers after 1894, led to a concentration and expansion of activities at Lerwick, Baltasound, Scalloway and Sandwick. The advent of steam drifters after 1900 also speeded on the centralisation of bases, for they required bunkers and water. Three steam drifters were bought by Shetlanders in 1906. The first motor boat for herring fishing was bought in 1908, and the full conversion to motor boats followed the end of the First World War.[1405]

Herring fishing was to Shetland what agricultural improvements with draining, liming and enclosing were to Orkney, though it had a greater intensity for the time being. In a very short time after the 1870s, 98 per cent of Shetland's exports consisted of herring produce, and the economy had become much more monolithic than in Orkney. The traditional work outlets, in cod and ling fishing, whaling and the merchant navy, were replaced by work at herring. Whereas the older forms of fishing left some periods free for work on the land, now increasing specialisation and the possibility of all the year employment meant

285. Boat-building in Orkney has a long tradition. In Stromness. Photo. W. Hourston. C78D.

that the land had less attention than before. Though women could get work at the curing stations, many had to stay at home and look after the crofts. Herring, therefore, exacerbated a situation that began to develop with the organisation of haaf fishing in the latter half of the eighteenth century.[1406]

Orkney also participated, however. There, herring fishing was based primarily on Stronsay, with Stromness taking second place. There were also smaller stations elsewhere, for example at Holm and Burray, where the net-warehouses still stand at the pier heads. Steam drifters built up the industry into a profitable but very seasonal activity in late July and early August, but most of the herring boats were not local. 'Orcadians either had not the capital necessary to go over from their half-decked sail-boats to steam drifters or preferred to put their money in farming. Indeed by the time the wild white clover culture prevailed, anyone who chose to devote himself to the sea was regarded as feckless or downright peculiar.' In 1936, the still unspecialised nature of Orkney fishing is indicated by the statistics, for 80 per cent of the fishermen were part-timers, most of whom also had small farms. After the war, however, there has been a greater concentration on fishing, especially for the highly profitable shellfish, but this development is in parallel with agricultural activities. Both industries are standing on their own feet.[1407]

Another aspect of the period was the extent of immigration. The great majority of immigrants who became permanent came from Banff. 'Having no ties of soil, almost all the fishing families which came to the islands took up residence in Lerwick, the only exception being one family in Scalloway. These people remained a relatively closed community following the pattern of their previous home fishing villages. They retained very strongly the Scottish form of speech so dissimilar to Shetland. Their descendants are still recognisable today by their speech and such surnames as Duthie, West, Wiseman, Watt and Sales, and they are still collectively regarded as Scots rather than Shetlanders by the islanders. Today the immigrant families make up almost the total number of Lerwick fishermen.' Seasonal migrants came in great numbers, though they made a less permanent impact. These were workers and fishermen engaged from May till the end of the season. In 1882, there were said to have been over 2000 incomers in Unst alone.[1408]

From this point on, the story of Shetland fishing is very much part of the story of fishing in Scotland and farther afield. It has been discussed by several writers.[1409] Apart from such sources, the direction from which the industry came to the Northern Isles is demonstrated by the concomitant terminology.

The fleet of herring-nets, which hung like a curtain in the sea, was slung from a head-rope or *back-rope* (cf. Norse *bakka*, a fishing line with many hooks; but perhaps simply English *back*) by short cords called *daffins* (origin uncertain: used in Moray, Caithness and Orkney) or *osels* (from wrong division of *a nossel*, Middle English *nostylle*, Old English *nos(t)le*, a band), a word used on the east coast from Shetland to Berwick. They were about 18 in. (46 cm) long. The side-ropes of the net were *gavels* or *gavel-ropes* (Old Scots *gavil(l)*, gable-end, 1387; Old Norse *gafl*) in Fife, North-East Scotland and Orkney, and the angle between these and the back-rope was the *klave* (Norwegian *klave*, wooden neck-yoke for animals, an angle-shaped figure, Old Norse *klafi*, forked stick, branks put on the neck of an animal), a term confined to Orkney and Caithness and clearly Norse in origin. The mesh was the *mask* (Old Scots *c.* 1575), a Scots word, though ultimately from Norse, used in Shetland before 1838; and in Orkney, a gauge-stick or measure of size for meshes in net-making was a *skunyal* (from Norwegian dialectal *skyndel*, weaver's shuttle, mesh-gauge). The Shetland sea-name for a net buoy, recorded before 1838, was *roiler*,[1410] apparently from Scots *roller*, something that rolls about. The terminology of the herring-net demonstrates unambiguously its Scottish origins, with a particular emphasis on North-East Scotland, though one or two terms show that the making of nets, not necessarily for herring, goes some way back in time in the Northern Isles. It is also true of ancillary industries such as coopering, that the terms used are almost entirely Scots. The coopering trade spread so instantaneously in the nineteenth century that the terminology of the various specialist tools and techniques is extremely uniform throughout the Scottish fishing towns.

70

The Sea Language of Fishermen
and the End of Norn

THOUGH the influence of Scottish speech and culture was being felt in the Northern Isles from the thirteenth century, when Scottish earls succeeded the Norse, the main impact came when the Scottish Crown took them over in the late fifteenth century.[1411] Scots was the language of administration as well as of the Church. According to Sir Thomas Craig in 1605, though nothing but Norn was spoken in the Northern Isles, the ministers were using English in the churches and were well enough understood. Scots became established quickly, and the first Scots document in Shetland, written by a Scots civil servant, dates from 1525.[1412] In Orkney, the earliest Scots charter dates from 1433, 35 years before the pledging of the isles to Scotland.[1413]

Norn (Old Scots, 1485; Old Norse *norrœna*, the Norwegian language), also called 'Norse', is the local development of Norwegian in the Northern Isles, acknowledged about 1680 to differ from Danish.[1414] No particular impression is given from seventeenth century sources, however, that there was a question of one language being deliberately superimposed upon and ousting another. It was a case of infiltration rather than substitution. The natives spoke Norse amongst themselves, and because of trading links could readily speak Low Dutch. Several of the udallers, many of them men of substance, spoke Scots, and some of the incomers learned to speak Norn.[1415] By the 1680s, it was noted that the people in South Dunrossness came mostly from Scotland and Orkney, and that their 'Language, Habit, Manners and Dispositions are almost the same with the Scotish'. In the less fertile north of the parish Norn was spoken by the natives amongst themselves, 'yet all of them speak the Scotish Tongue both more promptly & more properly, than generally they do in Scotland'. Overall, Norn was wearing out in comparison with the earlier period,[1416] though in Orkney there were areas like Harray where some people spoke nothing but Norn. One writer thought the Orcadians did not speak English with as much of an accent as in many parts of the North of Scotland. Norn was much better preserved in Shetland than in Orkney, and was so common still in the more northerly islands that it was the first language learned by the children. Many people, even servants, could speak good Dutch, and some could converse in English, Dutch and Norse. 'The Norse hath continued ever since the *Nor-*

vegians had these Isles in Possession, and in *Orkney* ... it is not quite extinct, tho there be by far more of it in *Zetland*, which many do commonly use.'[1417] The pattern is one of survival in the remoter areas, and of easy intermixture elsewhere, especially where incomers settled in any quantity.

In the eighteenth century, this pattern continued, with a steady weakening of Norn. English had become general in Shetland, though many still spoke Norn among themselves.[1418] In the 1790s, the people of Sandsting and Aithsting all understood English, 'though they could speak among themselves so as an Englishman could not understand them'. In Delting, 'the language is the same as in the Continent of Scotland. The inhabitants, however, have less of a provincial brogue than many parts of North Britain'. In Tingwall, Bressay, and Nesting, Norn had disappeared, though there were probably a few of the older people who could speak it.[1419] In Orkney, the disappearance came earlier. A witness from Stenness in the Pundlar Process case in the Court of Session in 1757 claimed that he 'remembers the *Norn* or *Norse* Language to have been vulgarly spoke by a good many People in the Main-land of Orkney; and that he knows some People, particularly three or four in the Parishes of *Harray* and *Firth*, who speak that Language pretty fluently, as far as he can judge, at this Day'. Norn was not uncommon amongst the older country folk.[1420] By the 1770s, there was hardly a single man in Orkney who could speak Norn. Even the songs had been lost, except for a few trifling ones, though in the 1720s Norn had been the main language in two of the Mainland parishes. By 1790, Norn had worn out in Harray.[1421]

The eighteenth century, therefore, saw the end of Norn as a consistent language, though several fragments have survived as fragments of conversations, rhymes, proverbs, riddles, snatches of songs, a burial formula, and the Lord's Prayer. These have been assembled by Jakobsen and by Marwick in their Norn dictionaries.[1422] As recently as 1958, a Norn verse was heard from George (Dodie) Isbister in Foula, which, written roughly phonetically, went:

> Ante pedu, sat a growla
> Sat a growla festa,
> Pirla moga, hench a boga,
> Settar alla nesta

This is evidently a fragment of the Eagle Song, of which Jakobsen also got fragments.[1423]

Related to the Norn language was the use of patronymics. In the Norse period, as in present-day Iceland, there were no true surnames, and patronymics were used of the type 'Garto Paulis douchter', 'Nichole Magnassoun', 'Nichole Johnsoun, son of Johannes of Caldbak'.[1424] In 1633, the natives were distinguished from the incomers by their lack of surnames, and in 1683 it was 'observable that the Names of the Descendants of the old Inhabitants, differ from the Names of others now numerous among them, for these only have a Name without a Sirname, save what is taken from their Father's Name, and by adding Son or Daughter thereunto ... If there be two Men or Women of the same Name, they use also to design them by the places where they ordinarily reside'.[1425] Patronymics lasted longer in Shetland than in Orkney. The first Orkney surnames to become permanent in the fourteenth and fifteenth centuries related closely to the designation of territorial, generally udal, land, and some of them were township names. Paplay, Ireland, Kirkness, Clouston, Flett, Linklater, Heddle and Rendall are examples, many of them belonging to the inland areas of Harray, Stenness and Firth. Land surnames are relatively few elsewhere in Orkney. South Ronaldsay, the greatest udal area next to the Mainland of Orkney, had most: Halcro, Berso or later Berstane, Windwick, Flaws, Norquoy and the obsolete Cara. It is to be assumed that such names indicate Norse descent, for an incoming Scot was more likely to have and to stick to his own surname. In the early stages of the mixture, some ambivalence is evident, for example in 1551 when a patronymic was used along with an estate name on the Scots model, such as James Williamson alias Holland son of William Swanson alias Holland. Occasionally, too, there was a reversion, when several branch families had the same surname. The solution to the confusion was to re-introduce patronymics, which then themselves became fixed surnames.

Studies of surnames in rentals and valuation rolls, and in the seventeenth century testaments, show that characteristically native names, such as Linklater, Foubister, Swanney, Manson and Drever in Orkney, were in a minority. In the North and South Isles of Orkney they constituted only a third to a quarter of the total, and only in the udal strongholds of the West Mainland, especially Harray, did they form more than half. The large numbers of some surnames amongst the 3000 listed in the Orkney testaments suggest extensive progenies from a comparative few. There are, for example, 90 Sinclairs, 80 Spences, 52 Cromarties, 51 Irvings, 45 Browns, 43 Craigies, 43 Louttits, 41 Mowats and 39 Garriochs. Of the originally Norse names, the most prolific were 60 Fletts, 52 Linklaters, 35 Inksters, 35 Rendalls, 31 Cursetters, 28 Halcros, 26 Kirknesses and 24 Isbisters. Servants' surnames had no special Norse emphasis by the seventeenth century.[1426] The patronymic system, therefore, died out much earlier than Norn did as a spoken language.

Dying out, however, is a relative term, for a considerable vocabulary has survived. Jakob Jakobsen's *Etymological Dictionary of the Norn Language in Shetland* recorded something like 10,000 words in 1908. In 1929, Hugh Marwick's *Orkney Norn* listed about 3000, and in Caithness about 500 were noted in 1950.[1427] The most remarkable area of survival is in the sea-language of fishermen. Round the coasts of Britain, the salmon, pig, rabbit, hare and minister were the chief subjects named by fishermen at sea in oblique terms. In the Northern Isles, however, something like 450 such terms have been recorded. Just as the difference in the numbers of Norn words in the two island groups marks differences in the strength of survival of the old Norn traditions, so also do the fishermen's terms, for Shetland has about 430 as against fewer than 20 from Orkney.

The Orkney names fall into the following groups:

Geographical features: *bairn*, a little hill (figurative use of the word for a child), *hog* (Norwegian dialectal *haug*, *hog*, Old Norse *haugr*, mound, hillock), a larger hill.

Atmospheric conditions: *fairweather*, *guidsweather*, thunder.

Religion: *burly* (Norwegian *byrleg*, Old Norse *byrligr*, promising, of wind) *hoose*, *munger-hoose* (Old Norse *munka-hús*, a monastery), a church.

Human beings: *pirrens* (Norwegian dialectal *piren*, sickly, weakly, thin), children.

Sea creatures: *hide*, a seal, *himsel*, *kleppy*, the halibut or turbot.

Fishing tools and equipment: *biter*, *ragger* (from English *rag*, to tear), a knife, *damp*, the end of a long-line, *horse-leg-been* and *keel-root*, the right- and left-hand oars in a boat, *klaran* (origin uncertain. Cf. Icelandic *klara*, rake for spreading dung, or Norwegian *kløronе*, the claws).

Fishing: *kan* (Old Scots *can*, ability, 1609), a superstitious term implying magic or skill, used in trying for fish. To fish 'on so-and-so's kan' might bring a good catch.

The majority are Norse, except *fairweather*, *hide* (= skin), *ragger*, *himsel* (the personal pronoun), and *kan*, probably all of Scots origin. *Guidsweather*, though compared by Marwick to Danish *guds-vejr* is just as likely to be Scots. It does not occur in Shetland. The frequent difficulty of deciding whether a particular word is Norse or Scots is a mark of the intimate blend of the two cultures in Orkney.

Of peculiar interest are the words *horse-leg-been* and *keel-root*. These terms may be Scots translations of the Norwegian place names Folafoten, in Hisöy, and Kjølrota, an off-lying skerry in the Sognefjord area, rationalising the transference of place names to the names of oars or rowing positions by suggesting their derivation from navigational directions by Vikings sailing these waters.[1428] If accepted, the coincidence is remarkable, and establishes a direct link between the two areas. However, Marwick has also heard the terms *owse-room* and *backber* for men rowing on the starboard and port sides, using the names for the parts of the boat in which they sat. It is possible that *horse-leg-been* and *keel-root* are corruptions of names of parts of the boat, or jocular terms of purely local significance, and not place names whose sense-transference in the manner suggested is unparalleled.

The Shetland material is too bulky for detailed treatment, but the following provides broad groupings with selected examples.

Geographical features: Included here are place names applied at sea to prominent landmarks, used as guides in reaching fishing grounds. The name may be altered only a little by a plural or diminutive ending, or by using a simple instead of a compound form. Sometimes the sea names belong to an earlier culture, or are in some way descriptive. Examples from North Yell include *Gord* or *Midgord* for Midbrake, *Leegord* for Houlland, *Reegord* for Brakon, *Laygord* for Toft, *Husebigd* for Torfhouse, *Seatersby* for Westafirth, and *Glippaby* for Gloup. These appear to reflect the earlier settlement pattern of a tightly knit Norse community, whilst the land names suggest changes due largely to scotticisation of language and forms of land holding and land use. Thus, there still remains at Westafirth the farm of Setter, from which *Seatersby* came, and above the Voe of Gloup lies Glippapund, no doubt the original pund (sheep enclosure) of the Gloup people, so that *Glippaby* was properly Gloup. The *-gord* (Old Norse *garðr*) names too suggest an outward spread from an original nucleus, in relation to which later farms were named. The fundamental nature of the group is further emphasised by terms like *bigg*, *bigd*, a farm or village, *bø* a farm, homefield, *fell*, a mountain or height, *glab*, a cleft, small valley, etc., all roots from which place names have been formed in considerable numbers.[1429]

Living creatures (excluding fish):

(a) Birds: the cormorant, eagle, and puffin, and the homely farmyard cock and hen which rejoice in twelve names between them. This is a more limited range than in the Faroe Islands, where bird fowling was, and is, of high economic importance.[1430]

(b) Farmyard animals: the sheep, ram, horse, mare, pig, and cow. The names *hokken*, *-ni*, *-ner*, a horse and *pertek*, a mare, deserve special attention since the former may be related to Dutch *hakkeneie*, a small horse, and the latter to Low German *perd*. The Dutchmen who visited Shetland in quantity during the great days of the herring fishing before its local development in the eighteenth century were fond of hiring Shetland ponies to run races for sport. Their language was well known, and the borrowing of words was easy.

(c) Pets and pests: the dog, for one of whose names, *bjenek*, Jakobsen suggests a Lappish origin, the cat, with twenty-one names mainly indicating scraping, mewing, or wailing, the mouse with sixteen names, including the ironically jocular *bohonnin*, from Old Norse *búhundr*, a watch dog, and the rat (rarely).

(d) Sea creatures: the otter, and seal.

(e) Human beings: father, mother, brother, father-in-law, mother-in-law, brother-in-law, sister-in-law, implying that the social organisation underlying the fishing teams was based on the extended family; a girl, a man, men or people in general (*foleks*), children, and a woman or wife. The latter was a *fru*, *fron*, *halihwiffer*, *hema*, *hemelt*, *hosper*, *hospra*, *hostan(i) kuna*, *søski* and *yemelt*, all Norse with a possibility here and there of Dutch or Low German influence, except for the Scots *hemelt*, *yemelt*, borrowed early to judge by the alternation *h/y* (from palatalisation of the initial h – i.e. h > hj > j).

Household and outdoor terms: The fireside is particularly prominent, the fire itself having thirteen names and the tongs eight. From the *festa* or *festin* (crook) over the fire hung the *grødek*, *grøta*, or *honger* (kettle, pot). To *vair de honger* was to turn the pot over the fire or to move fish and potatoes from one side of it to another when boiling. These things were very familiar to the men, who carried them to their fishing lodges and in their boats as part of the essential equipment. There were also names for the water bucket, churn, butter, sewing needle, scissors, spinning wheel, and box-bed.

Outside, bere and oats, the mill, and peat for fuel were all forbidden names. The name for a potato, *knubbi*, cannot antedate about 1750, when the crop began to appear in these islands.

Religion: one of the most widespread of fishermen's dislikes when at sea is the minister, whose noa names are *beniman, hoidin, loder, predikanter, pre-stengolva, singnar*, and *upstander*, or, in its older form, *upstaar*. The church was the *bønhus, bunek, byorg, kloster*, or *munger-hoose*, and preaching was *mulsin*. The Scots *black coat*, or some variant, was known but not used.

The sky and the weather: There are names for wind, rain, thunder, the stars, the moon, *globeren, glom, glunta, monen*, and the sun, *feger, foger, fogin, glid(a), shiner, sulin*.

Fishing: (a) Boats. The emphasis is on the primary functional features; the boat itself, *basek, far(lek), shar*, the oars, the thole, the mast, the sail, *duk, klut, skega, skye*, the baling scoop, the compass, *diacle, kokkel, legvise(r), righter, vigvise*, and the fog-horn, *honnek*, made of a cow's horn.

(b) The fishing grounds, including the sea itself, *dyup, hallost, halltott, l(y)og*, usually with the implication of deep-sea fishing grounds, surf and the noise it makes, and the sea-floor.

(c) Fishing equipment: baskets, buoys, bait or *nebert*, gathered *shusa-millabakka*, between the sea and the shore, the fishing line whose end had to be called the *arm, arvi*, or *damp*, sinkers of pebbles or stone fish hooks, the wooden V-shaped reel on which the line was wound, the reel or *bunki* on the gunwale for hauling in the line, the gaff, *huggiestaff, hudek, hun, hwadi, klepp, pikki*, the forked implement of wood or bone for getting hooks out of the fish's throat, the *gap-* or *gum-stick*, and the knife and whetstone.

In this connection there are a great many idiomatic expressions relating to fish nibbling at the bait, exhorting them to bite, the appearance of fish on a line being hauled, clearing a line stuck on the bottom, giving evasive answers about the numbers of fish caught, and so on. These may be almost pure Norse, or translations of Norse idioms, and it is in relation to the central act of the fisherman's life, the act of fishing itself, that the old sea-language is syntactically most complete.

(d) The fish. The generic term is *fisk* or *fusk*, and the names refer primarily to fish caught on the hand line, not in nets. Herring fishing has left no mark on the sea-language. Most prominent are the cod, *drolti, golti, kabbi, knabi, knavi, shukkollo*, the ling, *hersel', hulefer, hwida, longa-fish, mamsa, skudra*, and the halibut, *baldi(n), drengi, gloffi, himsel* (compare the feminine pronoun for the ling), *leger, pigvar*, and *plousi*. In addition the coalfish, cusk, dogfish, eel, grommet, mackerel, ray fish, shark, and whale, *fyedin, krekin* have sea-names.

(e) Fishermen's lodging and dress. The men occupied special dwellings at the stations in the fishing season, a boat's crew to each. These were called lodges ashore, but *hoids* or *høsleks* at sea.

Clothes in general are *claedin*, and individual items with sea-names were stockings, breeches, mittens, *dags, handibodeks, muliaks*, a hat, an outer coat, *furtail*, a skin coat, *skinfell* or *fübester*, and a flannel shirt or similar covering, *wily coat*. Shoes are *ifareks*, and waterproof sea-boots, to which the Shetlanders seem to have been partial, were *derteks*, *lers*, *stenglins*, *stenkels*, *stivalirs*, or *stavalirs*.

A higher proportion of these words are of Dutch or Low German origin than in any of the other groups, no doubt because of trade contacts with the Dutch fishing fleet, which was an element of great importance in the economy of the Low Countries from at least the twelfth century. No doubt sea-boots figured in the trading booths that clustered round the Shetland coasts in the seventeenth and eighteenth centuries.

An analysis of such names can tell us a good deal about the culture contacts, material culture, social and work organisation, and even the forms of land holding in the Northern Isles. Statistically, the considerable difference between Orkney and Shetland is emphasised, for Orkney, essentially a farming area, and heavily influenced from Scotland from at least the fourteenth century, retains a mere 4 per cent of the whole number.

Only a few of the names are Scots, Dutch, or Low German. The majority are Norse, and relate to the pre-industrial practical realities and everyday functioning and surroundings of a fisherman's world, with particular implications of magic and mystery in the terms used at that imponderable moment when the fish may or may not bite. They give the impression that they are in great measure survivals of the Old Norn language, maintained by tightly knit work groups of native Shetlanders in defiance of the incoming Scots speech (from which the majority of the land names come), just as the fishing communities of the Isle of Man for long retained their Gaelic at sea. As such, they provide invaluable clues to the material culture, work and attitudes of earlier generations.

But this is by no means all the story. They are also in the direct line of tradition out of which came the intricate system of kennings or circumlocutions that characterised Skaldic verse, and the alternative names that the dwarf Alvis attributed to men, gods, dwarfs, giants, etc. Indeed some of the Alvissmál names resemble Shetland tabu names, e.g. *fagrahvél*, 'fair wheel', *foger*, sun, *djúpan mar*, *dyup*, *mar*, sea, *forbrennir*, *brenner*, fire. The sea language of the Northern Isles of Scotland leads directly back to the mythology and habits of thought of the primitive culture of the Northern world, which, though forming part of an aspect of superstition of worldwide prevalence, could on occasion become sophisticated enough to form the stuff of poetry.[1431]

71

Conclusion

IN its original conception, this book was to have closed with a discussion of the social system of the people of the Northern Isles, their beliefs and customs, seasonal celebrations, weddings and funerals, nicknames, education and religion, their views of the world, all the things that make up the business of living as opposed to or in parallel with working. It soon became evident that the presentation of an adequate cross-section of the basic information on working life and organisation was more than enough for one book. The rest must remain for some other time. Nevertheless, the book as it stands is not about work, but about people. It tries to interpret settlement patterns, not primarily through documents but through the way people learned to live on and make use of the land and the shores and the seas around them. It is an approach to history through people and the things they did, the tools and equipment they used, the

286. Seamen of Papa Westray. Per Miss E. Sinclair. C5461.

287. Skeklers or guizers, dressed in straw, with straw hats, in Fetlar. 1.47.0.

houses they lived in, the stock they reared, the crops they grew, the food they ate. It has thrown into relief the remarkable range of differences between the two island groups. The linguistic element has been included with the specific purpose of pin-pointing what is indigenous and what is intrusive, and can serve as a key in examining the mixture of cultures, each with their special ingredients, that typify Orkney and Shetland.

It is a kind of book with a mix that has not hitherto appeared in Britain, though not uncommon in some other countries of Europe, where it will be recognised as a contribution to the subject that is now commonly known as 'European ethnology'. For purposes of identification, a subject must have a name. What the name is, is of less importance than the production, within the range of the discipline, of material as factually accurate and historically truthful as human fallibility allows. The *Northern Isles: Orkney and Shetland* is written in this spirit, as an act of faith. Vikings and Scots may come and go, haaf fishing and herring, kelp and agricultural improvements, may change the social structure and economy, oil will have its effect on the landscape and the people, but the essence that makes the islands what they are is indestructible.

References

1. *The Shape of Things*
1. O'Dell 1939. 1.
2. Nicolson 1975. 89–101.
3. Heineberg 1969. 17.
4. Brøgger 1929. 30.
5. O'Dell 1939. 270.
6. *Diplomatarium* 1907–13. I. 83.
7. Goodlad 1971. 74.
8. Monteith (1633) 1845. 24, 40, 41, 51; Smith 1673. IV. 253, 256; Martin (1695) 1884. 357, 385–6.
9. Campbell 1774. 670–1, 697.
10. Hay 1966. 122, 379–381.
11. Beenhakker 1973; Goodlad 1971. 81–6.
12. Barclay 1967. 65.
13. Neill 1806. 71; Henshall and Maxwell 1951–2. LXXXVI. 40.
14. Elder 1912.
15. Monipennie (1597) 1603. 9.

Farm and Township: Pattern of Settlement

2. *The Early Settlement*
16. Jønsson 1945. 9.
17. Curle 1938–9. 71–110; Childe 1942–3. 5–17; Hamilton 1956; Radford 1959; Small 1964–6. 225–48; Cruden 1965. 26–8; Small 1966; Small 1968. 62–70; Wilson and Moorhouse 1971. 137; Webster and Cherry 1972. 169; Ritchie 1974. 34; Maclaren 1974. 9–18.
18. Brøgger 1929. 66.
19. Hamilton 1956. 111.
20. Small 1966. 9; Webster and Cherry 1972. 169.
21. Ingstad 1970.
22. Ritchie 1974. 30, 32.
23. Clouston 1920. 23.
24. Spence 1920. 91–2; Marwick 1922–3. I. 22.
25. Marwick 1922–3. I. 54–5; Marwick 1924–5. III. 33.
26. Evidence summarised in Evans 1975. 4–5.
27. Marwick 1922–3. I. 22–3, 54; Marwick 1952. 3–5.
28. SND s.v. *treb*.
29. Þorsteinsson 1965. 208.
30. Brøgger 1930. 262, 264; Bjørkvik 1963. 643.
31. Lid 1958. 579–81; Þorsteinsson 1965. 209.

32. Anderson 1922.
33. Small, Thomas and Wilson 1973; cf. Lucas 1967. 172–229.
34. Duncan 1975. 82.
35. Benediktsson 1969. 287–91; Þorsteinsson 1965. 210.
36. Benediktsson 1969. 290; Steffensen 1968. 390–1.
37. Oftedal 1954. 363–409; Pálsson 1955. 13–14; Matras 1968. 91–2; Benediktsson 1969. 291.

3. *Consolidation of Settlement*
38. Sawyer 1962. 69–79; Foote and Wilson 1970. 232–54; Christensen 1968. 30–41.
39. Taylor 1938. 179, 188, 241, 250, 272, 284.
40. Olsen and Crumlin-Pedersen 1967. 73–174.
41. Marwick 1947. 19; Clouston 1930–1. 38–40; Taylor 1938. 353.
42. Small 1967–8. xvii/2–3. 149, Figs. 1–4; Dahl 1970. 63–69.
43. Holtsmark 1969. 234; Jónsson 1926. 176–90; Bellows 1923. 201–16; Foote 1975. 15–16.
44. Foote and Wilson 1970. 76; Lárusson 1965. 525–6.
45. Fenton 1968–9. 121.
46. Wainwright 1962. 158.
47. Duncan 1975. 577–80.
48. Taylor 1938. 151–2, 169, 181.
49. Taylor 1938. 143–4, 149, 157, 260–1; Clouston 1932. 33, 90.
50. DOST s.v. *outhall*; Dobie 1936. 452–3.
51. Marwick 1929 s.v. *udal*; Dobie 1936. 462; Robberstad 1967. 495–6.
52. Williamson 1948. 50.
53. Clouston 1932. 349; Bjørk 1975. 32.
54. Curle 1938–9. 79; Childe 1942–3. 5; RCAHMS 1946. 7, Fig. 65; Hamilton 1956. 94–5, 103.
55. Small 1971. 79.
56. Edmondston 1866; Cleasby and Vigfusson 1874 s.v. *heim-röst, röst*; Hammershaimb 1891 s.v.
    heimrustir; Aasen 1918; Bjørk 1975. 12.
57. Cleasby and Vigfusson 1874. s.v. *tún*.
58. Clouston 1920. 26; Marwick 1929. 192, 131; Clouston 1932. 346–60; Marwick 1939. ii. 36–7.
59. Hibbert 1822. 427; Marwick 1933–4. xii. 17; Thomson 1970. 176–7, 182.
60. Clouston 1920. 19–20, 23.
61. Clouston 1920. 36–7.
62. Clouston 1920. 23–4.
63. Donaldson 1954. 38, 99.
64. *Oppressions* 1859. 58.
65. Olsen *et al*. 1961. 697–710.
66. *Oppressions* (1575, 1578) 1859. 4, 58; Peterkin 1820. 13; Clouston (1507, 1578) 1914.
    79–143.
67. Cleasby and Vigfusson 1874; Marwick 1952. 240; Ståhl 1957. 25–6.
68. Hald 1957. 64–7.
69. Olsen 1928. 55–7. Ståhl 1957. 68.
70. Nicolaisen 1969. 14; Nicolaisen 1976. 92–4.
71. Ståhl 1957. 68; Nicolaisen 1969. 9–11.
72. Clouston 1932. 33, 162; Marwick 1952. 234–6; Bjørkvik 1975. 632.
73. Oftedal 1957. 371.
74. Clouston 1926–7. 41–4; Marwick 1929 s.v. *bow*; Clouston 1932. 157, 167–75; Olsen *et al*.
    1961. 700, 702–3.
75. Peterkin 1820. 30.
76. DOST s.v.
77. Clouston 1932. 154.
78. Clouston 1932. 178, 181.
79. Clouston 1932. 13–14; Marwick 1952. 37, 41, 227–8.

80. Marwick 1952. 288; Stewart 1965. 255.
81. Peterkin 1820. ii. 2.
82. Clouston 1914. 85.
83. Mooney 1952. 8, 23.
84. Clouston 1914. 322.
85. *Reg. Privy Seal* (1576) vii. 117/1; Clouston (1592) 1914. 167; Clouston (1694) 1919. 30; Johnston (1692) 1940. 164.
86. Peterkin (1595, 1614) ii, 41, 131; (1627) iii. 35; Clouston 1914, 84, 373–4.
87. Peterkin 1822. Appx. 17.
88. Clouston 1914. 143.
89. Clouston 1932. 266; Bjørk 1975. 33.
90. Clouston 1932. 347–9.
91. Marwick 1952. 229–31; Stewart 1965. 251–2; Nicolaisen 1969. 11–13.
92. Brøgger 1929. 77.
93. Dahl 1970. 71; Dahl 1970. 361–6.
94. Marwick 1922–3. 23; Marwick 1924–5. 36–7.

4. *Scattald and Hagi*
95. Jakobsen 1901. 64, 101–2; Bjørk 1975. 12–13, 16.
96. SND s.v.
97. Jakobsen (1908) 1928; SND s.v.
98. O'Dell (*c.* 1772) 1939. 240.
99. NSA 1845. xv. 64; Jakobsen 1897. 109; Jakobsen (1908) s.v. *hagri*; Saxby 1908. 269–70.
100. Hibbert 1822. 458; Neven (1667) 1933. 140–1.
101. Hibbert 1822. 458; Angus 1914; O'Dell (*c.* 1772) 1939. 242.
102. Reinton 1956. 98, 421.
103. Barry 1805. 224; Johnston (1771) 1910. 218; Jakobsen (1908) 1928 s.v. *gart*.
104. Cleasby and Vigfusson 1874; Neven (1667) 1933. 147.
105. Ståhl *et al*. 1961. 43–5.
106. Reinton 1956. 98, 420; Ståhl *et al*. 1961. 44; Bjørk 1975. 12.
107. Jakobsen (1908) 1928 s.v. *hemhoga, hoga*.
108. Jakobsen (1908) 1928; Aasen 1918.
109. Edmonston 1809. i. 149; Jamieson 1825; Jakobsen (1908) 1928 s.v. *hogalif*; Johnston 1910. iii/iii. 162–3, iii/iv. 217, iv/i. 34–5; 1911. iv/iv. 193; 1912. v/iii. 125, 126–8.
110. DOST files, per A J Aitken.
111. Cant 1975. 9.
112. Gifford (*c.* 1727) 1879. 78; *Oppressions* 1859. 46; Goudie 1892. xxvi. 201; *Reg. Privy Seal* vii. 75/1.
113. O'Dell (*c.* 1772) 1939. 240, 242–3.
114. Balfour 1860. 119; SND s.v. *tulbert*.
115. O'Dell (*c.* 1772) 1939. 239–40, 264.
116. Johnston 1910. 103–6.
117. Neven (1607) 1933. 141–2.
118. Bjørk 1975. 11.

5. *The Township and its Functioning*
119. Low (1778) 1915. 135; Smith 1914. 146; Whittington 1973. 536.
120. OSA 1793. vii. 398; Goudie 1889. 45; Clouston (1519) 1914. 93.
121. Clouston 1920. 26–7, 32.
122. Clouston 1920. 29–30.
123. Clouston 1914. 82, 84; Clouston 1920. 18–19, 30.
124. Clouston 1920. 30–1; *Session Papers, State of Process, Sinclair v. Sinclair* 1773. 9.

125. Clouston 1920. 19–20.
126. Shirreff 1814 b. Appx. 32–3.
127. OSA 1793. vii. 393.
128. OSA 1793. v. 195; Unst; Marwick 1952. 200–02.
129. Nicolson Papers, Oct. 1849; Clouston 1920. 21, 34–5.
130. Shirreff 1814 a. 65; Angus 1910. 10; Venables 1956. 25; Thomson 1970. 177.
131. Clouston 1920. 20; Marwick 1929 s.v. *uppa*.
132. Clouston 1925. xxii. 186.
133. *Session Papers, Graham v. Tyrie* 18 Jan. 1758. 10; Jamieson 1929. 74; Marwick 1929 s.v. *spell*; SND s.v. *speld*.
134. Angus 1910; Jamieson 1929. 71; Stewart 1965. 258; Thomson 1970. 177.
135. Marwick 1929; Bjørkvik *et al.* 1974. 173–7.
136. Jamieson 1929. 73; Venables 1956. 27.
137. *Nicolson Papers, Objections. c.* 1851.
138. Cf. Jakobsen (1908) 1928 s.v. *deld*; Angus 1910 s.v. *daal*.
139. NSA. 1845. xv. 96; Angus 1910; Thomson 1970. 178; SND s.v. *dello(w)*.
140. Angus 1910. 10–11.
141. Jakobsen (1908) 1928 s.v. *bødi*.
142. Edmondston 1866; Venables 1956. 27.
143. Jamieson 1929. 73.
144. *Reg. Great Seal* (1597) 182/i; Marwick 1929. 42, 229.
145. SND s.v.
146. Marwick 1929. 113–14.
147. Jakobsen (1908) 1928 s.v. *ger*; Firth (1920) 1974. 149; Marwick 1929 s.v. *geyr, garrick*.
148. Thomson 1970. 181.
149. Thomson 1970. 180; Whittington 1973. 539–40.
150. NSA 1845. xv. 109; Clouston 1920. 28–9.
151. Venables 1956. 22; Coull 1964. 141; Thomson 1970. 180–1.
152. Clouston 1925. xxii. 186; Marwick 1929. 83.
153. Thomson 1970. 181–3.
154. Sölch 1951/2. 1088.

6. *The End of Runrig*

155. Hepburn 1760. 12.
156. OSA 1798. xx. 250, 252–3.
157. Barry 1805. 29–30, 48; Teignmouth 1836. i. 270; NSA 1841. xv. 221; Pringle 1874. 10.
158. O'Dell in Stamp 1939.
159. NSA 1845 xv. 59, 185.
160. OSA 1792. ii. 565: Mid & South Yell; OSA 1793. iii. 414; Lerwick.
161. OSA 1793. vii. 392, 398.
162. *Ib.* 585.
163. NSA 1845 xv. 13, 43.
164. Evershed 1874. 217, 227.
165. O'Dell 1939. 42; Coull 1964. 141.
166. Draft-Scheme: covering letter dated 25 Sept. 1964.
167. APS 1695. ix. *c.* 69, 462.
168. OSA 1793. v. 407.
169. OSA 1795. xiv. 389, 390; OSA 1796. xvii. 225; OSA 1798. xx. 259.
170. Barry 1805. 30.
171. Barry 1805. 33, 42, 52, 54, 59, 61.
172. Forsyth 1808. v. 46.
173. Senior and Swan 1972. 43, 108.
174. NSA. 1845. xv. 6–7, 14, 26, 30, 60, 82, 84, 128, 152, 164, 197, 221.

175. O'Dell in Stamp 1939.
176. Forsyth 1808. 128; Wilson 1842. 268–9.

7. *Outsets and Outbreks*
177. Peterkin 1820. ɪɪ. 2.
178. Donaldson (1720) 1938. 90.
179. OSA. 1791. ɪ. 391.
180. OSA. 1792. ɪɪ. 569, 574.
181. OSA. 1793. vɪɪ. 393, 397.
182. OSA. 1793. vɪɪ. 581, 593–4.
183. OSA. 1793. v. 192.
184. OSA. 1793. vɪɪ. 549, 558.
185. OSA. 1794. x. 196–7, 199.
186. OSA. 1794. xɪɪɪ. 289.
187. OSA. 1794. xɪɪ. 355.
188. OSA. 1796. xvɪɪ. 499.
189. OSA. 1798. xx. 106, 115.
190. Kemp 1801. 8; Hall 1807. 527; Forsyth 1808. 126, 143–4; NSA. 1845. xv. 160.
191. NSA. 1845. xv. 13, 20, 28, 41–2, 44, 52, 66, 76–7, 88–9, 91–2, 94, 96, 117, 121–2.
192. Evershed 1874. 196–7, 228; Skirving 1874. 261.
193. Day 1918. 191; Hunter 1976. 161.

8. *Kelp*
194. Neill 1806. 28; Hossack 1900. 146.
195. Hepburn 1760. 18; Low (1774) 1879. 11, 19; Fea 1775. 45; Low (1778) 1920. 140.
196. Edmondston 1809. ɪɪ. 5; O'Dell 1939. 164.
197. OSA. 1791. ɪ. 390; 1793. ɪɪɪ. 416; 1793. v. 192; 1793. vɪɪ. 588; 1794. x. 196; Edmondston 1809. ɪɪ. 5.
198. Edmondston 1809. ɪ. 149; ɪɪ. 6; Shirreff 1814 b. 74; NSA. 1845. xv. 16, 134; Tudor 1883. 159.
199. Wallace 1693. 17.
200. OSA. 1793. vɪɪ. 454–5; Cross, Burness and North Ronaldsay.
201. Dennison 1891. v. 132; Hossack 1900. 147–8.
202. OSA. 1795. xɪv. 394–5.
203. OSA. 1793. v. 411–12; vɪɪ. 539–40, 553.
204. OSA. 1793. vɪɪ. 339, 455; 1795. xɪv. 126. 133, 315; 1795. xvɪ. 254, 435; 1796. xvɪɪ. 319; 1797. xɪx. 399–400, 418; 1798. xx. 249, 251, 266; 1795. 395–8; Jamieson 1800. 244; Hossack 1900. 149.
205. Barry 1805. 27, 32, 49–50, 52, 55, 57–8, 61–2; Neill 1806. 32.
206. Neill 1806. 7, 13; Forsyth 1808. v. 98, 105.
207. Shirreff 1814 a. 163–4, 174–5.
208. Wilson 1842. ɪɪ. 226.
209. *Home Industries* 1914. 173–4.
210. Cf. Gray. 1957. 124–41; Campbell 1965. 172–3.
211. *Home Industries* 1914. 173–4.
212. Robertson 1909. 241.
213. NSA 1845. xv. 7, 20, 23, 32, 63, 69, 91–2, 108–9, 111, 128, 145, 162, 164, 186–7; Traill 1823. 23.
214. Pringle 1874. 64; Tudor 1883. 363; *Home Industries* 1914. 41–2, 119; Dickinson 1963. 31.
215. *Orcadian* 9 July 1925.
216. Edmondston 1809. ɪɪ. 6.
217. Robertson, 1909. 22; SND s.v. *tari-*.

218. Marwick 1929.
219. Robertson 1908. 231–2.
220. Neill 1806. 29; Edmondston 1809. ii. 6; Robertson 1901. 235; *Home Industries* 1914. 122.
221. Jamieson 1800. 245; Neill 1806. 31.
222. Edmondston 1809. ii. 6; Tudor 1883. 363; Robertson 1909. 225–41; W. Swanney, *Oral information* 1964; Tulloch 1974. 106–15.

9. *Surveys and Surveyors*
223. *Orcadian* 15 Feb. 1973.
224. Graham 1968. Vol. 86. 17; Thomson 1970. 173.
225. *Midbrake Papers.*
226. MS Fetlar Excambion Correspondence 1881–2.
227. MS Report of Survey of the Town of Velzie, 1 March 1875.
228. *Letter*, Nicolson to Gifford, 9 Feb. 1846.
229. *Letters*, Gifford to Nicolson, 16 Feb., 5 March 1846; Nicolson to Gifford, 30 March 1846.
230. *Letter*, Gifford to Nicolson, 5 March 1846.
231. *Summons* 1845.
232. Lord Cuninghame, Interlocutor in causa Nicolson v. Gifford etc, 15 July 1845.
233. Minute by Pursuer, signed W. Sievwright, Lerwick, 8 May 1846; T. Irvine, Report of Survey of the Island of Papa Stour 31 Dec. 1866.
234. Minute by Arthur Gifford Esq. of Busta, Defender. Signed Rob. N. Spence, Lerwick, 9 May 1846.
235. Minute for the Defenders. Signed Archibald Greig, Lerwick, 9 May 1846.
236. Claim for A. Gifford – Defender. In Process of Division of the Island of Papa Stour. Signed Rob. N. Spence, Lerwick, 29 Sept. 1846.
237. Claim by Sir Arthur Nicolson – Signed Wm. Sievwright, Lerwick, 4 March 1847.
238. Claim for Rev. A. Nicoll and Jas. Irvine. Signed Archibald Greig, undated.
239. Report of Valuation, by Thos. Irvine of Midbrake, and (the Rev.) Peter Petersen, Vadlure, Walls, valuators ... 31 May 1847.
240. Minute for Sir Arthur Nicolson, 3 June 1848.
241. Report by T. Irvine, 11 June 1848.
242. Additional Claim for A. Gifford. Signed Rob. N. Spence, 1847.
243. Minute of Restriction and Amendment of Claim, signed by Wm. Sievwright; Additional Claim for A. Gifford, signed by Rob. N. Spence.
244. Proof in Causa of Division – signed by A. Ewanson, R. Bell, A. Nicoll (Clerk), Lerwick, 11 Dec. 1847.
245. *Ib.*, signed W. Henry etc.
246. *Ib.*, signed W. Georgeson etc.
247. *Ib.*, signed J. Mowat, Jnr. etc.
248. *Ib.* 3 March 1848.
249. *Ib.* 4 March 1848.
250. *Ib.* 4 March 1848.
251. *Ib.* 13 April 1848.
252. *Ib.* 2 May 1848.
253. *Interlocutor*, Lerwick 27 August 1849.
254. *Ib.* 27 August 1849.
255. MS Minute.
256. *Letter*, John Archibald Campbell to Messrs. Gordon Stewart and Cheyne, 9 August 1851.
257. Objections for Sir Arthur Nicolson, undated.
258. Note of Arable Grounds.
259. *Letters*, J A Campbell to Messrs. Gordon etc. 26 Nov., 1 Dec. 1853.
260. *Letter*, Cheyne to Campbell, 3 Dec. 1853.
261. Memorial for Counsel, 20 Nov. 1856.

262. *Letter*, Cheyne to Campbell, 13 Nov. 1856.
263. Interlocutor in causa Nicolson and Gifford, Edinburgh 3 Feb. 1857.
264. Edinburgh 22 May 1857.
265. *Letter*, Cheyne to Campbell, 1 July 1857.
266. Midbrake Papers, Bundle 388.
267. Letter, T M Adie to Sir Arthur Nicolson, 7 Sept. 1860.

10. *Dykes and Enclosures*
268. Saxby 1908. 268; SND s.v.
269. Shirreff 1814 a. 55.
270. OSA 1796. xvii. 226: Shapinsay; Jakobsen (1908) 1928; Venables 1956. 170–1.
271. *Ordnance Survey Name Books* No. 13. 206.
272. Marwick 1922–3. i. 22.
273. Leith 1926–7. v. 59–60.
274. Jamieson 1825. s.v. *ring*.
275. Campbell 1774. 666–7.
276. Low (1774) 1879. 40–1.
277. OSA 1791. i. 392: Delting; 1795. xv. 300: S. Ronaldsay; 1795. xvi. 252: Westray; 1798. xx.
     252: Evie and Rendall; 1798. xx. 269: St Andrews and Deerness.
278. OSA 1793. vii. 558; 1795. xiv. 328.
279. OSA 1795. xiv. 400–2.
280. OSA 1793. v. 202; OSA 1796. xvii. 231–2.
281. Barry 1805. 26, 50; Shirreff 1814 a. 56–7.
282. Shirreff 1814 b. 39–40; Pløyen (1835) 1896. 208; Wilson 1842. ii. 268–9; NSA 1845. xv. 3,
     13–14, 29, 48, 65.
283. Evershed 1874. 209–13, 215, 223, 228.
284. NSA 1845. xv. 14, 31, 35, 61, 96–8, 118, 128, 161–2, 197, 221.
285. Farrall 1874. 87–8.
286. Pringle 1874. 6, 10, 17–18, 23, 25, 27, 29, 31, 34–7, 38–42, 45–6, 49–50, 53, 56, 58, 63.
287. Mitchell 1897–8. xxxii. 28–9.
288. Smith *Correspondence* 1961.
289. Smith *Correspondence* 1961; Laurenson MS 1963.
290. Laurenson MS 1963.
291. Shirreff 1814 a. 58.
292. Edmondston 1866 s.v. *dyke-end*.
293. Pringle 1874. 25.
294. Edmondston 1866.
295. Shirreff 1814 b. Appx. 2.
296. Shirreff 1814 b. Appx. 5.

11. *Plantiecrues, Cabbage and Kail*
297. Barclay 1967. 118, 120; Martin 1884. 368, 373.
298. Wallace 1700. 35; Gifford 1786. 24.
299. Fea *MS Diary*.
300. OSA 1793. vii. 552; Neill 1806. 6; Jamieson 1887; Marwick 1929. 77.
301. OSA 1793. v. 408: Holm; Kemp 1801. 4; Neill 1806. 23.
302. Lockhart 1814. xxviii; Shirreff 1814 a. 80; NSA 1845. xv. 163; Smith 1883. 292–3.
303. Brown 1963.
304. Petrie 1963; Peterson, Fraser 1967.
305. NSA 1845. xv. 120; Skirving 1874. 244.
306. OSA 1793. v. 408; Evershed 1874. 200.
307. Henderson 1812. 118–19; Simpson 1969.

12. *The Finishing Touches: Drainage and Liming*

308. Shirreff 1814 a. 110.
309. Evershed 1874. 198–9.
310. Wilson 1842. ii. 268; NSA 1845. xv. 58, 61, 66, 77, 121, 128, 184; Pringle 1874. iv. 18, 34, 37, 41, 49–50, 52, 56, 58.
311. Tait *MS Diary* March 1923, Nov. 1926.
312. Shirreff 1814 b. 109–10.
313. Johnston 1910. iii. 162.
314. Pløyen (1839) 1894. 60.
315. *Midbrake Papers*, Bundle 3562, sheet 14.
316. O'Dell 1939. 173–4.

Homes and Working Places

13. *The Raw Resources*

317. OSA 1795. xiv. 136–7; 1795. xvi. 426; Barry 1805. 264; NSA 1845. xv. 17, 31, 119, 158; Wilson 1935. 148; Mooney 1953. i. 1–2; Miller and Luther-Davies 1968. 17–18.
318. Forsyth 1808. 138; NSA 1845. xv. 15, 29; O'Dell 1939. 174.
319. Trémarec 1772. 41–2; Marwick 1923–4. ii. 17.
320. Marwick 1939. Pt. ii. 48.
321. *Oppressions* 1859. 65.
322. Settle (1577) 1969 unpaginated.
323. *Oppressions* 1859. 97.
324. Donaldson 1954. 22.
325. Smith (1633) 1673. vi. 253; Monteith (1633) 1845. 24.
326. Brand (1683) 1701–3. 25; Marwick 1926–7. v. 72; Marwick 1936. Pt. i. 80.
327. Fraser 1934–5. xiii. 35–6; Fraser 1937–9. xv. 36.
328. Callander and Grant 1933–4. 223–4; Childe 1934. 148; Childe 1939. 36, 64; Stenberger 1943. 293; Wainwright 1962. 13; Henshall 1963. 83.
329. Stenberger 1943. 176; Dahl 1965. 138; Hoffmann 1966. 121, 123; Fenton 1978, 34.
330. Curle 1934–5. 265–321, Fig. 3; Fenton 1968. 84–103; Ritchie 1974. 33.

14. *The Longhouse*

331. Hamilton 1956. 94, 103, 158.
332. Small 1966. 9–11; Small 1966, 16–17; Small 1968. 68–9.
333. Nørlund 1936. 65–8, 75–7; Roussell 1941. 137, Fig. 84, 161, Fig. 98; Stenberger 1943. 205; Gestsson 1959. facing 32; Dahl 1965. 139; Eldjárn 1965. 10–19; Vebæk 1965. 114; Ingstad 1970. 109–54.
334. Hoffmann 1943. 54.
335. *Diplomatarium* 1907–42. ii. 90; Clouston 1914. 221.
336. Hall 1807. 526.
337. Hibbert 1822. 115.
338. Charlton (1834) 1935–46. 61–2; NSA 1845. xv. 21, 139.
339. NSA 1845. xv. 129, 181.
340. Barry 1805, 474.
341. Skirving 1774. 240; Roussell 1934. 52–7.
342. Hibbert 1822. 116.

15. *Twentieth Century Survivals: Some Detailed Examples*
343. Omond *c.* 1912. 8 and facing 14; Firth (1920) 1974, facing 19.
344. Clouston 1923. I. 11–19, 39–47; 1924. II. 7–14.
345. Clouston 1923. I. 15.
346. See Roussell 1934. 82.
347. Clouston 1923. I. 15.
348. Clouston 1923. I. 15.
349. Clouston 1914. 415; Roussell 1934. 95.
350. Clouston 1923. I. 13–14; Roussell 1934. 97.
351. Clouston 1923. I. 13–14; Roussell 1934. 96.
352. Clouston 1923. I. 17.
353. Leith *Correspondence* 1960.
354. Hamilton 1956. 190–3.
355. Roussell 1934. 87.
356. Fenton *MS Notebook*, Papa Stour 1967. 63–4; Bruce 1973. 18.
357. Roussell 1934. 53, 56, 59, 67, 69.

16. *Farms in General*
358. Fox 1951. 135.
359. Fenton *MS Notebook*, Orkney 1968.
360. Roussell 1934. 69.
361. Tait 1951. II. 77–82.
362. Fenton *MS Notebook*, Papa Stour 1967.

17. *Orkney Houses and Plenishings*
363. Taylor 1938. 155–6, 183–4, 242–4, 324, 338, 342.
364. Clouston 1914. 221–2.
365. *Diplomatarium* 1907–13. I. 111, 113.
366. Clouston 1914. 242.
367. Clouston 1920. XVII. 22–3.
368. Clouston 1914. 138.
369. Cf. Neill 1806. 3.
370. *Diplomatarium* 1908–42. III. 121.
371. Clouston 1932. 336–8; Johnston (1716) 1891. V. 187.
372. Clouston 1926–7. V. 9–11.
373. Macfarlane (1726) 1906–8. I. 143.
374. Marwick 1936. I. 145.
375. Settle (1577) 1969 unpaginated.
376. Barry 1805. Appx. IX. 474; see also *Acts* (1632) 1840. II. 208.
377. *Misc. Abbotsford Club* 1837. I. 155, 159; Low (1778) 1915. 135.
378. MacGillivray (1592–1638) 1953. I. 50.
379. Low (1773) 1923–4. II. 52.
380. Lucas 1956. 16–35.
381. Dennison 1884. 247–8
382. Fea *MS Diary*.
383. Mackaile in Barry 1805. 453.
384. Brand (1683) 1701–3. 21; Low (1774) 1879. 10; Marwick 1936. I. 54.
385. Fea *MS Diary* 30 Dec. 1766; *Report* 1884 Appx. A, LIX. 270–80.
386. Knox 1789. 139.
387. Fea 1775. 31.
388. OSA 1793. V. 410; Shirreff 1814 a. 141; NSA 1845. XV. 19, 107, 185.
389. Neill 1806. 3; Teignmouth 1836. I. 254; Pringle 1874. 54.

390. OSA 1795. xiv. 400; Dickson 1841. 131–2; NSA 1845. xv. 26, 129, 161.
391. Pringle 1874. 18, 24, 26–7.
392. NSA 1845. xv. 35–40, 107; Pringle 1874. 28–31, 34.
393. Pringle 1874. 42–3, 45, 46–52, 56, 58.
394. Scarth and Watt 1939. 6.
395. Neill 1806. 19–20; NSA 1845. xv. 163, 225; Pringle 1874. 27; Troup and Eunson 1967. 4.
396. Barry 1805. 351, 337; Forsyth 1808. v. 88; Shirreff 1814 a. 40, 150–1; Traill 1823. 23–4; Marwick 1929.
397. Maxwell (*c*. 1840) 1853. 297–8; Marwick 1929 s.v. *koly*.
398. Omond *c*. 1912. 8–9; Firth (1920) 1974. 8–13; Højrup 1960. 110–24.

18. *The Building Trade*

399. Craven 1911. 22–3, 47, 57–8.
400. Flett (1731–2). x. 51–2.
401. OSA 1793. v. 411; 1793. vii. 549; 1795. xiv. 319; 1795. xvi. 262, 434, 454; 1797. xix. 405.
402. OSA 1793. v. 411; 1793. vii. 485, 555; 1795. xvi. 431.
403. OSA 1791. i. 400; 1793. vii. 587, 594; 1794. x. 199–200; 1794. xii. 358; 1794. xiii. 287.

19. *Living Density*

404. NSA 1845. xv. 5.
405. OSA 1793. vii. 594.
406. *Ordnance Survey Name Books*, Fair Isle No. 11, 93.

20. *Shetland Houses and Plenishings*

407. Donaldson (1602–4) 1954. 4–5, 8, 11, 14, 20, 33, 70, 73, 75, 76.
408. *Acts* (1602–44) 1840. ii. 160.
409. Marr (*c*. 1680) 1908. 8.
410. Monteith (1633) 1845. 12–14, 24, 48–9.
411. Brand (1683) 1701. 70, 80–1, 86; Martin (*c*. 1695) 1884. 90, 384, 387, 390.
412. Low (1774) 1879. 91, 134.
413. Knox 1789. 140; OSA 1793. iii. 418.
414. OSA 1798. xx. 275; Kemp 1801. 16–17; Hall 1807. ii. 537; Edmondston 1809. ii. 27; NSA 1845. xv. 3.
415. Forsyth 1808. v. 129; Edmondston 1809. ii. 48–9; Shirreff 1814 b. 19; Maxwell (*c*. 1840) 1853. 144.
416. NSA 1845. xv. 14, 40, 43, 117, 121–2, 138–9.
417. *Midbrake Papers*, Bundle 391.
418. *Midbrake Papers*, Bundle 391.
419. *Midbrake Papers*, Bundle 392; NSA 1845. xv. 124: Sandsting and Aithsting.
420. Cowie 1871. 92; Skirving 1874. 240; Evershed 1874. 197, 202; Smith 1964. iv. 6.
421. Smith 1964. iv. 1–2, 4.
422. Smith 1964. iv. 6–8.
423. SND s.v. *lodie*.
424. Skirving 1874. 257–8; Evershed 1874. 210–12, 214, 223, 226.
425. *Letter*, Adie to Sir Arthur Nicolson, 7 Sept. 1860.
426. *Letter*, Rev. D. Webster to J A Campbell, 1864.
427. *Letter*, C. Arthurson to Lady Nicolson, 7 April 1876.
428. *Letter*, J M Aitken, builder, to C. Arthurson, 4 March 1879.
429. *Letters*, C. Arthurson to Lady Nicolson, 28 May 1881, 4 June 1881.
430. *List of Cash Paid out for Work etc.* 1881, 1883.
431. Day 1918. 190–5.

432. *Letters*, C. Arthurson to Lady Nicolson, 28 Oct. 1887, 23 March 1889.
433. Specification of Repairs on House of Still (and Aiths Bank House) – by J. Hutchison, Gen. Joiner and Builder, Lerwick, 9 July 1887.
434. Wilson *Correspondence* July 1963.
435. Laurenson *MS Notebook* 1963.

21. *Roofing Techniques*
436. Jakobsen (1908) 1928 s.v. *knokk*; Angus 1914 s.v. *nokkens*.
437. Eunson 1976. 15; Fair Isle.
438. Laurenson *MS Notebook* 1963.
439. Eunson 1976. 15.
440. Sibbald 1711. 3; Hibbert 1822. 114; Angus 1914.
441. Garrick 1960.
442. Seim 1947. 27; Fenton. 1970. 171.
443. Eunson 1976. 15; SND s.v.
444. Laurenson *MS Notebook* 1963; Eunson 1976. 15.
445. Jakobsen 1897. 46.
446. Roussell 1934. 57; Fenton 1961. iii/4. 27.
447. Laurenson *MS Notebook* 1963.
448. *Description* 1908. 7; Sibbald 1711. 3; Edmondston 1809. ii. 48; Pløyen (1839) 1894. 202; NSA 1845. xv. 138.
449. *Ordnance Survey Name Books*, Fetlar, No. 12, 34, 40, 62–3, 69, 85, 96, 117; North Yell No. 13, 27, 33, 35, 44, 121, 129, 146.
450. *Ib*. No. 13, 243, 252, 264, 266, 333, 335.
451. *Ib*. Fair Isle, No. 11, 1878. 93.
452. Fenton *MS Notebook* Fair Isle 1962. 1.
453. Shirreff 1814 a. 41; Smith 1837. 203.
454. Leask 1931. 63; Mooney 1953. i. 8.
455. Marwick 1922–3. i. 65; Firth (1920) 1974. 13–14.
456. Firth (1920) 1974. 13–14.
457. NSA 1845. xv. 179.
458. Marwick 1929.
459. Nicolson 1907. 73.
460. Garrick 1960.
461. Firth (1920) 1974. 31; Fenton 1961. iii/4. 24–5.
462. Fenton 1961. iii/4. 25–6.
463. NSA 1845. xv. 31. 119.
464. Low (1774) 1879. 2; OSA 1795. xiv. 136–7.
465. Scott & McMillan, Note, May 1964.
466. Jakobsen (1908) 1928; Marwick 1929.
467. Tait 1955. 30; SND s.v. *lungkiln*.
468. Ledingham 1837. 203; Smith 1882–3. xvii. 255–6.

22. *Sleeping Accommodation*
469. Macgillivray 1963. i. 50; Sigurðardóttir 1970. xv. 130.
470. Hibbert 1822. 538, 545; Charlton 1935–46. x. 61–2.
471. Dennison 1884. 274.
472. Erixon 1938. 70; McCourt 1956. Vol. 2. 27–34; Walton 1961. iii. 114–25.
473. Dennison 1884. 275.
474. Venables 1956. 7, 40.
475. Shirreff 1814 a. 53–5.

23. *The Hearth*
476. Stigum 1962. vii. 348–9.
477. Roussell 1934. 53, 55.
478. Nelson 1963.
479. Omond *c*. 1912. 8; Firth (1920) 1974. 8–9.
480. Omond *c*. 1912. 8; Firth (1920) 1974. 9.
481. Johnston *Notebook* 1961; Jakobsen (1908) 1928 s.v. *lipi*.
482. Low (1774) 1879. 180; Jakobsen (1908) 1928. cxv.
483. Firth (1920) 1974. 10; Berg, Steensberg, Eriksson 1965. x. 650–4.
484. NSA 1845. xv. 139.
485. Laurenson *MS Notebook* 1963.
486. Edmondston 1809. ii. 48; Pløyen (1839) 1896. 201; Evershed 1874. 202; Dietrichson & Meyer 1906. 193–4.
487. Laurenson *MS Notebook* 1963.
488. SND s.v. *rantree*.
489. Marwick 1929.
490. Fea *MS Diary*.

Fuel for the Fire

24. *Cow-dung and Seaweed.*
491. Ben in Barry 1805. 434.
492. Rundall 1849. 16; Settle 1969.
493. Monipennie (1597) 1603. 7; Brand (1683) 1701–3. 24–5; Aberdeen 1770; Fea 1787. 77; OSA 1793. vii. 486–8.
494. Fea 1787. 77; OSA 1793. vii 485–8; Barry 1805. 57; Neill 1806. 38.
495. MS. Addition to Campbell 1774; Shirreff 1814 a. 154; Donaldson, *Oral information*, 1977.
496. NSA 1845. xv. 102, 107; Gorrie 1868. 368–9; Pringle 1874. 33; J. Dearness per E. Marwick, 1972.
497. Miss B. Costie per E. Marwick, 1972.
498. Miss B. Skea per E. Marwick, 1972.
499. J. Dearness per E. Marwick, 1972.
500. Spence 1923–4. ii. 81; Fenton *MS Notebook*, Caithness, 1969.
501. Spence 1923–4. ii. 81; Marwick 1929.
502. Fenton 1972. 722–34.

25. *Peat and Turf in Orkney*
503. Taylor 1938. 141, 354.
504. SND s.v. *peat*.
505. Monipennie (1597) 1603. 7; Wallace 1700. 12; Low (1774) 1879. 197; Dickson 1841. vii. 116.
506. Fea *MS Diary*.
507. Brand (1683) 1701. 24–5.
508. Scott 1968. 145–6.
509. Monteith (1633) 1845. 7; Martin (*c*. 1695) 1884. 356; Low (1774) 1879, 12–13; OSA 1795. xv. 414.
510. NSA 1845. xv. 165, 168.
511. *Misc. Maitland Club* 1840. ii. 206, 214; OSA 1793. vii. 556; OSA 1797. xix. 395.
512. Low (1774) 1879. 1, 29, 42; OSA 1795. xiv. 132; OSA 1795. xvi. 250.
513. OSA 1795. xiv. 331, 414–15; OSA 1795. xvi. 264, 411, 419, 427, 449, 454; OSA 1797. xiv. 413.
514. Barry 1805. 37, 41, 52, 58; Neill 1806. 33, 38–9.
515. Shirreff 1814 a. 12, 39, 66, 152; NSA 1845. xv. 102, 107, 132, 154, 168, 189, 195.

26. *The Orkney—Edinburgh Peat Trade*
516. NSA 1845. xv. 162.
517. Marwick 1929; *The Orcadian* 16 Sept. 1971.
518. Johnston 1906–7. ɪ. 245.
519. Leask 1907–8. ɪ. 129–33.

27. *Peat Cutting in Orkney*
520. Leask 1907–8. ɪ. 134.
521. Leask 1907–8. ɪ. 134; Marwick 1929; Fenton 1970. 171–2, 178–9.
522. *Misc. Maitland Club* 1840. ɪɪ. 206; POAS 1922–3. ɪ. 65.
523. Firth (1920) 1974. 108; Spence 1923–4. ɪɪ. 80.
524. Firth (1920) 1974. 108; Spence 1923–4. ɪɪ. 80; Marwick 1929.
525. Johnston 1907–8. ɪ. 246.
526. *Misc. Maitland Club* 1840. ɪɪ. 148; Leask 1907–8. ɪ. 130.

28. *Peat in Shetland*
527. Brand (1683) 1701. 79; Low (1774) 1879. 149.
528. OSA 1792. ɪɪ. 574; 1793. v. 183, 194–5; 1794. xɪɪ. 358; 1798. xx. 112.
529. NSA 1845. xv. 20, 81, 138.
530. Letters, T M Adie to Lady Nicolson, 5 April, 28 April, 26 July 1881.
531. NSA 1845. xv. 3, 19, 52.
532. Shirreff 1814 b. 70.
533. Pløyen (1839) 1896. 20.
534. *Report* 1884. 22–4, 231.
535. Djurhuus (1781–2) 1976. 136–7, 139; Landt (*c*. 1798) 1810. 135; Williamson (1948) 1970. 61; av Skarði 1970. 67.
536. O'Dell 1939. 31, 36, 43, 45; Svensson 1955. 119–21; Venables 1956. 94; Eunson 1976. 28.
537. Jakobsen (1908) 1928.
538. Edmondston 1809. ɪ. 176–9; Hibbert 1822. 429–30; Cowie 1871. 166; Jamieson 1949. 213–14; Fenton and Laurenson 1964. 4–10; Fenton 1970. 170–1, 176–8.
539. Venables 1956. 19–21.
540. Evershed 1874. 203.

29. *The Peat Houses of Fetlar*
541. Fenton and Laurenson 1964. 19–26.

30. *Peat Charcoal*
542. Goudie (1790) 1889. 91.
543. Shirreff (1808) 1814 b. Appx. xɪv. 63.
544. *Midbrake Papers*, Bundle 387.
545. Ross 1885–6. 409; Bremner n.d.

Back Transport, Harness and Straw Working

31. *Horses and Ponies*
546. Boece 1527, Leslie 1579 in Brown 1893. 92, 157; Monipennie 1597. 3; MacGillivray (*c*. 1614–18) 1953. 49; Monteith (1633) 1711. 21; Brand (1683) 1701–3. 77–9; Gifford (1733) 1786. 16–17, 25; Trémarec 1772. 45.

547. *Orkney Testaments*; Monteith (1633) 1845. 22; *Diplomatarium* 1907–13. I. 72; for further evidence, see Fenton 1973. 15–18.

548. Shirreff 1814 a. 59; *Shetland Times* 24 March 1862; Goudie 1889. 56.

549. Brand (1683) 1701. 77–9; Anon. 1750. 9; Gifford (1733) 1786. 6.

550. Brand (1683) 1701. 77–9; OSA 1791. I. 393; 1793. v. 188; 1793. vII. 594–5; 1795. xIV. 650; 1798. xx. 107, 277–8.

551. Kemp 1801. 7–8; Forsyth 1808. v. 130–1; NSA 1845. xv. 45, 52, 81, 89, 125–6, 166.

552. O'Dell 1939. 83–4, 87–8; Dent and Goodal! 1962. 204.

553. O'Dell 1939. 87.

554. Fea 1775. 30; OSA 1793. v. 409; Holm; 1793. vII. 339: Rousay and Egilsay; 1793. vII. 454: Cross, Burness and North Ronaldsay; 1795. xIV. 129: Firth and Stenness; 1798. xx. 264: St Andrews and Deerness; 1798. xx. 249–50: Evie and Rendall; Sinclair 1795. 96; Barry 1805. 324–5; Shirreff 1814 a. 142.

555. Low (1773) 1923–4. II. 50; Barry 1805. 324–5.

556. Henderson 1812. 215–17, 238–9; JML 1909. 192–3.

557. NSA 1845. xv. 23; Johnston 1910. 74; JTSL 1910. 74–5.

558. OSA 1793. vII. 544: Kirkwall and St Ola; 1795. xIV. 322; Shirreff 1814 a. 144, Appx. 56; Scarth and Watt 1939. 16.

559. Marwick 1922–3. I. 65.

560. Shirreff 1814 a. 143–4; JTSL 1910. III. 75.

561. NSA 1845. xv. 61, 99, 145, 164; Farrall 1874. 85; Pringle 1874. 16; Scarth and Watt 1939. 16.

562. Barclay 1962. 23; Barclay 1967. 29–30, 70.

563. Donaldson (*c.* 1602) 1958. 33; Edmondston 1866.

564. Edmondston 1866; Donaldson 1954. 126; Donaldson 1958. 30; SND. s.v. *hest*.

565. OSA 1795. xv. 300; Dent and Goodall 1962. 201.

32. *Transport on Horseback*

566. Edmondston 1866; Marwick 1922–3. I. 65.

567. Landt (*c.* 1798) 1810. 278.

568. Johnston 1908. 246.

569. Aberdeen 1770 Estate Plan; Landt (*c.* 1798) 1810. 278; Johnston 1907–8. 246; Williamson (1948) 1970. 59; Fenton 1973. 126–34.

570. Marwick (1734) 1922–3. I. 65.

571. Fenton and Laurenson 1964. 10–14.

572. Omond *c.* 1912. 17; Firth (1920) 1974. 34–6.

573. *Orcadian* 9 Feb. 1961.

574. Jirlow 1937. II. 139; s.v. Skarði 1955. 32–60; 1956. 108–52; Rasmussen 1973. 416–18.

575. Aberdeen 1770 Estate Plan.

576. Omond *c.* 1912. 20; Klodnicki *et al.* 1975. vIII/2. 101–22.

577. Hibbert 1822. 431.

578. Omond *c.* 1912. 19; Firth (1920) 1974. 36; Fenton and Laurenson 1964. 10–17.

579. Hibbert 1822. 431; Edmondston 1866; Jakobsen (1908) 1928.

580. Johnston 1907–8. 246; Omond *c.* 1912. 20; Firth (1920) 1974. 36.

581. Omond *c.* 1912. 19–20.

582. Marwick (1716) 1936. I. 52; 1939. II. 53, 59–60.

583. Fea *MS Diary* 29 Oct., 1 Nov., 19 Nov. 1766 etc.

584. Barclay 1967. 27; Brand (1683) 1701. 28; Marwick (1727) 1936. I. 119.

Baskets and Ropes

33. *Domestic Baskets*
585. Omond *c*. 1912. 17; Firth (1920) 1974. 35–6.
586. Langskaill *Correspondence* 1 Feb. 1961.
587. Marwick 1929.
588. *Misc. Abbotsford Club* 1837. I. 178; Jakobsen (1908) 1928. s.v. *hovi*.
589. Omond *c*. 1912. 17–18; Marwick 1929.
590. Edmondston 1866; Jakobsen (1908) 1928; Angus 1914.
591. Edmondston 1866; Hunter 1952. 165.
592. Angus 1914; Jakobsen (1908) 1928.
593. Angus 1914; Marwick 1929; Nicolson 1931. 55; Donaldson, *Oral information*, 1977.
594. Neill 1806. 17; Spence 1923–4. II. 80.
595. Neill 1806. 17; Omond *c*. 1912. 18; Firth (1920) 1974. 15; Spence 1923–4. II. 80; Høeg 1975. 514.
596. Barry 1805. 467; Firth (1920) 1974. 15.
597. Fenton 1961. III/4. 24–5.
598. Edmondston MS 1961. 2.
599. Fea *MS Diary*.
600. Vedder 1832. 298; Dennison 1905. 34; Omond *c*.1912. 19; Firth (1920) 1974. 32; Marwick 1929; Leith *Correspondence* 18 Oct. 1960; Fenton 1961. III/4. 23; Scott 1968. 80.
601. Firth (1920) 1971. 105; Marwick (1734) 1922–3. I. 65; Spence 1923–4. II. 80.
602. Djurhuus (1781–2) 1976. 97, 99; Jakobsen (1908) 1928; Williamson (1948) 1970. 77; Nilson 1961. 56–61, 92, 155.

34. *Straw Plaiting and Straw-backed Orkney Chairs*
603. Neill 1806. 6, 71; Hall 1807. II. 518; Shirreff 1814 a. 163; 1814 b. 74; Firth (1920) 1974. 48.
604. *Report* 1914. 179–80.
605. NSA 1845. xv. 7, 20, 32, 62–3, 68–9, 75, 82, 129, 152, 215.
606. Gorrie 1868. 25; Pringle 1874. 6.
607. NSA 1845. xv. 4: Shetland.
608. NSA 1845. xv. 186; Freeman 1953.
609. Firth (1920) 1974. 48–50.
610. Dennison 1905. 41–2.
611. *Report* 1914. 109.

The Land and its Produce

35. *Seaweed Manure*
612. *Crofters' Commission Report* 1884. 278; Jackson 1948. 137, 142; Smith (1952) 1958. 77–8.
613. Johnston 1907–13. I. 61–4, 251–3.
614. *Reg. Mag. Sig.* 1883. 727/1; Mackaile in Barry 1805. 449; Peterkin 1820. III. 77; Brand (1683) 1701. 19; Wallace 1883. 42, comment added to 1700 edition; Pococke (1760) 1887. 149; Low (1774) 1879. 19; Rasmussen 1974. I. 395–6.
615. OSA 1793. VII. 452, 454: Cross, Burness and North Ronaldsay; Omond *c*. 1912. 6, 20.
616. OSA 1793. VII. 542; 1795. xvi. 253, 418, 420; 1796. xvii. 229; Forsyth 1808. v. 47; Traill 1823. 27.
617. OSA 1795. xvi. 253; NSA 1845. xv. 98, 146; Farrall 1874. 81; Scott 1968. 118.
618. Wallace (1700) 1883. 42; Gunn 1909. 230; Omond *c*. 1912. 6.
619. Leask 1907. I. 33–4.
620. Smith 1912. v. 4–5.
621. Marwick 1929.

622. Tait *MS Diaries.*
623. Donaldson (1602) 1954. 16; Brand (1683) 1701, 66; Gifford (*c.* 1725) 1879. 78; Anon. 1750. 9; Shirreff 1814 b. 55; *Crofters' Commission Report* 1884. Appx. A, LI, 231; Sandison 1968. 13.
624. Low (1774) 1879. 161–2; NSA 1845. xv. 158; Skirving 1874. 201–2; Fenton *MS Notebook, Papa Stour* 1967.
625. Fenton 1974. 147–86; Noble 1975. 80–3

36. *Turf and Animal Manure*

626. Martin (*c.* 1695) 1884. 355.
627. Low (1774) 1879. 81; OSA 1793. III. 586; 1793. v. 413: Holm; 1795. XIV. 127;NSA 1845. xv. 66–7: Tingwall, Whiteness and Weisdale; Skirving 1874. 243; *New Shetlander* 1949. No. 17, 2.
628. Low (1774) 1879. 161–2; OSA 1793. v. 182, 192; 1798. xx. 277: Tingwall; Forsyth 1808. v. 131; Evershed 1874. 201.
629. Darling 1945. 33.
630. Pococke (1760) 1887. 149; OSA 1793. VII. 542: Kirkwall and St Ola; 1795. XIV. 127: Firth and Stenness; Barry 1805. 352; Edmondston 1866.
631. Low (1774) 1879. 19: Flotta; OSA 1795. XVI. 420; 1796. XVII. 230; NSA 1845. xv. 13: Bressay, Burra, and Quarff; 1845. xv. 98; Evershed 1874. 201; Pringle 1874. 32, 42.
632. Marwick 1939. II. 19, 22.
633. Fea *MS Diary.*
634. Anon. 1750. 9; OSA 1793. VII. 586: Aithsting and Sandsting; 1795. xv. 302: South Ronaldsay and Burray; 1795. XVI. 260; Cowie 1871. 159.
635. OSA 1793. VII. 586; 1798. xx. 277; NSA 1845. xv. 43, 118; Evershed 1874. 201.
636. OSA 1793. VII. 585–6; 1795. XIV. 126: Firth and Stenness; 1795. XIV. 399, 651; 1795. XVI. 418, 420: Sandwick and Stromness; 1798. xx. 249.
637. Cf. Forsyth 1808. 47, 126–7.
638. NSA 1845. xv. 28, 43, 118, 120.
639. Farrall 1874. 81; Skirving 1874. 201–2; Evershed 1874. 200; Pringle 1874. 42; Smith 1958. 72–3.

37. *The Delling Spade*

640. *Deeds* 1840. II. 10; Donaldson (1602–4) 1954. 25; Marwick 1936. I. 135; Marwick 1922–3. I. 65.
641. Low (1774) 1879. 19, 28; OSA 1795. XIV. 403; 1795. xv. 301; 1798. xx. 277.
642. Low (1774) 1879. 97, 179; OSA 1791. I. 391–2; 1792. II. 574; 1793. v. 192; 1793. VII. 585–6, 593–4; 1794. x. 196–7; 1794. XII. 355; 1795. XIV. 651.
643. OSA 1793. VII. 383; Sinclair 1795. 251.
644. Kemp 1801. 6; Neill 1806. 74, 158; Hall 1807. II. 530; Forsyth 1808. v. 127; Shirreff 1814 b. 36; NSA 1845. xv. 44, 53, 91, 94, 117–18, 162.
645. Kemp 1801. 6; Tudor 1883. 149–50.
646. Angus 1914.
647. NSA 1865. xv. 77–8; Cowie 1871. 158–9; Russell 1887. 157–8; Jamieson 1949. 192–5.
648. Jakobsen (1908) 1928; Fenton 1970. 190.
649. NSA 1845. xv. 96; Edmondston 1866; SND s.v. *nattle.*
650. Fenton 1962–3. XCVI. 310.

38. *Plough Cultivation*

651. Stevenson 1960. 1.
652. Calder 1955–6. LXXXIX. 363.

653. *Ib*. 395.
654. Fenton 1962–3. xcvɪ. 265–8; Manning 1964. lɪv. 60.
655. Glob 1951. 58–70; Fenton 1968. 151–2; Lerche 1969. ɪ:2. 128; Fenton 1971–2. 70–1.
656. Fenton 1962–3. xcvɪ. 277–8; Steensberg 1963. 69–76; Lerche 1970. ɪ:3. 131–7, 144–5.
657. Donaldson 1954. 18, 109, 117; Clouston 1814. 182; *Misc. Abbotsford Club* 1833. ɪ. 138, 143; *Miscellany* 1840. ɪɪ. 206.
658. Monteith (1633) 1845. 18; Brand (1683) 1701. 19.
659. Terry 1902. 25; Marwick 1936. ɪɪ. 135, 140; Jakobsen (1908) 1928; Johnston (1732–5) 1911. ɪv. 121.
660. Barclay transcripts.
661. Fenton transcripts.
662. Marwick 1922–3. ɪ. 65.
663. Marwick 1934. 47–58.
664. Hepburn 1760. 10; Low 1924. ɪɪ. 53; Fenton 1962–3. 299.
665. Low (1774) 1879. 97; Campbell 1774. 666.
666. OSA 1791. ɪ. 391–2; 1793. v. 192–3, 393; 1793. vɪɪ. 393, 585–6.
667. OSA 1793. v. 409: Holm; 1793. vɪɪ. 339; 1795. xɪv. 318, 323, 331–2, 399; 1795. xv. 301–2: South Ronaldsay and Burray; 1795. xvɪ. 417–18; 1797. xɪx. 405, 408; 1798. xx. 249–50.
668. Jamieson 1825; NSA 1845. xv. 96; Sweet 1883. ɪ. 18; Jakobsen (1908) 1928; Donaldson 1954. 72.
669. OSA 1791. ɪ. 391–2; 1793. vɪɪ. 585–6; 1797. xɪx. 405.
670. OSA 1793. v. Frontispiece and 192–3; Shirreff 1814 a. facing 51; Hibbert 1822. Pl. vɪ. Fig. 20.
671. OSA 1795. xvɪ. 126, 417–18; Sinclair 1795. 226.
672. Low 1924. ɪɪ. 56.
673. Fenton 1976. 40–53.
674. Low (1774) 1879. 41; Fea *MS Diary* 22 Oct. 1779.
675. OSA 1793. v. 401; 1795. xv. 301, 401–2; 1795. xvɪ. 417–18; 1797. xɪx. 405; 1798. xx. 259.
676. Kemp 1801–6; *Letter* 1802. 3; *Letter* 1803. 12; Shirreff 1814 a. 35, 51. •
677. Barry 1805. 353, 356; Shirreff 1814 a. 40; 1814 b. 51–2; Traill 1823. 27; Fenton 1976. 38–43.
678. NSA 1845. xv. 21, 31, 60–1, 110, 145, 213.
679. Marwick (1903) 1936. 11–12.
680. NSA 1845. xv. 53, 58, 65, 78, 94, 115, 117.
681. NSA 1945. xv. 162.
682. Farrall 1874. 87; Pringle 1874. 54–5; Tudor 1883. 95.
683. Mitchell 1880. 94; Evershed 1874. 214; Skirving 1874. 245.
684. OSA 1793. v. 192–3: Unst; 1795. xv. 399; 1795. xvɪ. 417–18: Sandwick and Stromness; Barry 1805. 349; Shirreff 1814 a. 63; Omond *c*. 1912. 21; Firth (1920) 1974. 107.
685. SWRI 1966.
686. OSA 1793. vɪɪ. 585.
687. Marwick (1903) 1936. 6–11.
688. Shirreff 1814 a. 52.
689. OSA 1796. xvɪɪ. 228–9; 1797. xɪx. 408; Shirreff 1816 a. 51–2; Omond *c*. 1912. 19.
690. Shirreff 1814 a. 52; Marwick 1929.
691. *Orkney Herald* 10 April 1956, 6 August 1957; Spence 1956; *Orcadian* 1 April 1965.
692. Omond *c*. 1912. 21; Firth (1920) 1974. 106.
693. Marwick (1734) 1822–3. ɪ. 65; Hepburn 1756. 5; Fea *MS Diary* 21 April 1766.
694. OSA 1795. xvɪ. 254; 1798. xx. 260; Neill 1806. 158; Shirreff 1814 a. 52, 64; 1814 b. Appx. 19; NSA 1845. xv. 117.
695. OSA 1793. v. 409: Holm; 1795. xvɪ. 254: Westray; 1797. xɪx. 408: Orphir; NSA 1845. xv. 117; Gorrie 1868. 300; Omond *c*. 1912. 21; Firth (1920) 1974. 107.
696. Shirreff 1814 a. 53; Omond *c*. 1912. 21.

Draught Animals and Transport

39. *Oxen*
697. Boece in Brown, 1893. 93; Donaldson 1954. 108–9; Monteith 1845. 18, 21, 75; Gifford 1786. 24, 25 etc.
698. Marwick 1934. 48–53.
699. *Letter* 1760. 10; Campbell 1774. 666; OSA 1793. v. 409; 1795. xvi. 418; 1795. xv. 302; 1796. xvii. 229.
700. OSA 1795. xiv. 416; 1798. xx. 251.
701. Barry 1805. 322–3.
702. Barry 1805. 356; OSA 1793. vii. 544; Forsyth 1808. v. 48.
703. NSA 1845. xv. 164.
704. OSA 1793. v. 192; 1793. vii. 393, 585; 1798. xx. 277.
705. Sinclair 1795. 251.
706. Irvine 1814 in *Midbrake Papers.*
707. NSA 1845. xv. 65, 78, 117, 165.
708. OSA 1798. xx. 260.

40. *Wagons, Sleds and Carts*
709. Marwick 1939. ii. 22.
710. Marwick 1934. xii. 48–53.
711. Shirreff 1814 b. 36; Fenton 1976. 208.
712. H. Ritch 1961, per E. Simpson.
713. Fox 1931. 198, Pl. xvi; Berg 1935. 118; Simpson 1963. 160–8; Linklater, *Information* 1977.
714. Shirreff 1814 a. 53, Appx. 46–53.
715. Simpson 1963. 157.

Cereal Crops

41. *Grain Types and Trade*
716. Jessen & Helbæk 1949. 18; Murray 1970. 78, Table 147.
717. Calder 1955–6. 353–4; Wainwright 1962. 39, 48; *Radio-carbon* 1971. Vol. 13. 177.
718. Taylor 1938. 222.
719. Major 1521, Boece 1527, Leslie 1578 in Brown 1893. 48, 92, 157.
720. Monipennie 1597. 3; Ben in Barry 1805. 434; Monteith (1633) 1845. 12, 18, 71, 75; Brand (1683) 1701. 75–6; Martin (*c.* 1695) 1884. 371–2.
721. Monteith 1845. 6, 8; Brand (1683) 1701. 37; Low (1774) 1879. 24–5.
722. OSA 1792. v. 407–8; 1793. vii. 470, 474; 1796. xvii. 230; 1798. xx. 276.
723. Marwick 1936. i. 2, 5, 13–14, 20–3, 27, 37–9, 42, 47; 1939. ii. 12.
724. Marwick 1936. i. 66–7, 132.
725. *Ib.* 45, 64, 99–100, 106, 137.
726. Barclay transcripts.
727. Fenton transcripts.
728. Campbell 1774. 667, 686; OSA 1795. xiv. 126, 399; 1797. xix. 408–9; 1798. xx. 250.
729. Marwick (1734) 1922–3. i. 65; Fea 1775. 19; Fea 1787. 87.
730. Low (1774) 1879. 179; NSA 1845. xv. 158.
731. Low (1773) 1923–4. ii. 56–7; Low (1774) 1879. 81; OSA 1794. xiii. 281; 1796. xvii. 228; Mill 1889. 144.
732. OSA 1793. vii. 586; 1795. xvi. 415: Sandwick.
733. Neill 1806. 14, 74; Forsyth 1808. v. 46, 48.
734. NSA 1845. xv. 65, 93, 117–20, 158.
735. NSA 1845. xv. 6, 23, 98, 109, 164, 166, 182, 221–2.
736. NSA 1845. xv. 143–4.
737. Farrall 1874. 74; Pringle 1874. 21–2; Tait *MS Diary* 1925; Hewison 1954. ii. 14.

42. *Plucking, and Shearing with the Sickle*

738. Brand (1683) 1701. 73; NSA 1845. xv. 164; Spence 1923–4. ii. 78.

739. Brand (1683) 1701. 18; OSA 1793. v. 408: Holm; Barry 1805. 351.

740. Monteith (1633) 1845. 18; Fenton 1973/4. vii/1. 36.

741. OSA 1798. xx. 107: Walls and Sandness; 1798. xx. 277; Barry 1805. 351; Shirreff 1814 a. Appx. 50; NSA 1845. xv. 138; Farrall 1874. 87; Firth (1920) 1974. 48.

742. Marwick 1936. i. 140; Fea *MS Diary*; NSA 1845. xv. 145; *Crofters' Comm. Report* 1884. Appx. A, 270.

743. Jakobsen (1908) 1928; Marwick 1929; Firth (1920) 1974. 114; Marwick 1939. ii. 10.

744. Fenton 1976. 56–8.

745. Omond *c*. 1912. 21; Firth (1920) 1974. 144; Mrs Johnson *Correspondence*.

746. Omond *c*. 1912. 21; Firth (1920) 1974. 3; Marwick 1929.

747. *Old-Lore Misc.* 1920. viii. 15; Firth (1920) 1974. 115; Marwick 1929.

748. Martin (*c*. 1695) 1884. 368; Nicolson 1912. 122–3.

43. *The Scythe and Harvesting Machinery*

749. Monteith (1633) 1845. 18; NSA 1845. xv. 138: Sandsting and Aithsting; Edmondston 1866; Firth (1920) 1974. 113; Spence 1923–4. ii. 81; Marwick 1929; Eunson 1976. 23.

750. Shirreff 1814 a. 48, 50; Omond *c*. 1912. 6; Spence 1923–4. ii. 81.

751. SND s.v. *scy;* Irvine MS 1974. 7; Miller MS 1974. 6.

752. Tait *MS Diaries*.

753. Drever MS 1974. 5; Harcus MS 1974. 2; Irvine MS 1974. 7; Mackay MS 1974. 4; Manson MS 1975. 4; Miller MS 1974. 6; Linklater, *Information* 1977.

754. Barnes MS 1975. 11.

44. *Sheaves, Stooks and Stacks*

755. Low (1774) 1879. Facing xxii and 1; Barry 1805. 351; NSA 1845. xv. 21: Orphir; Omond *c*. 1912. 21; Firth (1920) 1974. 114; Fenton *MS Notebook*, Foula 1958. 12; Fenton 1976. 71.

756. Clouston 1914. 170–1; Barclay 1967. 38; Scott 1968. 65, 69; Mackintosh 1894. 250; Irvine MS 1974. 7.

757. NSA 1845. xv. 96; Omond *c*. 1912. 22.

758. *New Shetlander* 1949. No. 14. 29; Tait 1957. iii. 18; SND s.v. *affwinnin*.

759. Edmondston 1866; Jakobsen (1908) 1928; Marwick 1929.

760. Marwick (1747) 1934. xii. 49; NSA 1845. xv. 147: Lady; Pringle 1874. 245; Skirving 1874. 31.

761. Marwick 1929; *Orcadian* 13 Feb. 1930.

762. NSA 1845. xv. 22; Pringle 1874. 32; Eunson 1976. 26.

763. Fenton *MS Notebook*, Foula 1958. 12–14.

764. Fea *MS Diary* 3 Jan. 1767; Firth (1920) 1974. 114; Marwick 1929.

765. Tait *MS Diaries*.

766. *Misc. Maitland Club* (1632) 1840. ii. 208.

767. Shirreff 1814 a. 154; Farrall 1874. 75; Irvine MS 1974. 4.

768. Pringle 1874. 32; Fenton 1961. iii/4. 18–19; Manson MS 1975. 4.

769. Manson MS 1975. 4.

770. Firth (1920) 1974. 115; Marwick 1922–3. i. 28: Sanday; Osla 1962. 4.

771. Banks (1943) 1946. 10; Tait 1957. iii. 18.

772. *Folk-Lore* 1919. xxx. 131; Firth (1920) 1974. 115.

773. *Midbrake Papers*, Bundle 3562, Sheet 18, 19 Sept. 1826; Jokobsen (1908) 1928; Firth (1920) 1974. 115; Tait 1957. iii. 18.

45. *Threshing*

774. NSA 1845. xv. 95; Marwick 1929; Trotzig 1943. 115.
775. Johnson MS.
776. Omond *c*. 1912. 17; Firth (1920) 1974. 17.
777. Stephens 1844. III. 989.
778. Omond *c*. 1912. 14; Firth (1920) 1974. 17–18.
779. Omond *c*. 1912. 17.
780. Marwick 1929.
781. Johnson MS 1961.
782. Fenton *MS Notebook*, Fair Isle 1962. 20–1.
783. Marwick 1922–3. I. 65; Marwick 1933–4. 48; Marwick 1939. II. 139.
784. Fenton *MS Notebook*, North Ronaldsay 1964. 29.
785. Trotzig 1943. 35, 38, 42, 45, 49–50, 56–8, 66.
786. Henderson 1812. 153; Sutherland, *Oral information* 1969; Swanston, *Oral information* 1969.
787. Jakobsen (1908) 1928; Fenton *MS Notebook*, Fetlar 1963. 26–7, 37.
788. Fea *MS Diary*; Omond *c*. 1912, following 14. Firth (1920) 1974, facing 19.
789. Stout, *Tape-recording*, RL 1883.
790. Johnson *Correspondence* 26 Jan. 1962.
791. Omond *c*. 1912. 14–15, 17.
792. Firth (1920) 1974. 21–2; SND s.v. *hand trist*.
793. Traill 1823. 36; NSA 1845. xv. 90–1; Davidson 1936. XI; Fenton 1976. 83–7.
794. Hewison (1849–68) 1954. II. 18.
795. Farrall 1874. 86–7, 97; Pringle 1874. 25, 28, 35–6, 38–9, 53, 57; Skirving 1874. 210, 212, 256.
796. Tait *MS Diary* 22 March 1905, 15 Nov. 1907, 11 Jan. 1911, 1 April 1925, Memo. 1931; Leith and Spence 1977. 9–14.
797. Farrall 1874. 97; Scott 1968. 66; Leith and Spence 1977. 3–4.
798. Drever MS 1974. 5; Irvine MS 1974. 7; Leith and Spence 1977. 4–7.
799. Leith and Spence 1977. 7.

46. *Grain Storage and Winnowing*

800. Wallace (1693) 1700. 70; Low (1773) 1923–4. II. 57; Gorrie 1868. 301; Omond *c*. 1912. 14; Marwick 1929.
801. Shirreff 1814 a. 154–5.
802. Fenton 1978, forthcoming.
803. Marwick 1929.
804. Firth (1920) 1974. 23; Marwick 1929.
805. Edmondston 1866; Spence 1899. 172; Omond *c*. 1912. 17.
806. Low (1773) 1923–4. II. 57; Firth (1920) 1974. 22–3; Fenton *MS Notebook:* Fair Isle 1962. 21.
807. Leask 1910. III. 28.
808. Hepburn 1760. 11; OSA 1795. xv. 301; Marwick 1922–3. I. 65; Barry 1805. 351.
809. NSA 1845. xv. 119: Aithsting and Sandsting; Evershed 1874. 198.
810. Fea *MS Diary* 15 Dec. 1766, Nov. 1771; Omond *c*. 1912. 15; Firth (1920) 1974. 25; SND s.v. *rub*.
811. Edmondston 1866; Spence 1899. 182; Junda 1909. II. 79; Marwick 1929; SND s.v. *show*.

47. *Corn Drying and Corn Kilns*

812. Landt 1810. 286.
813. Curwen and Hatt (1946) 1961. 100.

814. *Misc. Abbotsford Club* 1837. I. 182; NSA 1845. XV. 96; Sands 1876–8. XII. 190; Mitchell 1880. 46; Jamieson 1825 s.v. *burston.*
815. Roussell 1934. 54, 56–7, 60, 62–3.
816. Djurhuus (1781–2). 1976. 342; NSA 1845. XV. 119.
817. SND s.v. *kilpinsten.*
818. Spence 1899. 170–1; Venables 1956. 66–7; Fenton *MS Notebook:* Papa Stour 1967.
819. Curle 1939. LXXIII. 95; Roussell 1934. 54, 60–1; Talve 1960. 375–9.
820. SND s.v. *sornie.*
821. Hamre 1950. 55; Rasmussen 1955. 147–8; Lockwood 1955. 20; Matras 1966. I. 795.
822. Talve 1960. 368; Fenton 1974. 251–2.
823. Landt 1810. 290; Hammershaimb 1891. II. s.v. *sodnur*; Williamson 1948. 207; Rasmussen 1955. 137–8, 140, 142.
824. Ropeid 1957. 279; Talve 1960. 279; Fenton 1974. 251.
825. Omond *c.* 1912. 15; Marwick 1929.
826. Marwick 1929; Fenton 1974. 254.
827. Fea *MS Diary.*
828. Firth (1920) 1974. 19.
829. Whitaker 1956–7. I. 168–70.
830. Firth (1920) 1974. 19; Roussell 1934. 92, 96.
831. Hamilton 1956. 190–2.
832. Roussell 1934. 87; Leask *Water Mills*, 197.
833. Gestsson 1959. 32–6, 86.
834. *RCAHMS Orkney and Shetland Inventory* 1946. I. 55–6.
835. *Misc. Abbotsford Club* 1837. I. 137; Fea *MS Diary.*
836. Omond *c.* 1912. 15; Firth (1920) 1974. 23–4.
837. Spence 1899. 191; Firth (1920) 1974. 126.

48. *Grinding the Grain*

838. Calder 1955–6. LXXXIX. 394–5; 1960–1. XCIV. 37, 42; Hamilton 1956. 16, 26; Wainwright 1962. 48–50.
839. Hamilton 1956. 71, 149–50, 182; Piggott 1961. 11.
840. *Misc. Abbotsford Club* 1837. I. 136, 154; Monteith (1633) 1845. 18.
841. Marwick (1698) 1936. I. 5.
842. Clouston 1924–5. III. 50.
843. Begg (1687) 1924–5. III. 63.
844. Low (1773) 1923–4. II. 57; Marwick (1723) 1922–3. I. 65.
845. OSA 1793. VII. 587; NSA 1845. XV. 115.
846. Fenton transcripts.
847. Shirreff 1814 b. 37–8; Clouston 1924–5. III. 71; Firth (1920) 1974. 27; Marwick 1929.
848. Omond *c.* 1912. 22–3; Firth (1920) 1974. 27.
849. Omond *c.* 1912. 23; Firth (1920) 1974. 26; Marwick 1929.
850. Barclay transcripts.
851. Fenton transcripts.
852. Marwick 1922–3. I. 65.
853. Firth (1920) 1974. 26–7; Scott 1968. 72–4.
854. Scott 1968. 75–8; Tulloch 1974. 162–9.
855. Jamieson 1825. s.v. *burston.*
856. Charlton 1913. VI. 179; Omond *c.* 1912. 23; Firth (1920) 1974. 27–8.
857. Spence 1923–4. II. 78.
858. Marwick 1929. s.v. *puffle.*
859. Firth (1920) 1974. 28–9.
860. Curwen 1944. 130 ff; White 1962. 80–1.
861. Lucas 1953; Fahy 1956. 47; Baillie 1975. Vol. 38, 28–30.

862. Brand (1683) 1701. 40.
863. Johnston 1907–13. I. 63–4, 252; Clouston 1924–5. III. 51–2.
864. Clouston 1914. 99–100; Clouston 1924–5. III. 51.
865. *Ib*. 74–5; *Ib*. 52–3.
866. *Oppressions* 1859. 10.
867. Clouston 1924–5. III. 65–70; Barclay 1967. 22; Brand (1683) 1701. 36.
868. Marwick 1922–3. I. 29; Marwick 1939. II. 37.
869. Fea *MS Diary*.
870. OSA 1793. v. 413; 1795. xvi. 262.
871. Clouston 1924–5. III. 71.
872. OSA 1793. v. 413; 1795. xv. 302; 1795. xvi. 262, 426, 455.
873. Leith 1934–5. XIII. 10, and facing.
874. NSA 1845. xv. 16, 46, 90–1, 108, 179, 198, 219–20; Pringle 1874. 33, 45.
875. Ellison MS 1884–1911.
876. Cruden 1946–7. LXXXI. 43–7; Cruden 1949. 1–4; Mrs Leith *Correspondence* 1961.
877. Omond 1909. 75–6; Spence 1909. 129–30.
878. Spence 1909. 130.
879. Scott (1822).
880. Low (1774) 1879. 74.
881. OSA 1793. v. 193–4; Neill 1806. 78; Henderson *c*. 1965. 45.
882. Evershed 1874. 197; Goudie 1886. 275.
883. Williamson 1946. xx. 88.
884. Lucas 1953.
885. Johnston 1910. 9–10.
886. Goudie 1904. 256–265; Firth (1920) 1974. 25; Dickenson and Straker. 1933. 208.
887. Henderson, *Oral information*, 1967.
888. Roussell 1934. 73.
889. Djurhuus 1976. 280; Landt (*c*. 1798) 1810. 293–4.

Root Crops and Gardening

49. *Turnips*

890. Wallace 1693. 35; Gifford (1733) 1786. 24.
891. OSA 1791. I. 386; 1793. VII. 392; 1794. XIII. 281.
892. OSA 1795. XIV. 320; 1795. XVI. 252, 419; 1798. XX. 260.
893. Barry 1805. 45, 358; Neill 1806. 15; Shirreff 1814 a. 74–5.
894. Shirreff 1814 a. 75–80.
895. NSA 1845. xv. 61, 98, 128, 145–6, 160, 164, 182, 184, 222.
896. NSA 1845. xv. 13–14, 21, 29, 47, 65, 79, 120, 163.
897. Hewison (1849–68) 1954. II. 15–16.
898. Farrall 1874. 74, 78, 80–1, 94–5.
899. Lawson (1836) 1842; Pringle 1874. 21, 26, 41–3; Evershed 1874. 213.
900. Feilberg 1910. I. 281.
901. SND s.v. *neep*.
902. Tait *MS Diary* 1923, 1924, 1928.
903. Senior and Swan 1972. 50, Appx. I, Tables 7–8.

50. *The Potato*

904. Low (1774) 1879. 23, 81, 97, 130, 162; Barry 1805. 358.
905. Fea *MS Diary*.
906. Low (1773) 1923–4. II. 57.
907. OSA 1798. xx. 276.

908. Neill 1806. 74; NSA 1845. xv. 144.
909. OSA 1793. vii. 586; 1798. xx. 287; NSA 1845. xv. 118.
910. NSA 1845. xv. 118–19.
911. OSA 1795. xvi. 419, 423; NSA 1845. xv. 89, 164.
912. Edmondston 1806.
913. Stewart, *Information* 1958.
914. Edmondston 1866; Jakobsen (1908) 1928.
915. Hewison 1954. ii. 13–14.
916. NSA 1845. xv. 6; Pringle 1874. 62.
917. Tait *MS Diaries*.
918. Firth (1920) 1974. 98–9; Fenton 1973. 4–5.

51. *Gardening*
919. Wallace (1693) 1883. 35; Gifford (1733) 1786. 24; Fea *MS Diary* 7–8 April; Campbell 1774. 667.
920. *Midbrake Papers* (1823–76), Bundle 3562.

52. *Hay and Grass*
921. Major in Brown 1893. 48; Monipennie (1597) 1603. 5; Monteith (1633) 1845. 51.
922. Monteith (1633) 1845. 4, 6, 8, 12, 15, 37–8, 42, 50, 57, 71–3; Campbell 1774. 690.
923. OSA 1794. x. 195, 197; 1795. xv. 300; 1795. xvi. 417; 1797. xix. 408.
924. Neill 1806. 46–7; Forsyth 1808. v. 41; NSA 1845. xv. 42, 65, 79, 89, 98, 138, 163–4, 182, 222; Høeg 1975. 313, 382, 450.
925. Edmondston 1866.
926. Fea *MS Diary* 12–13, 16 July 1774.
927. SND s.v. *skrivle*.
928. Shirreff 1814 a. 87–9; Farrall 1874. 80.
929. Venables 1956. 23.
930. Jakobsen (1908) 1928.
931. Spence 1923–4. ii. 81.

Cattle and Milk Products

53. *Cattle*
932. NSA 1845. xv. 123, 158; OSA 1793. vii. 393.
933. NSA 1845. xv. 123; Edmondston 1866; SND s.v. *lift*; Wills 1975. 426.
934. Kemp 1801. 5; Shirreff 1814 b. 47; NSA 1845. xv. 164; Edmonston 1866; *Midbrake Papers*, Bundle 388, Folder v, 1 April 1885.
935. OSA 1795. xiv. 131: Firth and Stenness; NSA 1845. xv. 124: Sandsting and Aithsting.
936. NSA 1845. xv. 124.
937. Forsyth 1808. v. 131; Shirreff 1814 b. 60.
938. Shirreff 1814 a. 126–8; Pløyen (1839) 1894. 70; NSA 1845. xv. 23.
939. Cowie 1871. 160.
940. Gifford (1733) 1786. 24; Campbell 1774. 690–1; OSA 1793. vii. 544; 1798. xx. 269: St Andrews and Deerness; Sinclair 1814. iii. 23–45.
941. Shirreff 1814 a. 126; Edmondston 1866; Cowie 1871. 160; Firth (1920) 1974. 120.
942. Edmondston 1866 s.v. *lendit, rieg*; *Shetland News* 4 Sept. 1897; Firth (1920) 1974. 118; Marwick 1929.
943. Spence 1899. 1976; Firth (1920) 1974. 118; SND s.v. *sholmit*.
944. Tait *MS Diaries*.

945. *Misc. Abbotsford Club* 1837. I. 155; Marwick 1923–4. II. 20; Laing 1818. 23; Cowie 1871. 160.
946. *Oppressions* 1859. 68; NSA 1845. xv. 130: Aithsting and Sandsting; Omond *c*. 1912. 4.
947. NSA 1845. xv. 124; Leask *Correspondence* 25 Aug. 1961; SND s.v. *grimek*.
948. Firth (1920) 1974. 105; Marwick 1929; Anderson *Correspondence* 4 Sept. 1961.
949. Farrall 1874. 99; Fenton 1969. 206.
950. Anon. 1750. 17, 23; Shirreff 1814 b. 61.
951. Wallace (1693) 1700. 14; Anon. 1750. 25; Pococke (1760) 1887. 139; Low (1774) 1879. 90; OSA 1798. xx. 251: Evie and Rendall.
952. Fea 1775. 9; OSA 1791. I. 392; 1793. VII. 593.
953. Omond *c*. 1912. 10; Saxby 1932. 172.
954. Edmondston and Saxby 1888. 132.
955. Anon. 1750. 25; Pococke (1760) 1887. 139; OSA 1793. VII. 536: Kirkwall and St Ola; 1795. XVI. 448: Sandwick and Stromness.
956. Shirreff 1814 a. Appx. 53–5.
957. Marwick 1929.
958. Edmondston 1866. s.v. *cutsy*; Jakobsen (1908) 1928 s.v. *söta*; *Svenska Landsmål* 1911. 341; T. 1912. V. 111; Bruce 1912. V. 52; Marwick 1929.
959. Forsyth 1808. V. 131; Shirreff 1814 b. 59; Laing 1818. 23; NSA 1845. xv. 124.
960. Donaldson (1602) 1954. 4–5; Monteith (1633) 1845. 17; OSA 1791. I. 400: Delting; Sinclair 1795. 248; Shirreff 1814 b. 60.
961. Monipennie 1818. 194.
962. Fenton 1975. 64, 69–70.
963. *Ib*. 70.
964. Groundwater MS.
965. Marwick 1929; Tait 1947. I. 87.
966. Omond *c*. 1912. 12; Firth (1920) 1974. 62.
967. Major in Brown 1893. 48; Brand (1683) 1701. 20; Fea 1775. 32–3; Low (*c*. 1795) 1813. 3; Forsyth 1808. v. 131; Marwick 1936. I. 148.
968. Fea *MS Diary*.
969. *Oppressions* 1859. 72.
970. Mackaile in Barry 1805. 449; Shirreff 1814 b. 60–1; SND (1838); NSA 1845. xv. 124; Spence 1923–4. II. 78.
971. Marwick (1747) 1933–4. XII. 51; SND (1838) s.v.; Firth (1920) 1974. 103.
972. Groundwater MS.
973. Low (1773) 1923–4. II. 54.
974. *Misc. Abbotsford Club 1837*. I. 144, 152.
975. Marwick 1922–3. I. 65; Marwick 1929.
976. Marwick 1933–4. XII. 51–2.
977. Monteith (1633) 1845. 47; Martin (*c*. 1695) 1884. 374; Anon. 1750. 16–17; Sinclair 1795. 248; DOST s.v. *bland*; NSA 1845. xv. 125: Standsting and Aithsting; Edmondston and Saxby 1888. 101; Saxby 1914. 70; Marwick 1929; Miss Wilson, *Information* 1963; Eunson 1976. 32.
978. Edmondston 1866; Saxby 1932. 167.
979. Jamieson 1825; Edmondston 1866; Edmondston and Saxby 1888. 101; Jakobsen (1908) 1928; Saxby 1914. XII. 71; Saxby 1932. 166–7; Eunson 1976. 32.

Sheep and Textiles

54. *Native Sheep and New Breeds*

980. Ryder 1967–8. 33; 1968. 130, 132–3, 140; Henshall 1963. 40.
981. *Misc. Maitland Club* (1604) 1840. II. 154: Whiteness and Weisdale; *Deeds* 1840. 10–12; Marwick 1939. II. 30.

982. Boece (1527) in Brown 1893. 92; Monipennie (1597) 1603. 10; Wallace (1693) 1700. 36; Martin (*c*. 1695) 1884. 355, 377; Irvine Sheep Book MS. 1829–77. 21.

983. OSA 1791. I. 393.

984. Neill 1792. 147; Marwick 1923. I. 65; O'Dell 1939. 55.

985. OSA 1795. XIV. 128; 1796. XVII. 314–15; NSA 1845. xv. 7, 99, 164; Farrall 1874. 84.

986. NSA 1845. xv. 28, 127–8; Shirreff 1814 b. 66.

987. Evershed 1874. 187, 207, 209–11, 214–15; Greig 1892. 13; O'Dell 1939. 31, 42.

988. Shirreff 1814 a. 133–4; Pringle 1874. 15, 20, 28, 43.

989. Monteith (1633) 1845. 46; Martin (*c*. 1695) 1884. 386; Anon. 1750. 25.

990. Evershed 1874. 207.

991. Tudor 1883. 158.

992. Jakobsen (1908) 1928.

993. OSA 1794. XII. 360: Northmavine.

994. Gifford (1733) 1786. 25; Hepburn 1760. 12.

995. Shirreff 1814 b. 63, Appx. 45; Eunson 1976. 38.

996. Cf. Shirreff 1814 b. 66–7.

997. NSA 1845. xv. 127–8; Jakobsen (1908) 1928.

998. Edmondston 1809. II. 223–4; Sinclair 1795. Appx. 31; Shirreff 1814 b. 65–6.

999. Laurenson *MS Notebook* 1965.

1000. *Misc. Maitland Club* 1840. II. 160, 162, 175; Monteith (1633) 1845. 22; Brand (1683) 1701. 76; Firth 1908. I. 307; Spence 1910. III. 25.

1001. *Misc. Maitland Club* (1612–23) 1840. II. 161, 174, 198; Monteith (1633) 1845. 22, 60; Brand (1683) 1701. 19; Wallace (1693) 1700. 72–3; Hibbert 1822. 437.

1002. Pococke (1760) 1887. 139; Brownrigg and Gaunt 1965. 47.

1003. Fea 1775. 34; OSA 1791. I. 392: Delting; 1795. XIV. 128: Firth and Stenness; NSA 1845. xv. 126.

1004. OSA 1793. v. 410: Holm; 1793. VII. 545: Kirkwall and St Ola; NSA 1845. xv. 183.

1005. NSA 1845. xv. 15, 126; Charlton (1832). VI. 190.

1006. Farrall 1874. 83.

1007. Monteith (1633) 1845. 46; Marwick 1936. I. 121.

1008. Brand (1683) 1700. 132; Wallace (1693) 1700. 14; Pococke (1760) 1887. 139; Low (1774) 1879. 51, 53; OSA 1798. xx. 263; Forsyth 1808. v. 141 in *Report* 1914. 15.

1009. Low (1774) 1879. 67–8, 103, 142; OSA 1793. III. 419.

1010. Fea 1775. 9; Fea 1787. 75; Knox 1789. 139.

1011. Fea 1787. 80; OSA 1793. VII. 396: Dunrossness.

1012. *Scotland Delineated* 1791. 32; OSA 1793. VII. 396: Dunrossness; 1793. VII. 588: Aithsting and Sandsting.

1013. OSA 1795. XVI. 434, 448.

1014. OSA 1794. x. 198: Bressay, Burra and Quarff; 1794. XII. 358, 364: Northmavine; 1795. XIV. 651: Fair Isle; 1795. xx. 280: Foula.

1015. OSA 1795. XIV. 319. 324–6.

1016. Kemp 1801. 10–13; Wilson 1842. II. 405; NSA 1845. xv. 116.

1017. Forsyth 1808. v. 93; NSA 1845. xv. 16, 21, 47, 76, 129; Evershed 1874. 198.

1018. *Report* 1914. 20; Nicolson 1931. 17.

1019. Edmondston 1809. I. 224; *Report* 1914. 36–7.

1020. Edmondston 1809. I. 224; Tudor 1883. 60; *Report* 1914. 37–8, 53.

1021. Angus 1914; *Report* 1914. 83–4.

1022. *Report* 1914. 85–6.

1023. Marwick 1922–3. I. 55–6.

1024. Barry 1867. xviii; Pringle 1874. 15; Firth (1920) 1974. 109; Marwick 1929; SND s.v. *cairie, keerie*.

1025. OSA 1793. VII. 471; Tudor 1883. 363.

1026. Marwick 1922–3. I. 90–1; Firth 1908. I. 307; *Misc. Maitland Club* 1840. II. 197.

1027. Firth 1907–8. I. 309; Omond *c*. 1912. 7.

1028. Tribe 1950. 107.

1029. Spence 1910. III. 22–7.

1030. Spence 1910. III, facing 24.

1031. Muir, *Oral information c.* 1963.

1032. Wallace (1693) 1883. 42; OSA 1793. VII. 544: Kirkwall and St Ola.

1033. Wilson 1842. II. 322; Donaldson 1954. 2, 51, 132, 134; Barclay 1967. 30.

1034. Jakobsen (1908) 1928; Bruce 1912. 52; Marwick 1929.

1035. *Northmavine Marks MS*; Marwick 1929.

1036. *Register of Marks.* 3–4, 6.

1037. Equal to 'Shetland': see Fenton 1973. Table I.

1038. Debes 1676; see also Tait 1954.

1039. *Oppressions* 1859. 67.

1040. Donaldson 1954. 7, 25, 53, 59, 92–3, 112, 117, 122, etc.

1041. Barclay 1962. 20–2.

1042. *Shetland Times* 19 April 1968.

1043. Firth 1907–8. I. 210.

1044. Johnston 1907–8. I. 164.

1045. Headrick 1807. 323–4; Donaldson 1954. 127.

1046. Pococke (1760) 1887. 140; Jakobsen (1908) 1928.

1047. Johnston 1911. IV. 4–5.

1048. *Ib.* 4–5.

1049. *Reg. Testaments* 11 May 1681, IX. Folio 16.

1050. Pococke (1760) 1887. 140; Firth 1907–8. I. 210.

1051. Johnston 1911. IV. 4–5.

1052. Marwick 1929.

1053. Smith 1913. VI. 4.

1054. Edmondston 1866; Spence 1899. 176; Jakobsen (1908) 1928; Angus 1914.

1055. *Irvine Sheep Book* 1829–77. 5.

1056. Johnston 1911. IV. 4.

1057. Jakobsen (1908) 1928.

1058. Firth 1907–8. I. 210; Firth (1920) 1974. 112; Marwick 1929 s.v. *aithken.*

1059. *General List* 1781; Freyr 1958. 136.

1060. Jamieson 1825; Maxwell 1880. 6; Johnston 1911. IV. 4; *Almanak* 1911. 81, Plate; Freyr 1958. 133; *Seyðamark* 1964. 4.

1061. Johnston 1907–8. I. 55; *Almanak* 1911. Plate; Freyr 1958. 135.

1062. Johnston 1907–8. I. 56; *Almanak* 1911. 81, Plate; Firth (1920) 1974. 110; Freyr 1958. 133; *Register of Marks* 9.

1063. *Almanak* 1911. 81, Plate; Freyr 1958. 133; *Seyðamark* 1964. 4.

1064. Jakobsen 1909 in Ryder 1965–6. 96; *Almanak* 1911. Plate.

1065. *Almanak* 1911. Plate; Anderson *Notebook* 1912–14. No. 2; Freyr 1958. 135.

1066. Firth 1907–8. I. 210.

1067. *Ib.*

1068. Pococke (1760) 1887. 140; *Northmavine Marks* MS. 1763; *Register of Marks* 5; Angus 1914 s.v. *kruk.*

1069. Johnston 1907–8. I. 56: Orphir.

1070. *Northmavine Marks MS.*, Eshaness, *c.* 1760, 1787, 1797.

1071. Jakobsen (1908) 1928.

1072. *Northmavine Marks MS.* 1789.

1073. Edmondston 1866.

1074. Edmondston 1866; Jakobsen (1908) 1928; Johnston 1911. IV. 4: Nesting; Angus 1914; *Register of Marks* 2.

1075. Djurhuus (1781–2) 1976, facing 232; Jakobsen 1909 in Ryder 1965–6. 96; *Almanak* 1911, Plate; Freyr 1958. 133.

1076. Jakobsen (1908) 1928; Angus 1914; Edmondston 1866.

1077. *Northmavine Marks MS* 1742, *c*. 1748; *Register of Marks* 1; Johnston 1911. IV. 4: Nesting.

1078. Johnston 1907–8. I. 165: Orphir; Spence 1910. III. facing 24; Johnston 1911. IV. 5; *Almanak* 1911, Plate; Firth (1920) 1974. 110; Freyr 1958. 133.

1079. *Register of Marks* 2, 14.

1080. Jakobsen (1908) 1928; Angus 1914.

1081. Irvine MSS. 395/1; *Irvine Sheep Book MS*. 1829–77; *Register of Marks* 5; Jakobsen (1908) 1928.

1082. Eunson 1976. 37.

1083. Marwick 1929.

1084. SND (*c*. 1838).

1085. Johnston 1907–8. I. 164; Marwick 1929.

1086. Djurhuus (1781–2) 1976, facing 230; Jakobsen (1908) 1928; *Almanak* 1911, Plate; Freyr 1958. 133.

1087. *Irvine MSS*. 395/4/2.

1088. Djurhuus (1781–2) 1976, facing 230; *Irvine Sheep Book MS* (1844) 1829–77. 95; Firth (1920) 1974. 110; Freyr 1958. 133; Berg 1966–7. 25.

1089. Edmondston 1866.

1090. Johnston 1907–8. I. 164: Orphir.

1091. *Irvine Sheep Book MS* 1829. 5; *Ib*. (1846) 114; Jakobsen (1908) 1928.

1092. Pococke (1760) 1887. 140.

1093. *Northmavine Marks MS* 1741, 1742; Pococke (1760) 1887. 140; Djurhuus (1781–2) 1976, facing 230 and 232; *Almanak* 1911, Plate; Anderson *MS Notebooks* No. 2. 1912–14.

1094. Johnston 1911. IV. 4.

1095. *Ib*.

1096. Djurhuus (1781–2) 1976, facing 232; *Register of Marks* 27; Spence 1910. III, facing 24; *Almanak* 1911, 81, Plate; Freyr 1958. 133; *Seyðamark* 1964. 4.

1097. Johnston (1813) 1911. IV. 4–5: Holm; Firth (1920) 1974. 110; Marwick 1929; Eunson 1976. 36.

1098. Spence 1910. III, facing 24.

1099. *Register of Marks* 1; *Almanak* 1911, Plate; Freyr 1958. 134; *Seyðamark* 1964. 3.

1100. Marwick 1929 s.v. *klow-sheer*.

1101. *Irvine Papers* 395/4/1; Djurhuus (1781–2) 1976, facing 230; Edmondston 1866; *Almanak* 1911. Plate; Freyr 1958. 134; *Seyðamark* 1964. 3.

1102. *Northmavine Marks MS*.

1103. Mackintosh (1808) 1887. 225; Johnston 1907–8. I. 56, 165; Marwick 1929.

1104. *Northmavine Marks MS* 1795; Hibbert (1822) 1891. 185; Freyr 1958. 135.

1105. Djurhuus (1781–2) 1976, facing 230; Edmondston 1866; *Almanak* 1911, Plate; Marwick 1929; Freyr 1958. 134; *Seyðamark* 1964. 3; Berg 1966–7. 24.

1106. *Register of Marks* 29; Edmondston 1866; Johnston 1911. IV. 4: Nesting; Jakobsen (1908) 1928; Angus 1914; Eunson 1976. 37.

1107. *Irvine Sheep Book MS* 1829–77. 5.

1108. Pococke (1760) 1887. 140.

1109. *Irvine Sheep Book MS* 1829–77. 37.

1110. *Register of Marks* 2, 10.

1111. *Ib*. 22; Johnston (1742) 1907–8. I. 55: Stromness; Eunson 1976. 36: Fair Isle.

55. *The Linen Trade in Orkney*

1112. Low (1774) 1879. 178; Wills 1975. 96–7.

1113. *Misc. Abbotsford Club* 1837. I. 174; Hepburn 1760. 13; Pococke (1760) 1887. 144.

1114. Low (1774) 1879. 50–1, 81; Fea 1775. 9, 46; Knox (1784) 1789. 140; Fea 1787. 76.

1115. OSA 1793, V. 408, 413; 1793, VII. 485, 536–8; 1794, XVII. 228–239; 1795. XIV. 134, 324, Appx. 651; 1795, XVI. 262, 434, 447–8; 1797. XIX. 405, 418.

1116. Barry 1805. 26, 34, 368–71.

1117. Shirreff 1814a. 46–55, 89.
1118. NSA 1845. xv. 65, 152.

Pigs, Rabbits and Geese

56. *Pigs*
1119. *Oppressions* 1859. 4, 46, 48; Monteith (1633) 1845, 47; Forsyth 1808, v. 63; Shirreff 1814a. 56, 145–6; 1814b. 67.
1120. Donaldson 1954. 115; Barclay (1615) 1967. 66; Marwick 1923–4. II. 20; Pococke (1760) 1887. 139; Farrall 1874. 86; Buckley and Harvie-Brown 1891.
1121. NSA 1845. xv. 128; Edmondston 1866; *Shetland News* 24 Dec. 1898; Jakobsen (1908) 1928; Marwick 1929; Laurenson MS 1967. 7.
1122. OSA 1793. v. 188; 1793. VII. 339, 471, 546, 595; 1795. XIV. 131, 416; 1795. XVI. 260, 430; 1796. XVIII. 314; 1797. XIX. 405; 1798. XX. 107, 251, 265.
1123. Wallace (1693) 1700. 14; Martin (c. 1695) 1884. 357; OSA 1795. XVI. 460; Shirreff 1814a. Appx. 53–5.
1124. NSA 1845. xv. 89, 128, 158, 168.
1125. NSA 1845. xv. 99, 164–5, 183; O'Dell 1939. 101; Scarth and Watt 1939. 20; Senior and Swan 1972. 50.
1126. Fenton 1973. 10–11.
1127. Edmondston MS 1970. 9; Fenton 1973. 104.
1128. Høeg 1975. 523; SND s.v. *murr*.
1129. Edmondston 1866; Jakobsen (1908) 1928.
1130. Laurenson MS 1972. 7.

57. *Rabbits*
1131. Wallace (1693) 1700. 10, 14, 36; Mackaile in Barry 1805. 449; Martin (c. 1695) 1884. 355, 357; Hepburn 1760. 18; Pococke (1760) 1887. 139; Low (1774) 1879. 42: OSA 1793. VII. 536: Kirkwall and St Ola; OSA 1795. XVI. 448: Sandwick and Stromness.
1132. *Misc. Maitland Club* 1840. II. 153; Barry 1805. 315–16.
1133. Fea *MS Diary*.
1134. Shirreff 1814a. 146–7, Appx. 53–5.
1135. NSA 1845. xv. 91, 164; Pringle 1874. 46.

58. *Geese*
1136. Anon. 1750. 25; Pococke (1760) 1887. 139; OSA 1795. XVI. 448; Shirreff 1814a. 147–8, Appx. 53–5.
1137. Marwick (1734) 1922–3. I. 65; Wilson 1842. II. 247; NSA 1845. xv. 142; Farrall 1874. 86; Pringle 1874. 10, 16.
1138. Pringle 1874. 158, 168; Evershed 1874. 209; Jakobsen (1908) 1928; Marwick 1929; Sabiston *Letter* Nov. 1961.
1139. Edmondston 1866; Jakobsen (1908) 1928; Miller 1967. Vol. 11, 218.
1140. Edmondston and Saxby 1888. 98; Scott 1968. 143; Fenton *MS Notebook*, Fetlar. 1963. 38.
1141. Højrup 1964. 109–15; Rasmussen 1966–7. 297; Genrup 1975.

The Shore and the Sea

59. *Wild Fowl*
1142. Johnston 1907–13. 210; Boece in Brown 1893. 92; Monipennie (1597) 1603. 3; *Misc. Maitland Club* (1615) 1840. II. 172.
1143. Monteith (1633) 1845. 8, 18, 23; Mackaile in Barry 1805. 449–50.

1144. Monteith (1633) 1845. 2, 41, 51; Mackaile in Barry 1805. 453; Donaldson, *Oral information* 1977.

1145. Brand (1683) 1701. 32; Wallace (1693) 1700. 14, 19, 73–4; Lockwood 1961. 32.

1146. Storå 1968. 164 ff.; see also Storå 1975. 128–242, for a description of a surviving but never used example in the Sjöhistoriska Museum in Turku, Finland.

1147. Brand (*c*. 1683) 1701–3. 23, 94; Martin (*c*. 1695) 1884. 374.

1148. Sibbald 1711. 5, 12, 15–16;Venables 1958. 110.

1149. Sibbald 1711. 22, 24, 31.

1150. Anon. 1750. 10–11.

1151. Anon. 1750. 46–7; Fea 1787. 91; OSA 1798. xx. 103–4, 264.

1152. Brand (1683) 1700. 153; Hibbert 1822. 418; Storå 1968. 167 ff.

1153. Fea 1787. 91; Laurenson, *Information* 1964.

1154. Knox 1789. 140; OSA 1793. vii. 536: Kirkwall and St Ola; 1795. vii. 447: Sandwick and Stromness; 1796. xvii. 322; 1798. xx. 100; Kemp 1801. 17; Forsyth 1808. v. 106–7; Edmondston 1809. ii. 20.

1155. NSA 1845. xv. 149.

1156. Lockwood 1961. 26.

1157. Neill 1806. 24–5; Nature Notes, *Orcadian* 23 Sept. 1971; Laurenson *Information* 1964.

1158. Edmondston 1809. ii. 253–4, 257–8.

1159. Shirreff 1814 a. Appx. 60.

1160. Shirreff 1814 a. Appx. 59; Jakobsen (1908) 1928; Angus 1914.

1161. Edmondston 1809. ii. 276–7; Henderson *Correspondence* 8 March 1972.

1162. Shirreff 1814 a. Appx. 59; Marwick 1929.

1163. Djurhuus (1781–2) 1976. 30; Edmondston 1809. ii. 274; Fraser 1863. 288; Saxby 1874. 312; Russell 1887. 69; Annandale 1905. 104, 112; Kolsrud 1976. 25, 27–30.

1164. Pennant 1784. i. xxix; OSA 1795. xx. 264; Jamieson 1825; Maxwell 1844. i. 248–9; Maxwell (*c*. 1840) 1853. 129–30; Edmondston 1866.

1165. Troup *Correspondence* 8 Aug. 1973.

1166. Trémarec 1792. 49; Annandale 1805. 98.

1167. Baldwin 1974. 65.

1168. M(arwick) 15 May 1975.

1169. Mooney 1972. 4; Hillson 1973. 36; Troup *Correspondence* 8 Aug. 1973.

1170. Mooney 1972. 4; Troup *Correspondence* 8 Aug. 1973.

1171. Dunn 1937. 88.

1172. Williamson 1946. 17.

1173. Marwick 1929; Lockwood 1961. 26.

1174. Marwick 1924–5. iii. 42; Marwick 1929.

1175. Williamson 1946. 19; Troup *Correspondence* July 1975.

1176. Carter *Correspondence* April 1977.

1177. *Scotsman*(?) 30 March 1863 in Irvine *Shet. Hist. Colls.* iii. 282–97; Lockhart 1902. iv. 207.

1178. *Shetland Times* Jan. 1876 in Irvine *Shet. Hist Colls.* iii. 342.

1179. Henderson *Correspondence* 8 March 1972.

1180. Laurenson *Letter* 13 Feb. 1964.

1181. Edmondston 1809. ii. 271.

60. *Seals and Otters*

1182. Mackaile in Barry 1805. 454; Low (1774) 1879. 1; OSA 1795. xvi. 436; Tudor 1883. 207.

1183. *Misc. Maitland Club* 1840. ii. 149; OSA 1793. vii. 454; Barry 1805. 317; Edmondston 1809. ii. 292–3; NSA 1845. xv. 106; Stoklund *et al*. 1960. v. 203, 205; Vilkuna *et al*. 1972. xvii. 690–1.

1184. Edmondston 1809. ii. 292; Edmondston and Saxby 1888. 107–15.

1185. Martin (*c*. 1695) 1884. 357; Knox 1789. 140; Shirreff 1814 a. Appx. 53–5.

1186. Brand (1683) 1701. 16; Martin (*c*. 1695) 1884. 369; Anon. 1750. 6; Barry 1805. 317; Dunn 1837. 13.
1187. Monteith (1633) 1845. 75; Low (1774) 1879. 197; Vilkuna *et al*. 1972. xvii. 695, 698.
1188. Brand (1683) 1701. 44; Barry 1805. 317; Edmondston and Saxby 1888. 121; Vilkuna *et al*. 1972. xvii. 698.
1189. Thompson, *Oral information* 1969; Yourston, *Oral information* 1972.
1190. Leask 1967–8. i. 320.
1191. Low (1774) 1879. 102; *Scots Magazine* May 1818. 429; Hibbert 1822. 586; Tudor 1883. 414; Marwick 1929.
1192. Tudor 1883. 365; Black 1903. 179 ff.; Dennison 1961. 61–6; Marwick 1975. 27–9, 113, 152–6.
1193. Wallace (1693) 1700. 14; Martin (*c*. 1695) 1884. 357; *Gentleman* 1758–9. 6–7; Low (1774) 1879. 129: Meikle Roe; Knox 1789. 140; Barry 1805. 317; Shirreff 1814 a. Appx. 55; Edmondston 1866; Venables 1956. 97.
1194. Russell 1887. 160; Venables 1956. 97; Laurenson *Letter* 13 Feb. 1964.
1195. Russell 1887. 160–1.

61. *Sillock, Piltock and Dogfish*
1196. James (*c*. 1614–18) 1953. i. 50.
1197. Firth (1920) 1974. 102.
1198. Morton Papers in Goodlad 1971. 77; Brand (1683) 1701. 74, 130, 135.
1199. Anon. 1750. 23–4; OSA 1791. i. 389–90: Delting; Edmondston 1809. i. 287; Shirreff 1814 a. Appx. 53–5; Goodlad 1971. 119.
1200. Brand (1683) 1701. 20, 135; Martin (*c*. 1695) 1884. 368.
1201. Low (1774) 1879. 19, 28–9, 197.
1202. Anon. 1787. 64, 66–7.
1203. Goodlad 1971. 138.
1204. Nicolson 1907. 64.
1205. Edmondston and Saxby 1888. 301.
1206. Scott 1968. 93–4.
1207. Laurenson *Information*.
1208. OSA 1791. i. 384–5; 1793. iii. 416; 1793. v. 190; 1794. x. 196; 1794. xii. 354.
1209. OSA 1793. v. 411; 1793. vii. 453; 1795. xiv. 138, 314; 1795. xvi. 260–1, 436; 1796. xvii. 239; 1797. xix. 398–9; 1798. xx. 263.
1210. Barry 1805. 27, 296; Neill 1806. 61–2, 78.
1211. NSA 1845. xv. 193–4, 220, 224.
1212. NSA 1845. xv. 22, 74, 88, 121–2, 160, 162–3.
1213. NSA 1845. xv. 58, 96, 101, 108, 171.
1214. Jakobsen (1908) 1928; Leask 1931. 280; Marwick 1929; Goodlad 1971. 38, 278–9.
1215. OSA 1792. ii. 574; Spence 1899. 34; *Shetland News* 21 Oct. 1899.
1216. Edmondston 1866; Spence 1899. 32; Jakobsen (1908) 1928.
1217. Monteith (1633) 1845. 23; Saxby 1932. 201; *New Shetlander* June–July 1947. 2.
1218. Edmondston and Saxby 1888. 299; Jakobsen (1908) 1928.
1219. Edmondston and Saxby 1888. 299; Tait 1955. 20, 26.
1220. Marwick 1929.
1221. Neill 1806. 92; *New Shetlander* June–July 1947. 2.
1222. Edmondston and Saxby 1888. 297–8.
1223. Robertson 1923–4. ii. 45.
1224. NSA 1845. xv. 122; Edmondston and Saxby 1888. 299; Barnard 1890, Plate xvii; Ellison MS 1884–1911; Marwick 1929; Venables 1956. 116.
1225. Edmondston and Saxby 1888. 299–300; Venables 1956. 116.
1226. Barnard 1890, Plate xvii.
1227. Edmondston and Saxby 1888. 300–1.

1228. Ellison MS 1884–1911.
1229. Fenton 1973. Vol. 17, 77–8.
1230. Edmondston and Saxby 1888. 302–3.
1231. Firth (1920) 1974. 101–2; Fenton 1975. 12.

62. *Shellfish and Lobsters*
1232. Peterkin 1820. II. 102; Mackaile in Barry 1805. 453; Wallace (1693) 1700. 42; Low (1774) 1879. 11; OSA 1794. x. 202; 1798. xx. 263; Barry 1805. 287; Neill 1806. 18; Tudor 1883. 104, 291; Peace *a.*1911. 110.
1233. NSA 1845. xv. 101; Edmondston 1820. 16; Edmondston 1866; McIntosh 1875. 62; Jakobsen (1908) 1928; Marwick 1929; Fenton 1978, forthcoming; SND s.v. *mussel*.
1234. Low (1774) 1879. 20; OSA 1798. xx. 263; Barry 1805. 286–7.
1235. Wallace (1693) 1700. 46.
1236. Low (1774) 1879. 159.
1237. Leask (1809) 1907–8. I. 320; Tudor 1883. 613; SND s.v. *wulk*.
1238. Barry 1805. 287; Hossack 1900. 147; Black 1903. 267; Leask 1907–8. I. 320; Fraser 1923–4. II. 29; *Press and Journal* 5 Feb. 1960.
1239. Barry 1805. 286; Goodlad 1971. 297–8; Miller 1976. 156–7.
1240. Low (1774) 1879. 20, 49; OSA 1795. xvI. 436; 1796. xvII. 319; 1797. xIx. 399–400.
1241. OSA 1798. xx. 99; Barry 1805. 40, 43, 52, 54, 58, 286.
1242. Forsyth 1808. v. 106; Wilson 1842. II. 230; NSA 1845. xv. 22, 31–2, 100, 164–5.
1243. Anderson 1834; Tudor 1883. 104; Goodlad 1971. 291–8; Miller 1976. 156–7.
1244. Edmondston 1809. I. 290.
1245. Thomas n.d. 7, 9; Fenton *MS Notebook:* North Ronaldsay 1964. 9–10.

63. *Whales and Whaling*
1246. Leslie 1578 in Brown 1893. 159.
1247. Gifford (1733) 1786.
1248. Edmondston 1809. II. 155–9; Johnston 1911. Iv. 119.
1249. Edmondston 1809. II. 159–74.
1250. Wills 1975. 12–15.
1251. Nicolson 1972. 169.
1252. OSA 1793. v. 190; Hibbert 1822. 421–4.
1253. Wilson 1842. II. 242.
1254. NSA 1845. xv. 88–9, 148–9, 163; Williamson (1948) 1970. 95–119; Rasmussen 1955. 26–7; Joensen 1976. 5–42.
1255. Gorrie 1868. 215–27; also in Gunn 1909. 242–7.
1256. Tudor 1883. 210–11, 283, 383, 490, 544.
1257. *Shetland Journal* 17 Nov. 1928; Williamson (1948) 1970. 116.
1258. Hibbert 1822. 425; NSA 1845. xv. 148; Tudor 1883. 415.
1259. Troup and Eunson 1967. 5–7.
1260. O'Dell 1939. 139–40; Nicolson 1972. 169; Wills 1975. 429–36.
1261. O'Dell 1939. 139–40; Troup and Eunson 1967. 7; Nicolson 1972. 169–70.
1262. O'Dell 1939. 140–1; Gordon 1959. 27–8; Anon. 1972. 12; Nicolson 1972. 170.
1263. Nicolson 1972. 171.

64. *Fishing Boats from Norway*
1264. Hamilton 1956. 114–15, Pl. xxI, 1, 2, 3, 4, 116; Koht 1962. 112–13.
1265. *Oppressions* 1859. 7, 66; Monipennie (1597) 1603. 9; Halcrow 1950. 68; Thowsen 1969. 149.
1266. Thowsen 1969. 149–50.
1267. *Misc Maitland Club* 1840. II. 150, 152; Clouston 1914. 265; Edmondston 1866.

1268. Monteith (1633) 1845. 23–4, 78; Terry 1902. 125.

1269. Brand (1683) 1701–3. 5, 73–4.

1270. Marwick 1926–7. v. 15; 1939. ii. 12, 53–9.

1271. Bruce 1931. xvii. 371; Halcrow 1950. 68; Thowsen 1969. 152–3, 155.

1272. Anon. 1750. 22–3; Anon. 1750 b. 13–15; Low (1774) 1879. 11, 79, 132–3, 141; Clouston 1914. 377; Anon. 1787. 36; Smyth 1929. 117–20.

1273. Fea *MS Diary*.

1274. OSA 1795. xiv. 107–8, 322.

1275. Thowsen 1969. 155–6.

1276. Bruce 1914. iv. 296.

1277. Sandison 1954. 11; Henderson 1969. 12.

1278. Pløyen (1839) 1894. 3–4, 23–4; Sandison 1954. 11; Henderson 1969. 12–13.

1279. OSA 1791. i. 387–8: Delting; 1793. iii. 415; 1793. v. 191; 1793. vii. 397, 589; 1794. x. 196; 1794. xii. 351, 358; 1795. xiv. 651; 1798. xx. 99, 102.

1280. OSA 1793. vii. 338; 1795. xiv. 319, 322, 325; 1796. xvii. 238–9, 319; 1797. xix. 399; 1798. xx. 252; Neill 1806. 61–2.

1281. Forsyth 1808. v. 140; Wilson 1842. ii. 279.

1282. NSA 1845. xv. 78–9, 173–4.

1283. *Ib*. 30–3.

1284. *Ib*. 4, 15, 46, 130.

65. *Yoles and Sixerns: Construction and Terminology*

1285. Smith (1633) 1673. vi. 256; *Description* 1907. 8–9, 41; Brand (1683) 1700. 73, 84–5, 128.

1286. Low (1774) 1879. 133; *Midbrake Papers*, Bundle 392; Sinclair 1795. 242; Shirreff 1814 b. 88; Halcrow 1950. 68.

1287. *Midbrake Papers*, Bundle 388, Folder vii.

1288. *Ib*.

1289. Shirreff 1814 b. 90.

1290. Henderson 1969. No. 89. 13–15; Goodlad 1971. 104.

1291. Shirreff 1814 b. Appx. 53; Laurenson 1962. No. 63. 21; 1963. No. 64. 25; 1963. No. 65. 22; 1963. No. 66. 8; WSI 1964. No. 71. 13–15; Henderson 1969. No. 91. 8–10; Laurenson 1965. No. 73. 17–18.

1292. Smith 1882–3. xvii. 298.

1293. Marwick 1929.

1294. Edmondston 1866.

1295. Jakobsen (1908) 1928; Spence 1910. iii. 37; Marwick 1929; Laurenson *MS Notebook*.

1296. Edmondston 1866.

1297. Sandison 1968. 12.

1298. Jakobsen (1908) 1928; Angus 1914.

1299. Edmondston 1866; Jakobsen (1908) 1928; Angus 1914; Marwick 1929.

1300. Edmondston 1866; Jakobsen (1908) 1928; Marwick 1929.

1301. Edmondston 1866; Bruce 1913. vi. 35; POAS xii. 50.

1302. Edmondston 1866; Jakobsen (1908) 1928; Angus 1914.

1303. Eunson 1976. 2.

1304. Marwick 1929.

1305. Edmondston 1866; SND s.v. *hinnie-spot*.

1306. Marwick 1929; Eunson 1976. 3.

1307. Edmondston 1866; Jakobsen (1908) 1928; Marwick 1929.

1308. Marwick 1929.

1309. Edmondston 1866; Jakobsen (1908) 1928; Angus 1914; Marwick 1929.

1310. Anson 1950. 100; Sandison 1954. 19.

1311. Edmondston 1866; Spence 1899. 137; Jakobsen (1908) 1928; Angus 1914; Marwick 1929; Sandison 1954. 19; Eunson 1976. 3–5.

1312. Christensen 1968. 49; Eunson 1976. 5; Thowsen 1969. 166 ff.

66. *Haaf Fishing*

1313. Edmondston 1809. I. 232–3; O'Dell 1939. 192; Wills 1975. 272 a.
1314. Tait 1947. 111–13.
1315. Trémarec 1772. 101; Anon. 1787. 37; Bruce 1931. 361, 365–6, 368, 370–1; Goodlad 1971. 94–5.
1316. Low (1774) 1879. 102, 120, 123, 133–4, 137–9, 141–2, 170; Donaldson 1954. 21.
1317. Anon. 1787. 39–42.
1318. *Ib*. 53–4, 56.
1319. Marwick 1929.
1320. Anon. 1787. 48–50, 57.
1321. OSA 1791. I. 387–9, 391–2, 394–5; 1793. III. 418; 1793. VII. 394, 397.
1322. OSA 1793. v. 190–1; 1793. VII. 583, 587, 589, 593; 1794. x. 196–7, 201.
1323. OSA 1794. XII. 351, 358–61; 1796. XVII. 499; 1798. xx. 99, 102, 280; Laurenson *MS Notebook*.
1324. OSA 1795. XVI. 435; 1796. XVII. 319.
1325. Kemp 1801. 8–10.
1326. Kemp 1801. 34; Edmondston 1809. I. 294 ff.; Hibbert 1822. 515–8; Goodlad 1971. 96–9; Wills 1975. 113.
1327. Edmondston 1809. I. 234–6.
1328. Low (1773) 1923–4. II. 54; Hibbert 1822. 509.
1329. Edmondston 1809. I. 238–40; Hibbert 1822. 510–11; Jakobsen (1908) 1928; Angus 1914; Laurenson *MS Notebook*.
1330. Edmondston 1866; Jakobsen (1908) 1928.
1331. Hibbert 1822. 510; Smith 1882–3. XVII. 297–8.
1332. Edmondston 1866; Tudor 1883. 132; Jakobsen (1908) 1928; Spence 1910. III. 36.
1333. Laurenson *MS Notebook*.
1334. Spence 1899. 134; Halcrow 1950. 70–2; Inkster, *Oral information*; Laurenson *MS Notebook*.
1335. Jakobsen (1908) 1928; Halcrow 1950. 71.
1336. Eunson 1976. 3.
1337. Spence 1899. 127; Spence 1910. III. 36–7; POAS. XII. 48; Halcrow 1950. 69.
1338. Hibbert 1822. 513.
1339. *Ib*. 240–1.
1340. Edmondston 1809. I. 241–52.
1341. Anon. 1787. 57–62.
1342. *Ib*.; Shirreff 1814 b. 90–1; Hibbert 1822. 519–20.
1343. Laurenson *MS Notebook*.
1344. Anon. 1787. 39; Donaldson 1954. 8.
1345. NSA 1845. xv. 170–2.
1346. *Ib*. 130–2; Laurenson *MS Notebook*.
1347. NSA 1845. xv. 4, 15, 30, 44, 46, 58, 60, 67, 78–9, 94, 96.
1348. Mather 1964. 19–21; Goodlad 1971. 106, 123–5.

67. *Handline Fishing, Tackle, Bait and Meiths*

1349. Shirreff 1814 b. 86–7; Hibbert 1822. 509.
1350. Macadam 1880–1. xv. 148–51.
1351. Spence 1899. 128; Stewart *Correspondence* 6 Oct 1962; Johnson *Correspondence*.
1352. Jakobsen (1908) 1928; Laurenson *MS Notebook*.
1353. Manson 1953. 13; Laurenson *MS Notebook*.
1354. Laurenson *MS Notebook*.
1355. NSA 1845. xv. 96; POAS 1922. 29.
1356. Edmondston 1866; Spence 1899. 130; Jakobsen (1908) 1928; Laurenson *MS Notebook*.

1357. Hibbert 1822. 508; Edmondston 1866; *Shetland News* 21 Oct. 1899; Jakobsen (1908) 1928; Eunson 1961. Vol. 5. 181–98; Goodlad 1971. 103; Laurenson *MS Notebook*.
1358. Laurenson *MS Notebook*.
1359. Jamieson 1825; Edmondston 1866; SND s.v. *skog*.
1360. Jakobsen 1897. 18.
1361. Edmondston 1866; Edmondston 1899. 128–9; Jakobsen (1908) 1928; Angus 1914.
1362. Marwick 1929.
1363. Laurenson *MS Notebook*.
1364. Edmondston 1866; Spence 1899. 244; Jakobsen (1908) 1928; Marwick 1929.
1365. Laurenson *MS Notebook*.
1366. Edmondston 1866; Jakobsen (1908) 1928; Angus 1914; Marwick 1929.
1367. Edmondston 1866; Spence 1899. 129; Jakobsen (1908) 1928; Marwick 1929; Scott 1968. 94; Stout *Correspondence* 13 April 1963.

68. *Cod Fishing*

1368. Boece, Leslie in Brown 1893. 93, 159; Settle (1577) 1969; *Deeds* 1840. 4; *Diplomatarium* 1907–13. I. 218–19; Platt 1932–3. LXVII. 135–6.
1369. DOST s.v. *gartling, girtling, greitling, grete lyne, grit lyne*.
1370. *Oppressions* 1859. 60, 65–6; Bull 1640–1720. v. 27 in Goodlad 1971. 59; Knox 1789. 326.
1371. Low (1774) 1879. 10; OSA 1793. VII. 551: Kirkwall and St Ola; 1795. XIV. 319; 1795. XVI. 442 ff: Sandwick and Stromness; 1797. XIX. 406–7: Orphir; 1798. XX. 265.
1372. Troup and Eunson 1967. 5–6.
1373. Teignmouth 1836. I. 234; Wilson 1842. II. 224–5; NSA 1845. XV. 74, 82, 100, 163.
1374. MacGillivray (*c*. 1614–18) 1953. I. 51; Scott 1968. 95–6. 101.
1375. NSA 1845. XV. 133.
1376. Tait 1947. IV. 86–91.
1377. NSA 1845. XV 133: Aithsting and Sandsting.
1378. *Ib*. 14, 16, 21, 78, 171.
1379. Tait 1947. IV. 115–17.
1380. Goodlad 1971. 129.
1381. Hibbert 1822. 520–2; O'Dell 1939. 123.
1382. Board of Trustees' Papers.
1383. Tudor 1883. 142; Halcrow 1950. 90; Goodlad 1971. 130, 132.
1384. Tudor 1883. 143; Goodlad 1971. 136–7.
1385. Pløyen (1839) 1894; Tudor 1883. 141; Degn 1929. 51; Goodlad 1971. 138; Joensen 1975. 20–1.
1386. Tudor 1883. 142; Goodlad 1971. 147–52.
1387. Goodlad 1971. 156–9.

69. *King Herring*

1388. Marwick 1926–7. v. 61.
1389. Brand (1683) 1701. 131–3; Wallace (1693) 1700. 38; Martin (*c*. 1695) 1884. 386; Barry 1805. 49; Forsyth 1808. v. 42–3; Goodlad 1971. 162–3.
1390. Gifford (1718) 1913. VI. 193–5.
1391. Macfarlane 1906–8. I. 142; Anon. 1750. 28; Knox (1784) 1789. 184, 272, 274.
1392. OSA 1791. I. 407–8; Kemp 1801. 29; Wilson 1842. II. 225, 230, 261, 280; NSA 1845. XV. 214.
1393. NSA 1845. XV. 22, 31, 74, 82, 163, 186, 194.
1394. NSA 1845. XV. 4–5, 16, 21, 30–2, 46–7, 54–5, 58, 67, 78, 94, 133–4, 172–3.
1395. Goodlad 1971. 168.
1396. Edmondston 1809. I. 281–2; Nicolson 1972. 133.
1397. Goodlad 1971. 174; Nicolson 1972. 134.

1398. Goodlad 1971. 175–8.
1399. Nicolson Papers.
1400. *Letters*, T M Adie to Lady Nicolson 5 April, 8 July 1881.
1401. *Letter*, C. Arthurson to Lady Nicolson *c*. 1881.
1402. Scott 1968. 98.
1403. Nicolson Papers.
1404. Nicolson 1972. 135.
1405. Goodlad 1971. 182–7; Nicolson 1972. 135–6.
1406. Goodlad 1971. 196–9.
1407. Tudor 1883. 104, 356; Miller 1976. 155–8.
1408. *Midbrake Papers*, Bundle 3562, Sheet 31; *Letter*, A. Sandison, Uyeasound, to J T Irvine, Oct. 1882; Goodlad 1971. 199–200.
1409. E.g. Heineberg (1969); Goodlad 1971. 162 ff.; Nicolson 1972. 133 ff.
1410. Edmondston 1866; Marwick 1929.

70. *The Sea Language of Fishermen and the End of Norn*

1411. Wainwright 1926. 190–1; Crawford 1969. 35–53.
1412. Terry 1902. 288–9; Murison 1954. 255.
1413. Marwick 1929. xxii.
1414. *Description* 1908. 64.
1415. *Monteith* (1633) 1845. 15–16; Donaldson 1958. 78–80.
1416. *Description* 1908. 4, 43–5.
1417. Brand (1683) 1701. 17, 69.
1418. Gifford (1733) 1786. 31–2.
1419. OSA 1791. I. 408; 1793. VII. 596; 1794. X. 203; 1796. XVII. 498; 1798. XX. 277; Neill 1806. 79.
1420. *Session Papers, Galloway v. Morton*. 12 Nov. 1757, 176; Marwick 1929. 226.
1421. Low (1773) 1923–4. II. 53; OSA 1795. XIV. 331.
1422. Jakobsen (1908) 1928. I. xci–cxvii; Marwick 1929. 226–7.
1423. Jakobsen (1908) 1928. cxii; Fenton *MS Notebook*, Foula 1958. 54.
1424. *Oppressions* (1576) 1859. 79, 83.
1425. Monteith (1633) 1845. 15–16; Brand (1683) 1701. 17, 69–70.
1426. Clouston 1923–4. II. 31–6; Marwick 1922–3. I. 56; Marwick 1926–7. V. 62, 73; Mooney 1931–2. X. 17–20 and 1932–3. XI. 19–26; Marwick 1932–3. XI. 32–43; Clouston 1932–3. XI. 59–65.
1427. Thorsen 1950. 230–8.
1428. Solheim 1947. 1–14.
1429. *Midbrake Papers*, Bundle 388.
1430. Lockwood 1955. 1–24; 1961. 60–71.
1431. Laurenson 1874. X. 711–16; Roeder 1904; Drever 1916. X. 235–40; Lundberg 1954. 221–9; Fenton 1968–9. 117–21.

Bibliography

Abbreviations

APS	Acts of the Parliament of Scotland
DOST	Dictionary of the Older Scottish Tongue
KLNM	Kulturhistoriskt Lexikon för Nordisk Medeltid
NMAS	National Museum of Antiquities of Scotland
NSA	New (Second) Statistical Account
Old-Lore Miscellany	Old-Lore Miscellany of Orkney, Shetland, Caithness and Sutherland
OSA	Old (First) Statistical Account
POAS	Proceedings of the Orkney Antiquarian Society
PSAS	Proceedings of the Society of Antiquaries of Scotland
SND	Scottish National Dictionary

Aasen, I. *Norsk Ordbog*. 1918.

Aberdeen, W. *MS Chart of the Orkney Islands*. 1770.

Acts and Statutes of the Lawting, Sheriff and Justice Courts, within Orkney and Zetland, from the year MDCII–MDCXLIV. In *Miscellany of the Maitland Club*. 1840. II. 137–216.

Anderson, A. *Correspondence* 4 Sept. 1961 (Fair Isle).

Anderson, A O. *Early Sources of Scottish History, 500–1286*. 1922. 2 Vols.

Anderson, G. and P. *Guide to the Highlands and Islands of Scotland, including Orkney and Zetland*. 1834.

Anderson, J D. Grazings Constable, Mangaster, Sullom, Shetland. *Notebooks. c.* 1943–5; 1912–14.

Angus, J S. *An Etymological Glossary of some Place-Names in Shetland*. 1910.

Angus, J S. *A Glossary of the Shetland Dialect*. 1914.

Annandale, N. *The Faroes and Iceland*. 1905.

Anon. *An Exact and Authentic Account of the ... White-Herring Fishery in Scotland*. 1750.

Anon. Olnafirth Voe and Valley. In *The New Shetlander*. No. 102. 1972. 12–13.

Anson, P F. *Scots Fisherfolk*. 1950.

Baillie, M G L. A Horizontal Mill of the Eighth Century AD at Drumard, Co. Derry. In *Ulster Journal of Archaeology*. 1975. Vol. 38. 25–32.

Baldwin, J R. Sea Bird Fowling in Scotland and Faroe. In *Folk Life*. 1974. Vol. 12. 60–103.

Balfour, D. *Odal Rights and Feudal Wrongs*. 1860.

Banks, Mrs M M. *British Calendar Customs. Orkney and Shetland* (The Folk-Lore Society). 1946.

Barclay, R S. *The Population of Orkney 1755–1961*. 1965.

Barclay, R S. *The Court Books of Orkney and Shetland 1614–1615* (Scottish History Society). 1967.

Barclay transcripts. Transcript of Orkney Testaments (publication forthcoming, Scottish Record Society).

Barnard, F. *Picturesque Life in Shetland.* 1890.

Barry, G. *The History of the Orkney Islands.* 1805.

Beenhakker, A J. *Hollanders in Shetland.* 1973.

Begg, J. The Bailie Courts of Orkney II. In *POAS.* 1924–5. III. 55–64.

Bellows. H A. *The Poetic Edda.* 1923.

Ben, Jo. Descriptio Insularum Orchadiarum. Appx. VII. In Barry G. *The History of the Orkney Islands.* 1805.

Benediktsson, J. Landnámabók. Some remarks on its value as a historical source. In *Saga-Book.* 1969. XVII/4. 275–92.

Berg, A., Steensberg, A. and Eriksson, M. Ljore. In *KLNM. 1965.* x. 650–3.

Berg, G. *Sledges and Wheeled Vehicles. Ethnological Studies from the Viewpoint of Sweden.* 1935.

Berg, G. Johannes Galejas märkebok och andra öländska märkeböcker. In *Kalmar läns fornminnesförenings årbok.* 1966/1967. 23–34.

Berg, G. Sheep and Cattle Marks in Scandinavia. In *Folk Life.* 1973. Vol. 11. 15–21.

Bjørk, E A. In Ewens, J. Jordfællesskab og Udskiftning paa Færøerne. Famien Bygd. (*Færoensia.* 1975. x).

Bjørkvik, H. Kolonisation: Norge. In *KLNM.* 1963. VII. 639–44.

Bjørkvik, H. Veitsle. In *KLNM.* 1975. XIX. 632–4.

Black, G F. *Examples of Printed Folk-lore Concerning the Orkney & Shetland Islands* (Folk-lore Society) 1903.

Brand, J. *A Brief Description of Orkney, Zetland, Pightland Firth and Caithness.* 1701–3.

Bremner, S. *North East Caithness Dialect List, MS.* nd.

Brøgger, A W. *Ancient Emigrants. A History of the Norse Settlements of Scotland.* 1929.

Brøgger, A W. *Den norske bosetningen på Shetland—Orknøyene.* 1930.

Brown, C. *Oral information,* Aith, Fetlar. 1963.

Brown, P H. *Scotland Before 1700 from Contemporary Documents.* 1893.

Brownrigg, D A. and Gaunt, D. Foula Sheep, their Wool and its Processing. 1965.

Bruce, I. *The Shetland Crofting Tradition.* (A dissertation offered for the degree of Bachelor of Arts with Honours in Architectural Studies at the School of Architecture, the University of Newcastle upon Tyne). Typescript. 1973.

Bruce, R H. The Sixern of Shetland. In *The Mariners' Mirror.* 1914. IV. 289–300.

Bruce, R S. Shetland Dialect. In *Old-Lore Miscellany.* 1912. v. 52.

Bruce, R S. Glimpses of Shetland Life, 1718–1753. II. In *Old-Lore Miscellany.* 1913. VI. 31–7.

Bruce, R S. The Haaf Fishing and Shetland Trading, 1730–5. In *The Mariners' Mirror.* 1931. XVII. 356–76.

Buckley, T E. and Harvie-Brown, J A. *A Vertebrate Fauna of the Orkney Islands.* 1891.

Calder, C S T. Report on the Discovery of Numerous Stone Age House-Sites in Shetland. In *PSAS.* 1955–6. LXXXIX. 340–97.

Calder, C S T. Excavations in Whalsay, Shetland, 1954–5. In *PSAS.* 1960–1. XCIV. 28–45.

Callander, J G. and Grant, W G. A long stalled chambered cairn or mausoleum, (Rousay type) near Midhowe, Rousay, Orkney. In *PSAS.* 1933–4. LXVIII. 320–50.

Campbell, J. *Political Survey of Great Britain.* 1774.

Campbell, R. *Scotland since 1707. The Rise of an Industrial Society.* 1965.

Cant, R G. *The Medieval Churches and Chapels of Shetland.* 1975.

Carter, J S. *Correspondence.* April 1977.

Charleson, M M. ed. *Orcadian Papers.* 1905.

Charlton, E. Journal of an Expedition to Shetland in 1834. v. In *Old-Lore Miscellany.* 1935–46. x. 55–71.

Childe, V G. *The Dawn of European Civilisation.* 1925. (5th ed. 1950).

Childe, V G. *New Light on the Most Ancient East.* 1934. (4th ed. 1952).

Childe, V G. Another Late Viking House at Freswick, Caithness. In *PSAS.* 1942–3. LXXVII. 5–17.

Christensen, A E. *Boats of the North. A History of Boat Building in Norway.* 1968.

Cleasby, R. and Vigfusson, G. *An Icelandic—English Dictionary.* 1874.

Clouston, J S. *Records of the Earldom of Orkney 1299–1614.* (Scottish History Society). 1914.

Clouston, J S. The Orkney Townships. In *Scottish Historical Review.* 1920. xvii. 16–45.

Clouston, J S. Old Orkney Houses, In *POAS.* 1923. i. 11–19; 39–47; 1924. ii. 7–14.

Clouston, J S. The People and Surnames of Orkney. In *POAS.* 1923–4. ii. 31–6.

Clouston, J S. The Orkney Lands. In *POAS.* 1923–4. ii. 61–8.

Clouston, J S. The Old Orkney Mills. In *POAS.* 1924–5. iii. 49–54, 65–71.

Clouston, J S. An Orkney 'Perambulation'. In *Scottish Historical Review.* 1925. xxii. 182–92.

Clouston, J S. An Old Kirkwall House. In *POAS.* 1926–7. v. 9–14.

Clouston, J S. The Orkney 'Bus'. In *POAS.* 1926–7. v. 41–49.

Clouston, J S. A Fresh View of the Settlement of Orkney. In *POAS.* 1930–1. ix. 35–40.

Clouston, J S. *A History of Orkney.* 1932.

Clouston, J S. The Origin of the Halcros. In *POAS.* 1932–3. xi. 59–65.

Costie, Miss B. per Marwick, E. 1972.

Coull, J R. Walls: A Shetland Crofting Parish. In *Scottish Geographical Magazine.* 1964. Vol. 80/3. 135–49.

Cowie, R. *Shetland and its Inhabitants.* 1871.

Craven, A. *Church Life in South Ronaldshay and Burray in the Seventeenth Century.* 1911.

Crawford, B E. The Pawning of Orkney and Shetland: a reconsideration of the events of 1460–9. In *The Scottish Historical Review.* 1969. xlviii, i: No. 145, 35–53.

Crawford, I A. Gual Gaidhealach: Peat Charcoal. In *Scottish Studies.* 1964. Vol. 8/1. 108–13.

Crawford, I A. Scot, Norseman and Gael. In *Scottish Archaeological Forum.* 1974. Vol. 6. 1–16.

Cruden, S. The Horizontal Water-Mill at Dounby. In *PSAS.* 1946–7. lxxxi. 43–7.

Cruden, S. *Click Mill, Dounby, Orkney* (HMSO). 1949.

Cruden, S. Excavations at Birsay, Orkney. In Small, A., ed. *The Fourth Viking Congress.* 1965.

Curle, A O. An Account of the Excavation of a Dwelling of the Viking Period at 'Jarlshof', Sumburgh, Shetland. In *PSAS.* 1934–5. lxix. 265–321.

Curle, A O. A Viking Settlement at Freswick, Caithness. In *PSAS.* 1938–9. lxxiii. 71–110.

Curwen, E C. The Problem of Early Water-mills. In *Antiquity.* 1944. xviii. 130–46.

Curwen, E C. and Hatt, G. *Plough and Pasture. The Early History of Farming.* 1961.

Dahl, S. *A Survey of Archaeological Investigations in the Faroes.* In Small, A., ed., *The Fourth Viking Congress.* 1965.

Dahl, S. Um ærgistaðir og ærgitoftir. In *Fróðskaparrit.* 1970. Vol. 18. 361–8.

Dahl, S. The Norse Settlement of the Faroe Islands. In *Medieval Archaeology.* 1970. xiv. 60–73.

Darling, F. Fraser. *Crofting Agriculture.* 1945.

Davidson, D. In *Journal of the Orkney Agricultural Discussion Society. 1936.* xi.

Day, J P. *Public Administration in the Highlands and Islands of Scotland.* 1918.

Dearness, J. per Marwick, E. 1972.

Debes, L J. *Faeroae and Faeroeae Reserata: That is a Description of the Islands and Inhabitants of Faeroe.* 1670. (English translation by J(ohn) S(terpin) 1676.)

Degn, A. *Oversigt over Fiskeriet og Monopolhandelen på Faerøerne.* 1929.

Dennison, W T. Remarks on the Agricultural Classes in the North Isles of Orkney. In *Report of Her Majesty's Commissioners of Enquiry into the Conditions of the Crofters and Cottars in the Highlands and Islands of Scotland.* 1884. 270–80.

Dennison, W T. Orkney Folklore. Sea Myths. In *The Scottish Antiquary.* 1891. v. 130–3.

Dennison, W T. Manufacture of Straw Articles in Orkney. In Charleson, M M., ed., *Orcadian Papers,* 1905. 32–42.

Dennison, W T. *Orkney Folklore and Tradition.* 1961.

Dent, A A. and Goodall, D M. *The Foals of Epona.* 1962.

Description. *Description of Ye Countrey of Zetland.* 1908.

Dickinson, C I. *British Seaweeds.* 1963.

Dickinson, H W. and Straker, E. The Shetland Water Mill. In *The Engineer*. 24 March 1933.

Dickson, J. Some Account of the Orkney Islands. In *Prize-Essays and Transactions of the Highland and Agricultural Society of Scotland*. 1841. XIII (New Series, VII). 115–36.

Dietrichson, L. and Meyer, J. *Monumenta Orcadica. The Norsemen in the Orkneys and the Monuments they have left*. 1906

Diplomatarium Orcadense et Hialtlandense. 1907 et seq.

Djurhuus, N. ed. J. Chr. Svabo. *Indberetninger fra en Reise i Færøe 1781 og 1782*. (Selskabet til Udgivelse af Færøske Kildeskrifter og Studier). 1976.

Dobie, W J. Udal Law. In *An Introductory Survey of the Sources and Literature of Scots Law*. (Stair Society). 1936. 445–60.

Dobie, W J. Allodial Law. In *An Introductory Survey of the Sources and Literature of Scots Law*. (Stair Society). 1936. 461–5.

Dodgshon, R. Runrig and the Communal Origins of Property in Land. In *The Juridical Review*. 1975. 189–208.

Donaldson, G. *Shetland Life under Earl Patrick*. 1958.

Donaldson, G. ed. *The Court Book of Shetland 1602–1604*. (Scottish Record Society). 1954.

Donaldson, J E. *Caithness in the 18th Century*. 1938.

Donnachie, I L. and Stewart, N K. Scottish Windmills – An Outline and Inventory. In *PSAS*. 1967. XCVIII. 276–99.

Draft Scheme. Covering letter of 25 Sept. 1964 to *Draft Scheme for the Reorganisation of the Townships in the Island of Fetlar, Zetland*. 1962. (typescript).

Drever, J. 'Taboo' Words among Shetland Fishermen. In *Old-Lore Miscellany*. 1916. x. 235–40.

Drever, J. MS 1974–5.

Duncan, A. *Scotland. The Making of the Kingdom*. 1975.

Dunn, R. *The Ornithologist's Guide to the Islands of Orkney and Shetland*. 1837.

Edmondston, A. *A View of the Ancient and Present State of the Zetland Islands*. 2 Vols. 1809.

Edmondston, A. *Observations on the Nature and Extent of the Cod Fishery*. 1820.

Edmondston, L D. MS. 1961.

Edmondston, L D. MS. 1970. 9.

Edmondston, T. *An Etymological Glossary of the Shetland and Orkney Dialect*. 1866.

Edmondston, B. and Saxby, J M E. *The Home of a Naturalist*. 1888.

Elder, J R. *The Royal Fishery Companies of the Seventeenth Century*. 1912.

Eldjárn, K. Two Medieval Farm Sites in Iceland and Some Remarks on Tephrochronology. In Small, A., ed. *The Fourth Viking Congress*. 1965.

Ellison, G. *Reminiscences of my Twenty Seven Visits to the Orkney Islands. 1884–1911*. MS. (Stromness Museum).

Erixon, S. *West European Connections and Culture Relations*. In *Folk-Liv*. 1939.

Eunson, J. The Fair Isle Fishing-Marks. In *Scottish Studies*. 1961. Vol. 5. 181–98.

Eunson, J. *Words, Phrases and Recollections from Fair Isle*. 1976.

Evans, E E. Highland landscapes: habitat and heritage. In Evans, J G., Limbrey, S., and Cleere, H., eds. *The Effect of Man on the Landscape (CBA. Research Report. No. 11)*. 1975. 1–5.

Evershed, H. On the Agriculture of the Islands of Shetland. In *Transactions of the Highland and Agricultural Society of Scotland*. 1874. (4th Ser.). VI.

Fahy, E M. A Horizontal Mill at Mashanaglass, Cork. In *Journal of the Cork Historical and Archaeological Society*. 1956. LXI. 13–57.

Fea, J. *The Present State of the Orkney Islands Considered*. 1775.

Fea, J. *Considerations on the Fisheries in the Scotch Islands*. 1787.

Fea, Patrick. *MS Diary*.

Feilberg, H F. *Dansk Bondeliv*. 1910. 2 Vols.

Fenton, A. Ropes and Rope-making in Scotland. In *Gwerin*. 1961. III/3 and 4. 1–15, 17–31.

Fenton, A. Early and Traditional Cultivating Implements in Scotland. In *PSAS*. 1962–3. XCVI. 264–317.

Fenton, A. Alternating Stone and Turf. An Obsolete Building Practice. In *Folk Life*. 1968. Vol. 6. 94–103.

Fenton, A. Plough and Spade in Dumfries and Galloway. In *Transactions of the Dumfriesshire and Galloway Natural History and Antiquarian Society*. 1968. XLV. 147–83.

Fenton, A. The Tabu Language of the Fishermen of Orkney and Shetland. In *Ethnologia Europaea*. 1968–9. II–III. 118–22.

Fenton, A. Paring and Burning and the Cutting of Turf and Peat in Scotland. In Gailey, A. and Fenton, A., eds. *The Spade in Northern and Atlantic Europe*. 1970. 155–93.

Fenton, A. Early Yoke Types in Britain. In *A Magyar Mezőgazdasági Múzeum Közleméńyei* 1971–1972. 69–75.

Fenton, A. *A Fuel of Necessity: Animal Manure*. In Ennen, E. and Wiegelmann, G., eds. *Festschrift Matthias Zender. Studien zu Volkskultur, Sprache und Landesgeschichte*. 1972. 722–34.

Fenton, A. Transport with Pack-Horse and Slide-Car in Scotland. In Fenton, A., Podolák, J. and Rasmussen, H., eds. *Land Transport in Europe*. (Nationalmuseet: Folkelivs Studier 4) 1973. 121–71.

Fenton, A. *The Various Names of Shetland*. 1973.

Fenton, A. Pork in the Rural Diet of Scotland. In Gantner, T. and Trümpy, H., eds. *Festschrift für Robert Wildhaber*. 1973. 98–110.

Fenton, A. Craig-Fishing in the Northern Isles of Scotland and Notes on the Poke-Net. In *Scottish Studies*. 1973. Vol. 17. 71–80.

Fenton, A. Sickle Scythe and Reaping Machine. In *Ethnologia Europaea*. 1973/4. VII, 1. 35–47.

Fenton, A. Seaweed Manure in Scotland. In *In Memoriam António Jorge Dias*. 1974. III. 147–86.

Fenton, A. Lexicography and Historical Interpretation. In Barrow, G W S., ed. *The Scottish Tradition. Essays in Honour of Ronald Gordon Cant*. 1974. 243–58.

Fenton, A. The Light and Improved Scots Plough and its Team. In O'Danachair, C., ed. *Folk and Farm. Essays in Honour at A. T. Lucas*. 1976. 40–53.

Fenton, A. *The Island Blackhouse (HMSO)*. 1978.

Fenton, A. Shellfish as Food and Bait. In Gunda, B. 1978. Forthcoming.

Fenton, A. A Note on Scottish Straw Rope Granaries. In Jasiewicz, Z., ed. *Tradition and Change. Essays in Honour of Professor József Burszta*. 1978. Forthcoming.

Fenton, A. Sheep in North Ronaldsay, Orkney. In Jenkins, J G., ed. *Studies in Folklife*. 1969. 206–33.

Fenton, A. *MS Notebook,* Foula, 1958.

Fenton, A. *MS Notebook,* Fair Isle, 1962.

Fenton, A. *MS Notebook,* Fetlar, 1963.

Fenton, A. *MS Notebook,* North Ronaldsay. 1964.

Fenton, A. *MS Notebook,* Papa Stour, 1967.

Fenton, A. *MS Notebook,* Orkney, 1968.

Fenton, A. *MS Notebook,* Caithness, 1969.

Fenton transcripts. Transcripts of Orkney testaments.

Fenton, A. and Laurenson, J J. Peat in Fetlar. In *Folk Life*. 1964. II. 3–26.

Firth, J. Sheep-Ca'ing in Orkney. In *Old-Lore Miscellany*. 1907–8. I. 307.

Firth, J. Sheep-Marks. In *Old-Lore Miscellany*. 1907–8. I. 210.

Firth, J. *Reminiscences of an Orkney Parish* (1920). 1974.

Flett, J. Kirkwall Incorporated Trades III. In *POAS*. 1931–2. X. 49–55.

Foote, P. Træl. In *KLNM*. 1975. XIX. 13–19.

Foote, P. and Wilson, D M. *The Viking Achievement*. 1970.

Forsyth, R. *The Beauties of Scotland*. 1805–1808. 5 Vols.

Fox, C. The Round Chimneyed Farm-Houses of Northern Pembrokeshire. In Grimes, W F., ed. *Aspects of Archaeology in Britain and Beyond*. 1951.

Fraser, J. Antiquities of Birsay Parish. In *POAS*. 1924–5. III. 21–30.

Fraser, J. Some Transactions of the Vice-Admiral Depute of Orkney in 1801–1803. In *POAS*. 1934–5. XIII.

Fraser, J. Old Shipwrecks and other Maritime Matters. In *POAS*. 1937–9. XV.

Fraser, W. *Oral information*, Papa Stour. 1967.
Frazer, J. In *Folk Lore*. 1919. xxx.
Freeman, C. *Luton and the Straw Hat Industry*. 1953.
Frimannslund, R. Utmark. In *KLNM*. 1975. xix. 383–4.

Garrick, G A. *Correspondence* 1960.
General List of All the Cattle Marks in the Parish of North Yell Exactly Coppied from A Book of Records keept by Mr. Alexr. Irvine of Papal and Compiled by him at Culeavoe 24th March 1781. copied 1813.
Genrup, K. *Gåsskötsel. En etnologisk studie med särskild hänsyn till skånska förhållanden*. (Skrifter från Folklivsarkivet i Lund nr. 16). 1975.
Gestsson, G. Gröf i Öræfum. In *Árbók hins Íslenzka Fornleifafélags*. 1959. 5–87.
Gifford, T. *Historical Description of the Zetland Islands*. 1786.
Glob, P V. *Ard og Plov i Nordens Oldtid (Jysk Arkæologisk Selskabs Skrifter* i). 1951.
Goodlad, C A. *Shetland Fishing Saga*. 1971.
Gordon, J J. A Voyage to the Greenland Whaling. In *The New Shetlander*. No. 52. 1959. 27–9.
Gorrie, D. *Summers and Winters in the Orkneys*. 1868.
Goudie, G. ed. *The Diary of the Reverend John Mill. Shetland 1740–1803*. (Scottish History Society). 1889.
Goudie, G. The Fouds, Lawrightmen, and Ranselmen of Shetland Parishes. In *PSAS*. 1892. xxvi. 189–212.
Goudic, G. *The Celtic and Scandinavian Antiquities of Shetland*. 1904.
Graham, A. *Archaeological Newsletter*. (Fourth Scottish Summer School of Archaeology) 1956.
G(raham), J J. Andrew Dishington Mathewson. In *The New Shetlander*. 1968. No. 86. 17–18, 27.
Gray, J A R. The Most Dangerous Occupation in the World. In *The Captain*.
Gray, M. *The Highland Economy 1750–1850*. 1957.
Greig, P W. *Annals of the Parish of Delting*. 1892.
Groundwater, Miss H. *Letters*.

Halcrow, A. *The Sail Fishermen of Shetland*. 1950.
Hald, K. – bol. In *KLNM*. 1957. ii. 64–7.
Hald, K. – by. In *KLNM*. 1957. ii. 381–7.
Hall, Rev. J. *Travels in Scotland*. ii. 1807.
Hamilton, J R C. *Excavations at Jarlshof, Shetland*. 1956.
Hammershaimb, V U. *Færøsk Anthologi*. 2 Vols. 1891.
Hamre, H. Ferøers Beskrifvelser, af Thomas Tarnovius. In *Færoensia*. 1950. ii.
Harcus, M M. MS 1974. 2.
Hay, D. *Europe in the Fourteenth and Fifteenth Centuries*. 1966.
Headrick J. *View of the Mineralogy, Agriculture, Manufactures and Fisheries of the Island of Arran*. 1807.
Heineberg, H. *Changes in the Economic-Geographical Structures of the Shetland Islands*. 1969.
Henderson, J. *General View of the Agriculture of Caithness*. 1812.
Henderson, J. *Information*, South Ronaldsay.
Henderson, T. *Oral information*. 1967.
Henderson, T. The Yoal and the Sixern. In *The New Shetlander*. No. 89. 1969. 12–15; No. 91. 1969. 8–10.
Henderson, T. *Correspondence*. 8 March 1972.
Henderson, T. Britain's Most Primitive Mill. In *Scotland's Magazine c*. 1965. 43–5.
Henshall, A S. Westness, Rousay. In *Discovery and Excavation – Scotland*. 1963. 40.
Henshall, A S. *The Chambered Tombs of Scotland*. 2 Vols. 1963 and 1972.
Hepburn, T. *Letter to a Gentleman from his Friend in Orkney*. 1760.
Hewison, W S. Holm Farm Diary 1849–68. In *Orkney Miscellany*. 1954. ii. 9–23.

Henshall, A S. and Maxwell, S. Clothing and other Articles from a late Seventeenth Century Grave at Gunnister, Shetland. In *PSAS*. 1951–2. LXXXVI. 30–40.

Hibbert, S. *A Description of the Shetland Islands*. 1822.

Hillson, R. Copinsay. The James Fisher Island. In *Scotland's Magazine*. February 1973. 35–7.

Høeg, O A. *Planter og tradisjon. Floraen i levende tale og tradisjon i Norge 1925–1973*. 1975.

Højrup, Ole. Låse of trae. In *Folkeliv og Kulturlevn*. 1960, 110–24.

Højrup, Ole. *Landbokvinden. Rok og Kærne. Grovbrød og Vadmel*. 1964.

Hoffmann, M. *Jærhuset* (Norsk Folkemuseum). 1943.

Hoffmann, M. Gamle fjøstyper belyst ved et material fra Sørvest-Norge. In *By og Bygd*. 1966. Vol. 18. 115–36.

Holtsmark, A. Rígsþula. In *KLNM*. 1969. XIV. 234–6.

Home Industries. *Report to the Board of Agriculture for Scotland on Home Industries in the Highlands and Islands*. 1914.

Hossack, B H. *Kirkwall in the Orkneys*. 1900.

Hovda, P. – by. In *KLNM*. 1957. II. 387–90.

Hunter, J. *Taen wi da Trow*. 1952.

Hunter, J. *The Making of the Crofting Community*. 1976.

I., W S. Muness Sixareens. In *The New Shetlander*. No. 71. 1964. 13–15.

Ingstad, A S. The Norse Settlement at L'Anse aux Meadows, Newfoundland. In *Acta Archaeologica*. 1970. XLI. 109–54.

Inkster, G. *Oral information*.

Irvine, J T. Note on Ocrigirt. In *Midbrake Papers,* Bundle 388, Folder v. 1 April 1885.

Irvine, J T. Zetlandic Memoranda. In *Midbrake Papers*. Bundle 394.

Irvine, T. Farming Notes in North Yell Shetland from 1823 to 1876. (*Midbrake Papers,* Bundle 3562).

Irvine MSS. 395/1.

Irvine Papers.

Irvine, W. MS 1974. 7.

Jackson, P. Scottish Seaweed Resources. In *Scottish Geographical Magazine*. 1948. Vol. 64/3. 136–44.

Jakobsen, J. *The Dialect and Place-Names of Shetland*. 1897.

Jakobsen, J. *Shetlandsøernes Stednavne*. 1901.

Jakobsen, J. *An Etymological Dictionary of the Norn Language in Shetland*. 1928.

Jameson, R. *Mineralogy of the Orkney Islands*. 1800.

Jamieson, J. *An Etymological Dictionary of the Scottish Language*. 1808, 1825, 1879–87.

Jamieson, P. Some Rig-names in Papa Stour, Shetland. In *Old-Lore Miscellany*. 1929. IX. 73–4.

Jamieson, P. *Letters on Shetland*. 1949.

Jessen, K. and Helbæk, H. Cereals in Great Britain and Ireland in prehistoric and early historic times. In *Kongelige Danske Videnskabets Selskab* (Biol. Skrift. III). 1949. 18.

Jirlow, R. Das Tragen mit dem Stirnband. In *Acta Ethnologica*. 1937. II. 137–48.

Joensen, J. Pauli. Pilot Whaling in the Faroe Islands. In *Ethnologia Scandinavica*. 1976. 5–42.

Johnson, J H. *Letters* and *Notebooks*.

Johnson, Mrs M., Quarff. *Correspondence*.

Johnston, A W. Orkney Jottings. In *Orkney and Shetland Miscellany*. 1907–8. I. 245–8.

Johnston, A W. Sheep-Marks. In *Orkney and Shetland Miscellany*. 1907–8. I. 164–5.

Johnston, A W. Orkney Horses. In *Old-Lore Miscellany*. 1910. III. 74.

Johnston, A W. Fetlar folk in 1716. In *Old-Lore Miscellany*. 1910. III. 103–6.

Johnston, A W. Grotti Finnie and Grottie Minnie. In *Old-Lore Miscellany*. 1910. III. 8–10.

Johnston, A W. Sheep-Marks. In *Old-Lore Miscellany*. 1907–8. I. 55–6, 164–5; 1911. IV. 4–5.

Johnston, A W. Teinds of Fetlar, Shetland, 1732–5. In *Old-Lore Miscellany*. 1911. IV. 119–22.

Johnston, A W. Scattald Marches of Unst in 1771. In *Old-Lore Miscellany*. 1910. III. 100–02; III. 162–3; III. 217–19; 1911. IV. 33–6; IV. 91–3; IV. 192–3; 1912. V. 125–9.

Johnston, A W., ed. *The Church in Orkney*. 1940.

Johnston, J G. The Hill Dyke. In *Scotland's Magazine*. Dec. 1952.

Johnston, T H. John Gow, the Pirate. In *The Scottish Antiquary*. 1891. v. 184–8.

Jónsson, F., ed. *Sæmundar-Edda, Eddukvæði*. 1926.

Jónsson, G., ed. *Egils Saga Skalla-Grímssonar* (Íslendinga sögur 4). 1945.

Junda. The Word 'Rüed'. In *Old-Lore Miscellany*. 1909. ii. 79.

Kemp, J. *Observations on the Islands of Shetland*. 1801.

Kjellberg, S T. Primitivt fångstliv. In *Från Stenålder till Rokoko. Studier tillägnade Otto Rydbeck den 25 Augusti 1937*. Lund 1937. 157–81.

Kłodnicki, Z. *et al*. 'Rezginia' in Europe. In *Ethnologia Europaea*. 1975. viii/2. 101–22.

Knox, J. *A View of the British Empire*. 1789.

Koht, H. *Sverre Soga*. 1962.

Kolsrud, K. Lundefangst. In *Norveg*. 1976. Vol. 19. 1–97.

L., J M. Orkney Horses. In *Old-Lore Miscellany*. 1909. ii. 192–3.

L., J T S. Orkney Horses. In *Old-Lore Miscellany*. 1910. iii. 74–5.

Laing, J. *Voyage to Spitzbergen*. 1818.

Laing, L R. *Orkney and Shetland: An Archaeological Guide*. 1974.

Laing, L R. *Settlement Types in Post-Roman Scotland* (British Archaeological Reports. 13). 1975.

Landt, G. *A Description of the Faroe Islands* (*c*. 1798). 1810.

Langskaill, J G. *Letter*. 1 Feb. 1961.

Lárusson, M M. Leysingi: Island. In *KLNM*. 1965. 525–6.

Laurenson, A. On certain Beliefs and Phrases of Shetland Fishermen. In *PSAS*. 1874. x. 711–16.

Laurenson, J. *MS Notebooks*.

Laurenson, J. The Sixern Days. In *The New Shetlander*. No. 63. 1962. 20–2; No. 64. 1963. 25–7; No. 65. 1963. 22–3; No. 66. 1963. 7–8; No. 68. 1964. 10–11; No. 69. 1964. 33–4; No. 70. 1964. 32–4.

Laurenson, J J. John Anderson of Klugen. A noted Fetlar haaf skipper. In *The New Shetlander*. No. 73. 1965.

Lawson, P. *The Agriculturists' Manual*. 1836. Supplement 1842.

Leask, Isabella J. *Correspondence*. 25 Aug. 1961.

Leask, John A. *Scottish Water Mills* (typescript thesis, Dundee College of Architecture).

Leask, J T S. Dividing Sea-Weed 100 Years Ago. In *Old-Lore Miscellany*. 1907–8. i. 33–4.

Leask, J T S. Orkney Dialect. In *Old-Lore Miscellany*. 1907–8. i. 317–28.

Leask, J T S. Tammy Hay and the Fairies. In *Old-Lore Miscellany*. 1910. iii. 28–33.

Leask, J T S. *A Peculiar People and other Orkney Tales*. 1931.

Leask, J T Smith. Shipping Peats from Orkney. In *Old-Lore Miscellany*. 1907–8. i. 129–34.

Leith, P. In *POAS*. 1926–7. v. 59–60.

Leith, P. The Smiths of Tormiston. In *POAS*. 1934–5. xiii. 9–13.

Leith, P K I. *Letters*.

Leith, Mrs P. *Letter*. 1961.

Leith, P. and Spence, S. *Orkney Threshing Mills*. (Scottish Vernacular Buildings Working Group). 1977.

Lerche, G. The Radio-carbon Dated Ploughing Implements. In *Tools and Tillage*. 1969. i:2. 128.

Lerche, G. The Ploughs of Medieval Denmark. In *Tools and Tillage*. 1970. i:3. 131–49.

Letter. *Letters by Landholders of Shetland to the Highland Society*. 1802.

Letter. *Letter respecting Shetland to the Highland Society*. 1803.

Lid, N. Eldviging I. In *KLNM*. 1958. iii. 579–81.

Linklater, R. *Information*. 1977.

Lockhart, J G. *Memoirs of the Life of Sir Walter Scott*. 7 Vols. 1837–8.

Lockwood, W B. Word Taboo in the Language of the Faroese Fishermen. In *Transactions of the Philological Society*. 1955. Vol. 102. 1–24.

Lockwood, W B. An Introduction to Modern Faroese. *Færoensia*. 1955. iv.

Lockwood, W B. *The Faroese Bird Names. Færoensia. 1961.* v.

Low, G. *Fauna Orcadensis* (1795). 1813.

Low, G. *A Tour through the Islands of Orkney and Shetland* (1774). 1879.

Low, G. Tour in Orkney, 1778. In *Old-Lore Miscellany*. 1920. VIII. 131–53.

Low, G. A Description of Orkney. 1733. In *POAS*. 1923–4. II. 49–58.

Lucas, A T. The Plundering and Burning of Churiber in Ireland, Seventh to Sixteenth Century. In *North Munster Studies*. 1967. 172–229.

Lucas, A T. The horizontal mill in Ireland. In *Journal of the Royal Society of Antiquaries of Ireland*. 1953. Vol. 83. 1–36.

Lucas, A T. Wattle and Straw Mat Doors in Ireland. In *Arctica* (Studia Ethnographica Upsaliensia XI) 1956. 16–35.

Lundberg, O. On the Shetland Sea Language as a Source of Old Norse Literature. In Simpson, W D., ed. *The Viking Congress, Lerwick, July 1950*. 1954. 221–9.

Macadam, W I. On the Use of the Spindle and Whorl by the Fishermen of the Present Day. In *PSAS*. 1880–1. XV. 148–51.

McCourt, D. The Outshot House-Type and its Distribution in County Londonderry. In *Ulster Folklife*. 1956. Vol. 2. 27–34.

Macfarlane, W. *Geographical Collections Relating to Scotland* (Scottish History Society). 1906–8. 3 Vols.

MacGillivray, E., ed. Richard James, 1592–1638, Description of Shetland, Orkney, etc. In *Orkney Miscellany*. 1953. I.

McIntosh. W C. *Marine Invertebrates and Fishes of St Andrews*. 1875.

Mackaile, M. A Short Relation of the Most Considerable Things in Orkney. In Barry 1805. Appx. VIII, 448–55, and in Macfarlane, 1906–8. III. 1–7.

Mackay, T. MS 1974. 4.

Mackintosh, W R. *Glimpses of Kirkwall and its People in the Olden Time*. 1887.

Mackintosh, W R. *Around the Orkney Peat-Fires*. (1894). 5th ed. 1949.

MacLaren, A. A Norse House on Drimore Machair, South Uist. In *Glasgow Archaeological Journal* 1974. Vol. 3. 9–18.

Manning, W. The Plough in Roman Britain. In *The Journal of Roman Studies*. 1964. LIV. 54–65.

Manson, B. Da last Sleekie Tows. In *The New Shetlander* 1953. No. 35. 13–14.

Manson, W. MS 1975. 4.

Marks. *The Marks or Characters on the people of Northmavine's Cattle*. MS. (NMAS Photocopy).

Martin, M. *Description of the Western Islands of Scotland*. 1884.

Marwick, E W. *The Folklore of Orkney and Shetland*. 1975.

Marwick, E W. Looking Around. In *The Orcadian*. 15 May 1975.

Marwick, G. *The Old Roman Plough*. 1936.

Marwick, H. The Place Names of North Ronaldsay. In *POAS*. 1922–3. I. 53–64.

Marwick, H. Antiquarian Notes on Sanday. In *POAS*. 1922–3. I. 21–7.

Marwick, H. A 1734 Orkney Inventory. In *POAS*. 1922–3. I. 65–6.

Marwick, H. Antiquarian Notes on Rousay. In *POAS*. 1923–4. II. 15–21.

Marwick, H. Antiquarian Notes on Papa Westray. In *POAS*. 1924–5. III. 36–46.

Marwick, H. A Record Miscellany I. In *POAS*. 1926–7. V. 37–40.

Marwick, H. Antiquarian Notes on Stronsay. In *POAS*. 1926–7. V. 61–83.

Marwick, H. *The Orkney Norn*. 1929.

Marwick, H. The Feas of Clestran. In *POAS*. 1931–2. X. 17–20.

Marwick, H. Impressions of Shetland. In *POAS*. 1933–4. XII. 13–18.

Marwick, H. Two Orkney Eighteenth Century Inventories. In *POAS* 1934. XII. 47–58.

Marwick, H. *Merchant Lairds of Long Ago*. 1936–39. Pts. I–II.

Marwick, H. *The Place-Names of Rousay*. 1947.

Marwick, H. *Orkney*. 1951.

Marwick, H. *Orkney Farm-Names*. 1952.

Mather, J Y. Boats and Boatmen of Orkney and Shetland. In *Scottish Studies*. 1964. Vol. 8. 19–32.

Matras, C. Points of Contact between Shetland and Faroes. In Niclasen, B., ed. *The Fifth Viking Congress*. 1968.

Matras, Chr. Dictionarium Færoense. Færøsk-dansk-latinsk ordbog, af J. C. Svabo. *Færoensia*. 1966. VII.

Maxwell, W H. *Wild Sports and Adventures*. 1853.

Midbrake Papers.

Miller, R. Land Use by Summer Shielings. In *Scottish Studies*. 1967. Vol. 11. 193–221.

Miller, R. *Orkney*. 1976.

Miller, R. and Luther-Davies, S. *Eday and Hoy. A Development Survey*. (Dept. of Geography, University of Glasgow). 1968.

Miller, T B. MS 1974. 6.

Miscellany. *Miscellany of the Abbotsford Club*. 1837. I.

Miscellany. *Miscellany of the Maitland Club* 1840. II.

Mitchell, A. *The Past in the Present: What is Civilisation?* 1880.

Mitchell, A. Note Regarding a Rude Stone Implement from Uyea, Shetland. In *PSAS*. 1897–8. XXXII. 28–9.

Monipennie, J. *Certeine Matters Concerning the Realme of Scotland* (1597). 1603.

Monteith, R. *Description of the Islands of Orkney and Zetland*. 1845.

Mooney, H. Running the Lee. In *The Orcadian*. 28 Sept. 1972. 4.

Mooney, H L. Early Records of the Free Church in Deerness. In *Orkney Miscellany*. 1953. I.

Mooney, J. The Kennedys in Orkney and Caithness. In *POAS*. 1931–2. x. 17–20, and 1932–3. xi. 19–26.

Mooney, J., ed. *Charters and other Records of the City and Royal Burgh of Kirkwall*. (Third Spalding Club). 1952.

Mooney, Dr R. per Marwick, E. in *The Orcadian*. 16 Sept. 1971.

MS Addition to Campbell, J. 1774. 1800.

Murray, J. *The First European Agriculture, a study of the Osteological and Botanical Evidence until 2000 BC*. 1970.

Nærstad, H. *Sameieretten til jord*. 1942.

Neill, P. *A Tour through some of the Islands of Orkney and Shetland*. 1806.

Nelson, G M. *Information*. 1963.

Neven, G. The Scattald Marches of Yell, Shetland, 1667. In *Old-Lore Miscellany*. 1933. IX. 140–8.

Nicolaisen, W F H. Norse Settlement in the Northern and Western Isles. In *Scottish Historical Review*. 1969. Vol. 48. 6–17.

Nicolaisen, W F H. *Scottish Place-Names*. 1976.

Nicolson, D B. Dialect. In Horne, J., ed. *The County of Caithness*. 1907.

Nicolson, J. Some Old-Time Shetland Customs. In *Old-Lore Miscellany*. 1912. v. 122–5.

Nicolson, J. *Shetland Incidents and Tales*. 1931.

Nicolson, J R. *Shetland*. 1972.

Nicolson, J R. *Shetland and Oil*. 1975.

Nicolson Papers. MS.

Nilson, A. *Studier i Svenskt Repslageri* (Nordiska Museets Handlingar 55). 1961.

Noble, R R. An End to 'Wrecking'. The Decline in the use of Seaweed as a Manure on Ayrshire Coastal Farms. In *Folk Life*. 1975. Vol. 13. 80–3.

Nørlund, P. *Viking Settlers in Greenland*, 1936.

O'Dell, A C. *The Historical Geography of the Shetland Islands*. 1939.

Oftedal, M. The Village Names of Lewis in the Outer Hebrides. In *Norsk tidsskrift for sprogvidenskap*. 1954. XVII. 363–409.

Oftedal, M. Busetnad. In *KLNM*. 1957. II. 370–3.

Olsen, G., *et al*. Hovedgård. In *KLNM*. 1961. VI. 697–710.

Olsen, M. *Ættegård og Helligdom*. 1926. Translated as *Farms and Fanes of Ancient Norway*. 1928.

Olsen, O. and Crumlin-Pedersen, O. The Skuldelev Ships. In *Acta Archaeologica*. 1967. xxxviii. 73–174.

Omond, J. Klik Mill, Millbrig, Birsay. In *Old-Lore Miscellany*. 1909. ii. 75–6, photos facing 75.

Omond, J. *Orkney Eighty Years Ago. c.* 1912.

Oppressions. *Oppressions of the Sixteenth Century in the Islands of Orkney and Zetland*. (Maitland Club). 1859.

Orcadian.

Ordnance Survey Name Books.

Osla. Whalsay ... Looking Back. In *The New Shetlander*. 1962. No. 63. 4–5, 26.

Pálsson, H. *Söngvar frá Suðureyjum.* 1955.

Peace, W M. *Hand-Book to The Orkney Islands. c.*1911.

Pennant, T. *Arctic Zoology.* 1784–7 (3rd ed.).

Peterkin, A. *Rentals of the Ancient Earldom and Bishoprick of Orkney.* 1820.

Peterkin, A. *Notes on Orkney and Zetland.* i. 1822.

Petersen, J. *Gamle Gårdsanlegg i Rogaland.* i–ii. 1929, 1935.

Peterson, G. *Oral information,* Papa Stour, 1967.

Petrie, W. *Oral information,* Fetlar, 1963.

Piggott, S. Native Economies and the Roman Occupation of North Britain. In Richmond, I.A., *Roman and Native in North Britain.* 1961. 1–27.

Platt, M I. Report on the Animal Bones from Jarlshof, Sumburgh, Shetland. In *PSAS.* 1932–3. lxvii. 127–36.

Pløyen, C. *Reminiscences of a Voyage to Shetland, Orkney and Shetland in the Summer of 1839.* 1894.

Pococke, R. *Tours in Scotland 1747, 1750, 1760.* (Scottish History Society). 1887.

Press and Journal.

Pringle, R O. On the Agriculture of the Islands of Orkney. In *Transactions of the Highland and Agricultural Society of Scotland.* 1874. (4th Series). vi. 1–68.

Radford, C A. Ralegh. *The Early Christian and Norse Settlements at Birsay, Orkney.* 1959.

Radio-carbon. 1971. Vol. 13.

Rasmussen, H. Korntørring og Tærskning pa Færøerne. In *Kuml.* 1955. 131–57.

Rasmussen, H. *Danish Peasant Culture.* 1955.

Rasmussen, H. Hausmarken und Viehmarken. In *Folk.* 1966/67. Vol. 8–9. 293–300.

Rasmussen, H. Traditional Ways and Means for Land Transport in the Faroe Islands. In Fenton, A., Podolák, J. and Rasmussen, H. *Land Transport in Europe.* 1973. 415–427.

Rasmussen, H. The Use of Seaweed in the Danish Farming Culture. A General View. In *In Memoriam António Jorge Dias.* 1974. i. 385–98.

RCAHMS. *Inventory of the Ancient Monuments of Orkney and Shetland.* 1946. 3 Vols.

Register of Marks (Yell), kept by John Spence of Stonganess, Alexander Irvine of Papil, Gilbert William Irvine of Midbrake, and Thomas Irvine of Midbrake.

Reg. Mag. Sig. Scot. *The Register of the Great Seal of Scotland.*

Reg. Privy Seal. *The Register of the Privy Seal of Scotland.*

Reinton, L. Alminding. In *KLNM.* 1956. i. 98–102.

Reinton, L. Beite. In *KLNM.* 1956. i. 420–3.

Report. *Report of Her Majesty's Commissioners of Enquiry into the Conditions of the Crofters and Cottars in the Highlands and Islands of Scotland.* 1884.

Report. *Report to the Board of Agriculture for Scotland on Home Industries in the Highlands and Islands.* 1914.

Richardson, J S. *The Broch of Gurness.* 1963.

Ritch, H. per E. Simpson. 1961.

Ritchie, A. Pict and Norseman in Northern Scotland. In *Scottish Archaeological Forum.* 1974. Vol. 6. 23–36.

Robberstad, K. Odelsrett. In *KLNM*. 1967. XII. 493–9.

Robertson, D J. Among the Kelpers. In Gunn, J. *The Orkney Book*. 1909. (orginally in Longman's Magazine).

Robertson, D J. Orkney Folk-Lore. In *POAS*. 1923–4. II. 37–46.

Roeder, C. *Manx Notes and Queries*. 1904.

Ropeid, A. Brygging. In *KLNM*. 1957. II. 279–81.

Ross, A. Old Highland Industries. In *Transactions of the Gaelic Society of Inverness*. 1885–6. Vol. 12. 387–415.

Roussell, A. *Norse Building Customs in the Scottish Isles*. 1934.

Roussell, A. *Farms and Churches in the Medieval Norse Settlements of Greenland* (Meddelelser om Grønland 89/1). 1941.

Royal Commission on the Ancient and Historical Monuments of Scotland, The. *Inventory of Orkney*. 1946.

Rundall, T., ed. *Narratives of Voyages towards The North-West* (Hakluyt Society). 1849.

Russell, J. *Three Years in Shetland*. 1887.

Ryder, M L. The History of Sheep in Scotland. In the *Bradford Textile Society Journal*. 1967–8. 33–48.

Ryder, M L. The Evolution of Scottish Breeds of Sheep. In *Scottish Studies*. 1968. Vol. 12. 127–67.

Sabiston, W. *Letter*. Nov. 1961.

Sandison, C. *The Sixareen and her Racing Descendants*. 1954.

Sandison, C. *Unst*. 1968.

Sands, J. Notes on the Antiquities of the Island of St Kilda. In *PSAS*. 1876–8. XII. 186–92.

Sawyer, P H. *The Age of the Vikings*. 1962.

Saxby, H L. *The Birds of Shetland*. 1874.

Saxby, J M E. Food of the Shetlanders Langsyne. In *Old-Lore Miscellany*. 1914. VII. 70–8.

Saxby, J M E. Shetland Phrase and Idiom II. In *Old-Lore Miscellany*. 1908. I. 267–74.

Scarth, R. and Watt, G. Agriculture of Orkney. In *Transactions of the Highland and Agricultural Society of Scotland*. (5th Series). 1939. 1–23.

Scott, M A. *Island Saga. The Story of North Ronaldsay*. 1968.

Scott, Mrs A. and McMillan, Mrs N F. *Notes on croft 'Gateside', North Ronaldsay, Orkney*. May 1964.

Seim, E. Hja Frendar på Fridaroy. In *Jol i Sunnfjord*. 1947.

Seim, E. Litt om Levemåten på Hjaltland Fyrr i tida. In *Årbok 1953–54 for Hordaland Landbruksmuseum*. 1954. 37–51.

Senior, W H. and Swan, W B. *Survey of Agriculture in Caithness Orkney and Shetland* (Highland Development Board Special Report 8). 1972.

Session Papers, Graham v. Tyrie (18 Jan. 1758).

Session Papers, State of Process, Sinclair v. Sinclair. 1773.

Settle, D. *Laste Voyage into the West and Northwest Regions* (1577). 1969 (unpaginated).

Seyðamark Serprent úr Álmanakkum. 1964.

Sheep Book of the late Mr. Thomas Irvine of Midbrake. 1829–77.

Sibbald, Sir R., ed. *Description of the Island of Orkney and Zetland by Robert Monteith*. 1845.

Sigurðardóttir, A. Seng. In *KLNM*. 1970. XV. 130–1.

Shirreff, J. *General View of the Agriculture of Orkney*. 1814 a.

Shirreff, J. *General View of the Agriculture of Shetland*. 1814 b.

Simpson, E J. Farm Carts and Waggons of the Orkney Islands. In *Scottish Studies*. 1963. VII. 154–69.

Simpson, M. *Oral information*, Thurso, 1969.

Sinclair, J. *General View of the Agriculture of the Northern Counties and Islands of Scotland*. 1795.

Sinclair, J. *General Report of the Agricultural State, and Political Circumstances of Scotland*. 1814. III. 23–45.

Skarði, J. av Føroyski leypurin. In *Fróðskaparrit*. 1955. Vol. 4. 32–60; 1956. Vol. 5. 108–52.

Skarði, J. av Faroese Cultivating and Peat Spades., In Gailey, A. and Fenton, A. *The Spade in Northern and Atlantic Europe*. 1970. 67–73.

Skea, Miss B. per Marwick, E. 1972.

Skirving, R. Scot. On the Agriculture of the Islands of Shetland. In *Transactions of the Highland and Agricultural Society of Scotland*. 1874. VI (4th Series). 229–64.

Small, A. Preliminary Notes on Excavations at Underhoull, Westing, Unst. In *The Aberdeen University Review*. 1963. XL.

Small, A. Excavations at Underhoull, Unst, Shetland. In *PSAS*. 1964–6. XCVIII. 225–48.

Small, A. *Excavations in Unst*. 1966.

Small, A. A Viking Longhouse in Unst, Shetland. In Niclasen B., ed. *The Fifth Viking Congress*. 1968. 62–70.

Small, A. The Distribution of Settlement in Shetland and Faroe in Viking Times. In *Saga Book of the Viking Society*. 1969. XVII. 145–55.

Small, A. The Viking Highlands, a Geographical View. In Meldrum, E., ed. *The Dark Ages in the Highlands*. 1971. 53–69.

Small, A., Thomas, C. and Wilson, D M. *St Ninian's Isle and its Treasure*. 2 Vols. 1973.

Smith, A M. *Manures and Fertilisers*. (1952). 1958.

Smith, Rev. C L. *Excursion through the Highlands and Isles of Scotland in 1835 and 1836*. 1837.

Smith, Captain J. *England's Improvement Revived*. 1673.

Smith, J A. Notes on Some Stone Implements, etc. from Shetland. In *PSAS*. 1882–3. XVII. 291–9.

Smith, M. Shetland Croft Houses and their Equipment. In *Shetland Folk Book*. 1964. IV. 1–8.

Smith, M C B. *Correspondence*. 1 May 1961.

Smith, W. Dividing Seaweed in Sandwick, Orkney. In *Old-Lore Miscellany*. 1912. V. 4–5.

Smith, W. Sheep-Marks, Orkney. In *Old-Lore Miscellany*. 1913. VI. 4.

Smith, W. Biggings. In *Old-Lore Miscellany*. 1914. VII. 146–7.

Smyth, H W. *Mast and Sail in Europe and Asia*. 1929.

Sölch, J. *Die Landschaften der Britischen Inseln*. 1951/2.

Solheim, S. Folafoten-Kjølrota. In *Maal og Minne*. 1947. 1–14.

Spence, J. *Shetland Folk-Lore*. 1899.

Spence, J. Klik Mills, Birsay, and the Fairies. In *Old-Lore Miscellany*. 1909. II. 129–32.

Spence, J. The Days of the Old Shetland Sixern. In *Old-Lore Miscellany*. 1910. III. 36–41.

Spence, J. The Kirk o Kirkgoe and the Picky Dykes of Birsa, Orkney. In *Old-Lore Miscellany*. 1920. VIII. 87–94.

Spence, J. Life and Work in Moorland Orcadia in Days of Old. In *POAS*. 1924. II. 77–82.

Spence, M. The Past in the Present. North Ronaldsay Sheep. In *Old-Lore Miscellany*. 1910. III. 22–7.

Spence, R. Orkney's Boy Ploughmen. In *Scotland's Magazine*. February 1956.

Ståhl, H. Bo. In *KLNM*. 1957. II. 25–8.

Ståhl, H. -bolstadh. In *KLNM*. 1957. II. 68–9.

Ståhl, H., *et al*. Hagh(i). In *KLNM*. 1961. VI. 43–5.

Stamp, D., ed. *The Land of Britain*. 1939–40.

Steensberg, A. Indborede sten og træpløkke som erstatning for beslag. In *Varbergs Museums Årsbok*. 1963. 69–76.

Steffensen, J. The physical anthropology of the Vikings. In *Journal of the Royal Anthropological Institute*. 1953. Vol. 83. 86–97.

Steffensen, J. Population: Island. In *KLNM*. 1968. XIII. 390–2.

Stenberger, M. *Forntida Gårdar i Island*. 1943.

Stephens, H. *Book of the Farm*. I–III. 1844.

Stevenson, R B K. Notes on Early Agriculture in Scotland. In *Agricultural History Review*. 1960. VIII/1. 1–4.

Stewart, J. Udal Law and Government in Shetland. In Simpson, W D., ed. *The Viking Congress, Lerwick, July 1950*. 1954.

Stewart, J. *Oral information*. 1958.

Stewart, J. *Correspondence*. 6 Oct. 1962.

Stewart, J. Shetland Farm Names. In Small, A. *The Fourth Viking Congress*. 1965. 247–66.

Stigum, H. Ildsted. In *KLNM*. 1962. VII. 348–51.

Stoklund, B. *et al.* Garn og garnfiskeri. In *KLNM*. 1960. V. 195–206.

Storå, Nils. *Massfångst av Sjöfågel i Nordeurasien.* (Acta Academiae Aboensis. Vol. 34. nr. 2). 1968.

Storå, N. Nät för sjöfågelfångst. In Bergengren, G., Henriksson, H. and Szabó, M. *Sista lasset in. Studier tillägnade Albert Eskeröd 9 maj 1974.* 1975. 129–42.

Stout, W. *Correspondence.* 13 April 1963.

Summons. *Summons of Declarator of Division of Runrig Lands and Commonty of Papa Stour, Sir Arthur Nicolson, Baronet, of Nicolson against Gifford, etc.* (Outer House) 29 April 1845.

Swannay, W. Vinkoin, North Ronaldsay. *Oral information.* 1964.

Sweet, H. ed. *King Alfred's Orosius.* 1883.

SWRI. Scottish Women's Rural Institutes. *Scalloway and District History.* Typescript. 1966.

T., J. Calls to Animals. In *Old-Lore Miscellany*. 1912. V. 111.

Tait, E S. Reid. The Mussel Scaap in Bressay Sound, 1813. In *The Hjaltland Miscellany*. 1947. IV. 86–91.

Tait, E S. Reid. Remonstrance by Thomas Gifford of Busta to and Agreement with the Inhabitants and Fishers of Northmavine, 1726. In *The Hjaltland Miscellany*. 1947. IV. 109–14.

Tait, E S. Reid. The Codling Hole, 1841. In *The Hjaltland Miscellany*. 1947. IV. 115–19.

Tait, E S. Reid. A Shetland Steading. In *Shetland Folk Book*. 1951. II. 77–82.

Tait, E S. Reid. Regulating Sheep 500 Years Ago. In *Shetland News*. 11 May 1954.

Tait, E S. Reid. *Some Notes on the Shetland Hanseatic Trade.* Lerwick. 1955.

Tait, E S. Reid. Some Notes on the Harvest and Harvest Customs in Bygone Days. In *Shetland Folk Book*. 1957. III. 17–19.

Tait, R W. Some Shetland Plant Names. In *The Shetland Folk Book*. 1947. I. 73–88.

Tait, W S. *MS Diaries.*

Talve, I. *Bastu och Torkhus i Nordeuropa.* (Nordiska Museets Handlingar: 53). 1960.

Taylor, A B. *The Orkneyinga Saga.* 1938.

Teignmouth, Lord. *Sketches of the Coasts and Island of Scotland and the Isle of Man.* 1836. 2 Vols.

Terry, C S., ed. Sir Thomas Craig. *De Unione Regnorum Britanniae Tractatus.* (Scottish History Society). 1902.

Terry, C S., ed. *The Cromwellian Union.* (Scottish Text Society). 1902.

Thomas, H J. *A Comparison of Some Methods used in Lobster and Crab Fishing.* (Marine Laboratory, Aberdeen). n.d.

Thompson, T. *Oral information.* 1969.

Thompson, W P L. Funzie, Fetlar: A Shetland Run-Rig Township in the Nineteenth Century. In *Scottish Geographical Magazine*. 1970. Vol. 86, 3. 170–85.

Thorsen, P. The Third Norn Dialect – That of Caithness. In Simpson, W D., ed. *The Viking Congress, Lerwick, July 1950*. 1954. 230–8.

Þorsteinsson, B. Landnám I. In *KLNM*. 1965. X. 208–10.

Thowsen, A. The Norwegian Export of Boats to Shetland, and its Influence upon Shetland Boatbuilding and Usage. In *Sjøfartshistorisk Årbok*. 1969. 145–203.

Traill, W. *Vindication of Orkney.* 1823.

Trémarec, Y J. de Kerguelen. *Relation d'un Voyage.* 1772.

Trotzig, D. *Slagan och andra tröskeredskap.* 1943.

Troup, J. MS.1973.2, and *Correspondence.* July 1975.

Troup, J A. and Eunson, F. *Stromness 150 Years a Burgh 1817–1967.* 1967.

Tudor, J R. *The Orkneys and Shetland.* 1883.

Tulloch, P A. *A Window on North Ronaldsay.* 1974.

Vebæk, C L. An Eleventh-Century Farmhouse in the Norse Colonies of Greenland. In Small, A., ed. *The Fourth Viking Congress*. 1965.

Vedder, D. *Tales and Sketches.* 1832.

Venables, U. *Life in Shetland*. 1956.

Vilkuna, K. *et al*. Säljakt. In *KLNM*. 1972. xvii. 686–703.

Wainwright, F T. *The Northern Isles*. 1962.

Wallace, J. *An Account of the Islands of Orkney*. 1700.

Walton, J. The Built-in Bed Tradition in North Yorkshire. In *Gwerin*. 1961. iii/3. 114–25.

Webster, L E. and Cherry, J. Medieval Britain in 1971. In *Medieval Archaeology*. 1972. xvi.

Whitaker, I. Two Hebridean Corn-Kilns. In *Gwerin*. 1956–7. i. 161–70.

Whitaker, I. The Harrow in Scotland. In *Scottish Studies*. 1958. Vol. 2. 149–65.

White, L. *Medieval Technology and Social Change*. 1962.

Whittington, G. Field Systems of Scotland. In Baker, A. and Butlin, R., eds. *Studies of Field Systems in the British Isles*. 1973.

Williamson, K. Birds in Faeroe Folk-lore. In *The North Western Naturalist*. March–June 1946. 7–19.

Williamson, K. Horizontal Water-mills of the Faeroe Islands. In *Antiquity*. 1946. xx. 83–91.

Williamson, K. *The Atlantic Islands* (1948). 1970.

Wills, J. The Uyea Whale Case. In *The New Shetlander*. No. 114. 1975. 12–15.

Wills, J W G. *Of Laird and Tenant*. Ph.D. Thesis, Edinburgh University. 1975.

Wilson, D M. and Moorhouse, S. Medieval Britain in 1970. In *Medieval Archaeology*. 1971. xv. 124–79.

Wilson, G G. *The Geology of the Orkneys* (HMSO). 1935.

Wilson, J. *A Voyage Round the Coasts of Scotland and the Isles*. 1842. 2 Vols.

Wilson, Miss Mary, Fair Isle. *Correspondence*. July 1963.

Yourston, J. *Oral information*. 1972.

Index and Glossary

Index and Glossary

This index has been designed to incorporate the glossary. All dialect words are listed in it, with references or cross-references to the subjects to which they refer. The captions to the illustrations are also referred to and the exact relationship between the text and the illustrations (which may serve more than one purpose) may be got by consulting the index.

F80 UREAD